Public Law

SECOND EDITION

Public Law is an ideal choice for all undergraduate and GDL students looking for a comprehensive yet accessible textbook on this area of law. The author's clear writing style, accessible tone, and focus on modern case law help bring the subject to life.

The book covers the key institutions, concepts, and legal rules of the United Kingdom's constitutional system, with the chapters arranged around four subjects: the foundations of the constitutional system; Constitutional Law; Administrative Law; and human rights. The book's central theme is that of state power, and the relationship between the state and the citizen.

The second edition has been revised to reflect recent key developments in Public Law, and now extensively explores, in addition to several other key chapter updates, the impact of the 2016 EU referendum, the 2017 General Election, and changes in devolution across England, Scotland, and Wales.

Clearly written and easy to use, *Public Law* enables students to fully engage with the topic and gain a profound understanding of this fundamental and exciting area.

The *Routledge Spotlights* series brings a modern, contemporary approach to the core curriculum for the LLB and GDL, which will help students:

- to move beyond an understanding of the law;
- to refine and develop the key skills of problem-solving, evaluation and critical reasoning, which are essential to assessment success;
- to discover sources and suggestions for taking your study further.

By focusing on recent case law and real–world examples, Routledge Spotlights will help you shed light on the law, understand how it operates in practice and gain a unique appreciation of the contemporary context of the subject.

This book is supported by a range of online resources developed to support your learning, keep you up-to-date and to help you prepare for assessments.

Michael Doherty is Principal Lecturer in Law a at Lancashire Law School.

SP🌞TLIGHTS

SHEDDING LIGHT ON THE LAW

Routledge Spotlights Series

A new textbook series designed to help you translate your knowledge of the law to assessment success.

AVAILABLE NOW:
EU Law, Gerard Conway
Equity & Trusts 2nd edition, Scott Atkins
Public Law, Michael Doherty
Contract Law, Tracey Hough and Ewan Kirk

FORTHCOMING TITLES:
English Legal System, Ryan Murphy

WWW.ROUTLEDGE.COM/CW/SPOTLIGHTS

SPOTLIGHTS
SHEDDING LIGHT ON THE LAW

Public Law

SECOND EDITION

MICHAEL DOHERTY

Routledge
Taylor & Francis Group

LONDON AND NEW YORK

Second edition published 2018
by Routledge
2 Park Square, Milton Park, Abingdon, Oxon OX14 4RN

and by Routledge
711 Third Avenue, New York, NY 10017

Routledge is an imprint of the Taylor & Francis Group, an informa business

© 2018 Michael Doherty

First edition published by Routledge 2015

British Library Cataloguing in Publication Data
A catalogue record for this book is available from the British Library

Library of Congress Cataloging-in-Publication Data
A catalog record for this title has been requested

ISBN: 978-1-138-50492-9 (hbk)
ISBN: 978-1-138-50493-6 (pbk)
ISBN: 978-1-315-14632-4 (ebk)

Typeset in Bembo, Bell Gothic and Avenir
by Apex CoVantage, LLC

Visit the companion website: www.routledge.com/cw/spotlights

Printed and bound by CPI Group (UK) Ltd, Croydon, CR0 4YY

DEDICATION

This book is dedicated to
my wonderful parents,
Owen and Rita Doherty,
and my darling wife,
Elizabeth Doherty.

CONTENTS

DETAILED CONTENTS

16   POLICE AND SECURITY POWERS   489

PREFACE TO THE FIRST EDITION

This book was written from a law teacher's perspective, and with law students very firmly in mind. It views its audience as being smart and motivated people who are approaching this subject for the first time. As Public Law is commonly a year one or Graduate Diploma in Law (GDL) subject, many readers will be approaching legal study for the first time.

The book is animated by a view that successful study is a union between skills and substance. There are some marvellous studies of Public Law which tend to focus on transmitting knowledge (although, of course, many do go on to pose questions and prompt further consideration). The focus here is both on what law students need *to know* about the topic and what they *can do* with that knowledge. This covers assessment (being the most immediate concern for many students) but goes beyond that.

There are two principal models of skills development: the stand-alone model where time is carved out of a busy curriculum to work specifically on development of particular skills, and the integrated model where students develop skills through the study of substantive material. My work on skills development over a number of years has convinced me that neither model, on its own, is the most effective option. We need to do both. Far too much skills development is lost because it is supposed to happen by implication of students simply being exposed to good teacher-researchers and good sources. An approach that is both stand-alone and integrated takes the time to explain the sorts of skills that students need to acquire to do well and how they might begin to acquire those skills. As skills development is a process not an event, these skills need to be explained and regularly practised in the context of the substantive material.

The 18 chapters are arranged around four broader subjects. Chapters 1–3 are foundational and contain important material for students who are new to legal study or relatively unfamiliar with the structure and institutions of the constitutional system. Chapters 4–11 cover Constitutional Law including sources of the UK constitution from legal rules (the supremacy of Parliament), to constitutional conventions (e.g. ministerial responsibility) and constitutional principles (the separation of powers and rule of law). It also examines the evolving process of devolution. Chapters 12–14 deal with Administrative Law, in particular judicial review, but also the role of the ombudsman and tribunals. Chapters 15–18 address human rights through the Human Rights Act 1998 and key issues of police powers, and freedoms of expression and assembly.

My thanks go to all my colleagues at Lancashire Law School and, in particular, to Rachel Nir, Ian Turner and Peter Kay. Professor Richard Taylor gave me my first permanent job as a law academic and over two decades later was the first person I turned to for advice on writing a textbook. Jane Anthony has been a supportive and marvellous Head of School. Professor Steven Wheatley is a former colleague, but one who is still a great friend and source of much wise counsel. Thanks also to the more than 20 cohorts of students who have put up with me and continue to provoke my interest in communicating the joys of Public Law.

The Association of Law Teachers has been a hugely important part of my professional life and many of the ideas here were prompted by papers from and discussions with ALT colleagues who are experts in pedagogy and passionate about teaching and learning. Particular inspirations have been Professor Phil Harris, Alison Bone, Professor Susan Marsnik, Professor Rebecca Huxley-Binns, Aidan O'Donnell and Brian Pillans.

I was so pleased when Routledge invited me to write this book and that it is a part of the Spotlights series. They have been a pleasure to work with, and thanks to Damian Mitchell and Emily Wells for their support and patience. The book would not exist without the work of Fiona Briden, a fine editor.

Thanks also to my parents, brothers and sisters. I always think that when you come from a large family you learn early and important lessons on equity, allocation, power and justice. They were, and are, a lot of fun to grow up with. The only downside to writing this book has been the evenings and weekends that I missed with my wife, Elizabeth.

MICHAEL DOHERTY
PRESTON
1 DECEMBER 2015

PREFACE TO THE SECOND EDITION

All the brilliant people who I mention above are still all brilliant and very dear to me. I would also like to thank the editorial staff at Routledge, particularly Rebecca Brennan, for commissioning this second edition.

It is two years since I completed writing the first edition of this text and in the world of Public Law they have been strange times. I never expected that updating and revising a Public Law text would be a modest undertaking, unlike in some other legal topics that proceed at a more sluggish pace. In some respects, however, the period from October 2015 to October 2017 has been the most tumultuous in my quarter of a century of teaching the subject.

The landscape has been dominated by Brexit; the referendum itself featuring all sorts of unusual sights including members of the same Cabinet publicly campaigning on different sides; the unexpected outcome of the referendum vote; changes to party leaders; despite the expectation of a fixed term under the Fixed-Term Parliament Act 2011, an early General Election; the first minority government since the 1970s; legal challenges before the Supreme Court with major consequences for supremacy of Parliament, prerogative powers, devolution, constitutional conventions and the relationship between Parliament and Government.

The backdrop, or complement, to this feverish constitutional activity has been a certain wildness in populist politics, a turning away from established methods of doing politics. Brexit was the herald for this, but it extends to Donald Trump in the White House, Boris Johnson in the Foreign Office, and far right and nationalist movements in European countries. As I write this, elected leaders of the Catalan Government are in jail on charges of rebellion against the Spanish state.

In other respects, Public Law has proceeded and evolved in its usual pragmatic engaging way. Earlier reforms such as the Judicial Appointments Commission and English Votes for English Law have been working their way through the system. There are still Church of England bishops and hereditary peers in the House of Lords. The Human Rights Act 1998 still stands, unrepealed, and prisoners still do not have the vote. Brexit has sucked up so much attention and energy that developments in other areas have been overshadowed or stalled. The useful reforms to the Ombudsman trailed in the first edition, for example, would surely have been completed by now if the process of exiting the EU had not come to dominate the agenda so fully.

Despite this, some reforms have been introduced. The Digital Economy Act 2017 has direct implications for freedom of expression (Chapter 17). The Investigatory Powers Act 2016 effects important changes in the security services (Chapter 16). There has been further devolution to Scotland, Wales and some English cities and counties (Chapter 11).

There has certainly been a blossoming of popular interest in the press and social media in constitutional matters. The counsel submissions before the Supreme Court in the *Miller* case were covered by the sorts of live blogs normally reserved for Ashes Tests or Champions League matches. There was live TV coverage of the delivery of the *Miller* judgment, and even wider celebrity for the advocate Lord Pannick. All this activity was complemented by great work from Public Law communicators trying to make seemingly bewildering or arcane issues relevant and understandable to the wider public, including: Professor Mark Elliot with his Public Law for Everyone blog; infographics and video explainers from RightsInfo; and David Allen Green with his Law and Policy tweets @davidallengreen. As we move closer to a cliff edge or a new and special relationship with the EU, interest in constitutional issues is only going to grow, and clear understanding of Public Law become even more important.

MICHAEL DOHERTY
PRESTON
6 NOVEMBER 2017

GUIDE TO THE SPOTLIGHTS SERIES

The Routledge Spotlights series is an exciting new textbook series that has been carefully developed to help give you a head start in your assessments. We've listened to lecturers and examiners to identify what it takes to succeed as a law student and we've used that to develop a brand new series of textbooks that combines detailed coverage of the law, together with carefully selected features designed to help you translate that knowledge into assessment success.

AS YOU READ

sections at the start of each chapter introduce you to the key questions and concepts that will be covered within the chapter to help you to focus your reading.

AS YOU REA

The focus of thi

■ Identify th

KEY LEARNING POINTS

throughout each chapter highlight important principles and definitions to aid understanding and consolidate your learning.

KEY LEARN

■ Collective
confider
respo

EXPLAINING THE LAW

brings the subject to life through the use of practical examples to provide valuable context to your learning.

EXPLAINII

Only one as
dismissal v
Parliam

ANALYSING THE LAW

invites you to consider your own response to legal dilemmas and debates. Critical thinking is key to assessment success and with this feature, our authors invite you to critique the law or evaluate conflicting arguments in a debate.

ANALYSIN

Take a mom
distinction.
Health S

APPLYING THE LAW

Problem questions will form a large part of your assessment and **Applying the law** allows you to develop your problem-solving skills by showing how the law can be applied to a given situation. Learn how to interpret the law and apply it to any problem question.

APPLYING

Imagine that
national cha
office tha

MAKING CONNECTIONS

will help you impress examiners, showing you how a topic fits into the bigger picture, not just of the wider subject but also across the legal curriculum.

MAKING CC
+ + + + + + + +
When you lo
of law, judic
operatio

POINTS TO REVIEW

bring together all of the principles and themes for the chapter, helping to reinforce your learning.

POINTS TO

- Tribunals car
- Their merits
- The Le

TAKING IT FURTHER

Reading widely impresses examiners! **Taking it further** provides annotated lists of journal articles, book chapters and useful websites for further reading which have been carefully selected to help you to demonstrate an enhanced understanding of the topic.

TAKING IT F

K McMillan and
not a law book
underpin mu
ook, an

GUIDE TO THE WEBSITE

LEGAL EXERCISES
to test knowledge and promote critical thinking, including exam/coursework questions and thinking points for further study and reflection.

MULTIPLE CHOICE QUESTIONS
for self-testing, helping you to diagnose where you might feel less confident about your knowledge so you can direct your revision time in the right direction.

REVISION ADVICE AND STUDY TIP PODCASTS
will help you to improve your performance and raise your grades.

KEY CASE FLASHCARDS
will help you to revise and remember the key cases and the legal principle they illustrate.

UPDATES
on cases and legislation will help you to stay on top of all the most important recent legal developments in the subject area.

TABLE OF CASES

TABLE OF STATUTES

TABLE OF EUROPEAN LEGISLATION

TABLE OF INTERNATIONAL LEGISLATION

TABLE OF STATUTORY INSTRUMENTS

1

CHAPTER 1
STUDYING PUBLIC LAW

Welcome to Public Law
You'll Never Leave

Hello, dear Public Law student, and welcome to a marvellous subject. The sign above highlights the fact that gaining an understanding of Public Law will not just help you pass your assessments with flying colours.[1] It will enrich your life. Years from now when you are

- watching some news item where Parliament is debating whether to send troops into some overseas conflict, or
- sitting with friends in a café who are wondering why 'bad people' have human rights, or
- trying to cope with a public official who is dealing with your reasonable request in an unreasonable manner,

I hope that your understanding, your perspective and your responses are informed by your appreciation of Public Law.

AS YOU READ

The focus of this chapter is academic skills. You should:

- Identify the key messages in relation to writing, researching and reasoning.

- Consider how you can carry these skills forward to effective study of Public Law and to your assessments.

---

1   You get extra 'pop culture reference' points for spotting that the image above is a nod to the town sign of Royston Vaisey, home of *The League of Gentlemen* (BBC TV). Weird, funny and truly fascinating, UK Public Law is a fair metaphor for the town.

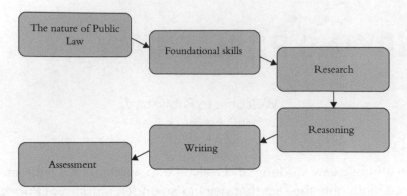

Figure 1.1 Structure of Chapter 1

1.1 THE NATURE OF PUBLIC LAW

Public Law is concerned with a wide range of issues, but some of its key questions are:

- How is the power of the state organised? This involves looking at, for example, who has the power to make law, or who has the power to adjudicate on legal disputes, and how these powers are shared between different parts of the state.
- Can the power of the state be limited by law? This involves looking at both theoretical approaches, for example the 'rule of law' and the 'separation of powers' and very concrete practical issues, such as whether an individual can legally prevent a local council from turning a much-loved beauty spot into a car park.
- What is the relationship between the individual and the state? This involves looking at the ability of people to legally challenge the actions of public authorities. It also includes the notion of 'rights', that the state should not have the capacity to interfere in certain fundamental activities of citizens, such as their right to free speech.

Public Law is a core subject on most law programmes. The Solicitors Regulation Authority includes many of the topics covered by this textbook in its Statement of Legal Knowledge, which is the knowledge that solicitors are required to demonstrate at the point of qualification. From 2020 it will be assessed as part of the new Solicitors Qualification Exam. The Bar Standards Board is retaining the need for a Qualifying Law Degree and the compulsory place on Public Law on that degree. In summary, one reason why you are studying Public Law is that the legal professions say that it is an essential part of becoming a lawyer.

Even if the professions made no sort of demand for Public Law to be studied, it would still be a core aspect of legal education.

- It truly is foundational – in the sense of building a foundation of concepts that you will take into other legal topics. Without a grounding in Public Law, it would be impossible to understand important aspects of, for example, EU Law, Family Law, Medical Law and Media Law.

- You *could in theory* be a practising lawyer ignorant of Public Law – but only if none of your clients ever had to deal with the police, local authorities, customs, immigration or tax authorities etc. In practice, such a body of clients does not exist.

You saw on the first page that Public Law links very readily to real life. Open any broadsheet newspaper on any day of the week, or watch TV news any night, and you will see something of constitutional importance and find that Public Law plays a central part in it. One piece of advice that Public Law teachers have been telling their students for many years is – read the newspapers. They illuminate your understanding and allow you to see interesting Public Law concepts in action.

In the last couple of days of drafting this second edition, in late October 2017, I noted down some of the stories that came on the radio when I was sat in my kitchen having my lunch. They included:

1   *Parliament debated a proposal to allow 16 and 17 year olds to vote in General Elections* – the electoral system is an important part of Public Law (see Chapter 3). Voting rights had been extended to 16 and 17 year olds first in the Scottish independence referendum of 2014 and then for Scottish Parliament elections from 2017. This proposal was supported by the Labour, SNP and Liberal Democrat parties but opposed by the Conservatives. A number of Conservative MPs talked for so long that the Commons was unable to move to a vote on the measures.
2   *Michael Fallon, the Secretary of State for Defence, resigned* – the Defence Secretary was one of the most senior politicians in the Government. There were two separate allegations of inappropriate sexual conduct which Fallon accepted had occurred. Further accusations, including of a more serious assault, were made in the two days after he resigned. It is an important constitutional convention that Government Ministers are responsible for their conduct and should resign if serious wrongdoing has occurred (see Chapter 4, Conventions, on Individual Ministerial Responsibility). The convention has developed over recent years so that it no longer seems to apply to consensual private sexual behaviour, but this restriction did not apply to Fallon, who accepted that he had committed sexual harassment.
3   *Spain imposed direct rule over Catalonia after its government issued a unilateral declaration of independence* – the Catalan government had conducted an independence referendum despite a ruling from the Spanish Supreme Court that this would be unlawful. The pro-independence result of that referendum led the Catalan government to declare that Catalonia was separating from Spain and would be an independent country. It supported this move with arguments based on democracy and the international law right of national self-determination. The central Spanish government triggered provisions of the national constitution dissolving the Catalan government and imposing direct rule, on the basis of the rule of law. There are number of Public Law concepts at play in this story: the rule of law, federalism, the supremacy of the constitution, the rights of 'nations' within a larger state, human rights of freedom of expression and democracy.

A random selection of stories on a couple of random days and almost all of them had very significant Public Law elements. So . . . welcome to Public Law; you'll never leave.

1.2 SUCCESSFUL STUDY

Effective study in any academic subject is a union between skills and substance. This applies particularly to legal study. The great American legal educator Karl Llewellyn said in 1948 that 'The essence of our lawyer's craft lies in skills . . . in practical, effective, persuasive, inventive skills for getting things done'.[2]

The Quality Assurance Agency (QAA) sets out in its 'benchmark statement' what any student graduating in law should be able to demonstrate. There are seven areas of performance, yet only one relates to legal knowledge. The other six cover application and problem-solving, research, critical thinking, autonomy and ability to learn, communication and literacy, and other key skills (e.g. IT and teamwork).

It can be argued that the purpose of higher education as a whole (what makes it 'higher' and therefore what makes graduates different from non-graduates) is to develop certain intellectual skills so that the graduate becomes an independent thinker. So, even for seemingly basic tasks it is never enough to just 'know'. Your examiner is not a mind reader, and to transmit knowledge you will need to analyse, summarise and communicate. Most Public Law assessment tasks will explicitly demand that you use a wider range of academic skills, such as research, writing and arguing. Most of the rest of this book is devoted to the substance of Public Law, although we have tried to integrate academic skills and assessment advice where it is helpful. This chapter focuses on study skills, although very much in the context of Public Law.

1.3 FOUNDATIONAL SKILLS

It does not matter how clever you are, but if you never make a note in a lecture or make time to write up coursework or prepare for an exam, you are not going to do well. Very good students have a strong foundation of skills that underpin not just their academic success but also make so many other aspects of their lives easier and more effective. The paradox is that we often do not give enough attention to these skills. We prefer to charge into the minutiae of prerogative powers, or mistake in a contract, or joint enterprise in Criminal Law, but if we do not have these foundational skills then the process of gaining legal expertise can become long, tiring and frustrating. So what are good foundations?

2   Karl N Llewellyn, 'The Current Crisis in Legal Education' (1948–49) 1 *Journal of Legal Education* 211.

1.3.1 TIME MANAGEMENT

In higher education, you are expected to adopt a mature and independent approach to your time management and to planning for lectures, workshops, reading, assignments, deadlines etc. This is one of the starkest differences from school and sixth-form education and one that some students struggle with.

Many people have written hundreds of pages on time management but the advice here is simple:

- Get a diary – if you do not already have one, then before you go any further, even to the next bullet point, get one. Do not stop for a cup of tea and think 'I must get around to getting a diary some time . . .'. Do it now. There is no effective way of juggling the competing demands on your time or of planning ahead to complete assessments if you do not have a diary. The format is entirely your preference – an A5 student organiser, a slim pocket diary, the calendar on your phone or an online diary (Google Calendar, Outlook) that you can access across devices. Whatever the format – get a diary.
- Put everything in it   some students possess a one-page A4 sheet called a 'timetable'. This does not contain your sports club fixtures, part-time work schedule, night out with friends or your coursework deadline in two weeks' time. (Your timetable tells you that you have acres of free time scattered luxuriously through the week – it is lying to you.) These other commitments might be in your head, but this is not the proper location to store this information. So what is the correct location? Yes – your diary. In particular, you need to pencil in chunks of time for your preparation for seminars and assessments, so that you are using your diary in a proactive way.
- Of course, you then need to follow it – but you have won half the battle by organising yourself this way.

If you already have all of this in hand, there is scope to take your time management and productivity further. The Getting Things Done system by David Allen is particularly recommended.[3]

1.3.2 NOTE-TAKING

Most law schools still operate on the basis of lectures followed by small group teaching, i.e. seminar, tutorial or workshop. Even those schools that have 'flipped' their learning and have online video recorded lectures still use lectures that you need to learn from, so you will need good note-taking skills. Most new students are unfamiliar with note-taking. You can find plenty of detailed guidance in the study skills books, so again the focus here is on simple tips.

1   In preparation for lectures, you should have printed off, or have available on your laptop, any lecture slides or handouts. You should read through the relevant sections of the module handbook and those slides/handouts in advance of the lecture.

---

3   D Allen, *Getting Things Done* (Paitkus, 2015).

2 Do not sit passively for the hour – first, you have got to develop a set of notes that will help you in future tasks and assessments. Any handouts or slides are designed merely to give you a framework, and the lecturer will provide further explanation and detail. A slide might for example have a case name and a key quote, but the lecturer might sketch in the facts of the case, the legal issue at stake, the arguments of the parties and the *ratio decidendi* of the judgment. If you do not have some of this detail in your notes, you will not recall it effectively. Secondly, lecturers think that their subjects are really fascinating and that they themselves are engaging and witty (and who are we to argue?), but lectures do not have the production values of even a basic TV documentary, i.e. unless you are actively engaged with the lecture, time will drag and you will lose focus. You need to use your brain and constantly ask, what is the key point? What do I need to jot down?

3 Develop your own shorthand – you cannot transcribe every word the lecturer says, and that is not the point of note-taking anyway. You need to supplement any existing slides/handouts with additional key points, useful facts, notes of things that you did not quite understand or further questions. Experience shows that for slides, printing them off at two or three slides per page gives you enough white space to make useful further notes. In addition, you will develop your own acronyms. Some suggestions are:

Govt	Government	CC	Constitutional Convention
Min	Minister	SofP	Supremacy of Parliament
H/C	House of Commons	SepofPow	Separation of Powers
H/L	House of Lords	RoL	Rule of Law
PM	Prime Minister	JR	Judicial Review
CivServ	Civil Servant	LA	Local Authority

4 Tidy them up afterwards – this does not have to take lots of time. If you find yourself writing out the whole set of notes again, you are not using your time well and need to revisit your strategy for making original notes in lectures. But at least part of what you note down in lectures is likely to be incomprehensible to you in a few weeks. Taking a few minutes in the week of the lecture to tidy up your writing will help your understanding both at that point and later. You can also get your coloured and highlighter pens out at this point and start to bring out a structure and key messages from your notes.

1.3.3 ORGANISATION

When we ask second-year students to reflect on one thing that they would have done differently in their first year to make their lives easier, 'organising materials' comes up time after time. They say that they started their first year with good intentions, but over the course of the year their notes and print-offs ended up in one folder, which became one small pile of papers on the corner of the desk, which turned into a large pile of papers on the floor. Many laptops have the digital equivalent of this pile of unsorted papers lurking on the hard drive.

Information management simply means organising your sources in a way that makes them accessible to you. That can mean a separate folder on your hard drive (e.g. 'Constitutional conventions coursework – sources') with each file named for its author and subject (e.g. 'Woodhouse – ministerial accountability 2003'). If you are printing off materials, then a separate ring binder organised the same way is useful. If you take notes rather than print a source, then, similarly, your notes should be titled with the author's name and filed the same way.

Take some time over this. Do it little and often. You will save yourself a heap of trouble, and when coursework or exams come along you will feel less stressed and more in control of your subject.

1.3.4 MOTIVATION AND ENGAGEMENT

There are a number of reasons why some, particularly first-year, students struggle with engagement and motivation. You may be away from home for the first time and have to adjust to a new city, new people and new responsibilities. You may become too enthralled by the stereotypical distractions of student life. For those students living at home, the law school may seem distant from their home lives. Mature students, having experienced life in the world of work without a degree, are often *very clear* as to what they want to achieve and why, but they have many competing demands and may feel different from the rest of their cohort. For the first-year student, the pressures of the post-graduation working world may seem a long way off and studying law, with its heavy reading schedule and technical language, may be a challenge. So what can you do about this?

1   Remember that you are not alone and that support from your tutors, law student society, students' union and other support services are readily available. Embrace the differences that university is making to your life. Think about the future and why you want to be here and who will be proud of you when you succeed.
2   Organisation and time management help immeasurably in staying focused on and comfortable with your studies.
3   'Year 1 does not count' – feel free to do whatever it takes, within the boundaries of both Civil and Criminal Law, to disabuse anyone peddling this false notion. Point out their error and tell them to stop them misleading themselves and others. Most degree programmes do not include first-year marks in the calculations of your overall degree classification. In every other way, your first year counts. It is a developmental year where you hone your academic and legal skills. If you coast through your first year, you will be making your mistakes in your second and third years. A good first year will be a springboard to greater success in later years. Graduate work may be some time off, but your career development needs to include work experience. The most important vacation schemes for law students recruit halfway through your second year, i.e. when the only things, from higher education, that you have to show potential employers are your first-year marks.
4   Study buddies – perhaps the single most powerful tool in keeping you motivated and engaged is your peer group. You help each other raise your games and your ambitions. You clarify things for each other, from the mundane ('where is the seminar sheet for our next class?') to the challenging ('do you understand the Wade/Laws disagreement on the implications of *Factortame*?'). These peer groups can arise naturally, but you can give them a kick-start and get the most benefit from them if you incorporate them into your study habits as a regular study group (duly entered into your diary). Make them happen and ask people who you like or respect to work with you.

A good group of friends at law school can transform what will be a worthy educational experience into a marvellous life experience.

Legal study is not easy. It is not designed to be and it ought not to be. Practising lawyers advise people on some of the most important decisions in their lives. Law graduates are sought by employers in other fields (business, finance, government) because of their rigour and intellectual abilities. You are well capable of succeeding. You have been admitted to a higher education course so you do belong here – focus on developing good academic habits and good friends, and you will have a most excellent time.

1.4 RESEARCH

'Effective legal research is central to the lawyer's role as problem solver.'[4] Law students need to be able to research and analyse the law from primary sources (legislation and cases) and secondary sources (mainly journals and books). They need to learn how to look at a problem or an issue and formulate research questions from it and then use authoritative and up to date resources to answer those questions. The next section outlines three types of research.

1.4.1 *BASIC RESEARCH* – RESEARCH WITH A READING LIST

You will often be provided, in lecture handouts and slides, with a range of references to relevant reading materials. In legal skills or legal methods courses you will have been shown how to find these resources using their references (e.g. case citations). The material could be in the library or in an online database. Your day-to-day work for seminars normally will involve this basic research. If you actually undertake this reading, learn how to handle legal materials quickly and how to extract the information you need, and then use it in your learning and your assessments you will go a long way on the road to success as a law student.

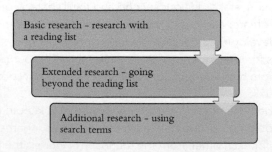

Basic research – research with a reading list

Extended research – going beyond the reading list

Additional research – using search terms

Figure 1.2 Types of research

4   D Stott, *Legal Research* (Cavendish, 1993).

In basic research, some of the work has been done for you. Your lecturer has sifted through the literature on a subject to highlight the most useful and relevant sources, and provided you with a reading list. As this is the material that has been highlighted by the people who will be marking your work, it would be *illogical* not to use the reading list as the basis for your research.

1.4.2 *EXTENDED RESEARCH* – RESEARCH GOING BEYOND THE READING LIST

Extended research involves using your reading list as a starting point for research rather than as an exhaustive list. Why would you undertake this type of research? It deepens your knowledge and understanding; it gives you something different from your classmates to say in seminars and assessments; it leads naturally to analysis and evaluation; it shows greater initiative and skill in research. These are among the most common assessment criteria, i.e. doing these things *really* helps your marks.

With hard-copy sources you can apply the 'paperchase' method to find further relevant material. Electronic databases are specifically designed to make this type of extended research easy and time-efficient by providing links between relevant materials.

Paperchase – all scholarly work uses references to show the author's awareness of relevant literature, to provide authority for their arguments and to indicate possible further reading. You can use these references to find additional sources that are relevant to the issue you are investigating. Once you find an additional source, it will *itself* contain lots of references to further material. You can link from source to source (or 'paperchase') to reach a potentially huge range of further sources.

APPLYING THE LAW – PAPERCHASE

Using this textbook as an example, Chapter 5, 'Constitutional conventions', discusses an important article by Diana Woodhouse ('The Reconstruction of Constitutional Accountability' [2002] *Public Law* 73). If you were writing a coursework on conventions or ministerial accountability, it would be good practice to use the citation in this textbook to find that Woodhouse article – the first link of the chain.

After locating that article, in the library or an online database (e.g. Westlaw) you will see that it contains further references to relevant material on constitutional conventions, for example in footnote 1, P Berberis, 'The New Public Management and Accountability' (1998) 76 *Public Administration* 3. Finding and using this source (the second link of the chain) will make your answer distinctive and show the marker that you have good research skills. Material from the Berberis article can help you deepen your analysis and build a well-argued conclusion. You can probably guess the next step? Yes, the Berberis article itself contains references to lots of other sources, so the only thing stopping you from going on and making other links in the chain will be your time, energy and the length of your assessment.

1.4.3 *ADDITIONAL RESEARCH* – USING GENERAL SEARCHES

This is where you use a search term, rather than an item from your reading list, as the basis for your research. This includes searching Westlaw or Lexis Library, and the use of Google etc.

The word *'additional'* is stressed above because far too often this is the main research method undertaken. Simply 'Googling' the broad subject of the assessment and using the results from the first page of hits is very poor practice. It does not show an understanding of what your markers are looking for and, in any case, using extended research will cover almost all of your research needs.

Additional research, if you decide you even need to undertake it, should start with attempts to find relevant formal sources from:

- The law databases (Westlaw, Lexis Library).
- Picking the best three or four sources from e.g. Westlaw effectively gives you a reading list. You can then use the 'extended research' method to find further decent sources.
- The general internet may have a *residual* role as a final stage in your research plan. It is the icing on the cake – not the cake itself!

The real skill for a modern law student in using 'additional research' to find the best research sources is in using *keyword searches* effectively, including filtering results so as to focus on the most relevant material. You can use the specific fields of the database – Westlaw, for example, has separate fields for cases, legislation, journals etc. In each field, there are options for basic search and advanced search. The advanced search enables you to narrow your results. When you get your results, you can search within those to find more relevant answers.

Boolean operators are also useful for keyword searches – most databases (and internet search engines) allow the use of Boolean logic to enable you to refine searches. Most databases will have an online guide or help page – e.g. Westlaw has a link to 'List of Connectors' on most search pages. The most used operators are:

- "Quote marks" – putting a term in double quote marks means that the databasesearches only for that whole term.
- AND – searching for *EU democracy* will return (on most databases) materials that mention the EU *or* democracy; searching for *EU AND democracy* will return only those sources that mention *both* EU and democracy.
- Root expander – to search for terms with multiple endings, use the '!' character. For example, *'object!'* will retrieve object, objected, objection, objecting, objectionable.

1.4.4 SEARCH ENGINES

Google is wonderful (and other search engines are available). It enables us to find all sorts of information within seconds, but just because it is very useful for getting train times or recipes for Lancashire hotpot does not make it ideal for conducting legal research. Here are some shortcomings:

- Very limited access to the sources your tutors (i.e. those assessing your work) are expecting you to look at – it cannot look into subscription-only digital resources, such as Lexis Library.
- No quality control – it does not list the best or most authoritative sources, just those that meet the criteria within Google's secretive algorithm. Weak or inaccurate sources may be very high in the search results.
- No guarantee of currency – i.e. the danger of using out-of-date material.

Google can be used as a last stage of your research method to identify other materials that may be *a useful supplement* to the formal legal research. You will, however, need to be alive to the dangers listed above and have an idea of what sorts of web resources can usefully contribute to your work. These are:

Public institutions – Government departments, e.g. the Ministry of Justice; Devolved administrations, e.g. the Scottish Government; Public bodies, e.g. HM Courts and Tribunals Service.[5]

Non-governmental organisations (pressure groups) – Liberty, for example, publishes authoritative policy reports in the field of human rights and civil liberties; JUSTICE is an all-party lawyers group to promote administrative, civil and criminal justice; the Public Law Project is a charity that seeks to improve access to Public Law remedies for disadvantaged people.[6]

Newspapers – Public Law teachers have traditionally been very keen on their students reading quality newspapers on a regular basis. It allows you to see how Public Law applies in the real world (see above). This desire continues in the modern digital era; the difference is that it is much easier to access this data. *The Times* has an excellent law section but you will need to subscribe. *The Guardian, Independent* and (most of the) *Telegraph* are free online.

1.4.4.1 BLOGS

A number of academics and research groups produce blogs. They are contemporary, written by experts and can be cited in your assessments. Two Public Law blogs stand out. First, the *UK Constitutional Law Association Blog*, whose strength lies in the breadth of expertise of its contributors. The second is *Public Law for Everyone* by Professor Mark Elliott. This is a brilliant individual sustained contribution to the public understanding of Public Law.

Twitter is also perfect for curating the internet and keeping up to date on Public Law developments. Elliott publishes an annual round-up of the best Twitter resources for Public Law students.[7] For any other internet source you need to be *very* confident that

---

5 Ministry of Justice, http://www.justice.gov.uk/; Scottish Government, http://www.gov.scot/; HM Courts and Tribunals Service, https://www.gov.uk/government/organisations/hm-courts-and-tribunals-service (last accessed 05/11/17).

6 Liberty, https://www.liberty-human-rights.org.uk/; JUSTICE, http://justice.org.uk/; Public Law Project, http://www.publiclawproject.org.uk/ (last accessed 05/11/17).

7 UK Constitutional Law Association, http://ukconstitutionallaw.org/blog/; Public Law for Everyone, http://publiclawforeveryone.com/; Mark Elliott's Blog and Twitter recommendations 2015/16, http://publiclawforeveryone.com/2013/09/16/new-law-student-who-to-follow-on-twitter-and-which-blogs-to-read/ (last accessed 05/11/17).

the material has been produced from an authoritative source and is up to date. If you are unsure – do not use the source. We live in an age of information overload and you will, using the methods outlined above, have access to more than enough relevant and authoritative information without undermining your work (and your marks) by reliance on inappropriate web sources. For all sources, but particularly for these public bodies, pressure groups and newspaper sources, you need to read the material critically, i.e. identify what the argument is, whether the supporting evidence is persuasive and why certain facts have been chosen or highlighted. A note on Wikipedia – there are some interesting debates in academic circles on the value of Wikipedia, but the consensus, and therefore the simple advice to follow, is that it is *not a valid source* to rely on or cite in academic work.

1.4.5 RESEARCH STRATEGY

For exam and coursework assessments, you need to read a *good range of sources*. There is no magic number of sources that you need to look at to feel that you have done 'enough', but you do need to consider as a minimum:

- Your textbook.
- Material identified as key reading for your seminars on the topic.
- Material identified by your tutor as key reading for the assessment.
- Primary sources (i.e. cases and legislation) that are central to answering the question.
- Some further reading that in your judgement puts you in a position to answer the question effectively.

Once you have read a good range of sources you need to *use them effectively* to gain credit for all that work. This means using authority to support your arguments; do not solely present your research in the form of quotations.

APPLYING THE LAW – ASSESSMENT ADVICE

There are three main ways of showing the reader that you have used an authority in your work.

Reporting – *As Professor Smith argues, conventions regulate important constitutional relationships.*[8]
Referencing – *Conventions regulate important constitutional relationships.*[9]
Quoting – *It has been argued that 'Conventions, regulating as they do fundamental relationships within the UK constitution, are key to understanding that constitution'.*[10]

---

8 Robert Smith, 'The Importance of Conventions' [2002] *Journal of Government Law* 55, 61.
9 Ibid.
10 Ibid.

1.4.6 PLAGIARISM

This is the practice of passing off other people's work as your own, and is a serious academic offence. If you are suspected of plagiarism you will be subject to an investigation. If found guilty, there are a range of serious sanctions that your university can impose on you. You will also have to explain the offence to the Solicitors' Regulatory Authority or the Bar Council later in your career. How can you make sure that you avoid any allegation of plagiarism in your own work? The simple answer is to *reference* your sources every time you use them to make a point, and to *cite* your sources accurately.

1.4.7 CITATION

You need to cite fully and precisely each time you use a source. Follow your law school's policy on citations. A number of law schools have adopted the Oxford University Standard for Citation of Legal Authorities (OSCOLA). If your school has no formal policy then consider using OSCOLA, as it can give you consistency and there are great support resources.[11]

You always need to provide a full **bibliography** at the end of your answer. This includes *everything that you have read* as preparation for the assessment (and *nothing that you have not looked at yourself*).

1.5 REASONING

McMillan and Weyers point out that 'The ability to think critically is probably the most transferable of the skills you will develop at university – and your future employers will expect you to be able to use it to tackle professional challenges'.[12]

The leading tool used to illustrate the different levels of reasoning skills that students are expected to use in higher education is called Bloom's taxonomy. This is outlined and applied in the substantive context of constitutions in Chapter 4. In summary, it explains that students start at the base of the pyramid of reasoning skills (remembering and understanding) and progressively develop abilities in the skills further up the hierarchy. To do well, you need to show that you can analyse, evaluate and create. More emphasis is placed on these skills in the later parts of your programme, but they enhance your work and your marks from the first day of law school.

So how do you demonstrate these sorts of reasoning skills? Again, the aim here is to give you some simple practical tips.

Get the basics right – if you properly follow the instructions in an assessment you will inevitably be demonstrating many of these skills. An assessment will never tell you to put

----

11 http://www.law.ox.ac.uk/publications/oscola.php (last accessed 05/11/17).
12 K McMillan and J Weyers, *The Study Skills Handbook* (Pearson, 2012) 121.

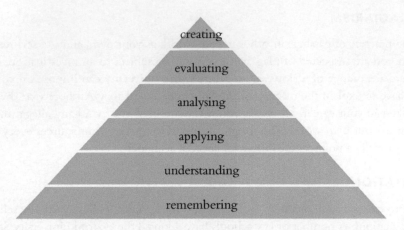

Figure 1.3 Bloom's taxonomy – as updated by Anderson and Krathwohl

down 'all you know' on a topic, which would only involve the bottom two skills. Anything asking you to 'discuss', 'consider', 'assess' etc will require you to undertake the higher reasoning skills. You will be selecting and analysing relevant source materials, evaluating the validity of any assertions, applying your knowledge to the terms of the question, creating your own conclusion and so forth.

Bring your sources together – reading a good range of sources and bringing together those different views and perspectives in your answer (often called synthesis) is an excellent form of reasoning.

Develop/strengthen an evaluative approach – There is no mystery to undertaking analysis (identifying the component parts of a source or argument) or evaluation (weighing how persuasive a reason or item of evidence is). Examples of what you can do to develop these aspects of your work are:

■ Comparing and contrasting – this could be comparing authors' views, contrasting approaches in different legal systems, comparing the legal position before and after a reform etc.
■ Using benchmarks – there may be some standard that you can compare the current law to, e.g. human rights standards, Law Commission proposals, general values of the legal system such as clarity, consistency, and impartiality.
■ Proposing alternatives – as long as these are linked to your analysis of what is wrong with the current position.

1.5.1 ARGUMENTS

The argument is the main mode of legal writing. It is what you produce when you answer an essay or problem question in a coursework or exam, or when you speak in a moot. Have you ever considered the purpose of an argument? What are you trying to do when you are putting an essay together? The objective of an argument is *to persuade*.

Arguments therefore contain:

> A conclusion – *What* am I trying to persuade the reader to accept?
> and
> Reasons – *How* am I trying to persuade the reader?

1.5.1.1 CONCLUSIONS

We are all familiar with what conclusions are; the key is to make yours as clear and persuasive as possible. A useful exercise in relation to every assessment (once you have done your research and reading) is to write down this question:

What is my conclusion?

And try to answer that in no more than a couple of sentences. Are you happy that it is clear and concise? Are you happy that this is what you want to really persuade the reader to accept? If so, this can help structure your work and form the basis for the written conclusion in your final draft. If not, rethink and rework it.

1.5.1.2 REASONS

'Understanding the evidence the author has for the conclusion drawn is as important as understanding the conclusion itself.'[13] Remember that the purpose of an argument is to persuade.

- The conclusion identifies *what* you want to persuade the reader of.
- The reasons are *how* you aim to persuade the reader.

Conclusions without reasons (or with weak or irrelevant reasons) are banal but, even worse, they fail to achieve their purpose, i.e. they do not persuade. Readers are best persuaded to accept a conclusion underpinned by strong and relevant reasons.

1.6 WRITING

1.6.1 PRESENTATION

Your law school may lay down specific requirements for presenting your work. Always follow those instructions very precisely. Unless it clashes with your law school requirements then it is good practice to:

- Use double or 1.5-line spacing.
- Use font size 11 or 12.

---

13 A Bradney and others, *How to Study Law*, 5th edn (Sweet & Maxwell, 2005) 145.

- Put all case names in italics.
- Number all pages.

For short quotes (less than two lines), include them in the body of your work. For longer quotes (more than two lines), add a space above and below the quote, and indent the quote, e.g.:

> Unquestionably, judicial review has caught the imagination of those affected by controversial public decisions (and perhaps more importantly their legal advisers) and the number of applications for judicial review continues to grow apace.

1.6.2 PROOF-READING

It is essential that the first draft of your work is not the version that you submit. A first draft is likely to contain spelling errors, grammatical errors, gaps in citation, incoherent passages of writing etc.

Spell-checking – the spell-check tool on your word processor is very useful, but it will not pick up all mistakes, e.g. *there/their*. The grammar-check tool will pick up some mistakes, but is less accurate than the spell-checker. You need to supplement these tools with careful proof-reading and revising.

You should leave time after you have finished a draft to revise it.

- You will proof your work more objectively if you leave time (even if it is just overnight) in between finishing writing and proof-reading.
- You will need time to make any revisions.

A useful tip on picking up grammar, coherence and writing style mistakes is to *read your work out loud*. This tends to make absurdities, or style mistakes such as very long sentences, really stand out.

1.6.3 COMMON ERRORS

Grammatical errors that regularly crop up include:

- Misuse of apostrophes, e.g. 'Judge's often argue . . .'
- Failing to put proper nouns in capital letters, e.g. 'the european commission'
- Mixing plural/singular, e.g. 'Defendants, in some cases, gives evidence of . . .'
- Mixing past/present, e.g. 'In the past, the House of Lords provides guidance . . .'

Common style errors include:

- Overlong paragraphs or sentences
- Contractions, e.g. *wasn't* rather than *was not*

- Slang/colloquialisms
- Use of the first person – e.g. '. . . therefore I conclude . . .'

1.7 ASSESSMENT

If you ever wonder (and you ought to) 'what am I being assessed on?' and 'what do I need to do to get a great mark?', then the answer lies in the assessment criteria. You need to familiarise yourself with them and consider for each assessment how you can effectively meet them. They are used by your tutors in grading your work and in feeding back to you what you need to do to improve your academic skills.

This chapter contains only very general guidance. In addition, you may receive subject-specific guidance in your Public Law module on e.g. the type of sources you will be expected to use or the structure to be adopted. This guidance comes from the people who will be marking your work. At the risk of stating the obvious, this subject guidance is valuable information and you need to ensure that you have observed it in your work.

Changes to teaching, learning and assessment practices have seen law teachers use a wider range of assessment types, including multiple choice questions, presentations, group work, portfolios and imaginative exercises such as completing a judicial review claim form. For any of these assessments, you need to follow the guidance of our tutors very closely. Despite these developments, the main assessment types on Public Law modules are coursework and examinations, both of which will pose essay-type and problem-type questions.

1.7.1 ESSAY QUESTIONS

A simple tip on approaching essay questions is APWP.

Analyse – Plan – Write – Polish

1.7.1.1 ANALYSE

Interpreting the question – if you do not address all the issues raised by the question, you will produce incomplete or irrelevant work. Make sure that your work answers the specific demands of the question through your 'interrogation' of its wording. Using key phrases from the question can help ensure that you are addressing the particular requirements of the question. To take a simple example:

The rule of law and the separation of powers are not significant features of the UK constitution. They are not consistently applied and do not perform key roles in limiting state power. Discuss.

The question contains key phrases, 'rule of law' and 'separation of powers' that identify the *subject matter* of the question. You will need to outline and illustrate these concepts. The other key phrases ('not significant features', 'not consistently applied', 'do not perform key roles') are *assertions*. You will need to think about whether these assertions are true and what evidence supports or contradicts them, e.g. is the separation of powers a significant feature of the UK constitution? What is the evidence for and against that proposition?

1.7.1.2 PLAN

You will need to plan the structure of your answer before you write the coursework. This will enable you to check that the structure is clear and logical, and that it addresses all the points raised by the question. It will also focus your further reading.

Introduction and conclusion – your introduction must indicate that you know what is required to answer the question and indicate how you will do so. Your conclusion must draw the threads of the argument together, summarise the answer and must not introduce new material or arguments. You may want to refer back to the terms of the question in your conclusion to show that you have stayed 'on track'.

Signposting the structure – your coursework needs to have a logical structure, with clearly distinct sections dealing with different aspects of the question. Unless you are told otherwise, you should not use numbered paragraphs and sub-paragraphs (as is common in reports), but it may be acceptable to use a limited number of headings. Otherwise, you should use linking phrases to produce a coherent narrative and to signpost the structure to the reader, e.g. 'Having outlined the traditional view of Parliamentary supremacy, the principal challenges to that view will be explored. First, the manner and form theory argues that . . .'

1.7.1.3 WRITE AND POLISH

See the guidance above on writing and proof-reading.

1.7.2 PROBLEM QUESTIONS

Problem questions are slightly less common in Public Law than in some other subjects such as Tort and Crime, but there is a good chance that you will be required to do some. The main assessment advice on problem questions in this book is integrated into Chapter 13, 'Grounds of judicial review', as this is where problem questions are most likely to be posed (although they also occur in human rights topics, and occasionally in other topics). To repeat its key message here, listen to your Public Law tutor on the approach they want you to take to problem questions, but commonly this will use the IRAC method. Remember that this involves:

> I – Issue: identify which issues arise from the problem scenario
> R – Rule: outline the relevant legal rules (from case law or statute)
> A – Application: apply those rules to the particular facts of the scenario
> C – Conclusion: answer the question, e.g. how would you advise your client?

1.7.3 EXAMS

Partly due to professional recognition reasons, exams remain as the most common method of assessment in Public Law. Again, refer to your tutor and to academic skills books for guidance, but some simple tips are:

Revision – you will need a schedule and to start as early as you can. There are lots of effective ways of revising, and in part it will depend on your preferred study style, but all effective methods involve actively engaging with your notes. Your first step will normally be consolidation, i.e. bringing your notes together from lectures, seminars and further reading and putting them into a coherent whole. You can then produce diagrams, mnemonics and flash cards. A particularly effective technique is condensing, i.e. working intensely with your 20–30 pages of notes to reduce them down to 5–6 sides whilst learning the detail behind the summary and then boiling down the 5–6 sides to one side of A4. This gives you a great visual map of the entire subject and by repetition and self-testing you can 'see' the detail behind the summary. The final stage in your revision should involve undertaking practice answers. You may be able to access past papers. Practice answers need to be done under exam conditions; you are honing your ability to write coherent, detailed answers in time-limited conditions with no notes.

1.7.3.1 COMMON ERRORS AND HOW TO AVOID THEM

- Fail to understand – i.e. simple factual mistakes. You avoid this through effective revision.
- Fail to write properly – you are writing under exam conditions, but all the rules and guidance on writing, grammar, structure and clarity (see above) are not just some academic hoops that tutors ask students to jump through. They allow one person to convey, in writing, their knowledge and understanding clearly to another person. If you do not pay attention to these features, then you will not be making the most of your hard work in revising the material.
- Fail to outline basic concepts – if you are doing a question e.g. on ouster clauses in judicial review, you know that you are going to have to outline what 'ouster clauses' are. Do not leave the process of deciding how you are going to do this and phrase this until you are sat in the examination hall. You can prepare some small building blocks of your answers in advance. You will need to deploy them flexibly and make sure they address the terms of the question, but doing this can increase your accuracy, detail and speed.
- Fail to use authority – the tutors assessing your work appreciate that you are writing exam answers without notes and they adjust their expectations. The similarities between coursework answers and exam answers, however, are stronger than the differences, including our expectation that you will use authority in your answers. You still need to use authority in exam answers. In a coursework, we would expect you to cite e.g. '*Attorney General v Fulham Corporation* [1921] 1 Ch 440', but in an exam, 'AG v Fulham Corp (1921)' would be good.
- Fail to provide detail – imagine that in an exam answer on the Human Rights Act 1998 you write two short sentences on section 3 of the HRA 1998. Is that enough? It depends on the context of the question, but the chances are – no. Your lecturer may have spent 20 minutes on this section alone, outlining its context, bringing out the different elements of the section, discussing its impact on judicial reasoning and illustrating its operation through case law examples. This textbook has 13 paragraphs, two detailed case outlines and reference to three further cases on section 3 of the

HRA. In your seminar on the subject, you will have been directed to further reading, e.g. a full article (D Nicol, 'Statutory Interpretation and Human Rights after Anderson' [2004] *Public Law* 274). Again, we know that you are pushed for time and writing without notes in exam conditions, but we do expect a good level of detail.

The chapter needs to finish, however, where we came in. Public Law is a fascinating and profoundly important subject – please enjoy it responsibly!

TAKING IT FURTHER

K McMillan and J Weyers, *The Study Skills Handbook* (Pearson, 2012) This is not a law book, but a key message from this chapter is that basic academic skills underpin much of academic success. This is the most practical general skills book, and if you refer to it through your programmes of study your academic life will be much improved.

E Finch and S Fafinski, *Legal Skills*, 4th edn (OUP, 2013) A very useful book-length treatment of material covered (very briefly, indeed) in this chapter and much more. This has a legal focus so is stronger than the McMillan and Weyers book on e.g. citation, use of legal sources and legal problem questions.

J Williams, 'New law student? Here's some advice from a recent law graduate', Public Law for Everyone blog, 2013, http://publiclawforeveryone.com/2013/10/15/new-law-student-heres-some-advice-from-a-recent-graduate/ This is in the form of a letter from a recent law graduate to his younger self – as a first-year law student setting out on his studies. It has some concise and very useful advice.

2

CHAPTER 2
INSTITUTIONS

This chapter has some rather particular objectives which govern its coverage and structure. The main objective is to give you a map. This will be largely textual, but it also includes diagrams. This mapping exercise aims to:

- introduce the main players in the drama that is Public Law
- map the structure of the state
- highlight the key relationships and processes.

It cannot afford then to get bogged down in detail, as you would not be able to see the wood for the trees. We will look at a *lot* of individual trees later, so the map is an overview – the whole of the wood.

The second group of objectives is to give you an understanding of the structure and functions of the executive (the Government, including the Prime Minister, Cabinet, the civil service and public bodies). It is rare to receive a Public Law assessment question solely on the Government or civil service. Nonetheless, examiners will assume that you are familiar with the composition and role of Government institutions when they are asking you about subjects such as the rule of law, separation of powers, prerogative powers, judicial review and human rights.

Some of you may already have a general sense of who does what and how things fit together in our constitutional system. Some of you will not. Do not worry; the broad outlines of the structure and the main roles of the players are easy enough to pick up – but do not skip this step. You can waste a great deal of time rereading material on later topics that is capable of being understood first time around if you know the structures and roles being discussed.

AS YOU READ

Many of the issues raised here are covered in depth in later chapters. When this is the case, there is a cross-reference and, usually, a simple recap. The chapter tries not to make assumptions about your previous knowledge, so some key concepts are simplified and basic terminology is explained. If you are already familiar with some of this, do not despair. There will be plenty of material to stretch your abilities in later chapters and you are still trying to get to grips with the general geography of the subject.

This is the key message to bear in mind as you read through this chapter. You should be aiming to get an overall picture of:

- Who does what in the UK state.
- A more detailed sense of what the role of the executive is, to help you develop a better understanding of later subjects.

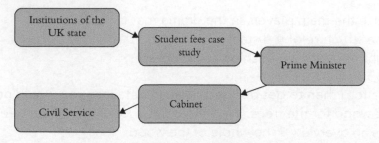

Figure 2.1 Structure of Chapter 2

2.1 ASSESSMENT TIPS

As explained above, specific questions on this area are rare, but the chapter will be very useful in helping you perform better in assessment of other topics. It addresses an issue that a number of Public Law students have raised over the years: their perception that this subject is abstract or divorced from the reality of their lives.

My colleagues who teach other subjects such as Contract Law or Criminal Law (the poor souls) have the disadvantage of dealing with material that is inherently less interesting than Public Law, but they do have one advantage. They can relate the legal rules of their subject to your daily life in a very accessible way. Contract Law teachers can get you to picture someone going into a shop to buy a chocolate bar so as to illuminate offer and acceptance. Criminal lawyers love to design hypothetical scenarios of various people aiming punches at each other to illustrate offences against the person.

Similar opportunities to ground Public Law in the realities of the daily life of their students are available to Public Law teachers, subject to two limits. First, you may all have the pleasure of receiving state benefits, getting student finance support and being issued with a driving licence and passport (and the pain of having to apply for all those things) plus, at some points in your life, brushes with the powers of public bodies such as the police, tax authorities, local authority planners etc. Some of you will join the public sector and exercise those powers. Not many of you though, I imagine, have current experience of explaining some Government scandal to the House of Commons or exercising prerogative powers to award honours to your friends. Secondly, to really get to grips with the law that relates to even those decisions that affect you directly, you need to understand who the public authorities are and the powers they are exercising.

So you will ultimately see (maybe not today, maybe not tomorrow, but soon and for the rest of your life) that Public Law surrounds you, affects so many elements of your day-to-day life, and structures so many important elements of the society you are living in. This process will be much easier if you can draw on the material in this chapter.

2.2 WHO'S WHO IN THE UK STATE (AND WHAT DO THEY DO?)

Many novels, of a certain vintage, have a list towards the very start of the book called *Dramatis Personae*. These are the players in the drama. The list is particularly useful in long engrossing novels with lots of characters; if you are halfway through and lose track of who is related to whom, you can flick back to the front and work out the relationships. So who are the *dramatis personae* of Public Law?

We will adopt the 'three branches' structure from the concept of the separation of powers – see Chapter 9. This divides the state into:

- A **legislative** branch whose main function is to make law.
- An **executive** branch whose main role is to both make policy and then implement (or execute) it.
- A **judicial** branch that applies the law to resolve legal disputes.

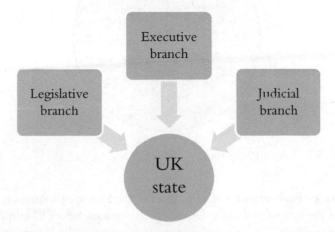

Figure 2.2 The three great branches of the state

2.3 LEGISLATIVE

The UK Parliament has three main components:

House of Commons – has 650 Members of Parliament chosen through General Elections which are normally held every five years. The MPs are organised into political parties. Their main roles are to make law (Acts of Parliament) by approving Bills proposed by the Government, and to try to hold the Government to account for its actions through questions and debates.

House of Lords – has around 800 peers (making it the second-largest legislative chamber in the world, after the National People's Congress of China). Most members are life peers appointed by the Government (in consultation with others), but there are still 26 bishops of the Church of England and up to 92 hereditary peers (who inherit their positions). Many members are arranged into political parties on similar lines to the House of Commons, but the House of Lords has a significant independent element. Its role is formally similar to the House of Commons – to pass laws and scrutinise Government actions. It has much less power than the Commons, but its greater independence and collective wisdom are thought to be strengths.

The Queen in Parliament – this is the third element of Parliament and involves the granting of the royal assent to Bills that have been passed by the other Houses. This step is needed for a Bill to become an Act of Parliament, but there is no personal discretion for the Queen, and assent is virtually automatic.

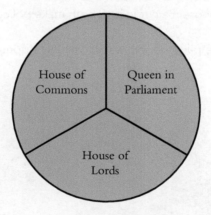

Figure 2.3 The elements of Parliament

Other elements of Parliament – the Speakers of the House of Commons and House of Lords administer Parliament and chair debates. Parliamentary Select Committees play a very important role in holding Government to account. They specialise in particular subjects and call witnesses, including ministers, to give evidence before them, and they publish influential reports.

Secondary legislation – the most important legal provisions are introduced in Acts of Parliament, but the largest volume of new legal rules is found in secondary legislation. The authority to make this lower level of legislation comes from Acts of Parliament that grant power to legislate to e.g. Government ministers via statutory instruments or local authorities through bye-laws.

2.4 EXECUTIVE

This branch includes the Government, civil service and public bodies.

Prime minister – is the leading political figure in the country. They are the leader of the political party or coalition that has the support of the House of Commons. Their role is to head the Government and to chair the Cabinet. They have wide powers of patronage (i.e. deciding who to appoint to important roles). They play a central role in policy-making and setting the legislative agenda. They represent the country in foreign affairs and direct the whole country's response to major events such as security threats from overseas.

Cabinet – is a group of around 22 senior ministers, including the Prime Minister, who decide major policy matters. Cabinet ministers will usually lead Government departments and so have a role in implementing policy, e.g. on defence or education.

Other ministers – outside of the cabinet there are ministers of state and parliamentary private secretaries. They work on policy matters and liaise with Parliament under the direction of the Prime Minister and the relevant cabinet minister.

Civil service – consists of around 500,000 administrative and professional staff who service central Government departments. This can involve helping ministers develop policies and legal proposals, delivering services directly to the public and general management of the public sector.

Public bodies – many public services (such as running prisons or granting passports) are not delivered by central Government departments themselves but by other public bodies. This category is very varied and covers hundreds of Government agencies and non-departmental public bodies. Private companies are now extensively involved in providing public services under contract, such as transporting prisoners to court hearings and undertaking assessment of those claiming disability benefits. The armed forces, police forces and customs officers are further examples of public bodies.

Local government – most of England has two layers of local government. County councils are responsible for services such as education and waste management, transport, social services and libraries. District councils regulate e.g. planning, public housing, waste collection and cemeteries. In some areas, these functions are exercised by a unitary authority. Large metropolitan areas (e.g. Birmingham), Scotland and Wales have single-tier or unitary authorities but they have similar responsibilities and powers to the two-tier system. London has its own arrangements but its local authorities, again, have similar duties and powers. Northern Ireland has a single tier of local government but with much more limited powers.

Local authorities play an important role in delivering public services. They derive their powers from statute and can make some local laws. They have elected members who are supported by local authority staff.

Overall, these relationships are not strictly hierarchical, but this visual does provide a sense of the numbers at each level and of the relative power relationships.

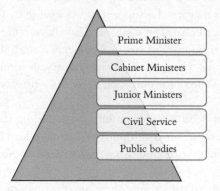

Prime Minister

Cabinet Ministers

Junior Ministers

Civil Service

Public bodies

Figure 2.4 The executive

2.5 JUDICIAL

Courts – you will cover the general courts hierarchy in detail in Lawyer's Skills, Legal System or a similar module. Of particular interest to Public Lawyers is the Administrative Division of the High Court, which hears legal claims against the Government and public bodies ('judicial review' actions). Public Law raises issues of great public importance, so the Court of Appeal and Supreme Court often decide Public Law cases.

Tribunals – hear a large volume of Public Law disputes on issues as varied as school admissions, welfare payments and release from mental health custody. In day-to-day practice, tribunals are arguably more important than courts in resolving Public Law issues. There is a first-tier tribunal divided into subject-specific chambers such as health, education and social care, social entitlement (covering e.g. child support), and tax. An upper tribunal hears appeals.

Personnel – these are the judges, magistrates and tribunal members that staff the judicial branch. They must, apart from magistrates and some tribunal panel members, be legally qualified. Of great importance from a Public Law perspective is that they are independent of Parliament and the executive. This independence is guaranteed by e.g. their security of tenure and their selection by an independent Judicial Appointments Commission.

European Court of Human Rights – is based in Strasbourg and hears cases brought by citizens against a state, alleging breach of the European Convention on Human Rights. It is unusual for international courts to allow access to private individuals. The judges come from 47 members of the Council of Europe. Its human rights judgments are not directly binding within the UK legal system, but UK courts are required to take them into account and in most (but not all) cases the Government and Parliament act to amend the law to give effect to a judgment.

2.6 OTHER INSTITUTIONS

There are some institutions that do not fall easily within this three-part division.

Ombudsmen – hear complaints about poor administration (rather than legal disputes) by public bodies including Government departments. They are part of the system of administrative justice but are not in the judicial branch. A very large proportion of their findings are accepted by public bodies, e.g. to pay compensation, to apologise, etc. There is a Parliamentary Ombudsman, and ombudsman services for local government and the devolved nations.

Monarch – in some senses the monarch is a part of all three branches (the Queen in Parliament, Her Majesty's Government, Her Majesty's Courts), but the Queen has very limited personal constitutional powers. Most of the legal powers that formally reside with the Queen (e.g. to grant mercy to prisoners) are in reality 'Crown prerogatives' exercised by the Government.

Devolved institutions – one of the most striking Public Law developments in recent decades has been the progress of devolution in Scotland, Wales and Northern Ireland. This means that these component parts of the United Kingdom have greater legal and policy powers over certain subjects. There is a Scottish Parliament and Assemblies for Wales and Northern Ireland, which have primary law-making powers. The Scottish Parliament can legislate on a range of issues including education, health and environmental protection, and it has tax-varying powers. The Welsh and Northern Irish Assemblies have similar but slightly more limited powers. Devolution has an executive as well as a legislative dimension. Each country has its own government to formulate and apply policies on devolved matters. Devolution in the UK is highly asymmetrical, meaning that powers differ from country to country and there is currently limited devolution in England.

European Union – at the time of writing the UK is still a part of the European Union, although the Brexit referendum result and the subsequent triggering of Article 50 means that it is set to depart the Union by the end of March 2019. The key institutions of the EU are discussed in detail in Chapter 8, 'Supremacy and the European Union'. In this mapping process, we will just pick out the fact, so long as the UK remains an EU Member State, EU law takes priority over conflicting national law, even over Acts of Parliament.

This is the landscape within which Public Law operates and the cast of characters who play the main roles.

2.7 CASE STUDY ON LAW AND POLICY IN THE UK STATE

One of the major aims of this book is that you do not simply *receive* information on a topic. It tries to highlight what you should *be able to do* with that knowledge and how to integrate subject knowledge with academic skills. This will help you with assessments, but more broadly it should help you develop a deeper understanding of the material. One of the key tools for doing this is simply to apply knowledge to a scenario.

This case study is on the legal and policy changes involved in raising student fees for higher education courses – I wanted to choose something of direct relevance to you. It is difficult to think of a more direct example of how Public Law and policy-making affect important aspects of your life. This focuses on the English position, as the university fees regime differs from country to country in the UK, but we do outline the differential position of Welsh, Scottish and Northern Irish residents in this chapter and there is a full chapter on devolution to look forward to later (Chapter 11, 'Devolution'). The devolved institutions have gone through similar processes of policy-making and legislating to establish their own fees regimes.

2.8 STUDENT FEES

Background – The Teaching and Higher Education Act 1998 introduced university tuition fees of £1,000 per year in England. The fee cap was raised by the Higher Education Act 2004 and fees had increased to around £3,300 per year by 2010. The Conservative Party election manifesto in 2010 committed the party, rather cagily, to considering implementing the Browne Review (see below), which had not yet been published. Infamously, the Liberal Democrats had not only made abolition of tuition fees a part of their manifesto, but most of their MPs had publicly signed a National Union of Students pledge that they would vote against any fee increases. Following the 2010 General Election, the Conservative and Liberal Democrat parties formed a coalition that held a majority in the House of Commons and therefore could form a Government.

The debates around student fees were complex and wide-ranging but took into account that the large expansion in student numbers of the previous 20 years had to be paid for, that universities needed more income to be able to compete with competitors on a global scale and that university graduates earned significantly more on average than those who did not attend university. It appeared that fears that fees would discourage applicants from poorer families had not been borne out in the previous 12 years. On the other hand, a larger rise in fees might have that effect on poorer applicants; society as a whole benefits from an educated workforce (and so should contribute to funding) and higher fees would place large debts on graduates for much of their working life.

The policy-making phase – we saw above that this is the role of Government.

A Cabinet minister, supported by junior ministers and civil servants, will take the lead on developing detailed policy proposals.

EXPLAINING THE LAW

The initial Coalition Agreement agreed to wait until a major independent review of university funding was published before producing fees proposals. This Browne Review was published later in the year and recommended the removal of the cap on student fees. The Government, in particular the Secretary of State for Business, Innovation and Skills (Vince Cable, now Sir Vince) and the Universities Minister (David Willetts) had to discuss the report, look at further research and formulate proposals to take to Parliament. They were advised by civil servants and special advisers. The proposal they developed had a significantly increased cap of £9,000 per annum, but more generous repayment terms for students.

The law-making phase – we have seen that this is primarily a role for Parliament but also that there is wide scope for ministers to make law through delegated legislation.

EXPLAINING THE LAW

The Higher Education Act 2004 already included powers to increase tuition fees, so the Government did not have to introduce a new Act of Parliament to put the policy into law – it could use secondary legislation. The changes did, however, have to be approved by votes in the House of Commons and House of Lords.

The proposals were approved with a majority of 21 in the House of Commons. Three junior members of the Government voted against the measures, and therefore had to resign under the convention of Collective Cabinet Responsibility (see below). The House of Lords also approved the proposals.

The policy implementing phase – we have seen that implementation is an executive function. It falls to Government and the civil service, but in practice it is often undertaken by public bodies or contracted out to private companies.

EXPLAINING THE LAW

The Student Loans Company (SLC) had been established in the 1990s to issue loans and collect repayments. It administers the Student Finance England system including loans to cover tuition fees. It is a public body and a Government-owned organisation (with part-ownership by the devolved administrations). It has a Chief Executive Officer and a Board, and operates under a framework agreement with a Government ministry. Since 2016 this is the Department for Education which has a continuing responsibility, e.g. for changes to interest rates on loans. In 2013–14, the SLC gave support to almost one million applicants and awarded loans or grants of £11,098 million.

Under the devolution settlement, higher education law and policy are controlled by the devolved administrations in Scotland, Wales and Northern Ireland. Each has taken a very different approach from the English policy on tuition fees questions. The Scottish Parliament abolished Scottish university fees for eligible Scottish domiciled students in 2000. Universities get their funding via direct grant from the Scottish Government. The Welsh Assembly allows Welsh universities to charge £9,000 in fees, but an eligible Welsh student pays £4,046 and the remainder is paid by the Welsh Government. The fees regime established by the Northern Ireland Assembly allows fees of £3,925 for Northern Irish students.

The control and review phase – this includes political, administrative and legal controls. We have seen that Parliament's duties include holding the Government to account, the Ombudsman plays a role in administrative justice and courts exercise legal controls.

Political controls – the Secretary of State for Education and the Minister for Universities will have to answer any questions about the fees regime at ministerial Question Time in the House of Commons. The Secretary of State is responsible under a constitutional convention of Individual Ministerial Responsibility for all that happens in their department. This responsibility extends, to some degree, to public bodies, so the minister would have to account for the operation of the Student Loans Company. The ministers could face more detailed and effective questioning by the House of Commons Select Committee on Education. This committee could also call in civil servants and staff of the SLC to give evidence. These political questions might cover the overall wisdom of the scheme, the impact on e.g. social mobility, and the operational effectiveness of the public body.

Administrative controls – these try to resolve disputes and promote good governance without recourse to litigation. The SLC has an internal complaints procedure. If this fails to resolve the issue, it can be escalated up to an independent assessor (appointed by the Department for Education), and there is a final formal appeal. In addition, those who feel they have suffered injustice as a result of maladministration by the SLC can complain to the Parliamentary Ombudsman who can investigate and recommend some form of recompense for affected individuals (see Chapter 14).

Legal controls – Judicial review is the main legal tool for challenging the actions of public bodies. The courts are limited to reviewing whether the public body has acted lawfully (rather than adjudging whether it has reached the right decision), but a successful action can quash an unlawful decision. The courts cannot judicially review Acts of Parliament, but the fees change was introduced by secondary legislation which can be challenged. There was such a challenge before the High Court in 2012, arguing that the rules breached human rights and equality laws. The courts found there were some limited procedural defects but refused to quash the rules.[1] Student Finance England have some discretion on how they exercise their powers, and if they act unlawfully in how they make a funding decision then that would be susceptible to judicial review.

Figure 2.5 Reviewing executive action

KEY LEARNING POINTS

- A wide range of institutions contribute to the constitutional system and the operation of the state.
- Most can be placed within one of three branches: legislative, executive or judicial.
- On a single subject, we can see the interplay between the different institutions so as to develop policy, put it into law, administer it and ensure that its operations are reviewed and held to account.

1 'Tuition fees case: Callum Hurley and Katy Moore lose', *BBC News*, 17 February 2012, http://www.bbc.co.uk/news/education-17069298 (last accessed 05/11/17).

2.9 THE STRUCTURE OF GOVERNMENT

The Government is at the head of the executive. Executive power is wide-ranging but at its heart is policy-making and policy implementing.

Policy-making, as we saw in the student fees example above, involves both research and evidenced-based approaches and the ability to give effect to one's political preferences. When the Government designs proposals to address an issue, any changes may be purely administrative and not involve legal reforms, or they may be within the remit of existing legal powers (for example a change of approach to planning applications for major supermarket developments). Some proposals, however, will involve changes to the law. In these cases, the Government will draft Bills, put them to Parliament, and with a compliant House of Commons and relatively weak House of Lords can normally expect to see them passed into legislation, i.e. in practice the Government is the most powerful part of the state.

Policy implementing, in an effective system, is the necessary counterpart to policy-making. Policy statements and even Acts of Parliament are empty words unless they are capable of being applied and enforced in the real world.

APPLYING THE LAW

A student fees and loans policy is useless unless there is some organisation like the Student Loans Company to assess, deliver and recover student loans. The same goes for a policy on the requirement for a driving licence (it requires a DVLA to issue licences, the police to investigate drivers who have no licence, the Crown Prosecution Service to bring charges before the courts). We can see, therefore, that policy implementing also includes enforcement activities, whether that is the police, or the Environment Agency addressing pollution incidents, or the Health and Safety Executive (which despite all the newspaper stories about 'health and safety gone mad' actually does a good job of stopping working people from getting seriously injured or killed in the workplace).

In Chapters 4 and 5 we point to the legal gap – one might say the gaping void – at the heart of the UK constitutional system. That is, the absence of legal regulation of the role of the Government and very particularly that of the Prime Minister and Cabinet. In Maitland's striking phrase, the law 'does not recognise [the executive] – knows nothing about it'. There seems to be a disconnect between:

■ How important these institutions are – the Prime Minister is the political leader of the whole country. Their role is set out below, but it includes setting the main policy and law agenda and responding to threats to national security from terrorism or war. The traditional label for our whole system of government is 'Cabinet Government'. This means that, you, I and the rest of the country are supposed to have the most important public-policy decisions affecting our lives decided by the members of the Cabinet sat in the Cabinet Room – how much tax we pay, the shape and operation of our educational and health services, etc.

AND

■ The absence of legal authorisations (granting powers) or legal controls (imposing limits or scrutiny requirements) or even recognition of these governmental institutions. The rare exceptions, for example the Ministerial and Other Salaries Act 1975 which mentions the Prime Minister and Cabinet only so that it can regulate their pay, illustrate rather than disprove the point.

2.10 PRIME MINISTER

Selection – the way in which Prime Ministers are chosen is covered in detail in Chapter 5, 'Constitutional conventions'. As a quick recap, the PM is appointed by the Queen but not as a matter of personal choice; it is governed by constitutional convention. The constitutional rule is that the leader of the political party that can command the confidence of the House of Commons has to be appointed as Prime Minister. 'Confidence' means that the party, or coalition, can command enough support to get the important parts of their programme accepted. Where there is a hung Parliament, i.e. no overall majority, then the parties are left to decide themselves what type of coalition to agree and who will lead it. In 2010, David Cameron and Nick Clegg, as leaders of the Conservative and Liberal Democrat parties, negotiated the key points of the agreement that would allow them to form a coalition with a combined majority of MPs. Once that agreement was announced, the Queen had to appoint Cameron as PM. Similarly, in 2017 when Theresa May informed the Queen that she had an agreement with the Democratic Unionist Party that would allow her to pass the important parts of her legislative programme, even as a minority government, then she had to be appointed Prime Minister.

It follows from the above and is clear by constitutional convention that the PM must be a member of the House of Commons. The last PM from the House of Lords was the Marquess of Salisbury (1895–1902), and it would now be constitutionally unacceptable to have a Prime Minister who was not from the elected chamber.

Role – the Prime Minister's role is, given their position as the leading political figure in the country, curiously hard to pin down. This is because we cannot point to a constitutional document that lists their legal powers. The PM actually has relatively few distinct legal powers. Their authority comes mainly through their political mandate (they led the party that won the election), through their public profile and the operation of their party machine and through patronage (i.e. powers of appointment).

The Prime Minister has the power to appoint all the other ministers of the Government. This extends to asking them to be reshuffled to another department, asking them to resign and, ultimately, to dismissing them. This is actually a Crown power (called a prerogative) but it is exercised wholly by the PM rather than by the Queen. There is no legal restraint on the power, and the only constitutional constraint is that a minister must be a Member of the House of Commons or House of Lords. This power of patronage also covers other appointments, such as senior civil servants, and the Parliamentary Ombudsman.

The Prime Minister manages the overall Government agenda and operations, including the structure of Government departments and the allocation of policy areas between those departments. Even a Prime Minister who is relatively weak (see below) is only weak *relative to other PMs*. In their relations with the Cabinet (who, remember, were all appointed by the Prime Minister) they can still set the agenda, sum up the meeting and decide which important decisions are to be taken outside of Cabinet (in a way that they can entirely control).

Prime Ministers issue instructions and set the tone on what is the 'public face' of the Government. This aspect of governing, i.e. its media messages and public relations, has grown in importance. Tony Blair's Director of Communications, Alastair Campbell, famously went to great lengths to ensure that Labour ministers and MPs were 'on message' with the Prime Minister's agenda. Ministers were required to work to tightly scripted messages so as to control the 'news cycle'. This process has been central to all governments since 1997 and was an important aspect of most of the preceding ones.

The Government has retained a limited but important store of legal powers that it does not derive from Parliament. These are the Crown prerogatives that were originally exercised by the Monarch. Which Government minister is responsible for exercising prerogative decisions depends on the subject matter (the Secretary of State for Justice will lead decisions on the prerogative of mercy), but the most important prerogative powers are largely in the hands of the PM. We have covered patronage and the appointment of ministers already, but the list also includes agreeing to international agreements, and foreign and diplomatic relations, and the award of honours.

APPLYING THE LAW

This is an illustration of the types of functions that the Prime Minister performs across a few days. The week in 2015, chosen at random, was busy and involved particularly important issues but is not so unusual as to be unrepresentative. This list is not at all exhaustive of the PM's commitments during this week.

28 November – Commonwealth Heads of Government Meeting, Malta, focusing on anti-extremism and corruption. Appointment of a new International Development Secretary following the resignation of Grant Shapps, who took responsibility for not addressing serious bullying within the party's youth wing.

29 November – Discussion with the President of the European Council on plans for renegotiation of EU rules, or their applicability to the UK, in advance of an in/out referendum on EU membership.

1 December – Speech to COP21 summit on climate change in Paris, potentially one of the most important international meetings in history. The PM will also have signed off on UK strategy in the negotiations. Cabinet meeting to agree the motion for the Syria debate.

2 December – 10-hour debate in the House of Commons on a motion to agree to a UK air campaign against Islamic State in Syria.

The Prime Minister does not have a Government department. Since departments, with their budgets, research staff and press officers can be a source of power, this could be seen as a disadvantage, but effective support is provided by the Cabinet Office and a Private Office. This is headed by a Chief of Staff and includes a Policy Unit, Strategy Unit and Press Office.

2.11 CABINET AND MINISTERS

The relationship between the Prime Minister and Cabinet is not governed at all by law and hardly at all by constitutional convention. It depends very strongly on variable factors such as individual personalities and the size of the Parliamentary majority. A 'strong' (which may be a polite way of saying 'domineering') PM such as Thatcher or Blair tends to reduce the role of Cabinet as a collective decision-making body. Margaret Thatcher gave early notice of her approach in 1979: 'As Prime Minister I cannot waste time having any internal arguments.'[2] A more collegiate (which may be a polite way of saying 'weaker') PM will tend to rely more on the input of Cabinet colleagues. This is the classic idea of the PM as *primus inter pares* (the first amongst equals), although the days of anyone genuinely believing that major policies are collectively decided by 20-odd people sat around an oval table in the Cabinet Room are long gone.

2.11.1 CABINET

In the vintage phrase of Walter Bagehot, the Cabinet is 'a hyphen which joins, a buckle which fastens the legislative part of the state to the executive part of the state'. Bagehot is pointing out that the Cabinet draws all of its membership from the legislative part of the state (Parliament), and it largely controls Parliament. This overlap or connection between

---

2   *The Observer*, 25 February 1979, as cited in A Carroll, *Constitutional and Administrative Law*, 6th edn (Longman, 2011) 237.

Cabinet and Parliament means that very broadly speaking (and whilst recognising the role of opposition parties and the House of Lords), the relationship can be seen as a joint venture. This constitutional arrangement is said to produce strong government capable of enacting its proposals as law. The situation contrasts with the US where the legislature (Congress) is formally separated from the executive (the President). This means that different political parties can control these different parts of the state, and if they disagree on important provisions (such as extending national debt), this can lead to the sort of deadlock which caused the shutdown of the whole US federal government for over two weeks in 2013.

The Haldane Committee 1918 (Cmnd 9230) saw the main role of Cabinet as making 'the final determination of policy to be submitted to Parliament'. But the real position is more complex and more fluid. We need to distinguish between decisions *made* by Cabinet and decisions made elsewhere and merely reported to or considered by Cabinet. The latter are much more common. Decisions wholly within the remit of individual departments tend to be made within that department and simply reported. There is a whole system of Cabinet Committees that can resolve interdepartmental disputes outside of the full Cabinet. Prime Ministers can develop policies through informal groups of favoured ministers (so-called sofa government).

There are also issues of time and process. The Cabinet tended to meet twice weekly, but Margaret Thatcher reduced this in the 1980s to a weekly meeting, and this is the more common practice now. There simply isn't time for Cabinet to debate and make decisions on most policy issues. The PM controls the Cabinet agenda, and Cabinet rarely votes on a proposal. The preference is for the PM to pick up on the feeling within the room and to summarise the outcome of a discussion. This gives further power to the PM.

Composition – there are no legal rules on the composition of Cabinet. Under the Ministerial and other Salaries Act 1975, only 22 people can be paid as Cabinet Ministers, including the PM. It is common to appoint some additional Cabinet attendees, but they have to get by without a Cabinet ministerial salary. By constitutional convention, Cabinet members must be Members of the Commons or the Lords.

It might be useful to give you a picture of the posts that hold full Cabinet positions (as of July 2017).[3] The titles of most of these positions are Secretary of State for . . . (e.g. Defence, Transport). Most of these people also lead Government departments, so the list also gives you an indication of the structure of government and the scope of its work.

In addition, there are eight people who may attend Cabinet, such the Chief Secretary to the Treasury.

How much choice does the PM have over appointments in practice? This list of positions does represent what we would expect to see, that is, the PM has some limited choice over

---

3   UK Government, 'Ministers', https://www.gov.uk/government/ministers (last accessed 05/11/17).

Prime Minister	First Secretary of State
Chancellor of the Exchequer	Home Secretary
Foreign Secretary	Exiting the European Union
Justice/Lord Chancellor	Defence
Work and Pensions	Health
International Trade	Education
Work and Pensions	International Development
Business, Energy and Industrial Strategy	Leader, House of Lords
Transport	Environment, Food and Rural Affairs
Northern Ireland	Scotland
Communities and Local Government	Wales
Chancellor of the Duchy of Lancaster	Digital, Culture, Media and Sport

Figure 2.6 Cabinet posts, 2017

Cabinet seats for less important roles, but it would be unthinkable to exclude not only the three great offices of state (Chancellor of the Exchequer, Foreign Secretary, Home Secretary) but also other important ministerial positions such as Health or Defence. There should also be some limited representation from the House of Lords (there was only one member of the House of Lords in the October 2017 Cabinet).

Of course, it is still up to the PM to choose whom they appoint to these positions, but even here they will not have a completely free hand. Certain colleagues will have such stature within the party that they will be difficult to avoid. There is a further need to have some balance between the differing political wings of the party and from different regions. The representation of women in Cabinet has been increasingly important; the figure of six women out of twenty-three Cabinet posts in 2017 still amounts to under-representation, but is some progress on most previous Cabinets.

The Cabinet is supported by the Cabinet Office. This might seem to be simple administrative support, but the Office has real power in its role in officially recording outcomes from Cabinet and in advising on aspects of the various Codes (Ministerial Code, Civil Service Code) that regulate the behaviour of those in Government.

EXPLAINING THE LAW – CABINET COMMITTEES

The Cabinet is the tip of the iceberg of governmental policy-making and decision-making, and, as well as those decisions taken entirely within a single department, there is a large volume of work undertaken by Cabinet Committees. This system has a complex structure, but recent Governments have at least published their number, membership and remit.[4] There are around 10 main committees or taskforces, some of which are chaired by the PM. The Economic Affairs Committee has the deceptively simple remit of considering 'issues relating to the economy'. It is chaired by the Chancellor of the Exchequer, contains most of the important Cabinet Ministers and takes hugely important decisions. Cabinet Committees take much of the burden of work away from Cabinet itself, whilst all of Government is bound by their decisions. The structure and composition of these committees is again within the patronage of the PM, and this adds to the power of their office.

2.11.2 MINISTERS

You might think that a rational system would be to call all members of Cabinet 'Ministers', so there would be a Finance Minister, a Home Affairs Minister etc. The UK constitutional system, as you will see, does not put great store by rational design, but has preferred organic and pragmatic evolution. The various offices have developed over centuries and many have retained their distinctive titles, so instead we have a Chancellor of the Exchequer and a Secretary of State for the Home Department, as well as curiosities such as the President of the Board of Trade (who doubles as the Business Secretary) and the Chancellor of the Duchy of Lancaster who has almost no departmental responsibilities.

There is a further curiosity. Acts of Parliament often grant powers to 'the Secretary of State', but the use of the definite article 'the' rather than the indefinite 'a' is misleading. Historically there was one post of Secretary of State, but it became the practice to appoint one person to handle internal affairs (which became the Home Secretary) and one for external affairs (which became the Foreign Secretary). There are now multiple Secretaries of State (e.g. for Justice, Education, Health, Defence). Powers are not granted to specific ministers, and whilst it may be obvious from the subject matter who is the most appropriate Secretary of State (e.g. schools → Education), the powers can be transferred by the PM between ministers without any legal change.

Figure 2.7 Ministers

4   UK Government, 'Cabinet Committees', https://www.gov.uk/government/publications/the-cabinet-committees-system-and-list-of-cabinet-committees (last accessed 05/11/17).

There are three main ranks of ministers.

- Cabinet ministers – have the highest ranking. They sit in Cabinet and normally lead major departments.
- Junior ministers – work under the direction of Cabinet ministers. They can be called Ministers of State or Under Secretaries of State. This middle rank includes some important responsibilities, such as the Ministers of State for Universities, for Schools, for Employment, for the Armed Forces.
- Parliamentary Private Secretaries (PPSs) – these are the most junior ministers whose main role is in liaising between Government departments and Parliament.

A limit is imposed by the House of Commons (Disqualification) Act 1975, so that only 95 ministers can come from the House of Commons. Ministers have an obligation to support Government proposals, so this rule seeks to limit the effects of block voting.

The duties and expected standards of conduct of ministers are set out in the Ministerial Code, the latest version of which was published in 2010 (revised in 2016).[5] This is not a legal document, but it includes rules that have the force of (non-legal) constitutional conventions. It lists some key principles:

- Collective responsibility for Government decisions.
- To account to Parliament for their department's policies, decisions and actions; to give accurate and truthful information to Parliament; and to be as open as possible with Parliament and the public.
- To require civil servants to give accurate and truthful evidence to Parliamentary committees; to uphold civil service impartiality; and not to use Government resources for party political purposes.
- To avoid conflicts of interest; and not to accept compromising gifts or hospitality; and to keep separate their ministerial and constituency MP roles.

2.11.3 GOVERNMENT DEPARTMENTS

There is flexibility as to the size and shape of Government departments and how they are led; there are 25 departments in central Government. They map fairly closely to the list of Cabinet posts outlined above. The most powerful single department is the Treasury because it has the main say on the budgets of all other departments. The Department for Work and Pensions is the largest department as measured by budget and number of employees. Again, their role is to assist ministers in formulating policies and then implementing them (although much of the delivery of public services has been delegated to other public bodies or private providers).

It is possible to have one minister heading multiple departments (this is always the case with the Chancellor of the Exchequer – the Treasury and HM Revenue and Customs), whilst

---

5   UK Government, 'Ministerial Code', https://www.gov.uk/government/publications/ministerial-code (last accessed 05/11/17).

bodies which do not seem to be departments (because they are not called the Department of X or Ministry of Y) can still be led by a Cabinet Minister, e.g. the Wales Office. There is no clear distinction between Government departments or any of the other myriad varieties of public body. Conceptually, it is all something of a mess. You might object that it works in practice, but one response to that could be that 'it works *to some extent* in practice'. A more regularised system of structuring Government may well work even better in practice.

Most of the powers of Government departments are granted to them by Acts of Parliament. The Department for Communities and Local Government, for example, exercises planning powers derived from the Town and Country Planning Acts. It can use these powers to issue guidance on e.g. wind farms, or to call in planning applications to be decided by departmental inspectors or the Secretary of State themselves.

EXPLAINING THE LAW – DELEGATED LEGISLATION

Parliament can also grant powers to Government ministers to make secondary or delegated legislation. Powers of delegated legislation are covered in the next chapter. The idea is that the parent Act of Parliament sets out the framework, objectives, criteria and processes of the particular scheme. Ministers can later fill out the details of the scheme by delegated legislation but must do so in a way that is consistent with the parent Act. For example, the Wildlife and Countryside Act 1981 protects various animal and plant species. The level of protection depends on the risk to the species which depends on many variables, in particular, the size and robustness of the species population. It would be unrealistic to amend the Act itself to address each change in population status of each protected species. The Act therefore gives the Secretary of State the power to update the lists of protected species in the Annexes to the Act via delegated legislation.

This is all entirely sensible, but delegated legislation can go further, and so-called Henry VIII clauses allow ministers to use delegated legislation to amend or even repeal Acts of Parliament. Elliott and Thomas give the example of the Civil Contingencies Act 2004 which allows ministers to make regulations in an emergency, where there is a threat of serious damage to the environment, to human welfare or to security. The regulations can e.g. authorise the destruction of property without compensation or prohibit travel, and can disapply any Act of Parliament (even one passed after 2004) to achieve this.[6] There is considerable unease about the width of these sorts of powers that could allow the executive to usurp the legislative function.

---

6   M Elliott and R Thomas, *Public Law*, 3rd edn (OUP, 2017) 143.

2.11.4 PUBLIC BODIES

We examined an example of a public body, the Student Loans Company, in the case study above. Again, there is no coherent category, or categories, of public body. They include public corporations, e.g. the BBC, and non-departmental public bodies, e.g. the Higher Education Funding Council. Other high-profile public bodies are the Benefits Agency, the Driver and Vehicle Licensing Agency, and the UK Passport Agency.

It was the case that central Government departments were very large and had multiple functions, especially in assisting policy-making and providing direct support to the minister. It was argued that it was therefore inefficient and cumbersome to make them responsible for implementing policy. A hugely influential report, 'Improving Management in Government: The Next Steps' (1988) recommended that implementation functions were split from central Government departments. They ought to be applied by agencies one step removed from the Government department. The continuing relationship between the department and the public body was to be managed under a framework document setting out performance objectives. Each next step agency would have a chief executive who would be responsible for meeting these objectives.

2.12 CONTROLS ON EXECUTIVE POWER

Writing in the 1970s, the leading Conservative politician, Lord Hailsham, said that the UK executive had become an 'elective dictatorship'.[7] He meant that whilst governments were subject to electoral approval every five years, in the intervening years there was a dangerous concentration of power, with very few effective checks and balances on Government action. Whilst this chapter is principally about mapping the institutions of the UK state and describing the executive in more detail, we should take the opportunity to assess Lord Hailsham's criticism, not least because it addresses a central theme of this whole book – the need for effective controls on state power. You will be exploring this theme in many subject areas where the power of the executive is an important consideration.

Because a person only gets to become Prime Minister if they lead the political party that can control a majority of votes in the House of Commons, it is written into the selection criteria for the Government that it is able to control and dominate Parliament.

The single largest factor that reinforces this control is party discipline. A very large majority of MPs in the ruling party can be relied upon to vote in support of Government measures for a very large proportion of the time. Government proposals are likely to broadly reflect their political preferences, but there is also the effect of natural loyalty to their party and to

---

7   Lord Hailsham, *The Dilemma of Democracy* (Collins, 1978).

their colleagues. Ambition and the possibility of advancement to a ministerial post further encourages loyalty, and the parties also use the whipping system. Whips are party officials who will encourage, cajole and even threaten MPs to vote in line with party wishes. The strength of the compulsion stretches from a free vote, where MPs are free to vote according to their conscience, to three-line whips where failure to obey party orders is a serious internal offence.

Despite the factors which concentrate power in the hands of the Government, and especially the Prime Minister, there are limits. A Prime Minister will ultimately need to retain the support of their fellow ministers and MPs, of their wider party and (to an admittedly vague degree) the citizens themselves. The most spectacular fall from grace in modern times was the rejection by the Conservative Party of their long-term, and electorally successful, leader Margaret Thatcher in 1990.

Whilst the UK constitutional system does concentrate power in the hands of Government, it also includes mechanisms for control and scrutiny of governmental actions:

Democratic and political controls – there is an official Opposition party and other political parties who will scrutinise the executive from within Parliament, and test proposals through Parliamentary debate. Governments have to be aware of the risk of backbench rebellion (their own MPs voting against them), whilst the House of Lords has limited powers but is more independent of Government and can delay proposals. The Prime Minister and other ministers are required to present themselves for questions before Parliament on a very regular basis (Prime Minister's Questions takes place each Wednesday at midday). Parliamentary Select Committees have emerged as an effective method of holding ministers to account and subjecting them to detailed investigation and questioning. Effective scrutiny requires access to Government data which is supported by the Freedom of Information Act 2000. More widely, a free press and free and fair elections are essential components of democratic and political controls.

Constitutional principles – although these are not directly enforceable in law, they can be very influential. The concept of the *rule of law* states that government is limited by law, that it must respect the law and must act with lawful authority. More broadly, the laws that governments rely on should be clear, open and prospective. The principle of the *separation of powers* provides that dangerous concentrations of power should be avoided and there should be a balance between the different powers that are held by the different parts of the state.

Administrative justice – this covers processes for examining Government action including internal appeals, the ombudsman services that can investigate complaints of poor administration, and tribunals that hear appeals against public bodies on legal issues.

Judicial review – these are legal proceedings where the courts hear allegations that ministers or public bodies have acted unlawfully, e.g. by going beyond their powers. They can be very effective because courts have the authority to quash executive decisions, but the basis for review is rather narrow.

2.13 CIVIL SERVICE

There is no satisfactory definition of the civil service or of civil servants. Perhaps the best working approach is that a civil servant is 'a servant of the Crown working in a civil capacity which is not: the holder of a political (or judicial) office'.[8] This approach excludes the police and armed forces (because they are not civil), local government and NHS staff (because they are not servants of the Crown) and ministers and judges (who hold political or judicial office). The civil service was only given a statutory basis by the Constitutional Reform and Governance Act 2010, but Crown prerogative legal powers are still important in its operations.

Employment status – civil servants are employed at the pleasure of the Crown under the royal prerogative. This means that they cannot normally sue under common law for breach of their employment contract, but if dismissed they do have the normal statutory rights to bring an action for unfair dismissal before an employment tribunal.

Civil Service Code 2007 – the most important aspects of the role and organisation of the civil service are its political impartiality and related principles, as outlined in the Civil Service Code.[9]

- Integrity – to use funds efficiently, and to uphold the law.
- Honesty – to refrain from knowingly misleading ministers, and to use funds only for the required purposes.
- Objectivity – to give evidence-based advice.
- Impartiality – not to favour particular interests, and to serve Government regardless of its political persuasion.

Civil servants are prohibited (to varying degrees) from taking part in political activity. This contrasts with the position in the US where senior civil servant posts change with the election of a new President.

Traditionally, civil servants had been protected from public blame for their actions. Their minister is formally responsible for everything that occurs in the department, including the actions of civil servants. This is the convention of Individual Ministerial Responsibility (IMR); civil servants are responsible to their Minister and the Minister is responsible to Parliament and the public. This convention has helped to preserve the neutrality of the civil service and avoid the public association of particular civil servants with particular political policies. This is important, as the same civil servants will have to serve ministers of a different political complexion if there is a change of Government.

---

8 HC 390-II (1992–3) 261, as quoted in A Bradley and K Ewing, *Constitutional and Administrative Law*, 15th edn (Pearson, 2011) 273.

9 UK Government, 'The Civil Service Code', https://www.gov.uk/government/publications/civil-service-code/the-civil-service-code (last accessed 05/11/17).

The way the IMR convention has developed, however, has implications for the civil service. Ministers now claim the right to assign blame for operational failures to individual civil servants (whilst retaining a duty to account for these failures to the House of Commons). This is called the policy/operations distinction. In 1995, the Home Secretary, Michael Howard, placed the blame for a series of prison escapes on to Derek Lewis who was the Chief Executive of the Prison Service. He went on to sack Mr Lewis. The second aspect of this change was the development of Next Step and other executive agencies. These have chief executives who are much more high profile than civil servants of the past. They must be the public face of their organisation and their responsibilities are spelt out more openly in the form of framework agreements.

APPLYING THE LAW

In 2007, a junior tax official sent a disc of information from Newcastle to London. It contained almost the entire UK database of child benefit information: the name, address and date of birth of millions of children. It never arrived. The Prime Minister (rather than the Chancellor of the Exchequer who is directly responsible) took Ministerial Responsibility for the incident, explained what had happened to Parliament and apologised to Parliament. The civil servant who sent the disc was not named and there is no public record of what happened to them, but the Chairman of HM Revenue and Customs resigned.

Under the Osmotherly Rules, chief executives and other civil servants are required to co-operate with Parliamentary Select Committees and give evidence on behalf of their minister. When the Cabinet Office receives a request to take evidence from a civil servant, 'the presumption should be that the minister will agree to meet such a request'.

2.13.1 SPECIAL ADVISERS

Whilst standard civil servants must be neutral, special advisers (SPADs) are political appointments; officially, they are temporary civil servants. They work for particular ministers and if the minister loses office, their employment automatically ends. They do work and provide advice that it would be inappropriate for civil servants to do: 'They add a political dimension to the advice and assistance available to Ministers while reinforcing the political impartiality of the permanent civil service by distinguishing the source of political advice and support.'[10] There usually is a limit of two SPADs per department.

Their role was recognised by section 15 of the Constitutional Reform and Governance Act 2010, which provided for a Code of Conduct for Special Advisers.[11] Integrating such

10 UK Government, 'Code of Conduct for Special Advisers', 2016 https://www.gov.uk/government/publications/
    special-advisers-code-of-conduct (last accessed 05/11/17)

11 Ibid.

political animals into the functioning of the civil service can create tensions. On 11 September 2001, as the news of the terrorist attacks on New York and Washington was breaking, a SPAD in the Department for Transport, Local Government and the Regions, Jo Moore, sent an email to the department press office saying that it was a good day to bury bad news and suggested sending out information on controversial changes to councillors' expenses that day. She resigned in 2003, after further controversies on communication strategy. Under section 8 of the Constitutional Reform and Governance Act 2010, SPADs cannot issue orders to or have management powers over the civil service, and the Code of Conduct says they should never have budgetary powers or exercise statutory powers.

POINTS TO REVIEW

■ The executive is led by the Prime Minister, who has few formal powers but in practice wields great authority.

■ Cabinet decides policy, but its role is often more formal and many real policy decisions are generated in departments and Cabinet Committees.

■ The Government also comprises junior ministers who are bound by Collective Cabinet Responsibility.

■ The civil service is politically neutral and required to work objectively and honestly.

TAKING IT FURTHER

How Government Works, https://www.gov.uk/government/how-government-works

This page itself is fairly basic, but its function is really as a front page for more detailed information including official websites and policy documents. It would be helpful to look at this to underline a key purpose of this chapter – gaining an understanding of the overall structure of Government.

T Daintith and A Page, *The Executive in the Constitution* (OUP, 1999) This is probably the best modern book-length treatment of the executive

The Ministerial Code & Civil Service Codes, https://www.gov.uk/government/publications/ministerial-code; https://www.gov.uk/government/publications/civil-service-code/the-civil-service-code.

It may not be the most obvious thing to do, but reading these two codes of conduct can give you a good insight into the work of ministers and civil servants and highlights the constitutional roles they perform.

3

CHAPTER 3
PARLIAMENT AND LEGISLATION

The single most common image of the British constitution, from textbook covers to YouTube videos, is the Palace of Westminster, home of the Parliament of the United Kingdom and, according the Victorian politician, John Bright, the mother of all Parliaments (although Icelanders and Manxmen may argue about that).

The proceedings of Parliament have a high profile in the public perception and understanding of Public Law processes. We rarely see laws being made beyond short news clips of the results of a close vote in the House of Commons. Yet Parliament is still the main stage, holding Prime Minister's Question Time, ministerial resignations and statements to the House in response to some crisis or atrocity. Parliament is also central to Public Law in its legislative capacity. Who has the authority to make law and how they make it are amongst the most important questions that a constitutional system can address.

AS YOU READ

In this chapter, we cover the electoral system, the life of Parliament, the composition and role of the House of Commons and House of Lords and the process for making law, including secondary legislation. In particular, you should:

- Note that the role and structure of Parliament is evolving.

- Assess the extent to which the law-making process is still dominated by Government.

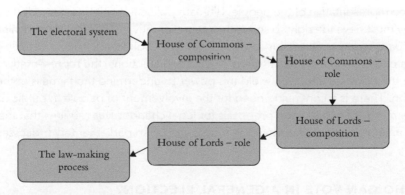

Figure 3.1 Structure of Chapter 3

3.1 ASSESSMENT TIPS

Whilst this is not the most common area within Public Law for stand-alone assessment questions, you may see questions on the electoral system or House of Lords reform. The mantra of this book, i.e. listen carefully to your Public Law teacher on all matters, applies very firmly in this case. To scope out the type of questions you may be facing, read any module guidance and look at past assessment questions. In any event, this material, just like that that in Chapter 2 'Institutions', underpins your understanding of so many other Public Law topics.

3.2 ELECTIONS

The UK electoral system, to a greater or lesser degree of efficiency and fairness, is democratic. This system also indirectly produces the Government and infuses the whole state, so that we can say that the UK is a democratic country. Democracy has its shortcomings; it tends towards factionalism, it can sometimes produce weak governance and it very commonly produces short-term thinking. Yet compared to the alternatives – absolute monarchies, military juntas, religious theocracies, one-party states – it is difficult to argue with the conclusion that democracy is the least-worst system of governance devised by humankind.

There are many flavours of democracy. They reflect the history and the cultural preferences of each country. This observation tells us that systems of democracy, like systems of law, are not natural states of affairs but are constructed by humans making decisions. The system of democracy in the UK is therefore as amenable to criticism and suggestions for improvement as any other artificial construction.

There are two main strands to democratic systems, and a genuine democracy needs to be healthy in both fields:

- Representative democracy – this is the idea that those who exercise power in a state must be representative of the people. Ultimate political legitimacy lies with the people, so they must have the right to select their representatives through free and fair elections.
- Participatory democracy – this says that leaving all political decisions to the representatives of the people is not sufficient. In between elections, the representatives might abuse their powers and even wield this power to undermine the fairness of the next election. There is a continuing need for the involvement of people in public discourse on the merits of policies and proposals for legal change. This requires that there be freedom of expression, freedom to protest, and open parliamentary processes.

3.2.1 WHO CAN VOTE IN A GENERAL ELECTION?

The UK has a system of *universal suffrage*, meaning that all adults have the right to vote in elections, although some limited restrictions remain.

EXPLAINING THE LAW

Imagine that you have used your time machine and gone back 200 years to around 1818. Suffrage is very limited, and the only holders of voting rights are men who own relatively substantial property. Most working people at this time do not own their homes and cannot vote. The franchise was extended to a wider range of males in the Reform Acts of 1832, 1867 and 1884, but the property qualification was not fully abolished until 1918. In addition to the narrow voting base, there were other problems; votes were not secret and so could be easily bought and sold and influenced by intimidation. There were rotten boroughs which were treated as the personal property of rich patrons to be passed on to their children or pawned off to a nominee.

If you went back 100 years to around 1918 then you have arrived at an exciting year. Most male householders can vote, but voting rights for some women are just being introduced; a successful result for the long and hard campaign of the suffragette movement. It is important to remember that these extensions of the franchise, like for working men before them, were not simply handed over by the ruling elite but fought for, tooth and nail. The Representation of the People Act 1918 stated that all men over 21 could vote (regardless of property) and, more fundamentally and for the first time, that women had the vote, but only for those aged 30 and above.

The Representation of the People Act 1928 equalised voting rights and allowed all women over the age of 21 to vote. The Family Law Reform Act 1969 lowered the voting age to 18 years. The Scottish independence referendum innovation of including 16- and 17-year-olds in the franchise appeared to work well. Indeed, it was extended to Scottish Parliament and local government elections by the Scottish Elections (Reduction of Voting Age) Act 2015. Attempts by the House of Lords similarly to lower the voting age for the EU Referendum were rejected by the Government and there are currently no plans to alter the voting age for General Elections.

Section 1 of the Representation of the People Act 2000 provides the test for who can vote in parliamentary general elections. A person is entitled to vote if he or she

- is registered in the constituency,
- is not subject to any legal incapacity,
- is a citizen of the Commonwealth or the Republic of Ireland, and
- is of voting age.

Legal incapacity includes being a member of the House of Lords, having been convicted of a recent electoral offence, struggling with mental disabilities if the person is incapable of making a reasoned judgement and being a convicted prisoner in detention.

If you, as a random example, were fortunate enough to have an Irish father, then he would have had the right to vote in every UK General Election since he took up residence in the UK. If you have the equal honour of a Spanish mother-in-law, then she would not have been entitled to vote in any UK General Elections, even if she had lived in the UK for 50 years.

APPLYING THE LAW – STUDENT VOTES

Most people have one place of residence, even if they work or vacation away from it for extended periods, so deciding which constituency they should be registered for is quite straightforward. A group of people who do not fit this model are students (at least those who live away from home). They have a 'home' address but reside for a majority of the year at their university address. Electoral law has accommodated the particular circumstances of students.

For students who want to cast a vote in their 'home' constituency, absence from their usual home address due to attendance at university will not disqualify them from registering at that home address.

The Court of Appeal in *Fox v Stirk* [1970] 2 QB 463 considered the position of students living in halls of residence. It held that people could register to vote where they were normally resident with a 'reasonable degree of permanence'. Therefore, a person could be resident in more than one place. As these students lived in the halls for at least half a year, they did have the necessary degree of permanence. Before you start to develop any cunning plans although, you should note that this only applies to *registration* and it is an offence to cast a vote more than once.

It seems that young people are the least likely to exercise their right to vote. Older people are the most likely. The Coalition Government of 2010–2015 committed itself to austerity policies of making large cuts in public spending, involving difficult choices as to who should bear the brunt of the measures. If you were a rational politician hoping for reelection, which age sector of society would you be least likely to impose cuts on? Yes – the sector who would have most influence over whether you were re-elected. Pension and other old-age benefits were largely protected from austerity, unlike university tuition fees, the Education Maintenance Allowance (for those aged 16–19) and restrictions on housing benefit for 18- to 21-year-olds.

In the 2017 General Election, the Labour Party attracted large numbers of votes from young people, in part due to policies attractive to students. It is still the case, however, that younger voters exercise their democratic rights less than older voters.

The legal incapacity of prisoners under the Representation of the People Act 2000 has generated a great deal of controversy.

> **KEY CASE** – *HIRST V UK (NO 2)* [2005] ECHR 681
>
> In this case, the European Court of Human Rights found that the blanket ban on any convicted person in detention from voting breached the European Convention on Human Rights, Protocol 1 Article 3. This Article commits Member States to 'free elections at reasonable intervals by secret ballot, under conditions which will ensure the free expression of the opinion of the people in the choice of the legislature'. This does not give an absolute right to vote, but the Court held that a complete ban applying to all prisoners was disproportionate. The solution would have been for the UK to adopt a limited ban, e.g. those sentenced to more than 24 months, and the chances are high that this would have been deemed lawful.

The judgment has not been accepted, however, and successive governments have either tried to delay thinking about it, ignored it or openly stated that they will not implement it. David Cameron said in 2011 that it made him 'physically ill' to contemplate having to give the vote to any prisoner,[1] and the House of Commons resoundingly rejected the notion. The European Court of Human Rights reiterated its stance that blanket bans are disproportionate in *Scoppola v Italy* (2013) 56 EHRR 19. The situation therefore is one of continuing stand-off between the UK Government and the European Court of Human Rights. In *R (on the application of Chester) v Secretary of State for Justice* [2013] UKSC 63, the Supreme Court found that it could only recognise this deadlock and that it was not its place to try to break it.

3.3 THE ELECTORAL SYSTEM

3.3.1 FIRST PAST THE POST

General Elections in the UK are held using the First Past the Post system (FPTP), sometimes called simple majority voting. The country is currently divided into 650 constituencies. Most constituencies have between 65,000 and 80,000 voters, although because the boundaries also try to follow natural divisions, some are larger or smaller; the Isle of Wight constituency has 108,000 voters.

---

1 A Hough, 'Prisoner vote – what MPs said in heated debate', *Daily Telegraph*, 11 February 2011, http://www.telegraph. co.uk/news/politics/8317485/Prisoner-vote-what-MPs-said-in-heated-debate.html (last accessed 05/11/17).

Each voter casts a single vote, and the candidate with the most votes wins the seat. There is no need for a candidate to obtain an overall majority of votes, e.g. if four parties are contesting a seat and the results are as depicted in this graph:

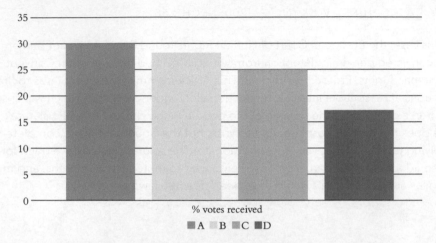

Figure 3.2 First past the post

Candidate A wins the seat even though they have less than one-third of the votes cast. If we extrapolate this to a national level, the issues are similar but more problematic. If candidate C was a member of a political party that fielded candidates in every constituency in the UK and each candidate also got 25 per cent of the vote, then that party would have the support of around 6 million voters and have won zero seats. This is not a fantastical calculation; in May 2015, UKIP obtained 3.8 million votes and won one seat. In February 1974, Labour gained 11.64 million votes as against the Conservatives' 11.87 million votes. Who won the election? It was Labour, with four more seats than the Conservatives.

FPTP is particularly harsh on smaller parties, who struggle to break through the 'winner takes it all' effect of this voting system. Constitutionally, this is important – a key idea underpinning the constitutional system is that political power and legitimacy lie with the people. This power is delegated by the people to state institutions to exercise on their behalf and in their interests. This delegation can only legitimately happen if people can choose their representatives to run these state institutions through an electoral system that fairly represents their preferences. So you might think it would be a central objective of any such system to represent those preferences accurately. In the UK, this is replaced by:

- First, a pragmatic belief that FPTP produces clear winners and strong governments. This recognises that more proportionate systems of voting result in smaller parties gaining seats, which reduces the likelihood of a single party winning more than half of the seats. This can produce weak and short-lived governments, although many Western democracies have stable governments under more proportionate voting systems. These tend to be coalitions, which may be formed after the election by secret negotiations and may include coalition partners that voters did not foresee and policies that privilege minority interests.

■ Secondly, a lack of popular interest in (or political will to adopt) alternative voting arrangements. The Liberal Democrats managed to include a referendum on electoral reform in their Coalition Agreement with the Conservatives in 2010. This was a nationwide referendum on a proposal to adopt an alternative voting system. This would have retained constituencies but allowed voters to rank candidates according to preference. If no single candidate wins 50 per cent of votes, then the second preferences of voters for weaker candidates are distributed. This is not exactly proportional, but at least the winning candidate has the acquiescence (or some expression of preference) from a majority of voters in a constituency. The referendum result was a clear rejection of the proposals: 67.9 per cent No, 32.1 per cent Yes, on a turnout of 42.2 per cent.

There are two significant reforms to the electoral system that are likely to be implemented before the 2022 General Election. First, a reduction in the number of constituencies (and therefore MPs) from 650 to 600, by section 11 of the Parliamentary Voting System and Constituencies Act 2011. Linked to this is a redrawing of the constituency boundaries to iron out some of the wide variations between their sizes and to recognise demographic changes, especially the large increase in population in London and the South East. This redrawing is due to be in place by 2018 under the Electoral Registration and Administration Act 2013.

3.4 THE UNITED KINGDOM PARLIAMENT

The Parliament of the United Kingdom, often called the Westminster Parliament, is bicameral, meaning that it has two houses or chambers. Many countries use this bicameral arrangement to spread power and to improve the scrutiny and revision of legislation. The members of the different chambers are selected through different electoral or appointment processes so as to avoid a duplication of political preferences and to provide a different perspective. The Westminster Parliament has three estates: the two chambers (House of Commons and House of Lords) and the Queen in Parliament.

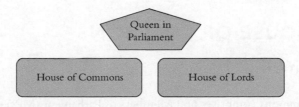

Figure 3.3 The elements of Parliament

3.4.1 LIFE OF A PARLIAMENT

For a century before 2011, the *maximum* life of a Parliament was five years, but the Government of the day could invoke prerogative powers to dissolve Parliament at any time before this maximum period. In practice, few Parliaments lived for five years. Where there was a minority Government or a small majority, then dissolution of Parliament and another election might follow in a few months (1974) or in one or two years (1950, 1964). Most Parliaments lasted for around four years.

This power to dissolve Parliament was used to try to gain a tactical advantage over the opposition, for example by calling an election during an economic upturn or after some popular tax cuts. The ability to plan strategy and finances for an election that only the Government had any advance warning of gave a real advantage to the incumbent on what ought to be a level playing field.

The normal life of a Parliament is now fixed at five years by the Fixed-term Parliaments Act 2011. As well as providing more equity as between the parties, this regularisation also provides more certainty in administrative and economic planning. The term can be extended by two months by the Prime Minister, with no legal need to specify the reason for an extension. The Act needed to provide for exceptions to this fixed term and allow for earlier elections in some circumstances, for example, where a Government collapsed through lack of support and no party or coalition can form an alternative Government. The Act states that an election within the five-year period can be triggered by a House of Commons motion on a two-thirds majority vote or on a motion of no confidence and where no alternative Government can be approved within 14 days.

It was not envisaged in 2011 that these exceptions would be much used, if at all. At almost the first test of the fixed-term system, however, an early election was called. Theresa May took over as Prime Minister following the resignation of David Cameron in 2016. She had no direct electoral mandate to be Prime Minister, although this is far from uncommon. Only half of prime ministers in the last 100 years have come to power in a General Election. May had a working majority of 12 seats but, in April 2017, said that it would be in the national interest to have a Government with a larger majority so as to drive the Brexit negotiations through more effectively. There were suspicions that May was responding to polling figures showing a large advantage over opposition parties and was trying to call the early election for political advantage – just the sort of thing that the Fixed-term Parliament Act was supposed to guard against. In this case, however, the Labour Party agreed to an early election and the required two-thirds majority was obtained.

3.5 THE HOUSE OF COMMONS

3.5.1 COMPOSITION

The House of Commons comprises 650 Members of Parliament (MPs) elected through the system outlined above. This is set to be reduced to 600 seats for the next General Election. Certain categories of people are disqualified from election to the Commons due to public policy and the need for some public office holders to be impartial. The list includes prisoners, (most) peers, children, bankrupts, psychiatric patients, foreigners (except Irish people), judges, civil servants, police or members of the armed forces (House of Commons Disqualification Act 1975).

You might think that resignation from the post of MP would be straightforward but the UK constitution, more than ever like some Disney version of Ruritania in this respect, insists that MPs cannot resign. An MP who wishes to relinquish their position must instead 'apply for the Chiltern Hundreds'. This means that they take up one of two archaic posts, Crown Steward and Bailiff of the three Chiltern Hundreds of Stoke, or Crown Steward and Bailiff of the Manor of Northstead. Their significance is that these are Crown Offices and so disqualify the holder from serving as an MP.

The chief officer of the House is the Speaker, who chairs debates and calls MPs to speak. They are notified of an MP's wish to speak either in advance through writing or in the chamber by an MP 'catching the Speaker's eye', i.e. standing up. The Speaker tries to maintain order in the House ('Order, order') and applies the rules, for example calling another MP a 'liar', a 'hypocrite' or a 'swine' is regarded as 'unparliamentary'[2] and the Speaker will suspend the user of such rough language unless they withdraw the remark. The Speaker is elected by MPs for the life of a Parliament. Even though they entered the House as a member of a party, their elevation to Speaker means they must resign from their party and stay politically neutral in all their dealings.

3.5.2 THE NATURE OF THE MP'S ROLE

Should an MP be the representative of their constituents or a functionary for their party? Winston Churchill asked, 'what is the use of sending members to the House of Commons who just say the popular thing of the moment?' and said that in a Parliamentary democracy we should not 'return tame, docile, subservient members'.[3] Churchill, of course, was none of those things, but his Parliamentary career as a serial rebel, switching parties more than once, is not a standard model for most MPs to emulate.

Members do need to represent their constituency. It is an interesting exercise to write to your MP (or visit them at a constituency clinic) on an issue that concerns you. From a large majority of MPs, you will get a considered, thoughtful response (even if it respectfully disagrees with you). If you have a genuine grievance, then it is very likely that the MP will use their time and energy to take the case up. It is a counterbalance to those who decry politicians as cynical and self-serving.

Their main role, however, is to support their party. In an era of party politics, they owe their position not to the voters' opinion of their merits as an individual but largely because they are the chosen candidate for a party. MPs support their party primarily by voting in line

---

2 Even if it happens to be true.
3 As quoted by A Carroll, *Constitutional and Administrative Law* (6th edn, Longman, 2011) 139.

with party wishes, as communicated through the party whip system, but also by showing support for other candidates in elections, and promoting party interests in interviews and the media.

We will see that Parliament has two main roles – law-making and holding the Government to account – and so MPs have this dual role. Typically, MPs of the majority party will support legislative proposals whilst opposition party MPs will test, challenge and oppose. In holding Government to account, MPs from all sides (excepting members of the Government) have a role to play in asking challenging questions, and in seeking explanations and assurances from ministers.

3.6 THE ROLE OF THE HOUSE OF COMMONS – SCRUTINY

You may think that the main role of the House of Commons is legislative; considering Bills is the core business of the House, and on any map of constitutional institutions Parliament is placed firmly in the legislative part of the state. In reality, its most important role is in holding Government to account.

Parliament does not independently come up with legislative proposals and then choose which ones are to be made into law; it processes the Government's legislative agenda. Elliott and Thomas say that 'it is more accurate to describe parliament not as law-making, but as a law–effecting, institution'.[4] The way in which the Commons carries out this law-effecting role is examined in the second half of this chapter, and here we will consider the more general role of the Commons in holding the executive to account for its policies and actions.

This scrutiny is underpinned by important constitutional conventions (these are explored in depth in Chapter 5). Collective Cabinet Responsibility provides that Government ministers are collectively responsible for Government decisions and actions. The convention is useful here in preventing a minister from disclaiming responsibility on the basis that they did not support a particular policy choice. MPs know that any answer they receive from a minister can be taken to represent the view of the Government as a whole.

Individual Ministerial Responsibility is even more important. It requires ministers to take responsibility for all the actions of their department and related public bodies, i.e. the Secretary of State for Work and Pensions cannot disclaim responsibility for 'fitness for work' assessments just because they are carried out by a private company on behalf of his department. The meaning of 'responsibility' is complex and contested, particularly in its

---

4   M Elliott and R Thomas, *Public Law* (3rd edn, OUP, 2017) 211.

relationship to culpability; taking responsibility for operational errors by civil servants is not the same thing as taking the blame for them. Nonetheless, it is clear that, in the words of the Ministerial Code, 'Ministers have a duty to Parliament to account, and be held to account, for the policies, decisions and actions of their departments and agencies'. This accountability involves explaining to Parliament what has gone wrong, why it has gone wrong, apologising if necessary and stating what the department is going to do to remedy the situation.

The Ministerial Code also provides that 'It is of paramount importance that Ministers give accurate and truthful information to Parliament, correcting any inadvertent error at the earliest opportunity', and that they should be as open as possible. The sanction for breaching this duty is that 'Ministers who knowingly mislead Parliament will be expected to offer their resignation to the Prime Minister'.

3.6.1 SCRUTINY AND DEMOCRACY

As discussed above, political authority and legitimacy lie with the people, but we could not have useful regular meetings with an assembly of 65 million people. It would be no way to take important decisions (referendums provide an interesting and highly occasional exception). It would be impossible to govern this way. There is, therefore, a need for representatives and institutions to take decisions and to run the country. They derive their authority and legitimacy from the people, so they ought to be using these powers only on our behalf and in our interests.

Representative democracy, as discussed above, means that the people choose who will run the most important parts of the state (Parliament and Government), but this only gives a snapshot, a very generalised view of people's wishes at five-year intervals. In the interim period, there is the risk of 'elective dictatorship' with an over-mighty executive always getting its way and not being immediately accountable for its actions. There is an ongoing need for participatory democracy, including freedom of expression and of the press, or a more formal role for public petitions. In the context of Parliament, we see the direct representatives of the people (MPs) hold to account the decision-making and the governing parts of the state (Government and public bodies).

The role of Parliament is limited to checking; the Government controls a majority in the House of Commons (or it would not be entitled to govern). The House cannot direct Government action, only subject it to questioning, criticism and publicity. JAG Griffiths compared Parliamentary control to the way the banks of a river control its flow rather than the way a driver controls their car.[5] We also need to see these questions as part of a 'continual general election campaign' between the parties.[6] The Opposition will criticise the

---

5   Cited in T T Arvind and L Stirton, 'Why the Judicial Power Project Is Wrong about *Anisminic*', U.K. Const. L. Blog (20 May 2016) (available at https://ukconstitutionallaw.org/).
6   M Elliott and R Thomas, *Public Law*, 3rd edn (OUP, 2017), 409.

Government to show its incompetence or its ignorance of the needs of 'ordinary people' or 'hard-working families' (or the political trope of the day) and to promote their alternative vision.

In exercising their functions, MPs enjoy rights and immunities under parliamentary privilege. Article 9 Bill of Rights 1689 provides that MPs have freedom of speech and that debates or proceedings in Parliament ought not to be impeached or questioned in any court. Parliament has exclusive cognisance, i.e. the legal authority to regulate its own affairs.

3.6.2 METHODS OF SCRUTINY

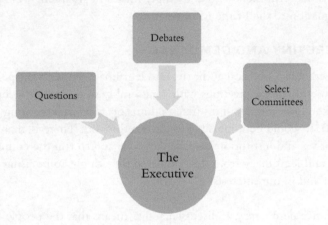

Figure 3.4 Methods of scrutiny

All of the methods of scrutiny are affected, mainly negatively, by the tribal nature of party politics. Most MPs are more interested in and committed to the interests of their party than in being some independent monitor of Government action. This means that scrutiny and critique from the Government backbenches can be partly (although not completely) controlled. Criticism from the Opposition benches can be partly (although not completely) ignored as ritualistic opposition rather than the exercise of a constitutional function of keeping limits on and accountability for state power. We have seen, however, that ministers have obligations to be open and honest in their response to the scrutiny role of Parliament. This role uses particular methods:

Questions to ministers – The most high-profile regular event in the week in Parliament is Prime Minister's Questions (PMQs) which take place each Wednesday for 30 minutes. The Prime Minister faces three to six questions from the leader of the Opposition and other questions from MPs chosen by random ballot. The Prime Minister normally faces 'untabled' questions, i.e. they have no advance notice, although they will be well briefed on possible topics and will often receive unthreatening questions from their own MPs ('Will the Prime Minister agree with me that the Government is doing a highly effective job of . . .'). PMQs seem to offer the possibility of seriously holding the head of Government to account, and scrutinising the executive in an unscripted and direct way. In practice, this is the noisiest and most tribal event of the week. Prime Ministers become adept at deflecting difficult questions and focus instead on reiterating their political messages of the week. Opposition leaders can sometimes make an impact at PMQs, but this is more a part of the 'continuous election campaign' than sober and detailed scrutiny.

Other ministers face their own Question Time on a rota, and each five weeks a minister will take oral questions. Oral questions provide the drama, but there is more detailed scrutiny carried out through the submission of written questions. MPs can submit questions to any minister, and unless it is ruled out of order it will be answered. It may be out of order because it does not relate to a minister's powers, it is *sub judice* (the subject of court proceedings) or the question has already been asked in the previous three months. A minister can also refuse to answer a question if the costs would be excessive (a test that is very much in the eye of the beholder), or if it relates to national security or international relations.

Debates – beyond the examination of legislation, there are debates on policy matters. These are mostly controlled by the Government, but there are around 20 Opposition Days each session where the opposition parties can choose the subject for debate, and some days for consideration of Private Members' Bills. The effect of debates is limited. They can involve MPs stating their established positions with little direct impact on policy, although by raising concerns there may be indirect effects on Government actions.

Select Committees – have emerged as the most effective vehicle for detailed scrutiny of the executive.

3.6.3 SCRUTINY AND SELECT COMMITTEES

Departmental Select Committees were established in 1979 and there is one for each Government department (see Chapter 2 for a list of departments). Their role is to 'examine the expenditure, administration and policy of the principal government departments' (Standing Order No 152(1)). They have a membership of around 12–15 MPs, whose appointment gives them some independence from direct governmental control. This is especially the case for committee chairs who are elected by their fellow committee members by secret ballot (rather than being selected by party whips). Membership roles are divided between the parties, and are limited by convention to backbench MPs.

The practice has been that Select Committee members are less partisan in committee than in the chamber of the House of Commons itself. MPs tend to invest time and energy into their committee work, and they choose areas where their interests lie. They develop subject expertise and closer working relationships with their political opponents on the committee.

This is one of the limited areas where a backbench MP can genuinely exercise some independent power.

APPLYING THE LAW – THE HOME AFFAIRS SELECT COMMITTEE

This House of Commons committee has 11 members that shadow the Home Office. A majority (six) are Conservative MPs. The Chair is the senior Labour politician, Yvette Cooper. In a typical month of April / May 2017, it:

- took evidence from the Europol Director on policing and security issues
- questioned Government ministers and social media company executives on hate crime; questioned ministers on the Police Funding Formula
- published reports on the failure of social media companies to take down illegal content; and on police misconduct and miscarriages of justice around the Orgreave confrontation in the 1980s miners' strike, and called on the Government to publish further information on Orgreave policing.[7]

Other important parliamentary committees include the Joint Human Rights Committee which draws its membership from both Houses and scrutinises proposals and Government actions to assess their consistency with human rights commitments. The influential Public Accounts Committee looks at the value for money of public spending and is supported by the National Audit Office and the Comptroller and Auditor General. It helps Parliament hold the Government to account on crucial issues on the expenditure of taxpayers' money.

We are, in this section on scrutiny, a long way from the shores of a purely legalistic approach. So much of what happens *depends* on variable factors: on the strength of the Government; on the personalities involved; on the nature of the issues; on the strength of political partisanship; on timing. We should not pretend that law is purely mechanistic or that many of these factors do not also have a presence in legal processes. It is clear, however, that whilst these scrutiny processes can be aided by a legal and institutional framework, they are highly contingent. Ultimately, however, scrutiny can exert *influence*. It can reduce the likelihood of bad ideas becoming proposals or of ill thought-out proposals becoming law. Government knows that it may have to explain and justify its executive and administrative operations in a public forum. Scrutiny can show Government what are the concerns of MPs (who are more in touch with the issues facing their constituents), and critical reports can influence future action.

---

7   The Home Affairs Select Committee, http://www.parliament.uk/business/committees/committees-a-z/commons-select/home-affairs-committee/ (last accessed 16/07/17).

3.7 THE HOUSE OF LORDS

The House of Lords is the second chamber of Parliament (although it is formally regarded as the 'upper chamber'). It has no direct democratic mandate. It was originally the dominant chamber and then for some time was on a reasonably even footing with the Commons. With the development of greater democracy through the nineteenth century, its status and relative power waned. This loss of status in favour of the Commons was codified after it lost the great constitutional battle with the Government and the House of Commons that resulted in the Parliament Act 1911. The House of Lords had an inbuilt and large Conservative Party majority through many decades, until the reforms in the House of Lords Act 1999.

3.7.1 COMPOSITION

The members of the House of Lords are called peers, of which there are over 803 (down from the remarkable peak of over 1,300 in 1999). There are three categories:

Hereditary peers – these peers inherited their titles, usually by being the eldest male in the line of their family. The award of hereditary peerage sharply declined in the twentieth century, and some hereditary lines die out, but in 1999 there were over 750 such peers. This category was not abolished but was reduced to a maximum of 92 by the House of Lords Act 1999; these 92 are elected from the small constituency of other hereditary peers. *Yes, you read that right.* In the twenty-first century in the second chamber of the Parliament of an advanced Western liberal democracy, there are 92 members who have seats in the legislature because one of their ancestors was given a reward at some point in history by the Monarch. They may be smart and socially conscious, or idiotic and morally bankrupt; their place does not depend on those virtues and is not barred by those shortcomings. It is an accident of birth that places them there.

Lords Spiritual – the UK is a multi-faith, and increasingly a no-faith, country, but the Lords Spiritual are the representatives only of the established Church: the archbishops of Canterbury and York and 24 other senior Church of England bishops. There is no place for the Chief Rabbi, or the Roman Catholic Archbishop of Westminster or representatives of British Muslims, or Methodists, or Hindus, or Presbyterians. The established churches of Wales and Scotland are similarly absent from the spiritual representation of the nation in the Lords.

Life peers – this category was established by the Life Peerages Act 1958. It allows the Government, using prerogative powers, to grant a person the honour of a peerage for the period of their life and which 'shall expire on his death'. The majority of peers in the Lords are life peers. The ability of a Government to appoint members to a chamber of Parliament that has powers to make law and a duty to hold that Government to account is, by its nature, bound to be controversial and ripe for low-level abuse and partisanship. There are no rules on the number of new peerages that can be created each year, and the Prime Minister still retains control of political appointments. It is the practice for each major political party to submit nominations and for the PM's recommendations to very broadly reflect the strength of the parties in the Commons. Most life peers have a political affiliation, and many are former MPs and ministers. Since 2000, an Appointments Commission has taken over the role of recommendations for non-party-political appointments, who become the independent 'cross-benchers' when they take their seats.

Until the House of Lords Reform Act 2014 only death could remove a member of the House of Lords. Now peers can voluntarily retire and under s 2 peers can be removed for failure to attend for a full parliamentary session, a fate that has happened to six Lords to date.

The post of Lord Speaker, elected by the Lords, presides over the business of the chamber but does not chair debates or (need to) keep order as the Commons Speaker does.

3.7.2 ROLE OF THE HOUSE OF LORDS

The work of the House of Lords reflects and complements that of the Commons, i.e. it is also involved in making law and holding the Government to account. Because it has no democratic mandate, its role is secondary to the Commons on both counts. Its advantages lie in its independence and its expertise. Its independence from Government dominance comes from the fact that, in particular since the 1999 reforms, there is a balance of power; no one party has an overall majority and there are a significant number of politically unaligned peers. The power of party discipline over political peers is also considerably weaker. These peers are not tied by the promise of promotion or threatened by the prospect of deselection from their seat. Loyalty to their party is a habit, but it will not override their conscience as readily as for members of the Commons. The Lords' expertise lies in the wealth of political experience of most of its members and from the eminence of its independent members, who have come from, and often still work in, different walks of life.

In relation to law-making, the Lords is principally a revising chamber. Less controversial Bills can be introduced in the Lords to help the workload of the Commons. The legislative process mirrors that of the Commons, explained in detail below. There are legal and political constraints on the Lords' ability to affect the outcome of the proposals that appear before them. The Parliament Acts 1911 and 1949 only allow the Lords a power of delay rather than veto. For Money Bills, which solely concern taxation or expenditure, this power of delay is no more than one month. For other Bills, the Lords can delay for one year. Rather than outright rejection, the Lords may deal with a proposal it dislikes by inserting amendments that alter the policy outcome. In this case there may be 'ping pong' between the chambers until agreement is reached or the Bill is forced through using the Parliament Act procedure.

The power of delay is not unimportant. It can cause problems for Governments, particularly towards the end of the life of a Parliament, and in practice Governments will try to balance an assertion of their right to govern with the need to make compromises on what might ultimately be a better solution. A keen self-awareness of their lack of a democratic mandate also means that the Lords exercise self-restraint in exercising what powers they have. Ultimately, they know their role is to advise and influence the law-making process.

Further controversy over the power of the chamber arose in 2015/16. The Lords delayed approval of secondary legislation on tax credits. It is rare for secondary legislation to be blocked, even though the parent Act had explicitly given veto powers to the Lords. The Parliament Act procedures do not apply to secondary legislation, so the Government had to claim the constitutional convention of financial privilege of the House of Commons. This means that when House of Commons clerks, in response to a Lords amendment, certify secondary legislation as having financial consequences then the Lords should not press for the amendment to be adopted.

Russell argues that the 1999 reforms to the composition of the Lords have emboldened the House of Lords and made conventions limiting its power 'increasingly fragile'.[8] The tax credits reforms ultimately went through unamended but the Government commissioned Lord Strathclyde to review whether further formal restrictions on the Lords' powers over secondary legislation were required. He recommended a complete abolition of its veto over statutory instruments but there are currently no plans to implement this into law.

The ability of the Lords to hold the Government to account is also affected by this lack of a democratic mandate. There are debates and ministerial questions, but whilst there are some Government ministers in the Lords, the most important ones are in 'the other place'. There is still, however, valuable scrutiny work undertaken by the Lords.

3.7.3 REFORM

Reform of the House of Lords has a venerable history, but actual progress has been halting and ad hoc. It seems that whilst there has been wide acknowledgement of the incongruity of an appointed (and still partially hereditary) chamber in the legislature, there has been fear of the impact of a powerful alternative chamber and a lack of political will to alter a body that does not make too much of a nuisance of itself.

The Preamble to the Parliament Act 1911 said, 'whereas it is intended to substitute for the House of Lords as it at present exists a Second Chamber constituted on a popular instead of hereditary basis, but such substitution cannot be immediately brought into operation'. The 1911 reforms were intended to be a stopgap in advance of an elected second chamber. It seems difficult to argue with the notion that any body of persons involved in making the primary law of the land ought to derive their authority from the people affected by those laws.

....

8 M Russell, 'The Lords, politics and finance' Constitution Unit Blog, 29 October 2015, https://constitution-unit. com/2015/10/29/the-lords-politics-and-finance/ (last accessed 05/11/17).

There are, however, some objections to this view. A key benefit of the Lords, within its limited scope of power, lies in its independence from the disciplines of party politics that allow the Government to dominate the operation of the Commons. If the second chamber was elected on the same basis (and at the same time) as the House of Commons, then it would a) just reflect the existing political make-up of the House of Commons and b) be organised on party lines as strictly as the House of Commons. Most second chambers in democratic parliaments are elected but on different voting systems and terms of office to reduce this problem, although party allegiances continue to affect the operation of these bodies. It is also necessary to establish a hierarchy between the chambers to avoid a deadlock or jurisdictional 'turf war'.

The UK could opt for something along these lines (e.g. a smaller body elected by proportional representation for seven-year terms with an effective but limited mandate). A preference has been emerging in more recent reform proposals, however, for a part-elected/part-appointed chamber. These include 50:50 and 80:20 elected/appointed proposals, but there has always been insufficient political will to promote any specific proposal seriously. As it has done for most of the past century, House of Lords reform remains on the table but with no definite action in sight.

KEY LEARNING POINTS

- Membership of the House of Lords is unusual and controversial.
- Its experience and independence from party control gives it strength.
- Its lack of a democratic mandate weakens its ability to exert control over Government.

3.8 THE LEGISLATIVE PROCESS

Each Government, when it enters office, has substantive policy objectives: to improve the economy, to promote employment, to reduce crime, to maintain and improve international relations, to improve education, transport, environmental protection etc. It has in its hands a number of levers of power with which to achieve these goals:

- Administrative and organisational power – through the operation of Government departments, civil service, public bodies, and powers of patronage.
- Financial power – to control budget deficits, growth packages, the disposition of public funds to departments, local government and the devolved institutions.
- Policy directing power – for example to renew diplomatic relations with a former enemy nation; to change planning policy without legislation, by ministerial directives or by requiring a change of approach to planning appeals.
- Media influence – to set the political agenda, to use the profile of Government to change perceptions of key themes and issues.

- Ultimately the ability to change laws and make new laws – by making Acts of Parliament, which is one of the most powerful tools in this toolkit.

Most Bills at the start of a five-year Parliament are based on proposals in the election manifesto. It is not a requirement either that these commitments are followed through by the Government or that any further proposals must have a basis in electoral promises. As Parliament goes through its lifespan, the legislative programme will be more and more a response to concerns that have arisen since the election.

There are a number of types of Acts of Parliament:

- Public Acts are proposed by the Government and are of general application.
- Private Members' Bills are brought forward by individual MPs chosen by ballot.
- Private Acts only apply to a particular scheme, company or public body.

Delegated legislation plays a very important role, but it is secondary rather than primary legislation.

3.8.1 PUBLIC ACTS

Public Acts are based on proposals from Government. There are around 30–40 Public Bills put before the House of Commons each year. Ministers often outline initial policy ideas in a Green Paper that invites consultation responses from the wider public. This can lead to more detailed legislative proposals in a White Paper where some aspects of the scheme are still up for discussion but the minister has committed to the general framework. Neither of these steps are required, however, and very specific proposals can go straight from Government departments into the legislative process. All proposals are submitted to the Parliamentary Counsel Office (PCO) which then turns them into parliamentary legislative language, although the PCO also has an objective to produce 'good law' that is more comprehensible to citizens.

Green Paper → White Paper → Draft Bill → 1st Reading

Figure 3.5 Possible (rather than required) stages in developing a Bill

We saw above that the Government dominates the law-making process and that Parliament's role is more law-effecting. This includes the scrutiny of legislation, and there is a tension between the facts that:

- Detailed and effective scrutiny ought to result in a significant number of amendments to initial proposals. Effective scrutiny could highlight technical defects of vagueness or inconsistency, or point out unintended or undesirable consequences.

- Parliament and especially the House of Commons is organised on political lines. Party discipline means that scrutiny can be brushed aside, with the proposal pushed through in its original form. A culture has developed where ministers see getting a proposal through the process without any amendments as a sign of strength (rather than of pig-headedness).

Even taking into account this dominance, the very fact of parliamentary scrutiny alters the legislative process. Defeat of a whole Bill is extremely rare, as is Parliament forcing an amendment on an unwilling Government, but the knowledge that the objectives, methods and details of the Bill will be subject to open review requires a minister to anticipate any problems and challenges.

Bills can be published in draft as part of the wider consultation process. This is strongly recommended by the House of Commons Modernisation Committee that says, 'Ministers are likely to be far more receptive to suggestions for change' at this draft stage and that 'it should lead to better legislation'.[9] It is disappointing, therefore, that this is still not the norm and most Bills are introduced directly to Parliament. Each Bill must go through a number of stages to become an Act.

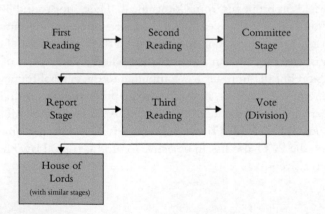

Figure 3.6 Legislative stages

First Reading – just the title of the Bill is laid before the House at this stage, with no debate or vote. The Bill is then published in full.

Second Reading – the minister sponsoring the proposal outlines the substantive benefits of the Bill to the House. This is followed by a debate on the overall merits of the Bill, but there is no chance to put forward specific amendments. The Opposition are invited to make a formal response and then there is a general debate.

---

9   The Legislative Process, 1997–8, HC 190.

Committee Stage – this is where proposals are examined in detail. This is not done by the whole House but by Public Bills Committees. These committees have around 20 members that reflect the political balance in the House, i.e. the Government will have a majority on every committee. Committees can propose amendments, but they tend to be minor changes to tidy up the Bill.

This stage seems, at first glance, to be the place where the real work of scrutiny can happen, through detailed line-by-line consideration of proposals away from the tribal politics of the House of Commons chamber. But the Committee Stage is, according to Elliott and Thomas, 'a dead letter'. They say that 'a government MP who goes on a committee with the genuine intention of scrutinising legislation may risk their career' and that the Government ensures that 'anyone who knows or cares about the legislation does not get on a committee in the first place'.[10] Most MPs from the Government party are simply instructed not to say anything.

This is clearly a part of the constitutional system that is failing. Successive Governments have not only been happy that it is failing, they have strived for and ensured that failure. We might, if we were romantic and a bit naïve, have an image of a Commons made up of maverick, independent, smart people who respond to each proposal according to their core beliefs and want to 'do the right thing'. That does not accord with the reality of our constitutional system, and yet, despite that dissonance, the real position is to some extent justifiable. We saw above that MPs are in the House primarily as a representative of their party. Governments might only be indirectly formed from the results of elections for the Commons, but the truth is that General Elections are battles between the political parties and their leaders. They are battles for the political authority to rule. If a successful party decides on a particular policy, then it ought to be able to put that policy into practice through legislation. This is not absolute, and must pay due regard to commitments to international obligations, human rights law, and the vague boundaries of political and public acceptability.

This is different, however, from saying that the Government has the right to ride roughshod over Parliament as a scrutinising institution. Whilst the general thrust of its proposals ought to be enacted, the details and the drafting ought to be further reviewed at this stage and, when flaws or unintended consequences are identified to be addressed through amendment.

Report Stage – the Public Bills Committee then reports back to the House on any amendments which can be accepted or rejected.

Third Reading – this is a short debate, rarely more than one hour, that focuses on changes since the Second Reading. The Bill is then sent to the House of Lords, which follows a very similar staged process.

----

10 M Elliott and R Thomas, *Public Law* (3rd edn, OUP, 2017) 220.

Reviewing this legislative process, we can see that whilst in structural terms it looks comprehensive and rigorous, in practice, some stages are largely a formality whilst other stages are prevented from providing genuine detailed scrutiny by the demands of party discipline.

Voting on Bills is also rather quaint. In most Parliaments (e.g. European Union, Scotland), voting is electronic. In the House of Commons, MPs walk through the 'Aye' or 'No' lobbies. They are counted by clerks and by MPs acting as tellers. The vote is called a division, and bells are rung through the Palace of Westminster and the MPs' main office accommodation in Portcullis House; the division bell is also connected to various pubs, clubs and restaurants in the immediate vicinity. MPs, wherever they are, then have eight minutes to get through the lobbies, so even those who have not heard any of the merits of the proposals being debated are called to vote.

Royal assent – the general rules on granting the royal assent are discussed in Chapter 5, 'Constitutional conventions'. Here, we can just note that the Queen must give the royal assent. In practical terms, she is not personally involved and the assent is merely pronounced.

The royal assent completes the process of a Bill becoming an Act of Parliament. When it comes into force depends on what the statute says. Some Acts take immediate effect; many either specify a later date or allow the minister to bring the provisions into force on an unspecified future date through a commencement order. In general, this is sensible, as it allows any necessary practical and administrative arrangements to be put in place and it is the minister who can arrange this and is best placed to see when the provisions can usefully be brought into force.

3.8.2 PRIVATE MEMBERS' BILLS

A Private Members' Bill ballot is held each year and the names of 20 MPs are drawn. These MPs have an opportunity to introduce a Bill to the Commons on a subject of their choice. Only the first ten names have any realistic chance of seeing their proposal become law, and this chance depends on whether the Government is happy to accept the proposal.

An MP might have their own particular interest that they can bring forward, but often those MPs who are lucky in the ballot are persuaded by lobbying to take up a cause or, more prosaically, but realistically, they can pick up a minor issue Bill from the Government's programme and be more assured of success.

APPLYING THE LAW – SUNBED REGULATION

A Private Members' Bill has almost no chance of succeeding without Government support, because the Government can limit the time available for debate or informally direct its members to block the Bill. If a proposal is regarded as a useful reform and not seriously inconsistent with Government views, then it has a reasonable chance of passing, for example the Sunbeds (Regulation) Act 2010. Julie Morgan, the MP for Cardiff North, having been picked out in the ballot, was contacted by Cancer Research UK, and her proposal to introduce safeguards in the sunbed industry, for the particular protection of young girls, was taken up by the Government.

Private Members' Bills seem like a small part of the legislative process, but in their willingness to take on sensitive or neglected issues, they can effect important social change, with examples including:

- Murder (Abolition of Death Penalty) Act 1965
- Sexual Offences Act 1967
- Termination of Pregnancy Act 1968
- Female Genital Mutilation Act 2004
- Forced Marriage (Civil Protection) Act 2007.

3.9 DELEGATED LEGISLATION

Delegated (or secondary) legislation developed in the nineteenth century and expanded as the role of the state expanded. The Donoughmore Committee 1932 found that delegated legislation is necessary because of limits on parliamentary time, but it needs safeguards.[11]

Delegated legislation takes a number of forms, including Orders in Council and local authority bye-laws. The category of most concern here is Statutory Instruments, where Acts of Parliament delegate the power to make secondary legislation to ministers. There are around 3,500 Statutory Instruments passed per annum and, in volume, they dwarf primary legislation.

The benefits and dangers of delegated legislation were examined in Chapter 2. In procedural terms, they often involve Parliament in one of two ways. This depends on the scrutiny procedure laid down in the parent Act.

- Negative resolution – this is the most common method for the Commons to have an oversight over how ministers are exercising delegated law-making powers. Instruments

---

11 Report of the Committee on Ministerial Powers, Cmnd 4060, 1932.

are laid before Parliament for 40 days, and if MPs bring forward and pass a negative resolution, the Statutory Instrument will have no effect. If no such resolution is passed then the law takes effect.

■ Affirmative resolution – this is considerably rarer and is used for more important or controversial instruments. It requires a positive vote on a resolution in the Commons (s.5 Statutory Instruments Act 1946).

The Joint Committee on Statutory Instruments has expressed dissatisfaction with these procedures. It argues that particular types of instruments need more detailed consideration by the House, for example instruments that attempt to exclude judicial review, that potentially go beyond the authority of the enabling Act or are an unusual or unexpected use of that power. There is currently no method for even identifying these problematic instruments.[12]

POINTS TO REVIEW

■ The law-making process is multi-stage, but revision and amendment is hampered by political partisanship.

■ There is considerable scope for improving the scrutiny and quality of legislative outputs.

TAKING IT FURTHER

House of Commons, 'Making laws', http://www.parliament.uk/about/how/laws/

If you need to take a step back and look at accessible material on the law-making process, the House of Commons resources are very useful. Once you have got a picture of the basics you will need to look at other sources, such as the ones below, for the detail you need to do well in assessments, but the links on this page can help you get a foundation of knowledge.

Cabinet Office, 'Guide to Making Legislation' (2015), https://www.gov.uk/government/publications/guide-to-making-legislation

This gives an interesting perspective on the law-making process. It is a guide to departmental teams on how to take a proposal all the way through the law-making process. It is very detailed, but if you focus on the first section and Chapters 2–4, you will get a good summary from a practical point of view.

12 Joint Committee on Statutory Instruments, http://www.parliament.uk/jcsi (last accessed 25/10/15).

House of Commons Select Committee on Political and Constitutional Reform, 'Ensuring standards in the quality of legislation', http://www.publications.parliament.uk/pa/cm201314/cmselect/cmpolcon/85/85.pdf

This identifies a range of problems with the law-making process and endorses Hansard Society recommendations for a Legislative Standards Committee. It can give you a sound critique of issues within the legislative process.

4

CHAPTER 4
CONSTITUTIONS

Constitutions establish and organise. Many institutions such as companies, charities and student law societies have constitutions to establish their existence, set up their internal structure and define their goals and powers. This is also the role of national constitutions. A constitution comprises the rules that establish the institutions of a state, allocate powers to those institutions and define the most important aspects of the relationship between the state and the individual. Just from this initial description you can see how important a constitution is. It establishes, to a greater or lesser degree, how a country is run. By laying down the most important aspects of the relationship between the state and citizen, it contributes to what kind of life citizens can lead.

A constitution is usually in the form of a single document. Whilst the UK has no such document, it is at least arguable that the UK does have some form of constitution, and we will explore its sources. In this chapter, we need to identify the nature and purpose of constitutions. By assessing the relative merits of the different approaches to constitutions, we can also consider whether the UK should adopt a codified constitution.

AS YOU READ

Much of this book is concerned with the detailed content of the UK constitution. In this chapter, we need to step back and look at constitutions as a concept or a legal tool. This involves looking at examples and approaches from different countries. Nevertheless, this all leads back to a consideration of the United Kingdom's constitutional system.

Students can sometimes have difficulty in getting a clear sense of what constitutions are. They can appear remote and abstract. They do not seem, at first glance, to have the direct role played in everyday life by, for example, simple contracts. The Contract Law teacher can lead their students into the subject through familiar scenarios of buying a bar of chocolate or a train ticket. The Public Law teacher needs to be more creative. Yet constitutions provide the structure, the overall architecture, of the legal systems and states in which we live. They are vitally important. One way of introducing yourself to the idea of a constitution is to find one that applies to your life and your activities on a much more local level.

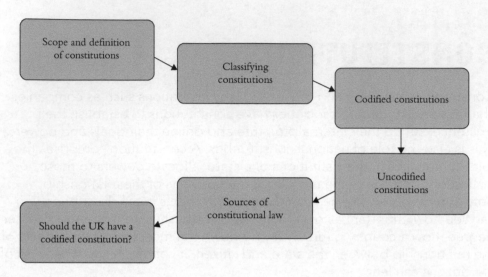

Figure 4.1 Structure of Chapter 4

4.1 THE SCOPE OF CONSTITUTIONAL LAW

As Barnett says, 'In lay terms, a constitution is a set of rules which governs an organisation'.[1] So most of the social, cultural, charitable or sporting groups that you belong to will have their own constitutions.

APPLYING THE LAW – STUDENT UNION CONSTITUTIONS

You are likely to belong to a students' union or some other sort of student body. Track down a copy of the student union constitution. You can normally do this online or by asking at your student union offices. If you cannot find the constitution of the organisation to which you belong (and it should be a matter of real concern and complaint if your union cannot supply this), then you can view a model constitution as suggested by the UK National Union of Students at http://www.nus.org.uk/PageFiles/673/Model-Constitution.pdf.

In relation to this constitution, consider:

■   What rights does the constitution give you as a member? (to vote, to stand for election etc)

---

1   H Barnett, *Constitutional and Administrative Law*, 11th edn (Routledge, 2016).

- What obligations does it impose on you as a member? (to abide by a Code of Conduct, etc)
- What institutions, offices and other positions does it set up? (an executive, council, Annual General Meeting etc)
- Is it based on some form of representative democracy? (elected officers, votes at AGMs, financial transparency, etc)

Even this simple exercise should start to reveal to you something of the nature of constitutions and the sorts of problems that they are designed to address. They seek to ensure that the institution is well-organised and efficient. They keep the operation of the institution in line with its stated aims and responsive to members' wishes. They are concerned with the abuse of power.

APPLYING THE LAW – DESIGNING A CONSTITUTION

In this scenario, there is a group of 100 people who want to establish a sports club (e.g. a tennis club). You know that members would be willing to pay an annual subscription of £100. There are currently no structures or organisation for the club. Some of the potential members approach you to draft a constitution for the sports club. In drafting this constitution there are a number of questions that you will need to address. These include:

(a) *What is the purpose of the organisation*? You are likely to include the sporting and recreational aims of the club in your constitution.

Many national constitutions have this sort of 'aims and objectives' preamble. The US Constitution of 1787 states that it was established by the people to, amongst other things, 'insure domestic tranquillity, provide for the common defence and promote the general welfare'. The Constitution of Brazil, drafted in 1988, outlines its purpose as:

to institute a Democratic State, for the purpose of ensuring the exercise of social and individual rights, liberty, security, well-being, development, equality and justice as supreme values of a fraternal, pluralist and unprejudiced society, founded on social harmony and committed, in the internal and international orders, to the peaceful settlement of disputes.

These general aims can be useful in a political sense of providing a purpose and sense of direction for the country and its institutions, and in a legal sense by helping with questions of interpretation. That is, laws should be interpreted as far as possible by judges to promote these purposes.

(b) *How is the organisation going to take decisions?* For significant decisions, such as whether to join a regional tennis league, you will probably want all of the members to have a say, through a general forum such as an annual general meeting. For day-to-day decisions, such as whether to update the website, and for the basic administration of the club, you will not want to have all 100 members sitting around the table debating the merits of an action and trying to reach a decision on it. You will need to have some sort of executive team or committee for this day-to-day administration. This might comprise a chair, a secretary and a treasurer. If the club expands, you might want to amend your constitution to provide for a membership secretary and a social secretary.

It is a central task of national constitutions to regulate this decision-making role and to set up the institutions that will make, implement and review these decisions. For a nation of millions of people, it is, in practice, very difficult to have the direct involvement of all citizens in decision-making. Only Switzerland uses direct referendums of its citizens on a regular basis. There have only ever been three UK-wide referendums. National constitutions, at least of the Western democratic model, set up a Parliament to represent the views of the people in taking significant decisions, but there is still a need for an executive (Government, civil service and public bodies) to administer the country on a day-to-day basis.

(c) *How is the organisation going to control the executive?* Having handed over significant powers to the executive officers, to exercise on behalf of the members, how do you ensure that these powers are exercised fairly and in response to members' needs? How do you prevent the abuse of power by those who exercise it? In your draft constitution, you will build in the methods for selecting these representative officers, usually through majority vote of all members in periodic elections. You will also want mechanisms to promote accountability and transparency. These may include an Annual General Meeting, the presentation of accounts and a treasurer's report, verification of finances by an independent auditor, and powers to remove people from office for misbehaviour.

This need for general organisation and limits on power are particularly important in relation to the nation state. If you are unhappy with the way your sports club is run, you can simply leave it. Short of emigrating, you cannot do this in relation to your country. The coercive powers that the nation state possesses (taxation, imprisonment, war) also underline the need for controls.

A key function of democratic constitutions is establishing processes to promote accountability. Democratic national constitutions will provide for periodic elections, and they often have limits on how long presidents or prime ministers can stay in office. They can outline procedures for dismissing senior office holders for crimes or other abuses of power (impeachment). They might give powers of scrutiny over the Government and civil servants to Parliament, for example through Prime Minister's Questions[2] and Parliamentary

---

2   You can watch Prime Minister's Questions on https://www.bbc.co.uk/iplayer/live/bbcparliament.

Select Committees. The constitution will normally provide for the courts to review the legality of official behaviour.

(d) *What are the main rights and responsibilities of members going to be?* For your sports club, this might include the right to play and to take part in competitions, and the right to vote and to attend meetings. You may outline responsibilities of mutual respect between club members, and obligations to avoid abuse or discriminatory behaviour.

National constitutions vary quite widely both in terms of what these rights and responsibilities are and whether they are included in the constitutional document itself. It is more common to include the main rights (e.g. the US Bill of Rights) than the main responsibilities (e.g. to pay taxes or to avoid criminal activity) which are left to ordinary legal provisions to regulate.

The constitutions of the clubs or societies that you belong to may seem, at first glance, to play a greater day-to-day role in your life than the national constitution. A national constitution is different, but it is largely a difference of degree and coverage rather than of essential nature; there are striking similarities, as outlined above. Both 'local' and national constitutions try to achieve comparable outcomes. It is useful to think of a constitution as a tool or a machine. It is constructed to achieve certain things.

APPLYING THE LAW – ANALYSING CONSTITUTIONS

Seeing a constitution as a legal tool has benefits for the development of your thinking skills. There is a tendency (often encouraged by the rulers) to see constitutions as an essential part of the fabric of the nation, as natural as its geography or climate. Regarding a constitution as a tool, just like any other legal rule chosen by humans, means seeing that the state did not *have to be* arranged in this particular way or did not have to adopt that particular form. We can evaluate these choices and see the consequences of choosing one form over another. Within this chapter we can only make a start on this task, but much of the rest of this book is concerned with the explanation and evaluation of the particular form and content of the UK constitution.

4.2 WHAT IS A CONSTITUTION?

The sections above helped you to see what a constitution is and what a constitution does, but it is useful to have a broad definition. There are many existing definitions to choose from, and the one here, from *Hood Phillips & Jackson*, is sufficiently broad to cover all the issues we want to discuss.

A constitution is 'the system of law, customs and conventions which define the composition and powers of organs of the state, and regulate the relations of the various state organs to one another and to the private citizen'.[3]

We will come back to the question of what form this system of law should take, in particular whether it needs to be codified into a single document. This definition, though, lets us arrive at three key elements of a constitution that we can use in our later analysis:

- Laws etc that define the composition and powers of organs of the state.
- Laws etc that regulate the relations of the various state organs to one another.
- Laws etc that regulate the relations of the various state organs to the private citizen.

4.3 CONSTITUTIONALISM

Most modern constitutions were developed in the context of a political and philosophical concept called *constitutionalism*. This has many facets, yet its basic content can be derived from considering a very practical issue.

ANALYSING THE LAW – THE PROBLEM OF STATE POWER

Imagine that in the middle of your next Public Law class a group of people burst into the room and say that they are going to take you away. If you struggle they will physically restrain you. They force you into the back of a van and take you to their base where they put you in a locked room for hours. This is, in substance (and subject to all sorts of justifications and constraints), a power that the state possesses, exercised as the process of arrest and detention through the state's police and security forces.

What would otherwise be a series of criminal acts (e.g. assault) and civil wrongs (e.g. false imprisonment) is transformed into the legitimate exercise of state power. What gives it this legitimacy? It cannot simply be any uniform the men are wearing or the sign on the building they take you to. These are merely symbols. There are many theories of the state and the legitimacy of state power, but most are derived from the notion that the constitution, *on behalf of the people*, establishes and legitimises the state powers. Public lawyers argue that, in return for this gift from the people to the state, the constitution

---

3   P Jackson and P Leopold, *O. Hood Phillips & Jackson Constitutional and Administrative Law* (8th edn, Sweet & Maxwell, 2001) 5.

must only grant limited and regulated powers to state organs and that the exercise of these powers is made accountable.

In the example above, therefore, constitutionalism requires that the police power to arrest and detain must be outlined in advance and in law. That law must have been made in the authorised manner, i.e. through being openly debated and approved in the Parliamentary process. In the UK, the power of arrest is normally limited by reasonable suspicion, which means that the police officer must have objective reasons (rather than a mere hunch) believe that the suspect has committed an offence before they can arrest. There are procedural safeguards: the reason for the arrest must be given, the arrestee must be taken to a designated police station, they must be informed of their right to legal advice, and only reasonable force may be used in the arrest. If there is an allegation of a breach of these safeguards, then there are practical mechanisms (complaints to an independent body; legal actions against the police) for investigating those allegations and providing redress for breaches.

Constitutionalism, therefore, 'suggests the limitation of power, the separation of powers, and the doctrine of responsible accountable government and the protection of individual rights and freedoms'.[4] As Lady Hale says, 'we have two constitutions – the legal and the political constitution. The first is represented by . . . concrete rules that the courts must and do apply when deciding real cases. The second is represented by such things as the way Parliamentarians behave, for example in response to the [Brexit] referendum'.[5]

Political constitutionalism puts its faith, primarily but not exclusively, in the political system to impose these limitations and to promote responsible government. The role of elections is crucial in making Government careful of exceeding its powers, but elections should not be the only method of making power accountable. Other safeguards such as freedom of information and a free press are also important. In political constitutionalism, power lies largely with the politicians and their need to maintain public support and consent.

Legal constitutionalism focuses more on the role of law and of the judiciary in defining and enforcing limitations on state power. This requires legal rules that are above the direct legal control of the Government and arguably have a higher status than the Parliament. The ultimate power in the state lies with these legal rules. The courts can have the final word on what these laws mean and cannot be overruled by Government or Parliament.

Political and legal constitutionalism are not mutually exclusive, and most states lie on a continuum that encompasses both methods. The UK has traditionally relied more on political constitutionalism. The development of judicial review and human rights legislation over the past half-century, though, has increased the role of legal constitutionalism.

---

4   Barnett, above n 1, 6.
5   Lady Hale, 'The United Kingdom Constitution on the move', Canadian Institute for Advanced Legal Studies lecture, 7 July 2017, www.supremecourt.uk/docs/speech-170707.pdf (last accessed 05/11/17).

4.4 CLASSIFYING CONSTITUTIONS

It is useful, in our task of becoming more familiar with constitutions, to identify a number of different types or classifications.

4.4.1 CODIFIED AND UNCODIFIED

The process of classifying constitutions tends to place them into one of two categories. These categories can have different labels. In your reading and your classes, you might see constitutions described as being written or unwritten; as taking the concrete or the abstract approach; or being constitutions in the narrow sense or the broad sense.

Each of these divisions is referring to a similar thing. The first terms (written, concrete, narrow) describe a situation where the fundamental laws have been separated out from the general pool of ordinary laws and collated in a single document (or set of documents) that is expressly called 'the constitution' of that country.

The second terms (unwritten, abstract, broad) refer to a situation where these fundamental rules, e.g. on the structure of the state and the powers of key institutions, are found in 'ordinary' laws and other types of rules. The constitutional rules are present, but they have not been collated into a single document.

For this reason, the terms 'codified' and 'uncodified' are preferred here. A problem with using the term 'unwritten constitution' is that it just seems an absurd notion. It also does not describe the reality of a situation where (almost all of) the rules *are* written, e.g. in Acts of Parliament. As Brazier says, 'The British Constitution is written, but it isn't codified into a single official document'.[6] You will need to be aware of the 'written/unwritten' distinction because you will read other sources that use this terminology, but the use of the 'codified/uncodified' terms avoids the strange situation of saying that 'much of the unwritten UK Constitution is written'.

EXPLAINING THE LAW – UNCODIFIED CONSTITUTIONS

Almost all countries in the world have a codified constitution. There are said to be only three states that take the uncodified approach: New Zealand, Israel and the UK.

New Zealand actually has a Constitution Act 1986 which states in the preamble that its purpose is to 'bring together into one enactment certain provisions of constitutional significance'. The Act, though, is not comprehensive and has no special legal authority compared to ordinary law. The Basic Laws of Israel were intended to form part of a single codified constitution but the process was never

6   R Brazier, 'How Near is a Written Constitution?' (2001) 52 *Northern Ireland Law Quarterly* 3.

completed. Most of the key legal rules on the organs of the state can be found in nine Basic Laws, though again there is no automatic precedence of the Basic Laws over ordinary laws.

To find the comprehensive constitutions of these countries, you would need to look at other legislative rules, court decisions and non-legal constitutional conventions, i.e. the sources of the constitution are not wholly codified. It would probably be more accurate, though, to describe the constitutions in New Zealand and Israel as lying on a spectrum between codified and uncodified.

By far the clearest example of the uncodified approach is the United Kingdom. We need to explore why the UK stands in such an isolated position.

4.5 WHY DOES THE UK NOT HAVE A CODIFIED CONSTITUTION?

Given the unusual nature of its constitution, it is worth asking why the UK does not have a codified constitution. The answer lies in historical continuity. Codified constitutions are normally adopted following some fundamental break with the previous regime, and they represent a fresh start for the country.

Examples include those constitutions drafted during or after revolutions, e.g. the US Constitution (1787) and the first French constitution (1791). The less violent but equally revolutionary changes in South Africa following the end of apartheid rule led to a wholly new codified constitution in 1996. This historical break can also arise from nations gaining their independence from colonial rule, e.g. Nigeria (1951, since replaced) and East Timor (2002), or secession from a larger state, e.g. South Sudan (2011).

It is often argued that the UK has had no such major break in its governance. This means that there has been 'an unusual degree of continuity in the governing institutions',[7] and so its system of government has evolved over the centuries. This explains why there has been no particular point when there was a need to sit down with a blank sheet of paper and decide on the structure of the state, its institutions and the fundamental rights of citizens.

Any historical account though needs to recognise that England *did* have a major revolution: the English Civil War (1642–1651). Following the defeat of the Royalist forces, an Instrument of Government was adopted in 1653. Although limited in scope, it could be called a codified constitution. It was replaced by a second codified constitution in 1657.

---

7   M Elliott and R Thomas, *Public Law* (3rd edn, OUP, 2017) 81.

On the Restoration of the monarchy in 1660, these constitutions were treated as being wholly illegitimate and the old monarchical system was regarded as having continued unbroken.

There have been major constitutional changes in the UK since then, not least the formation of the UK itself, through the Unions of England and Wales with Scotland and then with Ireland. The independence of most of Ireland, plus the effect of membership of the European Union, also radically changed the political structure of the United Kingdom in the last century. The ongoing devolutionary pressures in Scotland and Wales have already changed the nature of the relationship between the countries that make up the UK and may well change that relationship even further (see Chapter 11, 'Devolution'). It is only in recent years, though, that senior political figures have openly mooted the idea of a codified constitution for the UK.[8]

4.6 OTHER CLASSIFICATIONS

Each national constitution is unique and designed to suit the needs of that country (or at least its rulers). It is, however, possible to categorise constitutions in a number of additional ways. The most useful for the purpose of analysing the nature of constitutions and their functions are as follows.

4.6.1 MONARCHICAL/REPUBLICAN

On the face of it, this is a simple distinction between having either a president or a monarch as head of state. A president will typically be directly elected with significant powers in (at least) foreign affairs and internal policy-making. A monarch will typically have a figurehead role with no, or very little, political or legal authority. The distinction, though, is not quite so simple or so stark.

Some presidents have limited legal roles. This is the case in Germany and Ireland. These presidents perform something akin to the national figurehead role that monarchs perform in other countries. This figurehead function is supposed, to some extent, to apply to the US President. The substantive political power of the US President, though, restricts the viability of the Presidency being a unifying figurehead for all citizens and this has deteriorated in recent decades, particularly in the response of some sections of US society to the Obama presidency and (for different reasons) the Trump presidency.

Monarchical systems can co-exist with codified constitutions, and a significant number of Western liberal democracies retain monarchical systems, for example Spain, Netherlands, Denmark and Canada. Monarchs can be allocated residual or emergency powers under

---

8   Lord Scarman, *Why Britain Needs a Written Constitution* (Charter 88, 1992). Both Labour and Liberal Democrat parties have made electoral pledges to explore the suitability of a codified constitution for the UK.

these constitutions. Monarchs in other states, such as Saudi Arabia and Morocco, have huge legal and political power.

The UK, of course, has a monarchical system and a large number of important legal powers still reside (at least formally) with the Crown. We will see in Chapter 6, 'Royal prerogative', that these are largely exercised by Government ministers rather than by the Queen personally. It is arguable though that the Crown has some residual legal rights that can be exercised personally in very limited emergency situations, particularly where there is a threat to democracy.

4.6.2 FEDERAL/UNITARY

All states have some form of division between central and local government. Even France, the country most often cited as an example of a unitary state (though it is much less so now), has its *régions, départements* and *communes*. So what are the distinguishing features of a federal system? The key question is whether the regional and local units exercise their powers *as of right*, i.e. they are not reliant on a grant of power from central Government, and their powers derive directly from a constitution. States where local government powers are delegated from the central authority, with the possibility that the delegation will be reversed, are not true federal states. A federal constitution, with a higher authority than the central Government, will allocate powers, protect the competencies of the regional and local units and define the federal character of a state.

Although the division of powers between federal and regional units varies widely between states, some typical areas reserved for the national level include defence and foreign policy, whilst local competences may include planning and education.

Some federal systems have a uniform set of powers for each region, though they will then be exercised in different ways. A well-known example of this is the decision by the US state of Delaware to become a corporate haven. This involved exercising their local law-making powers under the US federal system to adopt company-friendly laws and light regulation. As a result, a majority of US public companies are now incorporated in Delaware. The formal scope of these local legislative powers, though, is the same for each US state. Other countries, such as Spain, have a variegated patchwork with different federal arrangements for different regions, often dependent on their political, cultural or linguistic distance from the 'centre'.

In the UK, power is devolved in a patchwork way to Scotland, Wales and Northern Ireland (see Chapter 11, 'Devolution'). In addition, there is an extensive system of local government and variation between the structure and powers of these local authorities, particularly the Mayor of London and the London Assembly (and now some large northern English cities such as Manchester).

All the powers of these bodies, and even the existence of the bodies themselves, are a product of statute or prerogative, that is, of law-making by the central law-maker. Power is granted from the centre and may be taken back. Under current conditions, this might seem to be purely theoretical in relation to some devolutions of power, especially in relation to Scotland, but also for the Assembly of Wales and the Mayor of London. It appears to be so politically unacceptable to withdraw power back to the centre from these institutions that it has to all intents and purposes been permanently devolved.

EXPLAINING THE LAW – DEVOLUTION OF POWER TO LOCAL AUTHORITIES

This idea that pulling power back to the centre is politically unthinkable is always contingent on political conditions and attitudes, and these can change. There are precedents for this. The Greater London Council (GLC), and its smaller predecessor, the London County Council, had operated a system of local government over London since 1889. The GLC became involved in increasingly bitter disputes with the Conservative Government in the early 1980s. As a result, the Government proposed the abolition of the GLC and this was achieved by the Local Government Act 1985.

The plasticity of these arrangements is further illustrated by the fact that power was devolved back to an overall London authority by the Greater London Authority Act 1999. This established the directly elected Mayor of London and London Assembly that exist today.

The withdrawal of power from the Northern Ireland Assembly by the Northern Ireland Constitution Act 1973, and the potential for direct Westminster rule as a consequence of the 2017 stalemate between the Northern Irish parties, is a further illustration that in the UK power can be both granted by the central authority and drawn back to the centre.

4.6.3 RIGID/FLEXIBLE

This distinction refers to how easy it is to change provisions of the constitution. Codified constitutions are normally designed to be protected from change and therefore they are often entrenched. This means that there are stringent, or at least more stringent, rules for amending constitutional laws than for normal laws.

Barnett describes the UK constitution as representing 'the height of flexibility'.[9] Any part of the UK constitutional system can be amended or abolished simply by passing an Act of Parliament. There is no requirement for a special majority or a referendum. The central role of constitutional conventions (which are non-legal rules of constitutional

---

9   Barnett, above n 1, 9.

behaviour – see Chapter 5) in the UK adds to this flexibility so that a person can act unconstitutionally without acting illegally and this behaviour is not capable of being judged by the courts. It also seems possible for politicians to change the content of constitutional conventions simply by acting differently from their predecessors.

It is important to grasp this general division between rigid and flexible constitutions, but again there is a more sophisticated understanding. There are many non-legal constraints on constitutional change in the UK, and many of the UK's constitutional features are remarkably durable in practice. In countries with seemingly rigid constitutions, the application of constitutional rules to citizens can be fluid and changing. Constitutions themselves can be amended or discarded with alarming frequency; France adopted 16 different constitutions between 1791 and 1958.

ANALYSING THE LAW – SHOOTINGS AND THE US SECOND AMENDMENT

The ability to respond to events by changing the legal duties of citizens is a sign of a flexible constitution.

In August 1987, a lone gunman in Hungerford in England killed 16 people and wounded 15 others using weapons, including semi-automatic rifles, which he legally owned. The Westminster Parliament responded by passing the Firearms (Amendment) Act 1988 which banned the private ownership of semi-automatic weapons. In March 1996, a gunman entered Dunblane Primary School, Scotland and killed 16 children and 1 adult. The killer used pistols and revolvers that he legally owned. Parliament again acted to restrict the rights of individuals to own firearms and effectively banned the private ownership of handguns through the Firearms (Amendment) Act 1997.

The most recent mass-shooting incident using legally owned firearms in the UK was the Cumbria shootings of June 2010. There was no legislative response to this, but gun control was reviewed further. David Cameron said, 'We should be clear that in this country we have some of the toughest gun control legislation anywhere in the world and we shouldn't make any kneejerk reaction to think that there is some instant legislative or regulatory answer'.[10] The key point for you to note from these episodes is that the UK Government and Parliament *could* act quickly to change the law and restrict individual rights.

In April 1999, 12 students and a teacher were killed by two students of Columbine High School, Colorado, USA. This only counts as the *fifth* worst school massacre in

10 J Miekle and H Carter, 'Cumbria shootings: government warns against rash changes to gun laws' *The Guardian* (3 June 2010), www.guardian.co.uk/uk/2010/jun/03/cumbria-shootings-theresa-may-gun-laws-review (last accessed 05/11/17).

the US, and there has been a seemingly endless cycle of mass shootings in the US. *The Guardian* reported that there had been around 1,000 mass shooting incidents in the US in 2012–15.[11]

The response to these shootings has often focused more on social and cultural issues such as bullying, video games and music than on gun control. President Trump has blamed failings in mental health provision rather than in gun control laws. An exception was Michael Moore's documentary *Bowling for Columbine*, which emphasised the lax controls over gun ownership in US law, and President Obama often expressed his deep anger and frustration at the continued deaths. What, however, has been the legislative response? It has been very limited. A key reason for this is the existence of the Second Amendment to the US Constitution, which states, 'A well-regulated militia being necessary to the security of a free state, the right of the people to keep and bear arms shall not be infringed'.

The right to bear arms is not absolute. There are restrictions imposed on felons and children, and there are some variations from state to state. The *constitutional* right to bear arms, though, limits the ability of state and federal law-makers to respond to incidents such as this by restricting individual rights to gun ownership, even if they wished to do so. Attempts by Senator Dianne Feinstein in 2015 to address the remarkable fact that individuals on the US terror watch list, who are forbidden from flying, have a right to purchase firearms were voted down by Senate Republicans.

Some scholars insist that the Second Amendment was not concerned with giving individuals a personal right to own firearms but only the right to do so as part of 'well-regulated militia'; nevertheless, the 'personal right' approach has been confirmed by the US Supreme Court and has become entrenched in political and social culture.

This illustrates a further aspect of entrenched constitutional rights. The law has exerted an influence on popular culture (there are around 90 guns per 100 Americans)[12] and these attitudes have in turn reinforced the status of the law. The firearms industry is lucrative and there are well-supported pressure groups – the National Rifle Association describes itself as the oldest civil rights organisation in the US and has over 4 million members. The US Constitution is entrenched legally through Article V (see below), but these social and political attitudes are equally important in making this a rigid part of the Constitution.

....

11 M Teague, 'Inglis, Florida: home to the 1,000th US mass shooting since Sandy Hook', *The Guardian* (11 October 2015), http://www.theguardian.com/world/2015/oct/11/mass-shooting-florida-1000th-sandy-hook (last accessed 05/11/17).

12 Graduate Institute of International Studies, Small Arms Survey, 2007: Guns and the City (Geneva, 2007).

4.7 CODIFIED CONSTITUTIONS

As we saw above, you have almost the whole world to choose from if you want to examine the nature and operation of codified constitutions. The US Constitution, though, is the most studied and debated constitution in the world. It was adopted in 1787 and followed the failure of the first US constitution, the Articles of Confederation and Perpetual Union. The document was drafted by delegates from 12 of the 13 states and then ratified by all 13 states. Its key purposes were to establish an effective federal government, to preserve the rights of the states and to give effect to some of the democratic ideals that had informed (together with more mercantile ambitions) the War of American Independence. The Constitution initially comprised only seven Articles which outlined the basic structure of the federal government and the relationship between the federal and state governments.

Shortly after the Constitution came into force, ten amendments were adopted. These became known as the Bill of Rights and provided for personal freedoms such as rights of trial by jury and protection from unreasonable search and seizure. There have been a further 17 amendments covering issues such as the abolition of slavery (Thirteenth Amendment, 1865), the prohibition of alcohol (Eighteenth Amendment, 1919; repealed by the Twenty-First Amendment, 1933) and the extension of voting rights to women (Nineteenth Amendment, 1920).

The first three Articles establish the structure of the federal state.

Figure 4.2 Structure of the US state

- Article I, Section 1 provides that 'All legislative powers herein granted shall be vested in a Congress of the United States, which shall consist of a Senate and House of Representatives'.
- Article II, Section 1 states that 'The executive power shall be vested in a President of the United States of America'.
- Article III, Section 1 says that 'The judicial power of the United States, shall be vested in one Supreme Court, and in such inferior courts as the Congress may from time to time ordain and establish'.

APPLYING THE LAW – THE US CONSTITUTION AS AN ARCHETYPAL CONSTITUTION

Compare these three Articles to the three key elements of constitutions identified by Hood Phillips & Jackson (above).

- Laws etc that define the composition and powers of organs of the state.
- Laws etc that regulate the relations of the various state organs to one another.
- Laws etc that regulate the relations of the various state organs to the private citizen.

The first element, to 'define the composition and powers of the organs of the state', is met by these Articles I–III that establish the bodies which exercise the power of the federal state. They also divide the three great legal powers of the nation state (*legislative*, to make law; *executive*, to apply the law; and *judicial*, to interpret the law and resolve legal disputes) and allocate them to separate institutions (legislative – Congress; executive – President; judicial – Supreme Court).

There are many ways in which the US Constitution addresses the second feature of constitutions, of regulating the relationship between different parts of state, and one example is impeachment of the president.

EXPLAINING THE LAW – IMPEACHMENT OF THE US PRESIDENT

Article II, Section 4 provides that 'The President, Vice President and all civil officers of the United States, shall be removed from office on impeachment for, and conviction of, treason, bribery, or other high crimes and misdemeanours'.

Impeachment is the formal process of charging the President, or other civil officer, with crimes etc and, if successful, is followed by the trial itself. The US Constitution gives the power of impeachment to the House of Representatives and the power of trial to the Senate. A conviction requires a two-thirds majority vote in the Senate.

Two US presidents have been impeached. Andrew Johnson was accused of breaching laws that protected the tenure of the Secretary of War in 1868. Bill Clinton was accused in 1998 of perjury and obstruction of justice over statements, made under oath, about his relationship with White House intern Monica Lewinsky. In both cases, the presidents were not convicted at the Senate trial, though Johnson survived by only a single vote.

The president who would almost certainly have been impeached *and* convicted was Richard Nixon. In 1972–73, President Nixon's involvement in a series of scandals involving phone tapping and the cover-up of a burglary attempt of the opposition headquarters (the Watergate scandal) became increasingly apparent. To avoid impeachment, Nixon resigned; he is the only US President to do so. At the time of writing, President Donald Trump has not been impeached.

These constitutional provisions illustrate a regulatory power that one part of the state (Congress) has over another part (President). The purpose is to prevent abuses of power, and the US Constitution provides a whole series of these checks and balances between the different parts of the state. Further examples include the presidential veto over Acts of Congress and that Justices of the Supreme Court are appointed by the President 'by and with the consent of the Senate'.

The third element of a constitution is to regulate the fundamental aspects of the relationship between the state and the individual. We have seen how the US Constitution does this in part through the Second Amendment and the right to bear arms. The Bill of Rights regulates other aspects of this relationship, most famously in the First Amendment. This states that 'Congress shall make no law . . . abridging the freedom of speech, or of the press; or the right of the people peaceably to assemble, and to petition the government for a redress of grievances'.

Free speech has a central place in US politics and culture, and is often regarded as the pre-eminent right. It is not absolute and there are the usual restrictions in relation to e.g. obscenity, national security, and threats of violence. *Brandenburg v Ohio*, 395 US 444 (1969) lays down the general test for legitimate limitations to freedom of expression: the state can only restrict expression where that expression 'is directed to inciting or producing imminent lawless action and is likely to incite or cause such action'.

4.8 CONSEQUENCES OF HAVING A CODIFIED CONSTITUTION

You can see from the example of the US Constitution that a codified constitution has all of the basic elements of a constitution. It establishes state institutions and endows them with power, and it regulates their relationship with each other and between the citizen and the state. There are some further consequences of adopting a codified constitution. These are that, normally:

- the constitution will be *entrenched*
- constitutional laws will have a *higher legal status* than ordinary laws.

Entrenchment means having stringent, or at least more stringent, procedures for amending constitutional laws than for changing ordinary laws. It is possible, though rare, for a constitution to provide for total entrenchment. This means that there is no legal mechanism for amending or repealing that provision.

EXPLAINING THE LAW – COMPLETE ENTRENCHMENT IN THE GERMAN BASIC LAW

The Basic Law of the Federal Republic of Germany contains a so-called eternity clause that indicates that any attempt to amend certain provisions of the Basic Law will be inadmissible. This clause protects provisions covering the dignity of people and fundamental human rights, democracy, the rule of law and the separation of powers.

A consequence of complete entrenchment is that these parts of the constitution cannot be altered by the German President, Chancellor, Parliament, courts, states or people (i.e. through referendum), whether they act individually or in concert. These unusual provisions can be explained by the historical context. The Basic Law was adopted in 1949 in the aftermath of the Second World War. The German people had seen the subversion of democratic controls by the Nazis under the old, more flexible Weimar Constitution. This was followed by a wholesale assault on human rights and human dignity under the Nazi regime. The framers of the Basic Law were the three main Western allies who had fought the Nazis, and the German leaders who had often been victims of the Nazi regime. Their desire to place the basic fundamentals of human rights and democracy beyond the scope of legal change is understandable.

The safeguard of *partial entrenchment* is much more common. This means that the constitutional provision *can* be changed but only by the special process outlined in the constitution. One example is Article V of the US Constitution. This provides that:

The Congress, whenever two thirds of both houses shall deem it necessary, shall propose amendments to this Constitution, or, on the application of the legislatures of two thirds of the several states, shall call a convention for proposing amendments, which, in either case, shall be valid to all intents and purposes, as part of this

Constitution, when ratified by the legislatures of three fourths of the several states, or by conventions in three fourths thereof, as the one or the other mode of ratification may be proposed by the Congress.

ANALYSING THE LAW – THINKING ABOUT ARTICLE V

You will often be asked to *analyse* and *evaluate* legal provisions as part of your studies and your assessments. These are different intellectual tasks. The most influential approach to identifying different reasoning skills has been Bloom's taxonomy from 1956. An updated categorisation was put forward by Anderson and Krathwohl in 2000.

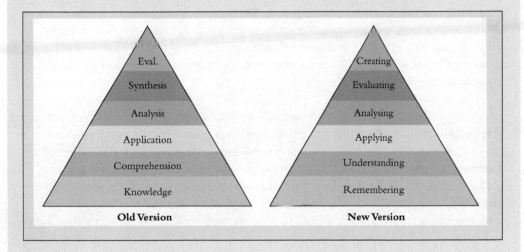

Figure 4.2.2

http://www.karenwalstraconsulting.com/home/index.php?ipkArticleID=15 (last accessed 05/11/17)

Analysing means identifying the component parts of a concept or a provision and finding how the parts relate to each other. Evaluating can be broadly summarised as making a judgement based on standards and criteria.

Bearing in mind the descriptions of these reasoning skills, analyse Article V.

Your *analysis* should identify that there are two possible procedures: (a) the proposal can come from Congress, with a two-thirds majority of both Houses; the proposal is then ratified by three-quarters of states; or (b) two-thirds of states can agree to call a convention (i.e. a meeting); a proposal from the convention is then ratified by three-quarters of states. If you can identify these elements in Article V, then you are undertaking legal analysis.

Your *evaluation* would almost certainly require further reading, and therefore involves research skills. You could focus on the *effectiveness* of the procedures as your standard and see that only the first procedure has been used in practice. You could evaluate Article V on the basis of the consequences for the *balance of power* between Congress and the states and decide that, whilst Congress has an important power of initiative, ultimately the decision on constitutional amendments lies with the states. You could evaluate the *practicality* of the constitutional amendment process and conclude that since it has only been successfully invoked 18 times (involving 27 amendments) in over 225 years, then the process can be applied, but that the high levels of consensus needed for change make it difficult.

APPLYING THE LAW – SHOW YOUR REASONING

The more you practise these thinking skills, the better you will become at them. These are often the skills that you need to increase your marks, and as you go through your degree you will need to demonstrate them to pick up first-class and high 2:1 marks. Being able to think about subjects in this way also simply makes the subjects more interesting.

The tip here is to be *explicit*. When you are analysing a case, a statutory provision or a legal principle (by identifying its component parts), state clearly that this is what you are doing. When you are evaluating some legal reform, against a standard of fairness, or openness, or efficiency, make it obvious what your standard is and that you are evaluating. This flags up to your tutor that you are engaged in these higher reasoning processes, that your conclusions are likely to be sound because they are well-reasoned and that you are doing your own thinking about a subject rather than just repeating the views of others.

The second key consequence of enshrining certain legal rules in a written constitution is that they can have a **higher legal status**, i.e. priority in case of conflict with an ordinary law. The South African Constitution of 1996 explicitly states this priority in Article 2: 'This Constitution is the supreme law of the Republic; law or conduct inconsistent with it is invalid'.

The US Constitution makes no provision for priority in case of conflict, but the question of the status of Constitutional Law soon arose before the Supreme Court in the case of *Marbury v Madison*, 5 US 137 (1803):

> If courts are to have regard to the Constitution, and the Constitution is superior to any ordinary act of the legislature, the Constitution, and not such ordinary act, must govern the case to which they both apply.

This gave the Constitution a higher legal status than ordinary law (including even the laws of Congress). The Supreme Court also found that resolution of any conflict between a constitutional law and an ordinary law was a process of legal interpretation and therefore it was a judicial function. The result was a power of judicial review, with judges able to declare invalid any ordinary laws that were inconsistent with the higher constitutional law.

4.9 THE UK SYSTEM IN COMPARISON WITH CODIFIED CONSTITUTIONS

As we shall see, the UK constitutional rules are scattered through a wide range of sources; it is the uncodified constitution *par excellence*. The UK constitutional system does not provide for either entrenchment or priority in case of conflict. Supremacy of Parliament means that any Act of Parliament, even one dealing with issues of fundamental constitutional importance, is made in the same way as a law dealing with more mundane matters. It can be amended or repealed in the same way as any other law, and therefore entrenchment does not seem to be possible (remember that entrenchment involves more stringent processes for amending constitutional rules).

Similarly, as there is no definitive list or collated group of 'constitutional laws', it is impossible to give any Act of Parliament a higher legal status, and therefore a priority in case of conflict, with any other Act. In these circumstances, a later Act will repeal an earlier statutory provision regardless of the constitutional significance of that earlier rule (see Chapter 7, 'Supremacy of Parliament').

APPLYING THE LAW – CONFLICTING STATUTES

Imagine that provisions of the Protection of Badgers Act 1992 (as a random example of a narrow ordinary law) conflict with provisions of the Act of Settlement 1701, one of the most important statutes in the UK constitutional system. How would the conflict be resolved?

The first thing to note would be that they were made the same way. Both statutes were agreed by the House of Commons and the House of Lords and then received the Royal Assent. There was no *special procedure* for making the constitutionally more important law. Secondly, you would not be able to find any mechanism that entrenches the Act of Settlement. It is subject to legal repeal or amendment in the same way as any other Act of Parliament. Third, the normal rule is that when there is an inconsistency between two statutory rules, then the earlier Act is impliedly repealed (i.e. ceases to have legal effect) to the extent that it is inconsistent. If the matter came before a court, therefore, the judges would have to say that the Protection of Badgers Act 1992 impliedly repealed the Act of Settlement 1701.

There is a different line of thought on this issue, stating that whilst constitutionally important Acts can be expressly repealed, it has become a new rule of statutory interpretation that they cannot be impliedly repealed. The status of this rule of construction is not entirely clear, but it shows that UK constitutional in still in flux even on major issues – see Chapter 7, Supremacy of Parliament.

It is natural, therefore, that questions arise as to whether the UK can be even said to have 'a constitution' at all. A number of, mainly British, constitutional writers have argued that the UK does have a constitution by reference to the notion of an uncodified, or unwritten, constitution.

4.10 UNCODIFIED CONSTITUTIONS

You cannot walk into a bookshop and buy a copy of 'the United Kingdom Constitution'. Doing an internet search of the phrase 'UK Constitution' might produce hundreds of thousands of results, but none of the links will take you to a document that *actually is* the constitution of the UK. Can you conclude from this that the UK does not possess a constitution? There are some scholars who argue that you should not reach this conclusion.

Essentially, these writers are arguing that the written constitution form, i.e. of codifying the most important constitutional rules into a single document and endowing those rules with a higher legal status, is not the only form that a constitution can take.

Colin Turpin states that a constitution is simply 'A body of rules, conventions and practices which regulate or qualify the organisation and operation of government in the UK'.[13] Similarly, K C Wheare defines a constitution as 'the whole system of government of a country, the collection of rules which establish and regulate or govern the government'.[14]

According to these definitions, a constitution must deal systematically with the institutions of government, their relations with each other and with the citizens. There is no requirement in these definitions for any special *form* for such rules; they *might be* collated in a single document or they *might be* found in multiple legal sources. As the content and not the form is the most important issue, the lack of a codified document does not prevent the existence of a constitution.

It is obvious that the UK has a whole range of rules 'which regulate or qualify the organisation and operation of government'. Much of this book is concerned with identifying and explaining these rules. Just one example to illustrate the existence of these rules is the formation of the Supreme Court of the United Kingdom (considered in

13 C Turpin, *British Government and the Constitution* (5th edn, Butterworths, 2002) 22.
14 K C Wheare, *Modern Constitutions* (2nd edn, OUP, 1966) 15.

depth in Chapter 9, 'Separation of powers'). The Supreme Court was established by the Constitutional Reform Act 2005 as the highest appellate court in the UK. It is the final court of appeal on all matters except for Scottish criminal appeals.

■ As we saw when looking at the US Constitution, establishing judicial institutions and allocating judicial power to them is a basic function of a constitution.
■ Similarly, there are rules which regulate the relationship of the Supreme Court to other parts of the state (e.g. preventing an overlap of membership between the Supreme Court and Parliament, setting out the limited role of the executive in the appointment of Supreme Court judges).
■ The relationship between this branch of the state and the citizen is defined, to some extent, by the rules on the jurisdiction of the Court which set out how and when citizens can access the Court.

4.11 OBJECTIONS TO THE UNCODIFIED APPROACH

There have long been other writers who have objected to this approach to defining constitutions. Their suspicion is that advocates of this uncodified, or abstract, approach are merely *describing* the system that happens to operate in the UK and then attaching the label 'constitution' to it. They are failing to identify the essence or the core criteria of what should qualify as a constitution. As Ridley says, 'Not to be left out of the world of constitutional democracies, British writers define constitution in a way that seems to give us one too . . . it simply shifts the ground, by using the word in an entirely different way'.[15] He responds directly to the assertion that the form of the constitution is not crucial by arguing that what is really important is that the constitution needs to be a special category of law.

Thomas Paine was an English radical of the eighteenth century who was a fierce critic of the English establishment system and a direct inspiration for both the American and French Revolutions. His retort to claims that there was an English constitution was 'A constitution is not a thing in name only, but in fact. It has not an ideal but a real existence; and wherever it cannot be produced in visible form, there is none'.[16]

He went on to argue that 'A Constitution is not the act of a government, but of a people constituting a government, and a government without a constitution is power without right'.[17] The key point he was communicating was that in the English system, any

---

15 F F Ridley, 'There is No British Constitution: A Dangerous Case of the Emperor's Clothes' [1988] *Parliamentary Affairs* 340.
16 T Paine, *Rights of Man*, 1790 (Dover, 2000).
17 Ibid.

constitutional rules that existed had been made by the Government. The Government itself (comprising, in this case, the King, the King's ministers and Parliament) had not been legitimately created by a constitution. The cart was before the horse.

This contrasted with the position in the US. The people's representatives (albeit limited to those of white men) had come together in a large meeting, a Constitutional Convention, to draft the constitution. In addition, the people's representatives at the state level had ratified this constitution. When it came into effect, it *created* the institutions of Government and endowed them with powers. The US Government did not create the constitution, rather it was a creature of that constitution and subject to its rules and limitations.

These points were developed further by Ridley. He echoed Paine's view that the UK does not have a constitution at all, merely a system of government. To justify this, he identified four essential characteristics of a constitution.

1(a) An existence prior to a system of government. This criterion is not met in the UK. We saw earlier that the UK, like the US and other countries, has a Supreme Court. This institution, though, was not created by a constitution but through a proposal from the Government of the day that was passed by Parliament as the part of the Constitutional Reform Act 2005. It was the *existing organs* of the system of government that decided to establish the Court, to define its composition and powers.

2(b) It establishes an authority outside and above the institutions it creates; power is attributed to the people. This criterion is not met. As Madgwich and Woodhouse say, there is no 'notion of an authority higher than the government of the day'.[18]

3(c) It contains a form of law which is superior to ordinary law because it originates in an authority higher than the legislature. We have already seen that, as a consequence of the supremacy of Parliament, the UK legal system does not recognise any higher form of law than ordinary Acts of Parliament.

4(d) It is entrenched, because its purpose is to limit the power of Government. Again, because of the continuing supremacy of Parliament, entrenching laws against future change does not seem to be legally possible within our current system.

According to this approach, the UK clearly does not meet the essential criteria and therefore does not have 'a constitution'. At this point, you would be forgiven for feeling a little exasperated (but surely also a little intrigued?). The UK does not have the sort of codified document that most of the rest of the world thinks of as embodying a constitution. There are some writers like Wheare, though, who argue that it is possible to identify a constitution from the many laws from diverse sources that deal with 'constitutional' issues even if they are not codified into a single document. This would mean that the UK does have a constitution. Then there are other writers, like Paine and Ridley, who argue that this uncodified approach is misconceived and that as the UK system does not match the

18 P Madgwich and D Woodhouse, *The Law and Politics of the Constitution of the United Kingdom* (Wheatsheaf, 1995) 75.

essential core characteristics of a 'constitution', then the UK simply does not have one. Is there a way out of this argument?

One possibility is to see this dispute as an argument about *definitions*. It focuses on the *label* to be attached to the governing system in a country. There are many times in law where the accuracy and clarity of definitions is crucial. In defining what amounts to the criminal offence of theft, for example, the statutory definition allows people to know what behaviour will be stigmatised as criminal and leave them exposed to punishment by the state; it needs to be as precise as possible. But is an all-encompassing, universally accepted single definition of 'constitution' as important here?

There are good reasons for thinking not.

ANALYSING THE LAW – KARL POPPER AND DEFINITIONS AS LABELS

Karl Popper was an Austrian philosopher of science and politics, who argued that Western political thought had fallen prey to the fault of 'essentialism' since the time of Aristotle. By this he meant that there was too much emphasis on debating the essential characteristics, or the definition, of particular concepts. He urged political thinkers (and by extension, us as students of Constitutional Law) to focus instead on problem-solving.

In the context of this chapter then, Popper's approach would be that the issue of what is the essence, or the objectively correct definition, of 'a constitution' is of secondary importance. The key question is, what are the problems and dangers inherent in systems of government and in how these Governments treat their citizens? The focus then moves to designing systems or tools that solve those problems and minimise those risks, whatever label you want to attach to those systems.

The evidence of history, and of different crises around the world in current times, shows us what some of the problems and risks are. They include systems of government that are inefficient and unstable; systems that lack transparency and that do not reflect the wishes of the people; systems where power is so concentrated in the hands of one person or one party that they can act without restraint; and systems that deny basic rights to their citizens and subject their citizens (and others) to ill-treatment and death.

So one way of proceeding with our evaluation is to see a constitution as a practical tool that can establish, or at least help to establish, an effective and responsive system of government, protect citizens from abuses of powers by institutions and, perhaps, articulate the fundamental values of the people.

4.12 PURPOSIVE APPROACH

If this purposive approach is going to be taken, then the immediate question is – what are the purposes of a constitution? There is no objectively correct answer to this. Popper would say that any conclusions on purposes should be subject to broad-based discussion so as to reach a consensus view. Following on from the previous section that outlined the dangers inherent in allowing wide powers to the state, we can say that a constitution ought to try to achieve the following:

1(a) To establish, allocate power to and impose limits on the main institutions of a state. We can link this to the earlier discussion of constitutionalism and the belief in limited government. If we had to pick out one *paramount purpose* of constitutions, then it would be to restrain the power of the state for the benefit of the people.

2(b) To make that system of government responsive to the wishes of the people. Sunstein argues that 'the central goal of a constitution is to create the preconditions for a well-functioning democratic order'.[19] Of course, not all states are democratic, or democratic in the way it is understood in Western societies. Their constitutions are drafted with little or no input from the people and to reflect the fundamental arrangements that the rulers want: dictatorship, one-party rule etc. The democratic purpose, though, is an ideal that we can use as a standard.

3(c) To reflect or articulate the fundamental values of the people. This is a more controversial objective. The fundamental values in a constitution may be those of the ruling elite rather than the people. Even if a provision on an ethical issue does reflect the views of a majority of people, enshrining it in the constitution may cause problems for those citizens who hold a different view. The 1937 Irish Constitution Article 41 said that 'No law shall be enacted providing for a dissolution of marriage'. This prohibition on divorce was confirmed by referendum in 1986, but it was seen as oppressive to those who did not share traditional Catholic views on divorce. It was removed by a constitutional amendment in 1996.

---

19 C Sunstein, *Designing Democracy: What Constitutions Do* (OUP, 2001) 6.

Taking this purposive approach, we can ask: does the UK have a system (whether we choose to label it 'a constitution' or not) that fulfils this purpose?

You can see immediately that a yes/no response to this question is unlikely to be satisfactory. The answer, though, even if it is nuanced (e.g. it fulfils these purposes partially, it is better in some areas than others), is likely to be reasonably practically useful. If the current UK system falls short of meeting these purposes, or if there are other models (and other constitutions) that seem better designed to meet these purposes, then we can critique the UK system and propose reforms. This 'fitness for purpose' approach can act as a benchmark for your evaluation.

By looking at the different sources of UK constitutional rules, we can assess to what extent the UK does have a system that meets these purposes.

4.13 SOURCES OF THE UK CONSTITUTION

An initial problem in identifying the sources of constitutional rules in an uncodified system is that it is difficult to draw distinctions between 'ordinary law' and 'constitutional law'. Most legal rules structure the relationship between the state and the individual in some way. The Consumer Rights Act 2015, for example, is primarily concerned with the relationship between the contracting parties themselves, but it still involves Government and Parliament establishing tests for what is an acceptable contract term. The state is laying down some basic (contractual) rights that citizens should enjoy and empowering a part of the state (the courts) to strike down contract terms that breach those rights. Yet we would not say that the Consumer Rights Act 2015 is a constitutional law – why not?

ANALYSING THE LAW – THE PROBLEM OF IDENTIFYING THE 'CONSTITUTIONAL'

Ridley states that 'In the context of the British legal system, the term constitutional law is thus literally meaningless'.[20] He also cites the leading Victorian jurist F W Maitland: 'there is hardly any department of law which does not, at one time or another, become of constitutional importance'.

Tony Wright MP, the former Chair of the Commons Public Accounts Committee, went even further (and surely too far) in saying to the House of Lords Select

20 Ridley, above n 15.

Committee on the Constitution, 'the constitution is . . . whatever it is at any one time and we make it up as we go along'.[21]

Perhaps the test put forward by Laws LJ in *Thoburn v Sunderland City Council* [2003] QB 151 can help move us beyond the rather despairing 'we make it up as we go along' approach. He argued that a constitutional statute was one which 'a) conditions the legal relationship between citizen and State in some general, overarching manner, or b) enlarges or diminishes the scope of what we would now regard as fundamental constitutional rights'. He gave examples including the Acts of Union, the European Communities Act 1972 and the Human Rights Act 1998.

As a formal test, though, it does throw up many questions: what amounts to a general, overarching aspect of the legal relationship? There is also an element of circularity to the idea of defining a 'constitutional' statute by its impact on a 'constitutional' right. Perhaps the better approach is a broad and pragmatic one. If a rule deals with an issue that is usually found in the written constitutions of similar countries, then it can be regarded as 'constitutional'.

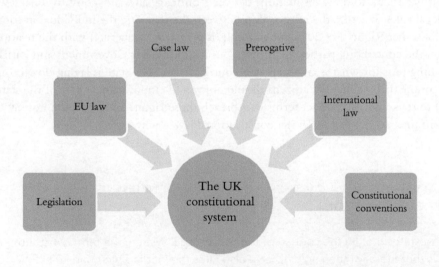

Figure 4.3 Sources of the UK constitution

4.13.1 LEGISLATION

This is the single most important source of constitutional rules. It provides many rules that fulfil the purposes of a constitution. We saw above how the Constitutional Reform Act 2005 'establishes, allocates power to and impose limits' on one of the main institutions of the

---

21 1st Report, HL of 2001–02, para 19.

state: the UK Supreme Court. The Parliament Acts 1911 and 1949 took away the veto of the House of Lords over the passage of legislation and limited its power to delay proposals. This is an example of legislation that imposes limits on one part of the state; a consequence is that a greater amount of power is allocated to the House of Commons. This is consistent with the 'democratic purpose' of a constitution, as it privileges the elected chamber over the unelected chamber.

EXPLAINING THE LAW – *HABEAS CORPUS*

There are many examples of statutes that restrain the power of the state for the benefit of the people. The ability of a court to require the release of a prisoner being unlawfully detained is found in the writ of *habeas corpus*. It is a powerful protection against oppressive state action. AV Dicey claimed that it was 'worth a hundred constitutional articles guaranteeing individual liberty'.[22] It can be traced back to Magna Carta 1215 and has been specifically protected by the Habeas Corpus Act 1679. The right has been suspended in times of war and other major crises such as the Troubles in Northern Ireland, but it has been reinforced by the general provisions of the Human Rights Act 1998.

A remarkable example of the protection that *habeas corpus* can provide is the case of Wolfe Tone. He was the leader of the United Irishmen and in 1798 led a revolution against British rule in Ireland in conjunction with the French. He was captured and sentenced to death by court martial. As he was not a soldier in the King's army, this court did not have proper jurisdiction to try him.

The Lord Chief Justice of Ireland was persuaded on the basis of the 'sacred and immutable principle of the constitution' to issue a writ of *habeas corpus* to prevent Wolfe Tone being executed. When the army officers holding him refused to comply with the writ on the basis that it was inconsistent with their orders from the Commander-in-Chief of the armed forces in Ireland, the court issued a further writ and threatened to arrest the army officers (*Wolfe Tone's Case* (1798) 27 State Trials 624). For a court to insist on the protection of the statutory rights of a dangerous revolutionary as against the demands of the armed forces is a rather astonishing illustration of the ability of law and independent courts to impose limits on state power.

One of the striking features of the UK constitutional system, though, is what is missing from this web of statutory regulation. You will search in vain for any Act that tells you how the Prime Minister is selected or what their principal duties and powers are.

---

22 A V Dicey, *Introduction to the Study of the Law of the Constitution*, 8th edn (Liberty Fund, 1982).

The UK is said to have a system of Cabinet Government, but there is no statute that establishes the Cabinet or defines its composition and powers. Some of the very few references to these offices in statute simply regulate how much they can be paid. There is a legal void at the heart of the constitutional system, but this is not the same thing as saying that these issues are unregulated. Many of these important constitutional relationships are controlled by non-legal rules called constitutional conventions (see Chapter 5, 'Constitutional conventions').

4.13.2 EUROPEAN UNION LAW

Membership of the European Union has had a major constitutional impact, not least because EU law directly enters the UK legal system and can be a source of constitutional rules on issues such as citizenship and equal rights. The final shape of Brexit will not be known until long after this edition is published, but it seems that the bulk of EU law will continue in force for many years after the UK has left the European Union.

4.13.3 CASE LAW

This can be a source of the constitution in two main ways. First, it is the courts that interpret and apply constitutional legislation. The Human Rights Act 1998 may set out a comprehensive scheme for rights protection, but it is only through the detailed application of those rights in the settlement of disputes before the courts that we see the actual scope of the rights and the precise restraint on state action.

Secondly, it is a source through the operation and evolution of common law and equity. Some of the most famous landmarks in the development of the UK constitutional system have involved the application of common law rules. In *Entick v Carrington* (1765) (discussed in detail in Chapter 10, 'Rule of law'), the courts used the common law tort of trespass to insist that public officials act in accordance with the law. In *Ridge v Baldwin* (1964), the equitable principle of the right to be heard was radically extended to cover a wide range of decisions of public bodies and has led to the development of a general duty of procedural fairness on all public bodies in their dealings with citizens. In *M v Home Office* (1993), the Court of Appeal decided that Government ministers were not covered by legal immunity and that if they disobeyed court orders they could be guilty of contempt of court in their personal and official capacities. As well as providing important rights to citizens, this case defines part of the relationship between different parts of the state: the judiciary and the executive.

4.13.4 ROYAL PREROGATIVE

This is a distinct part of the common law. On the face of it, the prerogative seems to keep very wide legal powers in the hands of the monarch. These cover, for example, the power of mercy to pardon convicted criminals, the power to declare war and the power to appoint the Prime Minister. In reality, the operation of these powers is governed by further constitutional rules, constitutional conventions (see below), which mean that the powers are exercised by Government ministers.

4.13.5 INTERNATIONAL AGREEMENTS

These are not normally a direct source of law or individual rights within the UK legal system. International treaties often require the Government, though, to introduce legislation of constitutional importance, such as the Geneva Conventions Act 1957. There is also a principle of statutory interpretation that the courts must try to interpret statutes in conformity with international obligations (*Cheney v Conn* [1968] 1 All ER 779).

4.13.6 CONSTITUTIONAL CONVENTIONS

These are non-legal rules of constitutional behaviour. They develop in all constitutional systems but play a more central role than usual in the UK (see **Chapter 5**, 'Constitutional conventions'). They regulate hugely important constitutional relationships such as how the prerogative power of selecting the Prime Minister is to be exercised. The responsibility of ministers to Parliament is governed by convention. The Sewell convention states that the Westminster Parliament will not legislate on devolved matters without seeking the consent of Scottish Parliament. The significant actions of the Crown, the Prime Minister, the Cabinet, MPs, civil servants and even judges are controlled, in part, by convention.

4.14 IS THE UK CONSTITUTION FIT FOR PURPOSE?

There is only scope for a quick overview in addressing this question. In relation to the first constitutional purpose of establishing, allocating and limiting state power, we have seen that statute provides many examples, but also that there are significant gaps. These gaps are filled by common law, prerogative powers and constitutional conventions, and the result is a complex but functioning system that largely does meet this purpose of establishing institutions and allocating power. It is still an open question as to whether this effectively limits state power.

In assessing this system, note that many of the constitutional changes over the past 15 years have been motivated by a belief that the system was not fulfilling this 'allocating and limiting' function as effectively as possible. These changes include the devolution of power to Scotland and Wales, the introduction of the Human Rights Act 1998 and the reforms to the office of Lord Chancellor. More recent changes and proposals, such as the Fixed-term Parliaments Act 2011, indicate that the constitutional system is a work in progress.

There are many examples of constitutional rules that promote democracy in the UK. Representative democracy is provided for by the Representation of the People Acts and the Political Parties, Elections and Referendums Act 2000. The Human Rights Act 1998 protects the basic rights necessary for democracy, such as freedom of expression. Parliamentary Select Committees and ministerial accountability, together with freedom of information laws, aim to make public bodies open and accountable. On the other hand, doubts remain over the fairness of the voting system and the effect of this on often-poor voter turnout. The funding of political parties makes them rely on donors and there have been serious concerns over the possible buying of access and influence.

There is no objective statement of the fundamental values that are articulated in the UK constitutional system, but a good argument can be made that equality (or at least the absence of discrimination) is a modern value of public life that commands very wide respect. This is reflected in the Equal Pay Act 1970, the Race Relations Acts, and the Equality Act 2010.

EXPLAINING THE LAW – SUCCESSION TO THE THRONE

Succession to the throne is governed by common law and the Act of Settlement 1701, and uses selection criteria that appear to be inconsistent with this commitment against discrimination, though there have been changes in the right direction in recent years. The first principle is heredity: that the office passes to a child of the current incumbent. This is not a principle that is acceptable for other public offices. You do not get to be Governor of the Bank of England because your parent once occupied that post. It must be accepted, however, that as long as the UK chooses to have a monarch as its head of state, then the heredity principle will remain.

The second selection principle is religious discrimination. The monarch must be in communion with the Church of England; so Jews, Sikhs, Muslims, Hindus and Baptists etc cannot be head of state. There was a further specific prohibition on anyone who 'professes the Popish religion' or who 'marries a papist' (i.e. a Catholic) from becoming head of state of the UK. The third selection principle was sex discrimination. Male children were higher in the line of succession than female children; Princess Anne is three places lower in the line than her younger brother Prince Edward.

In 2011, the Commonwealth Heads of Government Meeting agreed to abolish the precedence of male children and the bar on marriage to a Catholic. The requirement to be in communion with the Church of England (i.e. to be an Anglican) would remain. The changes were effected in the UK by the Succession to the Crown Act 2013.

Taking all of these sources together, it is clear that the UK has a comprehensive and sophisticated constitutional system. There are many aspects of the system that fulfil the purposes of a constitution in establishing institutions and granting them power and imposing limits on those powers. This in turn establishes fundamental aspects of the relationship between citizens and the state.

The ongoing dissatisfaction with the constitutional arrangements, though, has led to vigorous reform over recent decades. There has been a greater emphasis on legal constitutionalism and on making the UK's uncodified constitution approximate more closely the sort of arrangements (including human rights protections) found in codified constitutions.

4.15 BENEFITS AND PROBLEMS OF A CODIFIED CONSTITUTION

The apparent flexibility of uncodified constitutions provides both a potential strength and a potential weakness. We have seen some of the rigidity of codified constitutions illustrated by the Second Amendment of the US Constitution.

EXPLAINING THE LAW – THE PROPOSED ABOLITION OF THE LORD CHANCELLOR

The example of reform to the office of Lord Chancellor shows some problems in the very flexible UK system. In June 2003, Tony Blair's Prime Minister's Office issued a press release stating that the office of Lord Chancellor role would be abolished. It seems that there was no consultation, even within Government itself, of these changes. None of the other branches of the state affected by this proposed reform (the judiciary, the civil service, the House of Lords or the Crown) was consulted. The office of Lord Chancellor is over 700 years old and there are over 5,000 references to the post in legislation.

The Government back-tracked to some extent on these plans, and the office of Lord Chancellor was retained but substantially reformed. The fact that the Government, and in effect just the Prime Minister, thought that an important constitutional position could be abolished as though it was a minor administrative change shows some of the dangers of flexibility.

A codified constitution can entrench the fundamental principles of a state and more clearly demarcate the most fundamental rules. It also has a useful educative and symbolic role. Because it is consciously designed, it offers scope for a more complete separation of powers than a system that has evolved over a long period. In a planned constitution, it would be possible to address issues such as control of the executive and rebalancing of the Parliament/ Executive relationship as part of a broader reform package.

One of the key arguments against a codified constitution is that it just moves disputes from the political to the legal arena. In countries with codified constitutions, arguments

over constitutional issues are more often legal matters to be resolved by the courts. The
UK system has a combination of political and legal elements, and debates over appropriate
constitutional arrangements are more likely to be political. This has made it less likely
that unelected judges will decide constitutional questions. There has been a move in the
direction of more judicial involvement through the development of judicial review and the
Human Rights Act 1998, but a codified constitution would be a fundamental change.

4.16 SHOULD THE UK HAVE A CODIFIED CONSTITUTION?

There have been attempts by pressure groups and research bodies, for example the Institute
for Public Policy Research 1991, to draft a UK Constitution. These attempts illustrate the
feasibility of the idea, and a codified constitution has been (slightly tentatively) mooted by
Labour and Liberal Democrat politicians in recent years. There currently seems to be little
appetite for the adoption of a full codified constitution but the political climate can change
very quickly.

A codified constitutional settlement is not a prerequisite for constitutional reform. The
hotchpotch elements of reform seen over the last two decades have not been dependent
on a codified constitution and have arguably strengthened and improved the constitutional
system without inexorably leading to a codified constitution.[23] Many of the issues that the
UK constitutional system struggles with are very similar to those in countries with codified
constitutions: the balance between privacy and press freedom, the proportionate response
to terrorism, holding executive power to account. A codified constitution would not be a
panacea for these problems.

The hostility to the Human Rights Act 1998 from significant sections of the political and
public spectrum and the public rejection of electoral reform in 2011 do not show any
great desire for fundamental constitutional change. Given the cost and energy that would
be required to devise a UK codified constitution, it is unlikely that politicians will have it
towards the top of their agenda.

The process of drafting itself raises serious problems: who sits as part of the drafting
convention; how are delegates chosen; do you have only geographical representatives or
groups representing different interests such as trade unions, business organisations, religions,
charities? There would also be many difficult questions on the content of the constitution.
Since this is an opportunity, not quite to set the constitutional arrangements in stone, but
to protect these arrangements through entrenchment, many issues that are currently glossed
over (e.g. House of Lords reform) would need to be tackled and would be highly divisive.

23 Elliott and Thomas, above n 6, 82.

A codified constitution, even a comprehensive one, would not contain all of the constitutionally important rules. In the US, for example, to understand the right of freedom of expression your starting point would be the First Amendment to the Constitution, but you would also have to look at federal and state legislation and at decisions of the Supreme Court and other courts. As Barnett points out, the reality for citizens depends at least as much on the democratic process and the broader political processes that are acceptable within that state.[24]

Speaking extra-judicially in 2017, Lady Hale said '. . . we are unlikely to adopt a written constitution any time soon. This is not only because of the formidable obstacles to agreeing upon and formulating such a document and then enacting it; it is also because, as recent events have shown, the Constitution is in a state of flux, such that, even if it could be agreed upon, few would want to set it in stone'. She also thought that the inability of the UK Supreme Court, unlike other supreme courts, to strike down Acts of Parliament was 'as far as I am concerned, a very good thing!'[25]

Despite these formidable problems, the calls for a full codified constitution remain. Proponents say that such a constitution could be a vehicle for fairer elections, a stronger Parliament and a more accountable Government. They include arguments for further devolution, particularly for England. The underlying argument is that whilst the UK's constitutional system *does* fulfil the purposes of a constitution, a codified constitutional settlement could do so more effectively.

POINTS TO REVIEW

From this chapter; you should be able to:

- Outline the basic nature and different forms of constitutions, including the concept of constitutionalism.

- State the distinction between codified and uncodified constitutions and the legal consequences of the distinction, particularly for entrenchment and priority in case of conflict.

- Identify the different arguments as to whether or not the UK can be said to possess a constitution.

- Assess the value of a purposive approach to assessing constitutions.

- Recall and illustrate the sources of the UK constitution.

- Evaluate some of the key arguments on whether the UK should adopt a written constitution.

24 Barnett, above n 1, 9.

25 Lady Hale, The United Kingdom Constitution on the move' The Canadian Institute for Advanced Legal Studies' Cambridge Lectures, 7 July 2017, www.supremecourt.uk/docs/speech-170707.pdf (last accessed 05/11/17).

TAKING IT FURTHER

HM Government, 'The Governance of Britain', CM7170 www.official-documents.gov.uk/
document/cm71/7170/7170.pdf This is a very readable account of current constitutional
concerns within an historical context. These concerns include limiting the power of
the executive and making it more accountable, and reinvigorating democracy and
citizenship. It is a useful summary, but be aware that its proposals are those of a previous
Government.

V Bogdanor, 'Our new constitution' [2004] Law *Quarterly Review* 242 There are two
main uses to which you can put this article. First, as a summary and evaluation of the
constitutional changes between 1997 and 2004, in which case you will need to update
your research to take in more recent changes. Perhaps a more enduring purpose would
be to pick out Bogdanor's argument that these changes represent a 'new constitution'
and that they represent part of 'a long journey towards a codified constitution'. To place
more recent developments into the context of this argument would be a splendid piece of
scholarship for an undergraduate student.

N Barber, 'Against a written constitution' [2008] *Public Law* 11 Barber's starting point is
that the UK, with its stable system that works 'passably well', has the luxury of deciding
whether or not to adopt a codified constitution. He goes on, in a concise and punchy
article, to outline the three main hazards posed by codification. See if you can pick out the
three dangers and the arguments supporting them.

5

CHAPTER 5
CONSTITUTIONAL CONVENTIONS

As lawyers and law students we obviously, and understandably, concentrate on laws. Yet to understand the constitutional system of the UK we need to look beyond legal rules. There are important binding rules right at the heart of our constitutional system that are not laws; these are constitutional conventions.

Law students have an instinctive, or quickly acquired, idea of law as the archetype of a rule-based system. If you want to regulate something, use a law; if you want to require some conduct or prohibit some behaviour, then . . . use a law. But one of the fascinating things about conventions is that they broaden our horizons. They illustrate the existence of binding non legal rules and prompt us to consider whether they perform vital functions as well as, or even better than, laws.

You need to understand how constitutional conventions arise and, in particular, how they are binding (or *normative*). We will explore how they are different from both legal rules and mere habits. In this chapter, you will assess their role in the UK constitution and consider whether it would be better to replace them with legal rules.

We also explore, in depth, one of the most important conventions: Ministerial Responsibility. This plays a crucial role in making Government accountable for its actions.

AS YOU READ

- Identify the nature of conventions and how they have binding force.

- Assess their role in the UK constitution.

- Consider the developments that have occurred in the convention of Ministerial Responsibility.

- Evaluate whether conventional rules would be better replaced by legal rules.

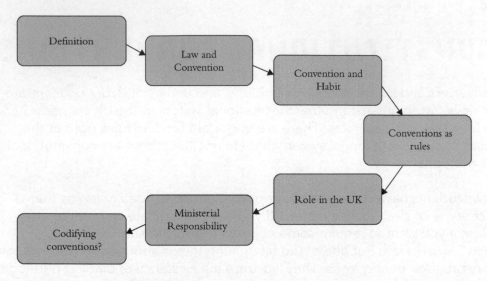

Figure 5.1 Structure of Chapter 5

5.1 CONSTITUTIONAL CHANGE

The process of regime change in a country can be a fraught one. You will have seen many examples from around the world of Presidents and Governments being forced from office by coup, armed insurrection and bloody civil war. There is an equally long (and perhaps even more depressing) history of failed attempts to oust a regime, with the defeated insurgents suffering terrible retribution. Unless there are clear, strict and widely accepted rules for transition from one governing regime to another, the result is likely to be disruption, violence and misery.

One of the most celebrated achievements of democracy (and therefore democratic constitutions) is that it facilitates this process of regime change in a regular, relatively stable and peaceful manner. So where are the rules governing change of Government in the UK constitution? You would search long and hard through the statute books and law reports and find almost nothing on this issue. There are laws on the requirements for elections for Parliament (e.g. the Representation of the People Act 2000) and the length of Parliaments (the Fixed-term Parliaments Act 2011), but these tell us about Parliament and not about the different branch of the state which is the UK Government. Where are the laws that tell us how the Prime Minister and the other Government ministers are chosen, or what their powers are, or crucially, how we can get rid of them without armed insurrection?

These laws simply do not exist, but that does not mean that it is a free-for-all or that the politicians, civil servants and Monarch just make it up as they go along. The process is governed by rules, but these are constitutional convention rules rather than legal rules.

APPLYING THE LAW – THE 1997 GENERAL ELECTION

On 1 May 1997, John Major, the Conservative Party leader, was the incumbent Prime Minister. The Conservatives lost the General Election held on that day, with Labour Party candidates winning 418 of the 659 seats in the House of Commons. The next morning, John Major went to Buckingham Palace to submit his resignation to the Queen. She accepted that resignation and shortly afterwards Tony Blair, the Labour Party leader, went to the palace. He was appointed as Prime Minister by the Queen and then went to 10 Downing Street to commence the Labour Government. There was a peaceful transition from one Government to another.

The Queen has the *legal right* to appoint absolutely whomever she wishes as Prime Minister. There is no legal requirement to even have a prime minister. According to the legal part of the constitution she could have appointed Prince Charles, or Lady Gaga, or nobody at all.

Yet, all of the main constitutional actors involved in this process in May 1997 (Queen, Conservative leader and Labour leader) knew precisely what they *had to* do in these circumstances. Other politicians, the civil servants and judges, all of the media and the public at large also knew that John Major was required to resign and that the Queen was required to appoint Tony Blair. This was a process governed not by whim or discretion but by strict and clear rules.

There were two aspects of the same constitutional convention operating in this example. First, that a Prime Minister who no longer has the confidence of the House of Commons (i.e. a majority) must resign. Secondly, that the Queen must appoint as Prime Minister the leader of the party that has the confidence of the House of Commons. Conventions are central to how the UK state operates, and we need to further explore the source and nature of these peculiar but important rules.

5.2 DEFINITION OF CONVENTIONS

A simple definition of constitutional conventions is provided by Geoffrey Marshall: 'non-legal rules of constitutional behaviour'.[1] Kenneth Wheare's definition is also useful in emphasising the binding nature of conventions and to whom they apply: 'By "convention" is meant a binding rule, a rule of behaviour accepted as obligatory by those concerned in the working of the Constitution'.[2]

---

1 G Marshall, *Constitutional Conventions* (OUP, 1984) 3.
2 KC Wheare, *Modern Constitutions*, 2nd edn (OUP, 1966) 122.

From these definitions, we can extract the following key features:

- Constitutional conventions are not legal rules, and must therefore be distinguishable from laws.
- Conventions are rules, and must therefore be distinguishable from mere habits or usages.
- Conventions are rules applying to those individuals, offices and institutions that operate within the constitutional system (what we can call 'constitutional actors').

5.3 DISTINGUISHING CONVENTIONS FROM LAWS

The first thing that you will need to be able to do is differentiate between laws and conventions. There are two main ways of doing this:

- Through the question of court enforcement
- Through the pedigree of the rule.

A V Dicey in his *Introduction to the Study of the Law of the Constitution* distinguishes law from convention on the basis of court enforceability:

> The one set of rules are in the strictest sense laws, since they are rules . . . whether enacted by statute or derived from the common law which *are enforced by the courts.*
> The other set of rules consist of conventions, understandings, habits or practices which, though they may regulate the conduct of . . . officials, are not in reality laws at all since they are *not enforced by the courts.*[3]

We can make some minor quibbles with this distinction. It would have been better to speak of laws as *capable* of being enforced rather *actually* enforced and it is not just the courts who enforce laws but also tribunals. Similarly, Government ministers exercise quasi-judicial functions. These are, however, still recognisably judicial functions; indeed, it is one of the defining features of a judicial function that it involves enforcing legal rules.

Rodney Brazier focuses on how the different types of rule are made, i.e. their pedigree. He says that conventions are 'not legal rules because they are not produced by legislation or the judicial process'.[4] There are a limited number of recognised ways for making a law, and for any legal rule it ought to be possible to pinpoint exactly how it was made and when it was

---

3   A V Dicey, *Introduction to the Study of the Law of the Constitution*, 8th edn (Liberty Fund, 1982) 23.
4   R Brazier, *Constitutional & Administrative Law* (Manchester UP, 1998).

made. We should be able to trace its pedigree to a specific piece of primary or secondary legislation or judicial statement of the common law. Constitutional conventions (as we shall see) are not made by these processes.

Sir Ivor Jennings was critical of the notion that there is a clear distinction between the two types of rules.[5] He argued that they are so similar that they should be put in the same broad category of 'constitutional rules'. The important issue for Jennings was not which sub-category a particular rule should be placed in but *compliance*, i.e. whether or not that rule was observed in the constitution. This stance is supported by DB Mitchell who pointed out that past practice is crucial to both law (particularly ancient legal custom) and convention.[6]

ANALYSING THE LAW – LAW/CONVENTION DISTINCTION

Should you accept Jennings's argument? There are reasons to be cautious about doing so. It is perfectly legitimate to have an umbrella term ('constitutional rules') that includes both types of rules, and even to point to some similarities between the two types of rules. This does not, however, erase the important differences between laws and conventions. It is true that the courts can recognise and acknowledge the existence of conventions, and there are arguments that this shades over into a sort of functional court enforcement. The overall evidence for this argument is rather shaky, however, and Dicey's basic distinction using court enforceability still holds true.

If the focus is 'compliance', then putting law and convention into one umbrella category risks glossing over the important differences in how the rules are enforced and how compliance is ensured.

As Turpin and Tomkins point out, 'those who are involved in observing the political process are aware of a difference between laws and conventions, and are rarely uncertain as to the category to which the particular rule belongs'.[7]

5.4 IDENTIFYING CONSTITUTIONAL CONVENTIONS

The approaches above are useful in identifying what constitutional conventions *are not*; they are not legal rules. Is there a more precise way of identifying what constitutional conventions *are*? Can they be distinguished from the mass of non-legal habits, understandings and practices that surround the constitution?

---

5 I Jennings, *The Law and the Constitution* (5th edn, London UP, 1959) 117.

6 D B Mitchell, *Constitutional Law* (2nd edn, W Green, 1968) 34.

7 C Turpin and A Tomkins, *British Government and the Constitution* (7th edn, Cambridge UP, 2012) 198.

One influential test was proposed by Jennings: 'We have to ask ourselves three questions: first, what are the precedents; secondly, did the actors in the precedents believe that they were bound by a rule; and thirdly, is there a reason for the rule?'[8]

So the Jennings test is:

- There are precedents.
- The constitutional actors believe they are bound by those precedents.
- There are reasons for the rule.

APPLYING THE LAW – APPOINTING THE PRIME MINISTER

In the example of the appointment of the Prime Minister referred to above, therefore:

- Precedent – it has been the accepted practice for around 200 years to appoint as PM the leader of the majority party following a General Election.
- Actors believe they are bound by those precedents – evidence of this can be found as far back as 1834 when the King was reluctantly persuaded to re-appoint Lord Melbourne as Prime Minister. His preferred choice, Robert Peel, had been unable to form a majority.
- Reasons for the rule – this promotes democracy and largely excludes the Monarch from exercising an inappropriately personal role in selecting the Prime Minister.

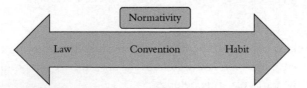

Figure 5.2 Normativity

This Jennings test for identifying conventions seeks to distinguish constitutional conventions from mere habits and traditions. The usefulness of this distinction has been challenged by Elliott and Thomas: 'In reality, the convention/tradition line is largely irrelevant'.[9] They argue that Jennings asked the questions in the wrong way. What is more important than the mere existence of precedent is its *extent*, and the feeling of obligation behind it. This is a question of degree. There is a spectrum of obligation, and a clear conventional rule with a long list of precedents and evidence of strong binding force is

8   Jennings, above n 5, 136.
9   M Elliott and R Thomas, *Public Law*, 3rd edn (OUP, 2017) 55.

more important and more akin to a legal rule. A weak convention is more akin to an implicit understanding or mere tradition.

This highlights a point that we return to below; conventions encompass a broad spectrum of rules. It is also a simplification to regard legal rules as operating like an on/off switch or a mathematical equation, but it is broadly true to say that if a legal rule applies to a situation, then the rule dictates (to some extent) the required outcome.

Some conventions operate in this prescriptive way; others do not. Some conventions have vague and contested boundaries. Some do not make it clear what is supposed to happen when the rule is breached. We are dealing with a broad category here.

The key aspect of the Jennings test is really the second criterion; the extent to which constitutional actors feel bound by the rule (the sense of obligation). This relates very strongly to the other criteria. Long consistent precedent (the first criterion) can contribute to the sense of obligation, but a short history of precedent is not necessarily fatal. The sense of obligation is reinforced, or undermined, by the quality or force of the reasons underpinning the rule (the third criterion).

The Jennings test has not been considered by the English courts but was accepted and applied by the Canadian Supreme Court in *Reference re Amendment of the Constitution of Canada* (1982) 125 DLR (3d) 1.

KEY LEARNING POINTS

....

- We can distinguish law from convention on the basis of court enforceability and the source of the rule.
- Conventions and laws have similar functions. They provide rules and prescribe conduct, but there are important differences in how they get people to comply with those rules.
- The Jennings test can be used to identify conventions, by focusing on the sense of obligation to follow the rule.

5.5 RELATIONSHIP BETWEEN LAWS AND CONVENTIONS

5.5.1 BREACH OF A CONVENTION IS NOT A BREACH OF THE LAW

It is sometimes argued that breach of a convention, whilst not unlawful in itself, will lead on to a breach of law. Dicey said that 'breach of . . . these conventions will almost immediately bring the offender into conflict with the courts and the law of the land'.[10]

....

10 Dicey, above n 3, 445.

As an example, the Triennial Act 1694 requires that 'Parliament shall be holden once in three years at the least', but constitutional convention says that Parliament must meet every year. If it did not, then any state powers that need annual renewal would automatically lapse, e.g. raising taxes or spending money on a standing army. The failure to abide by the convention would inevitably result in a breach of those legal rules on taxation and the army.

This example illustrates the point in relation to this particular rule, but the fact that, in practice, Parliament meets on many days over many months each year (normally 140–150 days per annum) shows that this is not the most important conventional rule. The broader allegation that breach of a convention *will* lead to breach of law is only true in a very limited number of cases. It cannot be regarded as a general characteristic of constitutional conventions.

5.5.2 BREACH OF A CONVENTION MAY LEAD TO ITS ENACTMENT IN LAW

EXPLAINING THE LAW – US PRESIDENT TERMS OF OFFICE

It had been an unwritten convention of the US Constitution dating back to Presidents Washington and Jefferson that the US President could serve no more than two terms in office (eight years). A number of subsequent Presidents had sought election for a third term but had failed to win sufficient support. This seemed to reinforce the existence and strength of the two-term rule. In 1940, President Franklin D Roosevelt obtained the approval of his party to seek a third term and was subsequently elected. He went on to win a fourth election in 1944 but died within months of the result.

The breach of the conventional rule in 1940 was justified by the global circumstances of the Second World War, which the US was to join by 1941. Nevertheless, there was some disquiet about the possibility of a President-for-life emerging which would run counter to the US Constitution's ideals of limited government. The result was the Twenty-second Amendment to the US Constitution, ratified in 1951. 'No person shall be elected to the office of the President more than twice'. The convention had failed to prevent a President from serving more than two terms, so it was replaced by a legal rule.

This is a particularly interesting example, as it shows that conventions can emerge in any sort of constitutional system. The US Constitution was designed to use legal rules to regulate the important relationships between constitutional actors (whereas the UK constitution is more of a mix of law, convention and politics). Even here, however, conventions emerged from the understandings, expectations and sense of obligation of those constitutional actors. Another US example is that members of the House of Representatives must not only live in the state that they represent (as required by law) but also in the district of the state that they represent, which is not legally required.

APPLYING THE LAW – THE PARLIAMENT ACT 1911

It was a well-established convention that the House of Lords would not prevent the passage of any Finance Bill (i.e. the Budget) that had been approved by the House of Commons. In 1909, the Liberal-dominated House of Commons had approved the 'Peoples' Budget'. This was a radical series of measures from the Chancellor David Lloyd George to raise more tax from the wealthy and increase social welfare through, for example, introducing the first old-age pensions. The Bill was rejected by the Conservative-dominated House of Lords. This was a breach of the convention.

On the basis of the US President example above, what would you expect to happen? Since the convention had failed to prevent the behaviour, then a legal prohibition was needed.

The Liberals dissolved Parliament and their subsequent victory in the General Election put so much political pressure on the Conservatives that the House of Lords eventually passed the disputed budget. The Liberal Government, however, was dissatisfied with the constitutional convention. It had failed to prevent the Lords acting unconstitutionally and there was no guarantee that a future House of Lords would abide by the rule any more faithfully.

ANALYSING THE LAW – PASSING THE PARLIAMENT ACT 1911

Can you see the problem facing any attempt to legally enact this rule? It would require an Act of Parliament, so think about the requirements for making an Act. An Act needs the approval of the House of Commons, the House of Lords and the Royal Assent. The Lords were, to put it mildly, unlikely to favour a Bill that restricted their powers.

The only way to force the Lords to accept the Bill would be to create a sufficient number of Liberal peers to outvote the Conservatives (or at least to threaten to do so). The power to create new peers, however, lay with the King, who was reluctant to get drawn into the political dispute without a further mandate from the people. Ultimately, the Liberals went back to the country again and marginally won another General Election. The Conservatives in the House of Lords, faced with the threat of losing their majority, reluctantly agreed to the restrictions and the Parliament Act 1911 was passed.

This Act limited the power of the House of Lords, which lost its power of veto over legislation and could only delay legislation for up to two years. This was reduced to one year by the Parliament Act 1949.

You need to pay particular attention to the word 'may' in the sub-heading above. There is no automatic connection between breach of a convention and its enactment as a legal rule. Whether or not to replace a convention with a law will be a political choice, largely in the hands of the Government. Breach of convention may result in no legal consequences whatsoever, even if this weakens the conventional rule.

5.5.2.1 THE COURTS CAN RECOGNISE BUT NOT ENFORCE CONVENTIONS

Judicial recognition has been the most discussed aspect of the relationship between law and convention. You will need to get a clear understanding of the *Jonathon Cape* case and of the differing academic interpretations of it.

KEY CASE – *ATTORNEY GENERAL V JONATHON CAPE LTD* [1976] QB 752

Richard Crossman was a Labour politician and member of the Cabinet from 1964 to 1970. He kept a diary with the intention of publishing it in full at a later date. It was clear that he knew that this would breach an established constitutional convention, but he wanted to challenge the secrecy at the heart of Government.

The convention was Collective Cabinet Responsibility which makes all Cabinet members collectively responsible for the decisions reached by Cabinet. A central aspect of this is that discussions within Cabinet must be confidential. Ministers are free to disagree in private, but once a decision is reached and announced then they must all publicly stand behind it.

Crossman intended to publish details of particular disagreements and outline the dissenting views of individual ministers in Cabinet. He died before publication, but his executors and publisher wanted to press ahead without the usual step of waiting for approval by the Cabinet Secretary. Publication of the diaries would amount to a breach of the convention, but what could be done about it? In particular, could a court prevent the publication? The Attorney General applied for an injunction to do so.

The defence argued that, whatever the constitutional convention says, 'there is no obligation enforceable at law to prevent the publication of Cabinet papers and proceedings . . .' and, furthermore, that 'the confidential character of Cabinet papers and discussions is based on a true convention . . . *an obligation founded in conscience only*' (Widgery CJ).

The court found that the Attorney General could rely on 'the developing equitable doctrine that a man shall not profit from the wrongful publication of information received by him in confidence'. This is the concept of breach of confidence. This legal rule had developed to restrain the unfair use of commercial secrets and had subsequently been extended by judges to cover confidential information in the domestic and family arena. The court considered whether it could be further extended to restrain the publication of 'public secrets' and concluded that potentially it could: 'when a Cabinet Minister receives information in confidence the improper publication of such information can be restrained by the court'.

Lord Widgery said there was an additional requirement in these circumstances, that the public interest required that the publication be restrained. On the facts, 11 years had passed since the events described and the intended publication date. Because of the passage of time, which included four general elections, the public interest did not require restraint of publication. The diaries could be (and were) published.

ANALYSING THE LAW – WAS THE COURT ENFORCING THE CONVENTION?

The court clearly *recognised* the existence of the constitutional convention in this case, but what does this tell us about the interrelationship between law and convention? Is it possible to argue that the court, in effect, enforced the convention? If so, this would undermine Dicey's attempt to distinguish between law and convention.

AG v Jonathon Cape is normally interpreted as an example of a court merely taking a convention into account. In doing so, the convention is just one of the facts of the case that may influence the application of law. Some commentators have taken this a step further and argued that this amounts to an indirect enforcement process.

Loveland suggests that differentiating a) enforcing conventions from b) merely recognising them may be a 'semantic distinction', and that 'we might argue that the court enforced a convention by cloaking it with a common law label'.[11]

It is argued here that the better view is that the court was enforcing the law and not the convention and that the distinction between the two remains valid. The legal concept of breach of confidence has three main elements:

- That information is obtained in circumstances imposing an obligation of confidence.
- That it has the necessary quality of confidence.
- That publication would cause damage to the applicant.

The convention was a crucial *factual* part of the case. It helped the court make a finding on the nature of the information (the Cabinet discussions) and the circumstances under which Mr Crossman had obtained it. It remains, however, just part of the factual background. In a similar way, the custom and practice in a particular industry can be recognised by the court. This does not create a new category of rules that courts are required to enforce.

The circumstances imposing an obligation of confidence can arise from a number of sources: agreement, relationship, implicit understanding, or constitutional convention. In *Shelley Films v Rex Features* [1994] EMLR 134, a photographer took pictures on the set of the film *Mary Shelley's Frankenstein*. There was a sign on the set prohibiting photography.

---

11 I Loveland, *Constitutional Law*, 6th edn (OUP, 2012) 268.

This fact led the court to find that attempting to publish the pictures would be a breach of confidence. This did not turn the film set sign into a species of legal rule or the production assistant who printed and posted the sign into a law-maker. The court was not recognising the sign and then enforcing it as though it were a law. This is more than a 'semantic distinction' – it is a real one.

If it was true that courts could, in effect albeit directly, enforce conventions, then we would expect to see more examples. It is only where there is a coincidental alignment between a law and a convention that a convention can be of any relevance to a court case. Even then it is not a free-standing right and only part of the factual background.

Furthermore, the courts have been consistent in their view that conventions are not some species of legal rule and that they cannot be enforced by the courts. Similarly, in *Reference re Amendment of the Constitution of Canada* (1982) 125 DLR (3d) 1, the Canadian Supreme Court used the Jennings test to establish the existence of a convention and found that the Canadian federal government was acting in breach of that convention but that the Court could not give legal effect to the conventional rule.

The constitutional convention that ministers are responsible for the actions of their department has been recognised by the courts on a number of occasions, e.g. *Carltona v Commissioners for Works* [1943] 2 All ER 560. In this and other cases, however, the position remains the same: conventions can be recognised and form part of the facts of the case. This can affect how the law applies to the particular circumstances of that case, but does not amount to court enforcement of constitutional conventions.

This approach was confirmed by the Supreme Court in in *Miller v Secretary of State for Exiting the European Union* [2017] UKSC 5, where it refused to give legal effect to the Sewel Convention (that the devolved legislatures would normally need to consent to changes to their powers). The Court found that judges were 'neither the parents nor the guardians of political conventions; they are merely observers'. Courts can 'recognise the operation of a political convention in the context of deciding a legal question' but cannot 'give legal rulings on its operation or scope, because those matters are determined in the political world'.

5.6 DISTINGUISHING CONVENTIONS FROM HABITS OR CUSTOMS

As we have seen above, constitutional conventions are widely accepted as a form of constitutional *rule*. These rules are different from mere customs or practices of the constitution, which means there must be some special distinguishing features of constitutional conventions that place them within this category of 'rule'.

EXPLAINING THE LAW – BLACK ROD

Black Rod, the Gentleman Usher of the Black Rod to give them their full title, is an officer of Parliament, and specifically of the House of Lords. Their role includes security and discipline within the House of Lords.

The highest profile function of Black Rod takes place during the State Opening of Parliament. They are instructed to go to the House of Commons and call MPs into the House of Lords chamber to hear the Queen's Speech. As they approach the House of Commons, the door is ceremonially slammed shut in their face. They knock on the door with their mace and permission is then given for them to enter. You can get a better understanding of the ceremony here: http://www.youtube.com/watch?v=h1bJ8nY2pcc.

The ceremony does contain important symbolism. It represents the liberty of the House of Commons from domination by the Monarch or the Lords. Is it, however, a constitutional convention? There is certainly a long precedent behind the ceremony, and the participants may feel that it is important to continue the ceremony. It is more difficult to identify a constitutionally important reason for Black Rod to act this way or to argue that those involved feel that they are obliged to act this way for constitutional, rather than symbolic or traditional, reasons.

Similarly, in the House of Commons the governing party traditionally sit on the benches to the right of the Speaker's Chair. If the seating arrangements changed, the Speaker and the parties would not feel that they were breaching a constitutionally significant rule.

The key distinguishing feature between constitutional conventions and mere habits, understanding or traditions is that conventions are regarded and acted upon as binding constitutional rules whilst habits are not. Marshall and Moodie define conventions as 'rules of constitutional behaviour which are considered to be binding by and upon those who operate the constitution but which are not enforced by the law courts'.[12] We explore where this binding force comes from in the next section.

5.7 HOW CONVENTIONS ARE MADE

In the past, most constitutional conventions arose from practice. Constitutional actors act a certain way in particular circumstances, e.g. appointing a Prime Minister after a General

---

12 G Marshall and C Moodie, *Some Problems of the Constitution* (5th edn, Hutchinson, 1971).

Election, and they have an implicit understanding of what is required. As we will see in the example in the next section, constitutional conventions normally emerge, much like social conventions or etiquette, from a combination of what people *do* in particular social/constitutional circumstances and what people *expect* should happen in those circumstances. These sorts of conventions are often completely unwritten.

Constitutional conventions can arise in other ways, however. They can simply be created, for example the convention that the UK Parliament will not normally legislate on a devolved matter without the consent of the devolved institutions in Northern Ireland, Wales or Scotland. This constitutional rule, called the Sewel Convention, did not emerge from practice or precedent. It was drafted from scratch and published in a Command Paper (an official Government publication; Cm 4444 (1999)).

Aileen McHarg explains that whilst 'conventions are typically thought of as the embodiment of constitutional custom or tradition; the product of a slow process of evolution', they can be created or declared.[13] Even with a declared convention (e.g. in relation to the devolved institutions), it is the response of the other constitutional actors to the asserted 'rule' (whether they act in accordance with it, whether they feel bound) that ultimately decides whether or not it actually becomes a constitutional convention.

5.8 HOW AND WHY CONSTITUTIONAL CONVENTIONS ARE BINDING

We saw above that Dicey argued that conventions are followed because their breach would lead to legal problems. But beyond the limited examples, e.g. tax collection powers needing annual legal renewal, this is not a convincing explanation for the general binding nature of conventions.

APPLYING THE LAW

This aspect of conventions, that they can be binding rules without legal pedigree or the possibility of court enforcement, is often puzzling to law students. You do need to get a firm grasp of this to really understand the nature of conventions. *Understanding* this binding nature will give you insights into the operation of particular conventions and in assessing the suitability of conventions for their constitutional role.

13 A McHarg, 'Reforming the United Kingdom Constitution: Law, Convention, Soft Law' [2008] *Modern Law Review* 853, 857.

To do this, we are initially stepping away from the constitutional sphere and looking at the operation of a social rule, or *social convention*.

APPLYING THE LAW – SOCIAL CONVENTIONS

Imagine that you are catching the bus into university to attend your Public Law lecture. You are understandably looking forward to it, and when the bus arrives you are relieved to see that there is one free seat at the front of the bus. The rest of the seats are taken.

At the next stop, a very elderly woman gets on the bus. She looks rather frail and is carrying a walking stick. Question – what do you do?

I really hope that your answer was along the lines of – 'I would stand up and offer her my seat' (anything else would be very disappointing). The further question is why you would act this way. You might say that it was something that you wanted to do. Yet, even if you felt tired and were looking forward to a relaxing journey, your behaviour would not change. Whether or not you *felt like* offering up your seat, you would.

This is an example of a social, rather than a constitutional, convention, yet it passes the Jennings test for identifying a convention:

- There is precedent. You will have seen this sort of behaviour and acted this way many times in the past.
- There is a sense of obligation. You do not just give up your seat on a whim. It is what you feel you *ought* to do in these circumstances.
- There are good reasons behind the convention. It shows respect for your elders, and it acknowledges that the elderly lady needs the seat more than you.

As with constitutional conventions, it is the internal sense of obligation that is the crucial factor here (although it is strongly reinforced by precedent and reason). You have an understanding of what is required of you, and the convention obliges you to act this way. In this sense, it is a *normative* rule, i.e. one that obliges particular action in a particular set of circumstances.

Failing to offer your seat, i.e. breaching the convention, will not automatically or necessarily result in a breach of the law (which was broadly Dicey's position). Jennings said that constitutional conventions are followed more because of the political difficulties that would follow from their breach. We can apply that here and argue that this social convention will also be observed because of the social difficulties that would follow a breach.

APPLYING THE LAW – BREACH OF CONVENTION

What would happen if you did not offer your seat? There may be a sense of unease or embarrassment. The other passengers may show their resentment through baleful stares or muttered comments or direct challenges complaining about your behaviour. There would be a social sanction of some sort.

Can you see how some conventions are quite similar to laws? Both are species of normative rules. Both are binding in the sense that they require us to act (or refrain from acting) in a certain way. For both, this normative force comes from an internal sense of obligation and from the possibility of external sanction if we breach the rule.

As you have been thinking about this scenario for a few minutes now, you may have an objection. There is often a sign by the front seats of a bus saying (something like), 'Please give up this seat to elderly or infirm passengers'. This is actually a great example of the non-legal codification of a convention. The sign does not turn the conventional rule into a legal rule; you will not be prosecuted in a court for breaching the rule in this sign. All it does is clarify and crystallise the obligation in the conventional rule.

APPLYING THE LAW – EVOLVING CONVENTIONS

Let us change the scenario slightly: imagine you are a young male Public Law student, the bus again is almost full and you take the last remaining seat which is right at the front. At the next stop, an able-bodied woman (she looks to be in her twenties or thirties) gets on the bus. Do you let her stand or offer your seat? The answer is less clear, but you would probably not offer your seat. You would very probably not offer her your seat simply on the basis that you are a man and she is a woman. My more mischievous students often say – 'It depends if you want to impress her!'

This, however, illustrates the point. You may offer to give up your seat for chivalrous or ineptly seductive purposes, but there is no shared social sense that you are *obliged* to give up your seat, as there was in the first scenario. Any action in these circumstances is not prescribed by a social convention.

If we transported the scenario back 50 or 60 years, however, the answer might well be different. From the development of mass public transport from the 1840s onwards, and for at least a century, it was a clear rule of social etiquette that a gentleman should give up his seat for a lady regardless of her age. So when did the social rule change? There was no specific time when this happened. We cannot say that from 1 September 1971 it became purely a matter of personal choice. The rule evolved, changed and ultimately disappeared.

This may be due to declining social standards of etiquette or, more likely, to a better understanding of the equality between men and women. The key point is that within the relevant community (public transport users) there was a change in perception of what was required and therefore the social rule changed.

This has been a long metaphor but it is important to draw out the key lessons on how conventions arise, operate and obtain their binding force. It is helpful to draw these lessons from a scenario that most of you will be very familiar with (or at least more personally familiar than the problem of who to appoint as your next Prime Minister). Those key lessons are:

- Conventional rules can be normative.
- This normative force comes from an internal sense of obligation and the possibility of external sanction.
- Conventional rules, based as they are on shared understandings, can arise, change and disappear without formal enactment, amendment or repeal.

APPLYING THE LAW – APPOINTING THE PRIME MINISTER

Think back to the opening example: the 1997 General Election when Tony Blair was appointed as Prime Minister. Why did the constitutional actors behave the way they did? We can now get a bit more under the skin of the scenario.

In the aftermath of the election, John Major did not submit his resignation to the Queen because of a sense of decency. The Queen did not accept the resignation and appoint Tony Blair because she preferred one political party rather than another. Tony Blair did not expect to be appointed because of some overweening sense of destiny. The shared understanding in this community (of constitutional actors) set the rules. This meant that each of the participants had an internal sense of obligation as to what they were required to do.

If the rule was breached and John Major refused to resign or the Queen refused to appoint Tony Blair, there would have been no legal breach. No court could have issued an injunction requiring the resignation or ordering the Queen to make the appointment. Yet this is a long way from saying that there would be no repercussions or other sorts of sanction for breach of the rule. The incumbent Prime Minister and the Monarch would face intense criticism; the pressure from other constitutional actors, from the media and from the people would be unrelenting. The sanction of political and public pressure would force them out of office. The constitutional crisis would prove hugely destructive for the incumbent Prime Minister and their party and their hopes of future electoral success. The Monarch would probably be forced to give up their remaining legal powers.

Legal rules are obeyed partly because of the punitive consequences that might follow a breach of the rule. These include injunctions, compensatory damages, fines and imprisonment. They are also obeyed, however, because of:

- A personal sense of morality – what is stopping you from walking out the classroom and assaulting people at random? (Hopefully) because you have an internal sense, regardless of its legal status, that such conduct would be wrong.
- A general moral sense of the need to obey the law – whether we completely approve of a particular law or not.
- The stigma of breaching societal norms.

These also apply, to a greater or lesser extent, to constitutional conventions.

Figure 5.3 The binding nature of conventions

KEY LEARNING POINTS

- Conventions are different from habits because they have normative force (require certain conduct in particular circumstances).
- This normative force comes from an internal sense of obligation and the possibility of external sanctions.

5.9 ROLE IN THE UK CONSTITUTION

Conventions regulate important aspects of the relationships between, amongst others;

- The Crown and the Government, e.g. the rule that ministers, in practice, exercise the Crown's legal powers of entering into international treaties.
- The two Houses of Parliament, e.g. the Salisbury/Addison convention that the House of Lords will not oppose Bills that that have been promised in an election manifesto.
- The parties in the House of Commons, e.g. the convention that a fair amount of time will be allocated for the Opposition to speak in debates; that the Speaker will act impartially as between the political parties.
- Ministers and judges, e.g. the convention that ministers will not criticise individual judges for individual judgments.

Sir Ivor Jennings described the contribution that conventions make to the UK constitution: 'A simple way to characterise conventions' constitutional function is that they provide the flesh which clothes the dry bones of the law; they make the legal constitution work; they keep in touch with the growth of ideas'.[14] Conventions can, in particular, play a positive role in promoting *efficiency, accountability* and *democracy*.

They can promote *efficiency* by providing the right mix of certainty and flexibility in the relations between different parts of the constitution. Politicians, civil servants and judges know broadly what is expected of them. Disagreements as to what the obligations are in particular circumstances need to be resolved politically rather than through the often long and tortuous process of litigation. As Jennings says, 'it enables the machinery of State to run more smoothly; and if it were not there friction would result'.[15]

For Geoffrey Marshall, 'the major purpose [of conventions] is to give effect to the principles of governmental *accountability* that constitute the structure of responsible government'.[16] We will see this in the detailed examination of Ministerial Responsibility in the next section. Many of the constitutional conventions relating to the Crown say that the powers are, in effect, exercised by ministers. Those ministers are then, again by convention, accountable to Parliament. The conventions on the parliamentary rights of the Opposition party and the impartial role of the Speaker in the Commons also support this accountability function.

It might seem strange to cite conventions, which are not made by any directly democratic process, as supporting *democracy*, but there are numerous examples of this effect. As Bradley and Ewing point out, 'The role of the monarch in the conduct of government has almost disappeared since the 18th century without a series of statutes removing one royal power after another'.[17] The transition from a largely undemocratic system to an imperfect but democratic one has been achieved by a mixture of law (e.g. extending voting rights to working men and to women) and convention. These conventions include the transfer of royal power to democratically accountable ministers.

EXPLAINING THE LAW – APPOINTING THE PRIME MINISTER

A further example is that since the early 1900s, the Prime Minister must be a member of the House of Commons rather than the House of Lords. In 1962, when the Conservative Party chose the fourteenth Earl of Home as their new leader, and therefore the new Prime Minister, he was a member of the House of Lords. He immediately disclaimed his earldom, became ordinary Sir Alec Douglas-Home and was selected for and elected in a safe Conservative seat for the House of Commons.

14 Jennings, above n 5.
15 Ibid., 136.
16 Marshall, above n 1, 18.
17 A Bradley and K Ewing, *Constitutional and Administrative Law*, 15th edn (Longman, 2011) 23.

In both 1923 and 1940, when there had been credible candidates for Prime Minister from both the Commons and the Lords, the candidate from the House of Commons was chosen. It has not been acceptable in the past century to appoint a Prime Minister who is unable to take part in debates or answer questions in the democratically elected chamber of Parliament.

These are all positive attributes of conventions, but they do not address the question of whether constitutional conventions are the best types of rules for promoting these positive attributes in a constitution. We will return to the issue of whether the shortcomings of conventions mean that legal rules could perform the required constitutional roles better, after we have examined a number of conventions in detail.

_____

5.10 CONVENTIONS IN PRACTICE: THE ROYAL ASSENT – A SIMPLE CONVENTION

It is a legal rule that for a Bill to become an Act of Parliament it must have been approved by both Houses of Parliament and received the royal assent. There is no *legal* obligation on the Monarch to give royal assent. If we based our view of the constitution solely on the legal position, it would seem that the Queen has a free hand to grant the royal assent or refuse to pass legislation. The Royal Assent Act 1967 only deals with the form of assent. The question of whether or not assent is given is still not regulated by law.

The constitutional rule, however, states that royal assent is given on the advice of ministers. In practice, this means that the royal assent is always given. This is a constitutional convention that is clear, normative and has a record of observance that most legal rules would envy.

APPLYING THE LAW – USING THE JENNINGS TEST

Let us apply the Jennings test for identifying a convention. Remember that this involves:

- Precedent.
- A sense of obligation.
- A reason for the rule.

The last time the royal assent was refused was by Queen Anne in relation to the Scottish Militia Bill 1708. The historical record seems to show that after its passage through the

Commons and Lords, the Government changed its mind on the wisdom of establishing a Scottish militia and 'advised' the Monarch to refuse royal assent so even this example shows ministers, and not the monarch herself, exercising the power. The development of the convention can more accurately be traced back even further to the new constitutional settlement of 1688 when Parliament gained ascendancy over the Crown. The precedent for the rule is in the dozens of Acts of Parliament passed every year, and the absence of any serious threat to withhold the royal assent for over 300 years.

The sense of obligation is slightly harder to identify, but it is not difficult to assert that amongst the hundreds of Acts passed in the last three centuries there will have been some that the monarch personally objected to, but felt obliged to assent to for constitutional reasons. Queen Elizabeth II has been very adept at not making her position apparent on partisan political issues. It would be reasonable to assume, however, that she gave her assent to the Hunting Bill 2004 due to a sense of constitutional obligation rather than any personal desire to put an end to fox hunting with dogs.

The reason for the rule is quite straightforward. An unelected monarch should not have a veto over legislation produced by a democratic process.

In human physiology, the appendix is a part of the intestinal system. For many years, it was thought that the appendix was a vestigial structure, i.e. it had previously performed a function but the human body had evolved so that the original function was lost. This is analogous to the royal assent. Through most of the history of the English monarchy it was a function of the monarch to approve or reject legislation. The UK constitution has evolved so that this function is no longer required or appropriate. The obvious question is, why retain it? Why not carry out surgery on the UK constitution and remove the functionless process?

More recent medical research on the appendix has shown that it is likely to perform some role in biological control and infection-fighting. It is not generally essential to human health but provides some benefits. Again, this is analogous to the royal assent, which is potentially a constitutional safeguard against tyranny. It would be unacceptable for democratic reasons for the Crown to use the royal assent for personal preference, especially to thwart the intention of the Commons. Those same democratic imperatives, however, would allow the monarch to veto any Bill that would radically undermine democracy, e.g. a Bill to take the vote from women. This would only be available in the most exceptional cases.

Loveland is sceptical about this alleged safeguard function, arguing that in the absence of a written constitution it is difficult to see what could be the objective basis for the Queen reaching the judgment that a Bill is so unconstitutional that she must refuse assent. He also points out the extreme unlikelihood of any such Bill being presented.[18] Royal assents,

18 Loveland, above n 11, 271.

and the possibility of withholding them, do exist in written constitutions, however, e.g. in Belgium and in Spain, and have been exercised.

Despite lingering doubts as to this 'ultimate safeguard' role, the constitutional convention is clear and simple. It could be replaced by a legal rule, e.g. similar to that in the Spanish Constitution, but it is difficult to identify much practical benefit or difference from doing so.

5.10.1 PARLIAMENTARY ASSENT TO WAR OR MILITARY DEPLOYMENT – AN EMERGING CONVENTION

Legally, the Queen has the power to declare war and deploy military forces. It is a long-established convention that this prerogative power is exercised by the Government. This is a further example of the exercise of a legal power being regulated by a constitutional convention. One concern with this constitutional arrangement was that it left crucial public decisions, whether to commit the country's armed forces to be ready to kill and be killed in pursuit of military and political objectives, entirely in the hands of Government. There was no legal or conventional requirement for the consent of Parliament.

The decision to commit the UK to the invasion of Iraq in 2003 was one of the most controversial decisions by a UK Government in decades. Estimates on the death toll as a result of the invasion and subsequent war vary widely between 600,000 and one million people. It was very difficult for Tony Blair as PM to build any kind of consensus for UK military involvement and the opposition was large and vocal. The Government decided in these circumstances to ask the House of Commons to approve a motion supporting military force to disarm Iraq. Did this action produce a new convention?

APPLYING THE LAW – APPLYING THE JENNINGS TEST

Apply the Jennings test to this emergent convention. The *reason* behind this practice is evident. Decisions of this magnitude need the widest possible authority. To exclude the directly elected chamber of Parliament from the decision-making process is undemocratic and reduces transparency and accountability.

The criteria of *precedent* and *sense of obligation* are harder to pin down. A House of Commons resolution from 2007 said that 'it is inconceivable that any Government would in practice depart from this precedent' and called for detailed proposals from Government on the Parliamentary role (HC Deb vol 460, col 582, 15 May 2007). The obligation, however, lies with the Government, so we need to identify whether *it* feels obliged to consult.

A Government consultation of 2007 discussed the possibility of requiring a House of Commons resolution, i.e. a written constitutional convention, or an enactment, i.e. turning it into a legal requirement.[19] In 2011, the Foreign Secretary announced his intention to enshrine the duty to consult Parliament into law. As of 2017, however, there has been no formal action by Government, and the House of Lords Select Committee on the Constitution describe the position as 'unclear'.[20]

Perhaps the best evidence comes from practice. Before the decision in March 2011 to commit British forces to enforcing a no-fly zone in the Libyan conflict, the Government put a motion to the House of Commons. This was approved. In 2015, the Government did not proceed with its intention to extend anti-ISIS air raids into Syria because it felt that it could not get a Commons majority. What would happen in the event of a 'No' vote in the Commons is still very uncertain. There is, however, strong evidence, from recent practice and Government statements, that a new constitutional convention has emerged.

5.11 MINISTERIAL RESPONSIBILITY – A COMPLEX CONVENTION

Ministerial responsibility has been chosen as an extended example of a convention for three reasons.

- It is the classic illustration of a 'political' convention. It is flexible, relatively complex and in the hands of the people supposedly governed by it.
- It is a hugely important topic in itself, what Loveland calls 'perhaps the most important non-legal rule within our constitution'.[21] Ministerial responsibility is a key feature of Public Law and governance in the UK. It fits with our abiding concern about constitutionalism and the limits on executive power.
- It is a consistently high-profile constitutional convention. Each year I (and other Public Law teachers) feel blessed. When the time comes to discuss ministerial responsibility, there is always a recent or ongoing ministerial difficulty, a scandal or a crisis of competence, with calls for the minister to take responsibility (often accompanied with calls for them to resign). The reality, of course, is not that these demands for accountability are arranged for the delight of Public Law teachers and the instruction of Public Law students, but that they are part of the day-to-day fabric of the constitutional system.

A simple and general definition of the convention is provided by Marshall and Moodie: 'Ministers are responsible for the general conduct of government; and ultimately, through

---

19 War Powers and Treaties: Limiting Executive Powers (CP 26/07).
20 www.parliament.uk/documents/lords-committees/constitution/CFEconstirightsofarmedforce.pdf (last accessed 05/11/17).
21 Loveland, above n 11, 263.

Parliament and parties, to the electorate'.[22] The doctrine has two limbs: collective cabinet responsibility and individual ministerial responsibility.

5.11.1 COLLECTIVE CABINET RESPONSIBILITY (CCR)

The UK is said to have a system of Cabinet Government, with the most important policy decisions made collectively by the Prime Minister and the (normally) 22–24 Cabinet Ministers. This is not always the case, and there is wide variation in practice depending on the issue and the character of the Prime Minister (see Chapter 2, 'Institutions'). The Cabinet meets each week in the Cabinet Room. The Ministerial Code, which collates and summarises the main obligations on Ministers, includes collective responsibility as a general principle of the Cabinet and states that all ministers are expected to follow it (para.1.1).

The convention was judicially recognised in the *Jonathan Cape* case, discussed above, where Lord Widgery described collective responsibility as 'the confidential character of those papers and proceedings derived from the convention of joint Cabinet responsibility whereby any policy decision reached by the Cabinet has to be supported thereafter by all members of the Cabinet whether they approve of it or not, unless they feel compelled to resign'. He continued, 'There may be no objection to a Minister disclosing (or leaking, as it was called) the fact that a Cabinet meeting had taken place, or, indeed, the decision taken, so long as the individual views of Ministers were not identified'.

APPLYING THE LAW – COLLECTIVE RESPONSIBILITY

Suppose that the Cabinet is considering a proposal to reduce the voting age in General Elections to 16 years. There are widely differing views held by Cabinet Ministers, but collectively a decision is made to reduce the voting age. What would be a useful constitutional rule to have in those circumstances, or to go back to the real basic issues, what dangers should a constitutional rule try to avoid or reduce?

The possible dangers of open disclosure of the differences include:

- The Government looks divided. This is not just a question of the political advantage for a Government of appearing to be united. Knowing precisely what the Government's position on any issue is helps the electorate in making their voting choices, helps markets to make financial decisions and helps foreign governments in international relations.
- Because of the dissenting voices, no clear policy emerges.
- Ministers who oppose the decision might disclaim responsibility for it. This would make it more difficult to hold the Government to account through Parliament and the media.
- Ministers might be reluctant to speak openly and honestly in Cabinet.

---

22 Marshall and Moodie, above n 12.

It is illuminating to go back to the decision to reduce the voting age from 21 to 18 made in 1968 (the reform came into force in 1970). The Crossman diaries (discussed in the *Jonathan Cape* case) revealed major disagreements within Cabinet on this issue. Yet, when a decision was made, the Bill was presented to Parliament with unanimous Government support. At the time, no minister made it known that they disagreed with the reform or refused to take responsibility for it. This indicates the two main strands of collective responsibility: unanimity and confidentiality.

5.11.2 UNANIMITY

'Decisions reached by the Cabinet or Ministerial Committees are binding on all members of the Government' (*Ministerial Code of Conduct*, 2010, para.2.1). 'Binding' means that no minister can publicly dissent from the decision or disclaim responsibility for it. Next time you are watching an interview with a Government minister on television, note how the interviewer rarely limits themselves to questions about the minister's specific area of responsibility. If, for example, there has been a major policy announcement on renewable energy and the Secretary of State for Justice is appearing on a Sunday morning politics programme, the interviewer will feel entitled to ask the minister about it. Even though energy policy is not part the Justice Minister's portfolio, they will support the policy and try to explain its benefits, regardless of their own private views on the issue. The Government is collectively responsible for Government decisions.

5.11.3 CONFIDENTIALITY

Collective responsibility requires that Ministers should be able to express their views frankly in the expectation that they can argue freely in private while maintaining a united front when decisions have been reached. This in turn requires that the privacy of opinions expressed in Cabinet and Ministerial Committees, including in correspondence, should be maintained.

(*Ministerial Code of Conduct*, 2010, para 2.1)

APPLYING THE LAW – CONFIDENTIALITY OF CABINET DISCUSSIONS

In the example above, the Justice Minister may be deeply opposed to the proposal on renewable energy. They are entitled to argue their position frankly and vigorously within the four walls of the Cabinet Room. Once a decision has been reached, however, they should not indicate that opposition. They must not express either their dissent or the views and positions of other Cabinet members.

The operation of these two strands means that a minister who disagrees with a policy must keep that disagreement confidential *and* publicly support the policy. If the minister is unable to do this, then they must resign. This will (largely) free them from both strands of the convention. They will be able to break ranks and state their opposition to a policy and explain the arguments and objections they presented within Cabinet discussions.

An example of this is the resignation of Robin Cook from his ministerial post in 2003. He strongly opposed the decision to go to war in Iraq. If he had opted to remain in Government, then he would not have been at liberty to express this opposition and, if questioned, would have been forced to state support and collective responsibility for the military action. Following his resignation, he could both oppose the Iraq decision and communicate what he had argued on this issue within Cabinet. In his widely admired resignation speech he stated, 'I cannot accept collective responsibility for the decision to commit Britain now to military action in Iraq without international agreement or domestic support'.

APPLYING THE LAW – THE PURPOSE OF COLLECTIVE RESPONSIBILITY

To go back to the exercise on lowering the voting age, then, we can see the purposes of the convention of Collective Cabinet Responsibility:

- To maintain confidence in the unified nature of government.
- To enhance the accountability of government as a whole.
- To provide stability.
- To reinforce political discipline and the power of the Prime Minister.

A further example of the convention in action that raises interesting questions about the basis for the rule is the resignation of Michael Heseltine, the Secretary of State for Defence, in what was known as the Westland Helicopters crisis in 1986. There was a dispute over who should be the preferred option (US or European) in the takeover bid of a British helicopter company. Heseltine supported the European option and felt that he was not being given sufficient time in Cabinet to argue for that option. He refused to submit to having his public statements cleared by Cabinet Office, walked out of a Cabinet meeting stating, 'I can no longer be a member of this Cabinet' and immediately announced his resignation to the press.

This raises an important issue: if the basis of collective responsibility is collective decision-making, then what if that basis disappears? Is it a pre-condition for the obligations of unanimity and confidentiality to apply to a minister that they have been able to fully participate in the decision, even if that simply means airing dissent within Cabinet?

The short answer appears to be no. The convention applies to all members of Government, including junior ministers who take no part in Cabinet discussions. Most Prime Ministers have chosen to take key decisions, e.g. on economic or national security issues, in smaller groups that may even include non-Cabinet members. Most Cabinet meetings are far too short (often as little as 30 minutes) for it to be a genuine forum for collective debate and decision-making. Recent Prime Ministers have preferred to use the Cabinet's time more for reporting decisions taken elsewhere. Nevertheless, there are limits to this, and there will still be an opportunity for a minister to raise in Cabinet concerns about decisions made in some other part of Government. Even dominant Prime Ministers will need to keep Cabinet members reasonably content about the link between Government decision-making and the Cabinet's collective responsibility for those decisions.

Unlike a legal rule, it seems that this particular convention can be suspended simply by Prime Ministerial diktat. In 1975, the Labour Government renegotiated the terms of membership of the European Economic Community (EEC) (what is now the European Union) and submitted the question of the UK's continued membership to a national referendum. The Cabinet was split, and ministers held very strong views on either side.

The Prime Minister, Harold Wilson, decided to suspend the operation of Collective Cabinet Responsibility on this issue for the duration of the referendum. This allowed the seven members of Cabinet who opposed EEC membership to publicly campaign for a 'No' vote. Even so, there were limits to the freedom of ministers. They could not oppose the official Government position whilst speaking officially in the House of Commons. One minister, Eric Heffer, was dismissed for breaching this restriction.

It does seem strange that an important constitutional rule can simply be waived. On a similar issue in 1979, the Prime Minister, James Callaghan, stated collective responsibility would always apply 'except in cases where I announce that it does not'. Widgery CJ in the *Jonathan Cape* case said: 'I find overwhelming evidence that the doctrine of joint responsibility is generally understood and practised and equally strong evidence that it is on occasion ignored'. In the campaigning for the EU referendum of June 2016, members of Cabinet were able to campaign openly and vigorously on either side of the Leave / Remain question. David Cameron said 'And, as indicated . . ., there will be a clear government position, but it will be open to individual ministers to take a different personal position while remaining part of the government'.[23]

Unanimity and confidentiality are also undermined by leaks to the press. The lobby system, whereby a privileged group of journalists got access to Government stories, often in return for not indicating the source of the story, was largely ended in 2002. Despite this, the classic formula of ministers subtly distancing themselves from decisions that they are not comfortable with through unattributed briefings does continue. When you read in a newspaper that 'sources close to the minister say that . . .', it is normally safe to assume that this is code for 'the minister says . . .'.

Some commentators have doubted whether it is even appropriate to regard Collective Cabinet Responsibility as a constitutional rule any more. Eric Barendt argued that 'the

---

23 N Watt, 'Eurosceptics force Cameron to give ministers free rein on EU referendum', *The Guardian*, 5 January 2016 https://www.theguardian.com/politics/2016/jan/05/eurosceptic-tories-force-cameron-announce-ministers-free-rein-eu-referendum (last accessed 05/11/17).

principles of Cabinet and ministerial solidarity and confidentiality now appear to be little more than political practices or usages which may be departed from whenever it is convenient to the government'.[24]

Arguably, this is going too far. The codification of the convention in the Ministerial Code (the 'rulebook' on how ministers carry out their duties) has helped to clarify and reinforce the obligations that the rule imposes. Perhaps the greatest 'stress test' for collective responsibility comes in coalition government. Expecting Cabinet Ministers from different parties, with different political ideologies and traditions and elected on the basis of different manifestos, to abide by the convention is a significant commitment.

The convention, however, largely held firm during the Coalition Government from 2010 to 2015. This was so even on the issue of student fees (as discussed in Chapter 2, 'Institutions'). The Liberal Democrats entered the election with a manifesto commitment to abolish fees and signed pledges to that effect. Yet Liberal Democrat Cabinet Ministers faced having to support a decision to allow fees to rise by almost 300 per cent in England.

Any anger or dissent from Liberal Democrat ministers was kept within the walls of the Cabinet Room. They publicly spoke of their disappointment that there was a need to reform student fees this way and claimed credit for the more progressive aspects of the policy. Ultimately, however, they were required to publicly support the policy and to vote in favour of it. This can be contrasted with the significant number of Liberal Democrat MPs, who were not in government and therefore not bound by the convention, who voted against the proposal. The fact that three Liberal Democrat ministerial aides resigned their posts rather than vote for the Bill is a graphic illustration of the continuing operation and strength of the conventional rule.

A recent illustration that the convention is often put the test but still remains relevant concerns leaks from the Cabinet seemingly aimed at undermining the Chancellor, Philip Hammond, in July 2017. Hammond complained that 'Cabinet meetings are supposed to be a private space when we are supposed to have serious discussions', leading the Prime Minister to criticise the leaks and remind her Cabinet of their duties.[25]

KEY LEARNING POINTS

- Collective Cabinet Responsibility imposes obligations of unanimity and confidentiality on Government ministers. It makes ministers collectively responsible for the decisions and actions of Government.
- Its function is to promote accountability and stability in Government.
- It can be suspended for particular topics and particular periods, but it continues to act as a normative constitutional rule.

24 E Barendt, *An Introduction to Constitutional Law* (OUP, 1998) 121.

25 G Parker, 'Philip Hammond accuses cabinet Brexiters of leaking against him' *Financial Times*, 16 July 2017, 3fe0c5b7eaa (last accessed 05/11/17) https://www.ft.com/content/3efb991a-6a0a-11e7-bfeb-3.

5.11.4 INDIVIDUAL MINISTERIAL RESPONSIBILITY (IMR)

Think of some of the big themes that have run through the opening chapters of this book: constitutionalism, the need for limited government, that those who exercise power must be made accountable (legally or politically) for those actions, and that there must be some way of ejecting those who abuse power or who have wholly lost the confidence of the people. Individual Ministerial Responsibility is a crucial tool at the heart of the constitutional system for promoting these aims.

Enoch Powell emphasised the central importance of Ministerial Responsibility 'without which the House [of Commons] scarcely has a real function or any real service that it can perform for the people whom it represents'.[26]

The convention was defined by Lord Morrison in 1964 as:

> a Minister is accountable to Parliament for anything he or his department does, if the action , , , is within the field of ministerial power or competence, the Minister is answerable to Parliament.[27]

IMR is often raised in the tempestuous environment of a scandal or administrative fiasco with calls from the press and opponents for the relevant minister to take responsibility and resign. But its role is both more mundane *and* more important than that. It underpins the daily work of Parliament and its Select Committees, including Prime Minister's Questions, other ministers' questions and investigations by Parliamentary committees. It can be a powerful tool to promote accountability and transparency.

APPLYING THE LAW

IMR can be a messy topic to study. Its boundaries, nature and, even, purpose are not entirely clear and there is a confused mass of practice from different ministers' conduct. All is not lost; one way of plotting a course through the subject and structuring your analysis is to impose a narrative on the discussion of IMR. Overall, the arch of the story presented here is that the convention has become both narrower and clearer (and that there are both positive and negative aspects to this development).

The story has three main sections:

- Changes to the scope of IMR.
- Changes to the nature of IMR, including the policy/operations distinction.
- Changes to the objectives of IMR, focusing on ministers' accountability rather than their responsibility.

---

26 House of Commons, HC Deb vol 53, col 1060, 9 February 1984.
27 Lord Morrison, *Government and Parliament*, 3rd edn (OUP, 1964) 332.

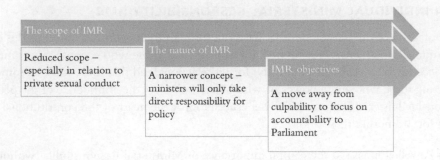

Figure 5.4 Evolution of IMR

5.11.5 QUESTIONS AS TO THE SCOPE OF THE CONVENTION

First, we need to examine the scope of the convention. Even when all is well and the policy and administration of a Government are error-free and yielding great results, IMR still has a role to play in promoting transparency and monitoring Government action. It is when things go wrong, however, that there is a particular requirement for a constitutional rule to shed light on the problem and stop each part of Government washing their hands of it.

These sorts of problems include *personal competence* and *errors of judgement* that impact on a minister's public functions. Estelle Morris resigned from the post of Secretary of State for Education in 2001. She explained that she did not feel up to the job of Secretary of State and had felt happier as a junior minister. This is a very unusual example of a minister evaluating their own personal competence and deciding of their own volition that they were not suited for the role. It is more common for others to reach the conclusion that the minister is not competent or has made serious errors of judgement, on which basis the minister is then sacked or (more commonly) persuaded to resign.

Peter Mandelson has the rare (but not unique) distinction of resigning from Cabinet for two separate errors of judgment. In 1998, he resigned as Secretary of State for Trade and Industry. He had accepted an interest-free loan to help buy a house from another member of Government and had not declared the loan in the Members' Register of Interests. After his return to the Cabinet, he had to resign again in 2001, over allegations that he had interfered in a passport application from an Indian businessman. He was later found not to have acted improperly, but the notion of ministers taking responsibility for their errors of judgement is wider than simple abuses of power.

There are more recent examples. Liam Fox resigned as Secretary of State for Defence in 2011 when it emerged that he had met his friend Adam Werrity on 18 foreign trips where he allowed Mr Werrity to attend meetings with military leaders and diplomats and had blurred the line between personal and professional responsibilities. Despite this, Fox returned to the Cabinet in 2016. Even more clear-cut is the resignation of Chris Huhne, the Energy Secretary, in 2012 following the decision to prosecute him for perverting the course of justice in relation to passing speeding penalty points to his wife (for which he was subsequently convicted and jailed).

The list of personal mistakes could go on, but it is uncontroversial to say that a minister should take responsibility for their own conduct as minister. Whether taking responsibility automatically equates with resignation is examined below. The more difficult questions relating to the scope of IMR are:

- To what extent do ministers have to take responsibility for things done by their Department and civil servants rather than by themselves (covered in the next section)?
- To what extent do ministers have to take constitutional responsibility for actions from their private life?

Chris Huhne's behaviour in persuading his wife to take speeding points that ought to have been his was not directly related to his public office or duties, but there is no doubt that his criminal conduct and dishonesty required his resignation. The aspects of private life that are most commonly at issue here are private sexual behaviour, and in particular marital infidelity.

Unacceptable sexual behaviour has been behind a number of high-profile resignations in the latter half of the last century, from John Profumo in 1963 (although that also involved national security issues and the cardinal sin of lying to the House of Commons), Lords Lambton and Jellicoe in 1973 (for liaisons with prostitutes) to Cecil Parkinson in 1983 (for an affair with his secretary). The last really high-profile resignation was Culture Secretary David Mellor in 1992. It was revealed that he had been having an extra-marital affair, which together with other minor allegations and a relentless press campaign led a reluctant Prime Minister to accept his resignation.

We can contrast these with the examples of Robin Cook (Foreign Secretary, 1999, revealed as having a number of extra-marital affairs and who had left his wife for his secretary) and John Prescott (Deputy Prime Minister, 2006, an affair with his secretary). In both cases, the Prime Minister quickly dismissed the stories as wholly irrelevant to their public functions and merely gossip relating to their private lives. There were only half-hearted calls for resignation from the press and Opposition.

It seems that the simple fact of marital infidelity will not now be sufficient to force a minister's resignation. Some might interpret this as a social change in public morals on the issue of fidelity or the sanctity of marriage, but there is probably a better way of understanding these examples.

Jaconelli argues that these examples of private sexual conduct are concerned with personal judgement or morals, rather than the operation of the constitution, and so they should not be classified as *constitutional* conventions.[28] The Scott Enquiry on Arms to Iraq (1996) also

---

28 J Jaconelli, 'The Nature of Constitutional Conventions' [1999] *Legal Studies* 24.

found that personal morality issues are outside of the operation of IMR and emphasised the constitutional quality of the convention.

Just as responsibility does not automatically equate to resignation, so not all ministerial resignations should be attributed to the operation of IMR. Hard and fast distinctions are quite difficult in this field. It is sometimes said that a minister's conduct in their private life tells us whether they are trustworthy in public office, but whether a minister's private sexual conduct requires their resignation is essentially a political question rather than the result of the application of a constitutional rule. It is argued here that this is a welcome development. The apparent scope of the convention is reduced, but in doing so it focuses on the more important constitutional role of the convention: to hold ministers to account for what they do as ministers.

5.11.6 QUESTIONS AS TO THE NATURE OF THE RESPONSIBILITY

IMR is sometimes seen as a resigning or a sacking convention, but we can question whether IMR *requires* a minister to go;

- if it is found that their department has committed serious errors, or
- only if they themselves have committed serious errors, or
- not at all (with resignation governed by other factors such as party support and pressure from the press)?

We have seen that taking responsibility for personal errors is a central part of IMR, and this can, for serious misjudgements, lead to resignation. There must, however, be a sliding scale of seriousness. Everyone makes mistakes, and automatic dismissal for any error would leave the Government ranks very thin. In 2013, Secretary of State for Education Michael Gove made critical comments on the historical ignorance of children. Despite asserting that the Department would promote evidence-based policies, it emerged that much of the data he used in the statements was derived from sources such as a poll for TV Gold and a Premier Inn hotel chain survey. This may be slip-shod and hypocritical, but taking responsibility for this ought not to entail dismissal. Lesser sanctions, including criticism and ridicule, seem more appropriate.

One enduring question, however, is what it means to take responsibility for the mistakes of others (e.g. civil servants). The Permanent Secretary to the Treasury has said, 'it has long been the established constitutional practice that the appropriate Minister of the Crown is responsible to Parliament for *every action* in pursuance of [their legal powers]'.[29] IMR clearly extends beyond a minister's own actions to encompass everything within the department's competence, but do we really expect a minister to resign for, even serious, errors made by civil servants?

---

29 2nd Report from the Public Service Committee, Ministerial Accountability and Responsibility, HC 313 1995/1996 –
    Sir Edward Bridges.

KEY CASE – *SIR THOMAS DUGDALE 1954 (THE CRICHEL DOWN AFFAIR)*

The Air Ministry acquired farm land in Devon in 1938. Following the Second World War, it was transferred to the Department for Agriculture. The original owners wanted to buy it back but they were refused the opportunity to do so, and the land was let to another tenant. There was a complaint and enquiry (Report of the Public Inquiry into the Disposal of Land at Crichel Down (Cmd 9176/1954)), which heavily criticised civil servants and found them guilty of maladministration. The Report did not directly criticise the minister, Sir Thomas Dugdale, or find that he had been personally involved in the case.

Dugdale responded by resigning, and he said to the House of Commons, 'I, as Minister, must accept full responsibility to Parliament for any mistakes and inefficiency of officials in my Department, just as, when my officials bring off any successes on my behalf, I take full credit for them' (HC Deb vol 530, col 1186, 20 July 1954).

This has often been presented (more by the media than by academic writers) as the classic or pure example of IMR. Many subsequent ministers have been criticised for failing to meet the demands of the 'honourable' benchmark set in this case. This is not necessarily a justified criticism.

The facts of the case are not quite as straightforward as they appeared. The original landowners had considerable influence, and it has subsequently come to light that Dugdale did have some knowledge of what his civil servants were doing at the time. More generally, Dugdale was unpopular with sections of his own party and had little support within Cabinet or from the Prime Minister.

There are very few examples of this sort of self-sacrifice either before or after Crichel Down. It is arguable that the resignation of Lord Carrington as Foreign Secretary following the Argentinean invasion of the Falkland Islands in 1982 is one such case. It is interesting to note that Carrington had been a junior minister in the Department for Agriculture at the time of Crichel Down and had his offer of resignation at that time turned down.

The idea that a minister should take responsibility, to the extent of resigning, for serious errors committed by civil servants has not been an accepted part of IMR for decades (if it ever was). Again, this seems sensible. Anything else would mean the Government would lose talented ministers, there would be constant disruption, it would be unfair to end someone's career in such circumstances and it may distract from the underlying problem within the department.

So, to recap:

- Ministers are responsible for everything that happens within their department.

- They ought not try to shift responsibility for any act within their department onto civil servants.
- The Crichel Down example is unrealistic, and ministers do not ordinarily resign for errors made by their civil servants.

So is there any coherent principle underlying these findings?

5.11.6.1 THE POLICY/OPERATIONS DISTINCTION

KEY CASE – *MAZE PRISON ESCAPE 1983*

James Prior was Secretary of State for Northern Ireland in 1983, at the time of a mass breakout of IRA prisoners from Maze prison. The prisoners included some of the most dangerous people in the country, and a prison guard died during the escape. Problems were identified with security systems at the jail, including the negligence of staff, but also with the supervision and oversight by the prison department in Northern Ireland.

Prior said he would resign if the report into the escapes showed that it was a 'result of some act of policy that was my responsibility'. When the report did not do so, he explained his refusal to resign to the House of Commons: 'In putting the emphasis that I did on the issue of "policy", I was not seeking to map out some new doctrine of ministerial responsibility . . . I do not accept . . . that there is any constitutional or other principle that requires ministerial resignations in the face of failure, either by others to carry out orders or procedures or by their supervisors to ensure that staff carried out those orders' (HC Deb vol 53, col 1060, 9 February 1984).

Speaking in the same debate, Enoch Powell called this distinction 'wholly fallacious'. It allows ministers to say, 'The policy was excellent and that was mine, but the execution was defective or disastrous and that was nothing to do with me', and 'there would be no political source to which the public could complain about administration or from which it could seek redress for failings of administration'.

There was a similar series of events in 1994 when the Home Secretary, Michael Howard, was pressed to take responsibility for a series of jail escapes. He refused to do so and instead sacked the Director of the Prison Service. He argued that there was a distinction between responsibility for a) the policy and b) the operations side of Government, along the same lines as Prior had in 1983. Ministers are directly responsible for the policies they adopt (and the sanction of dismissal still seems possible when a minister is sufficiently culpable for a dreadful policy). This direct responsibility does not apply, however, in relation to operational matters, i.e. how those policies are implemented by civil servants.

ANALYSING THE LAW – POLICY/OPERATIONS

Take a moment to consider Powell's criticism of Prior and the policy/operations distinction. What are the broad policy goals likely to be: 'Prisons are secure'; 'The Health Service will be effective'; 'The environment will be protected'. These are unimpeachably good, like voting for Mom and apple pie, as the American saying say.

Any problems are likely to occur on the point of delivery, and it may be much too easy for a minister to categorise this as an operational problem, thus freeing themselves of direct responsibility.

A further issue is that most Government policy is not implemented directly by Government departments any more. The operations of the state are largely handled by what are called 'next step agencies', e.g. the Prison Service or the Passport Office, and increasingly by private companies contracted to provide public services. There is an increasing distance between a minister's policy and its delivery to the public. The different layers of management can operate as a firewall between a controversy and a minister.

The leading writer on the subject, Diane Woodhouse, advises some caution in accepting the policy/operations distinction wholly on ministers' terms; it has:

> resulted in attempts by ministers to minimise expectations and distance themselves from culpability. Hence the employment of the distinction between 'policy' and 'operations', which implies that ministers cannot be expected to know anything about operational matters, and that between 'responsibility' and 'accountability', which implies that they therefore cannot be blamed for any operational error . . .[30]

In relation to Michael Howard, she argues that 'the Home Secretary became responsible for virtually nothing, the "cause" was tied to the responsibilities of the Director General, and managerial accountability was substituted for constitutional responsibility'.

The second part of this IMR narrative shows that ministers are responsible for a narrower range of actions. This does make the convention clearer, to some extent, but there is disquiet about allowing ministers to define the scope of their own constitutional responsibilities. This criticism goes to the heart of using constitutional conventions to regulate important matters. They can evolve through practice, and this practice is largely in the hands of the people who are supposed to be regulated by the rule. If ministers act in ways that are designed to protect themselves, does this change the constitutional rule? The answer (on the specific issue of IMR) lies in insisting on two features: supervisory responsibility and complete accountability, both explored below.

---

30 D Woodhouse, 'The Reconstruction of Constitutional Accountability' [2002] *Public Law* 73, 75.

5.11.7 MINISTERIAL RESPONSIBILITY OR ACCOUNTABILITY?

Much of the discussion around IMR focuses on the issue of resignations, but whilst 'the pursuit of Ministerial resignations is an important part of a process of enforcing political accountability, . . . too great a concentration on it obscures the wider importance of the day-to-day business of holding the executive to account in Parliament, to ensure that it is kept under proper democratic control'.[31] So what is missing from these discussions is a clearer focus on the purpose of the convention; what constitutional functions does it perform? This third part of this IMR story focuses on accountability.

The idea that resignation is a formal sanction that has a coherent relationship with breach of a formal constitutional rule of IMR has long been dismissed. Samuel Finer wrote in 1956 that:

> The convention implies a form of punishment for a delinquent Minister . . . loss of office. If each, or even very many charges of incompetence were habitually followed by the punishment, the remedy would be a very real one: its deterrent effect would be extremely great. In fact, that sequence is not only exceedingly rare, but arbitrary and unpredictable.

Instead, the sanction of loss of office 'is indiscriminate – which Ministers escape and which do not is decided neither by the circumstances of the offence nor by its gravity'.[32] Finer outlined three factors affecting who stays in office and who goes: that the minister is compliant; that the Prime Minister is firm; and that the party is clamorous.

We can add to this list the role of the Opposition and, in particular, the press. The key point remains that ministerial resignation is 'an informal and highly political affair. It cannot be reduced to firm rules and conventions'.[33]

EXPLAINING THE LAW – MISLEADING PARLIAMENT

Only one aspect of Ministerial Responsibility explicitly links the sanction of dismissal with breach of the convention. This is when a minister knowingly misleads Parliament. This was proposed in a House of Commons resolution in 1997 and later adopted by Government in the Ministerial Code: ministers must be 'as open as possible with Parliament and the public, refusing to provide information only when disclosure would not be in the public interest . . . [It is] of paramount importance that Ministers give accurate and truthful information to Parliament, correcting any inadvertent error at the earliest opportunity. Ministers who knowingly mislead Parliament will be expected to offer their resignation to the Prime Minister'.

---

31 2nd Report from the Public Service Committee, Ministerial Accountability and Responsibility, HC 313 1995/1996, para 31.

32 SE Finer, 'The Individual Responsibility of Ministers' (1956) 34 *Public Administration* 377, 393.

33 2nd Report from the Public Service Committee, above n 29, para 31.

A greater focus on the constitutional functions of IMR then is likely to produce a narrower, and in some ways less exciting, but more useful rule. Anthony Giddens argued that the convention really aims to:

- Secure information and explanation.
- Exert pressure for change.
- Attribute blame or praise.

That is, its aim was to give information but also to appear responsive to concerns.[34]

Woodhouse also argues that IMR has been reconstructed. It now involves ministers being accountable to Parliament, in the sense of having to give an account of all policies, all operational practices and mistakes and what is being done to remedy any failings.[35] From Giddens's list of functions it is the first two which are more important on a day-to-day basis.

APPLYING THE LAW – RESPONSIBILITY/ACCOUNTABILITY

Imagine that you are the branch manager of a clothes shop which is part of a national chain. If you make a serious error of judgement (such as failing to tell head office that you also work part-time for a rival clothes shop, or get convicted of conspiracy to pervert the course of justice), then you can expect to lose your job. This is similar to a minister being directly responsible for their own professional conduct.

You are responsible for certain aspects of the sales and marketing strategy at a local level (e.g. which clothing lines to particularly promote). What would your responsibility be for those decisions? It would be a direct responsibility. If your policies are a success, then you would expect credit for that. If they are not, you can expect criticism and review. If your policies are so bad that the head office questions your competence, then you may lose your job. This is similar to a minister being responsible for their own policies.

In addition, and running alongside this responsibility, you will be *accountable* for your policies, i.e. to give an account to head office of what you have done and why you have done it and what the results are. This accountability is a part of your role, whether clothing sales are going well or poorly. What is expected is complete transparency. If you fail to give a proper account, you can expect to be criticised, disciplined and even dismissed. This is similar to the duty on ministers to *account to Parliament* for their own policies and actions.

34 A Giddens, *The Constitution of Society* (Wiley, 1986).
35 Woodhouse, above n 28, 73.

So, to recap, ministers will be both directly responsible *and* accountable for what they themselves do in their conduct and policy-making. Transparency to Parliament is expected in accounting, not only for their own behaviour, but also for every action within their Department's area of responsibility. This still leaves the question of what direct responsibility ministers have for the actions of their civil servants.

APPLYING THE LAW – RESPONSIBILITY FOR THE MISDEEDS OF OTHERS

Back in the clothes shop, it appears that some of the staff in your branch have been stealing money from the tills. Is this your direct responsibility in the sense that you are immediately culpable for this and ought to offer your resignation? No. Just as a minister should not be dismissed just because a prison warder forgets to lock a door and a prisoner escapes, you are not immediately culpable for this. When someone calls from head office for an explanation, however, they would clearly not be satisfied with a response of, 'Well, I'm in charge of policy and this was purely an operational matter. It is not my responsibility'.

Your accountability duty covers everything within your branch. Even if you are not directly culpable, you will still need to find out what went wrong, why it went wrong, explain what you are going to do about the problem and what future measures you are putting in place to make sure the problem does not occur again, for example: 'I found that the money in the tills was not balancing the receipts. I observed all staff and saw two assistants taking money from the tills. I called the police and then dismissed them in accordance with the company policy. I am installing a CCTV camera to cover the tills'.

In a similar way, when something within a department's field of competence goes wrong, the minister must account to Parliament for that. They must be as transparent as possible in explaining what went wrong and why. They must outline what measures they are taking. This duty applies regardless of whether the minister is in any way directly responsible for the problem. In the prison escape examples, even if the fault lies wholly with the local operations in a specific prison, the minister still has a full duty to account for the errors.

APPLYING THE LAW – SUPERVISORY RESPONSIBILITY

Imagine that three months after the initial thefts from the shop, money starts going missing again from the tills. Someone from head office comes to investigate and finds that there are issues in the way you are supervising the shop (you did not get around to installing the CCTV, or you do not review the tapes, or you do not audit the till receipts properly). The primary fault, stealing money, still lies with someone else, but you are failing to carry out your supervisory responsibility. You can expect to be criticised, disciplined and even dismissed.

Similarly, ministers cannot disclaim supervisory responsibility. In the prison escapes, if the problems continue and this shows a minister's shortcomings in their ability to intervene and supervise their departmental operations effectively, then they can expect to be criticised, their career prospects damaged and even asked to resign.

5.12 POINTS TO NOTE

- IMR is not a rule that automatically requires dismissal from office. Dismissal is dependent on a range of other factors.
- Ministers are directly *responsible* for their own actions and policies and *accountable* for everything done in their department.
- Accountability involves investigating errors, explaining them to Parliament and putting in place measures to prevent future errors.
- Ministers have supervisory responsibility for the way in which their policies are delivered by civil servants.

5.13 THE ARMS TO IRAQ SCANDAL

One story sums up, more than most, the need for a clear and effective constitutional rule on Ministerial Responsibility. It should also dismiss any lingering notion that the Government will always act in the best interests of the public.

EXPLAINING THE LAW – MATRIX CHURCHILL

The Government announced in 1984 that it would not license the export of any military equipment to Iran or Iraq, in line with a UN resolution trying to limit the effects of the Iran–Iraq War. In 1988, three ministers changed the export policy in relation to Iraq. Loveland argues that 'It is scarcely credible to believe that this was done without Cabinet approval'.[36] The decision to change the rules was not communicated to Parliament or the public, almost certainly to avoid international and local embarrassment.

The directors of Matrix Churchill, a UK engineering company that was owned by Iraqi interests, sold equipment to Iraq with the support of the Department of Defence. This equipment had potential military uses. Customs and Excise were unaware of this

36 Loveland, above n 11, 291.

official encouragement or the change of export policy. They prosecuted the directors for breaching the export embargo.

At the directors' criminal trial, Government ministers tried to use public interest immunity (PII) certificates to prevent the relevant information, including the secret change of policy, being presented to the court. They falsely claimed this was on the grounds of a threat to national security. The attempt to use PII was rejected by the judge and the trial collapsed. One minister, Alan Clark, admitted to being 'economical with the *actualité*' (a nice way of saying 'dishonest') in his statements to Parliament.

Just take a moment to think about the gravity of what went on here. Government ministers were prepared to allow these people to be convicted and imprisoned rather than reveal politically embarrassing information, and had attempted to misuse a national security procedure to do so.

The aftermath of this scandal led to an independent inquiry – the Scott Inquiry. You may hope that the Government would have been shamed into decency, that they would try to clean their hands by adopting an open approach, by treating the Inquiry with respect. You would be mistaken. The Government obstructed the Inquiry and tried to weaken it. It forced the Inquiry to give it a full week's notice of its report. It scheduled the Parliamentary debate on the same day as publication (giving the Opposition almost no time to prepare for the debate).

The Scott Report said that there had been a failure of ministerial accountability. It explained that Governments:

do not submit with enthusiasm to the restraints of accountability . . . governments are little disposed to volunteer information that may expose them to criticism . . . The enforcement of accountability depends largely on the ability of Parliament to prise information from governments which are inclined to be defensively secretive where they are most vulnerable to challenge.

This brings us to the core value of IMR. There is a pressure within a democracy, with parties competing for the public's favour, for the governing party to present only its best face. This may involve public relations and spinning the presentation of both good and bad news at one end of the spectrum, through blaming others and shirking responsibility, right up to deliberately withholding information or misleading at the other end. A constitutional rule that pins down a minister's responsibility and accountability to Parliament, therefore, performs a vital constitutional function.

5.14 SHOULD ALL CONVENTIONS BE CODIFIED?

Codification here means the bringing together of all, or a sub-set of, constitutional conventions into a written document with no change to their legal status. It is different from the process of turning a conventional rule into a legal one – enactment. Australia undertook this codification process on a fairly comprehensive scale in the 1970s. There are more recent examples of partial codification in the UK, e.g. the Ministerial Code that brings together the conventions (and other understandings and expectations) that regulate ministerial conduct.

As Jaconelli notes, 'the formula records rather than creates, the convention'. They would be conventions even if they were not recorded. Even when they are recorded, it is the acceptance of what the rule is in the minds of the constitutional actors that makes the rule, rather than the written form. Nonetheless, recording can crystallise the shared understanding of the conventions' scope and interpretation.[37] McHarg agrees that it is 'the subsequent practice, rather than the initial statement, which . . . determine[s] both the status and the scope'.[38]

This takes us back to the definition of conventions and the process of how they arise. Irrespective of whether they are simply created and published in a Command Paper, or have evolved through a century of constitutional practice, it is the sense of obligation that is paramount. If a document is understood by the constitutional actors as merely providing a set of general guidelines rather than a binding rule, then it will not be a constitutional convention.

5.15 ENACTMENT

Would it be better to replace conventions with legal rules? On the plus side, this may promote greater certainty. The rules would have to be captured in the precise legal language used in statutes, and their subsequent meaning in different contexts could be clarified by judicial interpretation.

EXPLAINING THE LAW – THE PONSONBY RULE

The Ponsonby Rule was a constitutional convention that international treaties, which the Government wanted to ratify, should be laid before Parliament for at least 21 days. If there was significant demand for a debate, then the views of Parliament

---

37 J Jaconelli, 'Do Constitutional Conventions Bind?' [2005] *Cambridge Law Journal* 149, 169.
38 McHarg, above n 13, 859.

would be heard. The rule was unclear on the duties and rights of ministers if Parliament disapproved of the treaty.

This has been replaced by ss.20–25 Constitutional Reform and Governance Act 2010. This requires the minister to lay a copy of the treaty before Parliament. If Parliament resolves that the treaty should not be ratified, the minister can still proceed with ratification but must submit a statement to Parliament explaining why they are ratifying. Section 22 says that this procedure does not apply where a minister considers there to be 'exceptional circumstances'.

This provides a little more clarity to the rule, but the sanction for breaching s.20 is not clear. The courts are very reluctant to interfere with the internal workings of Parliament, and any remedy would probably lie within Parliament itself.

Elliott and Thomas argue that there should be no general or comprehensive process of enactment. Conventions already bind and the 'legal unenforceability of conventions is a good thing'. Conventions allow constitutional actors to deal with particular matters that are not always suitable for adjudication by a court.[39]

There are also doubts as to the practicality of wholesale enactment. There would be problems of identifying all relevant conventions and questions as to whether one particular political party in Government had the legitimacy to legally cast conventions in the mould of their choosing. If we go back to the source of conventions, i.e. social practice, you will see that further conventions would develop over time anyway. Conversely, a wholesale enactment would lose the flexibility that 'allows a congruous development of the constitution in response to experience and changes in society'.[40]

Munro recommends an ad hoc approach. Where obedience to a rule is important and where there is a risk of disobedience, then there are good reasons for enacting a convention as a legal rule.[41]

As ever, it seems that the UK constitution is proceeding on a pragmatic and ad hoc basis. Conventional rules will be enacted into law on a case-by-case basis when there is a particular reason to do so (and even then relatively rarely). Where conventions simply need to be clarified and made more precise, then they are grouped together in non-legal codes covering particular topics or personnel (Ministerial Code, Civil Service Code).

---

39 M Elliott and R Thomas, *Public Law*, 3rd edn (OUP, 2017) 63.
40 C Turpin and A Tomkins, *British Government and the Constitution*, 7th edn (Cambridge UP, 2011) 190.
41 C R Munro, *Studies in Constitutional Law* (Butterworths, 1999) 77.

POINTS TO REVIEW

- Conventions are non-legal rules of the constitution that regulate important constitutional relationships and powers.

- Conventions are different from laws both in the way they are created and in the fact that they cannot be enforced by the courts.

- They are different from habits because they are normative, i.e. they require certain conduct in certain circumstances. This normative force comes from an internal sense of obligation and the non-legal sanctions that would follow a breach of the rule.

- Constitutional conventions govern many of the powers of the Monarch, Prime Minister and Government and impose duties on ministers collectively to Cabinet and individually to Parliament.

TAKING IT FURTHER

J Jaconelli, 'Do constitutional conventions bind?' [2005] *Cambridge Law Journal* 14

This article explores the basis for saying that constitutional conventions are rules, that they bind. A very useful source if you want more depth and detailed arguments on the general nature of conventions.

N Barber, 'Laws and constitution conventions' (2009) 125 *Law Quarterly Review* 29

It is always useful to get contrasting views. Comparing a range of opinions is perhaps the easiest way of injecting critical evaluation into your work (although do not forget to build up to your own reasoned conclusion – 'The views of X are more persuasive because . . .'). This is an excellent article examining the relationships between law and convention. It differs from the stance taken in this chapter on the distinction between the two types of rule.

D Woodhouse, 'The Reconstruction of Constitutional Accountability' [2002] *Public Law* 73

This is still the best source for understanding the debates on what IMR really involves. Look out for Woodhouse's views on the policy/operations distinction and how she constructs an argument that ministers are accountable because of their constitutional role.

6

CHAPTER 6
ROYAL PREROGATIVE

It may seem strange to be devoting a whole chapter in a law textbook to the powers of the Crown. Surely, as the perception seems to be, the monarch has a largely ceremonial role in British public life? The Queen, however, is important because:

- She is formally the head of state – including being commander-in-chief of the armed forces.
- The monarchy is one of the estates of Parliament.
- Executive acts are done in her name by Her Majesty's Government.
- The courts are Her Majesty's courts, and justice is done in her name.

You will appreciate, of course, that the Queen does not personally decide on the disposition of the armed forces, on what legislation is passed, on what particular Government policies are adopted or on how any court case should be decided. So what is going on?

The answer lies in the concept of the royal prerogative. These are a bundle of disparate legal powers that are formally possessed by the Crown. Prerogatives are not granted by Parliament. They are not exercised personally by the Queen but, under constitutional convention, by the Government. They cover issues such as foreign relations and defence of the realm, some constitutional processes such as appointing ministers, granting of honours and mercy for those convicted of criminal offences.

As the Governance of Britain report says:

> In most modern democracies, the government's only powers are those granted to it by a written constitution or by the legislature. A distinguishing feature of the British constitution is the extent to which government continues to exercise a number of powers which were not granted to it by a written constitution, nor by Parliament, but are, rather, ancient prerogatives of the Crown.[1]

---

1 Governance of Britain, White Paper, Cm7170, 2007.

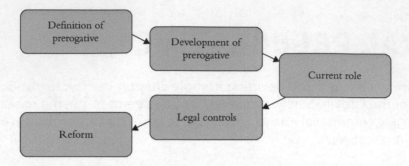

Figure 6.1 Structure of Chapter 6

AS YOU READ

The basic structure of this chapter is:

- Defining prerogative powers.
- Charting the development and current role of prerogative powers.
- The legal control of these powers.
- Reform.

You should be focusing on (a) picking up knowledge and (b) considering how you are going to use it. Like many areas of Public Law, the prerogative interacts with other topics, especially with the institutions of the constitution, rule of law and constitutional conventions, and judicial review. The chapter tries not to presume that you are already completely familiar with those topics and provides very short recaps – but you may need to cross-reference to get a deeper understanding. The ability to draw connections between different areas is a particularly effective way of showing examiners that you have thought carefully about the subject.

6.1 DEFINITION OF PREROGATIVE POWERS

A note on terminology: the 'monarch' is the person who is king or queen; the 'Crown' is a much broader term, 'which today personifies the executive government of the country' (*BBC v Johns* [1965] Ch 32). The exercise of royal prerogative powers is almost always in the hands of the Crown (i.e. central Government) rather than personally with the monarch.

So some of the key features of prerogative powers are that they are:

- Formally in the possession of the Crown.
- Not statutory (they derive from common law).

- Residual (their scope can be reduced but not increased).
- Exercised by Government.

There are two principal definitions of the prerogative. The seventeenth-century writer William Blackstone described it as '. . . that special pre-eminence which the King hath over and above all other persons, and out of the ordinary course of the common law, in right of his regal dignity'.[2]

For A V Dicey, the prerogative was '. . . the residue of discretionary or arbitrary authority, which at any time is legally left in the hands of the Crown . . . Every act which the executive government can lawfully do without the authority of an Act of Parliament is done in virtue of this prerogative'.[3]

There are differences between the two definitions. Look, in particular, at the second part of Dicey's definition. It seems to suggest that whenever Government does something under the authority of common law rather than statute (which could be something as simple as entering into a contract or buying land), then this is an exercise of prerogative power. This is not the best view. Look at the sub-clause in Blackstone's definition, i.e. powers which are 'out of the ordinary course of the common law'. Whilst prerogative powers might emanate from the same common law source, they are distinct from ordinary common law powers. Blackstone emphasised that if a power that the King enjoyed was 'in common with any of his subjects', then it was not a prerogative. A simple test is this: is this something that ordinary people are entitled to do under the common law? If the answer is yes, then it is not a prerogative power.

Courts have sometimes treated all non-statutory actions of Government as prerogative powers, but there is wider judicial support for Blackstone's view: 'Prerogative is, properly speaking, legal power which appertains to the Crown but not to its subjects' (*R v Secretary of State for Health, ex parte C* [2000] 1 FLR 627).

6.2 DEVELOPMENT OF THE PREROGATIVE

There was a question that ran through the centre of British history for at least 500 years. The consequences of the various answers threw up further challenges and questions that continue to the current day. The question was:

6.2.1 DOES THE KING RULE?

This focuses on whether the king has absolute power, the legal authority to have the final say on what is the law of the land.

---

2 Blackstone's Commentaries on the Laws of England 1765–69 http://avalon.law.yale.edu/subject_menus/blackstone. asp (last accessed 05/11/17).
3 A V Dicey, *Introduction to the Study of the Law of the Constitution* (8th edn Liberty Fund, 1982), 424.

Even the Norman kings ruled in consultation with a King's Council, and one of the reasons for the Magna Carta was the conflict between King John and his Council. The Tudor monarchs thought it politically wise to work with Parliament as far as possible.

The question of the monarch's legal powers was thrown into sharp relief during the reigns of the four Stuart kings (James I, Charles I and II, and James II). They believed in the 'divine right of kings'. This was the concept that kings obtained their earthly authority directly from God. Any attempts to limit the king's powers would therefore be a sacrilege and the King was entitled to assert absolute authority over political matters. Between 1603 and 1688, the Stuart kings used their personal prerogative power to summon and dissolve Parliament to try to force its obedience. The disputes between king and Parliament focused on tax-raising powers and imprisonment without trial. In 1629, Charles I dissolved Parliament and it was not summoned again for 11 years. During this time (the Eleven Years' Tyranny), King Charles ruled by personal decree.

KEY CASE – *CASE OF PROCLAMATIONS* [1610] EWHC KB J22

King James I considered that he had the power to alter the law without parliamentary consent by issuing royal proclamations. Most of these proclamations concerned his attempts to raise funds through taxes additional to those approved by Parliament.

The proclamations at issue in this case concerned a ban on new buildings in London and on the making of wheat starch. The House of Commons raised grievances against these proclamations as being against the law, and the Chief Justice of Common Pleas, Sir Edward Coke, was asked to provide a legal opinion.

After consulting with his fellow common law judges, Coke found that '. . . the King by his proclamation . . . cannot change any part of the common law, or statute law, or customs of the realm', and that 'the King hath no prerogative but that which the law of the land allows him'.

That is, the proclamations could not change the law because Parliament had not authorised it. The last sentence of the quote is crucial, because it is the courts who have the power to state what the law of the land is. Coke was not only asserting Parliamentary power; he was also making a claim for an independent judicial power.

Sir Edward Coke (pronounced Cook) was something of a hero of the common law and an important figure in the development of the British constitution. After serving the Crown very effectively as a prosecutor (he was Attorney General and chief prosecutor in the trial of Sir Walter Raleigh and of the Gunpowder Plot conspirators), he was appointed as a judge. He decided cases against King James's assertions of royal power (at risk to his liberty and even to his life) so often that he was transferred and then dismissed from office. He continued in public life as a politician and had a central role in drafting the Petition of Right, which laid out various rights and liberties and was a precursor to the Bill of Rights 1689. He seemed to have a number of virtues that lawyers like to think (sometimes wistfully) to be characteristic of their profession (and by implication themselves). He was scholarly and precise, reasoned and analytical, brave and independent. What makes his contribution still relevant to Public Law students today is his insistence that the law is an independent estate of the realm that can control the actions of the executive (then, the king; now, the Government) and even of Parliament (then, according to common right or reason; now, tentatively, according to democracy and the rule of law). He was also involved in our next case.

KEY CASE – *PROHIBITIONS DEL ROY (CASE OF PROHIBITIONS)*
[1607] EWHC J23 (KB)

King James I asserted the power to personally decide legal disputes in some circumstances. He said that the judges were merely his delegates in dispensing the King's justice. He attempted to adjudicate a property dispute between two individuals, which led to this case.

Edward Coke, speaking for the judges, said (and bear in mind this was directly to the king's face), 'the King in his own person cannot adjudge any case, either criminal . . . or betwixt party and party . . . but this ought to be determined and adjudged in some Court of Justice, according to the law and custom of England'. He argued that whilst the King was not subject to any individual, he was subject to the law. This law could not be declared or interpreted by the King because it 'demanded mastery of artificial reason . . . which requires long study and experience'. That is, only those who had studied and practised law were qualified to perform a judicial function.

Coke also passed a series of judgments that tried to limit the jurisdiction of various courts that the monarch had established by prerogative, such as the 'Star Chamber' and the Court of High Commission.

Taking the cases together, we can see that the monarch:

- Could not make new law (he did not possess legislative power and so was not part of that branch of the state) – *Proclamations*
- Did not possess adjudicative power to interpret the law and resolve legal disputes, so was not a part of the judicial branch – *Prohibitions*

These cases hemmed the monarch in, specifically into an executive role and, even then, only in so far as the king had specific executive legal powers as identified by the courts. This was intolerable to any monarch who thought they had been appointed by God. Following Coke's removal and a number of other changes, the pendulum swung back in the king's favour and his various assertions of power received some support from the courts.

6.2.2 THE MONARCHY STRIKES BACK

In *Darnel's Case (the Five Knights' Case)* [1627] 3 How St Tr 1, people had been imprisoned on the king's instructions, rather than by a court order or judicial sentence, for refusal to pay forced loans to support war. The court found that it could not interfere with the king's decision to imprison someone. This was reversed by Parliament in the Petition of Right 1628 and the Habeas Corpus Act 1640.

It was clear that the king could not impose direct taxation (e.g. income tax) without the consent of Parliament, but there were doubts about indirect taxation powers. The king could control trade and it was argued that this included a power to impose charges on imports and exports. It was found in *R v Hampden (the Ship Money Case)* [1637] 3 State Trials 835 that the king could impose a charge without parliamentary consent in times of emergency to defend the realm. This finding was again reversed by Parliament in the Ship Money Act 1640.

In *Godden v Hales* [1686], the question was whether King James II could exempt a Roman Catholic army officer from the legal requirements to swear allegiance to the Church of England. The court found he could and in sweeping terms said that 'the laws of England are the king's laws'; therefore, the king could dispense with penal law and could be the sole judge because power was not given to the king by the people but was part of the prerogative power which 'has not, and cannot, be taken away'.

These pro-royal prerogative cases, of course, straddle the period of civil war and the restoration of the monarchy. The seismic legal, political and religious disputes that ran through the seventeenth century were ultimately resolved when James II was separated from his Crown, but not from his head, in the Glorious Revolution of 1688. This led to the Bill of Rights 1689, which provided that:

- The powers of the Crown were controlled by law and 'there were no powers of the Crown that could not be taken away or controlled by statute'.
- The Crown had no right to raise tax either directly (e.g. income tax) or indirectly (e.g. through excise duties in ports).
- The Crown had no right to maintain a standing army.
- Parliament should meet regularly and had freedom of expression.
- The Crown had no right to suspend laws.

From this time onwards it was accepted that prerogative powers were residual, i.e. they could not be expanded. The limits of the prerogative powers were a question of law for the courts to define, whilst statutes took precedence and could limit or abolish prerogative powers.

6.3 CURRENT ROLE OF PREROGATIVE POWER

6.3.1 PERSONAL PREROGATIVES

It is sometimes said that there is a distinction between 'personal prerogatives', i.e. those that can be exercised according to the Queen's own wishes, and those that are exercisable by a minister in the name of the Crown. In particular, it has been suggested that the monarch has some limited discretion in whom to appoint as prime minister, and whether to give the royal assent. Blackburn says that this is 'a little corner of the constitution that is little understood and is routinely misunderstood'.[4]

The distinction is based on the notion that in some circumstances the Queen will be constitutionally entitled to exercise powers according to her own preferences, and even to depart from the 'advice' (which in this regal context is a polite word for 'instruction') of the Government. We examine the specific circumstances below, but we broadly follow the arguments of Professor Blackburn, who in his own words came to bury, not praise, the notion of personal prerogative.[5] There are almost no circumstances, within the bounds of probability, where the Queen can personally exercise choice over these prerogatives.

So what is left in the basket of *genuinely personal* prerogative (remember these are powers that *only* the Crown has in distinction to the public)? It is narrow, of limited importance and rather quirky.

APPLYING THE LAW – SWANS AND ROYAL GARTERS

The next time someone says to you that the Queen owns all the swans in England, you can dazzle them with your more precise Public Law knowledge. She does not own all the swans in England. By prerogative, as a relic of the monarch's old rights over all wild creatures, she retains the right to claim ownership of unmarked mute swans in open waters but only *actually owns* those individual swans that she has asserted ownership over.

This happens through an annual ceremony known as Swan Upping, where mute swans on the River Thames are caught, ringed for identification and released. Only those birds caught and marked by the Queen's Swan Uppers belong personally to her. Other swans on the Thames are claimed in the same process by the Worshipful Companies of Vintners and Dyers. Swans in other areas are either unowned or

---

4   R Blackburn, 'Monarchy and the Personal Prerogative [2004] *Public Law* 546, 546.
5   Ibid.

granted to particular families as hereditary rights. Similar prerogatives still exist over whales and sturgeon fish, but only once they have been caught.

Beyond this rather strange example, the Queen has some personal choice over the grant of some honours. This is limited to five specific types of honours, including the Order of the Garter and the Order of Merit.

Perhaps the most important benefit that the monarch enjoys is not a right but an immunity. It is a presumption of statutory interpretation that statutes do not apply to the Crown. This presumption can be overridden by clear intention and was severely limited by the Crown Proceedings Act 1947, but this immunity is still a residual principle of common law. The presumption applies to the Crown (i.e. central Government) rather than just to the monarch personally. Given the developing importance of the rule of law it is probably time that the presumption was reversed.

6.3.2 CROWN PREROGATIVES

The Annex to the Governance of Britain paper outlines a number of Government and civil service prerogatives:

- Justice and law & order – e.g. *nolle prosequi* (the power to stop prosecutions as exercised by the Attorney General in the name of the Crown), the prerogative of mercy (to reduce sentences or pardon offenders).
- Foreign affairs – e.g. the power to enter into international treaties, and to conduct diplomatic relations.
- Armed forces, war and emergency – e.g. to make military appointments.
- Miscellaneous – e.g. the power to dispense honours, such as knighthoods or OBEs (Order of the British Empire). These are granted by the Queen on the advice of the Prime Minister, who is independently advised by a Political Honours Scrutiny Committee.

Some of the most important prerogatives are not on this list; they are covered separately under 'other prerogative powers' as constitutional prerogatives and include powers to appoint ministers, to summon and prorogue (i.e. dissolve) Parliament, and to grant Royal Assent to Bills.

EXPLAINING THE LAW – PREROGATIVES AND CONVENTIONS

We need to pause briefly here, to recap on constitutional conventions (as covered in Chapter 5). You will not get a real understanding of the royal prerogative unless you can get to grips with the fact that the exercise of almost all prerogative powers is controlled by constitutional conventions.

Constitutional conventions are non-legal rules of the constitution. They are not enforced by the courts, but they nevertheless have binding force. This binding (or normative) force comes from two sources. For those people involved in constitutional decisions, conventions give them an internal sense of obligation: 'in this set of circumstances this is what I am obliged to do'. Secondly, there is the threat of external sanctions. These will not be legal sanctions, but can range from the relatively trivial (such as public criticism) to very serious (such as the end of a political career).

The simplest way of understanding the interaction of convention with prerogative is this:

> *whilst the legal position is that prerogative powers belong to the monarch, by constitutional convention they are exercised according to the wishes of the Government.*

Taking this into account, we can proceed to analyse some important prerogative powers through the lens of two issues:

- The extent to which the prerogative power is actually exercised according to the free choice of a Government minister, or is further controlled by some other rule.
- Any residual emergency or unusual circumstances where the monarch has some choice as to how to exercise the power.

6.3.3 ROYAL ASSENT

Creating an Act of Parliament requires the approval of the House of Commons, the approval of the House of Lords and the grant of the royal assent. The rules on granting royal assent are outlined in some detail in Chapter 5, 'Constitutional conventions'. The basic position is that the Queen, in law, has a choice as to whether to assent to a Bill or not, even if it has been passed by Commons and Lords. In practice, and on the basis of a very clear constitutional convention, she has no choice. Once a Bill has been approved by the Commons and Lords (or the equivalent Parliament Act procedure), then the monarch *has to* give royal assent.

So to address the issues. First, the prerogative power is not exercised according to the choice of a Government minister. It is completely governed by conventional rules rather than discretion. Theoretically, the Queen can withhold the consent on 'the advice of Ministers',

Key prerogatives
- Royal assent
- Ministerial appointments
- Dissolution of Parliament
- Foreign affairs
- War

Figure 6.2 Key prerogatives

and this is precisely what happened in 1708 when Queen Anne withheld consent for the Scottish Militia Bill on Government advice. Even in 1708 it was only a technical point; the Bill was to be replaced by something similar. There is no clear answer as to whether this could still occur in the modern day, but it is most unlikely.

On the second point, it has been argued that in an emergency, where some proposed legislation poses a serious threat to democracy or to the rule of law, then the monarch may have a right to withhold assent. (Blackburn vigorously disagrees that this right exists in any circumstances.[6]) The most definite thing that can be said about this potential residual right is that it would only be available under the most extreme circumstances – in Brazier's phrase, 'a permanent subversion of the democratic basis of the constitution'.[7] It could only be used to address a clear assault on the most fundamental features of democratic society and to arrest a slide into dictatorship.

6.3.4 APPOINTMENT OF MINISTERS

The strict legal position is that the Queen can appoint whomever she wants as Prime Minister. In 2015 she appointed David Cameron, but in theory she could have appointed Ed Miliband or Nick Clegg (or, indeed, David Beckham or Kim Kardashian, etc). Again, you should cross-reference to Chapter 5 on constitutional conventions for fuller details on the appointment of the Prime Minister.

As with royal assent, the prerogative power on appointment of the Prime Minister is governed by rule rather than choice, and, again, it is a constitutional convention. The conventional rule is that the Queen must appoint as Prime Minister the leader of the political party (or coalition of parties) that can command the confidence of the House of Commons. In simple terms, this 'confidence' means a majority of MPs who will support all or most of the Government's proposed legislation.

There are questions as to whether the Queen would have some element of personal choice in the circumstances of a hung Parliament or the sudden death/resignation of a prime minister. It is often said that the 'first past the post' electoral system produces clear winners and strong Governments, but this is not necessarily so. Elections in the 1920s, early 1970s and in 2010 produced hung Parliaments, i.e. where one party did not have an overall majority of seats. Even where there is a hung Parliament, there is no real personal choice for the Queen. The practice is that the incumbent Prime Minister is entitled to a first attempt to persuade other political parties to enter into a coalition, but in 2010 for example it was clear from the election result that the only viable way of producing a majority Government was a Conservative/Liberal Democrat coalition. Once the details of a coalition agreement had been worked out between the respective leaders, the Queen had no choice but to appoint David Cameron as her Prime Minister. The Queen can take no part in the negotiations to form a new Government or do anything to indicate a preference for any

---

6   Blackburn, above n.4, 552.
7   R Brazier, *Constitutional Practice* (2nd edn Clarendon, 1994) 190.

particular group of parties forming a coalition. Similarly, once Theresa May had told the Queen following the 2017 General Election that she had a confidence and supply agreement with the Democratic Unionist Party, and so could get most of her legislative agenda through as a minority government, then the Queen was duty bound to appoint her as PM.

As the leading parties now have both deputy leaders and clear internal processes to elect a successor in the circumstances of the sudden death or resignation of a prime minister, the Queen has no personal role to play. Once the Prime Minister is in post, then it is the PM who has a personal choice as to how to exercise the prerogative power of appointing other ministers.

6.3.5 DISSOLUTION OF PARLIAMENT

It used to be the case that the Queen dissolved Parliament on a request from the Prime Minister. Again, there was no personal choice for the monarch and it was entirely a decision for the Government.

This was an important governmental power that granted an advantage to incumbent Governments. Dissolution of Parliament triggers a general election and choosing the timing could benefit the Government. General elections are supposed to be fought on a (reasonably) level playing field, and the Fixed-term Parliaments Act 2011 was introduced to address this issue. The Act further reduces the role of prerogative powers in this area. The length of each Parliament and therefore the date of future General Elections is fixed by the Act, and the exceptions for invoking elections before the full five-year term lie with the House of Commons rather than Government or monarch.

6.3.6 FOREIGN AFFAIRS

A treaty is an agreement between sovereign nations. It is the main instrument for making international law, and treaties cover globally important issues such as human rights, prisoners of war, territorial claims and climate change. Agreeing to treaties falls squarely within the conduct of foreign relations, which is governed by the prerogative. The process for completing international treaties is normally two-fold. The representatives of each country sign the treaty but it does not come into force until it has been formally ratified by a proportion of the countries. Most democracies have some involvement from their legislature rather than just their Government in deciding whether to commit to that international obligation.

The position in the UK was that treaties were an expression of external sovereignty (rather than internal governance or democracy) and were therefore in the hands of the executive as a prerogative power. This was underlined by the fact that in the UK, as a dualist state, an international treaty will have no direct impact on domestic law unless Parliament passes an Act to give effect to it.

This position was mediated by a constitutional convention, the Ponsonby Rule 1924. This provided that after signing a treaty and at least 21 days before ratification, the Government would lay the text of the treaty before Parliament. The convention has been replaced by a statutory rule in section 20 of the Constitutional Reform and Governance Act 2010, which states that if the House of Commons passes a resolution against the ratification of a treaty, it cannot proceed. If the House of Lords passes a similar resolution, then the treaty can still proceed if a minister lays down a statement of reasons for ratification before Parliament. Note that there is still no need for a positive vote of approval from Parliament and there must be sufficient feeling against a treaty for MPs to demand, and find the time for, a vote on a resolution.

6.3.7 WAR

Committing the country to war against another nation is possibly the most serious decision that the state authorities can make. Formal declarations of war are distinctly unfashionable, but this power incorporates any deployment of armed forces to an overseas conflict. It is a prerogative power, and the choice lies in the hands of the Crown (i.e. the Prime Minister in consultation with other senior ministers) rather than the monarch. There is an emerging constitutional convention on parliamentary involvement in these decisions.

There were no votes or attempts to seek the approval of Parliament for e.g. the Falklands War 1982 or the first Gulf War in 1991. Tony Blair's Government committed the RAF to the Kosovo campaign without seeking parliamentary approval. It was the decision to join the invasion of Iraq in 2003 that provoked change. It was so hugely controversial that it was a political necessity rather than a legal or constitutional requirement to seek the approval of the House of Commons.

The House of Commons Select Committee on Public Administration called for parliamentary approval for war decisions to be a constitutional requirement.[8] The Government itself suggested in 2007 that it would support a House of Commons resolution stating that Government was required to consult Parliament before declaring war.[9] The issue was on the point of being resolved in favour of statutory regulation through the Constitutional Reform and Governance Bill 2010, which included draft provisions on prior approval by resolution of each House (with emergency exceptions). The final version of the Act that was passed did not include this proposal, so the exercise of this power remains in the hands of the Government. The decision not to proceed with airstrikes against ISIS in Syria in 2015 because the Government felt that it could not win the support of a majority in the House of Commons points to the strength of the emerging constitutional convention.

Is there a theme that unites these five examples? They vary quite widely, but a number of observations can be made.

- There is no single model of who is responsible for exercising prerogative powers, or for the involvement of Parliament in prerogative decisions.
- Blackburn was correct in downplaying the personal importance of the monarch in prerogative decisions in anything other than the most extreme circumstances.

8   Fourth Report 2003–4, HC 422.
9   Governance of Britain Green Paper, Cm 7170, 2007.

- The clear trend has been towards greater legal or political control and scrutiny of prerogative decisions. This can involve being largely replaced by statutory rules (dissolution of Parliament), new legal requirements for parliamentary scrutiny and possible veto (international treaties) or by emerging constitutional conventions on consultation with Parliament (war decisions).

6.4 LEGAL CONTROLS ON PREROGATIVE POWERS

6.4.1 BY STATUTE

We saw above in relation to the Fixed-term Parliaments Act 2011 that prerogative powers can be replaced by statutory rules, but what is the precise effect of such a statute on the continued existence of prerogative powers?

KEY CASE – *ATTORNEY GENERAL V DE KEYSER'S ROYAL HOTEL* [1920] AC 508

During the First World War, the Army Council requested that accommodation be found for the headquarters of the Royal Flying Corps. A Government department identified the De Keyser's Hotel as a suitable building. The Defence of the Realm Act 1914 gave powers to requisition property for public needs in a time of emergency. The Government purported to acquire the hotel through these powers.

The Act clearly required that compensation be paid to the owner of property acquired in this way. The Government later claimed to be acting under prerogative powers rather the Act and denied that it was required to pay any compensation to the owner. The Defence of the Realm Act 1914 did not expressly repeal the prerogative powers.

The House of Lords held that the Crown had no choice as to which power to avail itself of. The only lawful basis for its action was the Act and so it had to pay compensation. It could not use the prerogative power because that power was no longer available.

The key principle from the case was stated by Lord Atkinson. The statute 'abridges the royal prerogative while it is in force' and 'the prerogative to do that thing is in abeyance'. That is, the prerogative was not necessarily repealed – it does not automatically disappear forever from the body of law. If the statute itself is repealed, then there is a possibility that the prerogative, no longer 'abridged' or 'in abeyance', can spring back to life. Whether or not it does resurrect will depend on whether the prerogative was abolished by the statute through direct words or implication, or whether the prerogative has become obsolete (such as the power to press men into the service of the Royal Navy).

This approach was confirmed by the Supreme Court in *Miller v Secretary of State for Exiting the European Union* [2017] UKSC 5, where it was found that the effect of the European Communities Act 1972 was to displace the royal prerogative on conducting international relations when it came to notifying the EU of the UK's intention to withdraw.

The *Northumbria Police* case, discussed below, raises the possibility that a statute can simply limit the scope of, rather than utterly destroy, a prerogative, and that unless a statute provides exclusive rights to do a certain thing, then the prerogative can also run in parallel to the statutory power. A prerogative can be explicitly preserved as part of a statutory scheme (e.g. section 33(5) of the Immigration Act 1971: 'This Act shall not be taken to supersede or impair any power exercisable by Her Majesty in relation to aliens by virtue of Her prerogative').

KEY CASE – *LAKER AIRWAYS V DEPARTMENT OF TRADE* [1977] QB 643

Laker Airways was the easyJet or Ryanair of the 1970s, trying to shake up the established airline industry with new practices, although it faced an even tougher regulatory environment that sought to protect national airline carriers. It was seeking permission to establish a transatlantic route (which would have competed with British Airways).

There were two elements to the approval process for permission to operate commercial flights between the UK and US. First, Laker had received approval in 1973 for a *flight licence*, under the statutory scheme, from the Civil Aviation Authority. Secondly, its application for *designation as an airline* by the UK and US Governments under an international agreement (the Bermuda Agreement) had been approved, but was awaiting the US President's signature. A new Labour Government took a very different view of the Laker business and persuaded the US Government to withdraw its recommendation for approval. The Labour Government also used prerogative powers to give 'guidance' to the Civil Aviation Authority to withdraw the flight licence.

The Court of Appeal held that the 'guidance' was really a mandatory instruction and was unlawful. More broadly, where the exercise of statutory power relied on a parallel prerogative power, then the Crown could not frustrate the statute by withholding permission.

The House of Lords made a similar point in *R v Secretary of State for the Home Department, ex parte Fire Brigades Union* [1995] 2 AC 513. Parliament had spoken (as to the structure and content of a criminal injuries compensation scheme) in the Criminal Justice Act 1988 but left it up to the minister to decide when to introduce it. The Home Secretary then decided not to introduce the scheme at all. Rather than trying to repeal the Act, the minister tried to bypass Parliament and introduce a very different scheme via prerogative powers. This frustrated Parliament's intentions and was an abuse of the prerogative. The minister's scheme was quashed by the courts.

6.4.2 ISSUES OF EXISTENCE AND SCOPE

There is a marvellous and oft-quoted statement from the Court of Appeal in *BBC v Johns* [1965] Ch 32: 'It is 350 years and a civil war too late for the Queen's courts to broaden the prerogative'. The BBC had unsuccessfully claimed that its broadcasting activities were an exercise of the prerogative, and the Court found that the limits of prerogative power 'are now well-settled and incapable of extension'.

The courts have long been accustomed to ruling on the existence and scope of prerogative powers. This is uncontroversial and the more difficult issues have really been around the manner in which the courts have made these rulings, in particular in the following case.

KEY CASE – *R V SECRETARY OF STATE FOR THE HOME DEPARTMENT, EX PARTE NORTHUMBRIA POLICE AUTHORITY* [1989] 1 QB 26

It was the practice and the accepted legal position that the supply of equipment to police forces was the role of local police authorities. In 1986, the Home Secretary tried to bypass these arrangements and offer controversial riot control gear (CS gas and plastic baton rounds) directly to forces. He claimed that he had to the powers to do so under (a) the Police Act 1964 and (b) a royal prerogative power of keeping the peace.

The Court of Appeal held that (a) the Police Act 1964 did not establish exclusive rights for local police authorities to supply equipment, and the Home Secretary's arrangements could be regarded as an 'organisation' (which meant that it could supply equipment) under the Act, and (b) that there was a prerogative power to maintain the Queen's peace and to keep law and order. The prerogative could not be used where it would be incompatible with statute, but that was not the case here.

The great difficulty with this case is that a prerogative of 'keeping the peace' did not appear to exist before it was discovered here. The judgment provided an extensive survey of the literature but found that there was no mention of such a prerogative in the leading authorities on the subject (*Chitty on Prerogatives of the Crown,*

1820). Any prior judicial discussion of Crown powers had only stated that the Home Secretary had powers in the administration of justice.

The Court noted that there was a recognised prerogative to protect the realm from external threats, and then argued that there must be a parallel internal prerogative power, even though it had never been mentioned. Norse LJ supplemented this with a novel method of argument: 'the scarcity of references in the books to the prerogative of keeping the peace within the realm does not disprove that it exists. Rather, it may point to an unspoken assumption that it does.'

So, according to the Court of Appeal, a prerogative on an issue as lively, contentious and persistent as 'keeping the peace' that was unremarked upon by the courts and writers since 1688 was discovered in 1989 to be so obvious that there was no need to discuss or even mention it for three and half centuries. You can draw your own conclusions on the methodological soundness of that position. Barnett points out that 'the judge argued that the fact that no evidence existed was almost conclusive proof that [it] did exist' and argues that to uphold the minister's claim 'in the virtual absence of authority and precedent, and with little analysis, was remarkable'.[10]

There are also problems of consistency with other important cases. It is inconsistent with the principle from the great 'rule of law' case *Entick v Carrington* [1765] 19 Howells State Trials that 'if it is not in our books it is not the law'. This is an important principle in limiting supposed or assumed powers by the Crown. It is inconsistent with the approach in *De Keyser's* to situations where statute and prerogative deal with the same issue. Purchas LJ said in *Northumbria Police Authority* that it would take 'express and unequivocal terms' in a statute to deprive an individual from the benefit or protection of executive action, but casting this case as concerning individual rights rather than state power is simply mistaken.

The case of *Burmah Oil v Lord Advocate* [1965] AC 75 is an illustration of the courts deciding the scope of, and therefore limiting, a prerogative power. The case facts are discussed in depth in Chapter 10, 'Rule of law', but in summary, the army had destroyed property during wartime to stop it falling into the hands of the enemy. The Crown claimed (a) a prerogative right to destroy the property and (b) that the right could be exercised without any obligation to pay compensation.

The House of Lords examined the authorities and found that there was a prerogative power to do 'all those things in an emergency which are necessary for the conduct of the war' (Lord Reid). On the second question of whether there was a right to destroy such property without compensation, the Lords said no, the power did not extend that far.

---

10 H Barnett, *Constitutional and Administrative Law* (11th edn, Routledge, 2016) 105–06.

Burmah Oil was entitled to compensation, but if you have already read Chapter 10 you will know that there was an unusual postscript. The Government was worried about the cost of meeting potentially huge compensation claims and Parliament passed the War Damage Act 1965, which retrospectively took away these compensation rights. The Act leaves the prerogative power (to destroy property in certain circumstances in times of war) untouched; it merely takes away the associated rights to compensation.

It is also open to the courts to find that a prerogative power is broader than the Crown imagined, or that it has not been replaced by statute. In *R (on the application of Shields) v Secretary of State for Justice* [2008] EWHC 3102, the Justice Secretary thought that the power to issue a full pardon was not available to him because of the Repatriation of Prisoners Act 1984 and the Convention on the Transfer of Sentenced Persons 1983. The High Court held that the prerogative power of mercy did extend to cases such as this (where the individual had been convicted by a foreign court) and was available when they had been transferred to the UK under the international agreement.

6.4.3 EXERCISE OF PREROGATIVE POWERS AND THE COURTS

Traditionally the courts would not review how prerogative powers were actually exercised. This was an important gap in the judicial scrutiny of how the executive uses its legal powers. If an individual is legally mistreated by e.g. a minister through the exercise of *statutory powers*, then a claim for judicial review can be made. If that same individual was similarly mistreated by that same minister exercising *prerogative powers*, then there was no scope for judicial review or remedy.

Changes to this position were first seen in *R v Criminal Injuries Compensation Board, ex parte Lain* [1967] 2 QB 864, where the Court of Appeal found that the decisions of a body set up by prerogative could be reviewed by the courts. This was a useful development, but what about the direct exercise of prerogative powers by ministers themselves?

KEY CASE – *COUNCIL OF CIVIL SERVICE UNIONS V MINISTER FOR THE CIVIL SERVICE* [1985] AC 374

The case facts are outlined in detail in Chapter 13 on judicial review, but to recap briefly: the Prime Minister used prerogative powers (of organising the civil service) to ban membership of staff associations at the General Communications Headquarters (GCHQ). GCHQ is the third main branch of the security services and carries out electronic surveillance and interception of communications (e.g. of your texts and social media messages). Employees had the right to belong to these associations since the inception of GCHQ, and the associations had always been consulted on changes to working conditions.

The House of Lords accepted that there was a legitimate expectation that the staff associations would be consulted before this major change, and that this expectation had been breached. It found that even though the decision involved the exercise of prerogative powers, it was, in principle, reviewable. Ultimately, the Lords found that the Prime Minister's decision was taken on grounds of national security and it was not appropriate for the courts to review these grounds. The decision could not, therefore, be quashed.

The key significance of the case for the law on prerogative powers is two-fold. First, it established that decisions taken under powers provided by prerogative *could be* subject to judicial review. This closed that important gap. The second element of the judgment, however, limits the effect of this. Prerogative powers could only be reviewed if they were justiciable, i.e. on a subject where it was constitutionally appropriate for the courts to intervene. Rather than deciding this on a case-by-case basis, Lord Roskill set out a series of 'excluded categories' that the courts would not review. In relation to treaty-making, for example, he said, 'The courts are not the proper place wherein to determine whether a treaty should be concluded.' Lord Roskill's list of excluded categories also included the deployment of armed forces, the dissolution of Parliament, the appointment of ministers, the granting of honours and the grant of mercy. As you can see, this covers a great deal of the ground where prerogative powers are still relevant.

The inability of the courts to review decisions to sign international treaties is well established. In *Blackburn v Attorney General* [1971] 2 All ER 1380, Lord Denning said: 'The Treaty-making power of this country rests not in the courts, but in the Crown; that is, Her Majesty acting on the advice of her ministers . . . this cannot be challenged or questioned in the courts'. This was confirmed in a challenge to the Treaty on European Union in *R v Secretary of State for Foreign and Commonwealth Affairs, ex parte Rees-Mogg* [1994] QB 552. The applicant tried a slightly different line of argument, that the Treaty involved the abandonment, rather than the exercise, of prerogative powers. This was rejected by the Court of Appeal; ratification of the Treaty was an exercise of the foreign affairs prerogative and therefore incapable of review by the court. Even at a time when the courts have been moving away from a strict adherence to the 'excluded categories' approach (see below), challenges to foreign affairs decisions are seen as not suitable for court scrutiny (e.g. *Campaign for Nuclear Disarmament (CND) v Prime Minister* [2002] EWHC 2777, where the courts refused to make a declaration on the meaning of UN Security Council Resolution 1441, which gave Iraq 'a final opportunity to comply with its disarmament obligations').

The courts, however, have not held a strict adherence to the 'excluded categories' approach. In *R v Foreign Secretary, ex parte Everett* [1989] 1 QB 811 (on the issuing of passports), the Court of Appeal found that 'whether judicial review of the prerogative power is open depends upon the subject matter'. Matters of 'high policy', such as agreeing international treaties, would remain beyond the review of the courts, but 'the grant or refusal of a passport is in a quite different category. It is a matter of an administrative decision affecting the right of individuals and their freedom of travel.' So the more that a prerogative decision is like an ordinary administrative decision and less a question of high politics, the more likely it is that it will be subject to judicial review. It is the *subject matter* of the individual case rather than category which is important.

The prerogative of mercy is a further illustration of a departure from the 'excluded categories' approach. The central element of mercy is the power to pardon which removes the 'pains, penalties and punishment' from a conviction, but not the fact of the conviction itself. This a classic prerogative power where the Queen 'by constitutional convention exercises it in respect of England on the advice of the Home Secretary, to whom Her Majesty delegates her discretion' (*De Freitas v Benny* [1976] AC 239). In *De Freitas*, the Privy Council said that the mercy prerogative was not reviewable and mercy was mentioned in Lord Roskill's 'excluded categories'. This position changed in *Bentley*.

KEY CASE – *R V SECRETARY OF STATE FOR THE HOME DEPARTMENT, EX PARTE BENTLEY* [1993] 4 ALL ER 442

Chris Craig and Derek Bentley attempted to burgle a confectionary warehouse in November 1952. Craig had a revolver. They were seen entering the building and the police were called. The police captured Bentley, and called for Craig to hand over the gun. Bentley said to Craig, 'Let him have it, Chris'.[11] Craig immediately fired and injured a police officer. When reinforcements were sent in, Craig shot and killed Constable Sidney Miles.

The 16-year-old Craig fired the gun but was too young to hang. Bentley was 19, but had the mental age of an 11-year-old; he did not fire the gun and there was (and is) genuine uncertainty as to whether he was encouraging Craig to fire or to hand over the gun. But he was charged with murder, under the joint enterprise rule, convicted and sentenced to death. The jury recommended mercy for him, but the judge said there were no mitigating circumstances. The Home Secretary refused to exercise the prerogative of mercy despite considerable public and political pressure for leniency. Bentley was hanged in Wandsworth Prison in January 1953.

As part of a wide and long-running campaign to clear Bentley's name, a judicial review was brought by his sister, arguing that the Home Secretary ought to have recommended a posthumous pardon. The court accepted that it was 'probably

---

11 As referenced in the excellent song 'Let Him Dangle' by the excellent singer Elvis Costello.

right' that the criteria and policy adopted by the Home Secretary within the bounds of the prerogative power were beyond the scope of judicial review, but here the Home Secretary had failed to appreciate that the pardon could take a number of forms. That is, he made a legal error as to the scope and nature of the power. The decision was quashed and the Home Secretary was told to reconsider whether Bentley should receive a posthumous pardon, although the court could not direct the outcome of that decision.

The effect of the *Bentley* judgment, that the exercise of the prerogative of mercy could be reviewed by the courts, was confirmed in *R (on the application of Page) v Secretary of State for Justice* [2007] EWHC 2026. As a postscript, the Home Secretary issued a posthumous pardon to Bentley in respect of the death sentence in 1993. This did not remove the murder conviction, but the Court of Appeal later quashed the murder conviction on the grounds that the trial had been unfair due to faulty directions to the jury.

6.4.4 CASE STUDY: THE CHAGOS ISLANDS LITIGATION

The Chagos Islands are a group of small islands, south of the Maldives in the Indian Ocean. They were formed into a UK overseas territory, the British Indian Ocean Territory (BIOT), by an Order in Council 1965 (SI 1965/1920). An Order in Council is a way of legislating via prerogative that can be used to regulate dependent territories.

In 1971, the US requested the use of Diego Garcia (the largest island in the Chagos group) as a military base. In return for a discount on the purchase of US nuclear weapons, the UK entered into an agreement, requiring the compulsory expulsion of all the indigenous inhabitants of the islands. This legal order was also prerogative: the British Indian Ocean Territory Ordinance No.1 of 1971 made under the 1965 Order in Council.

In *R (on the application of Bancoult) v Foreign Secretary (Bancoult No 1)* [2001] QB 1067, the High Court quashed the 1971 Ordinance and ruled that the islanders' banishment from their homeland had been unlawful. It was outside of the purposes of the 1965 Order in Council (which authorised laws 'for the peace, order and good government of the territory'). The Government initially indicated that it would accept the judgment, but then in 2004 passed two further Orders in Council that permanently banned the islanders from ever returning. This led to further legal challenges.

In *R (on the application of Bancoult) v Foreign Secretary (Bancoult No 2)* [2008] UKHL 61, the Court of Appeal found that these 2004 Orders in Council could not be used to frustrate the previous court order. This was overturned on further appeal to the House of Lords. The majority in the Lords found that there was no breach of law and there was no legitimate expectation of a right of return. The minority in the Lords said the Orders were irrational and a breach of a representation that the islanders could return (which had created a legally enforceable expectation that they could).

So, following extensive litigation, the outcome was that the UK's attempts to ban a return for the Chagossian islanders was upheld. Yet, all of the judges felt able to review the exercise of prerogative power. The Foreign Secretary had argued that Orders in Council were akin to primary legislation and therefore beyond the scope of court review. This was rejected, even by the majority in the House of Lords. Lord Hoffmann said that such Orders do not share all the characteristics of Acts of Parliament and that he saw 'no reason why prerogative legislation should not be subject to review on ordinary principles of legality, irrationality and procedural impropriety in the same way as any other prerogative action'.

The majority in the Lords said that the courts could not assess whether any laws had been made 'for the peace, order and good government of the territory', as this was a purely political question (and therefore reversed parts of *Bancoult No 1*). Aside from this, we need to note that the issues in the cases were very much 'high policy'. As exercises of power in foreign affairs involving national security and the close relationship with the US, we would expect the courts to hold back from review, but the Government decisions were closely scrutinised and their legality assessed.

6.5 REFORM

As you will have seen as you read through this chapter, there are a number of problems with the prerogative. The powers often lack precision, and the relationship with statute can be complex. Bogdanor said: 'The extent and scope of the personal prerogatives are, however, unclear. It is difficult if not impossible to circumscribe them accurately'.[12]

The most significant problem, however, is that the use of prerogative powers circumvents Parliament. This has two facets. The first is that Governments, by availing themselves of prerogative powers, may not need to go to Parliament to seek statutory powers. This is what happened in the Chagos Islands saga. Any doubts as to whether the Government had the power to dispossess the islanders of their homes could have been avoided by proceeding by way of an Act of Parliament. This would have needed a full and public debate, which was something the Government wanted to avoid.

This leads us to the second point, that prerogative actions should be subject to greater scrutiny and control by Parliament. Again, the Chagos Islands saga illustrates this point. Foreign Office policy was to give as little information as possible to MPs, and information on what appears (at best) to be recent questionable behaviour, for example in establishing a nature reserve in the Chagos Islands, is more likely to appear through WikiLeaks than through Parliamentary scrutiny. A central function of Parliament is that it is supposed to be the democratic mandate for state action, and it therefore needs to be able to exert influence over and accountability from the executive. The problem was acknowledged by

---

12 V Bogdanor, *The Monarchy and the Constitution* (Clarendon, 1995), 75.

the Government in 2007: 'when the executive relies on the powers of the royal prerogative –
powers where government acts upon the monarch's authority – it is difficult for Parliament
to scrutinise and challenge government's actions'.[13]

The Governance of Britain White Paper (Cm 7170, 2007) advocated the wide replacement
of prerogative powers with statutory powers and Parliamentary control and scrutiny. The
Government would 'seek to surrender or limit powers which it considers should not, in a
modern democracy, be exercised exclusively by the executive'.

There are three main options for reform:

- Replace the prerogative power with a legal rule – for example the Fixed-term
  Parliaments Act 2011.
- Retain the prerogative power but formalise the legal requirements for Parliamentary
  consent – for example the Constitutional Reform and Governance Act 2010 on
  international treaties.
- Retain the prerogative power but formalise, by law or constitutional convention, the
  need for Parliamentary scrutiny of the exercise of the power – for example the emerging convention on use of the war prerogative.

6.6 ASSESSMENT ADVICE

Any assessment on this topic will tend to be an essay question. Typically, you will need to
be able to outline and discuss:

- The nature and development of prerogative powers.
- The current role of the major prerogative powers.
- The relationship between prerogative and statute.
- Judicial control and review of prerogative powers.
- The need for reform.

You will be aiming for high marks and, again, you can do this by moving beyond
description and introducing a critical edge to your work. You could do this by assessing
recent reforms, particularly in the Constitutional Reform and Governance Act 2010, and by
assessing the need for and options for further reform.

Potentially even more fruitful would be to use the rule of law as a critical benchmark. (For
which, of course, you need to be familiar with the material in Chapter 10, 'Rule of law'.)
You can outline that the rule of law prohibits of arbitrary power, and requires clarity and
certainty in legal rules, and for access to a court. In applying these ideas to prerogatives,

---

13 Governance of Britain Green Paper, Cm 7170, 2007.

you should recognise the progressive steps taken in cases such as the *GCHQ* case to open up prerogative powers to review and in *Bentley* and *Bancoult* to not be bound by excluded categories but to focus on the substance of the issues and the way in which individuals are affected. On the other hand, in practice the courts still show deference; *Northumbria Police Authority* is ripe for critique. *Bancoult No 2* shows that successful challenges to prerogative decisions are likely to be rare. The secrecy surrounding Foreign Office policy in the Chagos Islands and the inability of Parliament to subject it to effective scrutiny raise further rule of law concerns about arbitrary power impinging on fundamental rights.

POINTS TO REVIEW

- Prerogatives are the residue of special legal powers that the Crown possesses over and above all other persons.

- The monarch retains very few personal prerogatives, and most important powers (e.g. on mercy, foreign affairs, military deployment and honours) are exercised by Government ministers.

- Prerogatives can be controlled and displaced by statute, and the courts can rule on the existence and scope of prerogative powers and judicially review their exercise.

TAKING IT FURTHER

R Blackburn, 'Monarchy and the Personal Prerogative' [2004] *Public Law* 546 As well as enjoying Blackburn's confident and forthright attack on the views of his predecessor and contemporary 'senior academics', you can pick up further details on the scope and operation of important prerogatives. If you take up the invitation to use a 'rule of law' benchmark in your evaluation of prerogatives (see Assessment Advice above), then this would be a great source for views on the certainty of such powers.

R Brazier, '"Monarchy and the Personal Prerogative": a personal response to Professor Blackburn' [2005] *Public Law* 45 Good academics (and good law students) like an argument. Here, Brazier takes exception to how his views were represented by Blackburn and delivers a rather tart response. A nice example of academic debate and two pages that will give you a 'compare and contrast' from two leading writers.

Chagos Islands news stories, http://www.theguardian.com/world/chagos-islands This gathers together *The Guardian*'s coverage of the issue over the years and gives an insight into the ongoing human cost of the UK Government's actions.

7

CHAPTER 7
SUPREMACY OF PARLIAMENT

Who has the ultimate say over which laws govern your life? These laws regulate whether you are free to walk the streets and attend Public Law classes, how much you pay for those classes, whether you can post your views about Government powers on a social network and be free from state surveillance, the contract by which you bought this book and so many other things that contribute to your health, wealth and liberty. Deciding the question of who has this ultimate law-making power is one of the most important things that a constitution can do.

Constitutionalism, the concept which is the basis of much Constitutional Law, argues that there need to be strong legal limits on the power of the state. The single most important UK constitutional law, however, is parliamentary supremacy which states that Parliament is legally unlimited. It can make any law whatsoever and the courts are bound to obey and apply Acts of Parliament.

This chapter examines this traditional view of the supremacy of Parliament and goes on to examine a number of challenges to that traditional view, specifically from the Acts of Union between England and Scotland, the operation of the Parliament Acts, the manner and form theory and the notion of democratic or common law limits to supremacy.

It is very important to grasp that this is just the first part of a two-hander. To understand supremacy of Parliament properly, you need the full story. Rather than present you with a 25,000+ word chapter, that story has been broken into two parts. First is the story of the traditional view and a number of interesting, although arguably inconclusive, challenges to that view. Second is the story of, what has so far been, the main challenge to the traditional view of supremacy: membership of the European Union. The imminent withdrawal of the UK from the EU will have a very significant impact on this central pillar of the constitution.

AS YOU READ

- Identify the nature of the parliamentary supremacy rule.

- Identify the features of the traditional view.

- Assess the effectiveness of the challenges to the traditional view.

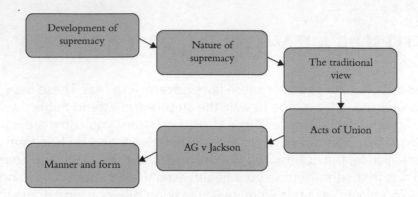

Figure 7.1 Structure of Chapter 7

7.1 THE TRADITIONAL VIEW OF SUPREMACY

By 'supremacy' we mean the highest form of law. This has a particularly striking aspect; if a supreme law conflicts with some other type of law, then the supreme law takes precedence. Ordinary laws that are inconsistent with supreme laws cannot take effect.

In states with a codified constitution, the constitution itself is normally considered supreme. An example of this *constitutional supremacy* is found in section 2 of the Constitution of South Africa: 'This Constitution is the supreme law of the Republic; law or conduct inconsistent with it is invalid'. The US Constitution has a supremacy clause. Article VI (2) states that the US Constitution (and federal statutes and international treaties) is the 'supreme law of the land'. Federal statutes, themselves, only have this character if they are consistent with the highest source of law – the US Constitution (*Marbury v Madison*, 5 US 137 (1803)). In the absence of a codified constitution, the UK has developed parliamentary, rather than constitutional, supremacy.

The traditional legal view of this supremacy, as outlined by AV Dicey, says that the Westminster Parliament is the supreme law-making body; it can make or unmake any law whatsoever and no other institution can override those laws.

We need to emphasise towards the start of this chapter that there *has* been some change to the traditional view. This is found in the statements of judges both within their judgments and speaking extra-judicially. This represents a change in the underlying theory of parliamentary supremacy but not as yet a change in practice. On a day-to-day basis, the courts continue to obey and apply Acts of Parliament.

7.2 A NOTE ON TERMINOLOGY

Many writers have used the term 'sovereignty of Parliament' rather than 'supremacy of Parliament'. This terminology, as used by Dicey, has been very influential, but in this text we use the term 'supremacy'. This is to more clearly distinguish this particular legal rule from related but distinct ideas of sovereignty. 'Sovereignty' is used in international law to refer to the independent authority of a state over a geographical area, e.g. the power of the sovereign state of Brazil to exercise authority over and make laws for the peoples and territory of Brazil. Sovereignty can also be used in a political sense to refer to the location of political power within a state, e.g. the political authority of a state ultimately lies with the people.

In almost every case when you see the phrase 'sovereignty of Parliament' in some other book or journal article, it means the same thing as the term 'supremacy of Parliament' as used here, and in most other modern accounts. Even this term of 'supremacy' is shorthand. It refers to the legislative supremacy of Parliament. To be even more precise, the legal rule only applies to Acts of Parliament and not to any other actions or resolutions of Parliament. It is therefore the legal supremacy of Acts of Parliament.

7.3 THE DEVELOPMENT OF PARLIAMENTARY SUPREMACY

Parliament has not always been supreme, and when the idea of parliamentary supremacy began to emerge, it was strongly contested. In *Dr Bonham's Case* (1610) 8 Co Rep 114, Chief Justice Coke asserted that 'When an Act of Parliament is against common right and reason, or repugnant, or impossible to be performed, the common law will control it, and adjudge such act to be void'.

Coke CJ is, in essence, arguing for the supremacy of the common law, that the common law provides for a higher power that can be called upon and exercised by common law judges to review and declare void Acts of Parliament. It is doubtful whether this was ever an entirely accurate picture of the relationship between the common law and Acts of Parliament, and in any case, the Glorious Revolution of 1688 resolved the conflict.

EXPLAINING THE LAW – THE GLORIOUS REVOLUTION

In 1688, King James II was forced from the throne, principally because of his support for Catholic rights. His daughter Mary, together with her husband, William of Orange, were invited by Parliament to take the throne. As part of this bargain, the new King and Queen had to accept the supremacy of Parliament. This new constitutional settlement, the Glorious Revolution, was enshrined in the Bill of Rights 1689.

Parpworth nicely sums up the outcome of the Glorious Revolution: 'It was Parliament which now held the purse strings. It was Parliament which now had responsibility for the security of the state. It was Parliament which now had legislative power. And it was to Acts of Parliament that the courts now owed obedience'.[1]

The Bill of Rights established Parliament as the highest law-making institution in the land. It also dealt with any remaining claims to monarchical supremacy, i.e. the ability of Monarchs to use prerogative power to make new law. The common law judges had to accept the political reality of this triumph of parliamentary power and acknowledge its legislative supremacy.

As Lord Templeman said in *M v Home Office and Another* (1994) 1 AC 377 HL, 'In the 17th century Parliament established its supremacy over the Crown as monarch, over the executive, and over the judiciary'.

The Bill of Rights 1689 did not include any explicit provision on supremacy of Parliament, and it is arguably an impossibility for legislation itself to establish supremacy; it has to come from some source above and beyond. The Bill of Rights did, however, recognise Parliament's authority through Article 9. This established parliamentary privilege which protects freedom of speech in Parliament so that it cannot be impeached or questioned in any court of law.

The status of supremacy following the Bill of Rights 1689 was relatively settled and uncontroversial. Lord Reid sums up this settled view in *Pickin v British Railways Board* [1974] AC 765: 'In earlier times, many lawyers seem to have believed that an Act of Parliament could be disregarded in so far as it was contrary to the law of God or the law of nature or natural justice, but since the supremacy of Parliament was fully demonstrated by the Revolution of 1688 any such idea has been obsolete'.

7.4 THE NATURE OF PARLIAMENTARY SUPREMACY

7.4.1 AS A FUNDAMENTAL CONSTITUTIONAL RULE

Supremacy is *the* fundamental legal rule of the UK legal system. Any other legal rule that you study, whether it is in Contract Law, in Family Law, or in Crime, gets its authority and

---

1   N Parpworth *Constitutional and Administrative Law*, (9th edn, OUP, 2016) 73.

its place within the legal system from the rule that Parliament is supreme. According to Dicey, it is 'the very keystone of the Constitution'.[2]

MAKING CONNECTIONS
+++++++++++++++++++

When you look at other key concepts in Public Law (separation of powers, the rule of law, judicial review, the Human Rights Act 1998), you will see that their role and operation are directly affected by this fundamental constitutional rule of supremacy. Many of the legal subjects that you study have this 'jigsaw' characteristic, that they only start to make real sense once a number of the pieces are in place. Land Law is a notable example.

In Public Law, each individual topic is comprehensible in itself, but if you treat each one as an isolated unit of information then you are only going to develop a basic understanding. To develop a deeper, more sophisticated understanding, you need to see the connections between issues. For example, a really good understanding of the legality principle in the rule of law recognises that Parliament can legally authorise any state action because Parliament can make any law whatsoever. Similarly, the rule of law provides a basis for some of the judicial warnings that they will not always give unconditional obedience to any Act of Parliament.

There are many cross-references in this book, but the more you make your own connections, the closer you will be to real mastery of the subject. This also shows engagement with the subject and strong analytical skills. Do not be shy about including these sorts of connections in your assessments (whilst also keeping a focus on the main topic).

The classic *definition of supremacy* comes from Dicey:

> The principle of Parliamentary sovereignty means neither more nor less than this: namely, that Parliament thus defined has, under the English constitution, the right to make or unmake any law whatever; and further, that no person or body is recognised by the law of England as having a right to override or set aside the legislation of Parliament.[3]

Dicey points out that this has a positive aspect, the right to make any law whatsoever, and a negative aspect, the incapacity of any other person or body to override an Act of Parliament. So supremacy is the most fundamental rule of the legal system, because it structures the hierarchy of rules within the legal system. This legal concept is akin to what the Austrian philosopher Hans Kelsen called the *Grundnorm*, i.e. a single underlying

---

2 A V Dicey, *Introduction to the Study of the Law of the Constitution* (8th edn, Liberty Fund, 1982).

3 Ibid, 39–40.

foundation to a legal system, and to the Yorkshire jurist H L A Hart's 'rule of recognition', i.e. a way of identifying what are the valid primary rules within a legal system.

7.4.2 SUPREMACY AS A COMMON LAW RULE

If supremacy of Parliament is the fundamental legal rule of the UK legal system, what *type* of legal rule is it? First, we need to discount it being a legislative rule. Wade argues that 'Legislation owes its authority to the rule: the rule does not owe its authority to legislation. To say that Parliament can change the rule, merely because it can change any other rule, is to put the cart before the horse'.[4]

As Barnett explains, 'the ultimate law maker cannot confer upon itself the ultimate power'.[5] It is too circular to say that Parliament is supreme because Parliament says that Parliament is supreme. It may assert that supremacy, but the rule really lies in the response of the other branches of the state, and particularly the judiciary, to that claim. The, seemingly paradoxical, consequence of this is that Parliament itself cannot make this particular legal rule.

There is judicial support for the view that supremacy is a common law rule. Lord Steyn said in *R (Jackson) v Attorney General* [2005] UKHL 56, 'It is a construct of the common law. The judges created this principle'. Similarly, Barnett argues that 'Sovereignty is the fundamental rule of the common law, for it is the judges who uphold Parliament's sovereignty. For as long as the judges accept the sovereignty of Parliament, sovereignty will remain the ultimate rule of the constitution'.[6]

This paints supremacy of Parliament as a malleable concept. For as long as the judges continue to treat Acts of Parliament as being supreme, then Parliament will still *be* legally supreme. If the judges stop treating Acts of Parliament as being supreme, then Parliament is no longer supreme. So whilst supremacy of Parliament is the fundamental feature of our constitutional system, it is not, according to this view, guaranteed to be a permanent feature. There is scope for the fundamental rule to change.

ANALYSING THE LAW

A syllogism is a powerful reasoning tool. It can provide logical rigour to your arguments. A classic example is:

- All men are mortal.
- Socrates is a man.
- Therefore, Socrates is mortal.

4   H W R Wade, 'The Legal Basis of Sovereignty' [1955] *Cambridge Law Journal* 172.
5   H Barnett, Constitutional and Administrative Law (11th edn, Routledge, 2016) 112.
6   Ibid., 112.

You will see that a syllogism starts with two *premises* from which the *conclusion* is inferred. Like most tools, syllogisms can be misused or badly constructed. One way of criticising a syllogism is to question the accuracy of the premises. Let us try to construct a syllogism on supremacy as a common law rule.

- Supremacy is a common law rule.
- Judges can develop and change common law rules.
- Supremacy can be developed and changed by judges.

You will probably already know (from your Legal System/Legal Method/Lawyer's Skills classes) that the second premise is true. The common law can evolve over time. This evolution takes place in the way the judges apply existing rules to new fact situations in the cases before them.

If the first premise is also true, then the conclusion must logically be true. We need to pin down very carefully, then, whether supremacy is simply a standard example of a common law rule, or something different.

Sir William Wade puts forward a subtly different view: 'The rule of judicial obedience is in one sense a rule of common law, but in another sense – which applies to no other rule of common law – it is the ultimate political fact upon which the whole system of legislation hangs'.[7] This means that supremacy can only change when the 'ultimate political facts' upon which the UK constitution rests change. That is, the rule is not a typical common law rule and is not subject to the ordinary process of common law development. Any change must be part of a bigger picture. Whilst judges may be an important part of that change, it is not entirely in their hands. There are good reasons for supporting this view.

Wade's 'ultimate political fact' argument has a closer fit to what has actually happened over the last three centuries, e.g. the courts recognising the authority of a new 'Parliament of Great Britain' following the union between Scotland and England in 1707, and more recent developments e.g. the implications of membership of the European Union and the ongoing Brexit process.

When the Parliamentary forces won the Civil War in 1649–52, the courts recognised that victory as a political fact and treated the new constitutional structure as the valid law-making structure. When the Monarchy was restored in 1660, the courts recognised *that* political fact and regarded as valid the new laws produced by the new political system. In 1688–89, the courts recognised that, after half a century of constitutional turmoil, the dominant political fact of the deal struck in the Glorious Revolution was that Parliament had emerged as the ultimate arbiter of what the general law of the land should be.

7   W Wade, *Constitutional Fundamentals* (Hamlyn, 1989).

Secondly, it is a general principle of the English legal system that the common law can be overridden by statute. This cannot be the case with the parliamentary supremacy rule, which cannot therefore be a standard common law rule. Third, if we regard supremacy of Parliament as the single foundational legal rule for the whole legal system (the *Grundnorm*, the rule of recognition) then it would be curious to find that it was just one typical example, with the same status and subject to the same processes, of a wide category of ordinary legal rules.

ASSESSMENT ADVICE: UNDERSTANDING THE UNDERLYING BASIS OF SUPREMACY

Do not worry of you are finding this section challenging; you will not be alone, and it is conceptually difficult, but it is worth getting to grips with. 'Understanding' is a key assessment criterion, but it is not an on/off concept. Markers do not simply decide whether you 'get it' or not. It is a qualitative criterion. Markers are looking for the depth and sophistication of your understanding. The more you understand the underlying basis of a concept, the deeper your understanding of the whole area. It also helps you apply the law better and evaluate it more effectively.

The argument presented here is that Wade gives us the most persuasive view of what type of legal rule supremacy is. As we will see, it also provides an explanation of recent challenges to the traditional view of supremacy. The differences of opinion in this section largely boil down to the idea that a) judges can develop the common law rule of parliamentary supremacy in the same way that they can develop any common law rule or b) that judges can only recognise bigger changes to the constitution, but that in recognising this 'ultimate political fact', they may be involved in changing parliamentary supremacy.

The crucial thing that you will notice from these differing viewpoints is that none of the writers or judges who have thought about the issue have concluded that supremacy of Parliament is immutable (i.e. free from the possibility of change). You are studying Public Law in an exciting time; the signs that change may actually be happening are becoming stronger.

7.4.3 SUPREMACY AS A RELATIONSHIP-DEFINING RULE

To refer back to Chapter 4, constitutions define the key relationships between branches of the state. What relationship is defined by supremacy? It is between Parliament and the judiciary. When the issues in a case are regulated by an Act of Parliament, then the court has no choice: it must apply the statutory rule to the facts. This is not a mechanistic process. The judges have some leeway in how they interpret the statute and how it is to be applied to the facts, but the option of deciding not to apply the statute is simply not open to them. In simple terms, judges must obey Acts of Parliament.

If you are stuck on some supremacy problem or puzzled by some conceptual aspect of supremacy, it a useful exercise to go back to this idea of *a relationship*. Supremacy defines the relationship between UK Acts of Parliament and UK courts. That relationship is one of obedience – the courts cannot override, but must apply, relevant Acts of Parliament.

Yet even on Wade's approach (which gives judges a more limited part in maintaining and potentially changing supremacy), judges have an important role to play in interpreting what the 'ultimate political facts' of the constitution are and then legally responding to those facts. In assessing whether any of the challenges to the traditional view of supremacy have been successful, we therefore need to keep a close eye on the judges. It is only by assessing whether they have changed their approach that we can decide if supremacy has been altered. As long as judges continue to treat Acts of Parliament as binding and unchallengeable, then supremacy is maintained (the 'ultimate political facts' are unchanged). If judges start to treat Acts of Parliament differently (as not applicable to certain situations, as being overridden by other principles) because the ultimate political facts of the constitution have changed, then we can conclude that the legal rule has changed.

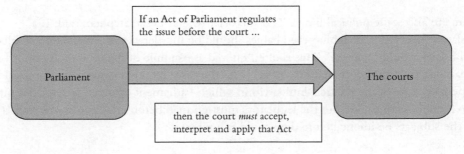

Figure 7.2 Relationship between Parliament and the courts

7.4.4 SUPREMACY AS A LEGAL, NOT A POLITICAL, RULE

EXPLAINING THE LAW   PRACTICAL LIMITS TO SUPREMACY

Suppose that Parliament passes an Act saying that:

■ the UK will enjoy long and balmy summers, or that,
■ the UK economy will have a healthy growth rate of 5 per cent per annum, or that,
■ all blue-eyed babies will be killed at birth.

When we talk about the supremacy of Parliament, we are really referring to its *legal supremacy*, and, as we saw earlier, this defines the constitutional relationship between Parliament and the courts.

This means that, whilst Parliament may be legally unlimited, it is still subject to a host of non-legal limitations. These include *practical limits*. If Parliament passed an Act that said British summers will be long, warm and dry, it would not stop the fact that any British summer may be short, cold and damp. The courts are obliged to obey Acts of Parliament; the weather is not. An Act saying that economic growth in the UK will be 5 per cent every year for the next five years would not in itself produce the changes in the global economic system needed to cause this growth. As a legal measure, it would be both legally valid and practically ineffective.

In 2017, the Australian Prime Minister, Malcolm Turnbull, was asked if the laws of mathematics (as applied to communications encryption tools in e.g. WhatsApp) would make his communications surveillance proposals ineffective. His reply that 'The laws of mathematics are very commendable, but the only law that applies in Australia is the law of Australia', provoked much mirth.[8]

There are also some political limits. The Victorian writer Leslie Stephens said: 'If a legislature decided that all blue-eyed babies should be murdered, the preservation of blue eyed babies would be illegal'. This is often quoted as example of the unlimited power of Parliament; in legal theory that may possibly be the case. Yet, in practice it simply would not happen, because of the political limits within which Parliament operates. Indeed, the quote from Stephens continues, 'but the legislators must go mad before they could pass such a law, and the subjects be idiotic before they could submit to it'.[9]

The MPs would not pass a 'blue-eyed baby killing' law regardless of whips and party discipline; the House of Lords would not pass it; the Queen would not grant Royal Assent; the Government would not propose it; the people would not accept it. These sorts of political constraints are perhaps the biggest limitation on the theoretical ability of Parliament to pass any conceivable law.

Lady Hale identified the Brexit referendum of 2016 as 'a further constraint on the sovereignty of Parliament'. She acknowledges that the vote was not legally binding, but points out that whilst a majority of MPs supported the Remain campaign, when called on to vote for a Bill to start the withdrawal process they 'felt constrained to do what the people wanted' and approved it.[10] This is really just a particularly strong example of the sorts of pragmatic political constraints on parliamentarians identified above rather a new category of limitations on Parliament itself.

---

8   N Evershed, 'Australia's plan to force tech giants to give up encrypted messages may not add up' The Guardian, 14 July 2017, https://www.theguardian.com/technology/2017/jul/14/forcing-facebook-google-to-give-police-access-to-encrypted-messages-doesnt-add-up (last accessed 05/11/17).

9   Stephens, as cited in Barnett, above n 5, 121.

10   Lady Hale, 'The United Kingdom constitution on the move', The Canadian Institute for Advanced Legal Studies' Cambridge Lecture 2017 www.supremecourt.uk/docs/speech-170707.pdf (last accessed 05/11/17).

The UK is part of an international legal community. International treaties have persuasive force, but do not bind Parliament. This means that whilst they can be used by the courts to aid their interpretation of statutes, they cannot be used to invalidate a statute: *Cheney v Conn* [1968] 1 All ER 779 states, 'What the statute itself enacts cannot be unlawful, because what the statute says is itself the law, and the highest form of law, that is known in this country'.

Nevertheless, the UK has committed itself in international law to a range of obligations, for example in United Nations and World Trade Organization treaties. Parliament could legislate in breach of those commitments, but the diplomatic, trade and political consequences of such a breach make it unlikely in practice.

7.4.5 ONLY ACTS OF PARLIAMENT ARE LEGALLY SUPREME

As Lord Templeman said in *M v Home Office and Another* [1994] 1 AC 377, 'Parliamentary supremacy over the judiciary is only exercisable by statute'. This means that any Parliamentary statement or action that is not in the specific form of an Act of Parliament will not attract this quality of supremacy.

The most important consequence of this is that secondary legislation is not supreme and can be judicially reviewed: *Manuel v Attorney General* [1983] Ch 77 states: 'Of course there is power to hold statutory instruments and other subordinate legislation ultra vires' (Sir Robert Megarry). This includes the many thousands of statutory instruments drafted by Government departments, and local authority bye-laws. If they are legally defective (i.e. ultra vires, see Chapter 13, 'Grounds of judicial review'), then the courts can declare them invalid using the judicial review procedure.

KEY CASE – RESOLUTIONS OF PARLIAMENT

In *Stockdale v Hansard* [1839] QB 21, the House of Commons directed Hansard, the parliamentary reporter, to produce a report accusing Stockdale of publishing obscene material. Stockdale sued for libel.

It was held that Parliament could not authorise the publication of defamatory statements through a mere direction, and that a House of Commons resolution could not alter the law. This distinction between Acts of Parliament and other statements was highlighted by the subsequent passage of the Parliamentary Papers Act 1840, which legally protected Hansard in a way that a simple resolution could not.

Similarly, in *Bowles v Bank of England* [1913] 1 Ch 57, the Bank of England imposed a tax on the plaintiff. The authority for this tax was in a budget resolution of the House of Commons. The court found that it was not permissible to impose the tax without the authority of Parliament, and that a resolution of one House did not have the same status as an Act of Parliament.

Proclamations of the Crown and international treaties are also examples of legal provisions that do not have this quality of supremacy.

7.4.6 THE ABSENCE OF LEGAL LIMITS

The absence of legal limits on the content of Acts of Parliament has led to Parliament exercising its supremacy in sometimes quite striking ways.

EXPLAINING THE LAW – THE LIFE OF PARLIAMENT

The life of Parliament (i.e. how long there is between General Elections) might seem to be a fundamental constitutional issue. Yet it has been changed, by ordinary Act of Parliament, on a number of occasions.

The maximum life of Parliament was set at three years by the Triennial Act 1694 and then extended to seven years by the Septennial Act 1715. This stayed in force until the Parliament Act 1911 set the maximum time to five years. The Fixed-term Parliaments Act 2011 changed the life of Parliament from a maximum term to a normal fixed term of five years.

Strictly following the five-year maximum would have required General Elections to be held in 1915 and 1940, times when the UK was involved in worldwide military conflict. Those elections were simply postponed by Parliament introducing Acts of Parliament to prolong its own life (e.g. the Prolongation of Parliament Act 1940 which was renewed annually during the period of the Second World War).

Parliament can also legislate to change the law retrospectively – to reach back into the past and change the legal obligations and relationships that existed at that time.

The classic example of this is *Burmah Oil Co Ltd v Lord Advocate* [1965] AC 75 and the War Damage Act 1965 (discussed in depth in Chapter 10, 'Rule of law'), but this is not a lone example. In *R v Londonderry Justices, ex parte Hume* (1970) 2 NI 91, the court considered the internment of suspects in Northern Ireland (i.e. arrest and detention without reasonable suspicion or criminal charge). The internment was carried out by British military personnel. They purported to be exercising powers under the Civil Authorities (Special Powers) Act 1922. It was held in this case, however, that the Act only gave powers of arrest to members of the local police force, the Royal Ulster Constabulary. The immediate response of Parliament was to enact the Northern Ireland Act 1972. This was passed within 48 hours of the Court of Appeal decision, and retrospectively conferred powers of arrest on the military personnel.

- Supremacy of Parliament is the fundamental rule of the UK legal systems. It means that Parliament can make or unmake any law, and the laws cannot be overridden by any other body.
- Supremacy is a unique type of common law rule that can only be changed in response to a change in the ultimate political facts of the UK system.
- Supremacy defines the relationship between the UK Parliament and the UK courts.
- There are a host of practical constraints on Parliament's law-making power but no legal limits.
- Only Acts of Parliament are supreme.

7.5 THE TRADITIONAL VIEW OF SUPREMACY

The traditional view of the supremacy of Parliament has held sway for most of the past three centuries. As we have seen, it was crystallised by Dicey in the classic statement that Parliament can make or unmake any law and that nobody has the right to set aside the legislation of Parliament.

We will explore the nature and consequences of this traditional view in three sections:

(1) That the courts will not question an Act of Parliament, discussed as part of the enrolled Bill rule.
(2) That no Parliament can bind either itself or its successors (continuing supremacy).
(3) That there is no necessary limit to the territorial extent of Acts of Parliament

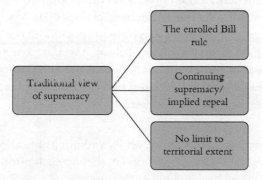

Figure 7.3 The traditional view of supremacy

7.5.1 NO COURT MAY QUESTION AN ACT OF PARLIAMENT – THE ENROLLED BILL RULE

The courts have traditionally been clear and consistent on what their duty is in relation to Acts of Parliament: *ex parte Canon Selwyn* (1872) 36 JP 54 states: 'An act of the legislature is superior to any court of law. We have only to administer the law as we find it and no court could pronounce a judgment as to the validity of an Act of Parliament'.

Similarly, Megarry VC said in *Manuel v AG* [1983] Ch 77 that 'once an instrument is recognised as being an Act of Parliament, no English court can refuse to obey it or question its validity'. The position seems very settled, but there have been attempts to argue that an Act of Parliament is invalid because of some defect in the manner in which it was made.

We saw in Chapter 3 how an Act of Parliament is made. At the simplest level, it involves the approval of the House of Commons, the approval of the House of Lords, and the Royal Assent. Of course, in practice the process of making an Act is much more complex. There are different readings and committee stages, involving time limits and notice requirements. Many of these detailed rules are set out in the Standing Orders of Parliament.

KEY CASE – *EDINBURGH AND DALKEITH RAILWAY CO V WAUCHOPE* (1842) 8 CL & FIN 710

The period from the 1830s to the 1840s was the first major period of railway building in the UK. To build a railway line and stations, you need to acquire particular parcels of land in particular places. This was accomplished through Acts of Parliament that authorised the compulsory purchase of that land. These were Private Acts that applied only to these individual companies and construction schemes.

The railway building scheme in this case involved paying fees to the landowner based on the tonnage of materials transported by rail across his land. A Private Act subsequently amended those rights, and Wauchope said that he had not been given personal notice of these proposed changes. He argued that a Private Act of Parliament could not extinguish private rights without notice. If the court had accepted and then acted on this legal claim, it would have meant the court declaring that the Act of Parliament was 'inoperative'. This particular ground of appeal was withdrawn before the case reached the House of Lords, but the Law Lords were nonetheless at pains to address it.

Lord Brougham described the claim as 'wholly without justification'. Lord Cottenham was keen to express his 'clear opinion upon it, that no such erroneous idea may exist in future'. Lord Campbell gave the fullest treatment to any notion that courts could declare an Act to be invalid or of no effect in a particular case:

> All that a court of justice can do is to look to the Parliamentary Roll: if from that it should appear that a Bill has passed both Houses and received the Royal Assent, no court of justice can inquire into the mode in which it was introduced into

Parliament, nor what was done previous to its introduction, or what passed in
Parliament during its progress in its various stages through both Houses.

The Parliamentary Roll was the official record of the legislation passed by Parliament. It was
a series of chests which held manuscript scrolls containing a copy of each Act. The position
now is that two master copies are made by the Queen's Printer, and then authenticated and
signed by the Clerk of Parliament. One copy is held by the Public Records Office and the
other in the House of Lords Library. There is therefore no ambiguity. If a dispute did arise
as to whether something genuinely was an Act of Parliament, then the court would not
embark on a detailed procedural review. If it is recorded in the official way as an Act of
Parliament, then the courts will simply obey and apply it.

KEY CASE – *BRITISH RAILWAYS BOARD V PICKIN* [1974] AC 765

Pickin was a railway enthusiast who was opposed to the extensive line closures
taking place in the late 1960s. He bought a strip of land adjoining a railway track
with a legal expectation that when the line was abandoned, the railway track land
would revert to him. This expectation was thwarted by the British Railways Act 1968
which allowed the British Railways Board to retain the land even after any railway line
had been closed down.

The usual approach is that the state pays compensation when it compulsorily takes
property rights from an individual. This Act, however, 'appears to take away without
compensation all rights of adjoining landowners to a reversion of land to them on
the closing down of any part of our railway system' (Lord Reid).

Pickin alleged that this part of the Act, favourable to the British Railways Board, had
been obtained by the board by fraudulently concealing information from Parliament
and thereby misleading Parliament. He asked the court to either expressly or
implicitly disregard the section of the Act. Lord Reid responded that 'The idea that a
Court is entitled to disregard a provision in an Act of Parliament on any ground must
seem strange and startling to anyone with any knowledge of the history and law of
our constitution'. And, further, that 'he is not entitled to go behind the Act'.

He summed up the duty of the judges:

The function of the court is to construe and apply the enactments of Parliament.
The court has no concern with the manner in which Parliament or its officers
carrying out its standing orders perform these functions.

This is really a separation of powers argument (see chapter 9, Separation of Powers) that the institutions must operate within their separate spheres. A second argument relates to the internal autonomy of Parliament; under Article 9 Bill of Rights 1689, the proceedings of Parliament ought not to be challenged in any court.

The consequence is that if Parliament has been misled, then it is up to Parliament itself to decide what it wants to do about the piece of legislation; whether to retain it, to amend or repeal it. This reiterates the point that when courts are faced with an Act of Parliament, they can only accept and apply it. Indeed, the point had been considered and dismissed much earlier in *Lee v Bude and Torrington Railway Company* (1870) LR 6 CP 576: 'If an Act has been obtained improperly, it is for the legislature to correct it by repealing it but so long as it exists as law, the courts are bound to obey it'.

7.5.2 PARLIAMENT CANNOT BIND EITHER ITSELF OR ITS SUCCESSORS

Every Parliament has the same supreme power in making or unmaking any Act of Parliament. Supremacy is therefore a *continuing* power. 'If an Act of Parliament had a clause in it that it should never be repealed, yet without question, the same power that made it, may repeal it' (Herbert CJ in *Godden v Hales* [1686] KB).

On the face of it, this seems to be a limitation on supremacy. It stops Parliament from successfully introducing a non-repealable measure, but this is actually a necessary consequence of that supremacy. Parliament must be able to change *any* of its existing laws or it would not be supreme.

APPLYING THE LAW – CONTINUING SUPREMACY

The National Assembly for Wales was established by the Government of Wales Act 1998. The Assembly can now be regarded as a fundamental part of our constitution. It sets up the constitutional relationship between different parts of the United Kingdom. Yet, according to this traditional view of supremacy, the Westminster Parliament must be able to pass an Act of Parliament that abolishes the Welsh Assembly *and* expect the courts to accept and apply that Act. This Act could be passed in the ordinary way with no need for special procedures or special majorities.

If Parliament is legally supreme to make or unmake any law, this must logically be true. You can refer back to the discussion of syllogisms above and present this as a syllogistic argument:

- Parliament can amend or repeal any Act of Parliament.
- The Government of Wales Act 1997 is an Act of Parliament.
- Parliament can amend or repeal the Government of Wales Act 1997.

If the Parliament of 1997 could pass an Act that was somehow protected from repeal or amendment by any later Parliament, then those later Parliaments would not be supreme. In this respect, supremacy is an all or nothing affair. If Parliament was entitled to repeal 99.99999 per cent of the laws but was incapable of e.g. abolishing the Welsh Assembly, then it would not be supreme. If this were the case, then the law that established the Welsh Assembly would have a higher status than Parliament. As Dicey says '. . . "limited sovereignty" . . . is a contradiction in terms'.[11] Supremacy is continuing and all Parliaments must have unlimited law-making power'.

7.5.3 EXPRESS AND IMPLIED REPEAL

The process of changing or abolishing existing statutes is called *repeal*. There are two ways in which Parliament can do this.

Express repeal is when a new Act of Parliament states that a previous Act is abolished. If Parliament does not want to repeal the whole of an earlier Act, but only some sections, it can expressly say so: 'Sections 1–3 of the Hypothetical Act 1996 are hereby repealed'.

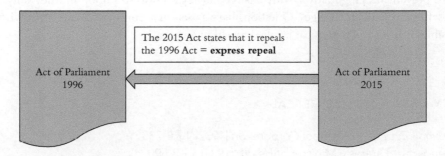

Figure 7.4 Express repeal

Implied repeal occurs where two statutes provide conflicting rules on the same subject, but the later rule does not expressly repeal the earlier rule.

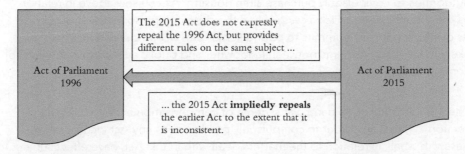

Figure 7.5 Implied repeal

----

11   [1885], at [68] as cited in Barnett, above n 5, 122.

Clearly, express repeal is neater and more certain, and parliamentary draftsmen try to identify all of the earlier inconsistent laws that need to be expressly repealed in a new piece of legislation, but it is possible for some provisions to slip through the net and have to be dealt with through implied repeal at a later stage.

ASSESSMENT ADVICE

The distinction between express and implied repeal is crucial to your understanding of supremacy. In particular, you will need to be familiar with it so as to understand the impact of the *Factortame* cases and the current role of EU law on the supremacy of the UK Parliament (covered in the next chapter).

Suppose the makers of an Act wanted to protect it from later implied repeal. They may want to prevent it being inadvertently changed or regard it as so important they only want purposeful and explicit changes. Questions have arisen in a number of cases as to whether it is possible to limit the process of implied repeal in any way.

KEY CASE – IMPLIED REPEAL

Vauxhall Estates v Liverpool Corporation [1932] 1 KB 733
Ellen Street Estates v Minister of Health [1934] 1 KB 590

At the end of the First World War, the British Prime Minister David Lloyd George promised that the returning troops would come back to 'homes fit for heroes'. The Acquisition of Land Act 1919 was a part of this commitment to demolish slum dwellings and replace them with more decent housing. It allowed local authorities to compulsorily purchase slum housing. As you saw above in relation to the *Wauchope* and *Pickin* cases, when the state compulsorily takes land from its owner, it normally commits to paying some form of compensation. There are likely to be disagreements between landowner and public authority on the level of compensation.

The 1919 Act laid out a particular scheme of compensation and also stated in section 7(1) that any order to compulsorily purchase, 'or any Act incorporated herewith, shall, in relation to the matters dealt with in this Act, have effect subject to this Act and so far as inconsistent with this Act those provisions shall cease to have or shall not have effect'.

It is possible to read this section as saying that any later inconsistent Act 'shall not have effect'.

Six years later, Parliament passed the Housing Act 1925. This, too, established a scheme allowing compulsory purchase by local authorities and requiring compensation to be paid to landowners. This was less generous than the 1919 scheme. The 1925 Act did not expressly repeal the 1919 Act and made no mention of it.

The question in these cases was, did the 1925 Act impliedly repeal the 1919 Act or did section 7(1) of the 1919 Act prevent this from happening? What the landowners wanted, of course, was the more generous compensation scheme to apply, and therefore asked the court to take the phrase 'shall not have legal effect' from the 1919 Act and interpret it as protecting the 1919 Act from implied repeal. How did the courts respond to such arguments?

There were similar facts, and ultimately the same problems, in both cases. The Divisional Court in *Vauxhall Estates* said that 'no Act of Parliament can effectively provide that no future Parliament shall interfere with its provisions' (Avory J).

In *Ellen Street Estates*, the Court of Appeal said, 'If in a subsequent Act, Parliament chooses to make it plain that the earlier statute is being to some extent repealed, effect must be given to that intention'. If you were acting for the landowners in this case, what part of this statement would you emphasise, so as to keep your argument alive? You would highlight '*chooses to make it plain*', so that we could argue that Parliament *can* choose to make it plain by expressly repealing a previous law, and anything less than that does not make plain Parliament's intentions. Unfortunately for this line of argument, the judgment also included this statement:

> The legislature cannot, according to our constitution, bind itself as to the form of subsequent legislation, and it is impossible for Parliament to enact that in a subsequent statute dealing with the same subject-matter there can be no implied repeal.
>
> (Maugham LJ)

Even if the drafters of the 1919 Act had been much more definite in trying to protect that Act from subsequent repeal, using terms such as 'this section shall not be subject to implied repeal', then all that any subsequent Parliament would have to do to amend or repeal that section is simply to introduce a new Act with different rules. This will impliedly repeal the older rule. So the traditional view insists that Parliament can change any existing legal rule either expressly or impliedly and that protection against implied repeal is impossible.

7.5.4 TERRITORIAL EXTENT

EXPLAINING THE LAW – EXTRA-TERRITORIAL EFFECT

Which geographical areas can the UK Parliament make law for? A common-sense answer might be 'Well . . . for the UK, of course!' Can the UK Parliament, however, legislate for what happens outside of this jurisdiction, on the high seas, in outer space, in other countries? The initially surprising answer is that Parliament *can* do this. It may legislate with extra-territorial effect and pass laws which affect the rights and duties of people outside the jurisdiction of the UK.

Sir Ivor Jennings came up with a deliberately provocative hypothetical example to illustrate this:

Parliamentary supremacy means that Parliament can legislate for all persons and all places. If it enacts that smoking in the streets of Paris is an offence, then it is an offence.[12]

APPLYING THE LAW – SMOKING IN THE STREETS OF PARIS

We need to consider this further. Suppose that Jennings's smoking law is in force and that two women are smoking on the streets of Paris – have they committed an offence? You might think that it depends on their nationality or on what the local laws say; but let us pose a very practical question. Would the French police arrest and charge these two women on the basis of the UK Act of Parliament? The answer is no. The UK law does not bind the French police, but does that mean that the women are not committing any offence?

If you remember, there was a top tip above on what to do if you are faced with a problem in applying supremacy of Parliament to any situation – think of supremacy as a rule that defines the relationship between Parliament and the courts; to be more precise, the relationship is between the *UK Parliament* on the one hand and the *UK courts* on the other. The content of this rule is that whatever the UK Parliament lays down in an Act of

---

12 I Jennings, *The Law and the Constitution* (5th edn, Hodder & Stoughton, 1959).

Parliament, the UK courts must accept and apply, with no power to declare it invalid (even if it goes beyond the jurisdiction of the UK).

So imagine that the two women are from Liverpool and have been on a weekend break to Paris and posted their holiday pictures on Instagram with a suitably helpful caption, 'Look at us smoking on the streets of Paris!!!' We accept that they would not be arrested by the French police, but if the UK police in Liverpool have evidence of this breach of UK law, they could decide to arrest them, and the Crown Prosecution Service may decide to prosecute them. If they appear before a UK court charged with an offence under this Act of Parliament, then the court has no choice but to apply the Act.

What if the two women smoking on the streets of Paris are not Liverpudlian but Parisian? Could they really be guilty of an offence if they are obeying the local laws in their home city? Again, we can agree that they would not be prosecuted in Paris, but what if they came to Liverpool for a brief cultural holiday? Again, if there is evidence of a breach of the UK statute, they could be arrested, prosecuted and brought before the court, and the UK court would have to apply the statute. As Jennings said, Parliament can legislate for all persons and all places.

Jennings' rather mischievous example tried to show that Acts of Parliament could have this extra-territorial effect even in highly unlikely scenarios. There are, however, many real life examples of statutes having extra-territorial effect. You should note that this is not the norm. Parliament does not ordinarily intend to legislate with effect outside of the UK jurisdiction, and the courts have an interpretive approach that means that statutes, unless clearly stated to the contrary, are read as only applying within the UK. Nevertheless, Parliament can make it clear that it is legislating for events outside of the UK borders.

An example is piracy. If the UK is going to address the problem of piracy, then it cannot limit the effect of its laws to the UK jurisdiction. The pirates are not going to helpfully stay within UK territorial waters, but are going to roam the high seas (i.e. outside of the ordinary jurisdiction of any nation state). Other interesting examples of extraterritorial laws include hijacking and treason.

KEY LEARNING POINTS

- The traditional view of supremacy says that Parliament can make or unmake any law and no other body has the power to override an Act.
- The enrolled Bill rule states that the courts will not look into the manner in which an Act has been passed. Any internal defects to the process must be addressed by Parliament itself.
- Parliament can amend or repeal any existing law. It is not possible to protect any statute against either express or implied repeal.
- Parliament can legislate with extra-territorial effect.

7.6 CHALLENGES TO THE TRADITIONAL VIEW

ASSESSMENT ADVICE

A typical assessment task here is to summarise the challenges to the traditional view of supremacy *and* to assess their effectiveness in altering the traditional view. There may be much to get through within a limited word count (coursework) or limited time (exams) and you may need to focus on particular challenges. You should, on this (as on all things), be guided by your Public Law teacher.

7.7 THE ACTS OF UNION

Before 1707, England (with Wales) and Scotland were separate, independent sovereign states. Each had their own head of state; however, since 1603 this position had been held by the same Monarch. This is akin to the position today where nations such as Australia, Canada and Jamaica have the same head of state (Queen Elizabeth II) but retain their independent sovereign status.

The two countries had their own legal systems, established religions and central and local government. Most importantly, they had separate Parliaments. The English Parliament emerged in the thirteenth century and met at Westminster, as the current Parliament does. The Parliament of Scotland met most commonly in Edinburgh and had also existed since the thirteenth century.

During 1705–1706, representatives of the Scottish and English Parliaments negotiated the terms of Union between the two countries, resulting in a Treaty of Union 1706. The English Parliament then passed the Union with Scotland Act 1706, whilst the Scottish Parliament passed the Union with England Act 1707. The new state, called 'Great Britain' came into being on 1 May 1707.

The Acts of Union are particularly significant for an understanding of the supremacy of Parliament because:

- They *created* the Parliament of Great Britain.
- They used the language of entrenchment (i.e. protection from repeal) for certain issues: Article 1 says: 'That the kingdoms of England and Scotland shall . . . for ever after be united . . .'.

So was the Westminster Parliament born unfree, subject to the limits set out in its foundational legal texts?

APPLYING THE LAW – ROYAL TITLES

A quick quiz question – how many British monarchs have been called Elizabeth? If you answered 'two' – sorry, try again.

Queen Elizabeth II is Queen of the United Kingdom of Great Britain and Northern Ireland. Queen Elizabeth I was monarch of a different political entity, England. The nation of Great Britain was not created until the union of England and Scotland in 1707, and the United Kingdom was formed by the further union with Ireland in 1800

Queen Elizabeth II's official title was settled by the Royal Titles Act 1953. This caused a grievance to, at least a few, Scots. For the English, this was their second queen called Elizabeth, but for the Scots, there had been no previous Queen Elizabeth. The royal title fails, therefore, to acknowledge the separate existence of Scotland as a sovereign state up to 1707 and fails to recognise that what happened in 1707 was Union between two independent sovereign states. This was the issue in *McCormick v Lord Advocate*.

KEY CASE – *MCCORMICK V LORD ADVOCATE* [1953] SC 396

McCormick was the Rector of Glasgow University and the other applicant was a law student of that university. They argued that the Royal Titles Act 1953 was unlawful. The Court of Session (a Scottish court) dismissed the substance of the claim as 'unsound and extravagant'. Lord Cooper, however, went on to say *obiter dicta*:

The principle of the unlimited sovereignty of Parliament is a distinctively English principle which has no counterpart in Scottish constitutional law . . . the question remains whether such a question is determinable as a justiciable issue in the Courts of either Scotland or England . . . I reserve my opinion with regard to the provisions relating expressly to this Court.

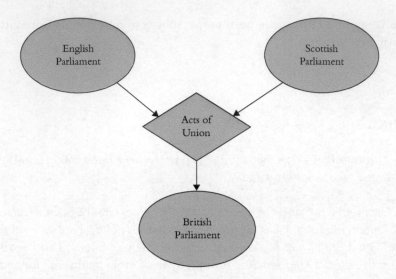

Figure 7.6 Acts of Union

The separate Parliaments of England and Scotland were the parents of the British
Parliament. They came together to create this new institution. On this view, the English
Parliament did not just carry on with a change of name and some new members from
Scotland, but rather, a wholly new institution was created. Lord Cooper is questioning
why this child, the new British Parliament, should have inherited all of its characteristics
from one parent (English Parliament) and none from the other parent (Scottish
Parliament).

A further strand to this argument looks at the procedures by which the new British
Parliament was created, i.e. that it was the Acts of Union that created the British Parliament.
The Acts came before the new Parliament and were its constitutive documents. In the same
way that written constitutions establish institutions and impose limits on them, the Acts of
Union can be seen as creating the British Parliament and subjecting it to the restrictions
contained in those Acts of Union. If this is the case, then the current Westminster
Parliament is still subject to these limitations. This is an elegant argument, but there is some
evidence to counter the notion that the Acts of Union limit the Westminster Parliament.

First, in *McCormick v Lord Advocate* itself, Lord Cooper went on to say, 'it has not been
shown that the Court of Session has authority to entertain the issue sought to be raised'. So
even if, as a matter of formal legal theory, there are limits on the Westminster Parliament,
a practical question is 'who can enforce those limits'? Lord Cooper was not ruling out the
possibility that this may be the courts but Applying the law is a normal judicial function.
By raising the question of whether the courts could enforce this (alleged) legal limit, he
seems to be more ruling it out that ruling it in.

If this court (or any other UK court) would not impose limits based on Union, then what
other institution would be competent to apply such limits to Parliament? Lord Cooper

may be talking about constitutional self-restraint of the *political* sectors of the constitution (Government and Parliament itself), but this would leave the *legal* rule of supremacy unaffected.

In *Gibson v Lord Advocate* [1970] 1 CMLR 563, the Court of Session took a similar approach when invited to invalidate an Act of Parliament on the grounds of a breach of the Acts of Union. In particular, it found that the question of whether a legal change was for the 'evident utility of the Scottish people' (as required by the Acts of Union) was essentially a political rather than a legal question. Nevertheless, it did raise a further flag of caution as to whether more fundamental aspects of the Union could be abolished.

The issue was raised more recently by Lord Hope in *Jackson v Attorney General* [2005] UKHL 56: 'the English principle of the absolute legislative sovereignty of Parliament . . . is being qualified . . . it may be said that the concept of a Parliament that is absolutely sovereign is not entirely in accord with reality'. Again this was *obiter dicta*, and whilst the *Jackson* case raises some hugely significant issues, the Acts of Union were not a key theme of the case.

Secondly, some provisions of the Acts of Union have already been amended or repealed by the Westminster Parliament. The Scottish Universities Act 1853 abolished the rule that professors at Scottish universities must be members of the established church. This changed the special position of the Church of Scotland which seemed to be protected by Union.

One counter-argument is that Scotland consented to these changes and therefore the Acts of Union could still be binding in the absence of that consent. This is not very convincing. It has never been clear how this consent has manifested itself.

Thirdly, the most fundamental provision of the Act of Union – that the Union will be forever – did not prevent plans for the Westminster Parliament to legislate for a breach of that Union. If there had been a positive vote for Scottish independence in the 2014 Referendum, the Union would have ended.

Fourthly, the experience of Union with Ireland provides further strong evidence that a strictly legalistic approach may not be appropriate to these questions. The Acts of Union with Ireland 1800 were similar to Scottish and English Union. They attempted to guarantee the position of the established Church of Ireland. Yet, this was disestablished by the Irish Church Act 1869. A legal challenge to this measure was dismissed as being not a justiciable matter, *Ex parte Selwyn* (1872) 36 JP 54, Lord Cockburn CJ: 'An Act of the legislature is superior in authority to any court of law. We have only to administer the law as we find it, and no court could pronounce a judgment as to the validity of an Act of Parliament'. The subsequent dissolution of the Union with Ireland shows the ineffectiveness of the, seemingly fundamental, statutory provision that the Union was to last forever.

The process of devolution is sometimes raised in the context of supremacy. In practice, this is a very important shift of law-making power from Westminster to the devolved legislatures. There seems, however, to be no impact on the traditional theory of supremacy. All the devolution legislation explicitly asserts the continuing right of the Westminster Parliament to legislate for those countries (section 107 Government of Wales Act 2006; section 28 Scotland Act 1998; section 5 Northern Ireland Act 1998).

KEY LEARNING POINTS
....

- The notion that the Acts of Union limit Parliament is an elegant argument and has some judicial support.
- This support, however, is in *obiter dicta* statements and there are doubts as to the justiciability of any claim; there is evidence of accepted historical change to elements of the Union, and a complete break-up of the Union seems legally possible.

7.8 THE PARLIAMENT ACTS

The circumstances leading to the enactment of the Parliament Act 1911 are explained in detail in Chapter 5, 'Constitutional conventions'. In short, a constitutional conflict between the Government and the House of Commons on one hand and the House of Lords on the other was resolved by a limitation of the Lords' powers. The Parliament Act 1911 allowed for a Bill to become an Act of Parliament without the approval of a majority of the Lords, which could only delay proposals for 24 months. This was further reduced to 12 months by the Parliament Act 1949.

As we saw above, parliamentary supremacy only applies to Acts of Parliament. Ordinarily, to create an Act of Parliament, a Bill must be approved by the House of Commons, approved by the House of Lords and receive the royal assent – what we can call, for shorthand purposes, the *standard procedure*. If the House of Lords refuses to approve a Bill, then under the conditions of the Parliament Act 1949, the Bill can nevertheless proceed to royal assent and become an Act of Parliament. We can call this the Parliament Act procedure (PA procedure).

The Parliament Act 1911 imposed only one express restriction on the use of this Parliament Act procedure: a Bill to extend the life of Parliament (section 2(1)). So when the Government wanted to delay the 1940 General Election, and extend the life of Parliament, it had no choice but the use the standard procedure and the Bill for the Prolongation of Parliament Act 1940 was approved by all three elements of Parliament. The key point for this part of the chapter is that the Parliament Act 1949 was itself made using the 'shortcut' PA procedure.

EXPLAINING THE LAW – THE PARLIAMENT ACT 1949

The Labour Government of 1949 was in a similar position to the Liberal Government of 1909. Following the 1945 General Election, there was a large Labour majority in the House of Commons trying to push through an ambitious legislative programme. This was being delayed and thwarted by a Conservative-dominated House of Lords. Unlike in 1909–1911, the 1949 Government did not have to endure a long constitutional crisis to force the House of Lords to agree to limit their own power. The Labour Government simply invoked the existing PA procedure to pass a law (the Parliament Act 1949) to further restrict the delaying powers of the House of Lords. It effectively reduced the power of the House of Lords to delay legislation from two years to one year.

So, to reiterate, this was a constitutional change effected by the 'shortcut' PA procedure. There have been only four other Acts passed using the 1949 PA procedure, including the Hunting Act 2004. This was a controversial piece of legislation, directed at banning fox hunting with dogs. It was strongly opposed in the House of Lords, and the Government eventually adopted the PA procedure to force it through.

An important question had emerged: the only express limitation on the laws that can be passed using the PA procedure is in section 2(1), but are there any *implied limits* on the sorts of constitutional change that are achieved by the PA procedure? There was a legal challenge to the use of the PA procedure to pass the Hunting Act 2004, and the judges explored these issues fully and made some interesting and potentially historic statements.

KEY CASE – *JACKSON AND OTHERS V ATTORNEY GENERAL* [2005] UKHL 56

The key claim in *Jackson* was that the Hunting Act 2004 is not a valid Act of Parliament because it was adopted under the Parliament Act 1949 procedure, and the 1949 Act itself is invalid. The Divisional Court dismissed the case, saying that the Parliament Act 1949 is entirely valid and so the Hunting Act 2004 was made according to a valid process.

The Court of Appeal did find that as well as the single express limitation on use of the PA procedure (section 2(1) extending the life of Parliament), there are implied

limitations meaning that major constitutional change cannot be effected using
the PA procedure. It was not Parliament's intention to take the House of Lords out
of the legislative process on questions of fundamental constitutional importance.
On the facts, the Court of Appeal decided that the Parliament Act 1949 was not a
major constitutional change. It was an amendment to a previous major change, and
as such, it could be validly made under the PA procedure. The real constitutional
importance of the case lies in the judgments of the Law Lords.

The House of Lords rejected the Court of Appeal's distinction between major and minor
constitutional change which had no basis within the 1949 Act itself. The Parliament Act
1949 was fully valid, and any Acts made using its procedure, including the Hunting Act
2004, were also fully valid.

It should also be pointed out that the PA procedure had already been used for major
constitutional change, without serious questions being raised. These include the most
contentious constitutional issue of its age (Home Rule for Ireland), retrospective criminal
legislation (War Crimes Act 1991) and how representative democracy operates (European
Elections Act 1999).

So, to recap:

- Court of Appeal – PA procedure could not be used to effect 'fundamental
  constitutional changes'.
- House of Lords – rejected the Court of Appeal distinction between 'modest' and 'fundamental change'. There was nothing in the Act to suggest further implied restrictions.

Some of the judges, however, took the opportunity (again speaking *obiter dicta*) to address
the question of whether there were some more general limitations on the supremacy of
Parliament.

7.8.1 RULE OF LAW LIMITS ON SUPREMACY

The Law Lords considered whether there are any wider limits on Parliament based on
broader notions of constitutionalism or the rule of law. The basis of any limits is not always
clearly explained, nor is the scope. All of the comments are *obiter dicta* and often speculative,
but, nonetheless, they are spectacular and almost revolutionary in nature. You need to bear
in mind what is at stake here. Supremacy of Parliament tells you who has the ultimate say
on the law of the land, on the rules that govern so many aspects of your life. The traditional
view on this issue has been the largely uncontested keystone of the whole constitutional
system for more than three centuries.

On the question of whether the Parliament Act procedure could be used to abolish the
House of Lords, Lord Steyn said:

I am deeply troubled by assenting to the validity of such an exorbitant assertion of government power in our bi-cameral system. It may be that such an issue would test the relative merits of strict legalism and constitutional principle in the courts at the most fundamental level . . . We do not in the United Kingdom have an uncontrolled constitution as the Attorney-General implausibly asserts.

Lords Carswell and Brown also flagged up, in a rather coded manner, that they would not pledge their unquestioning obedience to attempts to fundamentally change the constitution through the Parliament Act procedure. On the other hand, Lord Bingham restated the traditional view, that Parliament can make or unmake any law. Interestingly, many of the points made in the judgments are not explicitly limited to the Parliament Act procedure and any possible limits may apply to Parliament however it is constituted. Lord Steyn went on:

The classic account given by Dicey of the doctrine of the supremacy of Parliament, pure and absolute as it was, can now be seen to be out of place in the modern United Kingdom. Nevertheless, the supremacy of Parliament is still the general principle of our constitution. It is a construct of the common law. The judges created this principle. If that is so, it is not unthinkable that circumstances could arise when the courts may have to qualify a principle established on a different hypothesis of constitutionalism. In exceptional circumstances involving an attempt to abolish judicial review or the ordinary role of the courts, the [Supreme Court] may have to consider whether this is a constitutional fundamental which even a sovereign Parliament acting at the behest of a complaisant House of Commons cannot abolish.

This is a long quote, but an important one. He is asserting that:

■ The judges can change the traditional view of supremacy and no longer regard Acts as absolutely supreme.
■ The judges would be minded to impose some limits in some circumstances.

This is particularly interesting because Lord Steyn in a lecture in 1996 had said: 'Parliament asserts sovereign power. The courts acknowledge the sovereignty of Parliament. And in countless decisions the courts have declared the unqualified supremacy of Parliament. There are no exceptions'.[13] Clearly, his view on the constitutional principles changed. It is not absolutely clear why.

His judgment can be criticised in seeking the support of the devolution settlement and the Human Rights Act 1998 for his argument that a new legal order was being established. That may be the case, but specifically on the question of supremacy, they both make efforts to reaffirm, not limit, the power of Parliament to legislate on these matters. Nevertheless, the distance between this view and the traditional view of supremacy is rather startling.

....

13 Lord Steyn, Administrative Law Association Lecture (1996).

This takes us back to the start of this chapter: that Parliament is supreme because the judges treat Acts of Parliament as supreme, and if there comes a point when judges stop treating Acts as supreme, then the legal rule has changed. Lord Steyn did not say exactly what the limits were, or what the courts would do if those limits were reached. He did, however, give the examples listed in the quote above. Above all, the key point was made that the courts will not give Government/Parliament an unconditional guarantee that any and all constitutional change will be automatically applied by the courts.

Lord Hope takes a similar approach in asserting that the courts 'can void the acts of *any* organ of government, whether *legislative* or administrative, which exceed the limits of the power that organ derives from the law'. Emphasis has been added to bring out the (quietly revolutionary) points that:

- There are legal limits on Parliament.
- These limits can in practice as well as in theory be applied by the courts.

Lord Hope continues: 'Step by step, gradually but surely, the English principle of absolute legislative sovereignty of Parliament which Dicey derived from Coke and Blackstone is being qualified'. Yet, as Dicey said, limited sovereignty is a contradiction in terms. If Parliament's ability to legislate is limited, it must be limited by some rule or principle of higher status. Lord Hope indicates that 'the Rule of Law enforced by the courts is the ultimate controlling factor on which our constitution is based'.

> KEY LEARNING POINTS
> ....
>
> There are few definite limits that we can derive from the judgments in *Jackson* (e.g. of laws that will definitely be unacceptable), but it does indicate the potentially fluid nature of the judicial position on the legal rule of supremacy of Parliament itself.

7.9 MANNER AND FORM

RFV Heuston put forward a 'new view' of supremacy in 1961. He argued that:

- Parliament was unlimited as to the *subject matter* of legislation. It could introduce any new rule and amend or repeal any existing one, but
- Parliament was subject to restrictions as to the *manner and form* of legislation, i.e. rules on the composition and procedure for making Acts of Parliament were binding and could be enforced by the courts.

APPLYING THE LAW – THE NORTHERN IRELAND REFERENDUM

The Northern Ireland Act 1998 section 1 states: 'It is hereby declared that Northern Ireland in its entirety remains part of the United Kingdom and shall not cease to be so without the consent of a majority of the people of Northern Ireland voting in a poll'.

To use Heuston's language, the Act lays down a particular *manner and form* for changing the law on this specific issue. This raises some intriguing questions.

- Does this add a fourth element to Parliament (Commons, Lords, Royal Assent, referendum)?
- Can a later Parliament ignore the requirement?
- Would the courts declare any Act purporting to change the borders of Northern Ireland without a referendum to be invalid because it was not in the required manner and form?

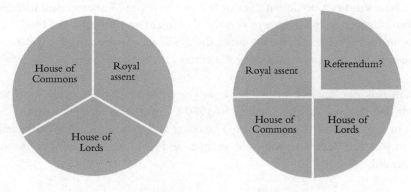

Figure 7.7 Does a referendum add a fourth stage to the law-making process?

One of the foundations of the manner and form theory is the existence of supportive Commonwealth case law.

KEY CASE – *HARRIS V MINISTER OF THE INTERIOR (1950) 22 SA 428*

This concerned the attempt of the South African Parliament to remove voting rights from black citizens in 1951, through the Separate Registration of Voters Act. The Act was passed using the ordinary procedure of simple majorities in both Houses. The South African Parliament, however, was created by the South Africa Act 1909 which included a provision, section 35, that protected the voting rights of black citizens. It provided that voting rights could only be removed by a two-thirds majority. This stipulation was simply ignored in 1951. The South African Supreme Court declared that the 1909 Act imposed binding restrictions and Parliament was not free to ignore the special majority requirement. The requirement to follow the particular manner and form for legislation on this issue was binding on subsequent Parliaments, even following independence from the UK.

Attorney General for New South Wales v Trethowan [1932] AC 526 raised similar issues. The state of New South Wales in Australia had two branches to its legislature (the Assembly and the Council). In 1929, the Constitution of NSW was amended so as to protect the Assembly. It required a referendum before a proposal to abolish the Assembly could be presented for Royal Assent. In 1930, following a change of Government, there was an attempt to abolish the Assembly without undertaking a referendum. It was held that this could not be a valid Act because it did not follow the required manner and form, i.e. the referendum. Central to the judgment was the Colonial Laws Validity Act 1865, an Act of the Westminster Parliament that established the NSW legislature and gave it power to make laws, subject to the legislation following the correct manner and form.

Similarly, in *Bribery Commissioners v Ranasinghe* [1965] AC 172, the Ceylon (now Sri Lanka) Parliament had ignored a requirement in its 1950 Constitution for a two-thirds majority to make changes to public organisations. The court said that the Ceylon Parliament was required to pass Acts following a specific manner and form, and by failing to do so the 1958 Act was invalid.

APPLYING THE LAW – NORTHERN IRELAND REFERENDUM

If you applied these cases directly to the Northern Ireland example, what would you conclude? If the cases are applicable, then the referendum requirement would have to be adhered to. This would mean an attempt by the Westminster Parliament to change the Northern Ireland border without a referendum could be prevented by the courts.

In *Ranasinghe*, the court made clear that these Commonwealth cases concern significantly different constitutional systems. All the legislatures in the Commonwealth cases were operating under the restrictions of the legal provisions that established them (South Africa Act 1909, Ceylon Constitution 1950). This is not the case in the UK where there is no such document. Any attempt to apply the Commonwealth cases in the UK runs up against the problem of the enrolled Bill rule. The courts in the UK seem to have made their position clear; they will not look behind the face of an Act of Parliament.

The best practical illustration of how the UK courts would address this question is from Megarry VC in *Manuel v Attorney General*: 'In the present case I have before me a copy of the Canada Act 1982 purporting to be published by her Majesty's Stationery Office . . . there has been no suggestion that the copy before me is not a true copy of the Act itself, or that it was not passed by the House of Commons and the House of Lords, or did not receive the Royal Assent'.

APPLYING THE LAW – NORTHERN IRELAND

Given the lack of applicability of the Commonwealth cases and the position of the UK courts as laid out in *Wauchope*, *Pickin* and *Manuel*, what would the UK courts do in the Northern Ireland example?

According to the enrolled Bill rule, the courts would not look into the procedures adopted in creating the Act. If a referendum was not undertaken, then the courts would regard it as a matter for Parliament and the wider political system to consider and address. The courts would not be competent to declare invalid an Act that was not accompanied by a referendum.

The manner and form argument seemed largely defunct until it was resurrected by Lord Steyn in *Jackson v Attorney General*:

Apart from the traditional method of law-making, Parliament acting as ordinarily constituted may functionally redistribute legislative power in different ways. For example, Parliament could for specific purposes provide for a two-thirds majority in the House of Commons and the House of Lords. This would involve a redefinition of Parliament for a specific purpose. Such redefinition could not be disregarded.

This is a very surprising statement. Lord Steyn does not indicate any limits to this power of redefinition. He seems comfortable with a requirement for a 66.6 per cent majority, which would grant a novel and significant power of partial entrenchment to Governments. Would a redefinition requiring a 95 per cent majority be respected or disregarded? If it was respected, this redefinition would effectively hand powers to the Government of the day to completely entrench any aspect of law.

This is an *obiter dictum* statement but, nevertheless, it represents a significant shift in judicial thinking (from one judge at least) on the manner and form question as it applies to the

Westminster Parliament. You should note, however, that it was only one marginal statement from one judge. In the same case, Lord Hope strongly dismisses the manner and form argument, and Lady Hale says that it is a question for another day. The weight of authority is still against the manner and form theory.

7.9.1 THE RULE OF RECOGNITION

Sir Ivor Jennings put forward a similar view, called the 'rule of recognition', that there are possible limitations on the procedures that Parliament can use to produce legislation.[14]

According to Jennings, this is a common law test. The standard rule of recognition is: consented to by Commons, Lords, Royal Assent. If a statute, however, prescribes a different way of making statute, e.g. requiring a referendum, then this is a new and alternative rule of recognition. As statute prevails over common law, the courts will be bound to accept this and apply the new rule: 'the legal sovereign may impose legal limitations upon itself, because its power to change the law includes the power to change the law affecting itself'.[15]

The problem is that this assumes that the 'rule of recognition' is just an ordinary common law rule. Ultimately, you need to go back to Wade's point that supremacy is not an ordinary common law rule. It is in a special category as the ultimate political fact of the Constitution. This leaves the supremacy of Parliament beyond the scope of legislative change. As Wade said, '. . . the "ultimate legal principle" is therefore a rule which is unique in being unchangeable by Parliament – it is changed by revolution, not by legislation; it lies in the keeping of the courts, and no Act of Parliament can take it from them'.[16]

KEY LEARNING POINTS

- The manner and form theory is supported by Commonwealth case law but not by the UK cases (with the exception of Lord Steyn's comments in *Jackson*).
- The courts must have some way of legally recognising an Act of Parliament, but the case law indicates that this is in accordance with the traditional view rather than granting Parliament a power to redefine itself or add manner and form requirements.

7.10 SHOULD PARLIAMENT BE LIMITED?

As critical thinkers, and part of the community of people thinking about these serious issues, we need to address not only what the law *is* but also what it *ought* to be. The

---

14   I Jennings, *The Law and the Constitution* (5th edn, Hodder & Stoughton, 1959).

15   Ibid.

16   W Wade, 'The Legal Basis of Sovereignty' [1955] *Cambridge Law Journal* 172.

conclusion reached in this chapter is that manner and form arguments do not represent a correct view of what the law of the UK constitution is. It is abundantly clear that a general manner and form process as outlined by Heuston is not a part of our constitutional arrangements. But ought it to be?

It is difficult to avoid a sense of hunger from some writers, that each potential procedural rule is seized upon as an opportunity to argue for a restriction of supremacy. Yet, to hand a general 'manner and form' power to Parliament (and therefore in effect to the Government) would, it is argued here, be a constitutional disaster.

It happens to be my personal view that Parliament ought not to do certain things, e.g. legislate for former colonies or pass legislation without, at least, considering whether it is consistent with the European Convention on Human Rights. But it is easy to imagine the sorts of things that some Governments might have considered so fundamental to UK interests that they should be protected by manner and form safeguards, e.g. the borders of UK or of the British Empire, the internal arrangements of the UK and devolution etc.

Accepting the manner and form theory or the rule of recognition would allow the Government of the day to construct, ad hoc and with no wider legitimacy, a body of higher Constitutional Law. This would be a patchwork representing sometimes the fundamental and eternal concerns of public life, and sometimes the petty and parochial obsessions of some people of a particular time.

This is not to say that the warning flags raised in the *Jackson* case are not welcome, or that some limits on Parliament would not enhance the constitution. Parliament ought not to have the power to limit itself, and this power should not be entirely in the hands of the judges, either. Again, going back to Wade's formulation of the nature of supremacy provides a persuasive explanation.

The argument proceeds like this:

- In 1688, the courts recognised the ultimate political fact that Parliament had won the constitutional battles of the previous half-century. They treated Acts of Parliament as supreme because Parliament had won the war.
- In the twenty-first century, the courts treat Parliament as supreme because it represents the voice of the people (democracy) and because we are governed by regular law (the rule of law). The ultimate political fact of the constitution then is that Parliament can make any law, subject only to these limits of democracy and the rule of law.

If Parliament made an extreme attack on e.g. democracy by trying to take the vote away from women or by abolishing freedom of expression, then this takes away the reason for the courts to obey Parliament. It goes beyond what Parliament is entitled to do, and in refusing to give effect to such laws, the courts would be recognising the ultimate historical fact of the constitution.

There is judicial support for thinking that this is what the law on supremacy *is* and also what it *ought to be*. Lord Hoffmann has stressed the democratic underpinning of supremacy: 'The principle of the sovereignty of Parliament, as it has been developed by the courts over the past 350 years, is founded upon the unique authority Parliament derives from its representative character' (*R (Bancoult) v Secretary of State for Foreign and Commonwealth Affairs (No 2)* [2008] UKHL 61).

Lord Steyn has said that the judges 'may have to consider whether judicial review is a constitutional fundamental which even a sovereign Parliament cannot abolish'.[17] Lord Woolf agreed that a parliamentary attempt to abolish judicial review (a foundation of the rule of law) would be 'unthinkable' and courts' responses would also have to be 'without precedent'.

> Some judges might choose to do so by saying that it was an unrebuttable presumption that Parliament could never intend such a result. I myself would consider there were advantages in making it clear that ultimately there are even limits on the supremacy of Parliament which it is the courts' inalienable responsibility to identify and uphold. They are limits of the most modest dimensions which I believe any democrat would accept. They are no more than are necessary to enable the Rule of Law to be preserved.[18]

Whatever the constitutional position is following Brexit then these common law notions of the relationship between the rule of law and supremacy are likely to increase in importance. We turn to the dominant issue in contemporary Public Law, the departure of the UK from the EU, in the next chapter.

POINTS TO REVIEW

- Supremacy of Parliament is the keystone of the constitution and the pre-eminent legal rule of the legal system.

- The traditional view of supremacy states that Parliament can make or unmake any law whatsoever and no other institution can override those laws.

- This means that the courts cannot look into how an Act was made (the enrolled Bill rule), that Parliament can impliedly repeal any law and legislate for all persons and all places.

- Some of the non-EU challenges to the traditional view (from the Acts of Union and the manner and form argument) are worthy of consideration but, in practice, lack a strong evidential base.

- Senior judges have indicated some potential limits based on constitutional principles of democracy and the rule of law; any limits would only apply in extreme circumstances.

---

17   Lord Steyn, Comments [2004] *Judicial Review* 107.
18   Lord Woolf, 'Droit Public – English Style' [1995] Public Law 57.

TAKING IT FURTHER

H W R Wade, 'The Basis of Legal Sovereignty' [1955] *Cambridge Law* Journal 17 Much of the analysis and evaluation in this chapter is based on Wade's view of the nature of supremacy. A good way for you to decide whether you agree with this approach is to go back to the original. It's not available through the online databases, so this is a good excuse to put some shoes on and get down to the library.

R Ekins, 'Acts of Parliament and the Parliament Acts' (2007) 123 *Law Quarterly Review* 9 This article examines the idea that the Parliament Acts are a type of manner and form procedure or have changed the rule of recognition. Try to identify whether Ekins thinks that the traditional view is undermined by the Parliament Acts.

J Jowell, 'Parliamentary sovereignty under the new constitutional hypothesis' [2006] *Public Law* 56 This explores in depth some of the ideas introduced in the latter parts of this chapter, especially the idea that there may be limits on Parliament founded in democracy (or legitimacy) and the rule of law.

UK Constitutional Law Group blog, https://ukconstitutionallaw.org/ and search for 'supremacy' A top assessment tip is to keep an eye on the UK Constitutional Law Group blog. You will get insightful discussion on recent developments that can enhance your work to great effect.

8

CHAPTER 8
SUPREMACY AND EUROPEAN LAW

The vote to leave the European Union in the June 2016 referendum has sent shock waves through the political, legal and constitutional structures of the UK. Things are changing day by day in the aftermath of the Leave vote, but at the time of writing (Autumn 2017), the *Miller* litigation clarified that only Parliament could authorise the Government to trigger Article 50 that would start a two-year process of leaving the EU.

That authorisation was given by Parliament in the European Union (Notification of Withdrawal) Act 2017, passed in March 2017 and on 29 March 2017 the formal notification of withdrawal was delivered to the EU.

The UK is therefore set to leave the European Union on or before 29 March 2019, unless some extension agreement is agreed as part of the ongoing negotiations.

The European Union (Withdrawal) Bill received its second reading in September 2017 but has not yet passed. It aims to incorporate all existing EU law into UK law and give ministers extensive powers to amend and repeal that body of law.

Negotiations have started and focus on financial arrangements, rights of EU & UK citizens and the border with the Republic of Ireland, with an intention to move onto trade relationships later in the talks. As of October 2017, the talks are not going very well.

Beyond that, the shape of Brexit remains very uncertain. Some commentators believe that Brexit can and will be stopped; some that transitional arrangements will keep the UK within the remit of EU law until 2021 or beyond; some that the UK is heading for a hard no-deal exit that will be a clean break from the body of EU law.

Writing at a time of such constitutional uncertainty poses a nice challenge to the textbook writer. If you are reading this second edition before April 2019 then the rules described in this chapter may be in their last days but will still be valid. After that time, and in the absence of a crystal ball, you should look at the companion website for updates to this chapter.

We also had to decide whether to retain the material on the institutions of the EU in the first part of this Chapter. It is still here. The institutions will continue making law that applies in the UK at least until March 2019 and potentially beyond. The UK may end up with a trading agreement with the EU that involves a continuing role (for many years) for EU law-making. This is why law students in non-EU countries, such as Norway and Switzerland, are required to study EU law and institutions in some depth.

The UK is a member of many international organisations, but its membership of the European Union is unique in the impact it has had on the UK constitution. EU law regulates a wide range of aspects of your life, from your employment rights and the permitted food additives in your breakfast this morning, to whether you can live and study in another EU country and the university fees that you can be charged for doing so.

Most international agreements and organisations simply impose rights and duties on nation states. The EU is different in the extent to which:

- It provides legal rights to individuals.
- Its laws are an integrated part of the legal system of each Member State.
- These laws take priority over inconsistent national laws.

The second half of the chapter follows on from Chapter 7 and considers the thorny issue of supremacy of Parliament. The traditional view of supremacy in the UK states that Acts of Parliament are the supreme source of law and the Westminster Parliament is the highest law-making authority. The EU view of supremacy is that EU law is supreme and takes precedence over any conflicting national law. It is impossible for both of these statements to be entirely true. At worst, one statement is simply wrong; at best, either (or both) statements need to be qualified. This is a nice conundrum for us to consider, and the answer (whilst not entirely straightforward) is very important for our understanding of UK Public Law.

If you are on a wider programme of legal study, you will most likely be studying European Union law either alongside or at a later date to Public Law. Your textbook for that module will be 250–500 pages long and, even so, will probably describe itself as mere introduction to the subject, i.e. EU law is a vast subject in its own right. In this chapter, we are just providing a *very* simple overview of the European Union and then focusing on its impact on our own object of attention: the UK constitution and system of Public Law.

AS YOU READ

- Develop an understanding of the reasons behind the formation and development of the European Union.

■ Form a picture of the institutional structure of the EU.

■ Follow how the Court of Justice of the EU developed the notion of the supremacy of EU law.

■ See how the UK judges have tried to resolve the clash between Westminster and EU claims to legal supremacy.

■ See how the process of Brexit has started and understand the implications of Brexit for supremacy of Parliament.

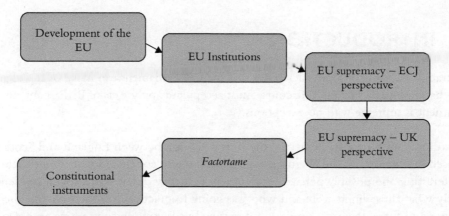

Figure 8.1 Structure of Chapter 8

A note on terminology – the European Union has gone through a number of incarnations over the past 60 years, and each version has had its own titles and terms. This can be a touch confusing. In this chapter, we will mainly use the modern terminology, but some of the older terms will be in quotations and other sources that you read.

■ What was the European Economic Community (EEC) → became (together with other organisations) the European Community (the EC) → which in turn developed into the European Union (EU)
■ What was 'Community law' → is now 'EU law'
■ What was the European Court of Justice (ECJ) → is now the Court of Justice of the European Union (CJEU)

To add to the challenges of studying the EU, the treaty Article numbers have been renumbered twice. Some provisions are known by three different Article numbers. We will leave the full joy of getting to grips with that to your EU Law module. Here we will simply give the latest version of the relevant treaties, which are either the Treaty on European Union (TEU) or the Treaty on the Functioning of the European Union (TFEU).

APPLYING THE LAW – ASSESSMENT ADVICE: EU OR ECHR?

One thing that you should never, ever do, on risk of hurting your grades quite painfully, is confuse European Union law with European Convention on Human Rights (ECHR) law. There is an increasing human rights dimension to EU law (including the EU acceding to the ECHR), but mixing this material up with talk of the Human Rights Act 1998 shows poor understanding of the subject and will leave a lot of irrelevant material in your answer.

8.1 INTRODUCTION

The traditional view of supremacy states that the UK Parliament can make or repeal any law whatsoever, and that the UK courts must accept and apply Acts of Parliament, i.e. that Parliament is supreme with no exceptions.

We explored, in Chapter 7, whether the Acts of Union between England and Scotland imposed restrictions on the Westminster Parliament and concluded that whilst there was an interesting and possibly persuasive argument that they did, it was difficult to identify exactly what those limits were and who was going to practically enforce them. The 'manner and form' theory is similarly interesting but lacking in substantive authority from UK law.

In relation to the Parliament Act procedures and the Hunting Act controversy explored in *Attorney General v Jackson*, some senior judges indicated that they will not give unconditional obedience to any Act of Parliament regardless of its content. Nevertheless, there is broad agreement that if these limitations do exist, they are only an ultimate safety valve that would only come into play in the most extreme circumstances. In the absence of a major crisis of democratic legitimacy, the courts will continue to obey and apply Acts of Parliament.

The major challenge to the traditional view of supremacy therefore has been the UK's membership of the European Union.

ANALYSING THE LAW – MEANING OF SUPREMACY

Are there any synonyms for supremacy? We could think of a few, such as ascendancy, superiority, pre-eminence. A simpler term is 'highest', and since 'supremacy' often refers to power or authority, we can call 'supremacy' the highest authority.

> Question – how many highest mountains can there be in a single mountain range? You have hopefully reached the only grammatically logical answer – 'one'. In the Himalayas, K2 is a very high mountain (8,611 metres) but it cannot be said to be the highest mountain in that range, because it is outranked by Mount Everest (8,848 metres).
>
> Question – how many highest sources of law can there be in a single legal system? Again, the answer must be 'one'.

Each legal system can have its own supreme source of law, but there cannot be multiple supreme sources within one legal system. At points in time there may be different contenders for the title of 'supreme source of law', but ultimately there will come a time when different laws lay down different rules covering the same issue (Law A says that you can do X; Law B says that doing X is forbidden). The resolution of this inconsistency must involve deciding to apply one law rather the other, and this tells us which law takes priority and has higher status (Law A *or* Law B, but not both). It is the courts who must resolve this sort of conflict.

The difficulty that we are going to address in this chapter is that a) the EU and national legal systems are connected, and EU law takes effect within national legal systems, and b) both EU law and UK statute law (Acts of Parliament) lay claim to being the supreme source of law within the UK legal system.

Using the analysis above, we can see that this is logically impossible. If two distinct types of law operate within the same legal system, they cannot both be supreme. There will ultimately be a clash between the two, and one type of law must be given precedence over the other.

8.2 THE DEVELOPMENT OF THE EUROPEAN UNION

EU law can be a challenging subject, with students having to learn a new legal vocabulary, different law-making and law-enforcing institutions and some novel concepts. It goes without saying that it is not quite as interesting as Public Law, but you will find it a stimulating and highly relevant subject.

Our aim in the next section is much more modest. It is to give you a very basic introduction to the institutions of the European Union. The subject of this book is the Public Law of the United Kingdom, and this focus extends to this chapter. The material covered allows you to see that the UK is a member of an international organisation that has autonomous institutions that can make laws independently of the wishes of an individual Member State, and that these laws can take effect within that Member State. We will explore the question of supremacy, i.e. what happens when these EU laws conflict with national laws, in detail in later sections.

8.2.1 WHAT IS THE EUROPEAN UNION FOR?

The European Union has grown from the original six Member States to an organisation with 28 members. These cover a majority of Western and central Europe. According to Article 3 TEU, 'The Union's aim is to promote peace'. The origins of the EU lie in the aftermath of the Second World War. The countries of Europe had been devastated for the second time in half a century. Their cities and economies lay in ruins.

The aims of providing lasting peace and economic recovery were closely intertwined. Reducing restrictions on trade between countries would make their economies more interdependent and make conflict less likely. This could also promote prosperity by increasing trade between the Member States. Those of you who did economics at school or college should refer back to Ricardo's theory of comparative advantage. Those of you who did not just need to know that economic theory says that international trade promotes efficiency, innovation and productivity both for the exporting and the importing countries.

From the outset, the European Union was intended to be a dynamic organisation. That is, it would not be reliant on all its Member States agreeing every action for every step of the way. Its institutions would have a life of their own and together would seek to promote peace and prosperity through 'an ever-closer union' of the peoples of Europe.

The principal method of achieving this more prosperous and peaceful Europe was through promoting economic integration by, first, directly removing the obvious barriers to trade and monitoring and enforcing those rules through independent institutions, and then, second, progressively reducing the less obvious barriers to trade. The direct barriers are addressed by the four freedoms (free movement of goods, services, people and capital). The indirect barriers can be addressed by harmonising products and processes.

APPLYING THE LAW – DEVELOPING AN INTERNAL MARKET

Imagine that three countries, Angland, Gaul and Teuton, want to reach an agreement to promote trade between them.

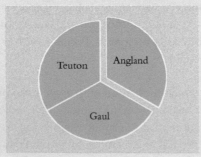

Figure 8.2

Digital radios are manufactured in all three countries. Radiobox Ltd is an Angland digital radio manufacturer that wants to sell its radios in the other two countries. What potential problems or barriers might face Radiobox, and how does the European Union deal with those barriers?

First, there may be *import limits*, e.g. that only 1,000 digital radios may be imported into Gaul each year. These sorts of quantitative restrictions are not allowed within the European Union. There may be *import tariffs*, e.g. that Radiobox must pay a tax of 20 per cent of the wholesale price to be allowed to export their radios to Teuton. This sort of import tariff is likely to make trade in radios between the countries uncompetitive, and is prohibited under EU law.

These useful, but relatively unambitious, measures can be achieved by a customs union or free trade area simply by agreement of the Member States. The agreement may set up a dispute resolution procedure or just leave resolution of any disputes to diplomatic processes, but there is no pressing need for law-making or law-enforcing institutions that are independent of the Member States.

The next level of integration says that to compete effectively, Radiobox may need sales and service centres in the other countries. To do this, they may need to *move capital and workers* to those countries, and be legally entitled to *offer those services*. Restrictions on the movement of foreign capital, services and workers are common in national laws, but are not permitted under EU law. This goes beyond a simple customs union, and these fundamental freedoms of movement are guaranteed by the EU Treaty.

Let us go further. There may be *regulatory differences* between the states, e.g. on health and safety requirements on small electrical products. If Radiobox can legally sell their Angland radios in Gaul, but need a separate production line to produce radios that meet the stricter product standards in Teuton, then their costs will be higher and efficiencies from trade will be lost. Ironing out these differences in national regulations, through institutions and law-making processes, can make international trade more effective.

Trying to equalise the *costs of production* involves going much further still. If the Radiobox factory in Angland can simply dump all their waste in the local river, whilst environmental laws in the other countries require expensive pollution treatment, then Radiobox has a 'costs of production' advantage. Harmonisation can help here, but involves going further and further into what might be regarded as national rather than international concerns.

Not everything that affects costs of production will be harmonised (e.g. countries might want to keep their laws on Sunday trading) and not every product feature will be harmonised (think of the cost of replacing every single three-pin electrical plug on every single electrical device in the UK with a two-pin plug used in other European countries, and then add the cost of changing every single electrical socket in every building in the UK!).

Transport costs impede trade, and the EU uses some of its budget to promote better and more integrated transport links. There are transaction costs and uncertainties that come from changing currency exchange rates; adopting a single currency (the Euro) can reduce those costs.

Very few of the actions following the formation of the EEC in 1957 have necessarily and automatically followed from these goals of peace and prosperity. At each stage of further integration and widening powers for the EU (many of which have been highly controversial), there has been a broad *political will* to develop this 'ever closer union'. There are many trading blocs in the world that have not felt the need to adopt a single currency or foreign and justice policies. Sceptics of the EU project in the UK and other states are suspicious that this closer union goes beyond trading and points inexorably to a European super-state and further losses of national sovereignty.

The activities of the Union are very broadly summed up in Article 3 TEU as including:

- An internal market free of internal tariffs.
- Free movement of goods, persons, services and capital.
- Common policies, including on agriculture and fisheries.
- Environmental, consumer and health protection.
- Promotion of external trade and development.

We are dealing with a complex body of law and institutions making difficult and controversial decisions on which rules to harmonise and which to leave to individual countries. In theory, you could leave this to individual countries to come together and agree on a case-by-case basis, leaving them to interpret what those standards mean and how to apply them within their own legal systems, and leaving enforcement up to the discretion of nation authorities. Disputes between nations could be decided by individual diplomatic discussion. Some aspects of the world trading system operate along these lines. The European Union has generally followed a more integrationist and centralising approach. Its Member States decided that they needed:

- A central executive organisation (the Commission) to propose new laws and make sure current laws were being applied across the states.
- A body to represent the voices of the Member States in the law-making process (the Council of Ministers). This started off with a consensus approach, i.e. each country had a veto. As the number of members grew, consensus became less likely and to avoid gridlock they moved to a majority voting system. This was crucial because, in doing so, Member States had agreed to be bound by particular laws even if they had opposed the proposals.
- Some directly democratic element (the European Parliament). All the Member States are functioning democracies, but as the Union takes decisions that impinge more and more directly on people within the countries of Europe, then a direct democratic voice is needed for legitimate decisions.
- A court to consistently interpret and enforce EU law (the Court of Justice).

There has been a transfer of sovereign rights to these institutions. Together they can make law that applies within Member State legal systems, including granting enforceable rights to individuals.

8.3 THE INSTITUTIONS OF THE EUROPEAN UNION

There are seven formal institutions of the European Union (Article 13 TEU). We will focus on the main five: the European Council, the Council of Ministers, the Commission, the Parliament and the Court. For each, we will examine its composition and main functions.

8.4 EUROPEAN COUNCIL

This had been a part of the Council of Ministers but was separated out as an independent institution by the Treaty of Lisbon.

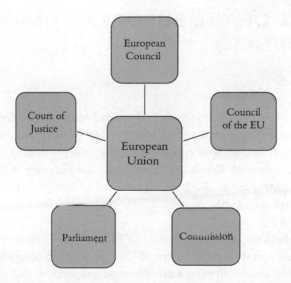

Figure 8.3 EU institutions

8.4.1 COMPOSITION

It is composed of the heads of state of the Member States (Theresa May for the UK, Angela Merkel for Germany, etc), the President of the European Council, and the President of the Commission. The EU Foreign Secretary also attends. This composition tells us that the European Council represents the views of the Member States on the highest level of policy and direction.

8.4.2 ROLE

It meets four times a year 'to provide the Union with the necessary impetus for its development and shall define the general policy directions and priorities' (Article 15(1) TEU).

EXPLAINING THE LAW – THE EUROPEAN COUNCIL'S ROLE

Developing a response to Brexit has obviously been a significant task for the European Council in 2017. It has also had to take a position on the Catalan independence crisis. The Council issued a declaration in February 2017 on external aspects of migration.

http://www.european-council.europa.eu/en/european-council/president/

8.5 COUNCIL OF THE EUROPEAN UNION (THE COUNCIL)

8.5.1 COMPOSITION

This is composed of ministerial representatives from each Member State depending on the subject matter. There is, therefore, no fixed membership. When the Environment configuration is meeting (as it does four times a year), then the environment ministers from each of the Member States attend. When the Agriculture and Fisheries configuration meets, then the agriculture ministers attend. Representatives need to have the authority to commit their state to specific actions and policies.

The Presidency rotates between the Governments of Member States each six months, which provides a, rather limited, agenda-setting power. With this rather shifting composition, there is a need for co-ordinated and continuing administration, preparation and negotiation. This is carried out by national civil servants and ambassadors seconded to work in the Permanent Representatives Committee (COREPER).

8.5.2 ROLE

The Council of Ministers acts as the voice of the Member States in EU policy and law-making. Law-making is the Council's prime function, but one that it shares with the Parliament, and to some extent the Commission. The Council also has some foreign policy and budgetary duties.

The Council votes on proposals to adopt laws. In most cases, it uses Qualified Majority Voting (QMV) (Article c4 TEU), although unanimity is still required in some areas such as aspects of employment law. QMV requires that a proposal gains the votes of:

- 55 per cent of Member States involving at least 15 Member States, and
- These Member States represent 65 per cent of the EU population.

This is complex, but there are two key messages. First, that no individual Member State has a veto over the adoption of legislation even though those laws will bind that Member State. The original position was that unanimity was required for most areas, i.e. that each individual state had a veto. As the Union grew, consensus became less likely and QMV has been extended to more and more subject areas. Unlike the EU, most international agreements allow states to either veto or opt out of new legal commitments. Secondly, most international agreements proceed on the basis of one state equals one vote, regardless of their size. The fact that QMV includes an EU population requirement shows that the EU is a Union not only of states but also of peoples.

EXPLAINING THE LAW – THE ROLE OF THE COUNCIL OF MINISTERS

As an illustration of this law-making role (which also includes policy-making and international relations), in October 2017, the Council confirmed support for new directives on the safety of passenger ferries including inspections of roll-on roll-off ferries. As an example of its international policy-making role it agreed the EU negotiating position on the use of forestry to address climate change targets under the Paris Climate Change agreement.

http://www.european-council.europa.eu/en/council-eu/

8.6 EUROPEAN COMMISSION

Under Article 17 TEU, the Commission shall be completely independent. It promotes the interests of the EU as a whole, rather than the separate interests of the Member States or political groupings.

8.6.1 COMPOSITION

The Commission is composed of:

A College of Commissioners – with one Commissioner from each of the 28 Member States. The Commissioners are 'chosen on the grounds of their general competence and whose independence is beyond doubt'. They are initially nominated by their Member State

Government but once appointed must not seek or take instructions from that Government. They are not representatives of the Member States. The post is held for a renewable five-year term.

A Commission President – nominated by the European Council and then elected by the Parliament. The President heads the Commission, distributes roles and has oversight of its general policy and legislative proposals.

Directorate-Generals – these are similar to national Government ministries in that they comprise civil servants who support the work of the Commissioners. They include subject areas such as Trade (a traditionally powerful DG), Environment and Energy and support services, such as translation. The Commission is huge by international organisation standards (around 25,000–30,000 staff), but tiny by national Government standards.

8.6.2 ROLE

The Commission has a number of functions beyond a general co-ordinating, executive and management role (Article 17 TEU):

- Legislative initiative – the Commission initiates all legislative acts in the Union. It can be subject to requests and influence from the Council and the Parliament, but it makes its own decisions on what legislative proposals go forward and on the first draft. This is a very important agenda-setting power.
- Guardian of the Treaties – it must, together with the Court, ensure that EU law is observed and enforced. Under Article 258 TFEU, it can bring enforcement actions against Member States for failure to implement EU law or for breaches of those laws.
- Budgetary powers – the Commission administers the EU budget (of around 140 billion euros). Revenues are raised through Member State contributions, external tariffs and VAT. Much of the expenditure is fixed (in the Common Agricultural Policy), but the Commission has some discretion in the spending of structural funds to aid development in poorer areas of the Union.

There is some oversight of the Commission's work, in part from the Court of Auditors, but principally from Parliament. In 1999, following allegations of waste and mismanagement, Parliament considered a motion of censure against the Commission. It did not pass by the required two-thirds majority, but the Commissioners nevertheless resigned en masse.

EXPLAINING THE LAW – THE COMMISSION'S ROLE

In October 2017, the Commission agreed 30 billion euro of investment in scientific innovation. It started a consultation on how to tax economic activity fairly in a digital economy. It agreed its 2018 work programme which includes a policy focus on job creation, a digital single market and progress on a trade deal with the USA, and completion of 66 legislative proposals.

http://ec.europa.eu/index_en.htm

8.7 EUROPEAN PARLIAMENT

The Parliament represents the direct political interests of the peoples of Europe.

8.7.1 COMPOSITION

There are currently 751 Members of the European Parliament (MEPs), and seats are distributed between states (very broadly) according to population. The most populous state, Germany (82 million inhabitants), has 96 seats; the UK (66 million) has 73 seats; Malta (0.4 million) has 6 seats.

The MEPs do not sit in national groups but rather in political ones. These range from far-left wing to far-right wing, and the two main groupings are the European People's Party (which is centre-right) and the Progressive Alliance of Socialists and Democrats (which is centre-left). This shows that the Parliament does not represent Member State interests but rather the political views of European people. For example, the second-largest grouping, the Socialists and Democrats, have MEPs from all 28 Member States, and these MEPs work together to promote centre-left political views from all those countries.

Of the main UK parties, Labour is in the Socialists and Democrats grouping, and the Liberal Democrats are in the Alliance of Liberals and Democrats for Europe. The Conservatives controversially left the European People's Party umbrella grouping, to join European Conservatives and Reformists (a more Eurosceptic group).

MEPs are elected every five years, and direct elections have been held since 1979. Elections must be proportionate but the detailed rules are left to each nation state. The UK is split into constituencies representing Scotland, Wales, Northern Ireland and the English regions, for example North West England which returns eight MEPs. Voting is by party list rather than individual candidates. Turnout in European Parliamentary elections has been a problem, with less than 50 per cent turnout across Europe.

8.7.2 ROLE

The Parliament's role was originally very limited. It was made up of delegates from national Parliaments and acted purely in an advisory capacity. Since direct elections were introduced in 1979, the Parliament has been able to claim to be the representative voice of the peoples of Europe, and with this its formal powers have grown, particularly in relation to law-making.

This is seen most clearly in the changes to the main legislative processes used over the last decades, and the way in which the Council of Ministers have had to progressively share more power with the Parliament.

- The original *consultation process* merely involved consulting the Parliament, which had no veto over proposals.
- The later *co-operation process* gave greater power to the Parliament with its approval of a proposal making it easier for the Council to adopt.
- The more recent *co-decision* process gives the Parliament an equal status to the Council, in that a proposal cannot become law without the consent of the Parliament.

The central role of the Parliament in the law-making process is confirmed by the Lisbon Treaty, which casts a version of co-decision as the 'ordinary legislative process'. The Parliament sits in plenary (whole session) around 12–14 times per year, and lots of preparatory work is done in committees.

Beyond law-making, the Parliament's other main role lies in supervision and accountability, particularly of the Commission. The Commission must respond to questions put by MEPs and supply an annual report. Parliament must confirm the appointment of Commissioners and can block their appointment. It can dismiss the whole Commission by a vote of censure with a two-thirds majority.

Other institutions, including the European Council and the Council of Ministers, need to report to the Parliament. The Parliament can also hold other institutions legally to account by bringing an action directly before the Court of Justice e.g. for infringement of the Treaty.

EXPLAINING THE LAW – THE ROLE OF THE PARLIAMENT

As an example of this law-making role, in October 2017, the Parliament agreed stricter rules to protect workers from exposure to carcinogens at work.

http://www.europarl.europa.eu/portal/

8.8 COURT OF JUSTICE

The original European Court of Justice has evolved into a, still relatively small, court system comprising the Court of Justice of the European Union, a General Court and an employment tribunal for EU employees.

8.8.1 COMPOSITION

There is one judge from each Member State in both the Court of Justice and the General Court. They normally sit in chambers of three or five. Each judge is nominated by their Member State and must be independent and impartial. They must have the same qualifications needed for the highest judicial office in their own country.

The Court is assisted by eight Advocates General, who provide reasoned opinions to the Court. These are in-depth reviews of the relevant legal position, assessment of the arguments of the parties and include a recommendation to the Court. This recommendation is followed in the majority of cases but is only advisory and the Court can (and occasionally does) depart from it.

8.8.2 ROLE

The Court's role is to interpret and apply the Treaty, to make sure that EU law is observed. This can happen through three main types of action:

- Direct actions under Article 258 TFEU – these are cases brought by the Commission against a Member State either for not properly implementing an EU law into its legal system, or for not observing that law in practice.
- Judicial reviews – these are allegations brought by an EU institution or a Member State that an institution of the EU (most commonly the Commission) has gone beyond its powers (TFEU Articles 263 and 265).
- Preliminary references under Article 267 TFEU – this is where a national court makes a reference to the Court of Justice seeking a ruling on the correct interpretation of a point of EU law. The Court aims for a consistent interpretation of EU law across all Member States. It can only provide a ruling on the meaning of the EU law, and the way that it is ultimately applied to the facts is still a matter for the national court.

The General Court has a particular jurisdiction on judicial reviews, and direct actions on subjects like competition law and agriculture.

The Court has been active and innovative throughout its history. It has developed some of the most important concepts in the development of the European Union and has often been at the forefront of the drive to 'an ever closer union of the peoples of Europe'. This includes the development of legal concepts such as the supremacy of EU law, the direct effect of a wide range of EU laws within Member State legal systems and new ways for individuals to enforce their EU law rights (indirect effect, state liability).

EXPLAINING THE LAW – THE COURT'S ROLE

In Case C-337/89 *Commission v UK (Drinking Water)*, the Court had to consider an allegation of both failure to implement and failure to observe EU law. The Drinking

Water Directive required maximum levels of certain pollutants (including nitrates) in drinking water supplies. The UK had not implemented the Directive in Scotland or Northern Ireland in the required time. The UK tried to plead internal difficulties but the Court refused to accept these and found a breach of EU law.

The Commission also alleged a breach of law in that the nitrate level had been exceeded in a number of supply areas in England. The UK argued that it was only under an obligation to take all practicable steps to improve water quality, not an absolute obligation to meet the quality standards. This was rejected by the Court, and it observed that the results outlined in EU law must be achieved. This illustrates the generally hard line that the Court has adopted to the enforcement of EU law.

http://europa.eu/about-eu/institutions-bodies/court-justice/

8.9 OTHER INSTITUTIONS

The other formal institutions outlined in the Lisbon Treaty are the European Central Bank which administers the Euro currency and the monetary policy of the Eurozone, and the Court of Auditors which provides financial audits of the use of the EU budget.

KEY LEARNING POINTS

- The EU has been primarily concerned with trade, but the objective of 'ever closer union' makes it dynamic and it is more integrated than other trading organisations.
- EU institutions are largely independent from the Member States.
- The institutions work together to make policy, create laws and then apply and enforce those laws.

8.10 SUPREMACY OF EU LAW – COURT OF JUSTICE PERSPECTIVE

The Court of Justice of the European Union asserts that EU law is supreme and takes precedence over national law in all circumstances. The original Treaty never explicitly said this, and even the Lisbon Treaty has no legal rule outlining this supremacy (although it does have a non–binding declaration). The development of supremacy, therefore, involved a considerable degree of judicial activism.

This supremacy was constructed from a number of elements, such as the broad Treaty objective of an 'ever closer union', the duty of Member States to apply EU law and the

Treaty description of a 'regulation' (a type of EU legal rule) as 'binding in its entirety and directly applicable in all Member States'. Nevertheless, it was the approach of the Court in a series of judgments that was the prime mover behind the development of the supremacy of EU law.

KEY CASE – *VAN GEND EN LOOS V NEDERLANDSE ADMINISTRATIE DER BELASTINGEN* [1963] ECR 1

This case was more concerned with whether EU law created rights for individuals that could be enforced within national legal systems ('direct effect'), but the judgment also raised the idea that the Member States had created a new legal order and thereby limited their sovereign rights. The Treaty was 'more than an agreement which merely creates mutual obligations between the contracting states', but rather it had 'created its own legal system' which . . . became an integral part of the legal systems of the Member States and which their courts are bound to apply'.

The Court pointed out that the Community had 'unlimited duration . . . its own institutions, its own personality, its own legal capacity and capacity of representation on the international plane'. This ultimately meant that 'the Member States have limited their sovereign rights, albeit within limited fields, and have created a body of law which binds both their nationals and themselves'.

There is no explicit message on supremacy here, but the implications of

(a) Member States being voluntarily bound by a body of EU law, and
(b) EU law giving enforceable rights to individuals within their country, and
(c) national courts being bound to apply EU law

does point towards a higher status for EU law as against national law.

KEY CASE – *COSTA V ENEL* (1964) ECR 585

The Italian Government nationalised power companies in 1962. Costa had been a shareholder in one of those companies, and considered that the nationalisation had infringed his legal rights under the EEC Treaty. The case proceeded slightly unusually, as Costa protested this alleged breach by refusing to pay his electricity bill. The nationalised electricity company sued him for the value of the bill (which was equivalent to less than £1).

The Italian court made a preliminary reference, i.e. asked a question of the Court of Justice as to whether the Italian law or the alleged Treaty right applied. The issue for the Italian court was that the nationalisation (1962) had taken place after the Treaty (1957). The normal rule in judicial interpretation is that a later law prevails over an earlier inconsistent law. On the substance of the case, the Court of Justice found that Costa had no individual rights under the Treaty, but went on to make a general statement about the status of EU law.

Under the 'terms and spirit of the Treaty', it was impossible for the states 'to accord precedence to a unilateral and subsequent measure' – i.e. give effect to a later national law that was inconsistent with EU law. The Court explained that 'The executive force of Community law cannot vary from one state to another in deference to subsequent domestic laws', and that 'the laws stemming from the Treaty . . . could not . . . be overridden by domestic legal provisions, however framed . . . without the legal basis of the Community itself being called into question'.

We need to pick out the significance of the word 'subsequent'. *Van Gend en Loos* made it clear that EU law took effect within national legal systems. According to typical practices across legal systems, this new law would impliedly repeal all existing national law that was inconsistent with it. The important implication of *Costa* is that if an inconsistent national law is introduced *after* the EU law, then this cannot take precedence over the earlier EU law; even a subsequent national law cannot impliedly repeal an existing EU law.

You might think that there must be some limit to this primacy of EU law, and it does only apply within the limited fields set out by the Treaty, i.e. those legal areas within the competence of the EU (trade, competition, agriculture, environment, etc). Within these fields, however, *Costa* said that EU law could not be overridden by domestic law, 'however framed'. What if the national law that conflicted with EU law had some special constitutional status? Can EU law take precedence even in those circumstances?

KEY CASE – *INTERNATIONALE HANDELSGESELLSCHAFT* (1970) ECR 1125

The case itself involves the operation of an agricultural regulatory regime – licences for the import and export of maize. The scheme, applied by the European Commission, was that if a company wanted to export maize, it had to apply for a licence that included a quota of the volume of produce, e.g. 100 tonnes. If the company did not use its full quota, then it had to make a penalty payment. That is, it was a scheme under which companies had to potentially forfeit property.

The German company in this case alleged that this scheme infringed their rights as guaranteed by the German national constitution, particularly their rights to property and the principle of proportionality. As we saw in Chapter 4, 'Constitutions', aspects of the German Basic Law are completely entrenched, i.e. regarded as so fundamental that they cannot be altered by the German parliament, Government, courts or peoples.

So there was an alleged conflict between a) fundamental entrenched German constitutional laws on the one hand and b) a rather mundane agricultural regulatory provision of EU law on the other hand. Which law took precedence? According to the Court of Justice, it was the EU law. It does not matter what the status of the national law is; if there is any conflict whatsoever between an applicable provision of EU law and a national law, then the national law must give way.

The Court explained that 'the validity of a Community measure or its effect within a Member State cannot be affected by allegations that it runs counter to either fundamental rights as formulated by the constitution of that state or the principles of the national constitutional structure'. Allowing exceptions for national constitutional rules would harm the uniformity and effectiveness of EU law.

This even extended to provisions of the German Basic Law which were completely entrenched. The Court tried to soften the blow (or defuse a major European constitutional crisis), by asserting that fundamental rights are a part of EU law and these rights are derived from national legal orders. There should, in practice, be no major inconsistencies between national fundamental rights and EU law, and in this particular case, it was ultimately found that the company's constitutional rights had not been breached by the EU law.

Whilst EU law supremacy had been judicially established, at least from the perspective of the Court of Justice, there remained questions of how to give this supremacy the widest possible effect. Most lower-level courts in most Member States would not have the power, according to their national constitutions, to override provisions of national legislation.

KEY CASE – *AMMINISTRAZIONE DELLE FINANZE DELLO STATO V SIMMENTHAL SPA* [1979] ECR 777

The case concerned whether health checks on foodstuffs imported from France into Italy amounted to an unlawful restriction on the free movement of goods. The significance of the case lies in the Court's explanation of the duty imposed on *all national courts* by the primacy of EU law.

The Court said that all institutions within a country must ensure that EU laws are fully and uniformly applied in Member States from the time they come into force.

This means that national courts do not have to wait for an inconsistent national law to be repealed by the national parliament. National courts, themselves, must set aside any provision of national law which may conflict with EU law, whether prior or subsequent to the EU rule.

So the obligation falls on national courts operating within national legal systems. 'Every national court' has to give priority to EU law (regardless of when the national and EU laws were passed). There is a related obligation on national parliaments to refrain from legislating in breach of EU law.

There was some discussion of whether to include this principle of EU law primacy in the Lisbon Treaty. It was ultimately decided not to do so, but to include a Declaration instead (Declaration 17). This is not legally operative but records the Member States' understanding of the existing legal position:

in accordance with well settled case law of the Court of Justice of the European Union, the Treaties and the law adopted by the Union on the basis of the Treaties have primacy over the law of Member States, under the conditions laid down by the said case law.

And:

At the time of the first judgment of this established case law (Costa/ENEL, 15 July 1964, Case 6/64) there was no mention of primacy in the treaty. It is still the case today. The fact that the principle of primacy will not be included in the future treaty shall not in any way change the existence of the principle and the existing case-law of the Court of Justice.

ANALYSING THE LAW – COMPETING SUPREMACIES

So from the point of view of the Court of Justice, EU law is simply and absolutely supreme, but do national courts share that attitude? If you think back to the previous chapter, you can see the problem for the UK constitution. If EU law is part of the UK legal system and has primacy over any provision of UK law, where does that leave the supremacy of the Westminster Parliament? The two sources of law might rub along together for a while, but there will ultimately come a time where both a UK Act of Parliament and an enforceable EU law seem to govern the same situation *and* lay down different rules. Applying both rules will be impossible, so the way in which the UK courts give precedence to one source of law over another will tell us much about where legal supremacy lies under the UK constitution.

8.11 EU LAW IN THE UK

The UK is a dualist country. This means that international obligations do not automatically become part of the domestic legal system. They only take effect domestically when there is some Act of Parliament (or secondary legislation) to translate them into national law: 'We take no notice of treaties until they are embodied in laws enacted by Parliament, and then only to the extent that Parliament tells us' (*Blackburn v Attorney General* [1971] 1 WLR 1037, per Lord Denning). EU law therefore required an Act of Parliament before it could apply within the UK legal systems. This was the European Communities Act 1972.

8.11.1 THE EUROPEAN COMMUNITIES ACT 1972

The ECA 1972 does not expressly say that EU law is supreme, and it is difficult to disentangle the enormously significant constitutional effects of ss.2 and 3 ECA 1972 from their complex and obscure wording. It seems that the UK Government did not want to baldly state 'EU law is part of our legal system and it is supreme'. Both the reception of EU law into the UK and its primacy over national law, however, can be derived from interpreting s.2(1), s.2(4) and s.3(1).

KEY STATUTE – THE EUROPEAN COMMUNITIES ACT 1972

Section 2

1(1) All rights from time to time created by the Treaties, are without further enactment to be given legal effect . . . and shall be recognised and available in law, and be enforced, allowed and followed accordingly . . .

2(4) . . . any enactment passed or to be passed, shall be construed and have effect subject to the foregoing provisions of this section.

Section 3

1(1) For the purposes of all legal proceedings any question as to the meaning or effect of any of the Treaties, or as to the validity, meaning or effect of any Community instrument, shall be treated as a question of law (and, if not referred to the European Court, be for determination as such in accordance with the principles laid down by and any relevant decision of the European Court).

Section 2(1) means that enforceable EU laws are to be given effect within the UK 'without further ado' (*Bulmer v Bollinger* [1974] Ch 401, per Lord Denning). The phrase 'from time to time created under the Treaties' means that future laws created by EU institutions after 1973 would also take effect in the UK without further ado. Section 2(1) is therefore *a gateway section*; it is the portal through which EU law enters the UK legal systems.

Section 2(4) is even more opaque. Looking at it, you would hardly imagine that it introduces the concept of another source of law having primacy over Westminster Acts of Parliament.

ANALYSING THE LAW – SECTION 2(4) ECA

> any enactment passed or to be passed, shall be construed and have effect subject to the foregoing provisions of this section

We need to break this subsection down into its constituent parts to make sense of it.

- ■ 'Any enactment' – including Acts of Parliament . . .
- ■ 'passed or to be passed' – applies to future Acts of Parliament . . .
- ■ 'shall be construed and have effect subject to' – can only be applied if . . .
- ■ 'the foregoing provisions of this section' – . . . they are consistent with enforceable EU law.

Section 3 ECA reinforces this message of the primacy of EU law. When UK courts are considering questions as to the meaning and effect, including the status of, EU law, they must act 'in accordance' with the relevant principles and decisions of the Court of Justice. We have just seen what these principles and decisions are – that EU law is supreme and takes precedence over national law.

APPLYING THE LAW – SECTION 3 ECA

Question – summarise the principles and decisions of the Court of Justice on the **effect** of EU law.
Answer – EU law takes precedence over national law, with no exceptions.
Question – summarise the principles and decisions of the Court of Justice on the **validity** of EU law.
Answer – the validity of EU law is not affected by inconsistent national laws, including constitutional rules.

The European Communities Act 1972 therefore gives a very strong steer to UK courts to give primacy to EU law over inconsistent UK law, but does not explicitly say *how* they are to do this, or what to make of the apparent clash with the 'keystone of the Constitution' – the traditional view of Parliamentary supremacy. We need to consider the response of the UK courts to this difficult challenge.

> **KEY LEARNING POINTS**
> ....
>
> - The supremacy of EU law was constructed by the Court of Justice.
> - This supremacy is absolute. There are no exceptions.
> - UK courts are required to give effect to this supremacy through provisions of the ECA 1972.

8.12 THE ISSUE OF SUPREMACY IN THE UK COURTS

The clash between the primacy of EU law and the traditional view of the supremacy of Parliament was always likely to be difficult to resolve. It is understandable, therefore, that the courts sought to find the consistencies between the two sources of law rather the differences, and to resolve any difficulties, as far as they could, through interpretation.

In *Garland v British Rail Engineering Ltd (No 2)* (1983) 2 AC 751, Lord Diplock expressed the traditional view that courts are to interpret Acts of Parliament as far as possible to be consistent with international obligations. This does not represent any radical extension of the pre-existing approach. In *Pickstone v Freemans Limited plc* [1989] AC 66, Lord Oliver went a step further by suggesting that courts must depart from the obvious meaning of words in a statute to give effect to EU law obligations. This active form of interpretation can resolve most issues, but judges from the 1970s onwards were also exploring the wider implications of the ECA 1972.

APPLYING THE LAW – EQUAL PAY

Both EU law and UK law have provisions on equal pay between men and women. UK law seemed to limit this requirement to where the man and woman are doing the *same work at the same time*. The EU law can be interpreted as requiring equal pay when the man and the woman are doing *equal work, even if this happens at different times.*

Imagine that Blakeburn Bus Company employs 100 bus drivers who all have the same roles and responsibilities. If the company pays its 25 women drivers less than its 75 men drivers, then this is clearly a breach of the equality laws of both the EU and the UK. If the company has one marketing director, a post previously held by a man, and they hire a woman to fill this post and pay her only 80 per cent of the previous salary, have they broken the equal pay laws? If we interpret the EU law as covering this situation (equal work in succession), but the UK law as not prohibiting this conduct (only applying to equal work at the same time), then which legal rule applies? Does the EU law take precedence over the UK law?

This was the scenario facing the Court of Appeal in a case that laid out important principles on the relationship between UK and EU law.

KEY CASE – *MACARTHYS V SMITH* [1979] 3 ALL ER 325

The defendant company was paying Mrs Smith less for her job as storeroom manager than the previous (male) manager.

'. . . the employers say that the woman and the man must be employed by the same employer on like work *at the same time*: whereas here Mrs Smith was employed on like work in succession to Mr McCullough and not at the same time as he. To solve this problem I propose to turn first to the principle of equal pay contained in the EEC Treaty, for that takes priority even over our own statute' (Lord Denning).

Lord Denning considered what would happen if the UK passed legislation which was inconsistent with the Treaty and concluded that 'the principles laid down in the Treaty are "without further enactment" to be given legal effect in the United Kingdom; and have priority over "any enactment passed or to be passed" by our Parliament'.

The first step should always be interpretation, but the courts would sometimes need to go beyond that: 'In construing our statute, we are entitled to look to the Treaty as an aid in its construction: and even more, not only as an aid, but as an overriding force. If on close inspection it should appear that our legislation is . . . inconsistent with Community law . . . then it is our bounden duty to give priority to Community law' (per Lord Denning).

On the facts, Lord Denning thought that the UK statute could reasonably easily be interpreted in a manner consistent with the EU law. The majority disagreed with him and required a reference to the Court of Justice. The Court answered that the EU law applied to the *Macarthys* situation, and the employer accepted defeat.

The position was clear in principle, that EU law took precedence over inconsistent UK law including Acts of Parliament. In practice, through the 1970s and much of the 1980s, the UK courts had been able to resolve any apparent differences between EU and UK law through a process of interpretation (i.e. finding that they were not inconsistent). No UK court had yet to undertake the constitutionally awkward process of actually declaring that a valid UK Act of Parliament could not apply to a situation before it, because some other law had primacy. Then came *Factortame*.

8.13 THE *FACTORTAME* CASES

Under the Common Fisheries Policy, each EU country has an annual quota of fish that its fishing fleets can take from their waters. The British quota had to be allocated between 'British' fishing vessels. A number of Spanish fishing vessel owners set up British companies and registered their ships as British vessels. These 'British' ships were then allocated a part of the British national quota, despite being owned and crewed by Spanish citizens, sailing out of Spanish ports and landing their catches back in Spain. This was known as 'quota hopping'. Take a moment to imagine any discussions about this practice between the British fishermen of Brixham, Fleetwood or Grimsby, and the British Government.

This led to the Merchant Shipping Act 1988, an Act of Parliament that imposed new requirements for registration of a British fishing vessel. These were, very broadly, that the vessel had to be controlled out of the UK and the owners/shareholders had to be at least 75 per cent British with residence in the UK. This did, however, seem to conflict with fundamental provisions of the Treaty, that there should be no discrimination between nationals of EU states on the grounds of their nationality, and that individuals had the right to set up businesses anywhere in the EU.

KEY CASE – *R V SECRETARY OF STATE FOR TRANSPORT, EX PARTE FACTORTAME (NO 1) [1990] 2 AC 85*

Resolving the case would take a number of years, so the Spanish fishermen asked the court for *interim relief*. This is where a court issues an order that protects the rights of a party during the time it takes for a final judgment to be made. In this case, granting the relief that the fishermen were asking for would have amounted to 'disapplying' the Merchant Shipping Act 1988. A problem for the applicants was that they were asking for something (a court order that an Act of Parliament did not apply) that did not seem to exist under UK law or the UK constitution. A problem for the UK court was that failing to grant the interim relief could mean that the fishermen's rights under the Treaty were not being protected.

The House of Lords decided that it could not grant the interim relief and made a preliminary reference to the Court of Justice.

APPLYING THE LAW

Go back to what you read above on the *Internationale Handelsgesellschaft* and *Simmenthal* cases and try to predict the outcome of this preliminary reference.

The *Internationale Handelsgesellschaft* case should tell you that any internal constitutional difficulties that the UK courts had in issuing interim relief against the Crown, or which had the effect of disapplying an Act of Parliament, would be of no real concern to the Court of Justice. The 'principles of the national constitutional structure' could have no effect on the validity of an EU law.

Simmenthal should show you that the national courts have responsibility for giving effect to the primacy of EU law. One way of resolving the conflict would be for the European Commission to put pressure on the UK Government to repeal the offending parts of the Merchant Shipping Act 1988, and for the UK Parliament to then do so (and something like this did eventually happen). Nevertheless, this does not take away from the obligation on the UK courts to give effect to the EU law from the time it comes into force.

So you should have worked out that the Court of Justice responded by stating that the national court must do whatever was required to protect rights under EU law, including granting interim relief that sets aside a national law. The House of Lords then had to apply this ruling to the facts of the case.

KEY CASE – *R V SECRETARY OF STATE FOR TRANSPORT EX PARTE FACTORTAME (NO 2)* [1991] 1 AC 603

The House of Lords accepted the ruling and granted interim relief to the Spanish fishermen. The historic effect of this was that, for the first time in the modern era, a UK court decided that it could not apply a valid UK Act of Parliament to the case before it.

Lord Bridge said that the supremacy of Community law over national law:

> . . . was certainly well established in the jurisprudence of the European Court of Justice long before the United Kingdom joined the Community. Thus, whatever limitation of its sovereignty Parliament accepted when it enacted the European

> Communities Act 1972 was entirely voluntary. Under the terms of the Act of 1972 it has always been clear that it was the duty of a United Kingdom court to override any rule of national law found to be in conflict with any directly enforceable rule of EU law.

Thus, the Merchant Shipping Act 1988 was 'disapplied'. There is a very important point to understand here. The Act was not found to be 'invalid' or 'void'. Only parts of the Act were disapplied, and only in the circumstances of this case. The Merchant Shipping Act 1988 was still a valid Act, and any provisions of the Act which did not breach EU law would have to be applied by the courts in relevant cases.

APPLYING THE LAW – DISAPPLYING STATUTES

Imagine that a group of Canadian fishermen tried to 'quota hop' by setting up British companies and registering their vessels as British so as to obtain a part of the UK quota. Would the UK courts be able to apply the Merchant Shipping Act 1988 rules on registration of vessels to the Canadians?

The answer is yes, and the UK courts would be obliged to do so. The Canadian fishermen have no rights under EU law. There is no conflicting EU law to which the UK courts have to give primacy. A valid UK Act of Parliament regulates the situation, and so (and you can go back to the sorts of statements made in e.g. *Pickin v British Railways Board*) the courts are obliged to obey and apply that Act.

8.13.1 ASSESSMENT ADVICE

A large majority of assessment questions (coursework, exam or presentation) on supremacy of Parliament will require you to cover the impact of the European Communities Act 1972 and *Factortame*. Too many assessment answers treat what we have covered so far as the end of the story, and conclude along the lines of – '*in Factortame the UK courts disapplied an Act of Parliament, therefore Westminster Parliament is no longer supreme*'.

We have not, however, reached the end of the story just yet. To reach the next level, you need to analyse the effects of *Factortame* and differentiate between its consequences on implied and express repeal. To reach this next level, you need to engage with some of the different academic views on the nature of the changes wrought by *Factortame*. Below, we introduce you to the 'revolution/evolution' debate between HWR Wade and Sir John Laws.

8.14 EU LAW AND EXPRESS/IMPLIED REPEAL

Let us remind ourselves of the normal rules on implied repeal of statutes. We would *expect* to see:

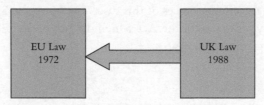

Inconsistent laws with no express reference to the earlier law

EU Law 1972

UK Law 1988

Normal rule? Later law *impliedly repeals* earlier law

Figure 8.4 Standard implied repeal process

The European Communities Act 1972 (ECA 1972) as interpreted and applied by the House of Lords in *Factortame* changes this. The EU Treaty provisions, which only take effect in the UK through this 1972 Act of Parliament, were not impliedly repealed by the 1988 Act of Parliament.

In *Factortame*, Lord Bridge said the ECA 1972 had 'precisely the same effect as if a section were incorporated' in the Merchant Shipping Act 1988 which 'enacted that the provisions with respect to registration of British fishing vessels were to be without prejudice to directly enforceable EU rights'. Lord Bridge's 'invisible section' instructed the courts to give priority to EU law in a conflict with a later Act of Parliament. Logically, this 'invisible section' must have been included in every single Act of Parliament passed since 1972.

What Lord Bridge says he is outlining here is a rule of interpretation (we will see below that Wade does not accept that this is what was really happening). The courts are generally concerned in statutory interpretation to give effect to the intentions of Parliament. Normally this is done by looking at the words in the Act, but membership of the EU is of such constitutional importance that it departs from this normal rule of interpretation. The courts need to understand the ongoing instruction from Parliament that it intends to legislate in accordance with EU law, and if an Act fails to achieve this then Parliament wants the courts to give precedence to EU law. The position now is:

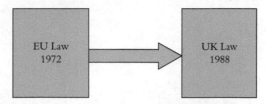

Inconsistent laws with no express reference to earlier law

EU Law 1972 → UK Law 1988

Following *Factortame, normal rules on implied repeal do not apply.* EC law will take precedence even over a later UK law.

Figure 8.5 Implied repeal following *Factortame*

8.14.1 EXPRESS REPEAL

This still leaves the question of what would happen if Parliament tried expressly to repeal an existing EU law.

APPLYING THE LAW

What if the Merchant Shipping Act 1988 had actually said, 'notwithstanding EU laws on non-discrimination . . .', or even, 'EU laws on non-discrimination are hereby repealed in the field of fishing vessel registration'?

You should be able to deduce the answer from what the *Factortame* case had to say about implied repeal. Lord Bridge was careful not to say that the UK courts were giving primacy to EU law because the Court of Justice had told them that EU law was supreme. He based his position on the intention of the UK Parliament. Parliament, in his view, had made it clear that it wanted the UK courts, on a day-to-day continuing basis, to give precedence to EU laws. The implication of this is that if Parliament clearly signalled a very different intention (by express repeal using explicit language), then the courts would obey that new instruction from Parliament.

On this account, the Westminster Parliament retains the ability to have the final say on any aspect of law in the UK. There would be very difficult practical and legal difficulties in the UK's relationship with the EU if Parliament decided to exercise this option, but in constitutional theory the position is the same as that explained by Lord Denning in 1979:

Thus far, I have assumed that our Parliament, whenever it passes legislation, intends to fulfil its obligations under the Treaty. If the time should come when our Parliament deliberately passes an Act with the intention of repudiating the Treaty or any provision in it or intentionally of acting inconsistently with it and says so in express terms then I should have thought that it would be the duty of our courts to follow the statute of our Parliament.

(*Macarthys v Smith* [1979] 3 All ER 325)

That is:

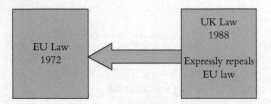

Following *Factortame*, courts recognise that *day-to-day* Parliament wishes them to give priority to EU law, BUT ultimately Parliament *retains the right to expressly repudiate EU law* and the courts will give effect to that ultimate intention.

Figure 8.6 Express repeal of EU law

This approach was reinforced by s.18 European Union Act 2011 which states that:

Directly applicable or directly effective EU law . . . falls to be recognised and available in law in the United Kingdom only by virtue of [the ECA 1972] or where it is required to be recognised and available in law by virtue of any other Act.

The key message from this rather abstruse provision is that EU law takes effect in the UK only because Parliament says that it does, with the direct implication that Parliament retains the power to change its mind and stop EU law having this effect.

KEY LEARNING POINTS

- The traditional rules on implied repeal have changed in respect to EU law. An EU law cannot be impliedly repealed by a later Act of Parliament.
- Parliament can still expressly repeal EU law, and the UK courts would give effect to that intention.

8.15 DIFFERING INTERPRETATIONS

There are two competing positions on interpreting the nature of the changes that have been wrought by the ECA 1972 and *Factortame*: the *revolution* and the *evolution* interpretations.

Wade argues that the changes are *revolutionary*. He points out that the normal rule under the UK constitution is that a later Act impliedly repeals an inconsistent earlier Act, and that the Treaty provisions entered the UK legal system through an Act of Parliament: the European Communities Act 1972. He describes *Factortame* as a 'constitutional revolution' because the 1972 Parliament has 'succeeded in binding the Parliament of 1988 and restricting its sovereignty, something that was supposed to be constitutionally impossible'.[1]

It is important to grasp that Wade is using 'revolution' in its technical sense, and not just as a description of a major change. Since allowing an earlier Parliament to bind a later Parliament was not legally possible under the UK constitution, then the courts have technically breached the existing constitutional order and put a new order in its place.

Laws adopts the *evolution* interpretation. He argues that the decision in *Factortame* merely provides 'a rule of construction for later statutes' and that this interpretive approach (derived from s.2(4) ECA 1972) 'cannot be abrogated by an implied repeal'.[2] He compares this to other situations where the courts will only be directed by express words in a statute, e.g. to impose criminal liability or retrospective effect.

In other words, the courts have taken the unique challenge of EU law primacy and absorbed it into their existing and established methods of interpreting statute. There are certain issues where Parliament's continuing intentions are clear (e.g. the courts have good reason to believe that Parliament does not intend to legislate with retrospective effect or extra-territorial effect) and the courts respect those continuing intentions. Similarly, the courts have very good reason to believe that Parliament has a continuing intention that the UK legal system is in accord with the UK's obligations under EU law.

ANALYSING THE LAW

Which position should you adopt? The best minds in UK Constitutional Law have debated this for some time and reached different conclusions, so please do not feel compelled to try to find a single 'right answer' yourself. What is important is that you understand the different positions outlined here and the reasons supporting them, and try to work out which position you feel is stronger.

Wade supports his revolution idea by pointing to the yawning gap between the great statements of principle from generations of judges on the traditional view of supremacy (that Parliament cannot bind itself) and the bare fact of what happened in *Factortame* (an earlier Parliament binding a later Parliament). He is also sceptical about

---

1   H W R Wade, 'Sovereignty – Revolution or Evolution?' [1996] *Law Quarterly Review* 568.
2   Sir John Laws, 'Law and Democracy' [1995] *Public Law* 57.

the language used in both the ECA and *Factortame*, arguing that both Parliament and the judges have shied away from acknowledging the scale of the changes.

For Laws, the evolution position is that *Factortame* is ultimately concerned with the interpretation of statute, and there are existing categories of laws where the UK courts will only be moved by express words in later statute. *Factortame* is an important evolution of these existing areas, but it is not a revolution. He finds support from the language used by Lord Bridge in the case itself.

The position adopted here leans more towards Wade's revolution interpretation than Laws' evolution approach. The Merchant Shipping Act 1988 was clear in its provisions. The only reasonable interpretation of that Act could be that it wanted to impose nationality and residence requirements. If it had been as unambiguous about imposing criminal liability (or retrospective effect or extra-territorial effect), then regardless of interpretive principles the courts would have applied the 1988 Act. The fact they did not shows that we are not dealing with the extension of an existing interpretive approach, but rather a whole new category. Saying that a clear and unconditional statute cannot be applied because of the existence of an earlier law goes beyond statutory interpretation and into the constitutional question of what source of law has supremacy within the UK legal system.

In the previous chapter, we were impressed with Wade's argument that in treating Acts of Parliament as supreme, the courts were recognising the 'ultimate political fact' of the constitution. That is arguably what has happened here. The courts have not simply extended existing approaches to interpreting statutes. Instead, in granting protection from implied repeal to EU law, they are recognising a new 'ultimate political fact'. Wade puts too much emphasis on the sole role of judges in this process, and it would be better to say that they are a part of a process (together with Parliament and the Government) of producing and recognising a revised 'ultimate political fact' of the UK constitution that takes account of our membership of the EU. In the same way, when Brexit occurs there will be a new ultimate political fact for the courts to absorb and respond to.

8.16 CONSTITUTIONAL STATUTES

The courts response to EU law represented a departure from the classical Diceyan view of statutes – that they all have exactly the same constitutional status. The judges in Factortame recognised that there could be forms of higher law which were protected from implied repeal. This raises a further question – does this category contain a single item (EU law) or could Acts of Parliament on other subjects fall into this protected category? Laws LJ, in his judicial capacity, has argued that there is indeed a wider concept of 'constitutional statutes'.

KEY CASE – *THOBURN V SUNDERLAND CITY COUNCIL* [2002] 1 CMLR 50

Thoburn, a Sunderland greengrocer, was charged with breaching EU regulations by displaying and selling his produce only in imperial measurements (pounds and ounces). The regulations required prominence for metric measures (kilos and grams) in the sale of goods. Thoburn, and the other 'metric martyrs' who had been prosecuted for breach of the regulation, argued that the Weights and Measures Act 1985 which allowed both metric and imperial measurements took precedence over EU regulations that took effect through the gateway of the ECA 1972.

It was held that there was no inconsistency between the rules, and the appeals were dismissed, but Laws LJ went on to consider, *obiter dicta*, the notion of a wider category of 'constitutional statutes':

We should recognise a hierarchy of Acts of Parliament: as it were 'ordinary' statutes and 'constitutional' statutes . . . Ordinary statutes may be impliedly repealed. Constitutional statutes may not.

(Laws LJ)

His argument was that the special status of the ECA 1972, in being protected from implied repeal (its status as a 'constitutional statute'), was derived from the approach of the UK judges. That is, its constitutional status comes from the UK common law rather than from an instruction from EU law or institutions. This status then is not necessarily confined to EU law issues; other statutes could be recognised by the common law as 'constitutional statutes'.

The next question is, what are constitutional statutes?

In my opinion a constitutional statute is one which (a) conditions the legal relationship between citizen and state in some general, overarching manner, or (b) enlarges or diminishes the scope of which we would now regard as fundamental rights . . . The special status of constitutional statutes follows the special status of constitutional rights.

(Laws LJ)

He gave examples of the Magna Carta, the Bill of Rights 1689, the Act of Union, the Reform Acts, the Human Rights Act 1998, the Scotland Act 1998 and the Government of Wales Act 1998. You must keep in mind that these comments are entirely *obiter dicta* from a Divisional Court and the case was not appealed. Lord Justice Laws (sitting in the Court of Appeal) reiterated the notion of constitutional statutes in *International Transport Roth v Secretary of State for the Home Department* [2002] EWCA Civ 158, but the concept did not seem to have attracted wider judicial support until the *HS2* case.

KEY CASE – *HS2 ACTION ALLIANCE V SECRETARY OF STATE FOR TRANSPORT* [2014] UKSC 3

The case concerned a challenge to the environmental impact assessment processes adopted for the high-speed rail line, HS2. The Supreme Court also examined the relationship between EU law, supremacy and constitutional instruments. Lords Mance and Neuberger said:

> The United Kingdom has no written constitution, but we have a number of constitutional instruments. They include Magna Carta, the Petition of Right 1628, the Bill of Rights and . . . the Act of Union 1707. The European Communities Act 1972, the Human Rights Act 1998 and the Constitutional Reform Act 2005 may now be added to this list. The common law itself also recognises certain principles as fundamental to the rule of law. It is, putting the point at its lowest, certainly arguable (and it is for United Kingdom law and courts to determine) that there may be fundamental principles, whether contained in other constitutional instruments or recognised at common law, of which Parliament when it enacted the European Communities Act 1972 did not either contemplate or authorise the abrogation.

This points to something beyond a simple resurrection of the 'constitutional statutes' idea, important though that is. First, the case was heard by the Supreme Court and the judgment of Lords Mance and Neuberger was agreed to by five of the other judges, rather than a single judgment in the High Court. The impact of *HS2* could be wider than *Thoburn*. Secondly, the judgment goes further than *Thoburn* in including common law principles within its category of special constitutional provisions. Thirdly, it seems to indicate a hierarchy within this constitutional category and places EU law lower in that hierarchy than the other constitutional provisions originating from UK law. All the statements were *obiter*, but in Elliott's view the case is profound because we can 'find the seeds – at the highest judicial level – of a vision of the British constitution substantially at odds with Diceyan orthodoxy'.[3]

KEY LEARNING POINTS

- The important constitutional changes made in the *Factortame* litigation can be regarded as either evolutionary or revolutionary.
- The revolution idea is arguably stronger.
- The idea of constitutional statutes looked to be withering away until *HS2*.

---

3   Mark Elliott, 'Reflections on the HS2 case: a hierarchy of domestic constitutional norms and the qualified primacy of EU law' (2014), http://ukconstitutionallaw.org/2014/01/23/mark-elliot-reflections-on-the-hs2-case-a-hierarchy-of-domestic-constitutional-norms-and-the-qualified-primacy-of-eu-law/ (last accessed 05/11/17).

8.17 BREXIT AND SUPREMACY

The referendum held on 23 June 2016 resulted in 51.9 per cent of voters in favour of leaving the European Union. The process of implementing this is still ongoing so this section will briefly outline how the first stages of the leave process have been undertaken, the legal challenge to the Government's preferred approach, and the draft Bill outlining how EU law is to be retained and interpreted following Brexit.

Article 50 Lisbon Treaty provides a power for Member State to leave the EU: 'Any member state may decide to withdraw from the Union in accordance with its own constitutional requirements'. The Supreme Court in *Miller v Secretary of State for Exiting the European Union* [2017] UKSC 5, was called upon to decide how the Article 50 notification could be done in accordance with the UK's own constitutional requirements.

The Government wanted to use it prerogative powers which would mean bypassing Parliament. Their argument was that withdrawing from an international agreement was an example *par excellence* of the conduct of foreign relations that fell firmly within the prerogative powers, i.e. exercisable by the Prime Minister without the need for Parliamentary approval. In the normal course of events withdrawal from a Treaty would be a prerogative process.

Miller argued that an Act of Parliament, the European Communities Act 1972, had conferred rights on people and that a decision to take away these EU legal rights could only be made by Parliament. It is a well-established principle that prerogative cannot be used to change the law or deprive people of statutory rights. The EU legal rights include rights which could be replaced by equivalent protections in UK law, such as workers' rights, and rights which could not survive exit, such as voting in European Parliament elections.

The Supreme Court, by a majority, was persuaded by Miller's arguments. It held that there was 'a new constitutional process for making law in the UK' and that EU law was now a source of law in the UK legal system. As such it could not be removed by the exercise of prerogative power.

The judgment in *Miller* meant that Government needed Parliamentary authorisation to proceed with an Article 50 notification. This was obtained through the European Union (Notification of Withdrawal) Act 2017. Attempts by the Lords to add amendments on protecting the rights of EU citizens living in the UK and on giving Parliament a vote on the outcome of the negotiations were defeated by the Government. The UK Permanent Representative to the European Union delivered the Government's letter of notification of intention to withdraw to the President of the European Council on 29 March 2017.

Attention then moved onto preparing for the legal consequences of Brexit. This was initially flagged as a 'Great Repeal Bill' but this titled was quietly dropped after it was pointed out that it would do the opposite of repealing a great number of laws. Over the years a huge volume of EU law had become part of the UK legal system. Repealing this whole body of law from the day of Brexit would have resulted in legal chaos and left many sectors of the economy without a regulatory regime. The aim of the European Union (Withdrawal) Bill therefore is continuity. It tries to provide time for necessary technical changes, e.g. setting up new authorities to regulate sectors previously regulated by EU bodies, and then allows Government to develop new substantive policies – the much vaunted 'taking back control'.

It was published in July 2017 and received its second reading in September 2017. It has three main elements:

a) Repeal of the European Communities Act 1972. This will give effect to the international law step of withdrawing from the EU, within internal UK law.
b) Incorporation of most existing EU law into UK law – this is to avoid a (whole series of) regulatory black holes. This new category of law will be called 'EU retained law'. It will include obligations from Directives that have been implemented into UK law, direct EU Regulations and some Treaty rights, e.g. on equal pay. The Bill also outlines how courts are to treat this 'retained EU law', which will keep its supreme status but only in relation to Acts of Parliament passed before the Brexit date. If there was a clash between a statute from 2012 and some element of retained EU law, then the courts would have to give priority to the EU retained law. If there was a future clash between a statute passed after Brexit, say in 2020, and a provision of EU retained law then the courts would have to apply the 2020 statute.
c) Gives broad powers to Ministers to amend, repeal and replace this EU retained law. These are, therefore, what are known as Henry VIII clauses. These are controversial because they give ministers the power to amend or repeal primary legislation with very minimal Parliamentary input or oversight. For practical reasons this is probably necessary, to some extent, but the proposals still amount to a huge transfer of power over law-making to the executive branch.

Elliott sums up the role of the Bill in usually forthright terms:

> In political terms, the Withdrawal Bill is being presented as the epitome of the taking back of control and the restoration of 'sovereignty' that has been so fetishized by some. But it actually demonstrates something very different. It serves as a stark reminder of the way in which the banal rhetoric that has characterised – and that continues to characterise – much of the political debate in this area is now beginning to meet brutal legal and constitutional reality. Some will doubtless find clause 1 of the Bill, which boldly proclaims that the European Communities Act will be repealed on 'exit day', intoxicating. They should make the most of it. Because the rest of the Bill palpably demonstrates that those drunk on the notion of taking back control need to face up to the fact that they – indeed, *we* – are in for one hell of a hangover.[4]

---

4   M Elliott, '1,000 words / The EU (Withdrawal) Bill', *Public Law for Everyone*, https://publiclawforeveryone. com/2017/07/14/1000-words-the-eu-withdrawal-bill/ (last accessed 05/11/17)

POINTS TO REVIEW

- The European Union has autonomous institutions that can make, administer and adjudge laws.

- The Court of Justice asserts the supremacy of EU law over any national law. As EU law can directly enter national legal systems, this poses a significant challenge to the traditional view of the power of the UK Parliament.

- The UK courts have accepted that, on a day-to-day basis, they need to give priority to EU law even if it conflicts with an Act of Parliament. The courts, however, say that UK Parliament retains the right to expressly repeal any commitment to EU law.

- The important constitutional changes made in the *Factortame* litigation can be regarded as either evolutionary or revolutionary, although the revolution idea is arguably stronger.

- Brexit will end the priority given to EU law in relation to Acts passed after the Brexit date.

- The idea of constitutional statutes, that there is a hierarchy of statutes, looked to be withering away until the *HS2* judgment.

TAKING IT FURTHER

H W R Wade, 'Sovereignty – Revolution or Evolution?' [1996] *Law Quarterly Review* 56 Concise and punchy analysis of *Factortame*. This is also a good example of how academic writers put forward their own views in a debate with rival perspectives, i.e. mostly respectfully but pretty forthrightly too (at one point, Wade describes a position taken by Laws as carrying us 'far from reality' and into 'cloud-cuckoo-land'!).

Sir John Laws, 'Law and Democracy' [1995] *Public Law* 57 This is a wide-ranging and typically thought-provoking review of the interrelationship between law and democracy and the implications for the judiciary. The section you really need to focus on is the sub-heading 'The imperative of higher-order law' (pp.84–90), where Laws explains why he disagrees with Wade's 'revolutionary' interpretation of *Factortame*.

M Elliott, '1,000 words / The EU (Withdrawal) Bill', *Public Law for Everyone*, https://publiclawforeveryone.com/2017/07/14/1000-words-the-eu-withdrawal-bill/ This is an accessible and concise summary of the Bill.

9

CHAPTER 9
SEPARATION OF POWERS

At its heart, Public Law is concerned with power, and in particular the abuse of power. As Lord Acton said in 1887, 'Power tends to corrupt and absolute power corrupts absolutely'.[1] The state possesses a huge amount of power: it can take money from our wages through taxation powers; it can take our liberty through imprisonment powers; it can send members of the armed forces to where they may have to kill or to be killed. The separation of powers is a principle of Public Law that seeks to prevent the abuse of power by insisting that the main types of state legal power are exercised by people and institutions that are separate from each other. It seeks to defuse the more dangerous aspects of power by diffusing power.

This chapter explores the close relationship in the UK constitution between the legislature (which makes laws) and the executive (which applies them). This relationship between two of the three branches of the state highlights the importance of the independence of the third branch, the judiciary (which interprets law and adjudicates legal disputes).

AS YOU READ

The general principle of the separation of powers itself is not the most difficult Public Law concept to grasp. The challenge is in understanding how the principle relates to the structure of the state in the UK. If you have a grasp of who does what within the UK constitutional system, then it is reasonably straightforward to apply the concept. Understanding the different interpretations of the concept is a little more complex. As you read you will have to reach a reasoned conclusion on whether the UK has an effective separation of power and whether there is scope for further reform.

By the end of this chapter you should be able to:

- explain the rationale behind the principle
- outline and assess recent reforms that have had a major impact on the separation of powers
- identify contemporary events and examples and show how they relate to the separation of powers.

---

1 Letter to Bishop Mandell Creighton, 1887.

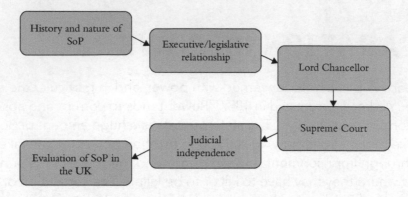

Figure 9.1 Structure of Chapter 9

9.1 INTRODUCTION

If we look at authoritarian and dictatorial countries, we see that a significant part of the legal power of the state is concentrated into the hands of one person. In other forms of oppressive government, the power is concentrated and controlled by a single political party, a single military group or a single religious leader. They may have some or all of the following powers: to make new laws, to repeal or suspend existing laws, to decide how the law should be applied, to decide whether or not to apply the law to their own actions or to the actions of their friends and allies, how the law should be interpreted, and whether to dismiss judges who interpret laws in ways that they disagree with.

APPLYING THE LAW – THE CONCENTRATION OF POWER IN NAZI GERMANY

Article 48 of the Constitution of the German Weimar Republic (1919–33) granted powers to the President to make emergency legislation. This was manipulated by Adolf Hitler and the Nazis to concentrate power into their hands.

The burning of the German Parliament (the Reichstag fire) in February 1933 provided the pretext for emergency action. Civil liberties, such as rights of assembly to protest and freedom of speech, were the first rights to be suspended. The legislative power of the state was then effectively transferred to the Chancellor (Hitler), and opposition parties were suppressed and then outlawed.

Hitler was dissatisfied with the way in which the regular courts dealt with the trials of those charged with the Reichstag fire and so set up a People's Court. This was staffed by Nazi judges and dealt with 'political offences' without the safeguards and restrictions applying in a normal criminal court. This centralised the three main legal powers of the state – to make, apply and interpret law – into the hands of one party and its leader.

Since a key purpose of modern liberal constitutions is to protect people from this type of oppression and dictatorship, these constitutions must inevitably be concerned about concentrations of power. In fact, written constitutions in many countries are deliberately designed to avoid this dangerous concentration and to distribute power to separate officials and institutions. The UK constitution has evolved to a position where this separation of powers is provided for in many, but not all, parts of the constitutional system.

9.2 SUMMARY OF THE SEPARATION OF POWERS

It is useful, at the outset, to provide a simple summary of the concept of the separation of powers. It states that there are three main categories of state legal power. These are:

- Legislative – the power to make laws.
- Executive – the power to implement, or to execute, laws.
- Judicial – the power to interpret law and adjudicate legal disputes.

The concept goes on to assert that to reduce the risk of an abuse of power, these three types of power should be exercised by separate people and institutions. There is obviously some more complexity to the concept and some more difficult questions on how it applies, but it is important to keep the basic concept in mind.

9.3 HISTORY

The separation of powers, as a tool for promoting good government, can be traced back to some of the earliest recorded political thought. Aristotle, writing in 350 BC, said that if the three elements in each constitution were separate then 'the constitution is bound to be well-arranged'.[2]

Legal historians have identified a concern with the balance or separation of power through much of the UK's constitutional history. The Magna Carta 1215 did not involve a separation of powers in the modern sense, but it provided that the king could not wield absolute power. The leading noblemen, the barons, could enforce legal restrictions on the king's power by taking his castles, and the Magna Carta sought to prevent tyranny by introducing checks and balances on some of the powers of the state.

This concern with balancing state power is evident in the work of English constitutional writers. Bolingbroke wrote in 1748 that 'in a constitution like ours, the safety of the whole

---

2   Aristotle, *Politics* (350 BC), http://classics.mit.edu/Aristotle/politics.html (last accessed 05/11/17).

depends on the balance of the parts'.[3] John Locke explained the dangers of a concentration of power as 'too great a temptation to human frailty, apt to grasp at power'.[4]

9.3.1 MONTESQUIEU

The modern concept of the separation of powers can be traced to the work of Baron Montesquieu in *L'Esprit des Lois* (*The Spirit of Laws*) 1748. Montesquieu was a French political writer who spent time in England studying its constitutional arrangements. By this time, there was some balance of power between the king and Parliament and some protection for the independence of the judiciary. Whilst the English constitution may not have measured up to his ideal of separation, it did inspire Montesquieu's vision.

Montesquieu firmly established the purpose of the separation of powers: to preserve liberty and prevent tyranny and the abuse of power. He also divided state functions into the three categories recognised today, stating that:

> All would be lost if the same man or the same body . . . exercised these three powers: that of making the laws, that of executing public resolutions, and that of judging the crimes and disputes of individuals.

Montesquieu's formulation was widely read during this period and directly influenced the design of the US Constitution in 1787.

9.4 THE THREE BRANCHES OF THE STATE

The US Constitution was drafted with the separation of powers very firmly in mind, so it is a prominent example of a 'separation of powers constitution'.

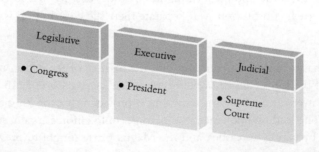

Figure 9.2 The three state branches in the US

3   Viscount Bolingbroke, *Political Writings*, ed. D. Armitage, (Cambridge UP, 1997).

4   J. Locke, Two Treatises of Government, 1689, http://www.gutenberg.org/ebooks/7370 (last accessed 05/11/17).

APPLYING THE LAW – LAW-MAKING, APPLICATION AND ADJUDICATION UNDER THE US CONSTITUTION

To see how this separation of institutions and functions works in practice, we can look at an example from wildlife protection law:

- In 1973, the US Congress, exercising its *legislative* power, passed a new law, the Endangered Species Act. This law imposed obligations on the executive branch. It regulated all federal executive agencies and, in particular, was applied by the Environmental Protection Agency as established by the US President.
- The Act required *executive* agencies to consult before taking action that threatens endangered species, and generally to act to protect endangered species.
- In 1978, there was a legal dispute on the meaning of the Act, and the *Tennessee Valley Authority v Hill*, 437 US 153 (1978) soon reached the Supreme Court. Federal agencies were involved in supporting a dam-building scheme that would have threatened a rare fish. The Court, exercising its *judicial* power, interpreted the Endangered Species Act 1973 as requiring executive agencies to terminate projects that jeopardise endangered species.

Although the UK does not have a written constitution and therefore cannot be said to have been designed in the same way, we can see that it has evolved a broadly similar structure.

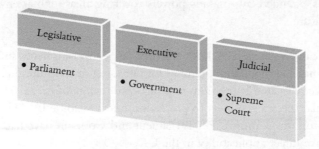

Figure 9.3 The three state branches in the UK

APPLYING THE LAW – LAW-MAKING, APPLICATION AND ADJUDICATION UNDER THE UK CONSTITUTION

To follow on from the US example, we can examine how the institutions of the UK constitutional system deal with wildlife protection law:

- The Westminster Parliament, as the *legislative* part of the state, makes a new law. In this case, the Wildlife and Countryside Act was passed by Parliament in 1981 and is still the main law on wildlife protection. It prohibits, for example, the killing of a listed wild animal or destroying its nest/shelter.

- The Act imposes duties on *executive* agencies, including the Environment Agency and Natural England, to apply the law including prosecuting wildlife crimes and taking action to preserve habitats.
- The courts, as part of the *judicial* branch, interpret the law in legal disputes. In *R (Fisher) v English Nature* [2003] EWHC 1599 (Admin), the High Court ruled that restricting the use of land to protect a rare bird species did not breach the landowner's human rights to possession of their property.

So we can see the operation of this basic separation of functions between the three different branches of the state in both the US and the UK constitutional systems. We see below that the situation is a little more complex than this and that there are overlaps between the branches, but it is useful first to outline in more detail the three branches of the state.

9.4.1 LEGISLATIVE BRANCH

Making law is the core of the legislative function, and as well as the power to make new laws, it includes the power to amend and repeal existing laws. The UK Parliament in Westminster is at the top of the legislative structure but many law-making powers have been delegated to other bodies. The Scottish Parliament can legislate on e.g. educational matters in Scotland. Following the 'yes' vote in the March 2011 referendum, the National Assembly for Wales now has extended law-making powers covering areas such as environment, education and culture.

Local authorities can pass local laws, known as bye-laws, covering issues such as access to parks and marinas and regulating premises for tattooing or acupuncture. Government ministers can make delegated legislation on a very wide range of issues, for example on whether a particular species is subject to protection under wildlife law. The institutions of the European Union (the Commission, Parliament and Council) have had the power to make laws that have direct applicability in the UK.

9.4.2 EXECUTIVE BRANCH

The executive power is more difficult to define. It has been described as 'the day-to-day control of the state . . . running the country'.[5] The executive category can be seen as residual, a catch-all that includes any governmental function that does not fall into the legislative or judicial categories. As well as implementing laws, the executive often also formulates proposals for new laws and develop policy more generally, e.g. in relation to foreign affairs. An example of this executive action is the UK Government's decision in March 2011 to vote in favour of UN Security Council Resolution 1973 to establish a

---

5   L Webley and H Samuels, *Complete Public Law* (3rd edn, OUP, 2015) 118.

no-fly zone over Libya and to take 'all necessary measures to protect civilians under attack', and then to be part of the military force taking action in Libya.

At the head of the executive is the Prime Minister, the Cabinet and the Government (see Chapter 2, 'Institutions'). Some of the Government's executive powers, e.g. the power to declare war, formally belong to the Crown but are exercised by ministers. Increasingly, executive powers are granted by statute.

The 'day-to-day running of the country' obviously involves a wide range of institutions, and the executive branch also includes civil servants, the police, customs officials and executive agencies, such as the Environment Agency and the Health and Safety Executive.

9.4.3 JUDICIAL BRANCH

The judicial function involves hearing and resolving legal disputes. Courts and tribunals have to interpret the law and decide how it applies to the facts of the particular dispute before them.

The court system has the principal responsibility for exercising this adjudicative power. The Supreme Court is at the apex of this system, and it includes the Court of Appeal, the High Court, county courts and magistrates' courts.

Tribunals were often set up as part of executive regulation schemes and linked to Government departments. Following the Tribunals, Courts and Enforcement Act 2007 the structure was rationalised, and they are more clearly separate from the executive branch and are more clearly judicial bodies. Some executive schemes make Government ministers responsible for legal adjudication. Whilst this may be a formal breach of the separation of powers, the minister must act in a judicial manner whilst exercising the judicial power.

9.5 THE LEGISLATIVE/EXECUTIVE RELATIONSHIP

This basic structure states that in the UK constitution, Parliament makes laws, the Government and public bodies execute the laws and the courts interpret and adjudicate these laws. Given this, it might seem obvious that the UK does have a separation of powers, but this is disputed by some academic writers.

W A Robson famously called the separation of powers 'that antique and rickety chariot . . . so long the favourite vehicle of writers on political science and constitutional law; the conveyance of fallacious ideas'.[6] Stanley de Smith called it 'an irrelevant distraction for the English law student and his [sic] teachers'.[7]

---

6   W A Robson, *Justice and Administrative Law* (2nd edn, Greenwood, 1947).
7   S A de Smith, 'The Separation of Powers in New Dress' (1966–67) 12 *McGill Law Journal* 491.

The weightiest piece of evidence supporting these very bold assertions was, and continues to be, the relationship between Parliament and Government. Essentially, all of the personnel of Government are drawn from the Houses of Parliament, whilst Government dominates Parliament and generally decides how Parliament exercises its law-making power. The influential Victorian writer Walter Bagehot called this 'the close union, the nearly complete fusion, of the executive and legislative powers'.[8]

This relationship is largely governed by constitutional conventions. The two most important here are:

1   All ministers, including the Prime Minister, must be Members of Parliament. This is a particularly firm convention. If a Prime Minister really wants to bring a person who is not currently an MP into their Government, then it has been the practice to arrange for that person to take the next available seat in a bye-election or to make them a peer in the House of Lords. It would simply be unacceptable to have someone who was not an MP holding ministerial office.

2   The Government is formed from the political party (or parties) that can control a majority of the votes in the House of Commons. Following the 2010 General Election, the Conservatives were the largest single party but did not have an overall majority. They could not form a Government until five days after the election when they had entered into a Coalition Agreement with the Liberal Democrats. It was only when they were in a position to control a majority of votes that the Coalition Government, with David Cameron as Prime Minister, could be formed. Similarly, in 2017 the minority Conservative Government was formed when Theresa May told the Queen that she had DUP support.

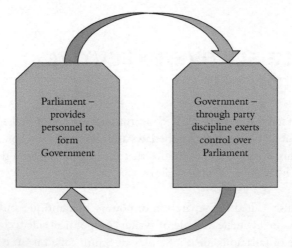

Figure 9.4 Government/Parliament relationship

8   W Bagehot, *The English Constitution* (2nd edn, J & A McLean, 1873).

The consequence of these conventions is a large overlap of personnel between the two branches and, more significantly, that the legislative branch does not exercise its law-making powers independently but under the control of the executive branch. This amounts to a serious breach of the separation of powers.

The House of Commons Disqualification Act 1975 does impose some limits on the personnel overlap. No more than 75 Government ministers can be drawn from the House of Commons (a smaller number come from the House of Lords). In practice, there are around an additional 40–50 parliamentary private secretaries (the first rung on the ministerial ladder) who technically are not ministers but who are subject to the discipline of being part of Government. The Government's control over voting in the House of Commons does not just come from directing how ministers should vote, but from party discipline. This means that MPs from the governing party will usually vote in the way that the party leaders tell them to. This is from a mixture of natural agreement, party loyalty and the threat of sanctions from party whips (e.g. suspension from the party).

It should be stressed that this control is not absolute. The Government must keep the support of a majority of MPs or it will fall. This happened in 1979 when the Labour Government of James Callaghan lost a 'vote of confidence' and Parliament was dissolved, leading to a general election. Governments must be able to get most of their legislative proposals through the House. Parliament also has a separate and more independent function of holding the Government to account through debates, questions and Select Committees.

In addition, Parliament has delegated wide powers to make law to Government ministers through the delegated legislation process. Most of these laws made by ministers and civil servants are formally approved by Parliament. In practice, however, there are far too many provisions (around 3,000 Statutory Instruments each year) for much genuine detailed scrutiny.

Overall then, the relationship between Parliament and the Government, with its overlapping personnel and dominance by ministers of the law-making process, is not consistent with the ideals of the separation of powers. Until recently, there were two further constitutional arrangements that undermined claims that the UK had a 'separation of powers constitution'. These were the role of the Lord Chancellor and the presence of senior judges in the House of Lords.

9.6 LORD CHANCELLOR

Before they were reformed in 2005, the varied duties of the Lord Chancellor were seen as a prime example of the lack of separation of power in the UK.

The Lord Chancellor is a Cabinet minister and, like all members of the Cabinet, they must be a Member of Parliament. The post is currently held by a member of the House of Commons, and this is likely to be the case for the foreseeable future. This is because the Lord Chancellor also holds the position of Secretary of State for Justice (who is responsible for politically sensitive issues such as prisons policy). The Lord Chancellor has responsibilities in relation to the administration of the courts and the judiciary. This means that there is an intercourse between the executive and the judicial branches. Beyond this, it is not immediately apparent why Public Law writers have given so much attention to the role of the Lord Chancellor, particularly as there are other ministers who actually exercise quasi-judicial functions.

The answer lies in history. You need to remember that this is an historical example of 'bad practice' and that the reform to the role of the Lord Chancellor actually illustrates a move to a clearer separation of powers in the contemporary constitution.

The post of Lord Chancellor goes back to the seventh century. It has historically been one of the most important positions in the Government, and has combined multiples roles in religious affairs, in operating courts and in administering policies. Up until the Constitutional Reform Act 2005, the duties of the Lord Chancellor could be summarised as follows:

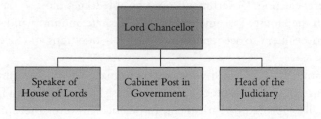

Figure 9.5 The Lord Chancellor pre-2006

We can immediately see that this was problematic for the separation of powers. The Lord Chancellor had important functions in all three branches:

- As Lord Speaker of the House of Lords, they would not only sit in the legislature but also act as the presiding officer arranging Parliamentary business.
- As a member of the Cabinet, they would head up a Government department and take an active role in executive decision-making at the highest level.
- As the head of the judiciary, the Lord Chancellor was a judge and could sit and hear cases in the Appellate Committee of the House of Lords.

This was the prime example of breach of the separation concept in the UK constitution: powers from all three branches unified in the body of a single person.

It should be mentioned that constitutional conventions and practices did operate to reduce the potentially negative effects of this unified power. As a member of the legislature and executive, the Lord Chancellor was not in a significantly different position to other members of the Government, who also sit as MPs, as outlined above. By convention, the Lord Chancellor would not sit as a judge in cases that involved the Government as a party or which were overtly political in nature.

Nevertheless, there were concerns about the judicial role of the Lord Chancellor. Article 6 of the European Convention on Human Rights requires that courts are 'independent and impartial'. The ability of a member of the executive to sit as a judge in the UK's highest court was potentially a breach of Article 6 ECHR. This difficulty became even more important following the incorporation of European Convention rights by the Human Rights Act 1998. In practice, it was increasingly uncommon for Lord Chancellors to hear judicial cases, and the last pre-reform Lord Chancellor, Lord Falconer, announced in 2003 that he would not sit as a judge.

Following an initial announcement that the office of Lord Chancellor would be abolished, it was decided to retain but substantially reform the post through the Constitutional Reform Act 2005. The position is now summed up by:

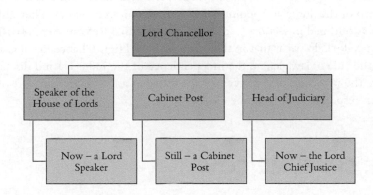

Figure 9.6 The Lord Chancellor's reduced role post-2006

So there is now a separate post of Lord Speaker who is elected by the members of the House of Lords and is expected to operate in a politically impartial manner, much like the Speaker of the House of Commons. This reduces the significance of the legislative/executive overlap. More importantly, the Lord Chancellor ceases to be a judge and cannot sit in any court. The role of head of the judiciary is transferred to the Lord Chief Justice.

9.6.1 ASSESSMENT ADVICE

To perform well in assessments, you will often have to go beyond describing legal changes and outline why those changes were made. Here, it may seem self-evident that the role of the Lord Chancellor was altered because of separation of powers concerns, but you need to be more certain that you are not making an assumption. Your reasoning will be stronger if you look for evidence that a particular principle or ideal (the separation of powers) was the motive for a particular change (the role of the Lord Chancellor). Fortunately, there is such clear evidence here. The Department for Constitutional Affairs White Paper that preceded the Constitutional Reform Act 2005 stated: 'The office of Lord Chancellor has become increasingly difficult to justify. The distinct roles of the Lord Chancellor need to be separated out and the relationship between the independent judiciary, the executive and the legislature needs to be clarified'.

The position now is that the Lord Chancellor is selected by the Prime Minister as outlined in section 2(1) of the Constitutional Reform Act 2005. They must be 'qualified by experience', which includes experience as a Minister, MP, legal practitioner or university law teacher. The Act, however, states that the Prime Minister only has to 'take into account' these criteria and they can take into account 'other relevant experience'. This means that whilst the Lord Chancellor is likely to be someone with a background in the legal profession, the Prime Minister is free to choose whom they wish. The last four Lord Chancellors have had no legal background (Chris Grayling, TV production; Michael Gove, journalism; Liz Truss, accounting; David Lidington, business). The statutory preference for a lawyer to hold this post must now be regarded as a dead letter, overborne by the political convenience.

The Lord Chancellor continues to appoint judges, but their discretion is severely restricted by the existence of the Judicial Appointment Commission (see below). They also have to swear an oath as outlined in section 17 of the Constitutional Reform Act 2005: 'I, [name of the Lord Chancellor], do swear that in the office of Lord High Chancellor of Great Britain I will respect the rule of law, defend the independence of the judiciary and discharge my duty to ensure the provision of resources for the efficient and effective support of the courts for which I am responsible. So help me God'.

9.7 THE SUPREME COURT

Until October 2009, the highest court in the land was physically located within the Palace of Westminster, the home of Parliament. It was formally a committee of the upper house of Parliament, and its judges were technically also members of the legislature. There were, however, important dividing lines between the work of the House of Lords (the court) and that of the House of Lords (the upper house of Parliament).

The Appellate Committee of the House of Lords, its full title, originally heard cases in the chamber of the House of Lords itself. After the Palace of Westminster was bombed during the Second World War, the Appellate Committee moved to a separate committee room and continued to use this for the rest of its existence. The judgments of the court continued to be given in the chamber of the House right up to 2009. This physical presence made it difficult to demonstrate the functional separation between Law Lords as judges and other Lords as legislators.

There was no legal restriction preventing *any* member of the Lords (to give a very hypothetical example, *Joseph and the Amazing Technicolor Dreamcoat* composer, Lord Andrew Lloyd-Webber) from sitting on the Appellate Committee. By a strictly observed constitutional convention, however, only the Lord Chancellor and the Law Lords sat on the Committee. There was a functional separation and only these highly experienced judges could perform the judicial function.

The Law Lords could sit in on the legislative debates of the House. They sat on the 'cross-benches', i.e. not aligned to any political party. Earlier judges would sometimes make contributions to debates (see below), but in the last decade of their existence, the Law Lords almost entirely ceased taking any part in the legislative work of the House. Overall, there was no real functional overlap between the judicial and legislative functions within the House of Lords. The Appellate Committee and the Law Lords were held in the highest regard, nationally and internationally, as independent and skilful judges.

Despite this, it was decided under the Constitutional Reform Act 2005 to replace the Appellate Committee with a Supreme Court of the United Kingdom, which has two main effects:

- First, the Supreme Court is physically separate from Parliament. The judges moved just across Parliament Square to the Middlesex Guildhall, but the physical location eloquently expresses the functional separation.
- Secondly, the Justices of the Supreme Court are not members of the House of Lords and cannot sit or vote in its legislative work. The gradual withdrawal of judges from legislative work is now formalised in law.

As with the Lord Chancellor above, we have evidence of what motivated these structural changes. The Government White Paper on the Constitutional Reform Bill stated, 'Our proposals rest on the separation of powers. The Law Lords will be taken out of the House of Lords and set up in a separate Supreme Court. There is an increasing need to underline the independence of the judicial system from both the executive and the legislature'.

The Supreme Court was not, however, given the power to judicially review legislation. This power to declare Acts of Parliament invalid, normally on the grounds that they breach some provision of a written constitution, is available to many supreme courts in different countries (e.g. the US).

KEY LEARNING POINTS

So far in this chapter, you should have:

- Picked up the basic shape of the separation of powers concept and how it developed.
- Seen that the overlap of functions between Parliament and Government supports arguments that the UK system is not based on a separation of powers.
- Understood that the Constitutional Reform Act 2005 has introduced changes that more clearly demarcate a separation of powers, particularly between the judicial branches and the other branches.

In the next section, we will focus on the need to preserve this independence of the judicial branch.

9.8 JUDICIAL INDEPENDENCE

One of the drafters of the US Constitution, Alexander Hamilton, described the judiciary as the 'least dangerous branch' of the state.[9] This was echoed by the House of Lords judge Lord Steyn who argued that the judges were 'the weakest branch'.[10] We can see evidence for this in the legal relationship between the courts and Parliament. This is governed by the supremacy of Parliament (see Chapters 7 and 8) which states that the courts are *obliged* to apply Acts of Parliament. In the words of Lord Diplock in *Duport Steels Ltd v Sirs* [1980] 1 All ER 529, 'it cannot be too strongly emphasised that the British Constitution, although largely unwritten, is firmly based on the separation of powers; Parliament makes the laws, the judiciary interpret them'.

If Parliament (or, more realistically, the Government that controls the law-making process) is unhappy with the way the courts have interpreted the law in any particular area, it can legislate. An example of this is the *Burmah Oil Company v Lord Advocate* [1965] AC 75 case discussed in Chapter 10, 'Rule of law'. The House of Lords had interpreted the prerogative power to destroy property in times of war as including a right to compensation for the owners of the property. The Government was concerned that this would open the floodgates to many further compensation claims and put undue pressure on the public finances. It put a Bill to reverse the effect of the court judgment through Parliament within a matter of weeks (the War Damage Act 1965). That is, if there are different views on what the law ought to be between the courts on one hand and Parliament on the other, then Parliament's view will prevail; the courts are relatively weak.

Yet, the significance of judicial power should not be underestimated. There was once a theory that judges do not make law, they merely declare it, i.e. they are just articulating in a specific case what Parliament said the law is or were discovering what the existing common law principles meant for the parties before them. This view has now been rejected, even by the judges themselves.[11]

When courts are called on to interpret Acts of Parliament, particularly in the higher courts, there are competing viable interpretations that they can choose from. This choice is a contribution to the law-making process, especially as it will bind future courts. Similarly, the common law is not simply discovered by courts. In applying existing legal principles to new

9 *The Federalist Papers*, 1788, http://www.gutenberg.org/ebooks/1404 (last accessed 05/11/17).

10 Lord Steyn, 'The Weakest and Least Dangerous Department of Government' [1997] *Public Law* 84.

11 Lord Reid, 'The Judge as Law-Maker' (1972) 12 *Journal of the Society of Public Teachers of Law* 22.

situations, the judges are directing the development of the common law. We can use this to critique Lord Diplock's statement in *Duport Steels* above. He was putting forward a very general view, but a closer analysis shows that judges are also important law-makers, albeit within the framework set by Parliament.

Beyond this general outline of judicial power, there are particular reasons for thinking that the judiciary play a crucial role in the constitutional system and for trying to ensure that this role is independent. In the judicial review process, courts hear claims that public bodies, including Government ministers and even the Prime Minister, have acted unlawfully. They must be formally and functionally separate from these executive bodies so as to assess the claims fairly, and to be seen to deal with them fairly. This process of Applying the law to other parts of the state and, if necessary imposing limits on state action, has developed widely with the growth of judicial review over the last 40 years, including the rights incorporated by the Human Rights Act 1998. These include Article 6 of the European Convention on Human Rights which states that:

> In the determination of his civil rights and obligations or of any criminal charge against him, everyone is entitled to a fair and public hearing within a reasonable time by an independent and impartial tribunal established by law.

Similarly, attempts by the Polish Government in 2017 to control the appointment of judges were criticised by the European Union. The proposals would have removed all supreme court judges apart from ones approved by the justice minister. The vice-president of the European Commission, Frans Timmermans, said 'Under these reforms judges will serve at the pleasure of political leaders, and be dependent upon them, from their appointment to their pension'. The Commission explored whether this amounts to a breach of fundamental rights that could lead to the suspension of Poland's voting rights in the EU, and the pressure led the Polish president to refuse to sign the measures.[12]

Finally, the 'almost complete fusion' of the legislative and executive branches in the UK constitutional system heightens the importance of judicial independence. If the separation of powers is going to play a role in the UK constitutional arrangements, then judicial independence is going to have to be both unambiguous and effective in preventing abuses of power.

Judicial independence is protected through a mixture of legal and conventional rules, but also by a clear understanding of its importance to the people working within the constitution, including vigilant protection by the judges themselves.

---

12 K Connelly, 'Poland's president to veto controversial laws amid protests' *The Guardian* (24 July 2017), https://www. theguardian.com/world/2017/jul/24/poland-president-to-veto-controversial-laws-amid-protests (last accessed 05/11/17).

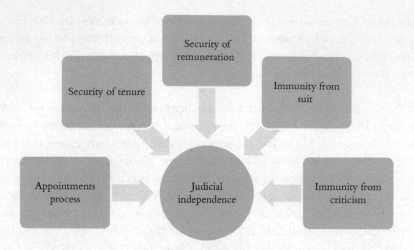

Figure 9.7 Factors supporting judicial independence

9.8.1 JUDICIAL APPOINTMENTS

If a Government was able to appoint whomever it wanted to the judiciary, the danger would be that it would abuse this power, for example by only appointing political allies or those who would follow its instructions.

Prior to the Constitutional Reform Act 2005, the process for appointing judges was very opaque. It was conducted largely by the Lord Chancellor and lacked both transparency and independence. Whilst there did not appear to be a problem *in substance* with the quality of judicial appointments, the process lacked *legitimacy*. It also lacked diversity. The political consequences of this were explored by JAG Griffith who argued that the very narrow social base that judges were drawn from led them to judgments that were conservative, supportive of the status quo and hostile to e.g. trade unions.[13] More recently, the largely 'male, pale and stale' character of the judiciary has been criticised as not reflecting the society that it serves.[14]

The Judicial Appointments Commission (JAC) was established by section 6 of the Constitutional Reform Act 2005 to select candidates to recommend to the Lord Chancellor. The Lord Chancellor still retains the formal power of appointment, but in the normal course of events it was expected (and it has been the case in practice) that the Commission's recommendations would be accepted, i.e. it is the JAC that decides who fills judicial posts.

---

13 J A Griffith, *The Politics of the Judiciary* (5th edn reissue, Fontana, 2010).

14 Council of Europe, European judicial systems – efficiency and quality of justice, 2016 https://www.coe.int/t/dghl/ cooperation/cepej/evaluation/default_2016_en.asp (last accessed 05/11/17), showing that the UK has one of the lowest proportions of women judges in Europe.

The Commissioners themselves are appointed on the recommendation of the Lord Chancellor. There is a requirement to have people from a range of backgrounds and not simply law. In 2017, for example, the Chairman Lord Ajay Kakkar has a background in medicine. Other lay members include a psychiatrist, an academic, and a civil servant. The Judicial Appointments Commission is relevant to the separation of powers in that it places some distance between the potentially sensitive issue of judicial appointments and the personal discretion of politicians.

9.8.2 SECURITY OF TENURE

If judges are to be independent, they cannot work with the fear that they will be sacked if they make judgments that displease the Government; they must have security of tenure.

APPLYING THE LAW – SECURITY OF TENURE IN PAKISTAN

In 2007, 60 of Pakistan's senior judges, including the Supreme Court Chief Justice, Iftikhar Chaudhry, were sacked by the Pakistani President, Pervez Musharraf. The Chief Justice had previously issued an order against the presidential decision to suspend the constitution and declare a state of emergency.

Whilst the President alleged that the Chief Justice was guilty of misbehaviour in a judicial office, it was widely believed that the dismissal was politically motivated. A judicial disciplinary hearing exonerated Mr Chaudhry, but the President nevertheless had him placed under house arrest.

There followed a mass protest led by the Lawyers Movement that fought for the re-instatement of Mr Chaudhry and the independence of the judiciary. Following a change in leadership in 2008, Mr Chaudhry was released and eventually re-instated to the Supreme Court in 2009. Pakistani lawyers and citizens had not been able to take security of tenure and judicial independence for granted and had to fight, often facing imprisonment and torture, for that constitutional principle.

Up until 1700, judges in England held office 'at the King's pleasure'. This meant that the king or his Government could dismiss judges for any reason. This was not just a theoretical possibility. From 1610, Chief Justice Edward Coke decided a number of cases that imposed limits on, and severely displeased, the king and Parliament. These included deciding that the courts could limit the king's prerogative (law-making) powers and that Parliament could not pass Acts that were 'against common right or reason'.[15] For this independence and assertion of judicial power, he was dismissed from judicial office in 1616.

---

15 *Case of Proclamations* (1611) 12 Co Rep 74; *Dr Bonham's Case* (1610) 8 Co Rep 114.

Since the Act of Settlement 1701, judges hold office 'during good behaviour'. The justices of the Supreme Court have this protection (under section 33 of the Constitutional Reform Act 2005), as do Court of Appeal, High Court and Crown Court judges (section 11(3) of the Senior Courts Act 1981). Less senior members of the judiciary, e.g. district judges and magistrates, can only be removed by the Lord Chancellor for incapacity or misbehaviour (section 22(5) of the Courts Act 1971). The key point for the separation of powers is that judges cannot be removed for political reasons.

It is possible to dismiss senior judges, but only by the Crown on an address (i.e. a vote) by both Houses of Parliament. This has happened only once since 1700. In 1830, a judge in Ireland was removed owing to allegations that he embezzled money paid into court. Misbehaviour will include criminal convictions, but errant judges and magistrates can normally be persuaded to resign before being dismissed, and a criminal conviction will not automatically trigger dismissal.

APPLYING THE LAW – JUDICIAL MISCONDUCT

Hilaire Barnett reports that six judges remained in office after being found guilty of drink-driving offences.[16] The practice in relation to drink-driving appears to be changing, however, possibly as a result of the increasing seriousness with which this crime is viewed. It is now seen as socially unacceptable and not just a technical illegality or minor misdemeanour.

The Office for Judicial Complaints reported in August 2011 that a Mental Health Tribunal judge had been removed from office by the Lord Chancellor and the Lord Chief Justice due to his conviction for driving after consuming excess alcohol and for not informing the President of the Tribunal about the criminal proceedings. This was treated as 'misbehaviour'.[17]

The Lord Chancellor can retire a judge if there is medical evidence of permanent infirmity from performance of their judicial duties and that that they are unable to resign because of incapacity. The retirement age for senior judges is 70 years, although this can be extended in the public interest up to 75 years.

A further development is the establishment of the Office for Judicial Complaints (OJC) in 2006, which can examine what judges do as part of their duties. The OJC, however, only has powers to investigate complaints relating to the personal behaviour of judges and magistrates. It cannot hear any complaint about the judicial decision itself, and therefore the key separation of powers protection, that a judge cannot be removed because their decisions are politically unpopular, remains in place.

---

16 H Barnett, *Constitutional and Administrative Law*, (11th edn, Routledge, 2016) 78.

17 Office for Judicial Complaints, http://judicialcomplaints.judiciary.gov.uk/docs/First_Tier_Tribunal_Judge_Michael_Marlow_-_OJC_Investigation_Statement_-_2611.pdf (last accessed 05/11/17).

9.8.3 SECURITY OF REMUNERATION

A further way in which an unscrupulous executive branch might try to put pressure on the judicial branch is through control of judges' pay. The Senior Courts Act 1981 protects against this by providing security of remuneration. Whilst judicial pay rates are determined by the executive, the Lord Chancellor can only increase, and not reduce, salaries. The salaries are paid out of the Consolidated Fund, which means that they are not subject to detailed approval by Parliament and cannot be withheld.

9.8.4 IMMUNITY FROM SUIT

Judges are protected from being sued for what they do as judges by both statute and common law. In the course of their duties, judges may do or say things that if done by other people may give rise to civil liability. Ordering people to be detained might result in claims of false imprisonment. Saying highly negative things about a person's character, in a summing up, might involve incorrect allegations that would, in other circumstances, result in a defamation action.

The Crown Proceedings Act 1947 forbids proceedings relating to actions done by a person discharging judicial responsibilities. Lord Denning, in *Sirros v Moore* [1975] QB 118, said that the immunity extended to every judge including lay magistrates if they honestly believed they were acting within their jurisdiction. Section 31 of the Courts Act 2003, however, only provides immunity to a magistrate 'in relation to a matter within his jurisdiction'.

ANALYSING THE LAW

What is the rationale for this seemingly generous immunity? In *Scott v Stanfield* (1868) LR 3 Ex 220, it was said that judges must act 'independently and freely, without favour and without fear'. The concern is that judges would be harassed by litigation from powerful individuals, companies and institutions.

An alternative view would stress that the separation of powers is concerned with the abuse of power and that an immunity or privilege such as this could be a shield for abuses by the courts themselves to take place. The court in *Scott v Stanfield* emphasised that the immunity was 'not for the protection of the corrupt or malicious judge, but for the benefit of the public'. Yet, the immunity does not depend on an absence of malice or corruption.

Someone aggrieved by what they perceive as judicial misconduct or negligence does have some other avenue for redress. They can complain to the Office for Judicial Complaints, and if they are not satisfied with that investigation, they can involve the Judicial Appointments and Conduct Ombudsman. The OJC cannot deal with everything that might otherwise be the subject of a civil action, but it can look at allegations of discrimination or inappropriate behaviour or comments. The complainant will not receive damages, but successful complaints are passed on to the Lord Chancellor and Lord Chief Justice, who have disciplinary powers. Irregularities may also be the basis for a successful appeal or judicial review before a higher court.

9.8.5 IMMUNITY FROM CRITICISM

In addition to these legal protections for judicial independence there are also rules of parliamentary practice and constitutional conventions that are supposed to protect judges from criticism by politicians. The rules of parliamentary practice (known as the Erskine May rules) state that MPs should not criticise judges unless it is part of a substantive motion. Ministers are subject to a conventional rule that prohibits them from criticism of individual judges and individual judicial decisions. The convention is not always observed.

APPLYING THE LAW – CRITICISM OF THE JUDICIARY

In 2003, Mr Justice Collins decided that six asylum seekers were entitled to welfare benefits even though they had not followed the asylum application rules as laid down by statute. He ruled that denying the benefits would amount to a breach of the European Convention on Human Rights.

The Government had only recently put these restrictions on benefits for asylums seekers through Parliament, and the Home Secretary David Blunkett reacted angrily. In a radio interview he said: 'Frankly, I'm personally fed up with having to deal with a situation where Parliament debates issues and the judges then overturn them. I don't want any mixed messages going out so I am making it absolutely clear today that we don't accept what Justice Collins has said'.

He was quickly rebuffed by Lord Woolf, the Lord Chief Justice, who argued that the judges were merely upholding the will of Parliament and were following their oath to apply and uphold the law, which included the Human Rights Act 1998. He echoed the structure and the purpose of the separation of powers in saying that the judges were 'protecting the public by ensuring that the Government complies with the laws made by Parliament'.

It was always understood that the Lord Chancellor would act as a restraining influence on colleagues who wanted to speak out about particular judges or decisions. The reform of the Lord Chancellor's role makes it more likely that they will be a career politician whose loyalties lie more firmly with their political colleagues and their wider political constituency. The legal duty on the Lord Chancellor under section 3 Constitutional Reform Act 2005 does apply here, but is not always upheld.

APPLYING THE LAW – 'ENEMIES OF THE PEOPLE'

Following the decision in the High Court in *R (Miller) v Secretary of State for Exiting the European Union* [2016] EWHC 2768 (Admin), the *Daily Mail* published a front-page headline branding the three High Court judges as 'Enemies of the People'. The response of the Lord Chancellor, Liz Truss, to this attack on the character of the judiciary was slow and weak. She later made a fuller statement that still refused to condemn what the Daily Mail had printed, on the basis that government ministers ought not to say what is acceptable for a newspaper to publish.

In March 2017, the Head of the Judiciary, Lord Thomas LCJ, gave evidence to the House of Lords Constitution Committee where he highlighted the particular constitutional duty of the Lord Chancellor to defend the judiciary from abuse and said that she was 'constitutionally absolutely wrong' in failing to fulfil that duty.[18] The consequent collapse in confidence in the Lord Chancellor from the wider legal community contributed to her being moved on to another ministerial post in June 2017.

9.8.6 CONSTITUTIONAL REFORM ACT 2005

We have seen that the Constitutional Reform Act 2005 had a particular objective of arranging constitutional roles to more closely adhere to the separation of powers. This includes reinforcing the independence of the judiciary through introducing general duties on ministers and specific duties for the Lord Chancellor.

All ministers and others with responsibility for the administration of justice 'must uphold the continued independence of the judiciary' (section 3(1)). Ministers must not 'seek to influence particular judicial decisions through any special access to the judiciary' (section 3(5)). In addition, under section 3(6) the Lord Chancellor must have regard to:

(a) The need to defend that independence.
(b) The need for the judiciary to have the support necessary to enable them to exercise their functions.
(c) The need for the public interest in regard to matters relating to the judiciary or otherwise to the administration of justice to be properly represented in decisions affecting those matters.

---

18 M Elliott, The Lord Chief Justice on the Lord Chancellor' *Public Law for Everyone* (22 March 2017), https://publiclaw foreveryone.com/2017/03/22/she-is-constitutionally-absolutely-wrong-the-lord-chief-justice-on-the-lord-chancel lor/ (last accessed 05/11/17).

9.8.7 JUDICIAL ATTITUDES

The courts have asserted the importance of the separation of powers, and the centrality of judicial independence to that concept, on numerous occasions. The classic statement is from Lord Diplock in *Duport Steels v Sirs*, as discussed above. A similar approach was taken by Lord Mustill in *R v Secretary of State for the Home Department, ex parte Fire Brigades Union* [1995] 2 AC 513, stating that: 'It is a feature of the peculiarly British conception of the separation of powers that Parliament, the executive and the courts have each their distinct and largely exclusive domain'. Lord Steyn later wrote that the constitutional protections for independence of the judiciary were total and effective.[19]

9.8.8 JUDICIAL INDEPENDENCE – CONCLUSION

This is the aspect of separation of powers that has the firmest footing in the UK constitution. It is the subject of a general statutory duty and specific legal protections. These are buttressed by rules of Parliamentary practice and constitutional conventions. Together, they seek to protect the independence of the judiciary from both direct assault and more insidious indirect pressures.

The legal and non-legal rules reflect a broader understanding from different parts of the constitutional system of the importance of judicial independence, and if those other branches are tempted to forget or downplay that independence, then the judiciary have shown themselves to be attentive and vigorous in protecting it.

The independence of the judiciary is the strongest card of those who argue that that a broadly effective but partial separation of powers exists in the UK. There are, however, some remaining questions on the boundaries between the judicial role and executive/legislative roles.

9.9 THE BOUNDARIES OF JUDICIAL POWER

9.9.1 ADJUDICATION BY THE EXECUTIVE

The European Court of Human Rights in *McGonnell v UK* (2000) 30 EHRR 289 examined the role of the Bailiff (a judicial post) in Guernsey. It found that the European Convention on Human Rights did not require states to follow any particular constitutional theory, including the separation of powers. Article 6 ECHR, however, did require that a tribunal be both independent and objectively impartial. As the Guernsey Bailiff had both judicial and executive/legislative powers and, importantly, this particular Bailiff was involved in making the law that he was later called on to adjudicate, this amounted to a breach of Article 6 of the ECHR.

---

19 Lord Steyn, 'Democracy, the Rule of Law and the Role of the Judges' [2006] *European Human Rights Law Review* 243.

Until 2000, UK politicians had a role in deciding how long someone under a life sentence stayed in jail. This practice could be criticised as an executive person exercising judicial power. Following the reasoning in *McGonnell*, this was not automatically a breach of Article 6 of the ECHR but there was a possibility of the Home Secretary being subject to influence from public opinion. This posed a real risk that they would act politically and not in the 'independent and impartial manner' as required by Article 6 of the ECHR. The sentencing power was reformed by section 60 of the Criminal Justice and Court Services Act 2000, and the early release provisions are now controlled by the courts.

Some regulatory schemes, e.g. planning, involve determining an individual's legal rights and make Government ministers or their civil servants responsible for adjudicating these rights. Following *McGonnell*, this raises questions about the independence and impartiality of the schemes. Bradley and Ewing argue that it can be difficult to say clearly and in advance whether a specific function should be seen as executive or judicial. They propose that 'decisions which are best made independently of political influence should be entrusted to the courts or tribunals, and decisions for which ministers should be responsible to parliament must be entrusted to executive departments or agencies'.[20]

In the *Alconbury* case, the House of Lords had to consider whether the planning powers of the Secretary of State for the Environment engaged Article 6 ECHR.[21] The court found that as these powers involved adjudicating on how owners could use their property, then the requirement for an independent and impartial tribunal did apply. The difficulty was that the Secretary of State would often be applying his own policies in deciding planning appeals. The process was ultimately found to be consistent with Article 6 ECHR but only because applicants could take their grievance further on to a court using the judicial review process.

APPLYING THE LAW – THE BSKYB TAKEOVER

In 2010–2011, Government ministers had to exercise a quasi-judicial role in the proposed takeover of BSkyB by News International. The decision was originally to have been made by the Business Secretary, Vince Cable. When it emerged, through recording of private comments, that Mr Cable wanted to 'declare war' on Rupert Murdoch and News International, it was clear that he could not demonstrate the required 'independence and impartiality'. The decision was passed to Jeremy Hunt, the Secretary of State for Culture, Media and Sport. He had to apply a test of plurality: that there would be sufficient diversity in media ownership. Rather than refer the decision to the Competition Commission, Mr Hunt indicated that he would accept undertakings to divide Sky News from BSkyB.

20 A Bradley and K Ewing, *Constitutional and Administrative Law* (15th edn, Longman, 2011) 86.
21 *R v Secretary of State for the Environment, Transport and the Regions, ex parte Alconbury* [2001] UKHL 23.

When the phone hacking scandal of 2011 became public, Mr Hunt had to take steps to maintain the appearance of impartiality. The Government, whilst expressing distaste for the actions of News International, stated that Mr Hunt's decision on the takeover had to be taken on the basis of the legal test alone. When MPs voted to condemn the role of News International in hacking murder victims and the families of dead soldiers, Mr Hunt had to abstain from that vote. Ultimately, News International's decision to withdraw their bid relieved the minister of having to make a decision.

It is a necessary and legitimate part of the Media Secretary's role to meet with media organisations, and there were a number of meetings between Mr Hunt and News International executives during the time when he was exercising this quasi-judicial role. Critics such as the Labour MP Tom Watson complained to the Cabinet Secretary about a number of 'unminuted, private, secret "informal" meetings'.[22] It is unthinkable that a 'judicial' judge would do this, and arguable that the independence and impartiality of all of these quasi-judicial decisions should be better protected.

9.9.2 JUDGES AND POLITICAL ACTIVITIES

If making sure that politicians do not become too involved in the judicial function is one side of a coin, then the other side is that judges should not become involved in politics.

It has long been a constitutional convention that judges should abstain from party politics, and it is now in the terms and conditions of employment for judges that they must forego any type of political activity. In the past, the Law Lords would occasionally take part in the legislative debates of the House of Lords and even propose amendments. Lord Scarman proposed a number of changes that became law, including one of the most important provisions in the law on criminal evidence: section 78 of the Police and Criminal Evidence Act 1984. This involvement has now ended with the creation of the Supreme Court. Judges are not allowed, under the House of (amended) Commons Disqualification Act 1975, to be members of the House of Commons.

9.9.3 JUDICIAL INQUIRIES

Judges are regularly appointed by the Government to head up inquiries. Following the phone hacking revelations of 2011, for example, a judicial inquiry was established and Lord Justice Leveson appointed to lead it.

Politicians are keen to appoint judges to chair inquiries because, as well as having skills in the scrutiny of witnesses and in handling large amounts of evidence, they have a reputation

---

22 'Jeremy Hunt is "knee deep in News Corp", claims Labour MP Tom Watson' *The Guardian*, 23 December 2010, http://www.guardian.co.uk/media/2010/dec/23/jeremy-hunt-news-corp-tom-watson-letter (last accessed 05/11/17).

for independence. This reputation helps the process of enquiry and the weight given to the conclusions. Yet, an overuse of judges for these purposes or placing judges in charge of politically highly sensitive matters brings a risk of undermining that very value of impartiality.

APPLYING THE LAW – THE BLOODY SUNDAY INQUIRIES

On 30 January 1972, 13 civil rights protesters were killed by troops of the Parachute Regiment on the streets of Derry, Northern Ireland. There were allegations that members of the IRA had infiltrated the march and had fired on the soldiers first. Lord Chief Justice Widgery was appointed to chair an inquiry into the event. His report was published only 11 weeks after the shootings.

The report largely exonerated the Parachute Regiment (although it concluded that some of their actions 'bordered on recklessness'). It found that the protests had created an atmosphere of danger, and that some of the marchers had been armed and had fired the first shots. The report was widely regarded in the Nationalist community as an establishment cover-up and as an insult to the dead protesters. In their eyes, it undermined the legitimacy of UK Government rule in Northern Ireland. From the separation of powers perspective, it is unfortunate that a judge was placed at the centre of such a sensitive and highly charged political issue. Having been drawn in, it is unfortunate that Lord Widgery discharged his responsibilities in this manner.

Campaigners in Ulster and elsewhere kept up the pressure to re-open the inquiry. They were eventually successful when the 'Bloody Sunday' Inquiry was established under another judge, Lord Saville, in 1998. In sharp contrast to its predecessor, the Saville Inquiry took 12 years to report. It concluded that the 'immediate responsibility' for the deaths lay with the soldiers who had undertaken 'unjustifiable firing' and had later lied to cover up their actions.

Although the Saville Report appeared to be a model of investigative rigour, it too was criticised by some for bias. It also kept Lord Saville from his judicial duties for some time. The two reports, in their different ways, illustrate the dangers for judicial independence of participation in these sorts of inquiries.

9.10 IS THERE A SEPARATION OF POWERS IN THE UK?

So, we have outlined information on various aspects of the separation of powers. What do you need to be able to do with that knowledge? Seminars and assessments will normally require you to be able to demonstrate an understanding of this material, to be able to summarise it effectively and illustrate your points with examples and authority.

It is common in seminars and assessments to ask students to consider whether there is an adequate separation of powers in the UK constitution or whether further reform is needed. This requires higher reasoning skills. You need to analyse the materials to see how they help you answer this sort of question, evaluate the competing arguments and create your own reasoned answer. How do you go about doing this?

To recap the main conclusions reached in this chapter so far:

- There is a close fusion between the legislative and executive branches,
- There is strong protection for judicial independence.
- The Constitutional Reform Act 2005 has placed institutional arrangements within a clearer separation of powers framework.

There are a number of possible approaches (and you are encouraged to come up with your own variation on any of these). The first is that there is no separation of powers or a very ineffective separation in the UK. This is the position taken by a number of academic writers. The second is that there is a broadly effective separation of powers, with judicial independence being the most crucial facet of the concept. This is the position of many judges.

There is a middle ground to this argument that acknowledges the importance of judicial independence and how effectively it is protected, and that recognises the seriousness of governmental domination of Parliament and the scope for a clearer separation of the legislative and executive branches.

In higher education, we are looking for you to reach a conclusion. Finishing an essay with a statement such as 'So in conclusion, there are different views on whether or not the UK has a separation of powers' is a weak conclusion. We are looking for you to read about and think about the different possible arguments and explain why one is more persuasive than the rest.

9.10.1 PURE VERSUS PARTIAL SEPARATION OF POWERS

Before we assess the different approaches, it is useful to distinguish between 'pure' and 'partial' conceptions of the separation of powers. Pure separation would involve each of the three branches having totally separate personnel and institutions. No person could exercise more than one type of power. In addition, no one branch of the state could exercise power or control over another branch.

There are a number of reasons for rejecting this as the most appropriate interpretation of the separation of powers. First, pure separation would not promote efficiency. Unless the three branches work together in some way, the state is unlikely to function well or even to survive.

Second, a pure separation of powers may not fulfil the purpose behind the concept any better than more mixed approaches. If no branch of the state can exercise control over another branch, then it cannot act to prevent abuse in that other branch. Each isolated part of the state might abuse its allocated portion of the state's power.

Even constitutions drafted with the separation of powers as a central theme do not have this 'pure' form. In the US Constitution, rather than isolation of the three branches there are a series of checks and balances. So, whilst the power to make law is granted to Congress, it must present the legislation to the President, who in effect has a veto power (Article 1). The US Supreme Court in *Marbury v Madison*, 5 US 137 (1803) interpreted the Constitution as giving the Court the power to declare invalid any law it regarded as unconstitutional.

The Justices of the Supreme Court are nominated by the President, but only 'by and with the advice and consent of the Senate' (Article 2). The President can also be removed from office by the Senate (the upper house of Congress) using the impeachment process in Article 4, for 'Treason, Bribery or other High Crimes and Misdemeanours' (see Chapter 4, 'Constitutions', for further details on the impeachment procedure).

APPLYING THE LAW – US PRESIDENTIAL IMPEACHMENTS

President Bill Clinton was impeached for perjury and obstruction of justice in 1998. The allegations were wide-ranging but focused on claims that President Clinton had lied under oath about his relationship with a White House intern, Monica Lewinsky. He famously stated that he did not have 'sexual relations' with Miss Lewinsky. There was evidence that they had engaged in oral sex and there was debate as to whether the President's statement therefore amounted to deliberate falsehood.

When the Senate voted on the impeachment, it divided along party lines (roughly 50:50) and the required two-thirds majority was not obtained.

President Richard Nixon resigned in 1974 over the Watergate scandal but would, in all likelihood, have been removed from office through impeachment if he had not resigned. The Watergate scandal involved a number of crimes committed by or on behalf of Republican Party aides, including putting political opponents under surveillance and breaking into the headquarters of the Democratic Party. Evidence emerged, in the 'smoking gun tape', that President Nixon had been told of these activities (after the event) and had been complicit in trying to block the investigation.

These illustrate the power of one branch of the state over another branch and how that can be used to scrutinise possible abuses of power.

Overall then, it is preferable to have a conception of the separation of powers that does not insist on complete isolation of each branch, but focuses on a distribution and balancing of power between different parts of the state to achieve the overall objective of preventing abuse of power.

9.10.2 THE 'NO SEPARATION OF POWERS' ARGUMENT

If you want to pursue this approach, then you will concentrate on the overlap between the executive and legislative branches. It would be useful to highlight that these are the most powerful parts of the state and that they can override the will of the judiciary. You could also note that many other constitutions at least try to separate the executive and legislative branches, whilst the UK system effectively staples them together.

The sorts of counter-arguments that you may have to address are that the academic writers (e.g. Robson, see above) may be using an unrealistically pure conception of the separation of powers, that it ignores the powerful protections for judicial independence and that these views were put forward before the important recent constitutional reforms. The consequences of taking this position are either that, a) like Bagehot, you welcome the close union between Parliament and Government as promoting efficiency and strong government, or b) that the UK unwritten constitution cannot support clear separation of powers and that wholesale reform including a written constitution is needed.

9.10.3 THE 'UK HAS A SEPARATION OF POWERS' ARGUMENT

This argument is largely a mirror image of the above. It focuses more on the importance of judicial independence and highlights the stringent protections for that independence. It accepts that there are some overlaps between the executive and legislative branches and focuses on the recent reforms and on how they have been explicitly based on a desire to establish a clearer separation of powers.

The possible counter-arguments are that this approach is rather naïve in ignoring the implications of governmental dominance of law-making and ignores the relative weakness of the judicial branch. This approach does not point to any need for major constitutional reform, and further evolution of law, convention and practice can reinforce and further strengthen the separation of powers.

9.10.4 THE 'MIDDLE GROUND' ARGUMENT

This self-evidently tries to balance the positive of judicial independence with the negative of legislative/executive fusion. One way of making this argument distinctive is by trying to sketch out a realistic understanding of how Parliaments and Governments are likely to be in close step with each other in modern liberal democracies.

Parliaments and Governments are chosen through the political electoral process. There are all sorts of variations between different systems, but the key is that those who make the law and those who lead the executive branch are chosen by methods of popular vote.

If the public leans in one direction (e.g. to the political left), then both the legislature and executive will be left-wing. If the public mood changes, then the personnel in both branches change.

People from both branches are in the profession of politics. They have a need to persuade the public to support them and they put forward their political ideology, programmes and specific proposals with this in mind. They are members of political parties which have the experience, structure, strategies and resources to make their candidates successful. In return, the party will demand loyalty and discipline. If both branches are controlled by politicians from the same party, then it is likely that they will act in a very co-ordinated manner.

M J C Vile denied that this overlap between legislative and executive branches was particularly problematic as long as it was accompanied by extensive checks and balances. The branches have never have been effectively separated and 'in every constitution they have continually influenced and acted upon each other'.[23]

You can develop this argument by noting that the UK constitution exacerbates this natural tendency to co-operation and co-ordination. Most constitutions make some effort to separate the processes, for example by holding elections for the different branches at different times or by using different electoral methods. As a result, in other countries, party discipline is often looser than in the UK and it is more common for the two branches to be controlled by politicians from different parties.

POINTS TO REVIEW

In this chapter, you should have:

- Picked up the basic shape of the separation of powers concept and how it developed.

- Seen that the overlap of functions between Parliament and Government supports arguments that the UK system is not based on the separation of powers.

- Understood that the Constitutional Reform Act 2005 has introduced changes that more clearly indicate a separation of powers, particularly between the judicial branches and the other branches.

- Grasped how the independence of the judiciary is protected by statute, convention and common understanding.

- Started to think about how you can move beyond description of the concept to an informed evaluation of its role in the UK constitutional system.

23 M Vile, *Constitutionalism and the Separation of Powers* (2nd edn, OUP, Liberty Fund, 1998) 47.

TAKING IT FURTHER

E Barendt, 'Separation of Powers and Constitutional Government' [1995] *Public Law* 599 This was an important article in re-starting the debate on the place of the separation of powers in the UK. One way of constructing an argument is to contrast the views of academic writers; you could make a very interesting contrast between what Barendt and Barber (see below) say on the values underpinning the concept.

N Barber, 'Prelude to the Separation of Powers' [2001] *Cambridge Law Journal* 59 This is perhaps the most challenging read of the sources listed here. You could focus on identifying the main arguments on a) the purpose of the separation of powers and b) whether there is a need for a definitive model of the concept.

R Benwell and O Gay, The Separation of Powers: Commons Library Standard Note (2011, House of Commons Library Briefing Papers), www.parliament.uk/briefing-papers/ SN06053.pdf This is a briefing note to MPs and is therefore is a very approachable summary. It is particularly strong on placing recent constitutional developments in the context of separation of powers. You could enhance your work by picking up on these examples.

D Woodhouse, 'The Constitutional Reform Act 2005 – Defending Judicial Independence the English Way' (2007) 5 *International Journal of Constitutional Law* 153 This article focuses on the Constitutional Reform Act 2005 changes. As you read this try to pick out *why* Woodhouse thinks that the statutory protection for judicial independence 'may be of little practical use'.

CHAPTER 10
THE RULE OF LAW

Here are some fundamental questions: why should people obey the law? Does the Government always need legal authority for its actions? Should public officials be bound by the same rules and subject to the same courts as ordinary citizens? Can oppressive dictatorships ever be said to be lawful? These are addressed by the constitutional principle of the rule of law. It is not in itself a legal rule but it organises a number of legal principles into a broad and powerful influence on the constitution. It outlines something of a paradox, that whilst the law is a powerful tool in the hands of the state, the need for lawful authority can be a powerful restraint on governmental abuses of citizens.

AS YOU READ

The meaning of the rule of law has been the subject of considerable debate. It is often described, even by some judges, as a particularly slippery and elusive concept. This chapter hopes to persuade you that this is not necessarily so. Each writer has their own particular take on the rule of law but, without unduly simplifying the approaches, we can place them into three categories. First, the **legality principle** states that Governments must act in accordance with the law. Secondly, the **formal school** adds the notion that laws should have certain characteristics (e.g. clarity) regardless of their content. Third, the **substantive school** argues that the rule of law additionally requires that the content of laws is consistent with human rights and human dignity.

In this chapter, you will need to understand these different approaches and be able to illustrate them and compare their strengths. You should not lose sight, however, of the important *practical* role that the rule of law plays in UK Public Law. Before you start you should view this video, with endorsement of the rule of law from the likes of Bill Gates and Archbishop Desmond Tutu: http://worldjusticeproject.org/endorsements

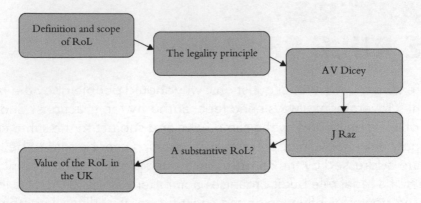

Figure 10.1 Structure of Chapter 10

10.1 INTRODUCTION

EXPLAINING THE LAW– WHAT DANGERS MAKE THE RULE
OF LAW SO IMPORTANT?

Imagine that Elizabeth makes some critical remarks about the rulers of a country. She
is abducted by state agents who refuse to tell Elizabeth's relatives where she is being
held or what law she has broken. When the relatives go to court, their application
fails because the Minister for Justice has informed the judge (without telling
Elizabeth's relatives) that a secret law was passed that morning by the President.
That law cannot be shown to the court but the Minister tells the judge that it covers
Elizabeth's past behaviour.

The police later confiscate all of Elizabeth's property. Her relatives cannot find any
law that authorises this. Their first application for a court order is rejected because
the Minister simply instructs the court to refuse them access and pays the judges a
bonus when they act on his orders. A different court agrees to hear the claim and
issues an order for the return of the property. The Minister commands the police to
ignore the court order.

This is a hypothetical scenario but it is also an amalgam of real life historical events. It
represents aspects of England at the time of Magna Carta 1215 and the Habeas Corpus Act
1679 and of Britain at the time of the *Entick v Carrington* case in 1765. It is a depressingly
familiar summary of the situation in dictatorships and totalitarian regimes from around the
world through recent centuries and right up to the present day. Some of the issues from
this scenario, such as refusing a prisoner access to a court, have been amongst the most
heated topics in recent decades in the Western liberal democracies of the UK and the US,
particularly in relation to responses to terrorism and the operation of Guantanamo Bay.

A bit of empathy never hurts in trying to understand the importance of legal protections, so go ahead and imagine that Elizabeth is one of your relatives. How are you likely to feel about your obligation to obey the laws of this state? What conclusions will you draw about the role of law within this country and the ability of law to control the Government?

In a state based on the rule of law, these things would simply not be allowed to happen. Public officials acting without lawful authority, secret and retrospective laws, governments controlling judges or instructing the police to ignore inconvenient court orders are all direct breaches of the principle of the rule of law.

As we go through the contested definitions of the rule of law and the subtle implications of one school of thought over another, you should keep this scenario in mind. Notice, in particular, that the rule of law has this core content in all its different guises and that it tries to prevent the sort of evils that some rulers are tempted into (or are hell-bent on doing).

EXPLAINING THE LAW – ZIMBABWE LAND REFORM

Southern Rhodesia was an apartheid state in southern Africa where black people were excluded from political and economic life by the white minority. A guerrilla war brought an end to the apartheid regime and the establishment of a new republic, Zimbabwe, in 1980. Zimbabwe is a signatory to numerous international agreements, including the International Covenant on Civil and Political Rights and the African Charter on Human and Peoples' Rights. These require the equal protection of the law and the independence of the judiciary.

The issue of land reform was a vexed one, and 20 years after the foundation of Zimbabwe, many large farms were still owned by white farmers. The ruling ZANU-PF party of the President, Robert Mugabe, sought to speed up the process of land redistribution. In the process they incited 'war veterans' to invade white-owned farms and evict the owners. These invasions were not legally authorised property transfers, and serious violence occurred, including murder. A Human Rights Watch study of 2002 reported allegations that the police and army were involved in assisting the land invasions and in the beating and torture of farm workers. The reluctance of the police to protect victims of violence was well reported.[1]

The farmers obtained court orders requiring the trespassers to leave. Ordinarily, the police would enforce such orders, but President Mugabe's Government instructed the police not to do so. This was part of the process of a country that had previously held a commitment to the rule of law now sliding into authoritarianism.

---

1 Human Rights Watch, 'Fast Track Land reform in Zimbabwe', http://www.hrw.org/reports/2002/zimbabwe/ ZimLand0302.pdf (last accessed 05/11/17).

10.2 DEFINITION AND SCOPE OF THE RULE OF LAW

There has been a good deal of worrying about the definition and scope of the term 'rule of law'. Barnett argues that 'Of all the constitutional concepts the rule of law is also the most subjective and value laden'.[2] Some commentators go further, and Shklar's declaration that the term is 'meaningless thanks to ideological abuse and general overuse' is often quoted.[3]

Yet to describe the principle as 'meaningless' is overstepping the mark. There is actually a good degree of consistency between the differing accounts of what the 'rule of law' means. You will see that the rule of law has a core meaning – the legality principle. Whilst this is limited in scope, it is hard-edged and has a defined legal content and mechanisms for securing legality. There is a penumbra of wider meaning that is subject to lively debate. It is generally accepted that this includes notions of natural justice, access to the courts and clarity and prospectivity in legal rules.

Writers have largely agreed on the core content of the rule of law and differ mainly on how wide the principle is. Some prefer a narrower formal approach, others agree that the rule of law requires these formal characteristics but also that there is a broader need for the *substance* of the legal rules to have a minimum content of fairness and equity. At its widest, these arguments say that the rule of law requires democracy, human rights and even social and cultural rights.

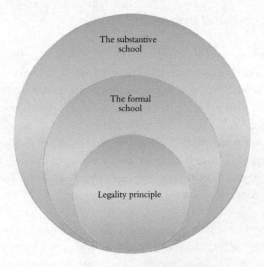

Figure 10.2 Different models of the scope of the rule of law

---

2   H Barnett, *Constitutional and Administrative Law* (11th edn, Routledge, 2016) 48.
3   J Shklar, 'Political Theory and the Rule of Law' in A Hutchinson and P Monahan (eds), *The Rule of Law: Ideal or Ideology* (Carswell, 1987) 1.

10.2.1 ASSESSMENT TIP

Do not let the contested nature of the concept put you off. Exploring these competing claims can be a very stimulating exercise, and (perhaps more important than debates on where the boundaries of the concept lie) the rule of law has crucial *functions* to perform. Jowell argues that the rule of law is defined in the course of its practical application[4] and when you see the work that the concept does, you will recognise its importance in the UK constitution.

10.2.2 THE RULE OF LAW AS A BENCHMARK

The rule of law can be used as a *benchmark* that allows scholars of Public Law (which now includes you) to evaluate and critique laws and constitutions. Proposals which do not measure up to the standards required by the rule of law can be criticised in those terms. This does not stop measures that breach the rule of law from being passed. Yet because there is such a widespread commitment to the rule of law these sorts of criticisms are very powerful and have resulted in proposals being dropped or amended.

The principle is particularly important in delivering constitutionalism, i.e. limited government and the prevention of abuse of state power. Most important amongst those who accept this function of the rule of law are the judges. They do not simply use the concept as a theoretical benchmark but also as a practical tool. The rule of law is a strong general principle that helps guide the development of the common law and a powerful presumption in statutory interpretation.

At its heart is the insistence on the supremacy of law over people, on a rules-based over a whim-based system. Its roots go deep into Western thought; Aristotle said, 'the rule of law is preferable to that of any individual', and English medieval writer Bracton wrote that 'the King ought not be subject to man but to God and the Law, because the law makes him King'.[5] It is also firmly embedded in the English constitutional system. The Magna Carta, signed in 1215, did not make any reference to the term 'rule of law' but it did provide some key rule of law protections:

- Chapter 39 – 'no freeman shall be taken or imprisoned . . . save by lawful judgement of his peers or by the law of the land'.
- Chapter 40 – to none will we sell, 'to none deny or delay, right or justice'.
- Chapter 45 – only those with knowledge of the law and 'minded to observe it rightly' will be appointed as judges.
- Chapters 52 and 55 – fines and confiscation of property must be in accordance with the law.

---

4 J Jowell, 'The Rule of Law's Long Arm: Uncommunicated Decisions' [2004] *Public Law* 246.
5 Bracton, *On the Laws and Customs of England*, c.1236.

10.3 THE RULE OF LAW IS NOT A RULE OF LAW

T R S Allan says: 'In the mouth of a British constitutional lawyer, the term "rule of law" seems to mean primarily a corpus of basic principles and values, which together lend some stability and coherence to the legal order'.[6] The rule of law is a principle of governance or an expression of state morality, albeit one that that can have powerful effects on how laws are made and interpreted. Its basis is not in formal legal sources, and there is no authoritative statement of its meaning in statute or case law.

The Constitutional Reform Act 2005 highlights its importance, stating in section 1 that 'This Act does not adversely affect the existing constitutional principle of the rule of law'. There is no attempt, however, to define the principle. The Act seems to recognise the importance of the rule of law as a pre-existing 'constitutional principle', but it does not help us to decide which formulation of the principle is the best one. Judges, as we will see, already use the rule of law in a wide and active manner. They probably did not need any further encouragement from statute to regard the rule of law as a constitutional principle. So what is the point of section 1 of the Constitutional Reform Act 2005?

The answer lies in the governmental reforms introduced by the Act (see Chapter 9, 'Separation of powers'). These initially put the existence of the office of Lord Chancellor in doubt. The Lord Chancellor was seen as the primary defender of the rule of law within Cabinet. The Lord Chancellor at the time of the passage of the Act, Lord Falconer, said that: 'The Government have no problem in accepting that the rule of law must and does guide the actions of Ministers and all public officials. It is also clear that Ministers and other public officials must comply with the law'.[7] Even though the office was reprieved, there are concerns that the new redefined Lord Chancellor (who is not necessarily a lawyer) will be less alive to the constitutional role of the rule of law than their predecessors.

10.3.1 OBEDIENCE TO THE LAW

The rule of law expresses a preference for a society ordered by law and order rather than anarchy. Whilst much of the focus of the rule of law is on the obligation of the Government and public bodies to abide by legal rules, this society ordered by law would be impossible if ordinary citizens did not obey the law.

APPLYING THE LAW – THE DEATH OF SOCRATES

Socrates was a philosopher in ancient Athens (c. 469BC–399BC). His philosophical approach did not expressly call for the overthrow of the government or the rejection of the accepted morals or religious beliefs of the city. His approach, however, was

6   T R S Allan, *Law Liberty and Justice: The Legal Foundations of British Constitutionalism* (OUP, 1995) 143.
7   Hansard HL, vol 667, col 738.

to constantly question things, including notions of justice, honour and bravery, and this in turn provoked and embarrassed the leaders of the city. He was charged with corrupting the minds of the youth of Athens, convicted and sentenced to death by poison.

Socrates' pupil, Plato, described the opportunity for Socrates to escape from prison and this unjust sentence, and his refusal to do so. Socrates chose to accept the death penalty and drank the poison. Why would he do so? Did he have an obligation to obey the law? Did this obligation even extend to laws that were oppressive and unjust?

Apply this to your life. Consider why you obey the law (if you do). Can you think of any legal restrictions that you obey but that you feel are unnecessary or unjust?

There are a number of reasons put forward by scholars for Socrates' resignation to his legal fate, including his feeling that the time was right for his death and that he had nothing to fear, but the key reason can be seen as an early version of what is known as *social contract theory*.

Socrates is reported to have said, 'do you imagine that a city can continue to exist and not be turned upside down, if the legal judgments which are pronounced in it have no force but are nullified and destroyed by private persons'.[8] Having chosen to continue to live in Athens, Socrates felt that he had entered into a sort of contract with the city. It would provide protection and order, and in return the citizen would provide obedience to the law.

Social contract theory provides a rationale for the obligation to obey the law and also an indication of the limits of that obligation. Thomas Hobbes and Jean-Jacques Rousseau came up with related ideas of why humans come together in civil society and the consequences that follow: individuals limit their own liberty and give some power to the state to rule over them. There are echoes of this in the House of Lords' judgment in *Heaton's Transport v Transport and General Workers Union* [1973] AC 15, where Lord Wilberforce said, 'The justification for the law, the courts and the rule of law is that they protect us from unfair and oppressive actions by others, but if we are to have that protection we must ourselves accept that the law applies to us too, and limits our freedom'.

Many social contract theories, however, go on to argue that when the state acts injuriously to the people, then the obligation of obedience is curtailed or suspended. There are obvious difficulties in identifying who gets to decide whether a law is unjust or not. Any civil disobedience should be proportionate to the injustice, and most theorists draw a line between non-violent resistance and violent acts.

---

8   Plato, *Crito* (CreateSpace, 2015), http://classics.mit.edu/Plato/crito.html (last accessed 05/11/17).

KEY LEARNING POINTS

....

- ■ The rule of law is an important constitutional principle rather than a single legal rule.
- ■ There are competing conceptions of the rule of law, but they can be used as a benchmark to assess Government action.

10.4 THE LEGALITY PRINCIPLE – GOVERNMENT ACCORDING TO THE LAW

'Legality' includes the idea that there are established institutions and established processes for making valid law. The rulers of a country cannot simply make up legal rules as and how they wish. For primary legislation (as we saw in Chapter 3, 'Parliament and legislation'), this involves Bills being submitted to Parliament, going through the various stages of debate and scrutiny, and being approved by the House of Commons, approved by the House of Lords and then receiving the royal assent.

Ultimately, it is the *judges* who police even this aspect of the rule of law (as we saw in Jennings's rule of recognition, Chapter 7, 'Supremacy of Parliament'). We can see this process even more clearly with secondary legislation, such as local authority bye-laws, where the courts can quash these purported legal rules on the basis that there was no lawful authority to make them or that the established procedures for law-making were not used.

The impact of the legality principle, however, does not fall heaviest on the legislature but on the executive. It requires that ministers and public officials act in accordance with the law and have lawful authority for their actions.

EXPLAINING THE LAW – *ENTICK V CARRINGTON* (1765) 19 ST TR 1029 (COURT OF COMMON PLEAS)

John Entick wrote pamphlets critical of the Government. The Secretary of State (a role broadly equivalent to the Home Secretary) ordered King's Messengers (the nearest modern equivalent would be the police) to seize his papers and gave them a warrant that purported to authorise their actions. They forcibly entered Entick's house, arrested him and took away his papers. Entick sued for trespass.

The King's Messengers claimed authority from a statute, but this did not authorise the warrant, so the argument shifted to state necessity. It was claimed that the defendant's writings were an attack on the state (an offence known as sedition) and therefore it was necessary for the state to defend itself. This necessity, it was argued, made the warrant lawful. Lord Camden, the judge in the Court of Common Pleas, dismissed this defence of state necessity and handed down one of the landmark judgments in English legal history:

> This power, so claimed by the Secretary of State, is not supported by one single citation from any law book extant . . . If it is the law, it will be found in our books. If it not to be found there, it is not law.
>
> By the laws of England any invasion of property, be it ever so minute, is a trespass. No man can set his foot upon my ground without my licence, but he is liable to an action.
>
> According to this reasoning, it is now incumbent upon the defendants to show the law by which this seizure is warranted. If that cannot be done it is a trespass . . . Where is the written law that gives any magistrates such a power? I can safely answer, there is none; and therefore it is too much for us without such authority to pronounce such a practice legal, which would be subversive of all the comforts of society.

This insistence that even public bodies must act according to the law and that even Government ministers could not simply extend their legal powers because they thought it necessary was highly unusual at the time.

At first glance, it might seem to impose substantive limits on state power, e.g. making it impossible to issue general warrants authorising arrest, search and seizure. By looking at subsequent developments, though, the scope of the principle in *Entick v Carrington* becomes clearer, in particular the rather narrow scope of the legality principle and its inability to prevent oppressive laws being passed becomes more apparent. This is especially so in the UK which does not have a written constitution and in which Parliament is supreme and legally entitled to make any law it wishes.

10.4.1 POWERS GRANTED BY PARLIAMENT

Section 20C of the Taxes and Management Act 1970 provides that: 'An officer of the Board [of the Inland Revenue] may enter premises, . . . on the issue of a warrant, and search them . . . may seize and remove any things whatsoever found there which he has reasonable cause to believe may be required as evidence for the purpose of proceedings . . .'

The reference to 'for the purpose of proceedings' might indicate that the warrant should state the particular offences which the company is suspected of. The section, however, does not expressly state a need for this. The danger that hovers over this is that state officials will be given the power to go on 'fishing expeditions', i.e. to search through property for evidence of wrongdoing without having to say beforehand what they suspect and why.

EXPLAINING THE LAW – *R V INLAND REVENUE COMMISSION, EX PARTE ROSSMINSTER LTD* (1980) AC 952

Rossminster Ltd was a company suspected by the Inland Revenue of committing some unspecified tax fraud. The Inland Revenue obtained warrants allowing them to enter and seize anything they thought might be relevant evidence of tax fraud. The warrant gave no particular details of what specific offences were suspected, and the warrant just followed the wording of section 20C of the Taxes and Management Act 1970. It was a general warrant.

Lord Denning in the Court of Appeal said:

> Once great power is granted there is a danger of it being abused. Rather than risk such abuse, it is, as I see it, the duty of the courts to construe such a statute so as to see that it encroaches as little as possible upon the liberties of the people of England.

> As a matter of construction of the statute and therefore of the warrant . . . in pursuance of our traditional role to protect the liberty of the individual – it is our duty to say that the warrant must particularise the specific offence which is charged.

On this basis the warrant was invalid, but this finding was reversed by the House of Lords who said: 'The Act authorises officers of the board of Inland Revenue, acting upon a search warrant, to enter premises by day or night, if necessary by force, and seize anything whatsoever reasonably believed to be evidence of an offence involving fraud in connection with tax . . .' and 'There is nothing in the statute to require the particular offence to be stated in the warrant. Since the provisions of the statute had been complied with, there was no violation of the principle of *Entick v Carrington*'. (Lord Scarman).

Lord Scarman was deeply troubled by the breadth of the power given by statute, describing it as 'a breathtaking inroad upon the individual's right of privacy and right of property'. Nevertheless, once a statute had granted the power to the public body, then as long as it operated within the bounds of that power, the legality principle was complied with. The legal principle is not breached if a Government gets their additional powers, no matter how intrusive or disproportionate, granted by Parliament. 'Legality' in this sense provides no substantive protection, merely requiring the state to 'jump through the hoop' of authorising its own actions.

One common interpretation of *Entick v Carrington* was that the law insisted that public bodies had authority for all of their actions, particularly those that interfered with the lives of citizens. The following case, however, cast doubt on even this limited protection.

APPLYING THE LAW – *MALONE V METROPOLITAN POLICE COMMISSIONER* [1979] CH 344

It emerged during the trial of Malone on charges of handling stolen goods that his phone had been tapped as part of the investigation. There was no statute at this time authorising the phone tapping. The physical process of tapping the phone took place at the telephone exchange rather than at Malone's home. Malone argued that his right to privacy had been infringed and that the trial should have been stopped.

Imagine that you are counsel for Malone. How would you use the previous authority of *Entick v Carrington* to support your client's claim?

10.4.2 ASSESSMENT TIP

You could use a process called reasoning by analogy. This is a typical form of reasoning used in the common law. You would argue that the relevant facts of the earlier case (*Entick*) are the same as the material facts in the current case (*Malone*) and therefore the legal finding, i.e. the ratio decidendi, from the earlier case is a precedent. Whether this is a binding or a persuasive precedent depends on other factors, principally the status of the court in the earlier case.

Using this approach, you could characterise *Entick v Carrington* as a case where public officials acted without lawful authority. In the absence of that authority, they were not entitled to interfere with the citizen's life in the way they did, and the court duly gave Entick a remedy. You would characterise the facts in *Malone* along similar lines – that the police had no authority to tap Malone's phone, that as the interference was without legal authority the police were not entitled to act this way, and that the court should give Malone a remedy (overturning the conviction).

This is essentially the argument that Malone's lawyers did use, and it was rejected. The judge, Megarry VC, stated that there was no general legally enforceable right to privacy in English law and that 'if the tapping of telephones by the Post Office at the request of the police can be carried out without any breach of the law, it does not require any statutory or common law power to justify it'.

As the phone tap involved no physical trespass to Malone's property or goods, it was not a breach of law. Public bodies did not need lawful authority for all of their actions, only those actions that would otherwise breach a citizen's legal rights. In this way *Entick* was distinguished from the facts in *Malone*. Entick had legal rights to his person, his goods and his home as recognised by the existing laws of trespass; Malone had no legal right to his privacy (at this time).

So where there is a recognised civil right in UK law, such as the right to be free from trespass to your property, then when the state makes 'great inroads' into those rights, at least it has to go through the open and (to some extent) accountable process of legislating. Where there is no recognised civil right, the state can use its huge power and resources to interfere with citizens' lives without being required to show lawful authority.

10.4.3 ASSESSING THE LEGALITY PRINCIPLE – DOES IT CONSTRAIN THE STATE?

Consider these points:

- Any law can be introduced or amended by legislation.
- Parliament can use legislation to authorise the actions of the state.
- The legality principle therefore does not impose any substantive restrictions.

Does the legality principle have any value?

Its value lies in the fact that it imposes procedural restrictions on the state. By forcing the Government to use *law* as the legitimate means of interfering with the lives of its citizens then it makes this process subject to the general characteristics of law. These are discussed in more depth below when we look at the work of Joseph Raz, but in the context of the UK system this has a number of consequences. When a Government wants to change or expand its powers it must (usually) get Parliament to pass an Act of Parliament. This is an open and public procedure. It calls for the proposals to be published and they must be explained by the minister and be subject to debate. They will be scrutinised by the Opposition and by Parliamentary Committees.

The Government will normally be able to rely on a majority in the House of Commons, but this is not guaranteed, particularly with controversial proposals. The House of Lords cannot veto legislation but can exercise a considerable moderating influence over controversial proposals and amend and delay measures. There is limited time in Parliament's law-making schedule, and Governments are wary of using this time on proposals that may fail.

The public nature of the process allows the press, pressure groups and public to contribute to debates on the desirability of the measures, and Governments take note of the strength of public feeling. Other normal and desirable characteristics of law, such as being general (not directed to a single person or even a single group) and prospective (not changing the legal character of past behaviour) also help in protecting citizens.

The following example illustrates some of the strengths of the legality principle and the difficulty that even Western liberal states with explicit commitments to the rule of law sometime have in meeting its standards.

EXPLAINING THE LAW – IN-DEPTH INTERROGATION IN
NORTHERN IRELAND

In 1971, the Troubles in Northern Ireland were causing serious loss of life. The
Northern Ireland Government's response was to introduce internment, i.e. detention
without trial. The internment itself had a legal basis: the Civil Authorities (Special
Powers) Act (Northern Ireland) 1922. Some of the 342 people arrested and interned
were subject to special interrogation practices that became known as the 'five
techniques' or in-depth interrogation.

Internees were subjected to hooding, constant 'white noise', deprivation of food and
water, deprivation of sleep and were forced to stand in 'pressure positions' for extended
periods. These techniques were applied by the police in Northern Ireland, but they
were trained by the British Army and senior UK Government intelligence officials.

There were a number of reports into these practices but Lord Parker, the Lord Chief
Justice, was particularly asked to look at the legality of the five techniques. The
Report concluded that 'There has been no dissent from the view that the procedures
are illegal alike by the law of England and the law of Northern Ireland . . . Only
Parliament can alter the law. The procedures were and are illegal'.[9]

One member of the Committee, Lord Gardiner, went further and issued a minority
report. He pointed out that the British Army did not seem to have considered
whether the techniques were lawful, and the police trained by the army simply
assumed that the army would not coach them in unlawful practices. He concluded
that the blame for the 'sorry story' lay with those who had introduced 'procedures
which were secret, illegal, not morally justifiable and alien to the traditions of what
I believe still to be the greatest democracy in the world'.

The UK Government responded immediately that use of the techniques would not
continue, and directives expressly prohibiting them were issued to the security services.

The role of the legality principle here is that it can help force such practices out into the
open and shine some light on them. If the UK Government wanted to authorise its security
forces to apply procedures that involve torture or, at best, inhuman and degrading treatment
(as the European Court of Human Rights thought it was: *Ireland v UK* (1978) 2 EHRR 25),
then it would have to persuade Parliament to pass a law to that effect in the open, contested
and closely scrutinised manner outlined above; not something that any Government would
be particularly keen to do.

---

9 Report of the Committee of Privy Councillors Appointed to Consider Authorised Procedures or the Interrogation
of Persons Suspected of Terrorism, Cmnd 4901, 1972.

KEY LEARNING POINTS

- The legality principle lies at the heart of the rule of law, requiring the state to have legal authority for its actions.
- This is more a procedural than a substantive limitation. The Government can get legal authority for its action by way of an Act of Parliament.
- This requirement is useful in making executive claims to power more public and transparent.

10.5 FORMAL AND SUBSTANTIVE CONCEPTIONS OF THE RULE OF LAW

Does the term 'rule of law' mean anything more than simple legality? In the scenario above, the UK Parliament *could* have passed an Act that authorised the use of inhuman and degrading interrogation techniques. As Parliament is legally supreme, it *could* state that the previously unlawful treatment was retrospectively lawful. It *could* declare that the techniques may only be used against Northern Irish Catholics. It *could* state that a minister can authorise other techniques (torture by electricity, waterboarding) without notifying the public. Anything authorised by the law would be consistent with this narrow concept of the legality principle, but could we really say that such a country observed the 'rule of law'? There are no mainstream writers on the subject who would answer 'yes'. They all have some extended notion of what the rule of law requires.

We can categorise these extended notions into formal and substantive schools of thought. The *formal school* focuses on, whether the law was made properly, by authorised persons using authorised procedures; the clarity of the law and whether it enables individuals to make informed decisions about their conduct; and whether the law only applies to future conduct.

The *substantive school* uses this formal conception as its starting point but goes further. It tries to use the rule of law as the basis for substantive rights. This would allow a critique of legal provisions as being 'good' or 'bad' laws depending on their content and their adherence to these substantive rights. We will discuss next what have been the two most influential versions of the formal school, from Albert Dicey and Joseph Raz.

10.6 DICEY AND THE RULE OF LAW

Albert V Dicey was the founding father of the academic subject of Public Law in the UK. In his classic *Introduction to the Study of the Constitution* (1885), he argued that the rule of law was a central pillar of the UK constitutional system and that it consists of three essential elements: no arbitrary law; equality before the law; and the constitution is the ordinary law of the land.

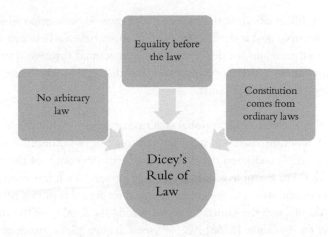

Figure 10.3 Dicey's rule of law

10.6.1 NO ARBITRARY LAW

Dicey said that 'No man is punishable or can be lawfully made to suffer in body or goods except for a distinct breach of law established in the ordinary legal manner before the ordinary Courts of the land'.[10] The idea here is that there is no arbitrary power and regular law predominates. 'Arbitrary' means power exercised on an unrestrained or personal whim and not according to a rational system. The Government cannot simply punish a person because it wishes to do so. Punishment can only follow a finding of guilt by a court of law.

Dicey went much further than this common-sense condemnation of arbitrary power and punishment. 'Discretion' means choice, and that a decision-maker can legitimately choose from a range of options. He argued that the rule of law is opposed to giving the state discretionary powers and equated discretionary powers with arbitrariness, saying that 'Government based on the exercise by persons in authority of wide, arbitrary, or discretionary powers of constraint' is contrary to the rule of law. This has the value of identifying a very wide or an unregulated discretion as a danger to individual liberty.

There are, however, serious objections to this aspect of Dicey's formulation. For example, police on their way to the scene of a violent crime may pass people committing speeding offences, driving through red lights or dropping litter. We would not expect the police to have a mechanistic duty to investigate, arrest and charge every offence they see in the order that they see it. They must have discretion to prioritise and even to overlook some offences. This was as true in Dicey's era as it is today, but, in addition, it is clear now that discretion is necessary in a modern state. The scope and volume of state activities mean that it is impossible for a state to address issues such as health and education provision, social welfare and care for the elderly and infirm, and environmental protection, without being able to exercise discretion.

10 A V Dicey, *Introduction to the Study of the Constitution* (8th edn, Liberty Fund, 1982).

Davis explains that 'Elimination of all discretionary power is both impossible and undesirable. The sensible goal is development of a proper balance between rule and discretion'.[11] It is better to aim for discretion that is structured through detailed procedures, open criteria, clear limits on the scope of power, and the right to challenge the lawfulness of the exercise of discretion before a court.

It is now a normal part of the constitutional system that ministers and public officials have choices as to what actions to take, e.g. what benefit to grant or withhold from a citizen. Whilst Dicey may simply condemn this, a more modern conception of the rule of law tries to control the power. For example, a statute can give powers to a minister to act 'as they see fit'. Rule of law concerns have led the courts to avoid reading this phrase literally and to say that such clauses do not stop the courts from examining the legality of the minister's actions (*Padfield v Minister for Agriculture* [1968] AC 997, see Chapter 13, 'Grounds of judicial review').

10.6.2 EQUALITY BEFORE THE LAW

Dicey said that 'No man is above the law but . . . that every man, whatever be his rank or condition, is subject to the ordinary law of the realm and amenable to the jurisdiction of the ordinary tribunals'. This means that Government is subject to the law, and public officials are subject to the same general laws as ordinary citizens. The law reports 'abound with cases in which officials have been brought before the courts, and made, in their personal capacity, liable to punishment, or to the payment of damages, for acts done in their official character but in excess of their lawful authority'.[12] Clearly, cases like *Entick v Carrington* were important to this line of reasoning.

There are, however, a wide range of exceptions. MPs have Parliamentary privilege; judges have immunity from being sued etc. Dicey allowed that there were exceptions. He mentioned the position of clergymen (of the Church of England) and soldiers who were subject to different bodies of laws and different courts, but perhaps underestimated the way in which each person has a unique set of legal rights and responsibilities. Nonetheless, the notion of equality before the law and that public officials are subject to the jurisdiction of the ordinary courts can be a powerful one, as the following case illustrates.

EXPLAINING THE LAW – *M V HOME OFFICE* [1994] 1 AC 377

M was a national of Zaire and claimed asylum in the UK. His application was refused and Home Office officials made plans to return him to Zaire, via Paris. An emergency application was made to a judge in chambers to judicially review the decision. The judge required that M be returned to the UK jurisdiction and noted that he had

---

11 K Davis, *Discretionary Justice* (5th edn, University of Illinois, 1971) 42.
12 Dicey, above n 10, 194.

received undertakings from Home Office lawyers that he would be returned from Paris. The undertakings were not understood (or not intended to be given) and M was put on to the Paris–Zaire flight. The judge made a mandatory order requiring his return to the UK. The Home Secretary received legal advice that the judge had exceeded his powers and decided not to act on the court order.

Ordinarily, if an individual refuses to obey a court order then they can face contempt of court proceedings. These are taken very seriously by the courts, and terms of imprisonment are often imposed for contempt. The difficulty here lay in the supposed immunity of the Crown from contempt of court proceedings. The Queen could not be guilty of contempt in the Queen's courts, and this immunity had been thought to extend to the Crown's ministers, i.e. the Government.

Lord Templeman made a crucial distinction between the Crown as Monarch and the Crown as executive (Government). He said, 'The judges cannot enforce the law against the Crown as monarch . . . but judges enforce the law against the Crown as executive, and against the individuals who from time to time represent the Crown'.

In a vivid echo of Dicey, he said, 'For the purpose of enforcing the law against all persons and institutions, including ministers in their official capacity and in their personal capacity, the courts are armed with coercive powers exercisable in proceedings for contempt of court' and rejected any notion that 'the executive obey the law as a matter of grace and not as a matter of necessity'. The House of Lords found in this case that the Secretary of State was guilty of contempt in his official rather than personal capacity and that a declaration of guilt was sufficient.

Dicey was hostile to the French style of Administrative Law, with its separate rules for state conduct and separate courts. He feared that the *droit administratif* and administrative courts would result in preferential treatment for public bodies and officials. In this he probably misunderstood the French system which simply recognised that public bodies have powers that private individuals do not and that these distinct powers need to be controlled by a distinct body of law.

There are so many exceptions to 'equality before the law' that Dicey cannot have meant that all citizens and Government officials should be subject to exactly the same rules. Therefore, the focus should be on the range of circumstances where Government officials can be subject to the jurisdiction of ordinary courts. The main vehicle for this is through judicial review (see Chapters 12 and 13).

Barnett admits that the scope of 'equality before the law' is contested, but that it is a positive contribution to Public Law and that 'to dismiss – as some writers do – this aspect of Dicey's exposition of the rule of law, is to deprive the student of the constitution of a valuable tool for analysis'.[13] The view taken here follows to some extent that of Jennings, who thought that rather too much has been loaded onto the term 'equality before the law',[14] but we would not want to deprive you, as a student of the constitution, of this valuable tool for enquiry and exploration.

10.6.3 ASSESSMENT TIP

In your seminars, when you prefer one view over another, your tutor may fire back a question ('why?', 'on what basis?') or a simple demand ('justify'). They are trying to get you to hone your thinking skills through these questions. The answer given here for departing, slightly and respectfully, from Barnett's view is that these issues can be dealt with better by considering Raz's formulation of the rule of law; that Raz's formulation has a firmer theoretical foundation and a greater contemporary relevance; and that the issues of access to the courts, natural justice, and the independence of the judiciary flow more logically from Raz's central thesis.

10.6.4 THE CONSTITUTION OF THE UK IS THE ORDINARY LAW OF THE LAND – LAWS CONCERNING THE LIBERTIES OF THE CITIZEN ARE JUDGE-MADE

Dicey's third element was that 'The general principles of the constitution are, with us, the result of judicial decisions determining the rights of private persons in particular cases before the courts'. This element emphasizes the failure of many written constitutions to limit abuses of power *in practice* and the contrasting English approach where individual rights are linked to a specific remedy available in the courts. This is linked to the idea of residual liberty – that British people have the right to do anything which is not prohibited – and a political tradition of Parliamentary restraint. The UK Parliament would hold back from interfering too readily or too extensively with the liberties of the British people.

Dicey was very sceptical of foreign constitutions where the 'security (such as it is) given to the rights of individuals results, or appears to result, from the general principles of the constitution'.[15] The two little asides in this quote are very telling. He felt that whilst written constitutions had wonderful sounding declarations of rights, in practice those rights were not delivered. The courts in those countries did not do the real practical work of English courts under a common law system of restraining abuses of governmental power. There was some evidence for this in the eighteenth century when the record of the UK on issues such as freedom of the press and freedom from arbitrary arrest compared favourably to other European countries.

The evidence now, however, has overtaken any approach that might have been defensible in the Victorian age. To continue to hold strictly to this view would misunderstand the effectiveness of general declarations of rights, such as the European Convention on

---

13 Barnett, above n.2, 69.

14 I Jennings, *The Law and the Constitution* (5th edn, Hodder & Stoughton, 1959).

15 Dicey, above n 10, 187.

Human Rights. Lord Bingham defends Dicey's third element by pointing out that the courts still have a central role in determining individual rights even under a general declaration of rights.[16]

10.6.5 PROBLEMS WITH DICEY

Dicey had very particular political views (including a lifelong opposition to granting votes to women). He was a Liberal Unionist who believed firmly in a *laissez faire* state. This means that he only saw a very limited role for public bodies, with the emphasis on individual liberty rather than on a state intervening to promote social goals such as health or the relief of poverty. We can accept that we all have our own political views, and accept that this may inform our evaluation of particular ideas and systems (even then it is better to be explicit about our perspective). The problem was that Dicey's work was primarily descriptive, and he allowed his political views to underplay some aspects (such as the role for discretion) and overplay others (such as the role of the courts in defending liberty). He described the rule of law in the UK constitution in a way which aligned with these political views.

There are other problems with taking a descriptive approach to the rule of law and basing it largely on one legal system. It will become less relevant as time passes, and it has limited use as a benchmark for evaluating other constitutions. The process should arguably be the other way around; a definition of the principle should be formulated and then a constitution can be described as meeting or failing to meet the relevant standard (*what ought to be*). Nevertheless, as Lord Bingham said, Dicey was 'effectively responsible for ensuring that no discussion of modern democratic government can properly omit reference to [the rule of law]'.[17]

10.7 JOSEPH RAZ

Joseph Raz outlined his ideas in 1977 in a hugely influential article 'The Rule of Law and its Virtue'.[18] He tried to overcome some of the difficulties inherent in Dicey's approach to the 'rule of law'; 'The Rule of Law should define what ought to be rather than what is'. In addition, he wanted to emphasise that the rule of law is a political ideal but only one of the virtues that a legal system might possess. He argued that one of the problems with the rule of law was that it had been confused with democracy, justice and fairness (this is explored in the critique of Raz below). For him, the concept ought to be as neutral as possible so that it could be used as an aspiration, a benchmark and an interpretive guide, in different times and different places.

---

16 Lord Bingham 'Dicey Revisited' [2002] *Public Law* 39, 51.

17 Ibid., 50.

18 J Raz, 'The Rule of Law and its Virtue' (1977) *Law Quarterly Review* 93.

EXPLAINING THE LAW– THE KNIFE METAPHOR

Raz had therefore set himself a difficult challenge, to arrive at a universal conception of the rule of law. To help illustrate his aims and methods he uses a metaphor: the metaphor of the knife. Answer these questions:

- What is the purpose of a knife?
- What general characteristics must a knife have to meet this purpose effectively?
- What sort of structure or design must a knife have to exhibit these characteristics?

Hopefully you decided that the purpose of a knife is *to cut*. Did you make any sort of moral judgement in deciding this? Probably not, and a knife can be used for good (slicing a cake) or for evil (stabbing someone through the heart). Its purpose as a tool is independent of the wider objective to which it is put.

The general characteristics that a knife needs to be able to cut effectively are sharpness and durability. Since its purpose is to allow *someone* to cut, then it also needs to be capable of being handled.

The structure and design of knives varies very widely, but they will include some sort of handle, some sort of blade, the blade will have one or two sharp edges, and the blade will be made of a material that either stays sharp or is capable of being sharpened.

APPLYING THE LAW – THE PURPOSE OF LAW

So let us apply this metaphorical structure to the social tool which is 'law'. What is the purpose of law? This is an interesting question for you as a law student to think about, independently of this question and this subject. For Raz, 'law should conform to standards designed to enable it effectively to guide action'.[19] So it is to allow people to know where they stand: to make decisions and know whether they are breaching the law.

We could argue that is not morally neutral. To allow individuals to plan their actions promotes their autonomy and protects human dignity. Yet, that is a necessary consequence of 'law directing human conduct'; it is not the same thing as saying that it has moral intention. The tool can be used to direct human behaviour in good ways (ensuring confidence in contractual agreements, protecting basic human rights) or in bad ways

---

19 J Raz, *The Authority of Law* (OUP, 1979) 218.

(allowing employers to exploit employees, directing state officials to undermine citizens' rights). Raz says that identifying this underlying purpose of law is a 'basic intuition' and it does not have a moral or ethical end as its starting point.

Let us move on to stage two and identify the characteristics that flow from this overall objective of guiding human behaviour. Raz argues that the most important characteristics are that laws should be prospective, open and clear and relatively stable. We cannot be guided by secret or obscure or confusing laws.

The third stage is to identify the underlying design that promotes these characteristics. They cannot be delivered in a vacuum, so a legal system having a certain structure or design is necessary. This legal system must have an independent judiciary and easily accessible courts that observe rules of natural justice. You cannot have clear laws if disputes as to the meaning of laws cannot be resolved by courts. It is interesting to note that Lon Fuller comes up with an almost identical list not on the basis of the morally neutral purpose of law but on his conception of the morality of law.

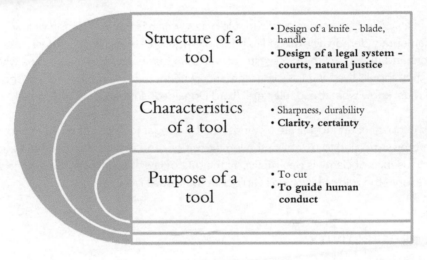

Figure 10.4 Raz's conception of the rule of law

10.8 CENTRAL CHARACTERISTICS

We will explore some of these core characteristics of law that allow it to guide human behaviour.

10.8.1 CLARITY

The European Court of Human Rights said in *Sunday Times v United Kingdom* (1979) 2 EHRR 245, 'a norm cannot be regarded as "law" unless it is formulated with sufficient precision to enable the citizen to regulate his conduct'. It is not a requirement that all laws are perfectly understandable by all lay people, but people should be able to find out where they stand, even if this means using a legal adviser to interpret the law and to guide them. As Lord Diplock found in *Black-Clawson International Ltd v Papierwerke Waldhof-Ascaffenberg AG* [1975] AC 591, 'The acceptance of the rule of law as a constitutional principle requires that a citizen, before committing himself to any course of action, should be able to know in advance what are the legal consequences that will flow from it'.

EXPLAINING THE LAW – *MERKUR ISLAND SHIPPING CORP V LAUGHTON AND OTHERS* [1983] 2 AC 570

This case concerned an action by the owners of a ship against the International Transport Workers Federation. It was a complex industrial dispute that led to a complex action. The court had to decide whether the union was tortiously liable for financial loss as a result of the strike and had to assess the interlocking effect of three separate Acts of Parliament.

The efficacy and maintenance of the rule of law, which is the foundation of any parliamentary democracy, has at least two prerequisites. First, people must understand that it is in their interests, as well as in that of the community as a whole, that they should live their lives in accordance with the rules and all the rules. Secondly, they must know what those rules are' (Lord Donaldson in the Court of Appeal).

British appeal court judges are amongst the best legal technicians in the world, yet even they struggled to establish the legal position, and expressed their frustration at this: 'Absence of clarity is destructive of the rule of law; it is unfair to those who wish to preserve the rule of law' (Lord Diplock in the House of Lords).

10.8.2 PROSPECTIVITY

Prospectivity means that laws should only apply to future conduct. If a statute comes into force on 1 April, it should only apply to conduct from 1 April onwards and not try to change the legal character of what you did in March, February or January. There is an instinctive moral dislike of retrospective legislation in that it offends against our ideas of fairness, but it also directly relates to Raz's formulation because a retrospective law cannot guide human conduct: from 1 April you cannot go back in time and change your actions from the preceding months. This is particularly important in Criminal Law, because of the sorts of sanctions that can be imposed, but it is also a very strong principle in Civil Law where established legal relationships may be severely disrupted by retrospective legal effects.

The courts actively use this element of the rule of law in their interpretation of statutes. There is a strong presumption that legislation is not retrospective, and this can only be overcome by express words in the statute. The courts must do everything they can short of 'doing violence to the language of the enactment' (*Re Athlumney* [1898] 2 QB 547, Wright J), to avoid retrospective effect.

In *Phillips v Eyre* (1870) LR 6 QB 1, an Indemnity Act was passed by the parliament of Jamaica which retrospectively took away rights to sue for acts such as assault and false imprisonment.

> Retrospective laws are contrary to the general principle that legislation by which the conduct of mankind is to be regulated ought to deal with future acts, and ought not to change the character of past transactions.
>
> (Willes J)

This highlights that the judicial hostility to retrospective legislation springs from the notion that the purpose of law is to guide conduct, as Raz argued. However, Willes J went on to say that the prohibition on retrospectivity is not absolute and there may be circumstances calling for 'special and exceptional remedy', and this is to be decided by Parliament. So it seems that retrospective legislation is permissible under the UK constitution, as further illustrated by the following case.

EXPLAINING THE LAW – *BURMAH OIL CO LTD V LORD ADVOCATE* [1965] AC 75

Property belonging to Burmah Oil had been destroyed by British forces during the Second World War to stop it falling into the hands of advancing Japanese forces. The House of Lords decided that these actions were covered by the prerogative of the Crown to lawfully wage war, but that the exercise of this legal power brought with it an obligation to pay compensation. The Government was deeply troubled by this judgment, and shortly afterwards Parliament passed the War Damage Act 1965: section 1(1) stated: 'No person shall be entitled at common law to receive from the Crown compensation in respect of damage to property caused (whether before or after the passing of this Act, within or outside the United Kingdom) by acts lawfully done by the Crown during a war in which the Sovereign was engaged'.

See if you can highlight the crucial words here – 'whether before or after the passing of this Act'. This retrospectively takes away legal entitlements that existed at the time the property was destroyed.

You might think that at least Burmah Oil, as opposed to other property owners, having fought through the courts to establish their entitlement to compensation, would be able to obtain that compensation, but section 1(2) of the War Damages Act stated that: 'Where any proceedings to recover at common law compensation in respect of such damage have been instituted before the passing of this Act, the court shall, on the application of any party, forthwith set aside or dismiss the proceedings'.

JUSTICE (an international human rights lawyers group) issued a report stating that 'The refusal to meet a legitimate claim for compensation affirmed by the highest court in the land . . . is in the view of JUSTICE an action inconsistent with the Rule of Law and a dangerous precedent for the future'.[20]

ANALYSING THE LAW – ACTING RETROSPECTIVELY

Imagine that you are a Cabinet Minister in the immediate aftermath of the *Burmah Oil* judgment. What do think are likely to be the competing arguments around the table?

The rule of law arguments have been set out above. Against them you would consider the costs of applying the judgement. The Government had already set aside money for a compensation scheme for war losses. The result of the case meant that this fund would have been wholly inadequate and large sums of additional taxpayers' money would need to be found. In relation to other property owners, there was no estimate of the bill, but it would have been huge. As a Government you are also responsible for finding the money for education, the NHS, national security etc. The point is that the rule of law is not an absolute; breaching it makes us a little queasy and states should only depart from prospectivity with the strongest possible justifications.

There would have been far less room for manoeuvre for the British Government if the case concerned Criminal Law. Article 7 European Convention on Human Rights states:

> No one shall be held guilty of any criminal offence on account of any act or omission which did not constitute a criminal offence under national or international law at the time when it was committed. Nor shall a heavier penalty be imposed than the one that was applicable at the time the criminal offence was committed.

This is a human rights prohibition on retrospective Criminal Law. Looking very carefully at Article 7, however, you will see that there does seem to be scope for retrospectively extending criminal liability in national law, but only if the action was a criminal offence in international law at the time it was committed. This allowed the UK to legislate consistently with Article 7 ECHR when it passed the War Crimes Act 1991. This Act allows proceedings for murder and manslaughter against a person in the UK irrespective of their nationality at the time of the alleged offence if a) it was committed during the time of the Second World War in Germany or under German occupation and b) it constituted a violation of the laws and customs of war. This is necessarily a very limited exception to the general prohibition.

Problems can be caused by the retrospective nature of **common law** developments. You will have seen from Public Law and your other subjects that the common law does not remain static. It evolves from case to case, applying existing principles to new situations.

---

20 C Turpin and A Tomkins, *British Government and the Constitution* (7th edn, Cambridge UP, 2011) 87.

This can result in a slow and gradual development or, in rare cases (e.g. the neighbour principle in tort from *Donoghue v Stevenson* [1932] AC 562), in great leaps forward. This process of development raises questions of whether people could know the legal consequences of their actions at the time they acted. If a court, ruling a number of years after the contested incidents, develops the common law in some appreciable way, then this potentially has retrospective effect.

EXPLAINING THE LAW – MARITAL RAPE AND RETROSPECTIVITY

It might surprise you to learn that up until 1991 there was no known offence in English law of a man raping his wife. If a man forced his wife into sexual intercourse without her consent, then there may have been general offences against the person, but not the sexual offence of rape. The wife was deemed from the time of her marriage to have generally consented to sexual intercourse with her husband. In a landmark ruling in *R v R* [1991] 4 All ER 401, the House of Lords decided that the defendant could be guilty of rape in relation to his wife. The 'rule of law' problem was that the offence seems to have been legally unknown at the time the actions took place in 1989.

There was a challenge to this development, on the basis of Article 7 ECHR, in *SW v UK and C v UK* (1995) 21 EHRR 404. The European Court of Human Rights rejected the claims on the basis that whilst it 'is unfair to expect citizens to live their lives according to laws which are unclear or are not even in existence when decisions or actions have to be taken by individuals . . . the development of criminal liability [in this case] was clearly defined and foreseeable . . . and [the case] continued a perceptible evolution of case law'.

The European Court of Human Rights noted that the 'marital rape' rule had been crumbling; a number of exceptions had developed over the years, e.g. where a couple were still married but legally separated. A husband in 1989 ought to have foreseen that non-consensual sex with his wife could be treated as rape. This is an unusual argument, and the substance of the issue (i.e. the appalling lack of effort by the UK Parliament to protect women from sexual assault by their husbands, and the lack of sympathy for husbands who physically coerce their wives into intercourse) surely influenced the outcome.

Subsequent courts have emphasised that whilst the 'requirement is for sufficient rather than absolute certainty', if the ambit of the common law is to be enlarged, it 'must be done step by step on a case by case basis and not in one large leap' (*R v Rimmington* [2006] 2 All ER 257 [HL]).

10.8.3 SECRET LAWS

Secret laws are rare; more common are secret military orders as seen in the 'Northern Ireland in-depth interrogation' example. The courts have also considered whether unpublished criteria on how laws are going to be applied are consistent with the rule of law.

In *Salih v Secretary of State for the Home Office* [2003] EWHC 2273, there was a scheme of discretionary support for accommodation for failed asylum seekers. The Minister's policy was not to inform failed asylum seekers of this scheme. Burton J said, 'It is a fundamental requisite of the rule of law that the law should be made known. The individual must be able to know of his legal rights and obligations'. The issue in *R v Secretary of State for the Home Department ex parte Anufrijeva* [2003] UKHL 36, was whether individuals had the right to be informed of decisions; '. . . a constitutional state must accord to individuals the right to know of a decision before their rights can be adversely affected. The antithesis of such a state was described by Kafka: a state where the rights of individuals are overridden by hole in the corner decisions or knocks on doors in the early hours. That is not our system' (Lord Steyn).

10.9 THE STRUCTURE AND DESIGN OF THE LEGAL SYSTEM

The third level of Raz's construct of the rule of law is to emphasize that a legal system must have certain features to be able to deliver clarity, openness, etc.

10.9.1 INDEPENDENCE OF THE JUDICIARY MUST BE GUARANTEED

The rule of law can only exist if there is redress for executive lawlessness. This is linked to the role of law in guiding human conduct in the sense that public bodies and officials must know that the law can be enforced against them and, conversely, that citizens know that they can rely on law rather than being dependent on the whim of public officials. This redress needs to come from courts and judges who are independent of the executive that they are holding to account.

The independence of the judiciary is explored in depth in Chapter 9, 'Separation of powers', but to summarise here: there are a range of legal and conventional protections for that independence. Judges have security of tenure (they cannot be sacked because of their judgments), security of salary (the executive cannot pressurise them through wage threats) and immunity from suit (they cannot be subject to harassment through being sued for what they do as a judge). The Constitutional Reform Act 2005 strengthened this independence by establishing a separate Supreme Court and making the judicial appointments process more transparent and much less reliant on executive discretion.

10.9.2 NATURAL JUSTICE

EXPLAINING THE LAW – *R V SECRETARY OF STATE FOR THE HOME DEPARTMENT, EX PARTE PIERSON* [1998] AC 539

Pierson was convicted of killing his parents and received two mandatory life sentences. At the time, the Home Secretary had the power to set his tariff (i.e. the punitive and deterrent element of his sentence). The Home Secretary set the tariff at 20 years. It later emerged (through another case that forced the Home Secretary to communicate his reasons for setting a particular tariff) that this tariff had been based on Pierson being guilty of a double premeditated murder. Pierson's lawyers argued that the murders were not premeditated and were part of a single incident. This was accepted by the Home Secretary, but he decided to keep the 20 years tariff in place.

Section 35(2) of the Criminal Justice Act 1991, stating that 'the Secretary of State may . . . release on licence a life prisoner who is not a discretionary life prisoner', was not ambiguous and gave a very wide and general power. Even so, rule of law principles had not been explicitly excluded by Parliament, and these included the principle that a sentence should not be retrospectively increased. This amounted to a limitation on the Home Secretary's power even if it was not a limitation stated in the statute: 'unless there is the clearest provision to the contrary, Parliament must be presumed not to legislate contrary to the rule of law. And the rule of law enforces minimum standards of fairness, both substantive and procedural'.

10.9.3 THE COURTS SHOULD BE EASILY ACCESSIBLE

Laws cannot guide behaviour if they cannot be enforced by courts. The same problem arises if people cannot access courts so as to receive a ruling on what the law means and how it applies to their particular circumstances. This requirement has a number of different facets.

It could be a question of jurisdiction. Governments sometimes try to prevent the courts from hearing challenges to the decisions of public bodies by inserting *ouster clauses* into legislation. If these were read literally by the courts, their jurisdiction to hear claims that a public body had acted unlawfully would be ousted. For rule of law reasons, the courts have consistently been hostile to ouster clauses and have used the rule of law as an interpretive aid in severely restricting the scope of ouster clauses (see Chapter 12 and *Anisminic v Foreign Compensation Commission*). Some judicial comment has gone further and suggested that it is impermissible under our constitution even for Parliament to try to stop people accessing courts (see Chapter 12). Similarly, the liberalisation of the rules on standing for judicial review (i.e. *who* has the ability to access a court to challenge unlawful action by a public body) has been achieved over the past 30 years not by legislation, but by judges motivated by rule of law concerns.

Secondly, there are questions of physical or practical access. This can encompass disability, and courts must make reasonable adjustments to allow disabled people to access courts, including disabled parking spaces near courts and hearing aid induction loops in court rooms.

In *R (Karas) v Secretary of State for the Home Department* [2006] EWHC 747 (Admin), the Home Office planned the deportation of a husband and his pregnant wife in such a way as to prevent them from obtaining or acting upon legal advice. They were to be spirited away quickly and with very little notice (less than 24 hours). Munby J said that this showed 'at best an unacceptable disregard by the Home Office of the rule of law, at worst an unacceptable disdain by the Home Office for the rule of law, which is as depressing as it ought to be concerning'. In *R v Lord Chancellor, ex parte Witham* [1997] 2 All ER 779, the High Court said, 'Access to the courts is a constitutional right; it can only be denied by the government if it persuades Parliament to pass legislation which specifically – in effect by express provision – permits the executive to turn people away from the court door' (Laws J).

The cost of accessing justice has long been an issue, but it has been brought into sharp focus by the deep cuts in legal aid following the Legal Aid, Sentencing and Punishment of Offenders Act 2012. In setting aside regulations on Employment Tribunal fees, the Supreme Court in *R (Unison) v Lord Chancellor* [2017] UKSC 51, found that excessively high court fees could breach the 'access to justice' requirements of the rule of law to such an extent that they would be unlawful.

Hickman points out that whilst this case addresses one costs issue in relation to employment tribunals, the expense of bringing public law cases remains; 'The irony that the right of access to justice has been developed in judicial review procedure, which fails its own test for ensuring access to justice, is not only unmistakable, but disgraceful'.[21] Zuckerman makes a more wide-ranging critique of costs and access to justice when he says that 'Access to justice is barred not only to those seeking judicial review but to every person who requires court assistance. Whether we are involved in disputes concerning family breakup, inheritance, child welfare, eviction, damages for breach of contract or for damage to property, all of us are denied affordable access to justice. This state of affairs undermines the rule of law'.[22]

10.10 DOES THE RULE OF LAW HAVE SUBSTANTIVE CONTENT?

Raz firmly believed that the rule of law:

> is not to be confused with democracy, justice, equality (before the law or otherwise), human rights of any kind or respect for the dignity of man. A non-democratic legal system, based on the denial of human rights, on extensive poverty, on racial segregation, sexual inequalities and religious persecution may, in principle, conform to the requirements of the Rule of Law better than any of the legal systems of the more enlightened western democracies.[23]

---

21 T Hickman, 'Public Law's Disgrace: Part 2' U.K. Const. L. Blog (26 October 2017), https://ukconstitutionallaw.org/ (last accessed 05/11/17).

22 A Zuckerman, 'The Law's Disgrace' U.K. Const. L. Blog (27 February 2017), https://ukconstitutionallaw.org/ (last accessed 05/11/17).

23 Raz, above n 19.

At the other end of the spectrum, the New Delhi Declaration 1959 from the International Commission of Jurists included social and economic rights and even cultural rights: 'the Rule of Law is a dynamic concept . . . which should be employed not only to safeguard and advance the civil and political rights of the individual in a free society, but also to establish social, economic, educational and cultural conditions under which his legitimate aspirations and dignity may be realised'.

Most writers agree that this is going too far and that it is unrealistic to expect the rule of law to be a vehicle for educational and cultural aspiration and dignity. On the other hand, there have been many, very distinguished, commentators who regard Raz's approach as too narrow and sterile. Sir Ivor Jennings argued for a definition broader than legality: 'it contains, something more, although it is not capable of precise definition. It is an attitude, an expression of liberal and democratic principles, in themselves vague when it is sought to analyse them, but clear enough in their results'.[24] This inability to pin down the boundaries of the substantive content of the rule of law has caused difficulties for other writers on the subject.

T R S Allan argues that the rule of law is aimed at the common good and that this necessarily requires adherence to the most basic features of human rights and human dignity, such as freedom of expression.[25] This tries to establish some of the environmental prerequisites for the rule of law to operate. It states that substance is inextricably bound up with formal characteristics and that they are part of the same functioning system.

Lord Bingham goes further than this basic minimum content but similarly has difficulty in explaining what particular human rights fall within the substantive content of the rule of law. Lord Bingham thought that the rule of law is based on a 'fundamental compact' between the individual and the state, with both parties sacrificing a 'measure of the freedom and power which they would otherwise enjoy'. This necessarily involves restrictions not just on the formal characteristics of law. Bingham accepts that there are different conceptions of human rights in different countries, but argues that the advantages of a broad interpretation of the rule of law outweigh these difficulties.[26]

The view taken here is that these problems ultimately lead back to Raz's limited but elegant solution. If the rule of law is to have serious critical force, to be a benchmark against which we can evaluate not just our legal system but legal systems generally, then it cannot be a catch-all for 'good things'. As Raz argues, it is not 'necessary or desirable to cloak the [conclusion on what is a just society] in the mantle of the rule of law'.[27] Raz goes further and says that the problem with loading too much onto the term 'rule of law' is that it becomes a contestable legal theory, i.e. you would need a complete social science conception of the world to justify it. Seeing the opposing sides (Spanish state authorities,

---

24 Jennings, above n 14, 48.
25 Allan, above n 6.
26 Lord Bingham, 'The Rule of Law' [2007] *Cambridge Law Journal* 67.
27 Raz, above n 19.

Catalan government) hurl the language of 'democracy' and 'rule of law' at each other in the Catalan independence crisis of October 2017, illustrates that when concepts are framed too broadly they cease to make useful contributions to debate.

Critics of the formal approach might say that it would not prevent a regime passing laws that permit human rights abuses and assaults on human dignity. But a theory of the rule of law would not *practically stop* this either, just allow commentators to condemn, on the basis of the rule of law, abuses that they could be condemning on other grounds anyway. Adherents of the formal school, such as Raz, are not prevented from holding views (or doing more active things) on human rights abuses.

There is also a danger of under-estimating the restrictions which the formal approach imposes. No state that has committed extensive human rights abuses has been able to be a 'rule of law' state. Nazi German laws allowed punishment according to the 'healthy instincts of the people' (breaching clarity requirements). Soviet laws subjecting every human freedom to the 'interests of the Communist Party' did *not* satisfy the formal school requirements. These regimes only had very tenuous claims to be 'rule of law states'. Apartheid-era South Africa did make more explicit claims to be based on the rule of law but was wracked by breaches of *habeas corpus*, extra-judicial state killing and lack of access to justice.

10.11 THE MODERN SIGNIFICANCE OF THE RULE OF LAW

In the UK constitutional system, principles and politics play a larger role in restraining Governments and preventing abuse than in countries with a written constitution, and this is true for the rule of law. The most important use of the rule of law in the hands of the judges is as an interpretive tool. As Lord Bingham said, 'the judges, in their role as . . . judgment-makers, are not free to dismiss the rule of law as meaningless verbiage, the jurisprudential equivalent of motherhood and apple pie, even if they were inclined to do so. They would be bound to construe a statute so that it did not infringe an existing constitutional principle, if it were reasonably possible to do so'.[28]

In *R v Horseferry Road Magistrates' Court, ex parte Bennett* [1994] 1 AC 42, Bennett was suspected of committing offences in the UK. It became known that he was in South Africa. Rather than commencing lawful extradition proceedings against him, he was taken by South African police (with UK authority collusion), put on flight to Heathrow airport, handcuffed to his seat, and arrested on his arrival into the UK. Could his trial be

---

28 Bingham, above n 24, 69.

stopped on the basis that the UK authorities had colluded in bringing him to the UK by unlawful means?

The House of Lords concluded that Bennett had been 'illegally abducted', and Lord Bridge said:

> When it is shown that the law enforcement agency responsible for bringing a prosecution has only been enabled to do so by participating in violations of international law and the laws of another state in order to secure the presence of the accused within the territorial jurisdiction of the court, I think that respect for the rule of law demands that the court take cognisance of that circumstance.

The previous practice of English courts was not particularly concerned with how evidence came to be obtained (or, how the suspect was brought before the court), but in *Bennett*, and on the basis of these rule of law concerns, the trial was stopped as an abuse of process.

This notion of the rule of law as an interpretive tool was also seen in *R (Evans) v Attorney-General* [2015] UKSC 21. The Prince of Wales has for a long time been sending confidential memos to Government departments giving his views on a range of policy matters; due to his scribbly handwriting, these are known as the 'black spider memos'. It was successfully argued before the Upper Tribunal that these should be released to the public. The Attorney General exercised his statutory power to issue a certificate ordering non-disclosure of this information on 'reasonable grounds'. This certificate was quashed by the Supreme Court on rule of law grounds. The statutory phrase 'reasonable grounds' seems very open-ended, but the Court found that it had to be read in a way that was consistent with the rule of law, including that judicial decisions cannot be set aside by executive order. Only where there was a demonstrable flaw in the judicial decision or a material change of circumstances would there be reasonable grounds.

Perhaps the last word in this chapter should go to Lord Hope who, in *R(Jackson) v Attorney-General* [2005] UKHL 56, said 'The rule of law enforced by the courts is the ultimate controlling factor on which our constitution is based'.

POINTS TO REVIEW

- Dicey's formulation of the rule of law has been very influential and still has useful elements, but becomes less relevant with the passage of time.

- Raz's conception of the rule of law has been criticised as sterile, but is a focused and well-constructed attempt to build a wider benchmark.

- The rule of law is a principle that exerts strong influence on the courts and others and performs a valuable function in limiting state power and promoting an equitable relationship between citizen and state.

TAKING IT FURTHER

M Elliott, 1,000 words/The Rule of Law, *Public Law for Everyone* https://publiclawforeveryone.com/2015/10/16/1000-words-the-rule-of-law/ One of Mark Elliott's estimable 1000 word summaries of key Public Law concepts.

J Raz, 'The Rule of Law and its Virtue' [1977] *Law Quarterly Review* 195 As you read this chapter, you may have noticed that it finds Raz's view of the rule of law to be persuasive. His original argument is laid out here in an elegant and subtle article.

Tom Bingham, *The Rule of Law* (Penguin, 2011) As a law student, if you buy one law book, beyond your recommended textbooks, make it this one. Lord Bingham was the leading British judge of his generation and was passionately concerned with the rule of law as the basis for a just society.

World Justice Project, http://worldjusticeproject.org/what-rule-law This takes a broad and accessible view of the rule of the law and, in particular, charts its impact on people. As the site says, 'everyday issues of safety, rights, justice, and governance affect us all; everyone is a stakeholder in the rule of law'.

CHAPTER 11
DEVOLUTION

What country do you live in? That probably seems like an easy question, but if you are a resident of the United Kingdom it is not entirely straightforward. We know that the United States of America is a sovereign country of states that are united – the clue is in the title. But what is the United Kingdom comprised of? Kingdoms? If you are reading these lines sat in Preston, or Coventry, or Plymouth, are you in the country of England or the UK? The answer is no more obvious if you are sat at a desk in Belfast, Edinburgh or Cardiff.

From the perspective of the international community the answer is easy. International law recognises sovereign states and the internal arrangements of these states are traditionally of little interest; to the international community you live in the United Kingdom. The internal arrangements of any country, however, are of the keenest interest to the Public Law lawyer. They say important things about the constitution of that country and address some of the key themes addressed in this book: where does power lie in a state; is it distributed or concentrated; what is the relationship between the governors and the governed?

Answering the question posed in the opening sentence involves semantics and definitions. If by 'country' we mean sovereign state, then, yes, you are in the United Kingdom.[1] That sovereign state comprises four constituent parts variously called countries, nations, provinces and principalities: England, Scotland, Wales and Northern Ireland. In this chapter, we will explore the constitutional position of each of these units, the powers that have been devolved to their administrations and their relationship with the United Kingdom.

AS YOU READ

Keep in mind that devolution means the transfer of power from the central power in a sovereign state to its constituent units. Some key themes of this chapter are:

- Mapping the devolution of power to Wales, Scotland and Northern Ireland.

- Examining the consequences of these devolution settlements to England.

- Noting devolution as a process rather than an event.

- Identifying the striking asymmetry of the UK's devolution arrangements.

---

1   Apologies, and hello, to readers outside of the UK.

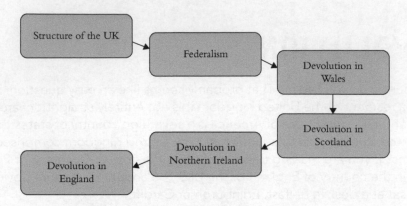

Figure 11.1 Structure of Chapter 11

11.1 THE STRUCTURE OF THE UK

11.1.1 TERMINOLOGY

The introductory section above alerted you to the fact that terminology is both vague and controversial in this field – a messy combination. We must do what we can to clarify what we can. Let us call each unit of the four units of the United Kingdom **'a nation'**. This means that:

- Great Britain: is a geographical entity that comprises the nations England, Wales and Scotland.
- United Kingdom: is a sovereign state that comprises Great Britain and Northern Ireland.

	Population (millions)	Population (%)
United Kingdom	63.3	100
England	53	83.9
Scotland	5.2	8.4
Wales	3	4.8
Northern Ireland	1.8	2.9

Figure 11.2 Demographics of the UK

The 'British Isles' is not a state but a wider geographical concept, which in some respects includes the Isle of Man and the Channel Islands. These islands are not a part of the United Kingdom. They are self-governing dependencies of the Crown, although they come under the umbrella of United Kingdom foreign policy for some issues.

11.1.2 WALES

England gained control of Wales by military conquest through the thirteenth century. Wales initially retained its own laws and language but was slowly assimilated into English laws and administration. The Act of Union 1536 was not an agreement between two independent nations – there was no Welsh Parliament. The Act regularised English arrangements over Wales and provided for Welsh representation at the Westminster Parliament.

England and Wales have been a single jurisdiction since then, and the integration of the legal system across the two nations is deep. From the early twentieth century, some administrative arrangements started to differentiate between Wales and England (e.g. the Welsh Department of the Board of Education) and there were some different laws on religion and language issues. The post of Minister for Welsh Affairs was created in 1951 but only as part of a wider portfolio (i.e. it was tacked on to another minister's main responsibilities). From 1964, however, there has been a Secretary of State for Wales, a Cabinet post, whose sole responsibility is administering Welsh affairs supported by a Government department: the Wales Office.

A rather limited devolution scheme was offered to the people of Wales under the Wales Act 1978. It was resoundingly rejected by them with only 12 per cent of the electorate voting in favour (amounting to 20 per cent of the votes cast). Further developments in devolution for Wales would depend on developments in Scotland.

11.1.3 SCOTLAND

Scots law, as the product of an independent country, developed separately from the English common law tradition. It is based on the continental European approach which took its principles directly from Roman law. After spending much of the preceding centuries at war or low-level reiving conflict, England and Scotland came under the same crown, that of James I (of England) and VI (of Scotland), in 1603.

The century that followed was one of the most tumultuous in British constitutional history, but by 1706–07, the two nations were ready to form a union. The Act of Union with Scotland 1706 and the Act of Union with England 1707, created a new sovereign state of 'Great Britain' with its new Parliament – the British Parliament. Despite Union, Scotland retained and was guaranteed the continued existence of the distinct Scottish legal, educational and religious systems. A range of separate administrative arrangements on e.g. health, education and prisons, continued and from 1885 there was a UK Government post of Secretary of State for Scotland, supported from 1945 by a Scottish Office.

When devolution of some powers was offered to Scotland in 1979, a small majority of those who voted were in favour. This did not, however, meet the requirement in the Scotland Act 1978 for 40 per cent of the overall eligible electorate to approve the proposals, rather than a simple majority of those who cast votes. In the 1997 referendum, under the Referendums (Scotland and Wales) Act 1997, 74 per cent of voters said 'Yes' to a devolved Scottish Parliament (on a 60 per cent turnout). A referendum on complete independence in 2014 returned a majority in favour of remaining as part of the UK.

11.1.4 NORTHERN IRELAND

We have nowhere near enough space in a book of this sort to do justice to the long, entangled and often bitter relations between Ireland and Great Britain (especially England). England asserted, with varying levels of effectiveness, control over Ireland from the twelfth century onwards. In the following centuries, there was a mixture of English laws and administrative arrangements together with Irish customs and Irish Parliament laws applying in different parts of the island. The existing problems of English dominance over Ireland were exacerbated in two particularly difficult ways:

- Religion – during the split of the English Crown from the Roman Catholic Church and the establishment of a Protestant state religion, Ireland stayed largely (and intensely) Roman Catholic.
- Large scale immigration of non-Catholics – this was mainly by Protestant Scots to the northern province of Ulster, in the seventeenth and eighteenth centuries.

The Act of Union 1800 between Great Britain and Ireland did not resolve these problems, and the 'Irish Question' of Home Rule or independence grew to be one of the dominant and most divisive issues of the late Victorian and Edwardian period. Home Rule was finally agreed to by the UK Parliament and Government in 1914, but postponed with the advent of the First World War. Irish rebels caused an Easter Rising in 1916, and through 1919–21 there was war either against the British or between rival Irish parties. A resolution of sorts was provided by the Government of Ireland Act 1920 and the Anglo-Irish Treaty 1922 involving:

- Partition of the island – six of the Ulster counties were separated from the political settlement for the rest of the island. The Act provided for one Parliament for Northern Ireland and one for the rest of Ireland.
- Self-governing status for the Irish Free State – which formally declared its independence from the United Kingdom as the sovereign state of Éire (later the Republic of Ireland) in 1937.

Northern Ireland remained as part of the United Kingdom. It possessed a Northern Ireland Parliament at Stormont with a significant degree of control over law and administration. Its more recent devolution history is bound up in the sectarian conflict that afflicted Northern Ireland in the last third of the twentieth century.

11.2 FEDERALISM

According to Turpin and Tomkins, the UK has neither a unitary nor a federal but a union constitution.[2] A *federal constitution* is one which divides power between a central federal

---

2   C Turpin and A Tomkins, *British Government and the Constitution*, 7th edn (Cambridge UP, 2011) 210.

government and the component parts (often called the states). A *unitary constitution* will have structures for local and regional government, but power ultimately resides at the centre, with any regional governments and legislatures subordinate to central authority.

A core feature of federations is that the balance between the federal and constituent parts of the state cannot be changed unilaterally by either party. Therefore, there must be a power over and above even that of the central Government, i.e. a codified constitution. This does not exist in the UK, and so the sort of federalism we see in the US, Australia and Germany does not seem possible.

The UK has often been thought of as a unitary state. This is a reasonable proposition because of the centrality of the supremacy of Parliament to UK constitutional arrangements. There has, however, always been a different legal system in Scotland, and there was a Parliament for Northern Ireland. In practice, the fact that the UK is a union of four nations (which retain quite distinct identities) and that, under current arrangements, three of those nations have their own legislatures and Governments, is too big a feature to ignore in categorising the UK constitution.

11.2.1 DEVOLUTION

In the best (or worst) traditions of the UK constitutional system, devolution has not been a planned approach to developing a federal state, or a coherent constitutional architecture; it has been a pragmatic response to particular pressures from particular nations.

Devolution brings some benefits. Central Government may be remote, and more local units of governance can reflect the wishes of the people more accurately. Where there is a disjuncture between the nation and the general political scene of the whole state, it can ensure that the preferences of the people of that nation have an impact on laws and policies as they apply to them. In 2015, only one Conservative MP was returned for Scotland, yet the Government of the United Kingdom that decides important Scottish issues, such as continuing to make Faslane (near Glasgow) the main home of the UK's nuclear weapons arsenal, was a Conservative one. We need to accept that a Government represents an aggregate of preferences that do not necessarily reflect the preferences in a particular county, town or locale, but major differences are important if each nation has retained a cultural and socio-political sense of its separateness from the centre. It could also be argued that central Government can be cumbersome and overloaded, and that devolved institutions can be more agile and responsive to the needs of their economy and people.

Devolution also brings potential problems. It can cause jurisdictional problems between different legal systems and institutions. Differences in the benefits provided to people in different nations can cause resentment in other parts of the state (see Scottish prescription charges and university fees). Rather than promoting the satisfaction of the people in devolved administrations with the level of freedom and self-governance they enjoy in the existing state framework, it can work to the detriment of that state. It can, in showing that a degree of self-governance works, promote a desire for and confidence in full independence.

11.2.2 ASYMMETRY

A symmetrical federal arrangement almost always begins with a blank sheet of paper and a desire to fit a complex and demanding set of circumstances into a coherent system. Whilst this has never happened in the UK, we should not be too scornful of the imbalanced, irregular, lop-sided system that the UK has arrived at. You should be in no doubt, however, as to the scale of this irregularity: 'Asymmetry runs through every clause and schedule of the devolution legislation, from the fundamentals of powers and functions down to the niceties of nomenclature'.[3]

As so often in the UK constitution, this can be ascribed to an attempt to pragmatically deal with demands within the existing constitutional system, rather than trying to redraft the whole constitution. This could be condemned as lacking vision but it is not an irrational response. Countries with written constitutions face the same pressures. Spain has a written constitution, but the Basque Country and Catalonia have greater powers than the other constituent parts (*autonomias*) as a pragmatic response to particular demands.

11.2.3 COORDINATION IN A UNION CONSTITUTION

One of the obvious dangers in a state where formal legal power is dispersed across different institutions and placed in different locations with different mandates is incoherence at a national level. There is a Memorandum of Understanding between the UK Government and the devolved administrations. This is a statement of political intent, i.e. it has no legal effects. The parties are making political commitments to communicate effectively and to involve the devolution administrations in UK external policy. As well as regular administrative liaison under agreed concordats, there is a Joint Ministerial Committee chaired by the UK Prime Minister which meets annually.

11.3 WALES

There are some underlying themes to the Welsh relationship with England and Great Britain:

- Devolution was slow to start, but has gathered momentum. After starting the devolution process with a more modest offer of powers than Scotland or Northern Ireland, the similarities with the other devolution schemes are now stronger than the differences, although some differences do remain.
- Culture plays a two-facing role in this relationship – the Welsh borders and, to some extent, Pembrokeshire have significant 'English' populations, whilst south Wales was closely integrated into the whole industrialisation of Britain and politically has been one of the wellsprings of the British Labour movement. On the other hand, and despite the much longer history of integration into an English-led state, the Welsh

---

3   Robert Hazell, *The State and the Nations* (Imprint Academic, 2002) 269, cited in Turpin and Tomkins above n 1, 220.

language has been remarkably durable – the most successful of any of the Gaelic languages – reinforced by Welsh-language TV and groups such as the Super Furry Animals.[4] Welsh national pride also runs through sport, especially rugby union.

Devolution has been something of a strange process in Wales. As noted above, devolution proposals in 1979 were decisively defeated, and through the following years there was no great demand for devolution in Wales. Devolution was ultimately part of a wider UK debate and demand led by the Scots, and the UK Government offer in 1997 reflected this by offering only administrative rather than legislative devolution.

Loveland calls the level of support in the 1997 Wales Referendum 'pathetically low'; only 50.3 per cent of voters said 'Yes' on a turnout of 51 per cent.[5] Some necessary context for this is given by Sir David Williams: 'There has never been an independent Welsh Parliament on an established basis and hence no overall executive government. Welsh law – at least in this millennium . . . has been English law . . . In this context, legislative devolution was "a giant leap" for many'.[6] The original Welsh devolution settlement was muddled, but whilst it did not seem like a satisfactory end point, it started a process.

11.4 THE NATIONAL ASSEMBLY FOR WALES

11.4.1 CYNULLIAD CENEDLAETHOL CYMRU

11.4.1.1 COMPOSITION

The Welsh Assembly was created by section 1 of the Government of Wales Act 1998. It has 60 Assembly Members (AMs), elected on what is called the Additional Member system. This is a mixture of 'first past the post' in constituencies (which return two-thirds of seats = 40) and proportional representation based on five regions and party lists (which return 20 seats). Voters can cast two votes, one in their constituency contest and one for the regional party list. The Assembly was set up to run on four-year terms, but under the Wales Act 2014 it now sits for a fixed term of five years and the elections are timed to avoid clashes with the UK General Elections.

11.4.1.2 POWERS

The Welsh Assembly originally had no legislative powers. It could only make delegated legislation, which is something your local council can do. The 1998 settlement gave the Assembly these sorts of powers over the whole nation of Wales and transferred some executive powers from the Welsh Office in Westminster, but it was not so different from existing systems of local government.

---

4   Whose top 20 album *Mwng* (2000) is wholly in the Welsh language. Gorky's Zygotic Mynci also played in the same brilliant vein.

5   I Loveland, *Constitutional Law* (6th edn, OUP, 2012) 436.

6   Sir David Williams, *Constitutional Reform in the United Kingdom* (Cambridge UP, 1998), cited in Turpin and Tomkins, above n 2, 246.

The Government of Wales Act 2006 (GoWA 2006) expanded these law-making powers and allowed for further strengthening of the Assembly, in three main ways:

- It widened the power to make secondary legislation.
- It granted the right to pass Assembly Measures on devolved matters. The Assembly could under section 94 of the GoWA 2006 'make any provision that could be made by Act of Parliament'. These Measures were a form of primary legislation but they needed the approval of the UK Government (and so fell short of the powers residing in Edinburgh and Belfast).
- It provided that the Assembly could have genuine primary law-making powers, under Part 4 of the GoWA 2006, but only if the people of Wales wanted them. The 2011 Referendum on this issue returned a positive result, so the Assembly can now pass Acts of the National Assembly. This replaces the power to pass Measures. The significance of 'primary' in this discussion is that Assembly Acts can amend and even repeal UK primary legislation.

This legislative power is wide but not unlimited. Assembly Acts can only apply to Wales and they must be consistent with EU and ECHR law. These limits are enforceable, and section 108 of the GoWA 2006 provides that: 'An Act of the Assembly is not law so far as any provision of the Act is outside of the Assembly's legislative competence'.

One important aspect of the Assembly's legislative competence was that it followed a *'conferred powers'* model; the Assembly only had power to make law on the particular subjects which are outlined in the legislation. Turpin and Tomkins stated that the list of competences had become 'so lengthy and complex that it has become difficult to navigate'.[7] These criticisms and arguments that the Welsh Assembly competencies were unjustly far more limited than those of the Scottish Parliament led to the Wales Act 2017. This means that the Assembly now operates on *'reserved matters'* rather than a conferred powers model. This is very similar to the Scottish Parliament and means that the Assembly can legislate on any issue unless it has been expressly reserved for the Westminster Parliament. The Act also extended competencies over the electoral system and other matters including oil and gas extraction.

Section 107 GoWA 2006 outlines the constitutional relationship of the Welsh Assembly with the Westminster Parliament: 'This Part does not affect the power of the Parliament of the United Kingdom to make laws for Wales'. This restates the traditional view of the supremacy of Parliament, but by convention Westminster will not legislate on a devolved matter without the consent of the Welsh Assembly. Any disputes over whether or not an Assembly Act is within the legislative competence of the Assembly may be decided by the courts, including the Supreme Court. The Wales Act 2017 also provided that the Assembly and Welsh Government are now permanent features of the UK constitution and can only be abolished with the consent of the Welsh people as expressed in a referendum.

---

7   Turpin and Tomkins, above n 2, 251.

Since the formation of a Welsh Government in 2006, the Assembly has had a role in holding the executive to account. It does this through similar methods to those used by the Westminster Parliament, outlined in Chapter 4, such as questions, debates and committees.

11.5 WELSH GOVERNMENT

Before 2006, executive powers were exercised by a committee of the Assembly, although this was treated in practice as a Government for Wales. The Welsh Government was formally established by section 45 of the Government of Wales Act 2006, and this more clearly separates the legislative and judicial functions. It is accountable to the Welsh Assembly and must retain the support of the Assembly or resign.

The Government is headed by a First Minister, selected because they are the leader of the largest party (or coalition) in the Assembly. Their main role is to develop policy and oversee implementation. The first minister appoints other ministers, who must be Assembly Members, to hold subject portfolios (on health, education, etc) A counsel general acts as the Government's legal adviser. There is a maximum of 12 ministers.

The Wales Office and Secretary of State for Wales continue to exist, although with a reduced role. This now focuses on liaison between the Westminster Government and the Welsh Assembly and Government.

The Welsh Government follows the usual role of Governments, particularly in the Westminster model, of developing proposals for legislation and using their party organisation and discipline to get them passed by the legislature. We can see the operation of this in the following:

EXPLAINING THE LAW – ORGAN DONATION

Whilst it is relatively commonplace for surgeons to save lives by undertaking organ transplants, using kidney, heart, liver and lung organs, the public-policy problems have always been about supply rather than demand. That is, transplants only work with healthy organs from recently deceased donors and waiting lists for transplant operations are long. The Welsh Government explained that in 2012/13, '36 people died in Wales whilst waiting for an organ transplant, as a donor could not be found'.[8]

8   Organ Donation Wales, http://organdonationwales.org/Organ-Donation-is-changing-in-Wales/why-change-the-system/?skip=1&lang=en (last accessed 05/11/17).

Organ donation in the UK has always been on an opt-in model, i.e. the presumption under UK law (Human Tissue Act 2004) is that a person does not consent to use of their organs. The easiest way to opt-in is to register with the NHS Organ Donor Register, but the presumption can also be overcome by expressing wishes in writing or by telling relatives.

International comparisons show that donation rates could be increased by up to 300 per cent with an opt-out system, i.e. the presumption is that people want to donate their organs after death, but they can register to the contrary (or otherwise let their wishes be known). A major departure from the existing UK model is the Human Transplantation (Wales) Act 2013, which came into force in December 2015, and adopts the opt-out model. This is an example of innovation and differentiation under a devolution settlement. The first edition of this text predicted that this could lead to legislative changes in other parts of the UK, and this has happened with Scotland introducing an opt-out model in 2017 and a consultation on similar proposals opening in England in October 2017.

Devolution continues to be a process rather than an event for Wales. Further reform in 2013 granted some wider financial powers, especially in relation to borrowing but also for fiscal powers to charge for public services. The Wales Act 2014 devolved further powers over some areas of taxation, particularly property taxes and the Wales Act 2017 continues this devolutionary trend.

11.6 SCOTLAND

The pressure for Scottish devolution did not dissipate after the failure to win sufficient support in the 1979 referendum, and divisions grew during the 1980s between a Conservative Westminster and an increasingly Conservative-less Scotland. In the early 1990s there was a broad-based consultative process called the Scottish Constitutional Convention that produced an influential report, 'Scotland's Parliament: Scotland's Right' (1995). The 1997 Referendum produced a 74.3 per cent Yes vote to establishing a Scottish Parliament, with 63.5 per cent agreeing that it should have tax-varying powers.

11.7 THE SCOTTISH PARLIAMENT

11.7.1 COMPOSITION

The Parliament in Edinburgh is comprised of 129 Members of the Scottish Parliament (MSPs). They are elected on an Additional Member system similar to the Welsh electoral system – a mix of constituency and regional lists, with each voter having two votes.

There are 73 constituencies, and regional lists produce 56 MSPs. This voting system is not perfectly proportional, i.e. the number of seats each party wins does not exactly match the percentage of the votes it obtained. It does, however, retain a key benefit of 'first past the post' – a strong link between an MSP and their constituency which helps them represent local issues. The regional list system helps reduce the disproportionality of 'first past the post' results, by making the election result reflect voters' preferences a bit more accurately. This is a compromise, but an honourable one that seems to work reasonably well. The Scottish Elections (Reduction of Voting Age) Act 2015 extends the right to vote in Scottish Parliament and local elections to 16- and 17-year-olds.

The Scottish Parliament was organised on four-year fixed terms, but again this has been changed to five years and elections avoid clashes with Westminster elections (Fixed-term Parliaments Act 2011). Unlike Wales, there is no prohibition on dual mandate, i.e. on a person being an MP and an MSP at the same time.

11.7.2 POWERS

The Scottish Parliament has, from its inception, had the power to pass primary legislation, called Acts of the Scottish Parliament. These can amend and repeal UK Acts of Parliament. Again, there are limits on the legislative competence of a devolved Parliament, and section 29 of the Scotland Act 1998 (SA 1998) states that: 'An Act of the Scottish Parliament is not law so far as any provision of the Act is outside the legislative competence of the Parliament'.

An Act will be outside of this competence if it tries to apply law to another country or is inconsistent with ECHR law. The competence uses a 'reserved matter' model. This means that the Scottish Parliament can (subject to the constraints already mentioned) make law on any matter, provided it is not listed as a subject reserved for the UK Parliament. These 'reserved matters' are listed in Schedule 5 Scotland Act 1998 under 11 main heads and include:

> Foreign affairs; defence and national security; some financial matters including currency and regulation of financial markets; aspects of trade and business including insolvency and competition; energy; transport; social security; immigration and nationality; and some criminal offences such as treason, misuse of drugs, firearms

In other words, the powers are wide but there are limits on the legislative competence of the Scottish Parliament. You will have already read enough law to realise that these sorts of jurisdictional boundaries inevitably throw up disputes. Real life issues are messy and do not neatly fall within the categories so precisely listed in the legislation. These risks were appreciated and addressed in the devolution settlement in a number of ways.

On the principle that it is better to stop proposals which are outside of the legislative competence before they reach the statute book, there are pre-legislative scrutiny processes. A minister introducing a Bill to Parliament must state that in their view the Bill is within legislative competence (section 31 SA 1998). This must, in effect, be confirmed by the presiding officer in Parliament (section 32 SA 1998). Under section 33 of the Scotland Act 1998: 'The Advocate General, the Lord Advocate or the Attorney General may refer the question of whether a Bill or any provision of a Bill would be within the legislative competence of the Parliament to the Supreme Court for decision'.

The Scotland Act 2012 devolved some further specific powers, e.g. in relation to drink-driving and speed limits. More significant, however, was the further devolution of some fiscal matters. The 1998 settlement allowed the Scottish Parliament to vary income tax levels by no more than 3 per cent (above or below) the UK rate. The Scotland Act 2012 gave full powers to the Scottish Parliament to set income tax levels. It also handed over powers on some property taxes and granted wider borrowing powers.

Maintaining good relations between the Westminster and Scottish Parliaments is important. Section 28(7) of the Scotland Act 1998 does not affect the power of the United Kingdom Parliament to make law for Scotland, but in practice there has been a division of labour. The UK Government indicated that it wanted to proceed via a constitutional convention. Unlike those conventional rules which emerge through practice (see Chapter 5, 'Constitutional conventions'), the Sewel Convention was drafted and negotiated between the parties. It is reflected in the Memorandum of Understanding between the Scottish and UK Governments and states that the UK Parliament will not legislate on devolved matters without the consent of the Scottish Parliament. There are often circumstances where it is sensible for this consent to be given, e.g. where Scotland considers that a UK-wide scheme would be more effective, or for minor and technical issues, the Scottish ministers will promote a Legislative Consent Motion, to be voted on by the Scottish Parliament, to allow the UK legislation to extend to Scotland on the specified matters. The legal status of the Sewel Convention was considered in the *Miller* case, see below.

11.8 THE SCOTTISH GOVERNMENT

This was originally called the Scottish Executive, but the Scotland Act 2012 effected a name change to 'Scottish Government'. The Government is led by a First Minister who is nominated by other MSPs. If a single party wins the election, then its leader will become First Minister. If a coalition is needed, then it would be the leader of the largest party in the coalition. The First Minister appoints a Deputy First Minister and other ministers, (who must all be drawn from the Scottish Parliament, following the Westminster model of government). There are eight cabinet secretaries (for e.g. Justice, Education and Lifelong Learning, and Health, Wellbeing and Sport), plus 13 junior ministers and two legal officers, the Lord Advocate and the Solicitor General.

The Scottish Government has the usual range of executive powers and functions, including policy-making, and applying laws, policies and budgets. It exercises all Government powers over devolved matters. The UK Government, therefore, has a continuing but much reduced role, exercised by the Secretary of State for Scotland and the Scottish Office.

The most high-profile of the Scottish Government and Parliament policies have been university fees (discussed in Chapter 2, 'Institutions'), social care charges and prescription charges.

EXPLAINING THE LAW – PRESCRIPTION CHARGES

Prescription charges were introduced in the UK in the 1950s so that patients contributed to the costs of the medicines prescribed to them. Of the four nations in the UK, prescription charges only remain in England. The basic charge is £8.20 per item, although there are very wide exemptions for children, for people with low incomes and for certain medical conditions. The Scottish Government made it a policy object to abolish these charges in 2011 and this was implemented via the National Health Service (Free Prescription and Charges for Drugs and Appliances) (Scotland) Regulations 2011.

There are continuing concerns over the cost of the policy, but Michael Matheson, the Minister for Public Health, reiterated Scottish Government support in 2014: 'It remains our firm belief that healthcare should be free at the point of use – the founding principle of the NHS. Free prescriptions are consistent with our ambitions for a socially just society for the people of Scotland, and we remain committed to this policy'.[9]

11.8.1 INDEPENDENCE REFERENDUM

When the Scottish Parliament was created, Labour had been the dominant force in Scottish politics for decades. It won the largest number of seats in the first two elections to the Parliament and formed the Scottish Government in coalition with the Liberal Democrats. By the 2007 election, the Scottish National Party (47 seats) had overtaken Labour (46 seats). The SNP formed a minority Government and by 2011 was strong enough to win an outright majority and form a majority Government. The UK Government could not ignore this remarkable swing towards a party whose core policy was, and is, to seek independence from the United Kingdom. This produced the Edinburgh Agreement 2012 between the Scottish and UK Governments setting out the process for an independence referendum, and the Scottish Independence Referendum Act 2013 was passed by the Scottish Parliament. This set the voting date for September 2014 and the question to be voted on was:

'Should Scotland be an independent country?'

9   Scottish Government, http://news.scotland.gov.uk/News/Free-prescriptions-f8b.aspx (last accessed 05/11/17).

Eligibility to vote was based on residency in Scotland rather than national identity (so excluding Scots living in England and elsewhere) and introduced the innovation of extending the franchise to 16- and 17-year-olds (Scottish Independence Referendum (Franchise) Act 2013).

After a lively campaign that included some predictions of a very close result or even a narrow victory for the independence campaign, the outcome was 45 per cent Yes, 55 per cent No. The Union between Scotland and the rest of the UK had been preserved, but concessions had been made by the No campaign on devolution of further powers: so-called Devo-Max. Many factors influenced the voting patterns, but these included constitutional concerns about the currency that an independent Scotland would use, membership of NATO, and most importantly – membership of the European Union. There were vigorous debates as to whether, in the event of a 'Yes' vote and independence, Scotland would be treated as a new country or an automatic successor to the rights of EU membership it previously enjoyed as a part of the UK. If it was regarded as a wholly new sovereign state, it would probably have had to go through the full application process to join the EU. In consequence, it would be required to accept the Schengen Agreement on the free movement of persons without border controls (with implications for the land border with England) and to sign up for adoption of the Euro currency.

The 'Devo-Max' offer that impacted on the latter stages of the referendum campaign was examined by the Smith Commission 2014. There were continuing disputes between the Scottish and UK Governments on important details of the scheme but broad agreement was reached and led to the Scotland Act 2016 which provided:

- A commitment that the Scottish Parliament and Government are permanent features of the constitutional system.
- Full devolution of the arrangements over the Scottish Parliament, including the electoral process.
- Devolution of further tax-setting powers and powers over welfare benefits.

We noted above that there are still Scottish features in the UK Government (a Secretary of State for Scotland and Scottish Office), but more constitutionally difficult is the presence in the House of Commons of 59 Scottish MPs who can vote on matters affecting England alone. This is called the 'West Lothian Question' or 'English Votes for English Laws' (EVEL) and is examined below.

11.9 NORTHERN IRELAND

Any discussion of constitutional arrangements in Northern Ireland takes place in the shadow of Anglo-Irish history, summarised very briefly above. We left that summary with the establishment of a Northern Ireland Parliament which first met in 1921. This institution lasted until 1972 when, together with the Northern Ireland Government, it was suspended. Northern Ireland was governed by direct rule from Westminster for most of the following 30 years.

The Northern Ireland Parliament was dominated by Ulster Unionists who were generally Protestant and believed staunchly in continued union with Great Britain. On the opposing side were the Nationalists who were generally Catholic and who sought a united Ireland.[10] The Northern Ireland institutions carried out systemic discrimination against Catholics, especially in relation to jobs and housing, but also in fixing election arrangements to their own advantage (a process known as gerrymandering). In the late 1960s, a civil rights movement modelled on the campaigns in US southern states developed, but its failure amid hostility from the state forces of Northern Ireland led to the Troubles. This was the conflict that spanned almost 30 years, based mainly in Northern Ireland but with violent effects in mainland UK, the Republic of Ireland and beyond. It resulted in over 3,500 deaths, many more injuries, and it blighted the lives of countless thousands more.

There were many attempts at peace in the intervening years, many futile but some such as the Anglo-Irish Treaty 1985 produced small but appreciable gains. In 1995, the IRA called a ceasefire and this led to the 1998 Belfast Agreement, often called the Good Friday Agreement. This sketched out a legal framework for power-sharing between the different communities in a devolved administration that would be committed to peaceful solutions. It was passed as the Northern Ireland Act 1998 (NIA 1998) and started with a double commitment, that:

- 'Northern Ireland in its entirety remains part of the United Kingdom and shall not cease to be so without the consent of a majority of the people of Northern Ireland'.
- 'But if the wish expressed by a majority in such a poll is that Northern Ireland should cease to be part of the United Kingdom and form part of a united Ireland,' then effect would be given to that wish (section 1 NIA 1998).

As Elliott and Thomas explain, this was 'a highly bespoke solution to the specific problems facing Northern Ireland . . . in a sharply divided community, devolved government would only be perceived as legitimate . . . if it enjoyed the support of both Nationalists and Unionists'.[11] The Agreement set up a three-part structure:

- Northern Ireland Assembly, which would produce a Northern Ireland Executive.
- North/South Ministerial Council, comprising representatives from the Northern Ireland Executive and the Irish Government with participants at ministerial level. It agrees actions in a number of areas of co-operation often involving cross-border issues, such as the environment, tourism (e.g. on shared inland waterways), transport planning and trade.
- British-Irish Council, an intergovernmental organisation with a membership of the heads of Government (variously styled Prime Minister, First Minister, Chief Minister and *Taoiseach*) of the UK, Ireland, Northern Ireland, Scotland and Wales; it also includes the Isle of Man and the Channel Islands. It has suitably lofty goals of promoting harmonious

---

10   There are admitted and obvious simplifications in this brief account.
11   M Elliott and R Thomas, *Public Law* (3rd edn, OUP, 2017) 305.

and mutually beneficial development amongst 'the people of these islands', but also discusses and, where possible, co-ordinates policy responses to issues such as energy and the environment.

11.10 NORTHERN IRELAND ASSEMBLY

11.10.1 COMPOSITION

As with the other devolved legislatures, the Assembly has moved from a four- to a five-year fixed term (Northern Ireland (Miscellaneous Provisions) Act 2014). The Assembly had 108 Members of the Legislative Assembly (MLAs), a relatively large number for such a small population. This was reduced to 90 members in the 2017 election. Voting is by single transferable vote, returning six members per constituency. This again tries to balance the strengths of 'first past the post' (strong constituency link) with the need for a more proportionate relationship between votes and seats. There is no dual mandate, so Assembly Members cannot hold seats in other Parliaments, including the Irish Parliament, the *Dail Eireann*.

11.10.2 POWERS

The Assembly has the power to make primary legislation, and again the UK Parliament retains the right to make law for Northern Ireland (section 5 NIA 1998). Under section 6 of the NIA 1998, it cannot legislate for matters outside of Northern Ireland, or inconsistently with EU or ECHR law. The devolution arrangements use the 'reserved matters' model that we saw in relation to the Scottish Parliament, with similar content, i.e. issues such as defence, immigration, international relations are reserved to the UK Parliament. There are additional limitations on the Northern Ireland Assembly. It cannot discriminate against people 'on the ground of religious belief or political opinion', and the Act entrenches the Human Rights Act 1998 in the constitutional arrangements. Policing was originally regarded as too sensitive a subject for the Assembly to handle, but policing and justice were devolved in 2010. It has the usual provision that measures outside of the legislative competence of the Assembly are not law and has similar pre-legislative scrutiny processes to the Scottish Parliament.

11.11 NORTHERN IRELAND EXECUTIVE

The executive branch of Northern Irish devolution is the Executive Committee comprising a First Minister, Deputy First Minister and Northern Ireland Ministers, whose number is limited to 10 (section 20 NIA 1998).

Scotland also has a post of Deputy First Minister (DFM), but this office in Northern Ireland is pivotal to the whole power-sharing basis of the devolution settlement. Following an election, the parties must consult and put forward nominations for a First Minister and

DFM to be elected by the Assembly. The crucial feature is that the FM and DFM are put forward as a *package*. This package must attract a majority of both Unionist and Nationalist votes, and this ensures that the executive branch must be a co-operative enterprise involving both communities. The other ministerial posts are then allocated in proportion to the strength of the parties in the Assembly.

Ministers must take a pledge of office as set out in Schedule 4 NIA 1998. This commits them to observe a Code of Conduct and a duty of good faith, including

- 'commitment to non-violence and exclusively peaceful and democratic means';
- 'to serve all the people of Northern Ireland equally, and to act in accordance with the general obligations on government to promote equality and prevent discrimination'; and
- 'to promote the interests of the whole community represented in the Northern Ireland Assembly towards the goal of a shared future'.

The Assembly has powers to remove ministers from office if it resolves that a minister no longer has the confidence of the Assembly because they are 'not committed to non-violence and exclusively peaceful and democratic means' (section 30 NIA 1998). Similar powers apply in relation to the commitment of whole political parties to peaceful means.

The peace process has not been easy, and the UK Government has had to intermittently suspend the operation of the Assembly and Executive, including through much of 2000–07, but the parties continued to make difficult but valuable progress during this time. This led to a complete cessation of hostilities by the IRA in 2005, including independent verification that they had decommissioned their arsenal of weapons. Under the St Andrews Agreement 2006, the Assembly and Executive were restarted and the following two administrations did serve their full terms.

Problems resurfaced in 2015, with renewed paramilitary violence leading to the First Minister temporarily stepping down, but the 2016 elections proceeded in the standard manner. The response of First Minister, Arlene Foster, to a scandal over a renewable heat incentive scheme then led the deputy First Minister, Martin McGuiness, to resign. Under the power-sharing scheme this triggered the removal of the First Minister which in turn triggered the dissolution of the Assembly in January 2017. Further elections were held in March 2017 but Sinn Féin refused to nominate a new deputy First Minister so the Executive could not be formed. There have been talks and threats to impose direct rule from Westminster, but the stalemate continues.

11.12 BREXIT AND DEVOLUTION

The 2016 referendum on leaving the European Union has a number of implications for the devolution arrangements. The overall result for the UK (and Gibraltar) was 51.9 per cent of voters in favour of leaving the EU, but the breakdown of votes in the constituent nations varied widely. A majority of voters in England and Wales voted for Leave (53.3 per cent and 52.5 per cent respectively), but Leaver voters were in the minority in Northern Ireland and Scotland (44.2 per cent and 38 per cent respectively).

The devolved legislatures claimed they have a veto over decisions to change their powers, including any decision to leave the EU. This was considered in the case of *Miller v Secretary of State for Exiting the European Union* [2017] UKSC 5 (discussed in detail in Chapter 8, Supremacy and European Law). This argument was based on the Sewel Convention that the Westminster Parliament would normally only legislate on a matter within the competence of the Scottish Parliament with the consent of the Scottish Parliament, and the fact that the convention was now recognised in statute; section 28(8) Scotland Act 1998 (as inserted by the Scotland Act 2016): 'it is recognised that the Parliament of the United Kingdom will not normally legislate with regard to devolved matters without the consent of the Scottish Parliament'.

We saw in Chapter 6 Prerogative, that the courts can recognise political conventions but not enforce them as though they were legal rules. The Supreme Court found that recognition of the convention in the Scotland Act 2016 had not turned the Sewel Convention into a legal rule and so its application and consequences were questions for the political rather than the judicial part of the state.

The specific element of the devolved legislatures power that will be directly affected by Brexit is that currently they are prohibited from legislating in a way which is inconsistent with EU law. Once this restriction is removed it seems to open up the prospect of much wider powers for the devolved bodies. They could, for example, develop approaches to agriculture, fisheries, the environment that would differ greatly from the English position. This effect of Brexit is addressed in the European Union (Withdrawal) Bill. It proposes that central Government has full control of this process. The powers will not flow automatically from Brussels to Edinburgh, Belfast or Cardiff, and it will be up to Government in Westminster to decide to what extent these powers will be devolved.

With the UK and Ireland both being members of the European Union's single market and the ending of the Troubles in the 1990s, the border between the two countries has become very soft. Certainly, the experience of crossing the border in recent decades is worlds away (in a wholly positive way) from the experience in the 1970s and 1980s. Brexit, however, will mean that the Northern Ireland/Republic of Ireland border will become an external border of the European Union and Single Market. There are concerns that this will reintroduce a 'hard border' with customs checks and even the possibility of immigration border controls. The Irish border is one of three initial issues being addressed in the UK/EU negotiations but as of late October 2017 there is no indications of how the challenges will be met.

The 2014 Scottish independence referendum was described as a being a once in a generation decision for the Scottish people, but Brexit raises questions about the potential for a second independence referendum. As we saw above a large majority of Scots voted to remain in the European Union. The prospect of the Scottish people being dragged out of the EU and losing their concrete rights and wider identity as EU citizens because their views have been outweighed by their English neighbours seems to be a recipe for renewed independence demands. Thus far, such demands have been muted. The 2017 General Election saw a retreat from the (admittedly incredible) high water mark of success for the Scottish National Party and even saw an increase in Conservative representation in Scotland.

11.13 ENGLAND

Note that whilst there are four nations in the UK, only three of them have their own legislature. The Westminster Parliament is a Parliament for the whole of the United Kingdom and not for England alone. This raises questions of the need for English Votes for English Law (EVEL), aka the West Lothian Question. The relative success of devolution in the three nations has brought about interest in regional devolution within England as a counter to the economic and political domination of London and the South East. As with national devolution, it is hoped that this will give other cities and regions an opportunity to articulate different priorities and a chance to give effect to those priorities.

11.13.1 EVEL

We saw in Chapter 2 that devolution of education matters has resulted in four different regimes for university tuition fees, and above we saw the significant differences in health law and policy. As power over health is devolved to the administrations in Edinburgh, Cardiff and Belfast, this means that when the UK Parliament is legislating on health matters (including the NHS) it can only do so in relation to England. Yet who debates and votes on these legal proposals? It is all MPs, regardless of what constituency they represent. Scottish people know that decisions which affect them on their health provision or access to education will be made by their political representatives. They can make their preferences known through the ballot box and hold politicians to account for their policy choices. English voters face the prospect of decisions on these important matters being voted on by MPs whose constituents are unaffected by the proposal. This was a paradox, or injustice, raised by the MP for West Lothian, Tam Dalyell, in 1978 and has been known as the West Lothian Question. The focus now is not simply Anglo–Scottish, as it also applies to Welsh and Northern Irish MPs, and the issue is commonly called English Votes for English Laws, or EVEL.

One obvious answer would be an English Parliament. This has little support. England has over 80 per cent of the population and over 80 per cent of the MPs in the UK, so it could be argued that there is little need for special arrangements to articulate the needs of such a dominant partner. An English Parliament could result in effective redundancy for Westminster. There would be the cost of building and running a new Parliament building outside of London. It would not simply be a legislature, either; we saw in the Welsh example that legislatures spawn governments. There would be a de facto English Government in competition with a UK Government. The notion that England is too large a partner for a fully federal approach was raised as long ago as 1973: 'A federation consisting of four units – England, Scotland, Wales and Northern Ireland – would be so unbalanced as to be unworkable'.[12]

Nevertheless, the McKay Commission in 2013 found considerable dissatisfaction amongst English voters with current arrangements and recommended a principle that 'decisions at the UK level with a separate and distinct effect for England . . . should normally be taken only with the consent of a majority of MPs for constituencies in England'.[13] It favoured a political procedural method of achieving this consent. Parliament would publicise the break-down of votes by geographical constituency (England, Scotland, Wales, Northern Ireland) which would make it politically difficult for a Government to impose English-only laws without the consent of a majority of English MPs. The Commission's idea was that a strong constitutional convention would emerge along the lines of the Sewel Convention.

The option taken by the UK Government is more radical than this. This momentous constitutional change was achieved not through wide public debate and primary legislation, but through the House of Commons agreeing a motion to change its Standing Orders (i.e. its internal procedural rules) in October 2015. The process is rather complex,[14] but in summary:

- The Speaker can certify a Bill (or parts of it) as being English-only.
- The Bill will be considered at Committee Stage only by English MPs.
- There will be a Legislative Grand Committee (England) made up of all English MPs who can agree to put a Bill to the whole House (note that this is in effect a veto).
- At the third reading, there will be a 'double majority' process – the whole House votes, but an England-only Bill will need a majority of both the whole House and of English MPs.

The EVEL procedure has operated relatively quietly since its introduction which may be a sign that it has not been unduly contentious. In its first year of operation, the Speaker certified nine Bills as being English-only. Gover and Kenny found that none of the certification decisions caused controversy. They do go on to criticise EVEL for not effectively creating an 'English voice' in the law-making process, with Legislative Grand Committees being 'almost

12   Report of the Royal Commission on the Constitution, Cmnd 5460/1973 (The Kilbrandon Report).
13   Report of the Commission on the Consequences of Devolution for the House of Commons (2013).
14   UK Government, Explanatory Guide to EVEL, https://www.gov.uk/government/publications/english-votes-for-english-laws-proposed-changes/english-votes-for-english-laws-an-explanatory-guide-to-proposals (last accessed 05/11/17).

entirely perfunctory'.[15] This lack of visibility may also indicate that EVEL has not succeeded in fully addressing the concerns about a lop-sided devolution arrangement.

11.13.2 METROPOLITAN AND REGIONAL DEVOLUTION

Since 2000, London has had a Greater London Authority (GLA) and a Mayor. The Mayor has no tax-raising powers, but can generate income independently of central Government through e.g. the congestion charge. The Mayor and GLA have an executive and policy role in e.g. transport, planning, economic development, environment and waste. The list is similar to local authority powers, but the practical difference is in the scale and profile of the London administration. It administers for a population of around 8.5 million, which is larger than any of the devolved nations and reflects London's economic, political and cultural power.

There were proposals in 2003 for regional devolution across eight regions of England. These would have created elected assemblies. There was limited enthusiasm for the proposals, and the first proposal, for the North-east region, was strongly rejected in a local referendum, causing further plans to be shelved.

The idea of regional devolution in England was resurrected by the Chancellor, George Osborne, within his wider 'Northern powerhouse' concept. Initial activity focused on Manchester ('Devo-Manc'), but has been extended. The devolution to a Greater Manchester Combined Authority and an elected mayor included greater powers over transport, fire services and policing. The real significance of the scheme, however, is two-fold:

- Control over a local NHS budget of £6 billion which will be integrated with social care.
- Some control of property taxes, in particular being allowed to keep 100 per cent of business rates growth.

This is clearly a model of executive, and not legislative, devolution, but the Government is talking of this devolution scheme as 'a process'.[16] The Cities and Local Government Act 2016 made more general provision for regional devolution. It allows for directly elected mayors (who would take over the duties of Police and Crime Commissioners for their areas) and the devolution of executive powers in relation to transport, housing, education and economic development. This does not automatically apply across England and there must first be a 'devolution deal' agreed between Government and the cities or counties to create Combined Authorities. There are currently eight Combined Authorities that have devolution deals, including Greater Manchester, Liverpool, Sheffield, West Yorkshire, West Midlands and Cornwall.

....

15   D Gover and M Kenny, 'Finding good in EVEL (Centre on Constitutional Change, 2016).

16   UK Government, 'Further devolution to the Greater Manchester Combined Authority and directly-elected Mayor', https://www.gov.uk/government/uploads/system/uploads/attachment_data/file/443087/Greater_Manchester_Further_Devolution.pdf (last accessed 05/11/17).

POINTS TO REVIEW

- The United Kingdom comprises four nations, each of which has had a devolution of powers from 'the centre'. These devolution arrangements are deeply asymmetrical.

- Wales, Scotland and Northern Ireland have devolved legislatures which possess powers to make primary legislation within each nation on issues which are conferred by (Wales) or not reserved to Westminster (Scotland and Northern Ireland).

- Wales, Scotland and Northern Ireland have executives to govern on devolved issues and to administer the laws and policies of each nation.

- Devolution is much less developed in England, but the introduction of EVEL and the start of regional devolution are signs of an evolving structure.

TAKING IT FURTHER

Devolution – *Public Law* journal The journal *Public Law* produces short updates on developments in devolution on a regular basis. They could really help you show initiative in incorporating contemporary developments in your work. The best way to access them is through Westlaw. Go to the Journals tab – Advanced search – enter "Public Law" in the Journal Title box, and Devolution in the 'Article' title box.

N Walker, 'Our constitutional unsettlement' [2014] *Public Law* 529 This is an ambitious article that is not limited to discussing devolution. The devolution process, however, is an important part of Walker's thesis, that a fluid unsettled constitution is not necessarily pathological and may be a 'least-worst' solution to the diverse pressures with the constitutional system.

UK Government, Explanatory Guide to EVEL, https://www.gov.uk/government/publications/english-votes-for-english-laws-proposed-changes/english-votes-for-english-laws-an-explanatory-guide-to-proposals The English Votes for English Laws process was agreed in the very last stages of this book being written. It could have a significant impact on devolutionary pressures throughout the Union, so it would be worth your whilst keeping an eye on developments.

CHAPTER 12
JUDICIAL REVIEW – ACCESS TO JUSTICE

Public bodies exercise powers that have a direct impact on your life. A very short illustrative list could include decisions about medical treatments, how you use your home, your access to benefits (including student financing), your tax liability and whether you can vote, marry, or travel abroad on a passport. These are decisions which are all relatively individual and direct to you. In addition, public bodies take decisions that profoundly affect the society in which you live, such as whether to build a high-speed rail link across the country, whether to commit to low-carbon energy generation, whether to privatise NHS services.

These decisions must be made in line with various rules. The rules can be derived from the Act of Parliament that granted the power to the public body or more generally from the common law. When something goes legally wrong in the way the public body has reached a decision, then judicial review is the key legal procedure for challenging that decision before the courts.

AS YOU READ

You should be able to:

- Understand the nature and purpose of judicial review.

- Outline the effect of ouster clauses.

- Assess whether a claimant would have standing (*locus standi*) to bring a judicial review claim.

Discussion of judicial review will be central to our exploration of Administrative Law. Most of the previous chapters have focused on the Constitutional Law elements of Public Law, i.e. concerned with the structure of the constitution of the state and the broad questions of how state power is allocated and controlled. Administrative Law is closely related to this but is more precise; it is located in specific procedures and particular disputes. It is more concerned with questions of what happens when an individual has a specific legal grievance with the state.

There are two chapters on judicial review. In this first, we are going to look at:

- The nature of judicial review.
- The procedure for making a claim.

- When it is available.
- When it can be excluded.

In the next chapter, we will examine the grounds of judicial review, i.e. the ways in which a public body can be shown to have acted unlawfully. In a judicial review action, once the rules of procedure are complied with, the claimants need to successfully demonstrate at least one of the grounds of review to the court.

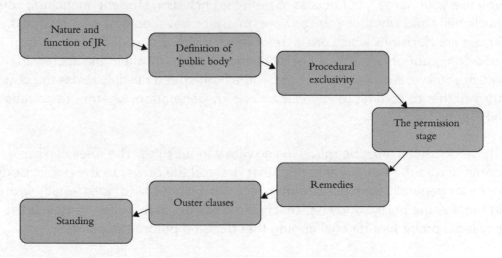

Figure 12.1 Structure of Chapter 12?

APPLYING THE LAW – PUBLIC DECISIONS AFFECT PRIVATE LIVES

Imagine that the Department for Transport (DFT) has decided on the route of a new high-speed rail link. The line will go past the end of your garden, within 50 metres of your house. It will carry trains going over 200 miles an hour for 18 hours a day, seven days a week.

The DFT had initially promised to consult with all affected parties, but did not consult with you. You know that the Public Health department of the local university submitted a research report to the DFT on the impact of high-speed rail noise on the mental and physical health of people living close to rail lines. The report is not even mentioned in the DFT decision.

The DFT were given powers by statute to compensate property owners affected by the development of the rail line, but have a strict policy that this power will only be used for properties directly in the way of the proposed line and not for neighbouring properties.

Your initial feelings may be that you are the underdog in any 'David versus Goliath' challenge to the DFT decisions. You are an ordinary householder who has been very badly treated by a major Government department over a multi-billion pound, decades-long infrastructure project. Is there any way, in law, to challenge these decisions? The answer is yes – through a claim for judicial review.

12.1 THE ROLE AND FUNCTION OF JUDICIAL REVIEW

We are, once again, concerned with the control of power, and with courts examining how public bodies exercise power. The focus is on executive power; this includes decisions made by great bodies of state, such as the Home Office, right the way down to your local city or town council. Prerogative powers can, generally, be subject to judicial review. Judicial review is also available to challenge the legality of delegated legislation, e.g. statutory instruments created by Government Ministers, but primary legislation (Acts of Parliament) cannot be questioned through the judicial review process.

Judicial review examines the legality of the decision and not its merits. 'Judicial review . . . does not allow the court of review to examine the evidence with a view to forming its own view about the substantial merits of the case' (Lord Clyde, *Reid v Secretary of State for Scotland* [1999] 2 AC 512). As Laws LJ explained in *R v Somerset County Council, ex parte Fewings* [1995] 1 All ER 513, the court 'does not ask itself the question, "is this decision right or wrong?"'

So the court is not concerned with whether the Department for Transport's choice of rail line is a good decision. Whether it is good transport policy, whether it is good economics, whether it is environmentally responsible are questions that are allocated to different parts of the state. It is for the Government to come up with the broad policy, Parliament to approve it and the public body (such as the Department for Transport) to apply the powers. For these aspects of the decision, Government and Parliament must be politically accountable. Judicial review simply tries to ensure that for the legality of the decision that the public body is *legally accountable*.

Some students really like it when the Public Law syllabus moves on to judicial review. It is legalistic in the sense that it involves applying statutory rules, and the development of common law principles through cases. It is, compared to the sweeping principles of Constitutional Law, more akin to the type of legal study you undertake in other substantive modules (e.g. Contract). On the other hand, some students struggle with judicial review because they never develop an overall picture of what the review process actually involves. It is important, therefore, to develop this coherent picture.

Judicial review is not limited to the review of statutory powers but in a large majority of cases the starting

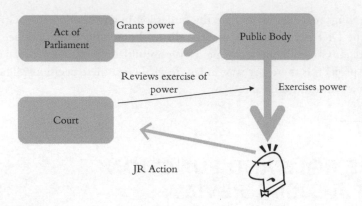

Figure 12.2 The operation of judicial review

point is an Act of Parliament. Parliament passes an Act that establishes a public body and *grants it powers*, or amends the powers granted to an existing public body. For example, an Act of Parliament may grant the power to decide the route of new rail lines to the Department for Transport. It may go on to give the DFT discretion on when to make compensation payments to those affected.

So, Parliament empowers public bodies and those public bodies *exercise their powers* in their day-to-day dealings with citizens. Public bodies may exercise powers in ways which are unlawful, by going beyond the scope of those powers or exercising the powers in some legally flawed manner. For example, the DFT may fail to consult when it was legally obliged to do so. It may fail to take into account some research that was legally relevant to reaching its decision. In those circumstances, an aggrieved person or group can take their complaint to court through a *judicial review claim*. For example, as an affected property owner you could ask the court to quash the DFT decision because of the lack of consultation.

The court will *review the exercise of power*. If it finds that any of the grounds of judicial review are present (such as a breach of a legitimate expectation that you will be consulted, or failure to take into account all relevant considerations), then it can decide to quash the DFT decision. Note that the court is *not* reviewing the *grant of power* by the Act of Parliament, because it cannot review primary legislation; its focus is on the way in which the powers were *exercised*.

12.2 RELATIONSHIP TO CONSTITUTIONAL ISSUES

Constitutional law and Administrative Law do not exist in separate compartments. The nature and purpose of judicial review are products of some of the constitutional ideas we looked at in earlier chapters, and judicial review illustrates important aspects of Constitutional Law.

12.2.1 SUPREMACY OF PARLIAMENT

In judicial review, the court is not reviewing the validity of an Act of Parliament. The traditional view of Parliamentary supremacy tells us that this is not possible and that courts can only accept and apply Acts of Parliament. Judicial review actually supports supremacy. When Parliament grants power to a public body, the grant is made subject to certain limits which are found in the Act. In a judicial review action, the court is requiring respect for those statutory limits and so is giving effect to the intention of Parliament.

12.2.2 SEPARATION OF POWERS

Judicial review illustrates the separation of powers. Parliament in making the law is exercising its *legislative function*; the public body, such as the Department for Transport as part of the executive, and is applying the law (an *executive function*); if there is an allegation of unlawful exercise of powers, then that goes to the court which carries out its *judicial function* of interpreting the law and resolving legal disputes. This also explains why this procedure is limited to *review*. The courts may not be best placed, in comparison with the technical and economic expertise available to Government departments, to decide the merits of policy decisions. The courts also do not have the same democratic authority to decide what is in the best public interest on broad political and economic issues.

12.2.3 RULE OF LAW

Judicial review is one of the principal vehicles for the rule of law. The rule of law can seem like an abstract concept, but judicial review gives it flesh and bone. The legality principle says that the state must operate in accordance with the law, and that it must have lawful authority for its actions; but what happens if it does not? Judicial review is not the only mechanism for holding the state to the rule of law. Civil actions can be brought, for example, against the police when an officer oversteps their authority, but the most important procedure is judicial review. If there is no lawful authority for a public body decision, then the court can quash that decision and require the public body to operate within the bounds of the law.

We saw in Chapter 10 that A V Dicey was very concerned about the existence of discretionary powers. He thought that their existence undermined the rule of law and could be equated with arbitrary power. With the expansion of state activity through the last century, this view is no longer practicable. The modern state needs discretion. One way of addressing Diceyan concerns, however, is through *supervision of the discretion* (the choices that public bodies make). This can be done politically through e.g. Parliamentary Select Committees and questions to ministers, and legally through judicial review.

Joseph Raz argued that a legal system needed to have a certain structure (including access to justice and natural justice) so that it could demonstrate the characteristics (such as clarity), needed for law to do its job of guiding human behaviour. We will see in this chapter how access to justice has been an abiding concern in judicial review whilst natural justice (e.g. the absence of bias) is an important ground of judicial review.

12.3 ACCESS TO JUSTICE

One of the objectives of this textbook is to help you develop your reasoning skills. In this chapter, we will try to do this by using a particular principle, access to justice, as a benchmark. Using this benchmark allows us to go beyond describing the procedure of applying for judicial review and on to evaluate that procedure. We can assess how the procedure has developed, the state of the current law and proposals for reform.

Evaluating against a benchmark is a useful way of demonstrating higher reasoning skills to your tutors. Many coursework and exam questions will explicitly require you to 'critically evaluate'. Using a benchmark is not the only way of doing this. Alternatives include to compare and contrast, to identify tensions within a system and to assess the socio-economic consequences of legal decisions. Using a benchmark, however, can be a relatively simple way of strengthening the evaluative aspects of your work. It is important to explicitly identify what your benchmark is (as we are doing here). It is also important to justify its use. In this case, access to justice is a relevant benchmark. It is a crucial feature of the rule of law, as outlined above, which has been a noticeable feature of judicial thinking on judicial review. It has been a motive for, and justification of, many developments in judicial review procedure. When the state is being subject to legal scrutiny and having its decisions quashed, the temptation is to use its dominant power to exclude or limit access to those review procedures. A number of Governments have succumbed to that temptation, and recent proposals, e.g. the Grayling 'reform' proposals of 2014, have been criticised on the same basis.

In the next section, we will examine the situations where judicial review is available, by identifying:

- Who a judicial review claim can be brought against – what is a public body?
- Whether there are other ways of accessing justice – the impact of alternative remedies.
- Whether a claimant is required to use the judicial review path – procedural exclusivity.

12.4 WHAT IS A PUBLIC BODY?

Judicial review is a Public Law procedure. It is not available for private law disputes and, as such, it cannot be used against bodies which exercise no public functions. So how can the law distinguish between a public and a private body? It is often a straightforward question; most public bodies are established by statute. Examples include local authorities, the Independent Police Complaints Commission which was set up by the Police Reform Act 2002, Her Majesty's Passport Office which was established by the Identity Cards Act 2006, and the Environment Agency which was established under the Environment Act 1995. These bodies also derive their powers from statute.

There are, however, institutions that play an important role in our public life, and carry out regulatory roles, which were not set up by statute. They are often charities or the self-regulation body for a particular industry, commercial or sporting sector. In most cases, they will be treated as private bodies, but there are circumstances where the courts will categorise some of their functions as 'public'.

KEY CASE – *R V CITY PANEL ON TAKEOVERS AND MERGERS, EX PARTE DATAFIN* [1987] QB 815

The body at the centre of this case was the City Panel on Takeovers and Mergers, established in 1968 by the financial institutions of the City of London. Its main role is to apply the City Code on Takeovers and Mergers which seeks to ensure that shareholders are treated equally during takeovers.[1]

In the following 20 years, it became 'woven into the fabric' of City financial regulation. As Lord Donaldson said, 'the panel is a truly remarkable body, performing its function without visible means of legal support. But the operative word is "visible" . . . invisible or indirect legal support there is in abundance'. It could make decisions with direct impacts on statutory functions, such as the listing of shares on the Stock Exchange. Did this make it a public body for the purpose of judicial review?

The approach of the courts up to this point was focused very much on the source of power; was the body established by statute and exercising statutory powers? But Lord Donaldson stated:

> I do not agree that the source of the power is the sole test whether a body is subject to judicial review . . . If the source of power is a statute then clearly the body in question will be subject . . . if, at the other end of the scale, the source of the power is contractual then clearly the body is not subject . . . in between these extremes there is an area in which it is helpful to look not just at the source of the power but at the nature of the power.

The City Panel was exercising 'Public Law type' powers and carrying out governmental functions, because:

- It had a compulsory jurisdiction – if you wanted to do business in the City of London then you had to abide by City Panel rulings.
- It exercised powers that had their basis on statute.

---

1 The Takeover Panel, 'About the Panel', http://www.thetakeoverpanel.org.uk/structure (last accessed 03/11/17). The Panel was given a direct statutory underpinning in 2006.

- The 'but for' test – but for the existence of the City Panel, would the state have to intervene? In this case the answer was unambiguously positive. If the Panel did not exist, then the Government would have had to either establish a new body by statute to exercise its functions or extend the functions of some existing body, such as the Bank of England or the Monopolies and Mergers Commission. The Panel regulated issues that were of governmental concern, issues that could not be left unregulated by the state.

This seemed to point the way to a wider scope for judicial review; a more extensive range of bodies could be subject to judicial review actions. The courts in subsequent cases, however, have emphasised the limiting aspects of *Datafin*.

KEY CASE – *R V DISCIPLINARY COMMITTEE OF THE JOCKEY CLUB, EX PARTE AGA KHAN* [1993] 2 ALL ER 853

The Aga Khan was a famous race horse owner. One of his horses won the Oakes at Epsom – one of the classic races of the year. The horse was disqualified by the Jockey Club, the organisation that ran horse racing in the UK; (it was replaced by the British Horseracing Authority in 2007). The Jockey Club was established by Royal Charter, regulated a significant national activity and had compulsory jurisdiction. If you want to race horses in the UK, then you had to submit to the authority of the Jockey Club.

The court found that the Jockey Club was not a public body for the purposes of judicial review. It was not part of a scheme of state regulation, barely mentioned in statute and not given any significant statutory power: 'the Jockey Club effectively regulates a significant national activity, exercising powers which affect the public . . . it is not in its origin, its history, its constitution or its membership a public body . . . the powers which it exercises over those who agree to be bound by the Rules of Racing derive from the agreement of the parties and give rise to private rights'.

So the Aga Khan had a contractual relationship with the Jockey Club, and if he wanted redress then he would have to pursue a private law action.

The judges were divided on the application of the 'but for' test. Lord Hoffmann thought the Government would not be obliged or inclined to intervene in horse racing in the absence of the Jockey Club, whilst Lord Bingham considered that if it did not exist, then the Government would 'probably be driven to create a public body' to regulate horse racing. This contrasts with *R v Football Association Ltd, ex parte Football League* [1992] 2 All ER 833, where Rose LJ thought there would be no need for Government intervention to directly regulate particular sports, and that commercial interests were more likely to play any organisational and regulatory role.

In relation to access to justice, the approach outlined in *Aga Khan* means that in most cases, an aggrieved person should still be able to access a court. A key question is: how did this body come to be in a position to make decisions affecting this individual? If it is not through Public Law powers, then it is most likely to be through some contractual relationship. If the case is against a body that has no particular authority over and above what a private individual or private company would have, then the relationship can be governed by private law, e.g. of tort or property.

The current approach of the courts now derives from *R v Chief Rabbi of the United Hebrew Congregation, ex parte Wachmann* [1993] 2 All ER 249:

> To attract the court's supervisory jurisdiction there must be not merely a public but potentially a governmental interest in the decision-making power in question . . . where non-governmental bodies have been held to be reviewable, they have generally been operating as an integral part of a regulatory system . . . supported by statutory powers and penalties clearly indicative of governmental concern.
>
> (Simon Brown J)

So the test has two elements. The body must be:

- Operating as an integral part of a regulatory system.
- Supported by statutory powers and penalties clearly indicative of governmental concern.

Claims of a breach of European Convention rights under the Human Rights Act 1998 are subject to a similar restriction. They can only be brought against a 'public authority' (s.6 Human Rights Act 1998). Whilst there are similarities with the approach of the courts in ordinary judicial review claims, as outlined above, the procedures are not integrated. Human rights claims will be considered in Chapter 15.

12.5 ALTERNATIVE REMEDIES

Judicial review is not available when Parliament has provided some alternative remedy. It is fairly common for an Act of Parliament setting up a governmental scheme to include a right of appeal to a court, tribunal or inspector. Where this right of appeal exists, an individual must exercise it and will not be allowed to proceed directly to a judicial review claim (*R v Epping and Harlow General Commissioners, ex parte Goldstraw* [1983] 3 All ER 257).

How does this affect our principal benchmark of access to justice? Appeals will often provide better access to justice. An appeal does not simply consider the legality of the decision, but can also revisit the merits. In practical terms of cost, time and complexity, an appeal is often more accessible then judicial review.

12.6 PROCEDURAL EXCLUSIVITY

Once a special procedure for judicial review claims was established by the Senior Courts Act 1977, the question arose of what types of actions *had to* use this procedure. In particular, could the public interest restrictions within the judicial review procedure (e.g. time limits, discretionary remedies) be circumvented by raising Public Law issues in ordinary legal proceedings? The question was answered by the House of Lords in *O'Reilly v Mackman*. Unfortunately, the answer raised more questions than it resolved.

KEY CASE – *O'REILLY V MACKMAN* [1983] 2 AC 237

A number of prisoners were charged with offences against prison discipline following riots at Hull prison. The Board of Prison Visitors upheld the charges and imposed various penalties (i.e. these were public body decisions). The prisoners sought a court order to nullify the decisions, claiming a breach of natural justice (i.e. on Public Law grounds). These actions were brought by ordinary writ rather than through the judicial review procedure.

The House of Lords overturned the judgments of the High Court and Court of Appeal that claimants had a choice as to which type of procedure to use. The Law Lords stated that trying to enforce Public Law rights through ordinary procedures, rather than judicial review, was an abuse of process.

This meant that there would be *procedural exclusivity*: the judicial review procedure was exclusively for Public Law claims, and Public Law claims had to be brought exclusively under the judicial review procedure. This raised a number of issues. The procedural exclusivity outlined in *O'Reilly v Mackman* was only intended to be a 'general rule', that is, it was envisaged that there would be exceptions. What were those exceptions?

Two broad exceptions emerged from the (rather large) number of cases that followed: collateral issues and defences.

1(a) Collateral issue – real life can be a messy business and does not present problems that fall neatly into the categories that are, by necessity, established in law. A single dispute might contain elements of both public and private law.

KEY CASE – *ROY V KENSINGTON AND CHELSEA AND WESTMINSTER FAMILY PRACTITIONER COMMITTEE* [1992] 1 AC 624

Dr Roy was a GP employed in part by the NHS with his pay set by regulations. The Family Practitioner Committee (FPC) had Public Law powers to reduce pay if it considered that a GP was not devoting sufficient time to NHS work. The FPC decided to reduce Dr Roy's pay. He argued that he had been underpaid on his contract with the FPC and sued, in private law, for the additional pay. The FPC argued that this was a Public Law dispute.

The House of Lords held that the Public Law decision by the FPC was a part of the case, but that Dr Roy had some private law rights at stake in his dispute with the FPC. He was entitled to sue the FPC for breach of contract using ordinary litigation procedures, because the Public Law issues were a collateral part of the case.

Notice the language here. Following the general principle of procedural exclusivity in *O'Reilly v Mackman*, one might have expected that there would be an exception only where a Public Law issue was *merely ancillary or subsidiary* to a private law action, i.e. a very minor part of a predominantly private law action. The use of the word *collateral*, which means accompanying, parallel or running alongside rather than necessarily subordinate, shows that from an early stage, the courts have been retreating from a strict procedural approach. Their concern has not been to preserve the purity of the categories. The courts have just noted that the different procedures for bringing a dispute to court have different rules and different aims. They are alive to the fact that giving a complete choice to people as to what procedure to use could result in an abuse of process, and preventing such abuses has been their key consideration.

This was underlined by the Court of Appeal in *Mercury Communications Ltd v Director General of Telecommunications* [1996] 1 WLR 48. There will be some disputes where bringing an action in *either* judicial review *or* the ordinary procedure is possible. It is also possible for a case to be transferred by a judge into and out of judicial review. You might think that these procedural issues are rather abstract (and even some judges would not disagree with you – Lord Woolf in *Clark* below called them 'arid questions'). By looking at a particular issue, however, we can see that the distinct procedures do make a difference. The amount of time that you have to bring a claim is often of huge practical importance.

- Judicial review claim – the claim must be brought promptly, and in any event within three months (Civil Procedure Rules, Order 54(5)).
- Ordinary action – the typical period for bring a claim in contract or tort under the Limitation Act 1980 is six years.

This was one of the issues in the following case.

KEY CASE – *CLARK V UNIVERSITY OF LINCOLNSHIRE AND HUMBERSIDE* [2000] 1 WLR 1988

A student sued her university for breach of contract over a finding of plagiarism. She commenced her action around two years after the plagiarism decision. The university said that she ought to have brought her challenge by way of judicial review, and therefore 'promptly and in any event within three months'. It asserted that framing her challenge to the plagiarism decision as a breach of contract allowed her to circumvent the time limit and was an abuse of process.

The Court of Appeal held that Clark could bring a claim in contract based on a bundle of public and private law issues. Even if it may have been more suitable to bring an action by judicial review, the court will not strike out a claim unless it is, over and above that fact, an abuse of process.

The other side of the coin is that there will be circumstances where the procedural exclusivity rule still needs to be applied, i.e. where a Public Law decision has a wider impact on the interests of third parties or on effective administration by public bodies. *Clark* could be seen as a dispute between one student and one university about a decision that had very limited consequences for the wider public. Planning decisions on the other hand can significantly impact on the interests of third parties, and public bodies need to have confidence to act on their decisions, e.g. on whether to demolish a building, without waiting six years to see if there is a legal challenge (as underlined in *Stancliffe Stone Co Ltd v Peak District National Park Authority* [2005] EWCA Civ 241).

The judgment in *Clark* goes a long way to resolving any access to justice concerns that the *O'Reilly v Mackman* principle might produce. The main danger is that if an individual mistakenly challenges a Public Law decision through the wrong procedure and has their claim struck out, they will be too late to commence a judicial review. Even if the public body has acted unlawfully and their interests have been affected, they will not be able to access any remedy. Giving judges a discretion to only strike out claims when they are, for broader reasons, an abuse of process reduces the scope for injustice and promote access to justice.

1(b) As a defence – a claim that a public body decision is unlawful can be used as part of a defence in both civil and criminal cases.

KEY CASE – *WANDSWORTH LONDON BOROUGH COUNCIL V WINDER* [1985] AC 461

Winder was sued by the Council for rent arrears. His defence included an allegation that the attempt to raise rents by the Council, under the Housing Act 1957, was unlawful. The Council argued that he ought to have challenged their actions under the judicial review procedure. The House of Lords held that this was not an abuse of process. A defendant being sued on the basis of potentially unlawful decisions could challenge those decisions as part of their defence.

This ability to use the unlawfulness of public body decisions as a shield against actions is not limited to civil cases. In *Boddington v British Transport Police* [1999] 2 AC 143, the House of Lords confirmed that the principle from *Winder* applied equally in criminal cases.

KEY LEARNING POINTS

- Judicial review only examines the legality and not the merits of public decisions.
- Judicial review is only available against public bodies. This includes non-statutory bodies that are part of a scheme of governmental regulation and exercising public powers.
- If alternative remedies are available, they must be used in preference to judicial review.
- The general rule in *O'Reilly v Mackman* means there ought to be procedural exclusivity – Public Law claims need to be brought through judicial review.
- The general rule of procedural exclusivity is subject to broad exceptions for collateral challenges and as a defence.

12.7 WHAT IS THE PROCEDURE FOR APPLYING FOR A JUDICIAL REVIEW?

In a claim for judicial review, there is:

- The **permission stage** which serves as a sieve or filter.
- The **substantive hearing** is where the claimant presents their detailed evidence and must establish the grounds for their complaint.

This procedure is governed by section 31 of the Senior Courts Act 1981, and Part 54 of the Civil Procedure Rules 2000 (CPR).

12.7.1 PRE-ACTION PROTOCOL

The Pre-Action Protocol for Judicial Review came into force in 2002.[2] It requires the parties to consider alternative dispute resolution (ADR) before the litigation process starts. They may need to show evidence of this to the court, and failing to do so may impact on case management and costs. The protocol involves:

- Letter from claimant – to identify the basis of the dispute and request a response (normally within 14 days).
- The judicial review claim normally cannot start until the response date has passed.
- The response letter from the public body might concede the claim, in full or in part, or explain the decision further.

---

2   Ministry of Justice, 'Pre-Action Protocol', http://www.justice.gov.uk/courts/procedure-rules/civil/protocol/prot_jrv (last accessed 03/11/17).

The benefits are that it should help to resolve the dispute before litigation starts and, if not, it will inform both sides of the basis of the claim and the defence.

12.8 PERMISSION STAGE

Up to the Bowman reforms in 2000, this was called the leave stage and was *ex parte*, meaning that only the claimant addressed the judge. Since 2000, it is called the permission stage and is *inter partes*, meaning that both sides are involved. Permission is dealt with by a judge sitting alone in chambers and is a paper-based process. There is still some limited scope for short oral hearings in open court but these are much less common than before the Bowman reforms. A claimant must complete the Judicial Review Claim Form which must be served on the other party as well as filed with the Court.

APPLYING THE LAW – THE JUDICIAL REVIEW CLAIM FORM

In undergraduate legal education, you do not often look at court forms. There are good general reasons for this. Legal education is a general liberal education that is useful to all those who undertake it, including the significant proportion who do not become legal practitioners. The detailed processes on how to initiate litigation are generally best left to the vocational stages of legal training (e.g. the Legal Practice Course, the Bar Professional Training Course). Nevertheless, it is occasionally instructive to look at the practicalities of law in action. The Judicial Review Claim Form is Form N461: http://hmctsformfinder.justice.gov.uk/HMCTS/GetForm. do?court_forms_id=594.

Have a look at the form. It illustrates: the need to identify the defendant and other interested parties, details of the decision to be reviewed, that you have complied with the pre-action protocol, the details of the grounds on which you seek to challenge a decision, and the remedy you are seeking.

You cannot require a legal review of a decision merely because you disagree with it. You need to articulate what the legal grounds of your complaint are. If there is no legal basis for your complaint, then the claim will be filtered out at this stage.

If a judge, on looking at the information in form N461 and reading the counter-argument from the defendant, does not see a valid claim, i.e. 'an arguable ground for judicial review having a realistic prospect of success' (*Sharma v Brown-Antoine* [2006] UKPC 57), they will refuse permission. Under section 31(6) of the Senior Courts Act 1981, the court may also refuse permission if the granting of relief 'would be likely to cause substantial hardship to, or substantially prejudice the rights of, any person or would be detrimental to good administration'.

12.8.1 TIME LIMITS

Section 31(6) Senior Courts Act 1981 allows a court to refuse permission if there has been *undue delay* in making a claim. Rule 54(5) of the Civil Procedure Rules states that a claim should be made:

> promptly, and in any event not later than three months after the grounds to make the claim first arose.

The House of Lords in *R v Dairy Produce Quota Tribunal for England and Wales, ex parte Caswell* [1990] 2 AC 738 explained that failing to satisfy the test in CPR Rule 54(5) would amount to undue delay for the purposes of section 31(6) of the Senior Courts Act 1981. The time limit can be extended under the CPR for 'good reason'.

APPLYING THE LAW – ASSESSMENT ADVICE

What is the time limit for bringing a judicial review? Many Public Law students will say 'three months'. This will get the person marking your work reaching for their red pen (or their digital equivalent) to put a cross on your paper. The test is *promptly* and in any event within three months. It is a difference that matters. If you go into practice and a client comes to you with a judicial review problem and you say, 'we have three months in which to make a claim', then even though the courts will rarely block a claim made within three months, you are being negligent.

KEY CASE – *R V INDEPENDENT TELEVISION COMMISSION, EX PARTE TV NI LTD* [1991] TIMES LAW REPORTS 606

The Independent Television Commission awarded a TV franchise to a rival of TV NI Ltd. TV NI brought a judicial review claim within three months of the decision. The claim was rejected for not meeting the time limit test. In cases involving the interests of third parties, the claim must be brought with the 'utmost promptitude because so many third parties are affected by the decision and are entitled to act on it unless they have clear and prompt notice that a decision is being challenged'.

Third parties, including sometimes the wider public, act on the basis of public body decisions. In this case, the third party was the winner of the TV franchise, Ulster TV. Following its successful bid, it would immediately begin to renew contracts, recommission programmes, hire studio space, etc. It had to rely on the public body decision.

12.8.2 STANDING

Standing, sometimes called '*locus standi*', is your right to challenge a public body decision before the Administrative Court – your connection to the thing you are complaining about. It is considered in detail below.

12.8.3 OPERATION OF THE PERMISSION STAGE

The operation of the permission stage in judicial review has been controversial. There is no permission requirement in Contract or Tort Law. It is argued that there is a need to protect public bodies from being harassed by frivolous or vexatious law suits. Flooding a public body with legal challenges will hold up its work and take resources away from the public services it is intended to provide. Whilst the need for the existence of some sort of filter is broadly accepted, its practical operation has been subject to detailed scrutiny, in particular by Bondy and Sunkin. Their research found that in 2006 only 22% of judicial review applications received permission to proceed, down from 58% only a decade previously.[3]

The leading test in the early years of the reformed judicial review procedure was from Lord Diplock in the *Fleet Street Casuals* case (1982): 'If, on a quick perusal of the material then available, the court thinks that it discloses what might on further consideration turn out to be an arguable case' then permission ought to be granted.[4] The language used by the judiciary became progressively less generous through the 1980s and 1990s, and sought to exclude cases where the evidence at the permission stage did not *already show* an arguable case. The Bowman reforms of 2000 also reduced the number of permissions granted by reducing oral hearings and by allowing defendants to respond to allegations. Bondy and Sunkin point out that this reduction is not necessarily all negative in that the involvement of defendants allows for a much higher number of cases to be settled. They go on to argue, however, that clearer criteria would help those advising claimants, and (together with a more experienced core of Administrative Law judges) address the problem of inconsistency between judges.[5]

12.9 REMEDIES

There are four main remedies available in judicial review proceedings:

- Quashing order – quashes the decision of the public body. This is the most common remedy granted in judicial review actions. It allows a fresh decision to be made by the public body.
- Mandatory order – requires a public body to act in accordance with the law and its statutory duties.
- Prohibiting order – focuses on the future and orders the public body to refrain from acting in a way which would breach the law. It is used most frequently in relation to

---

3   V Bondy and M Sunkin, 'Accessing Judicial Review' [2008] *Public Law* 647.

4   *IRC v National Federation the Self-Employed and Small Businesses* [1982] AC 617.

5   V Bondy and M Sunkin, 'The Dynamics of Judicial Review Litigation' [2009], http://www.publiclawproject.org.uk/resources/9/the-dynamics-of-judicial-review-litigation (last accessed 03/11/17).

asylum and immigration claims, e.g. prohibiting the immigration authorities from deporting an asylum seeker.

■ A declaration – simply declares what is the legal position between the parties and provides no specific relief to the claimant beyond that. It might seem like a rather strange 'remedy', in that it does not compel any particular action, but it is useful as it lets the public body know clearly the legal position. They are used mostly in relation to central Government on the basis that ministers can be assumed to abide by declarations.

In addition, injunctions and damages are general legal remedies that are also available in judicial review actions. Injunctions allow a court to issue instructions to prevent the infringement of a person's legal rights. They are not often used in judicial review because they are so similar to prohibiting orders, but they are useful where the claimant is seeking interim relief (i.e. protection of their interests by the court pending the outcome of the full case). Interim injunctions can be granted, whilst interim prohibiting orders cannot. The award of damages is possible but rare. The focus in judicial review claims is on stopping unlawful decisions being made or quashing unlawful actions rather than on compensation for losses.

12.9.1 REMEDIES ARE DISCRETIONARY

A distinctive feature of remedies in judicial review proceedings is that they are discretionary. You can: go to court, pass the permission stage, make your argument that the public body has acted unlawfully, have the court accept that argument and *still* not get the remedy that you require. It is open to the court, on Public Law grounds, to refuse to grant you a remedy. This is quite unusual, but it does happen, for example where the claimant has acted in bad faith, or where there is undue delay that affects third parties. The discretion reinforces the fact that this is a Public Law procedure, concerned with broader issues than just the legal relations between the parties. Private law does not allow the same judicial discretion over remedies. If you litigate a breach of contract issue and persuade the court that a breach of contract has caused you some harm, then you are entitled to a remedy.

Access to a remedy was further restricted, as part of wider hostility to judicial review from the Coalition Government, by the Criminal Justice and Courts Act 2015 which directed courts not to refuse to grant relief where it is highly likely that the outcome for the claimant would not have been substantially different if the conduct complained of had not occurred.

12.9.2 WHAT IS A SUCCESSFUL ACTION?

Even if you go to court, pass the permission stage, make some good legal arguments, get the court to agree that the public body has acted unlawfully *and* to award you a remedy, that still might not provide you with the ultimate outcome that you wanted when you started the claim.

APPLYING THE LAW – THE LIMITED UTILITY OF JUDICIAL REVIEWS

Go back to the problem scenario at the beginning of this chapter: the decision by the Department for Transport to place a new high-speed rail line very close to your house.

You might consider that the failure to consult with you is a legal flaw in the decision-making process used by DFT. A lack of consultation can result in the decision being unlawful (as we will see in the next chapter), so you apply for a judicial review and are successful. The court grants you the remedy that you want, which is a quashing order that quashes the decision on the route of the rail line. You celebrate with your fellow campaigners on the steps of the Administrative Court and have your picture on the front page of the local newspaper.

It would, however, still be open to the DFT to revisit its decision on the rail route. One of the options it can consider is to adopt the original route going just past your house.

As long as the DFT undertakes consultation with all relevant parties (including you), it can come to the conclusion that, whilst the views of local residents are relevant, on balance they are outweighed by the economic benefits of the original route.

Remember the key learning point – judicial review is concerned with the legality of the decision-making process not its merits. As long as the DFT has reached this new decision in a lawful manner then it cannot be quashed by judicial review action. The route can lawfully go ahead.

The remainder of this chapter will consider two key issues, ouster clauses and standing to bring a judicial review claim. In the discussion keep in mind the idea of access to justice. This benchmark has been central to the development of the law and links the judicial attitude to both issues.

12.10 OUSTER CLAUSES

Ouster clauses are provisions in an Act of Parliament (or secondary legislation) that try to oust the jurisdiction of the courts to hear claims in judicial review on particular issues.

Why would a Government try to insert these sorts of clauses into a statute? The answer is not a mystery; there are many circumstances where people do not like their decisions to be questioned. It can be inconvenient and costly to defend allegations. It can slow down the decision–making process and, ultimately, if it is found that your decision is unlawful, it can be very embarrassing. There is, then, a real temptation for a Government to try to insulate its schemes and projects from challenge through judicial review. As Andrew Le Sueur says:

Judicial review can inconvenience government. Indeed, that is one of its main purposes – to ensure that public bodies give appropriate priority to principles of legality over competing policy goals (such as speedy decision-making and economy with resources).[6]

Ouster clauses are problematic, and you need to understand why. The key problem is that they limit access to justice. Ouster clauses prevent individuals from accessing courts even when they think that they have been dealt with in an unlawful manner by the state. The rule of law requires that public bodies act in accordance with the law and on the basis of legal authority. What ouster clauses say (in effect) is that even if a public body has acted outside of the general principles of the law then there is no scope for legally challenging that unlawful decision.

It is the judges who have the primary responsibility for protecting the rule of law. So from the outset we would expect to see judicial hostility to ousters. The Lord Chancellor also has constitutional duties to protect the rule of law under the Constitutional Reform Act 2005 and it could be argued that the Lord Chancellor *should* oppose the use of ouster clauses in political discussions within Government.

On the basis of this hostility, simple attempts to oust judicial review by 'finality clauses' have been unsuccessful. Lord Denning in *R v Medical Appeal Tribunal ex parte Gilmore* [1957] 1 QB 574 said that statutory phrases that decisions of a public body 'shall be final' just meant that there is no right of appeal and did not exclude judicial review. More ambitious attempts to completely oust jurisdiction have not fared better.

KEY CASE – *ANISMINIC LTD V FOREIGN COMPENSATION COMMISSION* [1969] 2 AC 147

The case involved an action against the Foreign Compensation Commission (FCC), a public body established to deal with compensation claims by UK companies/owners for losses they had suffered from seizure of their overseas assets. If the UK Government was able to obtain compensation from the foreign Government, then the FCC could hear claims from affected companies and distribute the funds.

It is clear that the distribution of a limited pot of compensation money amongst competing claims is going to be a very controversial process, so when the FCC was established by the Foreign Compensation Act 1950 the Government inserted an ouster clause.

---

6   A Le Sueur, 'Three Strikes and It's Out? The Government's Strategy to Oust Judicial Review from Immigration and Asylum Decision-making' [2004] *Public Law* 225.

Section 4(4) – 'The determination by the Commission of any application made to them under this Act shall not be called into question in any court of law'.

Anisminic Ltd was a mining company that had its assets in Egypt seized by the Egyptian Government in 1956. The UK Government negotiated a Treaty with Egypt for the payment of compensation. Anisminic applied to the FCC for a share of the compensation and had its claim rejected. It sought a judicial review of how the FCC had dealt with its claim.

APPLYING THE LAW

Imagine that you are the legal adviser for Anisminic Ltd. What is the immediate problem facing your claim? It is the ouster clause in section 4 of the Foreign Compensation Act 1950. You might know that the courts are hostile to ouster clauses but the basic tenet of supremacy of Parliament still holds true: the courts must accept and apply any relevant Act of Parliament. Can you see any way around the ouster clause?

On appeal, the Law Lords ultimately decided that section 4 of the Foreign Compensation Act did not apply to this particular dispute and the jurisdiction of the court was not ousted. It could hear the claim in judicial review and it quashed the FCC decision. How was this achievable given that the Act seems very straightforward in excluding jurisdiction?

Some explanations of the *Anisminic* case focus on the issue of 'error of jurisdiction'. This is a rather arcane area of law, a distinction as to the type of legal error committed by a public body that is so serious that it takes the public body beyond the jurisdiction granted to it by Parliament. Largely due to *Anisminic* the distinction is no longer applied. Whilst 'error of jurisdiction' was important at the time, these accounts do not focus on the *key technique* which the Law Lords used to give effect to their hostility to ouster clauses.

The Law Lords applied their interpretive skills to the word 'determination' in section 4 of the Act. Lord Pearce noted that section 4 only extended to 'determinations' by the FCC and this 'meant a real determination, not a purported determination'. A decision or other action based on a legal error was not a real 'determination' under section 4. If it did not fall into the category of a 'determination', then the section 4 ouster did not apply, and the court could hear the case.

The Law Lords said that Parliament cannot have intended section 4 to extend to legally flawed actions, and Lord Wilberforce asserted that the Court was 'carrying out the intention of Parliament'. It is difficult to accept that this *genuinely was* the intention of Parliament, but by ascribing this intention the judges could ostensibly stay within the judicial function of merely interpreting and applying, rather than rewriting, legislation.

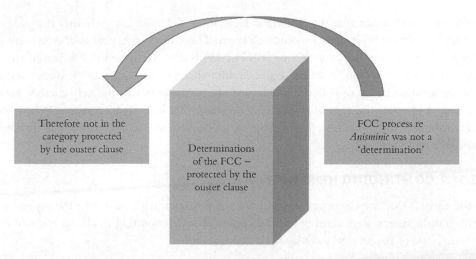

Figure 12.3 Anisminic

12.11 TIME LIMIT CLAUSES

- A quick question for you – what is the normal time limit for judicial review actions?
- If you said 'three months', then close but *not quite* – have a look at the section above. The test is *promptly*, and in any event within three months.

Even stricter time limits are possible for particular statutory schemes. These are typically six weeks long and are common in schemes for the compulsory purchase of land.

KEY CASE – *SMITH V EAST ELLOE DISTRICT COUNCIL* [1956] AC 736

Mrs Smith had some property compulsorily purchased by East Elloe District Council under the Acquisition of Land (Authorisation Procedure) Act 1946. This provided a time limit of six weeks in which an aggrieved person could challenge a compulsory purchase order, and prevented any other sort of legal challenge. *Six years* later she brought an action. She had discovered evidence that led her to believe that there had been bad faith and even fraud in the Council's actions, and launched a judicial review to quash the purchase order. Was the very strict time limit applicable here? The House of Lords ultimately decided that it was.

This approach to time limit clauses has been consistently followed by the courts, but it does *not* mean that these strict time limit clauses will automatically be applied regardless of the facts of the case. In *Smith*, the House of Lords decision was a 3:2 split and the majority were only willing to let the time limit clause apply because Mrs Smith had an alternative avenue to justice: a private law action against the clerk of the Council. In the absence of an alternative, it is not clear that the Lords would have applied the time limit.

There was some doubt after the landmark decision in *Anisminic* as to whether this judicial acceptance of time limit clauses would still apply. The Court of Appeal in *R v Secretary of State for the Environment, ex parte Ostler* [1977] 1 WLR 258 confirmed that it would and that claims out of time would be struck out. The difference between a complete ouster and a time limit clause is one of policy. Time limit restrictions do not completely exclude access to justice and cover the sorts of Public Law decisions that have wider impacts. Public bodies and third-party individuals need to be able to act on land use decisions and start making physical alterations.

12.11.1 CONTINUING HOSTILITY

In the early 2000s, the Government was concerned that individuals within the asylum and immigration system were abusing judicial review claims, by putting in claims without any realistic hope of success just to delay their deportation.

There was evidence in support of this concern. A majority of judicial review claims, over 61%, were made in relation to asylum and immigration and a large proportion of these were dismissed. There was therefore some rational basis for the Government's proposed action of introducing a clause in the Asylum and Immigration (Treatment of Claimants, etc) Bill 2003, even if it was careless of constitutional principle. The section was described by the Government itself as 'an ouster clause' (which is not something that Governments ordinarily do). The section stated:

The Asylum and Immigration (Treatment of Claimants, etc.) Bill 2003, s 108A

(1) No court shall have any supervisory or other jurisdiction in relation to the Tribunal.
(2) No court may entertain proceedings for questioning . . . any determination, decision or other action of the Tribunal

Notice that this discussion is about the Bill, i.e. the proposal, rather than the final version of the Act. If it had been passed, would this ouster clause have been judge-proof? It seems that whoever drafted this clause had been present, awake and alert during their Public Law classes, at least on the day when they covered *Anisminic*. The clause seems designed, in the light of the judicial creativity in *Anisminic*, to close off all avenues whereby the judges could circumvent the ouster clause whilst still declaring allegiance to the intention of Parliament.

APPLYING THE LAW – CIRCUMVENTING OUSTER CLAUSES

If you were advising in an asylum case, can you think of ways to persuade a court not to apply this ouster clause to your client's case?

Some parts are easy. The clause states that 'no court may entertain proceedings for questioning any determination'. You would just ask the court to apply *Anisminic* and say that an action based on a legal error is not a 'determination', it is a nullity and Parliament cannot have intended the clause to cover it. You can dispose of the word 'decision' in the same way. When it comes to 'any other action', the strain of being loyal to the Act starts to show more clearly, but you could argue that a nullity is not an 'action' authorised by statute.

That leaves this part of the section as rather meaningless, but that is not your concern. You want an interpretation that is tenable and that suits your client. You might also feel (and point out to the court) that your preferred interpretation accords with wider notions about access to justice, separation of powers, and the rule of law.

The first part of the ouster clause is much more difficult. Judicial review *is* 'supervisory jurisdiction'. Judges would not be able to circumvent the first part of the ouster clause whilst maintaining any sort of credible appearance that they were upholding that keystone of the constitution – supremacy of Parliament.

The Bill was not passed in this form due to a strong coalition of opposition. From the political front, Liberal Democrat MP Simon Hughes said:

The Government have a perverse and obsessive belief that going to court for a judicial review of administrative decisions is a hindrance to government. However, whether one is dealing with immigration, asylum or any other matter, it is fundamental to our constitution that the court, not Ministers, is the place of last resort. In a country with no written constitution, it is vital that the independent judiciary at all levels makes decisions on the law and the facts.[7]

This opposition was backed up by external pressure from the legal profession and beyond. Crucially, there was also vigorous opposition from the judges. Lord Donaldson wrote that:

Had they successfully pursued the ouster clause then we certainly should have been in a very interesting constitutional crisis . . . we would simply have to say: 'We [the judges] are an independent estate of the realm and it's not open to the legislature to put us out of business. And so we shall simply ignore your ouster clause.[8]

This is an astonishing statement. It indicates that judges would refuse to apply a relevant statute to a dispute in a case before them. If forced to choose between the supremacy of statute and the demands of the rule of law and separation of powers, the judiciary would choose the latter.

----

7   Simon Hughes MP (Lib Dem), Standing Committee E (21 May 2002), col 367.
8   Lord Donaldson, quote from 'Judges reveal anger over curbs on power', *The Guardian* (26 April 2005), http://politics.guardian.co.uk/election/story/0,15803,1470398,00.html (last accessed 03/11/17).

There is a proviso that Lord Donaldson had retired by the time he made this statement. It is a wider truism that people who have retired (or who are approaching retirement) feel much freer to say things about the institutions they have belonged to. This is doubly the case with judges who have responsibilities not to get entangled in political arguments whilst they are still serving. Other judges have been slightly more restrained in their language, but have let it be known that introducing ouster clauses such as this will provoke serious constitutional crises. In *R(Jackson) v Attorney General* [2005] UKHL 56, Lady Hale said that any attempt to 'subvert the rule of law by removing governmental action affecting the rights of the individual from all judicial scrutiny' could be rejected by the courts. Writing to The Times in 1969 to address the furore following the Anisminic judgment, HWR Wade said 'If legal rights cannot be brought before the courts, the rule of law collapses. The judges, well understanding this, have for 300 years firmly set their faces against such provisions and have, to put it bluntly, refused to apply them'.[9]

These cases and the example of the Asylum and Immigration Bill show us the depth of the hostility of judges to these ouster clauses and the reason for that hostility: the need to defend the rule of law with its insistence on access to justice and on judicial scrutiny of unlawful state action.

12.12 STANDING

Standing (or *locus standi*) is the legal test that indicates who can bring a judicial review action to challenge a decision. Section 31(3) of the Senior Courts Act 1981 provides that the court shall not grant leave to apply for judicial review 'unless it considers that the claimant has a *sufficient interest* in the matter to which the claim relates'.

The key phrase is 'sufficient interest', and the test is intended to act as a filter. This is a *single test*, i.e. there are no formal separate categories recognised by law, but we can pick out some typical examples and see that the 'sufficient interest' test applies to them in slightly different ways.

12.12.1 INDIVIDUAL INTEREST

Most judicial review claims are brought by individuals who have been directly affected by a particular decision of a public body. They have some sort of interest that has been adversely affected. Examples could include:

- A homeowner aggrieved that the local authority has granted planning permission for a waste incinerator opposite her home. This adversely affects the value of her home and she may also be concerned about the impact on her health.
- An asylum seeker whose asylum application is rejected. This decision directly affects a whole range of her interests from health, to finance, to family life.

---

9   T T Arvind and L Stirton, 'Why the Judicial Power Project Is Wrong about *Anisminic*', U.K. Const. L. Blog (20 May 2016), https://ukconstitutionallaw.org/ (last accessed 03/11/17).

These sorts of claims are relatively unproblematic from the point of view of standing. Such individuals clearly have a 'sufficient interest' in the contested decision. The 'individual' can be an organisation and companies in this, as in other areas of law, are treated as (corporate) individuals.

12.12.2 ASSOCIATIONAL STANDING

This term was developed by Peter Cane to cover a group (e.g. a trade union, professional association, sporting federation) bringing a claim on behalf of (the interests of) identifiable individuals who are its members. The key aspect is that each, or some, of the individuals within that association would have an individual interest in the contested decision.

KEY CASE – *R V LIVERPOOL CORPORATION, EX PARTE LIVERPOOL TAXI FLEET OPERATORS' ASSOCIATION* [1972] 2 QB 299

Liverpool Corporation had initially assured the taxi association that they would be consulted before any decision to increase the number of taxi licences issued in the city. This was then followed up with a public promise that there would be no imminent increase in taxi numbers, and then confirmed in a letter to the taxi association. A few months later, and with no warning or consultation, the Corporation increased the number of licences.

An individual taxi driver would have standing to challenge this decision because of the impact on their business. The Association could act both on its own behalf, and on behalf of its affected members.

Similarly, in *Royal College of Nursing v Department of Health and Social Security* [1981] AC 800, the Department of Health issued a new circular on whether it was lawful for nurses to take part in certain abortion procedures without supervision by a doctor. There was no consultation, and this clearly affected individual nurses. The action was brought by the Royal College of Nursing, and it was accepted that they were an association representing members who had been individually affected.

Cane puts forward two requirements for associational standing to be legitimate:

- Are members of the association individually affected? If so,
- Does the association sufficiently represent their interests on this issue?[10]

Again, this form of standing is rarely problematic.

---

10 P Cane, 'Standing up for the Public' [1995] *Public Law* 276.

12.12.3 PUBLIC INTEREST STANDING

What if a person (or more commonly a group) wants to challenge a potentially unlawful decision by a public body when they are not personally affected by that decision? For some policy decisions, e.g. on climate change policy, they might be indirectly affected by the global effects of any decision but no more than the rest of the populace. The very existence of the standing test in section 31 of the Senior Courts Act 1981 tells us that not *everybody* (or *every group*) can access a court to judicially review *any* decision made by *any* public body. If it is a filter, then it has to filter out some claims. Simply saying that you are 'interested' in a particular issue, such as climate change or the protection of endangered species or child poverty, does not seem like an effective claim to 'sufficient interest'. That would deprive the 'sufficient interest' test of any objective value and allow anyone to challenge anything.

For these reasons, it has traditionally been difficult for individuals or non-governmental organisations (such as pressure groups) to challenge public decisions in the wider public interest. A model of judicial review, and thereby a test of standing, based on the idea of protecting individual interests does not easily accommodate these public interest challenges. The leading case on standing signalled a change in the nature of judicial review.

KEY CASE – *INLAND REVENUE COMMISSIONERS V NATIONAL FEDERATION OF SELF-EMPLOYED AND SMALL BUSINESSES LTD* [1982] AC 617 (COMMONLY CALLED THE *FLEET STREET CASUALS* CASE)

The case concerned employment practices amongst print workers on Fleet Street in central London, back when most national newspapers were based there. Many of the print staff worked on a casual basis. They would work a night shift, receive a pay docket and take it to the wages office to be paid in cash. The pay docket required them to indicate their names and address for tax purposes. It became common practice amongst the print workers to put down false names and addresses to avoid tax. The case also has a second nickname, the *Mickey Mouse* case, because some print workers became so blasé about the practice that they put down joke names.

The Inland Revenue moved to stop this abuse and decided that to get an effective tax collection process in place they would need the co-operation of the employers and the unions. To reach this agreement they undertook not to investigate any tax offences from previous years. This upset the National Federation whose members had not been granted such generous treatment.

The House of Lords ultimately found that the National Federation did not have standing to challenge the Inland Revenue decision. As a general principle, no single taxpayer had a sufficient interest in how the Revenue assessed the tax liability of any other individual. The real significance of the case, however, lies in what the Law Lords said more generally about the nature of the standing test.

Up until this time, the main approach of the courts was to (in effect) ask 'Who are you and what does this decision have to do with you?' The focus was on identity and the effect of the decision on personal interests. Lord Wilberforce said, however, that 'The question of sufficient interest cannot . . . be considered in the abstract, or as an isolated point: it must be taken together with the legal and factual context'.

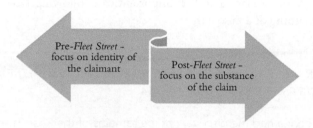

Figure 12.4 The impact of *Fleet Street Casuals* on the law of standing

An equally important question for the court then is 'What is the complaint?' Is it about some serious issue? Does the claimant, on the face of it, have evidence that the public body has acted unlawfully? Almost regardless of who is bringing this complaint, is there a public interest in the court assessing whether the public body has broken the law? This has a number of implications:

- Procedural operation of standing – at the permission stage, standing can only be a threshold test and a very low hurdle to clear. If the court is looking at the merits of the claim as well as the identity of the claimant, then it will only be in a position really to examine this once the evidence has been submitted, i.e. at the substantive hearing. The relatively limited amount of information that has to be included in the initial claim to the court and the fact that the judge decides permission simply on the basis of these papers means that only obvious busybodies ought to be excluded at this point.
- The nature of judicial review – *Fleet Street Casuals* seems to indicate that, at least as much as protecting personal interests, the purpose of judicial review is to examine coherent allegations of unlawful conduct by public bodies, i.e. these are very much rule of law and Public Law concerns. If a public body may have acted unlawfully, the courts will want to permit the allegations to come to court, hear the evidence and quash public body actions that are ultimately found to be unlawful.

As Lord Diplock said, 'it would be a grave lacuna in our system of public law if a pressure group or single public-spirited taxpayer, were prevented by outdated technical rules of standing from bringing the matter to the attention of the court to *vindicate the rule of law*'.

This ought not to (and does not) negatively affect standing for claims brought on the basis of individual interest or associational interest. It does, however, have implications for public interest standing. If claimants do not need to show a direct impact to their personal rights or interests, but rather focus on bringing evidence of public body unlawful behaviour to the attention of the courts, then it will be easier for public interest claims to obtain standing. If your complaint has substance, then the courts want to hear it and are much less concerned with your identity.

We will now look at the implications of *Fleet Street Casuals* and how this has played out through the subsequent case law. This first important case following *Fleet Street Casuals* was widely seen as something of a false start.

KEY CASE – *R V SECRETARY OF STATE FOR ENVIRONMENT, EX PARTE ROSE THEATRE TRUST CO* [1990] 1 ALL ER 754

The case itself concerned the discovery of the remains of the Rose Theatre on the South Bank, London. This was important because it was the first Elizabethan theatre in Bankside and had hosted the first productions of important playwrights, in particular some of Shakespeare's early plays. As, arguably, the greatest playwright in history and England's greatest single contribution to world culture, many people had an interest in the preservation of historical sites linked to Shakespeare's work.
A proposal to build a car park and office building over the top of the theatre remains was being considered. The local authority refused to grant listed building status and the Secretary of State for the Environment refused to grant historical monument status under the Ancient Monuments and Archaeological Areas Act 1979.

A judicial review claim was brought by the Rose Theatre Trust, an association comprising actors, historians, archaeologists and other concerned parties who came together for the express purpose of challenging this decision and protecting the site. The Trust was refused standing.

Mr Justice Schiemann, in deciding the question of standing, made a conscious effort to apply the judgment of the House of Lords in *Fleet Street Casuals*. He picked out and applied a number of propositions:

- Not every member of the public can complain about any possible breach by a public body. Logically this must be true. There *is* a test of sufficient interest which is intended to act as a filter. That test must mean something.
- Merely to assert that you have an interest does not necessarily mean that you satisfy the legal test of sufficient interest. Again, this is sound reasoning, otherwise anyone could assert an interest in anything and the sufficient interest test would become meaningless.
- A quick mathematics question for you – what is 1000 x 0? Good lawyers in practice need to be numerate, so hopefully your answer was zero. Schiemann J made the same point here. If a number of people, each of whom has no sufficient interest in the contested decision, come together, then their organisation does not possess any

more interest than they had as a disparate group of insufficiently interested individuals. The individuals who comprised the Rose Theatre Trust did not individually have any financial, professional or other interests directly affected by designation of the site, so an aggregate of those interests was still not sufficient. (Contrast the position here with e.g. *Royal College of Nursing*. Each individual nurse had sufficient interest, so an association representing those interests would definitely have standing.)

The judgment was criticised for missing the big picture. Schiemann J had picked out aspects of the speeches in *Fleet Street Casuals*, but the key message; that the merits of the claim were an important, if not dominant, feature, was not identified and applied in *Rose Theatre Trust*. The courts developed a better understanding of that key message in two cases from the mid–1990s.

KEY CASE – *R V HM INSPECTORATE OF POLLUTION, EX PARTE GREENPEACE (NO 2)* [1994] 1 WLR 570

The Inspectorate of Pollution varied the authorisation for the discharge of radioactive waste from the Sellafield nuclear reprocessing site in Cumbria. This public body decision was challenged by Greenpeace. Mr Justice Otton granted standing to Greenpeace, based on a number of grounds:

- Local membership – Greenpeace had a very large general membership but particularly importantly had 2,500 members in the area.
- Health issues – releasing more radioactive material into the environment potentially increases the risks to the health of those local people. There were allegations of a heightened risk of leukaemia.

Taking these first two points together means that there were 2,500 Greenpeace members who individually would have a sufficient interest. When Greenpeace is acting on their behalf, it is acting in an associational way. This way of showing standing already existed and had been accepted by the courts; it adds nothing to the existing approaches. However, Otton J went on:

- Serious allegation – this was worthy of determination by the court. A potentially unlawful decision by a public body allowing more radioactive material into the environment with allegations that this would increase cancer risks is, by any measure, a serious allegation.
- Respected organisation – Greenpeace had consultative status with the United Nations and other international organisations concerned with the environment.
- Expertise and resources – Greenpeace was able to present a difficult and complex case. The case involved environmental and epidemiological evidence (e.g. on leukaemia clusters, background levels of radiation, causal links) and complex legal argument. Greenpeace had access to relevant scientific and legal expertise and sufficient resources to mount a challenge.

Putting all these things together, the court found that Greenpeace was 'the best placed challenger'. Go back to *Fleet Street Casuals* and consider the purpose of judicial review. It is for the courts to examine coherent allegations of unlawful conduct by public bodies, without focusing too much on who is bringing the complaint. These final three grounds have a stronger public interest flavour. Otton J does still examine the identity of the claimant, but to identify if the claimant is well placed to effectively bring the allegation to the court in the wider public interest rather than to find some personal right or interest that has been infringed:

> if I were to deny standing to Greenpeace, those it represents might not have an effective way to bring the issues before the court . . . a less well informed challenge might be mounted which would stretch unnecessarily the court's resources and would not afford the court the assistance it requires in order to do justice between the parties.

> (Otton J)

The next case takes the development of the law a little further, in that there was no question of the pressure group being granted standing on an associational basis. If it was to have sufficient interest, it would have to be purely on public interest grounds.

KEY CASE – *R V SECRETARY OF STATE FOR FOREIGN AND COMMONWEALTH AFFAIRS, EX PARTE WORLD DEVELOPMENT MOVEMENT* [1995] 1 WLR 386

We explained at the beginning of this chapter that the starting point of a judicial review action is often an Act of Parliament. The Act may set up a public body, endow it with power and impose limits on that power. This was the case here. The Overseas Development and Co-operation Act 1980, allowed the UK Government to give financial aid to other countries, but only for *development purposes*. That is, the power was granted for a particular purpose, and we will see in the next chapter that using power for an improper purpose is unlawful.

There was a proposal to support the construction of a hydro-electric project in Malaysia, the Pergau Dam. The proposal was internally examined by civil servants from the Overseas Development Administration who concluded that there would be *no development value* from supporting the construction of the dam, and any funding would be an abuse of the development programme. Nevertheless, the Government went ahead and provided funding.

The allegation from the World Development Movement was that the UK Government funding was a 'sweetener' (i.e. an incentive) in a major arms deal that the Malaysian Government was concluding with UK arms companies. That allegation was found to be true. This was use of public power for an improper purpose, and therefore an unlawful abuse of power. An important question was whether the World Development Movement (a small pressure group based in London) had standing. Compared to *Greenpeace*, there was no locality issue. No members of the World Development Movement would be personally affected by this decision; none of their health, property or other interests would be damaged. If the judge had followed *Rose Theatre*, he would have concluded that each of the members of the group had zero personal interest and merely coming together in a group was no more than the sum of their parts.

The court, however, granted standing to the World Development Movement and did so explicitly on public interest and rule of law grounds. Rose LJ found that it was a coherent and serious allegation. The World Development Movement was a respected organisation, with over 25 years at the forefront of international development concerns. It had real expertise. Crucially, there would be no other likely challenger; think back to the time limit test (promptly and in any event three months). No other challenger would mean that the Government would not be legally accountable for unlawfully misusing large sums of public money allocated for development purposes.

Rose LJ stressed the importance of 'vindicating the rule of law':

standing should not be treated as a preliminary issue, but must be taken in the factual context of the whole case . . . furthermore, the merits of the challenge are an important, if not dominant, factor when considering standing.

The current state of the law on standing is best summed up by the decision in *ex parte Dixon* (see below). In both *Greenpeace* and *World Development Movement*, important developments though they were, there was still a great deal of emphasis on the status, prestige and expertise of the claimants. If the key message from *Fleet Street Casuals* is followed through to its fullest extent, then there should not be an emphasis on the *identity* of the claimant.

KEY CASE – *R V SOMERSET COUNTY COUNCIL, EX PARTE DIXON* [1997] *JPL* 1030

Somerset County Council gave permission for the reopening of a quarry. As a consequence, there would be noise, dust and an increase in traffic, so *some* individuals would suffer impacts to their personal interests.

The judicial review claim was brought by an individual, Mr Dixon, rather than a group. Dixon had no property or other personal rights affected. He argued, however, that he had a greater interest than the general public in this particular public decision, on the basis that:

- He was a member of the local parish council.
- He was a candidate in the local district council elections.
- He was a member of environmental organisations concerned with the Somerset countryside.

The court rejected those arguments and found that he had *no greater interest* than the general public, but nevertheless (and here is the key relevance of this case) granted him standing. The Court said that judicial review is 'not, at base, about rights . . . it is about wrongs – that is to say, misuses of public power'.

Standing therefore has become a very low hurdle. You ought to be granted standing unless your claim is seen as vexatious or you are perceived as a busybody, i.e. someone who is not genuinely concerned with the legality of this particular decision but is using the litigation process to otherwise harass and obstruct the public body.

This line of cases also highlights the link between the judicial approach to both standing and ouster clauses. For standing, the courts have taken the statutory term 'sufficient interest' and interpreted it very widely so as to exclude very few claims. For ouster clauses, whatever the statutory formula, the courts have given them highly restrictive interpretations to limit their effect and ensure that they do not prevent judicial review claims. The judges are motivated by the same concerns: the rule of law, access to justice and preventing public bodies from getting away with unlawful behaviour.

12.13 HUMAN RIGHTS CLAIMS

The Human Rights Act 1998 gives citizens the possibility of bringing a form of judicial review action against public authorities to directly vindicate their European Convention human rights (s.7 Human Rights Act 1998). Some writers therefore closely integrate their discussion of human rights actions and ordinary judicial review claims. The approach taken here respectfully differs. The two types of action have different rules both in their procedure (e.g. on standing and time limits) and substance (e.g. the basis on which public decisions are scrutinised by courts). Just as importantly, they are different in their underlying nature. As we have just seen, ordinary judicial review is more concerned with public wrongs than private rights; human rights claims are inherently about breaches of individual rights.

There may be scope for a unification of the two types of action (which in itself shows their separation), but this process lacks obvious benefits and could cause conceptual confusion.

To avoid this confusion, you will find discussion of human rights actions under section 7 of the Human Rights Act 1998 in Chapter 15.

_____

POINTS TO REVIEW

This chapter has discussed:

- The nature of judicial review and its relationship to constitution principles.

- The availability of judicial review, including the concept of a public body, the availability of alternative remedies and procedural exclusivity.
- The procedure for making a judicial review claim.
- Ouster clauses, highlighting judicial hostility to them.
- Standing, including the generous approach adopted by the courts.

To move beyond description, we have used the principle of access to justice as a benchmark. Even though this has been done in a relatively simple way, it has, hopefully, enabled you to analyse and evaluate the topic better. It allows us to see the broad consistency in the approach of the courts to issues of standing and ouster clauses, and highlights areas where there is scope for improvement (e.g. Bondy and Sunkin's work on the permission stage).

APPLYING THE LAW – ASSESSMENT ADVICE

Assessment of this topic generally falls within two categories.

First, it can be assessed, in coursework or exam, through **an essay question**. Follow the general advice on essay questions covered in Chapter 1 and in any guidance from your tutor or law school. Typically, this will encourage you to use a good range of sources, show sound understanding of the material, structure and write your work clearly and precisely, cite your sources and use authority and evidence to support your answer – all good advice.

You will typically also need to demonstrate analysis and evaluation to obtain better marks. Analysis involves breaking down a topic into its component parts, or identifying the elements of a broader concept. You can do this in a number of ways, such as clearly structuring your discussion to show the different stages of the claim procedure, or the development of the law on particular issues (e.g. *O'Reilly v Mackman*, ouster clauses, standing).

Evaluation can involve making judgements and weighing the evidence. You need to establish on what basis you are making judgements and what point you are making when you weigh the evidence. This will often be provided by the essay question itself, asking you to deal with an assertion that the courts' approach has been 'generous' or 'restrictive', 'consistent' or 'confused'. For these questions you will need to organise the issues and evidence (from this chapter and your further reading) and reach a reasoned conclusion on the extent to which the evidence justifies the view that the courts have been e.g. 'generous'. In the absence of any benchmark in the question, you could follow the access to justice theme adopted here, or explore an alternative evaluation based on the further reading outlined below.

Secondly, the material (particularly on the procedure for making a claim, and standing) can be assessed as part of a broader **judicial review problem question**. This will require you to apply the law on procedure and standing to a problem scenario, which will also cover the grounds of judicial review. The focus of these questions is more on the grounds of review, and so we will return to this type of assessment in the next chapter.

TAKING IT FURTHER

Public Law Project (PLP) resources

- 'Introduction to judicial review', http://www.publiclawproject.org.uk/introduction-to-judicial-review
- 'Guide to judicial review procedure', http://www.publiclawproject.org.uk/resources/114/guide-to-judicial-review-procedure

The PLP, a UK charity working for access to justice in Public Law matters, produces some rather brilliant short guides to aspects of judicial review; very good introductory material from a law in action perspective.

A Le Sueur, 'Three Strikes and It's Out? The UK Government's Strategy to Oust Judicial Review from Immigration and Asylum Decision-making' [2004] *Public Law* 22 Again, this is a relatively short article that nevertheless gives you great insight into the competing tensions (between Government and the courts) when an ouster clause is proposed.

V Bondy and M Sunkin, 'The Dynamics of Judicial Review Litigation' [2009] http://www.publiclawproject.org.uk/resources/9/the-dynamics-of-judicial-review-litigation

This is a long (86 pages) research project from the Public Law Project. It is full of original and insightful research. If you wanted to focus on one section, then Section 4 – Permission is probably the most relevant. You could use material from this report in a constructive way to give a distinctive (and strongly law in action) perspective to your work.

T Hickman, 'Public Law's Disgrace', UK Constitutional Law Blog, 9 February 2017 https://ukconstitutionallaw.org/2017/02/09/tom-hickman-public-laws-disgrace/. This could be seen to follow on from Bondy and Sunkin's work in looking at the real-world practicalities of bringing a judicial review action. It focuses on the enormous difficulties, for a majority of the population, in funding judicial review actions.

CHAPTER 13
GROUNDS OF JUDICIAL REVIEW

In the last chapter, we looked at the framework of judicial review, examining its nature and relationship to Constitutional Law; which bodies can be subject to judicial review and the procedure for making a claim; attempts to limit review through ouster clauses; and standing to bring a claim. In this chapter, we are looking at the content of judicial review actions. If the preceding chapter described the bones of judicial review, then this is the meat.

The grounds of judicial review identify the different ways that public bodies can be found to have acted unlawfully. Courts must be satisfied that at least one of the grounds of judicial review is made out by the claimant before they will consider quashing the decision, or granting any other remedy.

There are a number of grounds, but they are helpfully organised into three broad categories. Your mission is to be able to understand and summarise the legal principle of each ground, discuss any ambiguities and difficulties, illustrate the grounds with case law authority and be able to apply them to resolve problems.

AS YOU READ

At the end of this chapter you should be able to:

- identify and discuss the three types of grounds for judicial review

- illustrate those grounds with examples and authority

- apply those grounds to a problem scenario.

One of the important messages from the last chapter was that judicial review is not an appeals process. It is a review of the *legality* of the decision: whether the public body has acted unlawfully. This chapter explores the various grounds of judicial review, i.e. the different ways in which public bodies can be found to have acted unlawfully.

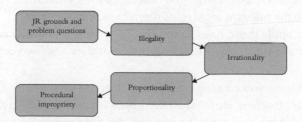

Figure 13.1 Structure of Chapter 13

A NOTE ON CATEGORISATION

There are numerous grounds of judicial review, so it is useful to attempt to organise them in a conceptual framework. There is no definitive terminology, and some judges and authors use different terms. The most common practice, however, is to use the clear and rational categorisation provided by Lord Diplock in *Council for Civil Service Unions v Minister for Civil Service* [1985] AC 374 (the *GCHQ* case). He outlined a three-fold division of the grounds:

- Illegality – the public body acting beyond its power, or in some other way abusing its discretionary powers.
- Irrationality – acting in defiance of logic so that no rational public body could have arrived at the same decision.
- Procedural impropriety – either breach of a particular statutory procedure or breach of a wider duty of procedural fairness.

The individual grounds fall within these categories. They are not mutually exclusive, and a single dispute between an individual and a public body may involve a number of grounds.

In your wider reading, you may come across something called *Wednesbury* unreasonableness. Until the 1980s this was the language used to categorise the judicial review grounds. It has been superseded by the *GCHQ* categories outlined above, although some commentators and judges persist with the old terminology. A very rough equivalence between the two systems (so that you have some context) is:

- unreasonableness in the narrow sense = irrationality
- unreasonableness in the wider sense = illegality
- the maxims of natural justice = procedural impropriety.

ASSESSMENT GUIDANCE

This topic is very commonly assessed by problem scenarios. You need to refer back to Chapter 1 for general guidance on answering problems. Some law schools or your individual Public Law tutor might want you to use the IRAC method. Remember that this involves:

I – Issue: identify which issues arise from the problem scenario
R – Rule: outline the relevant legal rules (from case law or statute)
A – Application: apply those rules to the particular facts of the scenario
C – Conclusion: answer the question, e.g. how would you advise your client?

Not all tutors will want you to adopt this formal method of answering problem questions. Some law teachers regard the IRAC method as too restrictive and repetitive. As ever, please be guided by your tutor. In any case, the fundamentals of answering problem questions remain the same. You will always need to be able to identify the legal issues, state what the relevant legal provisions are (including legal authority) and apply them to the problem scenario.

A central aim of this book is to help you not just pass your Public Law course but to excel. So how can you perform particularly well on judicial review problem questions? Some top tips:

- *Comprehensiveness and focus* – you need to be able to identify all the relevant grounds and then focus only on these grounds. In problem questions, students sometimes make the mistake of covering all the grounds that they can remember.
- *Detail and authority* – for each of the grounds covered in this chapter we will provide the legal principle and some case-law illustrations. There may be some discussion of the development of the principle and examination of areas of uncertainty around the JR ground. You need to aim to get a good level of detail into your answer. Going beyond your lecture materials and using additional authorities from this or other sources shows initiative.
- *Application* – there is scope for some real subtlety in the application phase. Applying the grounds to the facts of the problem scenario is rarely a mechanistic process. The best advice is to really know your stuff and then to *think*. In particular, think about whether the facts of the scenario are materially the same as those of a relevant case. If there are differences (there often are), then are they legally significant? This process of drawing out similarities and differences between authorities is a key component of common law reasoning.
- *Conclusion and advice* – the assessment task in problem questions is almost always to advise a client. In judicial review problems, you will typically have to advise an individual or company who has had difficulties with a public body and wants to know whether they can bring a claim to review the actions of that body. So do not forget to advise them! Some students, unfortunately, do not conclude their answers particularly effectively. As a minimum, you need to restate the grounds on which you might bring a claim and actually advise the client on whether or not a claim can be brought. A good way of going further is to not simply identify the grounds (analysis) but to weigh the strength of your claim (evaluation). If you have identified e.g. five possible grounds but think that you have a much stronger claim in relation to two of those, then say so.

This is a typical problem scenario.

The (hypothetical) Market Trading Act 2001 allows local councils to grant and revoke licences 'as they see fit', so as to promote trade on markets in their area. Sleepyton Council has delegated its powers under this Act to its Licensing Committee. The Committee has further delegated powers to revoke licences to its markets manager.

The council has adopted an objective that Sleepyton will be 'the most organic town in England' on the basis that 'organic farming is the only ethical way to care for the land'. On the basis of this objective, the Licensing Committee has drafted a policy of refusing all new applications for licences to trade in non-organic produce.

Elizabeth Orchard applies for a market trader's licence to sell non-organic fruit and vegetables. Her application is rejected on the grounds that it is not consistent with the policy.

George Hogg has operated a butcher's stall on Sleepyton Market for 20 years. He has never sold organic produce. In response to the increasing promotion of organic produce, he puts up a poster on his stall saying 'Non-organic sausages – the original, the cheapest and the best!' The markets manager orders him to remove the poster as it is 'inconsistent with the ethos and image of Sleepyton Market'. When he refuses, the markets manager revokes his licence. Hogg appeals to the Licensing Committee, which grants him an oral hearing but rejects his appeal. The hearing is chaired by Councillor Brownbread, who is also the regional chair of the Organic Soil Campaign.

Advise Orchard and Hogg on the possibility of judicial review proceedings.

We will come back to this scenario at various points in the chapter. At the outset, however, you could give an indication of how you are going to approach identifying and applying the grounds. You could structure your answer based on how the different grounds naturally arise in the problem scenario or use the pre-existing three-fold structure from the *GCHQ* case. Either is fine, although we adopt the latter approach here.

As part of your advice to the clients, you need to mention some of the procedural issues covered in the last chapter. Given the typical word count constraints for coursework and time constraints for exam questions, this will necessarily be brief so that you can concentrate on the grounds of review. You could mention the time limit (promptly and in any event three months), the need to go through a permission stage and the requirement of standing (sufficient interest). In our scenario, as Orchard and Hogg are both the subjects of individual decisions by a public body then there is no problem at all in showing a sufficient interest.

13.1 ILLEGALITY

Vires means power. *Ultra* means outside or beyond. *Intra* means within. So *ultra vires* is a decision made beyond the power granted by statute. A decision within the power granted by statute is *intra vires*. **Simple ultra vires** arises where the relevant legislation does not contain the necessary power for the particular action carried out by the public body, e.g. where a statute confers power on a public body to do *A* but not to do *B*. If the public body does *B*, then it is acting ultra vires, beyond its power.

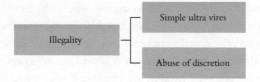

Figure 13.2 Basic division of the illegality ground

For example, the Passport Office is granted powers by statute to issue passports. If it issues a passport to an applicant, then it is acting intra vires. If the Passport Office tries to issue an immigration visa (and there is nothing within statute to authorise this), or a driving licence, or a wedding certificate, then that is ultra vires.

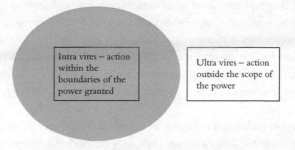

Figure 13.3 Intra and ultra vires

The second kind of illegality is where the relevant legislation permits the public body to use its discretion to make a particular decision, but the *way* in which the public body exercises its power breaches the relevant principles. This kind of illegality is often termed an **abuse of discretion**.

13.1.1 ULTRA VIRES

KEY CASE – *ATTORNEY GENERAL V FULHAM CORPORATION* [1921] 1 CH 440

Local authorities were empowered by the Baths and Wash-houses Acts 1846–1878 to establish wash-houses. At this time, most houses did not have adequate clothes washing facilities. The function of wash-houses was that local residents could come and wash their clothes using the facilities provided. A key feature was that the residents would wash and dry the clothes *themselves*. Fulham Corporation decided to take this a step further. It established a service where local residents could bring their clothes to the washhouse, leave their clothes with the staff, and for a small fee have them washed and ready for collection later.

A local ratepayer complained that Fulham Corporation had gone beyond their remit and had, in effect, opened up a laundry on a (subsidised) commercial basis. The court agreed and found that the Corporation had simply acted beyond its powers.

Sometimes it is reasonably straightforward to decide where the boundaries of power are. Sometimes it is not so straightforward: 'When a public body's conduct is challenged as *ultra vires* or contrary to statute, the court's attention focuses on the Act which is claimed to be the source of its authority. Often an answer is found by interpreting that Act'.[1] *Powers which are reasonably incidental* to the exercise of a public body's main functions may also be impliedly granted.

KEY CASE – *R V RICHMOND-UPON-THAMES COUNCIL, EX PARTE MCCARTHY AND STONE* [1992] 2 AC 48

Planning law provides powers to local authorities to decide which land developments can go ahead, and what conditions apply. Planning law is rather complex and once a planning application is submitted it must be processed and decided by the planning authority in a relatively short period of time. It is, therefore, often a good idea for the developer and the planning authority to have some sort of informal discussion before a planning application is submitted, to resolve issues and allow developers to amend proposals that are clearly going to be unacceptable.

Planning legislation makes no mention of informal consultations or pre-planning application negotiations. They are not expressly authorised. Richmond-upon-Thames Council decided that it would be useful to provide time for these informal consultations and encourage developers to engage with them. The planning officers' time in undertaking these consultations cost the council money and it decided to recoup some of this through a £25 charge. A building developer, McCarthy & Stone, challenged this decision, and there were two questions that the court had to answer:

- Were the informal consultations ultra vires? The answer was no. Even though they were not expressly authorised by statute, they were *conducive to* or *reasonably incidental* to the main power. The actions were therefore impliedly authorised by statute.
- Was the £25 charge ultra vires? The court answered that it was beyond the power granted by statute. Our constitutional system does not allow public bodies to impose new taxes or charges upon the public without the consent of Parliament. This goes back to the Bill of Rights 1689 and the great constitutional struggles between the King and Parliament of the seventeenth century.

Statute, therefore, does not have to list every conceivable action that a public body might need to undertake to carry out its principal functions. Anything which is conducive to or reasonably incidental to a power that is expressly granted by statute is implicitly authorised by that same statute.

---

1   A Bradley and K Ewing, *Constitutional and Administrative Law* (15th edn, Longman, 2011) 671.

13.1.1.1 MIXED MOTIVES

What if the public body, in taking a particular decision, is motivated by a number of considerations and some of those considerations are within the scope of the Act and some are outside of that power? This is known as acting on mixed motives.

KEY CASE – *WESTMINSTER CORPORATION V LONDON AND NORTH WESTERN RAILWAY CO* [1905] AC 426

The traffic in Westminster was as busy in the early twentieth century as it is today, and it was not particularly easy or safe for pedestrians to cross the road. Local authorities of this time were not authorised to build pedestrian subways. They were, however, empowered under public health legislation to build public toilets.

Westminster Corporation decided to build a public toilet under the road that could be accessed from both sides of the street. This allowed pedestrians to use the stairs and path under the road without taking advantage of the public toilet and, in effect, created a pedestrian subway. The railway company challenged this action and said that the mixed motives underlying the development made it ultra vires.

The court held that mixed motives in themselves would not make the action unlawful.

> It is not enough to show that the corporation contemplated that the public might use the subway as a means of crossing the street. In order to make out a case of bad faith it must be shown that the corporation constructed the subway as a means of crossing the street *under the colour and pretence* of providing public conveniences not really wanted.

> (Lord Macnaghten)

This is going to be difficult for a claimant to do in the absence of some council meeting minutes or other document outlining their own subterfuge or bad faith.

APPLYING THE LAW

In our problem scenario, 'The (hypothetical) Market Trading Act 2001 allows local councils to grant and revoke licences "as they see fit", so as to promote trade on markets in their area'; we can see that there is no real issue of simple ultra vires. The council has received powers to grant and revoke market licences and that is precisely what it has done in relation to Orchard and Hogg. In an assessment, you could simply omit discussion of this ground or, at most, include a very brief statement along the lines of the previous sentence.

13.2 ABUSE OF DISCRETION

The second branch of illegality is abuse of discretion. Discretion involves choice. As Bradley and Ewing explain, it is 'the possibility of choosing between several decisions or courses of action, each of which may be lawful'.[2] In planning law, for example, a local authority planning committee has a number of options as to how it decides a planning application to build a block of student residences. It can: approve the application with no conditions; grant permission subject to conditions (e.g. on access, parking, height of the building, landscaping etc); or reject the application. Each of these options is potentially lawful and the authority has a discretion to choose between them.

13.2.1 REASONABLENESS AND SUBJECTIVELY WORDED DISCRETION

Statutes may grant powers to public bodies to exercise their powers 'as they see fit'. How can a court intervene to control this seemingly absolute discretion? On the face of it, as long as the public body stays within the boundaries of the power granted by statute, then any legal challenge would fail. The public body could respond to any challenge by arguing – 'The statute says that I can act as I see fit and . . . I acted as I saw fit. I was therefore in accordance with the law' – the courts, however, have been reluctant to accept this position.

KEY CASE – *PADFIELD V MINISTER OF AGRICULTURE* [1968] 2 WLR 92

The Minister of Agriculture used powers under the Agricultural Marketing Act 1958 to set up a milk marketing scheme. The Act gave him power, as he directs, to pass on complaints about the scheme to a committee of investigation. The Minister refused to do so in this case and when challenged he claimed that the statute gave him a complete discretion arguing that the phrase 'as he directs' meant he could exercise the power as he saw fit.

The House of Lords disagreed and found that 'our law would be very defective if persons aggrieved were not entitled to the protection of the court' where a public body misconstrues its powers or uses its discretion to frustrate the objectives of the Act.

Parliament must have conferred the discretion with the intention that it should be used to promote the policy and objects of the Act; the policy and objects of the Act must be determined by construing the Act as a whole and construction is always a matter of law for the court.

(Lord Reid)

---

2   Bradley and Ewing, above n 1, 673.

So no matter how widely worded the discretionary powers are, the courts can always review the exercise of those powers.

APPLYING THE LAW

In our problem question, 'The (hypothetical) Market Trading Act 2001 allows local councils to grant and revoke licences "as they see fit", so as to promote trade on markets in their area'; this prompts discussion of the Padfield principle. You could outline the principle that even very broad discretionary powers can be subject to judicial review. Applying *Padfield* can simply involve stating that the courts will still look at whether Sleepyton Council has exercised the power 'to promote the policy and objects of the Act'.

13.3 FAILURE TO EXERCISE DISCRETION

Exercising discretion involves making a choice. Even a very broadly drafted discretionary power, of the sort used in *Padfield*, therefore imposes an obligation on a public body. It must identify a range of possible outcomes and choose between them. Failing to carry out that process is unlawful: 'It is a well-established principle of law, that if a person or public body is entrusted by Parliament with discretionary powers to be exercised for the public purpose, those persons or bodies cannot divest themselves of those powers and duties' (*Birkdale District Electricity Supply Co Ltd v Southport Corporation* [1926] AC 355). This failure, or divesting, can happen in two main ways: through replacing a choice with a strict rule (fettering discretion) and by passing the power on to some other body (delegation of discretion).

13.3.1 FETTERING DISCRETION

A public body might adopt a policy on how it will exercise its powers that is unlawful because it is so strict and unbending that it replaces a choice with a rule. This can arise particularly where the public body is receiving applications (e.g. for licences, permissions or funding) from the public. The discretionary power has to be exercised in relation to *each* application, i.e. a genuine choice must be made. As Lord Browne-Wilkinson said in *R v Secretary of State for the Home Department, ex parte Venables* [1998] AC 407: 'The person on whom the power is conferred cannot fetter the future exercise of his discretion by committing himself now as to the way in which he will exercise his future power'.

KEY CASE – *SAGNATA INVESTMENTS V NORWICH CORPORATION* [1971] 2 QB 614

The Betting, Gaming and Lotteries Act 1963 provided that permits for amusements with prizes (amusement arcades) could be granted 'at the discretion of the local authority'. Norwich Corporation adopted a general policy that it would not grant licences for amusement arcades. Sagnata applied for a licence for an amusement arcade and this was rejected.

The court found that 'the licensing committee have decided that they will not grant a permit for *any* amusement place with prizes in the City of Norwich, and the reasons they give for *this* refusal would apply to *any* application'. There was 'evidence before the recorder to the effect that they had rejected the application solely on the basis of the policy decision'.

The Court of Appeal held that the corporation had acted illegally because, in the exercise of its powers, it had adopted a policy which was so rigid in application it meant that it was not truly exercising its discretion at all.

The courts have recognised, however, that there are significant benefits for public bodies in adopting policies on how they will exercise discretionary powers:

- Efficiency – public bodies often receive large volumes of applications. To ask officials to sit down afresh with each one and treat it in isolation from all other applications is unrealistic. A policy can both speed up and guide the process.
- Consistency – it is a general principle that like cases should be treated alike. If there are multiple people in an organisation dealing with applications, then the only way in which the public body can produce any sort of consistent result is through quite detailed policies.
- Transparency – publicising how discretionary powers are going to be normally exercised makes it easier to hold public bodies to account and helps the public. Published policies can illuminate what sorts of issues need to be addressed and what is likely to result in a successful (or unsuccessful) application.

'These considerations do not preclude the person on whom the power is conferred from developing and applying a policy as to the approach which he will adopt in the generality of cases' and only 'an inflexible and invariable policy' will be unlawful (*R v Secretary of State for the Home Department, ex parte Venables* [1998], Lord Browne-Wilkinson).

KEY CASE – *BRITISH OXYGEN CO LTD V MINISTER OF TECHNOLOGY* [1971] AC 610

The Minister of Technology had discretion to subsidise industrial investments. He adopted a policy of only subsiding purchases of items with a value of £25 and over. The British Oxygen Company purchased hundreds of thousands of gas bottles which cost no more than £20 each, although the overall spend was £4 million. Its application for a subsidy was rejected, in line with the policy.

The House of Lords stated that the key question is, does the policy exclude discretion? Where a policy is in place, the applicant must have the chance to argue that the policy should be departed from in their particular case, and the public body must genuinely examine that claim. The public body must not 'shut its ears to an application'. On the facts, the company had extensive discussions with the ministry, and their concerns had been considered but ultimately rejected. So even quite strict general policies are permissible, if it is possible for an applicant to argue for a departure from that policy.

Public bodies will also unlawfully fetter their discretion if they enter into a contract or other sort of agreement that replaces their choice with an obligation. In *Stringer v Minister for Housing and Local Government* [1970] 1 WLR 1281, an agreement between local planning authorities and the Jodrell Bank radio telescope directorate to discourage physical development in the vicinity of the radio telescope in Cheshire was quashed, because it required the planning authorities to always reject certain types of planning applications.

APPLYING THE LAW

From our problem scenario: 'On the basis of this objective, the Licensing Committee has drafted a policy of refusing all new applications for licences to trade in non-organic produce. Elizabeth Orchard applies for a market trader's licence to sell non-organic fruit and vegetables. Her application is rejected on the grounds that it is not consistent with the policy'. This part of the problem raises the issue of fettering discretion. Again, state the general principle, perhaps using the quote from *ex parte Venables*. Applying the rule will involve some discussion of the scope for adopting strict policies, in accordance with *ex parte British Oxygen Company*, but the case most on point with our problem is *Sagnata*. You can make a direct comparison between the apparently inflexible rule that all amusement arcade applications would be rejected in *Sagnata* (plus the finding that the reasons given for the refusal of Sagnata's application would apply to *any* application), with Orchard's application for a market licence.

13.3.2 DELEGATION OF DISCRETION

The second way in which a public body can fail to exercise discretion is by passing the power on to somebody else. The general principle, therefore, is that discretionary power should only be exercised by those to whom it is given. This notion is grounded in the intention of Parliament. When Parliament establishes a public body, it endows that specific body (as opposed to other organisations) with specific powers. Respecting the intentions of Parliament involves preventing the powers being passed on to others.

KEY CASE – *VINE V NATIONAL DOCK LABOUR BOARD* [1957] AC 488

The National Dock Labour Board was granted various powers to regulate and operate docks. There were separate boards for the major docking cities (e.g. Liverpool, Glasgow, Hull) and the national board delegated some of those powers to its local boards.

In this case, the South Coast Dock Labour Board *further delegated* some powers down to the level of an individual manager. The manager then exercised disciplinary powers in relation to Vine, who argued that this was an unlawful delegation of power. The court agreed and quashed the decision. There are two main legal principles flowing from the case.

The first level of delegation, from the national to the local board, *was expressly authorised* by statute. Courts can look at the whole regulatory scheme set up by an Act and see if some ability to delegate (particularly within the organisation) is expressly or impliedly authorised in that scheme. The second level of delegation (to the manager) was *not expressly or impliedly authorised* by statute. In reaching this decision, the court took into account the nature of the powers and the level of the manager within the regulatory scheme. Judicial-type or disciplinary powers were not normally suitable for delegation. Some statutes expressly authorise delegation, e.g. section 101 of the Local Government Act 1972 allows local authorities to delegate powers to internal committees and officers.

KEY CASE – *CARLTONA LTD V COMMISSIONERS FOR WORKS* [1943] 2 ALL ER 560

The Commissioners for Works was a Government ministry that had powers to requisition property. Carltona Ltd was faced with the requisition of its factory and noticed that the power seemed to have been exercised by a civil servant rather than the Commissioners. As the Defence (General) Regulations 1939 only authorised the Commissioners to exercise this power, Carltona alleged that this was an unlawful delegation.

The court found that the delegation *was lawful*. Ministers have general powers to delegate to civil servants. It was implied by the statute, owing to:

- Reasons of practicality – ministers have a wide range of statutory powers that have to be exercised in very many instances. It is simply not realistic to expect a minister to exercise those powers personally in each case. Parliament must be taken to intend that powers can be delegated down to civil servants.
- Constitutional principle – the courts recognised a constitutional convention.

In Chapter 5, 'Constitutional conventions', you will recall the case of *Attorney General v Jonathan Cape* [1976] QB 752, where the court recognised but did not enforce the constitutional convention of Collective Cabinet Responsibility. The same process happened in *Carltona*, where the convention was Individual Ministerial Responsibility. The court recognised that the convention existed and that it governed the relationship between ministers and civil servants. The court could accept the idea that ministers can extensively delegate their powers, because constitutionally the minister is still responsible for those actions.

APPLYING THE LAW

The problem question continues: 'Sleepyton Council has delegated its powers under this Act to its Licensing Committee. The Committee has further delegated powers to revoke licences to its Markets Manager'. You can identify the issue of delegation of power. The legal principle, as illustrated in *Vine v National Dock Labour Board*, is that discretionary power should only be exercised by those to whom it is given, and unless the delegation is expressly or impliedly authorised by statute then it is unlawful. Applying the principle will lead you to section 101 of the Local Government Act 1972 that expressly allows local authorities to delegate powers to internal committees and officers.

There is some scope for discussing the difference between *Vine* where there was a sub-delegation of disciplinary-type powers not envisaged by statute, and the present case where there is express statutory authorisation for the delegation (Local Government Act). Whilst delegation of the general power from the Council to its Licensing Committee is clearly lawful, it is arguable that the further delegation of disciplinary powers to an individual manager is unlawful, on the basis of *Vine*.

13.4 EXERCISING DISCRETION UNLAWFULLY

The courts can still intervene if the public body actually does exercise its discretion within the scope of the powers given to it by the legislation. If the Passport Office, for example, is granted power to issue (or refuse to issue) passports and for a particular individual case it refuses a passport application, then this does not necessarily close off judicial review. There is still scope for a public body to act unlawfully in these circumstances, and it may illegally abuse its discretion through breaching the relevancy rule or by acting for an improper purpose.

13.4.1 THE RELEVANCY RULE

A decision-maker must only take into account relevant considerations and must discount any irrelevant ones. Some statutes indicate what is relevant to the exercise of a power, but normally it is a question of interpretation for the court. We saw above in the *Padfield* case that no matter how wide the discretion given to a public body, it must be exercised within the overall purpose of the statute, which means the action must be based on relevant factors. The general principle here then is that discretion must be:

- exercised on the basis of all the relevant considerations, and
- without taking into account any irrelevant considerations.

KEY CASE – *R V EALING COUNCIL, EX PARTE TIMES NEWSPAPERS LTD* (1986) 85 LGR 316

When Rupert Murdoch took over *The Times* newspaper in the mid-1980s, he moved the physical production of the newspaper from Fleet Street to Wapping in East London. It was a very controversial move, and widely seen as an attack on the print trade unions. The result was a very long and bitter industrial dispute.

A number of organisations, including Ealing Council, wanted to show their support for the print workers in this dispute. The council decided to cancel its subscriptions, including public library subscriptions, to *The Times*. That decision was challenged by Times Newspapers Ltd for breach of the relevancy rule.

The court had to examine the relevant statute to see the duty of the local authority and therefore which factors were relevant. The Public Libraries and Museums Act 1964 provided that the duty was to provide 'a comprehensive and efficient library service'. This leaves local authorities with a very wide discretion. It is their choice as to what books, journals and newspapers they buy. Whether they regard purchasing e.g. a new J K Rowling novel as supporting a comprehensive and efficient library service is a decision that has been primarily allocated to each local authority.

This is, however, subject (amongst other things) to the relevancy rule. When a local authority is making a choice, it must take into account only considerations which are relevant, and exclude from library purchasing decisions factors which are not relevant. The court, in this case, found that there had been a breach of the relevancy rule.

The court found that Ealing Council had not based its decision on an assessment that *The Times* was no longer a good newspaper, or that it was no longer needed by library users (which would have been relevant considerations). The council had been solely swayed by the industrial policy of the newspaper company and this was not relevant to library purchasing decisions.

KEY CASE – *R V PORT TALBOT BOROUGH COUNCIL, EX PARTE JONES* [1988] 2 ALL ER 207

Mrs Kingdom was a local councillor in Port Talbot, and part of the ruling Labour Party. She applied to be rehoused by the council housing services. Even though she was not at risk of homelessness, and was a single person, she was pushed right to the top of the council housing list and was allocated a three-bedroom house in the council ward that she represented.

This decision was challenged, and the council argued that her status as a councillor *was* relevant to their housing allocation decision, because:

- She needed a larger house, so that she had the space to carry out her duties as a councillor, e.g. having meetings with local people.
- She needed to live in the council ward that she represented.
- There was no immediate prospect of a smaller property becoming available in that ward.

The court completely rejected those submissions. Her status as a councillor was simply irrelevant to decisions by the council on housing and homelessness. Her role as a councillor was the main factor in the decision and therefore that decision was quashed.

On the face of it, this seems to give courts very extensive powers to interfere with the decisions of public bodies. Often it will be a matter of opinion as to what is relevant or irrelevant in any decision. Consider the thought processes in buying a new mobile phone. Factors such as cost and appearance may be common, but you might be swayed by details such as availability of accessories and the quality of the camera. Your friend may base their decisions more on technical specifications including battery life, operating systems and reviews from specialist websites. You would not expect your friend to have the power to interfere in your choice because *you* have not included in your exercise of discretion all of the factors that *they* consider relevant.

The courts have recognised the dangers of taking too interventionist an approach to this ground, on the basis of constitutional principles such as the separation of powers. Under our constitutional arrangements, the discretion, on library purchasing or granting social housing etc, has been allocated by statute to the executive – the public body.

The court's role is merely to review the legality of the decisions and it needs to be aware that there may well be differences of opinion as what is considered relevant. The courts, therefore, will only intervene if a decision:

- Completely excludes a consideration that ought to have been an important part of the decision-making process, or
- Is strongly based on factors which are clearly not relevant.

Further, it is the public body (and not the court) that decides what *weight* to give a particular factor in its decision-making.

13.4.2 IMPROPER PURPOSE

The general principle is that powers can only be used for the purpose, or purposes, for which they were granted.

A simple illustration of this is the Australian case of *Municipal Council of Sydney v Campbell* [1925] AC 338. Statute gave the Corporation powers to compulsorily purchase land, and indicated the purpose of the power: to improve or remodel any portion of the city, i.e. an urban development purpose. In this case, the Corporation received advice that if it compulsorily acquired property on the outskirts of the city (for which it would have to pay current market values) and then resold the property on the open market once it had improved road access, then it would make a significant profit. This was using the power for property speculation rather than urban development.

The key element of this judicial review ground is that the powers have been granted for one purpose and used for a very different purpose, yet often a statute will not indicate what the specific purpose of a discretionary power is. In these cases, the courts need to look at the whole statute and the whole regulatory scheme and find what the overall purpose is.

KEY CASE – *WHEELER V LEICESTER CITY COUNCIL* [1985] AC 1054

Leicester City Council decided to ban Leicester Rugby Football Club from using its recreation grounds for training, using powers to regulate access to those recreational facilities under the Open Spaces Act 1906. The rugby club alleged that these powers had been used for an improper purpose, although the Act did not indicate the purpose for which the powers had been granted.

The facts are complex but interesting. The apartheid regime in South Africa (that operated from the 1940s up to 1994) was based on racial classification. Many aspects of life, such as where you lived, what work you could do and who you could marry, were regulated on racial grounds. The black majority were horribly oppressed by this regime and it attracted widespread international opposition. In the Gleneagles Agreement on sporting contacts with South Africa (1977), the Commonwealth Governments agreed to uphold a sports boycott of the apartheid regime, but some rugby union members breached this boycott. In 1984, a so-called rebel tour of South Africa took place which included some players from the Leicester club.

Note that rugby union at this time was an amateur sport and the players were not employees of the club. The council asked the rugby club to publicly condemn the involvement of their players in the tour and to give affirmative answers to a number of questions about the sporting boycott. The club refused and was banned from a recreation ground that they had previously used for training.

There was nothing in the Open Spaces Act 1906 to indicate that its powers could be used for these purposes, but, on the other hand, local authorities have wide-ranging duties under race relations law to promote good race relations in their area. The council pointed out that Leicester had an ethnic minority population of over 25 per cent. The issue of the engagement by a key symbol of the city of Leicester with a racist regime involving breach of an internationally agreed sporting boycott was a genuine race relations issue.

The House of Lords agreed that the Race Relations Act duty was relevant, but found against the council on the basis that it had used its powers for an improper purpose. Lord Roskill said the council was trying to 'force acceptance by the club of their own policy on their own terms' and punishing them for failing to 'wholeheartedly align themselves with the council on a controversial issue'. The rugby club publicly stated that it *did* condemn apartheid but that there were a range of legitimate views on how to seek its end. Most people thought the best way of pressing for change in South Africa was through a process of isolation, whilst others thought that constructive engagement could be effective. From this range of legitimate points of view, the council wanted the rugby club to publicly agree with their specific stance.

Lord Templeman went even further than his colleagues, saying 'the laws of this country are not like the laws of Nazi Germany. A private individual or private organisation cannot be obliged to display zeal in the pursuit of an objective sought by a public authority'. This language goes too far. Comparing the well-intentioned, although ultimately unlawful, efforts of a local authority to promote racial harmony in furtherance of its wider statutory duties with state actions in Nazi Germany is disproportionate. Nevertheless, the decision itself is well-founded. For a public body to go to a private organisation and say, 'out of all the possible acceptable political stances on this issue, we require you to agree with our stance, or we shall use our public powers to punish you' is not a legitimate use of state power.

KEY CASE – *R V SOMERSET CC, EX PARTE FEWINGS* [1995] 3 ALL ER 20

Fewings was involved in stag hunting, an activity similar to fox hunting where hunters on horseback, with a pack of hunting dogs, catch and kill a stag for their entertainment. This took place on common land in Somerset. This is land which has no single owner but is controlled by the local authority. Somerset County Council had powers under section 120 of the Local Government Act 1972 to regulate access to and management of common land 'for the benefit, improvement or development of their area'. This phrase in section 120 of the LGA 1972 indicates the purposes which the power can be used for.

At a council meeting, a decision was taken to ban the stag hunters from accessing the common land. The record of the debates showed that this decision was taken for purely ethical reasons. The councillors regarded stag hunting as cruel and were using their powers to signal their disapproval of the activity and to make it harder to undertake within the county of Somerset.

The High Court found that using land management powers as a vehicle for the councillors' ethical concerns about a lawful (at the time) activity breached the improper purpose ground. The decision 'must objectively relate to the preservation or betterment of the area's amenities. It must not spring from, nor be fuelled by, ethical perceptions of the councillors about the rights and wrongs of hunting'.

The decision was upheld on appeal, although on slightly different grounds. Ethical concerns were not necessarily irrelevant, but the council had not considered the overall effect of any ban on the common land.

There are two further minor grounds:

- **Bad faith**, i.e. dishonesty – can invalidate a public body decision. Such allegations are rare and need to be supported by compelling evidence.
- **Breach of a fiduciary duty** – local authorities (although not central Government) are under a duty to spend their resources in a financially responsible way and for the benefit of the whole community. There are some notorious cases. In *Prescott v Birmingham Corporation* [1955] Ch 210, a free public transport scheme for pensioners was struck down as not based on ordinary business principles because the Corporation was not at liberty (in its use of public resources) to favour a particular section of the community on benevolent or philanthropic grounds. In *Roberts v Hopwood* [1925] AC 578, Poplar Borough Council decided to pay its workers a decent salary (even if this was above the market level) and to pay its male and female workers equal wages. This was 'a flagrant violation' of the fiduciary duty and the councillors 'had allowed themselves to be guided in preference by some eccentric principles of socialistic philanthropy, or by feminist ambition to secure equality of the sexes in the matter of wages'.

APPLYING THE LAW

Our problem includes the statement that 'The Council has adopted an objective that Sleepyton will be "the most organic town in England" on the basis that "organic farming is the only ethical way to care for the land"', and there are a range of decisions made on the basis of this objective. This prompts discussion of both the relevancy rule and improper purpose. Again, you need to state the general rule for each, supported by authorities such as *ex parte Times Newspapers* and *Wheeler*.

The starting point for applying these grounds is back in the first sentence of the problem, where it outlines the main purpose of the Act: to promote trade on markets in their area. You could argue that the council is using its 'organic town' objective to restrict trade for ethical reasons rather than to promote trade, and therefore using powers for an improper purpose and based on an irrelevant consideration. The counter-argument from the council may be that having a distinct organic identity will promote trade (and that it is within the acceptable range of objectives that they can use the powers for). As long as the council has considered the overall benefits for trade, then, according to the Court of Appeal decision in *ex parte Fewings*, ethical considerations *can* play a part in the council's decision-making.

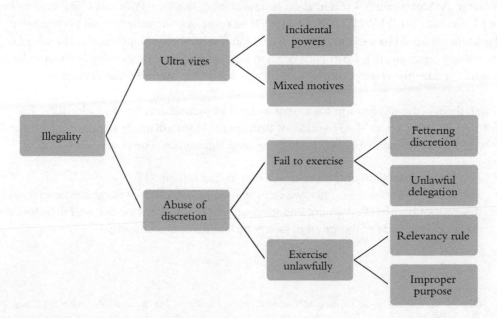

Figure 13.4 Map of the grounds of illegality

13.5 IRRATIONALITY

This is the second major group of grounds identified by Lord Diplock in the *GCHQ* case. The modern test comes from the case itself – a decision will be irrational if it is:

> so outrageous in its defiance of logic or of accepted moral standards that no sensible person who had applied his mind to the question to be decided would have arrived at it.
> *(CCSU v Minister for the Civil Service* [1985] AC 374, Lord Diplock)

The older test of *Wednesbury* unreasonableness in the narrow sense was that a decision would be unlawful if it was 'so unreasonable that no reasonable authority could ever have come to it' (*Associated Provincial Picture Houses Ltd v Wednesbury Corporation* [1948] 1 KB 223, Lord Greene).

Take a few moments to look again at the language used in these formulations. What does the language tell you about the nature of this ground? You will see that the concept of irrationality does not cover slightly unusual or mildly eccentric decisions. The language indicates how high a hurdle this is for the claimant and how rare a finding of irrationality is going to be. When the Association of British Bookmakers decided not to judicially review proposals to reduce the maximum stake on fixed-odds betting machines in 2017, one industry source was reported as saying 'You've got to virtually prove that the secretary of state was insane at the time of making the decision'.[3]

There is good reason for this very high threshold. One of the key messages of these chapters is that judicial review is not an appeal process. The court should not be concerned with the *merits* of a policy decision, only with its *legality* and the lawfulness of the process of reaching that decision. As Stuart-Smith J said in *R (on the application of Rhodes) v Police and Crime Commissioner for Lincolnshire* [2013] EWHC 1009 (Admin), 'The court must not interfere simply because it thinks that it would have made a different decision if it had been the primary decision-maker', yet when a court says that a particular decision is so lacking in rationality that it ought to be quashed, it takes the court perilously close to a review of the merits of that decision.

What, then, is the justification for a separate head of judicial review of irrationality? It is justified by reference to 'the intention of Parliament', that Parliament does not intend the powers it has granted to a public body to be used irrationally. The courts are *not saying*:

- This is a bad decision and we disagree with it, *but rather,*
- This is such a bad decision that we cannot imagine any rational person making it, and this cannot be what Parliament intended when it granted this power, and therefore the decision is outside of the grant of power by statute and is unlawful.

---

3   R Davies, 'Bookmakers braced for fixed-odds terminal betting restrictions' *The Guardian* (29 October 2017), https://www.theguardian.com/uk-news/2017/oct/29/bookmakers-braced-fixed-odds-betting-terminal-restrictions-fobt (last accessed 03/11/17), with a hat tip to @PaulFScott for spotting this.

Whilst this provides a foundation for the ground of irrationality, it also tightly circumscribes its scope. If Parliament *has* considered a policy and expressly or impliedly approved it, then it seems impossible for the courts to find that the policy is so irrational that Parliament cannot have intended that outcome. The type of decision, and how political it is, can also limit the scope of this ground.

Light scrutiny – some types of decisions, e.g. allocating financial resources, can be subject to only a very light level of scrutiny.

KEY CASE – *NOTTINGHAMSHIRE CC V SECRETARY OF STATE FOR THE ENVIRONMENT* [1986] AC 240

In the mid-1980s when there were regular disputes between local and central Government, the Secretary of State for the Environment imposed restrictions on the budgets on 'high-spending' councils. Nottinghamshire County Council argued that the decision was irrational because its budget had been set at an unfairly low level, and the finance rules were disproportionately disadvantageous to a small number of authorities.

The court rejected the claim for two main reasons:

- The type of decision – it was a matter of *high policy*. The allocation of finite financial resources to different areas was a political function *par excellence*. It is exactly the sort of thing that the Government and other executive bodies, rather than the courts, are best equipped to do.
- The implicit approval of Parliament – the financial restrictions had been placed before the House of Commons and approved by resolution of the House. This is not the same as legislation (it involves only one House, and scrutiny is limited), but the Commons had the opportunity to intervene and to say that the finance rules were nor rational, and did not do so. It would be difficult in these circumstances for the court to say that this decision was so outrageous in its defiance of logic that Parliament could never have intended to authorise the action.

Lord Scarman explained: 'I cannot accept that it is constitutionally appropriate, save in exceptional circumstances, for the courts to intervene on the ground of "reasonableness" to quash guidance framed by the Secretary of State and approved by the House of Commons'.

When this issue of constitutional appropriateness arises in relation to national security or international relations issues, it is often called 'deference'. In *R (Campaign Against the Arms Trade) v Secretary of State for International Trade* [2017] EWHC 1726 (QB), for example, the High Court rejected a challenge to a decision authorising the export of arms to Saudi Arabia. The claimants had argued that a Government finding that such arms would not be used by Saudi Arabia in its conflict in Yemen in a manner that breaches of international humanitarian law, was irrational. The High Court pointed to the 'considerable specialised knowledge' of the Government and that this was really a matter of political judgement.[4]

Anxious scrutiny – conversely, decisions which affect fundamental rights will be subject to 'anxious scrutiny', i.e. the courts will look in more detail at the decision-making process and require clearer justification for the action taken. Questions of broad economic policy are largely beyond the remit of the courts, but defending fundamental rights is at the heart of the judicial function. Judges feel much better equipped, and more clearly constitutionally authorised, to intervene.

KEY CASE – *R V MINISTRY OF DEFENCE, EX PARTE SMITH* [1996] 2 WLR 305

The Ministry of Defence had a strict policy that gay and lesbian people could not join the armed forces. If serving personnel were found to be gay or lesbian they would be discharged, regardless of whether or not they were sexually active. A number of former members of the armed forces, who had good service records, were dismissed solely on the grounds of their sexual orientation. There was no allegation that their sexual orientation had any impact on how they carried out their professional duties, or that they had engaged in any sexual activity on armed forces premises.

The judges in the case made their own feelings on the ban reasonably clear. They thought it inappropriate and based on very slender justification. However, the Court of Appeal did not find that the Ministry of Defence had acted irrationally. The continuation of the ban was supported by a survey of existing armed forces members, but more significantly, the ban had been considered by Parliament four times in the previous decade and had remained in place. Again, it would be difficult to argue that Parliament could not have intended the Ministry of Defence to use its powers this way.

> The more substantial the interference with human rights, the more the court would require by way of justification before it was satisfied that the decision was reasonable. The existing policy could not be stigmatised as irrational . . . it was supported by both Houses of Parliament and by those whom the Ministry properly looked to for professional advice.
>
> (Bingham MR)

---

4   See D Lock, 'Questions Regarding Judicial Deference in *R (Campaign Against the Arms Trade) v Secretary of State for International Trade*' U.K. Const. L. Blog (20 July 2017), https://ukconstitutionallaw.org/ (last accessed 03/11/17).

Even in this case, where the Government action involved interference with the most intimate aspects of a citizen's private life, where the court subjected the decision to anxious scrutiny and where there was justifiable scepticism as to the validity of the justifications for the ban, the court did not feel able to strike down the policy as irrational. As a postscript, the ban was ended in 2000 following a successful challenge for breach of Article 8 ECHR, the right to a private life, before the European Court of Human Rights (*Smith v UK* (2000) 29 EHRR 493). See below for an application of these grounds to the problem scenario.

13.6 PROPORTIONALITY

Lord Diplock in the *GCHQ* case left open the possibility that the grounds could be added to by future developments and, in particular, suggested that the principle of proportionality might develop in this way.

EXPLAINING THE LAW

Imagine that your law school is concerned about cheating in exams, and thinks that students may be taking notes into examinations. It introduces a policy of strip searching all exam candidates before they are allowing into the exam hall.

- Is the objective (to prevent exam cheating) appropriate? Yes.
- Would the proposed actions help to achieve that objective? Yes.

So what is the problem? The problem is that the action is disproportionate. It goes too far. To use the classic metaphor, it uses a sledgehammer to crack a nut.

Proportionality, according to Lord Steyn in *R v Secretary of State for the Home Department, ex parte Daly* [2001] UKHL 26 means that the courts need to:

- Assess the balance which the decision-maker has struck.
- Direct attention to the relative weight accorded to the interests.
- Subject the decision (if necessary) to an intense review, even going further than the anxious scrutiny test from *ex parte Smith*.

Applied to the strip-search example, we can see that the balance of the law school action is wrong and insufficient weight has been given to principles of privacy and dignity. Looking at the three points from *ex parte Daly*, you should note that proportionality has the potential for the courts to step more fully, compared to the irrationality test, into the field of reviewing the merits of a decision.

The courts had found that some notion of the need for proportionate action was inherent in the common law (relating to excessive punishments, *R v Barnsley Metropolitan Borough Council, ex parte Hook* [1976] 3 All ER 452). In the leading pre-Human Rights Act case, however, the House of Lords said there was 'at present no basis upon which the proportionality doctrine applied by the European Court can be followed by the courts of this country' (*R v Secretary of State for the Home Department, ex parte Brind* [1991] 1 AC 696, Lord Ackner). The position is different following the introduction of the Human Rights Act 1998. Lord Steyn in *ex parte Daly* said that most cases would be decided the same way under irrationality or proportionality, but that proportionality did entail more intense review of the public body action. Proportionality is still not comprehensively available in all Public Law complaints but can be applied in cases involving European Union law, and claims for breach of a European Convention or common law right. The Supreme Court have indicated that when a case involves particularly important consequences for the claimant then they can apply proportionality principles even beyond these categories (*Pham v Secretary of State for the Home Department* [2015] UKSC 19).

APPLYING THE LAW

Coming back to our problem question, there is a limited amount to discuss under this section. Rejecting and revoking market licences on the basis of an organic policy does not fall within the type of action that is 'so outrageous in its defiance of logic or of accepted moral standards that no sensible person who had applied his mind to the question to be decided would have arrived at it', in accordance with *GCHQ*. There is a potential line of argument that in restricting how George Hogg advertises his wares, the council is limiting his freedom of expression, which would bring both the *Ex parte Smith* 'anxious scrutiny' and the more intense review of proportionality into play. Even so, this would not be the strongest basis for a judicial review of the council's decision.

13.7 PROCEDURAL IMPROPRIETY

The third group of grounds identified by Lord Diplock in the *GCHQ* case was procedural impropriety. This covers three main areas:

- breach of statutory procedures
- legitimate expectation
- breach of a general duty of procedural fairness (including natural justice).

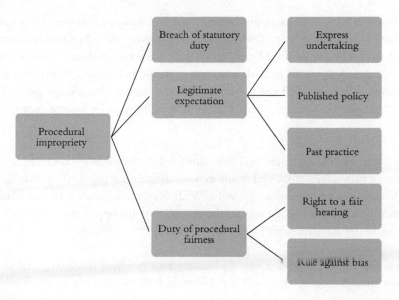

Figure 13.5 Map of procedural impropriety

13.7.1 BREACH OF STATUTORY PROCEDURES

Failure to comply with a procedure laid down by statute *may* invalidate a decision. Let us examine a scenario that ought never to arise in *your* university life.

APPLYING THE LAW – PLAGIARISM PROCEDURES

Universities have regulations as to the conduct of students, including rules on plagiarism and academic dishonesty. The substantive rules, e.g. the identification of plagiarism as an academic offence, will normally be accompanied by procedural rules. Typically, these will cover issues such as: the student will be notified of an allegation in writing, they will have an opportunity to attend a hearing, and they can be accompanied by a friend or Student Union representative.

You should be able to find the rules of academic misconduct and plagiarism that apply within your educational establishment and identify which of those rules provide procedural safeguards.

Failure to follow these rules will be a procedural defect, and may give rise to an internal appeal within the institution. Similarly, many statutes impose these sorts of procedural rules on public bodies. Failing to follow such rules may lead to a procedural impropriety and a successful judicial review of the decision.

Local authorities have very extensive powers to e.g. regulate planning. They can
decide what is built and where. These substantive powers are subject to quite extensive
procedural rules. There are time limits on dealing with the application, duties to publicise
the application and duties to consult with other public bodies (e.g. Environment Agency,
the Highways Authority) and the public. It is important to identify the general principle
here. It is that failure to comply with a procedure laid down by statute may invalidate
a decision.

The crucial word is 'may'. Failure will not automatically invalidate a decision, and so not
all breaches of procedural rules will result in a decision being quashed. In *R v Immigration
Appeal Tribunal, ex parte Jeyeanthan* [2000] 1 WLR 354, Lord Woolf said that courts would
consider whether there had been substantial compliance (as opposed to strict compliance),
and what were the consequences of non-compliance.

A complete failure to publicise a major planning proposal will result in an invalid decision,
but a minor breach (e.g. if a site notice publicising a proposal is placed on the wrong
lamppost) relating to a minor development is much less likely to be quashed. In each case,
the court will look at the type of the breach, the consequences of the breach and the
impact on the public.

13.7.2 LEGITIMATE EXPECTATION

A legitimate expectation will arise in the mind of the complainant wherever they have been
led to understand, by words or actions of the decision-maker, that certain procedures, e.g.
consultation, will be followed in reaching a decision.

In a private law relationship, you may want to enter into an agreement with someone. If
they are promising you some product or service and you want to rely on that promise,
what legal mechanism is available to you? Hopefully you were able to identify the answer as
'contract' (although I understand if Contract Law is not your favourite subject). If you want
to hold somebody to their word, to rely on their promise, then Contract Law provides a
tool for doing so.

This mechanism is not available in relation to Public Law powers. If a public body tries to
enter into a contract governing how it will exercise its discretionary powers, then that will
not be a lawful contract (as noted in the *Stringer* case above). So how do we citizens rely on
the statements and promises of our public bodies? The mechanism developed by the courts
from the 1960s onwards is called 'legitimate expectation'. There are three ways in which a
legitimate expectation can arise:

- express undertaking
- published policy
- past practice.

13.7.2.1 EXPRESS UNDERTAKING
Schmidt was the case that first established the concept of legitimate expectation within the UK.

> **KEY CASE** – *SCHMIDT V SECRETARY OF STATE FOR HOME AFFAIRS* [1969] 2 CH 149
>
> A group of American students was given leave to stay in the UK so as to study at a Scientology college. The Government was then persuaded that Scientology was socially harmful, and in following that new policy the Home Secretary rejected the students' applications to extend their time in the UK. Lord Denning explained that there was a need to distinguish between:
>
> - aliens whose leave to remain in the UK had expired (including the applicants in this case), who had no legitimate expectation of any specific outcome or procedure. They could be ordered to leave the country with no further hearing and
> - aliens whose leave had been prematurely terminated by the Home Office, i.e. the promise to allow someone to stay in the UK for a set period of time had been withdrawn. In these circumstances, a legitimate expectation would arise.
>
> It would be unfair to deprive them of their permission to stay without a hearing.

Similarly, in *R v Liverpool Corporation, ex parte Liverpool Taxi Fleet Operators Association* [1972] 2 QB 299, the taxi association received a direct undertaking from the local authority as to the number of taxi licences in the city. It was held that 'the corporation were not at liberty to disregard their undertaking. They were bound by it so long as it was not in conflict with their statutory duty'.

It is important to notice that the right granted by the legitimate expectation in *Schmidt* was not a *substantive right* to remain for the full period but only a *procedural right* not to be deprived of that permission without a hearing. In *Ex parte Liverpool Taxi Fleet Operators Association*, despite the fact that a substantive promise had been made, the legitimate expectation produced only a procedural right to be consulted on increases to taxi license numbers.

The vast majority of legitimate expectation cases have given rise to procedural rights. *R v North East Devon Health Authority, ex parte Coughlan* [2001] QB 213 is the principal exception. A patient was given a promise that she could live for as long as she chose in a specific NHS facility. To renege on that promise, on the specific facts of the case, would amount to an abuse of power. This is very rare and will be limited to where a very specific promise has been made to a very limited number of people who have acted on that promise, where the situation is more akin to a contract than to normal policy statements.

13.7.2.2 TAKING ACCOUNT OF A PUBLISHED POLICY

Public bodies often publish information through leaflets, websites etc, giving an indication of how they are going to exercise their powers. This is particularly relevant when there is a statement of who will be consulted before a decision is taken and the criteria that will be taken into account in deciding applications. These statements can give rise to a legitimate expectation.

KEY CASE – *R V HOME SECRETARY, EX PARTE KHAN* [1984] 1 WLR 1337

Mr and Mrs Khan were Pakistani nationals who had permanent leave to remain in the UK. They wanted to adopt a child from Pakistan and bring it to the UK. Mr Khan completed the application for this process on the basis of the criteria published in Home Office guidance. In the time between him sending in his application and it being decided, the Home Office changed their approach to such applications. The Home Office rejected his application on the basis of the new criteria, which were not published at the time Khan completed his application.

It was held that Khan had a legitimate expectation that the decision would be made on the basis of the published criteria. The Home Office were not entitled to base their decision on a factor (the ability of the natural parents to care for the child) that was not mentioned in the initial guidance.

13.7.2.3 PAST PRACTICE

Consistent past practice can give rise to an expectation that the practice will continue in the future. The General Communications Headquarters (GCHQ) is a part of the UK intelligence services. It is where the UK Government can listen in to your phone conversations, read your social media messages and look at your webcam communications.

KEY CASE – *COUNCIL OF CIVIL SERVICE UNIONS V MINISTER FOR THE CIVIL SERVICE* [1985] AC 374

GCHQ has been operating in different guises since 1947, and from that time staff had been allowed to join staff associations. These were not exactly trade unions but the associations were allied to the trade union movement. Since 1947, any change to working terms and conditions had been put to the staff associations for consultation. There had been a long and unbroken chain of past practice.

In 1984, Prime Minister Margaret Thatcher, as Minister for the Civil Service, banned GCHQ staff from belonging to any staff association. The decision, which had immediate effect, was not subject to any consultation. It was a major change to staff working conditions, and so the consistent and long-standing practice of consultation had been broken. One consequence was that 14 people refused to give up their membership and were dismissed.

The Council of Civil Service Unions alleged that the invariable practice of consultation had given rise to a legitimate expectation that the staff associations would continue to be consulted before changes were made. To clarify, there was no absolute substantive right for membership of the associations to continue. If there had been proper consultation on the proposal to ban membership, then this would not have breached any legitimate expectation.

The House of Lords agreed that there was a legitimate expectation arising from the consistent past practice and that it had been breached by the actions of the Prime Minister.

The court, however, refused to quash the decision, on grounds of national security. It found that the Government and Prime Minister were in the best position to assess whether the decision was required to defend national security and that the court would not second-guess the Prime Minister on that question.

13.8 THE DUTY OF PROCEDURAL FAIRNESS

The general duty on public bodies to act procedurally fairly is a development from the principles of natural justice. There are two rules associated with natural justice:

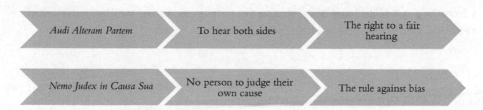

Figure 13.6 The maxims of natural justice

These now form part of an overarching **duty to adopt fair procedures**.

The maxims of natural justice have their roots deep in the common law. Since the 1960s, they have become absorbed within an overarching duty of procedural fairness. In the exercise of their powers and their dealings with the public, public bodies have a general duty to adopt fair procedures. If you see the phrase 'a general duty of fairness' you need to understand that it only refers to having fair procedures, not that the outcome will be substantively fair. The pivotal case for the evolution of maxims of natural justice into a general duty of procedural fairness was *Ridge v Baldwin*.

13.8.1 THE RIGHT TO A FAIR HEARING

KEY CASE – *RIDGE V BALDWIN* [1964] AC 40

Ridge was the Chief Constable of Brighton Police Force. He was charged with conspiracy to obstruct the course of justice and faced a high-profile trial at the Old Bailey. He was acquitted, but in his summing up the judge was very critical of Ridge and alleged that he had not shown the qualities of leadership required for his office. Shortly afterwards, the Brighton Watch Committee met and dismissed him, using powers under the Municipal Corporations Act 1882. He was given no notice of the meeting and therefore no opportunity:

- to hear the allegations and evidence against him
- to challenge those allegations and evidence
- to make his own representations.

The difficulty facing Ridge in challenging this decision was that up to this point the right to a fair hearing had only been required for judicial or judicial-type proceedings. Most of the cases concerned magistrates' courts, but the maxim also applied e.g. to tribunals. Administrative proceedings, such as whether to dismiss a Chief Constable, seemed to be outside of the scope of the right.

The Court of Appeal rejected the claim on the basis of that existing approach: 'the defendants were acting in an administrative or executive capacity just as they did when they appointed him'. The House of Lords, however, found that natural justice required that notice of a hearing should have been given.

You need to understand why the Law Lords departed from the previous limitations. Imagine that you are facing a judicial–type proceeding, e.g. in the magistrates' court, that could impose some sanction on you. What if you did not receive notice of the trial hearing, did not know what you were alleged to have done, did not have any chance to examine to allegations against you or the evidence on which those allegations were based, and did not have the chance to address the court or have a lawyer speak for you? Would you consider that the state was dealing with you in a fair manner? Obviously not.

Yet, Ridge in his case was also suffering a serious sanction, albeit through an administrative procedure. The categorisation of the decision as judicial or non–judicial was not the crucial aspect of the process *for him*. The House of Lords ultimately agreed. Limiting the right to a fair hearing to judicial proceedings was framing the issue in the wrong way. What was more important was the impact of the Public Law decision on the individual. There can be administrative decisions that have a major impact on an individual, and there is a need to ensure the fairness of those processes. Ridge had lost his job, what was left of his reputation and, crucially, his pension rights. There had been a breach of natural justice.

What is involved in a fair hearing depends very much on the circumstances. For the most serious decisions it may involve:

- the opportunity to know the case against you
- the opportunity to state your case
- the opportunity to comment on all the material considered
- that no party should communicate with the decision-maker behind the other's back
- the right to an oral hearing
- the right to representation.

This gold standard of procedural fairness does not apply to all Public Law decisions. As Lord Bridges said in *Lloyd v McMahon* [1987] AC 625, the rules of natural justice are 'not engraved on tablets of stone', and what procedural fairness demands depends on:

- the character of the decision-making body
- the kind of decision it has to make
- the statutory framework in which it operates.

There are high-volume processes (i.e. where the public body receives lots of applications) where it would be unrealistic to require these elaborate and costly processes and decisions where the impact on the individual is more minor. Decisions that have a major impact on the status quo, e.g. taking away someone's home or their livelihood, are more serious than an application relating to a new home or a new career. Even for these less impactful decisions, there are still requirements of procedural fairness: to know the criteria that will be used in the decision and to be informed both of the decision and (often, but not always) the reasons for it.

13.8.2 THE RULE AGAINST BIAS

The rule against bias is strict: it is not necessary to show actual bias on the part of the decision-maker. Under this second maxim, we clearly expect that decision-makers exercising Public Law powers on our behalf and affecting our interests are not biased. The rule against bias takes a little more explanation, however, and in particular is concerned with protecting the general public's perception of the integrity of public body decision-making: the 'appearance of the matter is just as important as the reality' (*ex parte Pinochet* (see below), Lord Nolan).

The rule is particularly strict where the judge, or decision-maker, has any *direct pecuniary interest* in the outcome of the decision. Pecuniary means financial or otherwise relating to money.

KEY CASE – *DIMES V GRAND JUNCTION CANAL* [1852] 3 HL CAS 759

This was an ordinary civil dispute between a private individual and a private company. The case came before the Lord Chancellor, Lord Cottenham. It was later discovered that the Lord Chancellor had a financial stake, a substantial shareholding, in the canal company. There was no allegation of actual bias or that the Lord Chancellor was even aware of his shareholdings, but the decision was quashed. The Lord Chancellor ought to have recused himself, i.e. stepped down from acting as a judge in this particular case.

This is an automatic disqualification rule. Whenever a judge or other decision-maker has any type of financial interest in the outcome of a decision before them, they should have no involvement in the outcome of that process. The rule against bias can also apply to a judge/decision-maker having a **direct non-pecuniary interest** in the outcome of the case, or where they have close involvement with a cause central to the decision.

KEY CASE – *R V BOW ST MAGISTRATES, EX PARTE PINOCHET UGARTE (NO 2)* [2000] 1 AC 119

General Augusto Pinochet came to power in a military coup in Chile in 1973, which overthrew the democratically elected socialist Government in an action that was supported by the US CIA. Once in power, Pinochet instituted a regime of severe repression of political opposition, including the widespread use of torture (of over 30,000 people) and murder of dissidents (estimated at over 2,000 crimes). Many of these actions, such as the 'disappearance' of activists by Government-controlled murder squads, were committed with no legal basis.

General Pinochet was a close personal friend of the former British Prime Minister Margaret Thatcher. In 1998, he was visiting the UK to receive medical treatment and to visit Lady Thatcher. The authorities received a warrant from a Spanish magistrate for his arrest and extradition to Spain for involvement in the murder of a Spanish diplomat and 94 counts of torture of Spanish nationals. In ordinary circumstances, the warrant would have been executed and Pinochet would have faced extradition to stand trial in Spain. The complicating factor was the existence of *state immunity*. This is a concept of international law that says that heads of state of a country cannot be held liable, in Civil or Criminal Law, for what they do as head of state. The immunity is regarded as necessary, as a general rule, to allow for international diplomacy.

Human rights groups had been campaigning for some time for a limitation of state immunity for allegations of crimes against humanity, which include torture. This was the legal issue that appeared before the appeal courts. Ultimately, the House of Lords, in a landmark human rights judgment, decided that state immunity did not protect a head of state from facing allegations of crimes against humanity.

The procedures adopted by the House of Lords, however, breached the rule against bias. The leading human rights organisation, Amnesty International, was allowed to give evidence of Pinochet's connections to murder and torture, and therefore became a party to the legal proceedings. One of the Law Lords hearing the case, Lord Hoffmann, was a non-executive director of a charitable arm of Amnesty International. He had no sort of pecuniary interest at stake in the case. Nevertheless, it was decided that 'promotion of a cause in which he was involved together with one of the parties' was sufficient to invalidate the judgment.

13.8.2.1 THE GENERAL TEST FOR BIAS

The cases above outline where the judge or decision-maker should be automatically disqualified from hearing the case, but there is also a general test for the rule against bias. In *R v Gough* [1993] AC 646, the House of Lords framed the test as a 'real danger of bias' so as to focus on the possibility rather than the probability that bias had occurred. An adjustment was made in *Re Medicants and Related Classes of Goods (No 2)* [2001] 1 WLR 700, where it was made clear that the test must be from the perspective of 'a fair-minded and informed observer'. The House of Lords returned to the test in *Porter v Magill*.

KEY CASE – *PORTER V MAGILL* [2002] 2 WLR 37

If local counsellors knowingly act unlawfully and this causes financial loss to the authority, then the councillor can be surcharged, i.e. forced to pay the amount of money they caused the council to lose. The District Auditor imposed a surcharge of £15 million pounds on Porter and her deputy. Porter alleged that the auditor was biased, and the House of Lords, applying this test, rejected her appeal.

The general test for assessing bias in public decision-making was that 'the fair-minded and informed observer, having considered the facts would conclude that there was a real possibility that the tribunal was biased', Lord Hope. The key is whether there is an objective 'real possibility' of bias.

The test applies to executive and administrative decisions as well as judicial proceedings. This potentially causes problems for politicians involved in executive decision-making. Unlike judges, they are expected to broadcast their opinions on a wide range of subjects that they may later have to make decisions on. In practice, the courts will take this into account, and Elliott and Thomas outline how politicians are permitted to have a predisposition in favour of a particular policy, as long as they do not 'lapse into predetermination'.[5]

---

5   M Elliott and R Thomas, *Public Law* (3rd edn, OUP, 2017) 535.

The case of *Porter v Magill* is instructive in other ways. One sometimes gets the impression teaching Public Law that students consider some of our concerns about abuse of public power to be fanciful or overblown. In the UK, we live in a democracy that (more or less) reflects the will of the people and (for better or worse) holds those in power to account. This is broadly true, and there is a very respectable argument that some public lawyers (in their enthusiasm for legal controls) give insufficient weight to the benefits of the democratic and political accountability that operates in the UK. Nevertheless, there are examples of abuse of power that are so outrageous that they demonstrate the necessity of vigilance (whether through *legal or political* mechanisms) and for very careful scrutiny of how public power is exercised. *Porter* is one of these.

Dame Shirley Porter was Conservative leader of Westminster Council in the 1980s, widely held up as a flagship council, a beacon of what local authorities could achieve. It was discovered that she had been abusing local authority powers over council housing to try to influence the outcome of elections. On the premise that people in council housing were more likely to vote Labour than Conservative, she ordered (against legal advice) that sales of council houses to private tenants would take place mainly in marginal wards.

The result was that many properties remained empty for extended periods of time including during election periods. Attempts were also made to move homeless people out of marginal wards. The attempt to use housing policy so as to influence election results is in itself offensive, but she did so by leaving social housing empty at a time when homelessness levels were very high, particularly in central London. For people to be forced to sleep in cardboard boxes on the street whilst perfectly decent property was purposely left empty, so as to fix election results, was an appalling and corrupt abuse of power.

APPLYING THE LAW – THE PROBLEM SCENARIO AND PROCEDURAL IMPROPRIETY

Returning to the problem scenario, we are told that following the revocation of his licence, George Hogg is granted a hearing. We are not told of any particular statutory procedures in the Act. There have been no promises from the council on procedures, so legitimate expectation does not seem to be an issue. We may speculate that after 20 years of trading on the market Hogg has acquired expectations in a similar way to the workers in the *GCHQ* case, but there are differences. In *GCHQ*, a particular procedure (consultation) was followed each time there were changes. There is nothing here to suggest that there has been a history of consultation, and, in general, students should be wary of reading too much into problem scenarios. There is normally enough to deal with without inventing new issues.

It is worth briefly comparing Hogg and Orchard. As Hogg is subject to a decision that severely affects the status quo, i.e. a long-established business, he is entitled to a higher level of procedural fairness than Orchard. Whilst it was prudent for the Licensing Committee to grant him an oral hearing, it would not necessarily be required to do so for an application for a new licence from Orchard.

The key issue is obviously – 'The hearing is chaired by Councillor Brownbread, who is also the regional chair of the Organic Soil Campaign' and the rule against bias. At first glance, this may look like a straightforward application of *ex parte Pinochet*. Whilst the facts are similar, there are material differences. In *Pinochet*, Lord Hoffmann had a close involvement with a cause central to the case, but the real issue was that he was promoting that cause *together with one of the parties to the case*. Here the Organic Soil Campaign is not a party to the decision or the appeal. We need to apply the general test from *Porter v Magill*; is there an objective real possibility of bias? The application of the test is arguable. We need to keep in mind that Brownbread is a politician and therefore can legitimately show support for particular policies. We would need to show, perhaps by reference to the strictness of the policy on new applications to the market, that Brownbread was predetermined to find against all non-organic stallholders, or that overall his work with the Campaign is such that an informed and reasonable member of the public would consider there to be a real possibility of bias. This may not be a particularly straightforward task.

POINTS TO REVIEW

This chapter has discussed the grounds of judicial review, as categorised by Lord Diplock in the *GCHQ* case.

Under the heading of **illegality**, we explored the *Padfield* principle that even very wide discretionary powers can still be subject to review. Illegality can result from a public body simply acting beyond the scope of its powers, i.e. ultra vires. It can also occur when a public body fails to exercise a discretion that has been granted to it, by replacing it with an overly strict policy (fettering discretion) or by passing the power on to someone else (delegating discretion). The way in which a public body exercises its discretion can also be illegal if the body breaches the relevancy rule (taking into account irrelevant considerations, or failing to consider relevant ones) or uses the power for an improper purpose.

Under the heading of **irrationality**, we discussed the very high hurdle that claimants had to clear before they could show that a public body had acted 'in defiance of logic'. This is due to the proximity of irrationality to a review of the merits of the decision. The factors that make a successful claim less likely include the nature of the decision (whether it is a question of 'high policy') and whether the decision has been expressly or tacitly approved by Parliament. Conversely, where the decision intrudes into individual rights, then the courts will subject the decision to 'anxious scrutiny'. Proportionality, which is applicable in European Union and human rights cases, requires the court to assess the balance between the competing interests and to subject the decision to more intense review.

Under the heading of **procedural impropriety**, we examined the ways in which public bodies sometimes adopt unlawful and unfair procedures. These include breach of procedures laid down by statute, although this does not automatically invalidate a decision. Legitimate expectation, which arises when the decision-maker has led an individual to believe that a particular process will be adopted, can also be binding on the public body. Beyond this, there is an overall duty to adopt fair procedures. This has its roots in the maxims of natural justice: that there is a right to a fair hearing (the requirements for which vary widely according to the type of decision) and the rule against bias.

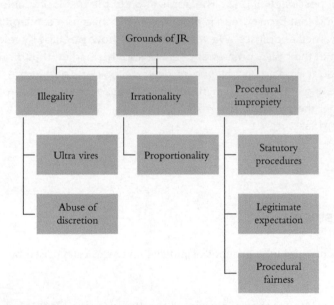

Figure 13.7 Map of judicial review grounds

ASSESSMENT ADVICE

Throughout the chapter we have focused not simply on an explanation of the differing grounds, but also on how you might be called on to apply them in answering problem questions. In your conclusion to the Orchard and Hogg problem, you could quickly recap the grounds that you have considered: delegation of discretion; fettering discretion; relevancy rule and improper purpose; irrationality/proportionality; and the rule against bias. It is good practice to show that you can weigh the strength of each claim. The strongest element of Orchard's claim would be the fettering discretion ground where the *Sagnata* case provides clear support. Hogg has a less obvious strong suit, but there may be substance in a claim of possible bias and tying a freedom of expression argument to a proportionality claim.

TAKING IT FURTHER

Public Law Project, 'An Introduction to Judicial Review', 2013, http://www.publiclawproject.
org.uk/resources/6/an-introduction-to-judicial-review

For a very simple guide to the grounds that places them in the context of the whole
judicial review procedure, and from a practical perspective.

There are a range of excellent detailed analyses and arguments for reform of specific
grounds, in articles such as:

C Forsyth, 'Legitimate Expectations Revisited' [2011] *Judicial Review* 429

P Walker, 'What's Wrong with Irrationality' [1995] *Public Law* 556

A Olowofoyeku, 'Bias and the Informed Observer' [2009] *Cambridge Law Journal* 388

Treasury Solicitors Department, *The Judge Over Your Shoulder,* 5th edn, 2016, https://
www.gov.uk/government/publications/judge-over-your-shoulder

A very interesting publication, known in the civil service as JOYS. Since 1987 it has been
guiding civil servants on how judicial review might affect their work. The introduction
states that: 'Its purpose is not "How to survive Judicial Review", but rather to inform and
improve the quality of administrative decision-making – though, if we are successful, that
should have the incidental effect of making decisions less vulnerable to Judicial Review'.

JOYS gives a fascinating practical insight into, and very clear explanation of, the grounds.
The case examples are particularly illuminating.

14

CHAPTER 14
OMBUDSMAN AND TRIBUNALS

Visions of an unaccountable bureaucracy, uncontrolled either by political transparency or the rule of law, can be the stuff of horror, as in Kafka's *The Trial*, or Terry Gilliam's film *Brazil*. British variations on this theme are gentler, but very pervasive, and the classic Ealing comedies of the 1940s–60s, such as *Passport to Pimlico* and *Whisky Galore*, feature a range of petty, faceless, intrusive and unaccountable bureaucrats.

Charles Dickens provided some early satire on the dangers of state bureaucracy in *Little Dorrit*: 'No public business of any kind could possibly be done at any time without the acquiescence of the Circumlocution Office. Its finger was in the largest public pie, and in the smallest public tart. It was equally impossible to do the plainest right and to undo the plainest wrong without the express authority of the Circumlocution Office'.

Despite the grimly comedic tone of these artistic visions of bureaucracy, public bodies make millions of life-affecting and life-changing decisions in relation to citizens each year. When they get it wrong, those citizens need to be able to access administrative justice. The obvious starting point is to look to the courts system, but in a majority of cases we need to look elsewhere because (a) the courts cannot be involved because the complaint is not a legal one, or (b) the courts are not the most appropriate means of addressing the complaint.

This point was made by the then Parliamentary Ombudsman, Ann Abraham, in 2011, whilst noting the valuable role of the courts:

> Yet citizens are just as likely, if not more likely, to come across administrative justice issues in their ordinary lives than civil or even family justice issues. The outcomes of decision making by a wide-range of public bodies on a daily basis affect family incomes, jobs, healthcare, housing, education and much, much more.

To illustrate the point – in 2010 in England and Wales:

> There were around 63,000 hearings/trials dealing with civil justice matters;
> There were over 200,000 criminal justice hearings/trials;
> There were over **650,000** administrative justice hearings – of which over 275,000 were about social security and child support.[1]

---

1   A Abraham, 'Parliamentary Ombudsman and Administrative Justice: Shaping the next 50 years' JUSTICE Tom Sargant Memorial Lecture 2011, http://justice.org.uk/ombudsmen-administrative-justice/ (last accessed 03/11/17).

In 2013, tribunals received 867,338 cases,[2] and the use of tribunals and complaints to ombudsmen are the most important elements in providing administrative justice as between the citizen and the state.

AS YOU READ

You should consider:

- The ability of ombudsmen and tribunals to deliver justice in a relatively quick and efficient way.

- Issues around access to the justice schemes and the scope of their jurisdiction.

- Their relationship to the court system.

14.1 ASSESSMENT TIPS

You will normally face essay-type questions on this subject, and you should refer back to Chapter 1 for advice on how to approach and complete these sorts of questions. There is one additional point to be made here. Active and efficient research is an integral part of performing well in your law assessments. You need to be able to identify and use authoritative sources to inform your understanding and provide authority for your reasoning. A large majority of this research should be from recognised sources. You can access primary sources of legislation and case law through the online databases that your law school subscribes to (Westlaw and/or Lexis). You can access good secondary sources

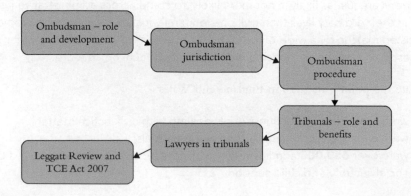

Figure 14.1 Structure of Chapter 14

---

2   Annual Report, HM Courts and Tribunals Service 2014–15.

of books and journals through your recommended textbook, the library and also through Westlaw/Lexis and other online databases.

The key message is that you should normally give Google (or other general search engines) a miss. Its usefulness in legal research is residual and limited. Use it to find recent stories from quality newspapers, quality legal blogs such as Public Law for Everyone and the UK Constitutional Law Association blog,[3] and not much else. One exception is official institutions and publications. These are particularly useful for this topic, and you would do yourself a real favour by reviewing the sites of the Parliamentary Ombudsman and the HM Courts and Tribunals Service before undertaking any assessment. They can give you excellent insights, up-to-date information and evidence your initiative in researching beyond your formal reading list.

14.2 OMBUDSMEN

The former Parliamentary Ombudsman Ann Abraham gives a typical example of the sort of complaint received by ombudsmen.[4]

APPLYING THE LAW – ADMINISTRATIVE MISTAKES

Ms M's address details were held by a number of different Government agencies, including, unsurprisingly, HM Revenue & Customs, the Child Support Agency and the Department for Work and Pensions. In 2006 her personal details were wrongly changed on one Government agency's computer system to show her living at her former partner's address. In fact, she had never lived there. With alarming efficiency, these false personal details instantaneously spread across an entire network of Government computer systems and before long had fallen into the hands of her former partner. As a result, her child support entitlement was incorrectly reassessed and reduced without her knowledge.

When my office investigated Ms M's complaint we found it likely that her details had been incorrectly changed by the Tax Credit Office and then passed to other agencies' computer systems by the linked-in computer network. But none of the bodies involved would accept responsibility, preferring instead to pass the buck to one another and, somewhat chillingly, arguing that since the mistake had been

3   Public Law for Everyone, http://publiclawforeveryone.com/; UK Constitutional Law Association, http://ukconstitu tionallaw.org/blog/ (last accessed 03/11/17).
4   Abraham, above n 1.

made by 'the system' there was nothing they could do about it. We disagreed and recommended that HMRC pay her £2,000 compensation and correct the false entry on 'the system'.

Just as importantly, we also recommended that the three agencies concerned work with the Cabinet Office to decide how to respond in future to complaints of this sort which cross organisational boundaries. And that the Cabinet Office take steps to ensure that lessons are learned from Ms M's experience and that appropriate guidance is disseminated to all Government departments.

One of the overall themes of this book is that of power and the state and the need to establish a fair balance between the mighty state and the ordinary person. In recommending the establishment of a UK ombudsman, Lord Shawcross wrote in 1961 that:

With the existence of a great bureaucracy there are inevitably occasions, not insignificant in number, when through error or indifference, injustice is done . . . too often the little man, the ordinary humble citizen, is incapable of asserting himself . . . The little man has become too used to being pushed around; it rarely occurs to him that there is any appeal from what 'they have decided'.[5]

There is a need for limits on state power and for mechanisms to prevent abuse of that power. The focus in other chapters has been on a mix of legal and political constraints provided in the UK's uncodified constitution, for example the constitutional accountability of Ministers to Parliament, or legal claims under the judicial review procedure. This leaves a gap, however, of situations where the public body is not necessarily breaching the law, or politically momentous constitutional rules are not at stake, but where public bodies are not treating citizens well and there are negative human impacts. This may involve, for example, delayed welfare payments, or a failure to respond to a reasonable request for information.

The report that ultimately led to the establishment of the UK Parliamentary Ombudsman describes the sort of situations that the Ombudsman would be uniquely placed to help: 'relatively minor complaints, not sufficient in themselves to attract public interest, but nevertheless of great importance to the individuals concerned'.[6]

The best way for you to get a sense of the type of problems that the various ombudsmen deal with is by looking at the case summaries on their websites. The Parliamentary Ombudsman had produced a nice video summary of one example, where a Mrs G suffered loss as a result of an error by the Legal Services Commission and the Commission refused to fully reimburse her: https://www.youtube.com/watch?v=R2__c8qBpSQ.

----

5   JUSTICE, 'The citizen and the Administration' (1961) (known as the Whyatt Report); foreword by Lord Shawcross.
6   Ibid., para.76.

This is a typical case but not the only type. There are many complaints to the Health Ombudsman which, by their nature, involve very serious quality of life issues and even life or death decisions. The Parliamentary Ombudsman can reveal systemic failures affecting thousands of people.

These failures come under the heading of **maladministration** rather than illegality. The role of the ombudsman is broadly to help citizens suffering from the effects of poor administration and to improve the quality of public body operations. Bradley and Ewing sum this up as 'On one view, the essence of the ombudsman idea for the ordinary person is accessibility, flexibility, informality and humanity. On another view, the Ombudsman provides an authoritative means of "judging" the conduct of faceless officials and bureaucracies, thus helping to develop *systems* of administration that are both humane and effective'.[7]

Administrative justice can be said to carry out two roles: first, to deliver justice to the individual and, second, as a consequence, to keep public bodies in line and 'on their toes' and contribute to the development of good governance. Judicial review can achieve things, but the ombudsman's role is far more explicit and direct in addressing this second role of promoting good administrative practice. The ombudsman can and does make wider recommendations on e.g. communicating with the public and administering compensation schemes. Dame Julie Mellor, former Parliamentary Ombudsman, explains that people who approach the Ombudsman generally want three things:

(a)   an explanation for what went wrong,
(b)   an apology and
(c)   to prevent it happening to someone else.

In preventing the maladministration from happening again, the ombudsman can contribute to creating an effective and responsive public service, and Mellor talks about an ongoing and collaborative relationship with Parliament and public bodies.[8]

14.3 OMBUDSMAN – DEVELOPMENT AND ROLE

The ombudsman is a Scandinavian idea. The first ombudsman was created in Sweden over 200 years ago, followed by Finland and Denmark (whose ombudsman had a strong influence on the adoption of the position in the UK). The creation of an ombudsman in New Zealand in 1962 showed it could work within a Westminster-style system of government. The influential Whyatt Report in 1961 reviewed all the existing ombudsman schemes and recommended a complaints system along the lines eventually adopted, but it was not until the Parliamentary Commissioner Act 1967 (PCA 1967) that the office was created.

---

7   A Bradley and K Ewing, *Constitutional and Administrative Law* (15th edn, Longman, 2011) 659.
8   J Mellor, 'The Constitutional Role of the Parliamentary and Health Service Ombudsman', speech at UCL Constitution Unit (17 April 2013), https://vimeo.com/64628880 (last accessed 03/11/17).

There has subsequently been a proliferation of ombudsman roles for different parts of the state, and the principles have been adopted to resolve conflicts and handle complaints in the commercial world as well (for example financial services ombudsmen, a Removal Industry Ombudsman Scheme). These ombudsmen are intended to be complementary to the existing system for addressing grievances, including court action, tribunals and political means such as a direct complaint to a minister.

As we outline the role and operations of the Parliamentary Ombudsman we need to keep in mind the alleged benefits of the role and possible shortcomings of the particular ombudsman model adopted in the UK. The key benefits are cost, accessibility, flexible procedures, and independence. The key potential shortcomings are around the jurisdiction of the ombudsman, the MP filter, the lack of enforcement powers and the sketchiness of the central concept of 'maladministration'.

The location of the ombudsman in the scheme of the UK constitutional system is interesting. It occupies 'a novel place in the constitution alongside other non-political, non-legal and non-executive branches of the state designed to improve and uphold the accountability and integrity of Government'.[9] The most important of the ombudsman schemes, the Parliamentary Ombudsman, was created as an extension of Parliament, not part of the executive, but Mellor places it in the middle of the three great branches of state (legislative, executive, judicial). Ultimately, its location needs to be defined by its role, which according to the Prime Minister who introduced it, Harold Wilson, is 'to humanise the administration and to improve relations between Westminster on one hand and the individual citizen on the other'.[10]

14.4 THE PARLIAMENTARY OMBUDSMAN

There was some nervousness in the 1960s about the wholesale import of a foreign constitutional concept, so the ombudsman was formally styled as the Parliamentary Commissioner for Administration. This is still the official title of the office, but it has been commonly known as the Parliamentary Ombudsman for years, and this is the title used in all reports and communications by the Parliamentary Ombudsman themselves: so this is the term adopted here.

The Parliamentary Ombudsman is appointed by the Crown (i.e. by Government but with consultation with Parliament) for a period of seven years. The Ombudsman's role is to investigate complaints that individuals have been treated unfairly or have received poor service from Government departments, other public organisations or the NHS in England.[11]

---

9 T Buck, R Kirkham and B Thompson, 'Time for a "Leggatt-style" Review of the Ombudsman System' [2011] *Public Law* 20, 22.

10 Mellor, above n 8.

11 Parliamentary Ombudsman, 'Who We Are', http://www.ombudsman.org.uk/about-us/who-we-are/the-ombudsman (last accessed 03/11/17).

Health matters and the NHS were originally outside of the Parliamentary Ombudsman scheme. A health ombudsman scheme was created in 1993,[12] but has always been held by the same person and in practice is now fully integrated with the work of the Parliamentary Ombudsman and their office.

14.5 JURISDICTION

The Parliamentary Ombudsman has power to investigate complaints, relating to a very wide range of Government departments and statutory and prerogative public bodies, including for example the Environment Agency, the Higher Education Funding Council and the Child Support Agency (section 5 PCA 1967). Rather than using a general test of what is a 'public body' or 'public authority', as happens in judicial review and human rights law, the relevant bodies are simply listed in a Schedule to the PCA 1967. This has the advantage of side-stepping the very difficult definitional questions that have dogged the public/private divide in other areas, but it does mean that the Schedule needs constant updating to keep pace with changes in institutional arrangements. In practical terms, you can simply go the Ombudsman website and see if the body you want to complain about is on their list.[13]

14.5.1 LIMITS ON JURISDICTION

There are certain institutions and issues that cannot be investigated by the Parliamentary Ombudsman. Two of the most important limits, on devolved matters in Scotland, Wales and Northern Ireland and in relation to local authorities, are due to the existence of separate ombudsmen schemes. There are other jurisdictional limits based on the sensitive nature of the institution or issue. The Ombudsman cannot hear complaints about international relations, extradition, action taken to investigate crime or protect national security, disciplinary and personnel matters in the civil service and armed forces, or the granting of honours (section 5(3) PCA 1967). Specific bodies including the Prime Minister's Office and Cabinet Office, the Bank of England and tribunals are beyond the Ombudsman's jurisdiction.

The Ombudsman cannot conduct an investigation where the person aggrieved has, or had, a right of appeal or reference to a tribunal or to a remedy through court proceedings (section 5(2) PCA 1967). This limit could cause problems. The Ombudsman is a possible avenue to justice and is easy to access and free. It seems unfair to prevent an individual from using this service because they have a right to use a court that is useless or very difficult for them, on the basis of the cost, complexity and time involved in much litigation. The limitation in section 5 of the Act is interpreted flexibly. Where a legal action would be disproportionately lengthy or expensive in relation to the harm suffered, then the Ombudsman will be willing to deal with the complaint. The basic question is whether a

---

12 Health Service Commissioners Act 1993.

13 Parliamentary Ombudsman, 'How to Complain', https://www.ombudsman.org.uk/making-complaint (last accessed 03/11/17).

court would be the more appropriate forum for a complaint to proceed (*R v Commissioner for Local Administration, ex parte Croydon London Borough Council* [1989] 1 All ER 1033).

The availability of other types of avenues to justice is also relevant. These are not formal limits on jurisdiction but they influence whether the Ombudsman will choose to investigate a complaint. The Ombudsman Assessment Code says it will consider if another agency would be better placed to deal with the complaint, e.g. Independent Police Complaints Commission or General Medical Council. Further, a person 'should' (or 'must') complain first to the public body, and where there is an opportunity for a second internal review of the complaint (a 'second tier'), as there is for e.g. the Child Support Agency and JobCentre Plus, then this must be taken.[14]

Complaints must be brought within a time limit of 12 months from the date when the person first had 'notice of the matters alleged in the complaint', i.e. from when they became aware of the issue rather than when the cause for complaint arose (section 6(3) PCA 1967). There is a 'special circumstances' exception.

One of the most important limits on the jurisdiction of the Ombudsman is that the complaint must be one of maladministration causing injustice and *not* about the merits of the decision. This leads to many complaints being rejected.

Jurisdictional limits	Other ombudsman schemes	Devolved institutions; local government
	Sensitive subject matter	International relations; extradition; national security; honours
	Alternative remedy	Right of appeal to a court or tribunal
	Discretion to reject	Another agency is better placed; internal review options
	Nature of the role	Only investigate maladministration not merits

Figure 14.2 Jurisdictional limits

14.5.2 THE MP FILTER

As things stand, the Parliamentary Ombudsman can only receive complaints that have been referred by a Member of Parliament – the MP filter. Section 5(1) of the PCA 1967 states that the Ombudsman must first check to see if 'a written complaint is duly made to [an MP] by a member of the public who claims to have suffered injustice in consequence of maladministration'. You cannot complain directly to the Parliamentary Ombudsman.

....

14 Parliamentary Ombudsman, 'How we deal with complaints', https://www.ombudsman.org.uk/making-complaint/how-we-deal-complaints (last accessed 03/11/17).

The MP filter is an anachronism and the numerous calls to abolish it are finally being acted upon. A draft Public Service Ombudsman Bill was published in December 2016, containing provisions to end the MP filter. If and when the Bill is passed, it will allow complainants to go directly to the Ombudsman. MPs will still potentially be involved, as they can be authorised by the complainant to act on their behalf. As of October 2017, however, no timetable for proceeding with the Bill has been published and there is a risk that the Bill will be pushed down the list of political priorities as Brexit comes closer.

The filter was only ever intended to be a temporary measure of around five years to allow MPs, public bodies and the general public to adjust to the new roles, yet it is still in place almost 50 years later. Its durability can be explained by the fact that some MPs have been keen to retain this role as it keeps them in touch with the issues affecting their constituents which they can then champion. It does allow an MP to try to resolve the matter for their constituent e.g. through direct communication with the relevant body or through raising the matter with ministers. More cynically, it allows MPs to take credit for resolving disputes when the 'behind the scenes' work has been done by the Ombudsman; the practice up until 2002 was for the Ombudsman to send the report to the MP who would have the sole honour of delivering the solution to their constituent. Governments may also be reluctant to remove the filter and widen access to a process that scrutinises the executive.

The weight of opinion and argument is firmly against retention. It is bureaucratic, and the character and views of a particular MP can influence whether a constituent feels able to approach them and whether they are willing to pass a complaint on to the Ombudsman. Mellor estimates that 'at least 20% more people would come to us if there was direct access as well'. This is based on the experience of removing similar filters in relation to other ombudsman schemes.[15]

The Ombudsman's report on direct access pointed out that 'Redress systems should not be designed for the ease and comfort of the bodies complained about, for political representatives, or even those, like the ombudsman and courts, who make decisions about disputes. They should be designed with [the public] in mind'.[16]

14.6 PARLIAMENTARY OMBUDSMAN – PROCEDURE

The Ombudsman must decide if the complaint is within their jurisdiction and whether a full formal investigation is necessary. In practice, there is an emphasis on local resolution and on 'putting it right' in ways which are flexible and focused on the needs of the

---

15 Mellor, above n 8.

16 Report on the consultation on direct access to the Parliamentary Ombudsman (2011), https://www.ombudsman.org. uk/publications/consultation-responses (last accessed 03/11/17).

complainant. The Ombudsman Assessment Code says: 'We also look to getting complaints resolved quickly without the need to investigate whenever possible'. The Ombudsman will depart from this flexible resolution and undertake a full formal investigation depending on the facts or, where there is an issue of potentially avoidable death, wider public interest or serious failures.[17]

The departments and persons concerned must be given 'an opportunity to comment on any allegations contained in the complaint' (section 7 PCA 1967). Under section 8 of the PCA 1967 the Ombudsman can *require* bodies and persons (including ministers) 'to furnish information or produce documents relevant to the investigation', and obstructing the Ombudsman in the performance of their functions is treated in the same way as a contempt of court (section 9).

The investigative method is private and inquisitorial, and so is very different to court proceedings. The Ombudsman sends their finalised reports to the MP and to the body and persons concerned in the complaint. They can also lay a special report before Parliament if injustices have been caused by maladministration 'and that the injustice has not been, or will not be, remedied' (section 10 PCA 1967).

Kirkham and Thompson have raised concerns that this 'ombudsman model' of investigation is under threat from judicial review challenges to ombudsman reports.[18] They cite, in particular, *JR55 v Northern Ireland Commissioner for Complaints* [2016] UKSC 22. Their fears that the Northern Ireland Court of Appeal judgment against the Commissioner would be upheld by the Supreme Court were borne out. The Supreme Court, however, stressed that their findings were limited to the special circumstances of the Northern Ireland scheme and did not apply to UK Parliamentary Ombudsman, (aside from some more general comments on the need for ombudsmen to base any recommendation for financial recompense on a rational basis.) The distinctive 'ombudsman model' was clearly recognised in *Miller v Parliamentary and Health Service Ombudsman* [2016] EWHC 2981 (Admin), where the Administrative Court confirmed that the Health Service Ombudsman could recommend compensation. It also rejected arguments that would have imposed a more legalistic approach on ombudsman investigation methods, such as applying legal tests of medical culpability.

14.6.1 ENFORCEMENT

There is no power to enforce the findings or recommendations in Ombudsman reports. In the usual course of events, the Ombudsman findings are accepted and acted upon by the public body. The Ombudsman can suggest but not order a change of decision or other remedy (such as an ex gratia payment), and where a specific remedy is recommended, then this is granted, in Mellor's estimate, 99.99 per cent of the time.[19] Even in the absence

17 Parliamentary Ombudsman Assessment Code, above n 14.

18 R Kirkham and B Thompson, 'Judicial Neutering of the Powers of the Ombudsman' U.K. Const. L. Blog (10 Nov 2015), https://ukconstitutionallaw.org/ (last accessed 03/11/17).

19 Mellor, above n 8.

of systemic recommendations, the expectation will be that the organisation will take due notice of the finding of maladministration and make whatever changes are needed to avoid a similar finding in the future.

Public bodies, however, do not always accept the Ombudsman's findings or recommendations. The role of the Department for Work and Pensions in the winding up of some final salary occupational pension schemes caused some tension between the Government and the Ombudsman. The failure of the pension schemes affected up to 125,000 people who suffered often very significant losses. They claimed that the Secretary of State had provided poor and misleading information which amounted to maladministration. The Ombudsman investigated and laid a special report before Parliament agreeing that there was maladministration and recommending some recompense for those affected. The Secretary of State rejected most of these findings and refused to pay out to the people affected. This was challenged through judicial review.

KEY CASE – *R (BRADLEY) V WORK AND PENSIONS SECRETARY* [2008] EWCA CIV 36

The Court of Appeal held that there was nothing in the PCA 1967 that required the minister (or any public body) to accept the Ombudsman's findings on maladministration. The minister could prefer their own view, but any rejection of the Ombudsman findings had to be rational and this required the minister to provide a reason. In this case, the minister had not provided adequate reasons for rejecting some of the findings, and in relation to these findings had acted irrationally.

The House of Commons Public Administration Select Committee is a further lever to promote the acceptance and application of the Ombudsman's findings. It holds the Parliamentary Ombudsman to account, but can also call on ministers and others to account for any failure or delay in accepting and applying recommendations. It is accepted that imposing a legal obligation on public bodies to accept findings and recommendations would be unwise; it is better to focus on making the political levers more formal and more effective.

Abraham has discussed the need to 'resist the onslaught of judicialisation',[20] and if an adversarial relationship developed between the Ombudsman and public bodies that would undermine many of the flexible problem-solving benefits of the scheme. After the Department for Agriculture initially rejected some findings on complaints about a farm payments scheme, the chair of the Public Administration Select Committee said, 'These arguments at times seem to be based on a misunderstanding, and at other times

---

20 Abraham, above n 1.

seem to be predicated on taking an adversarial rather than a common-sense, compassionate approach to people who have undoubtedly suffered injustice as a result of the Department's administrative failings'.[21] Ultimately, the department responded to the Select Committee's promptings and acted in line with the Ombudsman recommendation. The Public Administration Select Committee recommended in 2009 that Government resistance to accepting or implementing an Ombudsman report should trigger a three-hour Commons debate, but this has not been adopted.

14.6.2 MALADMINISTRATION

There is no definition of 'maladministration' in statute, although it is clearly wider than the legal grounds for judicial review. In the Japanese internment case, the claimants brought a judicial review action (*R (Association of British Civilian Internees: Far East Region) v Secretary of State for Defence* [2003] EWCA Civ 473) on grounds of breach of a legitimate expectation. The court found that the Government announcement of a compensation scheme was not sufficiently precise to generate a legitimate expectation, and so the legal action failed. Those affected by the shortcomings in the scheme complained to the Ombudsman, who concluded that there had been maladministration in the Ministry of Defence.

The most widely quoted approach is the non-definitive outline given by Richard Crossman, the minister who introduced the role in 1967: 'including bias, neglect, inattention, delay, incompetence, ineptitude, perversity, turpitude, arbitrariness and so on'.[22] Maladministration is found in the way in which decisions are taken and people are treated as part of that process, rather than the outcome of the decision and its merits, and the Act confirms that the Ombudsman cannot 'question the merits of a decision taken without maladministration' (section 12(3) PCA 1967).

The term is vague and opaque, and this may be a barrier to public engagement with the ombudsman scheme. The Ombudsman has attempted to demarcate and demystify the term by spelling out six principles of good administration:[23]

1   Getting it right.
2   Being customer-focused.
3   Being open and accountable.
4   Acting fairly and proportionately.
5   Putting things right.
6   Seeking continuous improvement.

---

21 Defra's response to the Ombudsman's report on the Single Payment Scheme HC 331 (2009–2010). Letter from Tony Wright, chair of PASC (4 February 2010), as cited in Buck, Kirkham and Thompson, above n 9.

22 Official Reports HC 734 col 51.

23 Parliamentary Ombudsman, 'Principles of Good Administration', http://www.ombudsman.org.uk/improving-public-service/ombudsmansprinciples/principles-of-good-administration (last accessed 03/11/17).

This list illuminates the constitutional role of the Ombudsman, lying in the space between the main branches of the state. The need to act 'fairly and proportionately', for example, is a classic legal concept. The way in which it is applied by the Ombudsman will differ from judicial applications, but will have the same roots. The objective of 'being customer-focused' is very much in the administrative realm (and is really the language of consumer relationships) covering e.g. rudeness. The office of the Ombudsman, in its role of promoting good governance and reducing complaints, has also produced good practice guides on 'good complaint handling' and 'principles for remedy'. Abrahams describes this as carving out a distinctive niche that complements other forms of remedy and accountability and creates 'the foundations of what might be described as a form of "Ombudsprudence" in which principles not rules are normative'.[24]

14.6.3 INJUSTICE

The Ombudsman focuses on maladministration that causes injustice, but this is interpreted very broadly. Whilst it might be impolite and a source of frustration if a public body does not keep you informed of progress when they are handling a decision with important effects on your life, you could not normally have any remedy for that in a court of law. The Ombudsman's jurisdiction, however, covers 'the sense of outrage aroused by unfair or incompetent administration, even though the complainant has suffered no actual *loss*' (*R v Parliamentary Commissioner for Administration, ex parte Balchin (No 1)* [1997] JPL 917).

14.7 OTHER OMBUDSMEN

Local Government – the Local Government Act 1972 established a Commission for Local Administration in England. This is now known as the Local Government Ombudsman (LGO). There are three LGO ombudsmen covering geographical areas of England. Their work also covers police authorities and other local public bodies that work in partnership with local authorities. Citizens can complain directly to the LGO but must first notify the relevant local authority. The LGO can recommend a remedy but not enforce it. LGOs deal with a diverse range of issues, but most complaints are around housing, education admissions and adult social care. Section 31 Local Government Act 1972 makes it clear that, as for the Parliamentary Ombudsman, the public bodies need only to take note of reports that highlight maladministration that has caused *injustice*.

The devolution ombudsmen – there are separate ombudsmen schemes for the devolved institutions in Scotland, Wales and Northern Ireland. The Scottish Public Service Ombudsman covers all devolved issues including the Scottish Executive. There is a Public Service Ombudsman for Wales, and an Assembly Ombudsman for Northern Ireland. A key feature of these schemes is that they are integrated (the Northern Irish one only partially), meaning they cover both national/assembly matters and all local government issues.

---

24 Abrahams, above n 1.

Public sector – There are a range of other public sector ombudsmen covering sectors such as legal services, information, and pensions.

14.8 REFORM

The Ombudsman system, in its varying forms, has clearly contributed a great deal to administrative justice and the promotion of good governance over the last half-century. There is, however, scope for useful reform. We saw above that there are significant areas of public activity that are outside of the jurisdiction of the Parliamentary Ombudsman, many of which were written into the scheme back in the 1960s when there was anxiety about the place of an ombudsman in the UK constitutional system. Those fears are allayed and a review of jurisdiction is overdue. There is also fragmentation and overlap in the number of different ombudsman schemes operating in the public sector. This was partially addressed by the requirement for better co-operation and co-ordination under the Regulatory Reform (Collaboration etc between Ombudsmen) Order 2007 (SI 2007/1889), but this reduces rather than eliminates difficulties.

As noted above, further reforms do seem to be in train. The Public Services Ombudsman Bill, announced in the Queen's Speech in May 2015, was published in draft in December 2016. It proposes integrating the offices and functions of the Parliamentary Ombudsman with the Local Government Ombudsmen into a single Public Services Ombudsman. If the Bill had followed the other recommendations of the Gordon Review, it would have granted this single Public Service Ombudsman an extended jurisdiction, covering some of the excluded areas, and including 'any organisation delivering public services on behalf of a public body'.[25] The draft Bill, however, retains the jurisdictional limit to 'designated authorities' and retains a large list of 'excluded matters' (Schedule 4).

One important recommendation in the Gordon Report was to grant the Ombudsman 'own initiative' powers, i.e. they could launch their own investigations. This power would be most important for those who are less likely to be able to make a coherent written complaint themselves: people in psychiatric hospital, children in immigration custody, etc. As seen in the Jimmy Saville scandals and more contemporary sexual grooming cases, some of those most in need, and who are often hard to reach, have been given low status and betrayed by the failures of administrative bodies (and those governmental bodies that decide their priorities and funding levels). Abrahams argues that 'The ability to . . . seize the initiative, to catch a whiff of scandal and run with it, is now a necessity not a luxury, especially if social justice is to reach some of the most vulnerable and marginalised people in society'.[26] It is disappointing therefore that the draft Bill does not adopt this and would restrict the Ombudsman to responding to complaints from the public.

---

25 The Gordon Review, 'Better to Serve the Public: Proposals to restructure, reform, renew and reinvigorate public service ombudsmen', https://www.gov.uk/government/publications/governance-review-of-the-local-government-ombudsman-service (last accessed 03/11/17).

26 Abrahams, above n 1.

- Ombudsmen have an important role in administrative justice distinct from other branches.
- The Parliamentary Ombudsman investigates public bodies on findings of maladministration causing injustice.
- Their jurisdiction is subject to quite wide exceptions and an MP filter, with further issues around enforcement of findings.
- Reform of the MP filter and a more integrated ombudsman service are likely to be introduced.

14.9 TRIBUNALS

Here is just one example of what tribunals do.

The UK has committed itself in international law to providing support for refugees. When someone arrives in the UK seeking asylum on the basis of fear of persecution in their home country, they can, if they have followed all of the correct procedures, ask for **asylum support**. This will give them housing and some money whilst they are waiting to find out if their asylum application has been successful. It also gives them access to the NHS and schooling for their children.

The Asylum Support chamber is part of the First-tier Tribunal. Its role is to hear appeals against Home Office decisions to reject a claim for asylum support or cancel existing asylum support.

APPLYING THE LAW – CASE ASA/02/12/5224[27]

The appellant was an asylum seeker from the Democratic Republic of Congo, who had independent medical evidence outlining the physical and mental injuries supporting his claims that he had been tortured in his home country. The Home Office has a dispersal policy to stop an over-concentration of asylum seekers in London, and the internal recommendation was that he be sent to Birmingham. He could mix with other Congolese people and speakers of his language, Lingala. The Home Office then further dispersed him to Wrexham in North Wales, where there were no other people from his country or language group. He suffered an assault and robbery incident, which was probably directed at him because of his race or asylum-seeker status.

---

27 Case Report, Asylum Support Tribunal, http://www.asylum-support-tribunal.gov.uk/public/view.aspx?ID=7395 (last accessed 03/11/17).

The medical evidence said that his isolation in Wrexham was adding to his mental problems. He temporarily left Wrexham to return to Birmingham for 'respite' from his attack. Leaving an allocated address without permission is a lawful ground for the Home Office to withdraw asylum support, which is what the Home Office did. This decision left him with no money, nowhere to live and no means of making money (as asylum seekers cannot work).

He appealed the decision to the Tribunal. The Home Office had given no reasons for his move to Wrexham, which went against their own internal advice. The Tribunal Chair looked at the merits of the decision and decided that the Home Office had got it wrong. He remitted the decision back to them but directed that the appellant's asylum support should be restored and that the Home Office should support his stay in Birmingham (or another area with a Congolese/Lingala community).

There are some key issues to bear in mind, and explore during assessments, including their independence, coherence and status, but the overarching issue for us as Public Law students is this: does the tribunal system contribute as effectively as it could to resolving problems that arise between citizens and the state?

The significance of tribunals to this fundamental relationship is highlighted by Elliott and Thomas who said, 'When viewed collectively, tribunals comprise the most important component of the legal system for ensuring legality in respect of the mass of front-line decision-making that characterises modern government'.[28]

14.10 THE ROLE OF TRIBUNALS

APPLYING THE LAW – DEFINING TRIBUNALS

A tribunal is a body which is permanent, and adjudicatory, i.e. it resolves disputes as to law and fact and makes decisions which are binding on the parties. Think about this definition: isn't this really what courts are and what they do? This definition gives us an indication of the nature and role of tribunals but does not adequately distinguish them from what seem to be a distinct group of institution – the courts.

In *Attorney General v BBC* [1981] AC 303, the House of Lords said, 'I would identify a court . . . as a body established by law to exercise . . . the judicial power of the state.

28 M Elliott and R Thomas, *Public Law* (3rd edn, OUP, 2017) 683.

In this context judicial power is to be contrasted with legislative and executive (i.e. administrative) power. If the body under review is established for a purely legislative or administrative purpose, it is part of the legislative or administrative system of the state, even though it has to perform duties which are judicial in character'.

Does this help? A tribunal can be a body carrying out judicial-type functions, but it is not a court because it is part of the administrative system of the state. This seems a process of designation, or labelling, rather than a fundamental difference.

As Adler says, 'there is a degree of overlap between courts and tribunals in that some tribunals, e.g. employment tribunals, have characteristics that are commonly associated with courts and some courts, e.g. small claims courts, have characteristics that are commonly associated with tribunals'.[29] There are some differences. Tribunals tend to be more specialist than the generalist courts (although this is a matter of degree – there are e.g. family and administrative court divisions). Tribunals tend to be simpler, cheaper and less adversarial than courts with fewer applicants having legal representation.

The main role of the courts in administrative justice is in reviewing the *legality* of public body decisions, so it is important to remember that tribunals are *appeal* bodies, i.e. they can look at the merits of the decision (though some have judicial review jurisdiction). We can see this in the Congolese asylum support case. The tribunal was not limited to assessing the lawfulness of the Home Office decision; it could decide that the initial decision-maker had got their decision wrong. This is not something that the courts can do in judicial review proceedings.

14.11 DEVELOPMENT

The first tribunals were introduced in the eighteenth century, but the most important trigger to their development has always been an expansion of the state. Histories of tribunals often highlights the controls introduced during the Second World War, the subsequent rationing of resources and then the introduction of the welfare state by the 1945–51 Labour administration. The expansion of the state, however, really started much earlier in the century and was accompanied by a large increase in the number and remit of tribunals. These tribunals were needed because of the greater interaction between citizens and state. As the state was providing more entitlements, such as old-age pensions and imposing greater controls, such as land-use planning controls, then the scope for, and volume of, legal disputes increased.

---

29 M Adler, 'Recent developments in the tribunals world' cited in Elliott and Thomas, above n 28, 724.

For a long time, the development of tribunals was very piecemeal. As a new statutory scheme was developed, for example on agricultural subsidies, then a new specific tribunal would be established to hear disputes arising from that scheme. There was no template, so each tribunal would have its own jurisdiction, rules of composition and procedures. These questions were normally decided by the relevant Government department that would go on to administer and fund 'their' tribunal.

The range of areas where tribunals have operated is very diverse (there is still a Pathogens Access Appeals Commission) but the main areas have been health, welfare, immigration and asylum, tax, employment and pensions. Our focus in this half of the chapter is on the large majority of tribunals that handle 'administrative justice', i.e. disputes between the citizen and state, rather than the minority, particularly employment tribunals, which deal with disputes between individuals.

14.11.1 THE FRANKS REPORT

Following rising concerns about the quality and integrity of public body decision-making in the 1950s, as illuminated by the Crichel Down affair (see Chapter 5, 'Constitutional conventions'), the Committee on Administrative Tribunals and Enquiries was established. It published its report, universally called the Franks Report, in 1957,[30] which identified three principal and linked characteristics.

- Openness – required 'the publicity of proceedings and knowledge of the essential reasoning underlying the decisions'.
- Fairness – meant 'the adoption of a clear procedure which enables parties to know their rights, to present their case fully and to know the case which they have to meet'.
- Impartiality – was 'the freedom of tribunals from the influence, real or apparent, of departments concerned with the subject-matter of their decisions'.

The Franks Report said that 'tribunals should be independent, accessible, prompt, expert, informal, and cheap'. It recommended wider (but not universal) rights of appeal from tribunals, on a point of law, to the High Court.

14.12 BENEFITS OF TRIBUNALS

Tribunals deal with legal disputes. These are very diverse. Many cases are not particularly factually complex or involve difficult questions of legal interpretation, however tribunals deal with one of the most complex and high-stakes legal questions – asylum – which involves deciding whether someone claiming persecution can find asylum in the UK or have to be returned to their home country where, they allege, they are at risk of serious

---

30 Cmnd 218.

harm or death. Whether the parents of a child with a serious disability can require their local authority to provide special education support is sometimes terribly difficult to establish both on (contested versions of) the facts and the vexed legal question of whether the public decision-maker has reached the right decision. That is, many of these disputes could very naturally be heard in a court. What is it about tribunals that make them a better forum for some types of disputes?

Cost – Tribunals, unlike courts, have no direct fees for bringing a case. It is very unusual for any costs order to be made (i.e. requiring the losing party to pay the representation costs of the winning party). This is a result of the reduced need for legal representation in tribunals, but also of their speed and informality.

Speed – if your welfare benefits have been sanctioned and you are searching for the nearest food bank so that you can feed your children for the coming week, then the speed in which you challenge that decision becomes of central importance. The supposedly higher quality of justice that results from formal exchanges of evidence, advice by legal professionals and adjudication in one of Her Majesty's courts of law fades in priority. This need for speed is just as relevant to e.g. mental health and care standards, which includes restricting people from working with or caring for children or vulnerable adults. The relative speed of tribunals (which is far from perfect but is as subject to resource constraints as any other part of the public sector) can be attributed to their specialisation and informal procedure.

Informality – you can probably see by now that these benefits are highly interrelated. You should note, therefore, that changing one attribute of tribunals is more than likely to have implications for these other attributes, for example the wider use of lawyers. The relative informality of tribunals can be a characteristic of their physical environment; they are less imposing and intimidating than courts, which are often designed to express the full majesty of the law. It is seen in the clothes that tribunal members wear, and in the buildings and the rooms where hearings take place. Procedures are also less formal, e.g. tribunals do not make witnesses take oaths, and they try to directly involve the applicant in the proceedings.

The level of formality varies amongst tribunals, e.g. it is a part of the ingrained culture of the Asylum and Immigration Tribunal to be adversarial and legal representation is more common. Others adopt a more discursive round-table approach where the applicant can participate without specialist representation.

Elliott and Thomas argue that this informality can be 'a trap for unwary appellants'.[31] Ultimately, a tribunal is involved in a legal process of establishing material facts, identifying legal rules and ensuring that the law is applied correctly to the facts. It is not about dispensing justice (whatever that might appear to be in the eyes of the tribunal) regardless of the law.

---

31 Elliott and Thomas, above n 28, 706.

Accessibility – informality is also linked to accessibility. The Leggatt Report said that 'It should never be forgotten that tribunals exist for users, and not the other way round', so tribunals need to be 'understandable, unthreatening, and useful to users'. There are still problems around citizens' knowledge of appeal rights, and the whole process can still seem very daunting. There is the need to gather evidence, the prospect of 'taking on' a Government department, and the uncertain costs of time and energy, together with a suspicion (often unfounded) that a challenge will not make much practical difference in the end.

To promote accessibility, the Traffic Penalty Tribunal has used phone hearings for some time. It has also produced videos demonstrating the process of applying to the Tribunal and giving 'real world' examples of the sorts of things that it can deal with and how in appropriate cases it can help citizens.[32] Whilst most other tribunals, e.g. the Asylum Support chamber, have produced textual run-throughs of the process, they lag behind the willingness of the Traffic Penalty Tribunal to reach out to those who may be entitled to use their services.

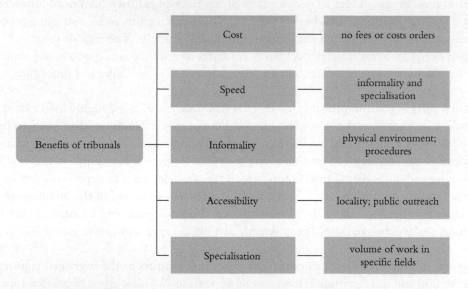

Figure 14.3 The benefits of tribunals

Specialisation – each tribunal or tribunal chamber has a relatively narrow subject matter, and the tribunal members build up a deep understanding of the law and practice within that field. Some tribunal members have specialist subject knowledge, e.g. mental health. A wider consequence of the work of tribunals is that they reduce the volume of cases before the courts, so allowing the higher courts to focus on what they are specialist in – deciding difficult questions of legal interpretation in cases of wider public importance.

---

32 Traffic Penalty Tribunal, https://www.trafficpenaltytribunal.gov.uk/ (last accessed 02/11/17).

14.13 THE ROLE OF LAWYERS?

Questions arise as to whether lawyers have any role to play in tribunal justice. There seem to be strong arguments for their inclusion when the stakes are high for the applicant. Mental health tribunals decide questions of liberty. Asylum and immigration tribunals decide whether someone is genuinely fleeing persecution, risk of serious harm and even death in their home country or whether they ought to be returned to that country.

Many areas of the substantive Administrative Law that tribunals apply are complex, making it very challenging for some applicants to adequately represent themselves. The appellant will almost always be unfamiliar with the processes and language used in the tribunal process. In some cases, it will be impossible for the appellant to present their case and follow the proceedings properly, particularly in mental health, immigration and child cases.

The defendant, usually a Government department or public body, will be familiar with the process, context and even the personnel of the tribunal. Importantly, they will know the law in what is ultimately a legal adjudication process. They are used to defending claims, know the types of arguments presented by applicants and come to know the best ways of countering those. Even when a department is not legally represented, it will often use an internal reporting officer, someone with experience of the administrative field and the specifics of the tribunal process. This can leave a serious imbalance as between the applicant and the public body.

On the other hand, making it the norm that applicants have legal representation in tribunals would be in some respects counter-productive and in other respects impossible. Many of the benefits of tribunals identified above would be undermined. Processes would become more formal and legalistic, and proceedings would be slower. The overwhelming difficulty is cost. Tribunals hear a huge number of cases, so who would pay for the lawyers? Legal aid budgets, at their height, would never have been able to cover the cost, and those budgets have been cut very hard. Legal aid has never generally been available in tribunal cases, with some exceptions for asylum and immigration claims.

Whether or not there is a need for legal representation is intimately linked to the procedures adopted by the tribunal. An adversarial approach and culture is one where

- the parties bear the responsibility for presenting their own cases, and
- the focus is on beating their opponent's case, whilst
- the tribunal members do not intervene but simply weight how persuaded they are by the competing legal arguments.

This approach results in a greater need for legal representation. Tribunals had mostly been adversarial in their approach and this caused problems for unrepresented clients, because adversarialism raises serious 'equality of arms' issues.

The Leggatt Review (see below) was generally hostile to the notion of legal representation in tribunals (with strict exceptions), arguing that widespread representation would be disastrous for the distinctive and positive features of tribunals. It thought that it was the responsibility of the tribunal itself to arrange proceedings so that unrepresented appellants did not suffer and could present their case effectively.

Leggatt said that tribunals were 'intended to provide a simple, accessible system of justice where users can represent themselves. So it is discouraging to note the growing perception that they cannot. Every effort should be made to reduce the number of cases in which legal representation is needed'. This was a call for a move away from an adversarial approach to an *enabling approach*, involving the tribunal itself taking responsibility for the provision of information, for assistance from chairmen to users on presenting their case, and for providing comprehensible decisions. Representation is different from legal advice, and Leggatt recognised that pre-hearing advice could be very helpful and called for support for voluntary advice groups.[33]

The more enabling approach adopted by tribunals after the Leggatt Review, and subsequent reforms, seem to be making a difference. Influential research by Genn and Genn in the early 1990s had identified a 'representation premium', i.e. the positive difference that legal representation makes,[34] but a more recent survey by Adler for the Administrative Justice and Tribunals Council showed that this representation premium is now quite low.[35]

14.14 LEGGATT REVIEW
AND THE NEW SYSTEM

In 2000, the Government commissioned a review of the operation of tribunals. This reported in 2001 as the Leggatt Review of Tribunals – 'Tribunals for Users, One System One Service'.[36] By the time of the Review there were 70 different administrative tribunals, dealing with nearly one million cases a year, 'but of these 70 tribunals only 20 each hear more than 500 cases a year and many are defunct. Their quality varies from excellent to inadequate'. The Review was tasked with producing recommendations for 'fair, timely, proportionate and effective arrangements', consistency with the European Convention on Human Rights and that tribunals 'constitute a coherent structure for the delivery of administrative justice'.

The Leggatt Review was unusually penetrating and forceful in its investigation and recommendations, and Leggatt said that his objectives were:

- To make the 70 tribunals into one Tribunals System.
- To render the tribunals independent of their sponsoring departments by having them administered by one Tribunals Service.

33 The Leggatt Review (2001), ss 4 and 7, http://webarchive.nationalarchives.gov.uk/+/http://www.tribunals-review. org.uk/ (last accessed 03/11/17).

34 Cited in M Adler, 'Tribunals Ain't What They Used to Be' *Adjust Newsletter* (March 2009).

35 Ibid.

36 Leggatt Review, above n 33.

- To improve the training of chairmen and members in the interpersonal skills peculiarly required by tribunals.
- To enable unrepresented users to participate effectively and without apprehension in tribunal proceedings.

Perhaps the central finding of the Review was that tribunals 'are not independent of the departments that sponsor them'. It identified the fact that many tribunals received administrative support and financial resources from Government departments. As long as these were involved in setting tribunal procedures and housing tribunals in their own buildings, then 'the tribunal neither appears to be independent, nor is it independent in fact'.

This is consistent with a distinction between impartiality and independence identified by the courts in *Gillies v Secretary of State for Work and Pensions* [2006] UKHL 2. Impartiality is the way in which tribunals actually decide particular cases, whilst independence relates to how free tribunals are from the executive branch in their structure and organisation. There was a more pressing need, after the introduction of the Human Rights Act 1998, under Article 6 ECHR for independence from the sponsoring Government department.

Leggatt also found that 'because they are many and disparate, there is a considerable waste of resources in managing them, and they achieve no economies of scale'. Taking the issues of coherence and independence together meant that there was a need for a separate administrative support service. This should be within the Lord Chancellor's Department (which is now incorporated into the Department of Justice). As well as efficiencies, a single service could improve the profile and prestige of tribunals as distinct from courts.

14.15 TRIBUNALS, COURTS AND ENFORCEMENT ACT 2007

The Leggatt Review recommendations formed the basis for the Government White Paper, 'Transforming Public Services: Complaints, Redress and Tribunals' (CM 6243), which in turn led to the Tribunals, Courts and Enforcement Act 2007 (TCEA 2007). This Act integrated most existing tribunals into a two-tier structure.

The First-tier Tribunal has seven chambers and hears appeals of administrative decisions on issues such as tax assessments by HM Revenue and Customs, whether a person can be detained under the Mental Health Acts, and disputes about social security payments (including income support, Jobseeker's Allowance, Incapacity Benefit and the State Pension). There is a separate chamber for Immigration and Asylum cases. The General Regulatory Chamber has a wide jurisdiction covering issues such as appeals against decisions of the Charity Commission, licensing decisions by the Gambling Commission and civil sanctions imposed by the Environment Agency.

The **Upper Tribunal** has four chambers: Administrative Appeals, Immigration and Asylum, Land, and Tax and Chancery. Under section 11 of the TCEA 2007, there is a right of appeal from a First-tier Tribunal decision to the Upper Tribunal, but only on a point of law, e.g. failing to give adequate reasons for the decision.

Some other tribunals continue to exist outside of this structure, for example the Employment Tribunal and Employment Appeal Tribunal, which are concerned with civil rather than administrative (i.e. citizen vs state) cases. The Special Immigration Appeals Commission is not incorporated into the two-tier system because its work usually relates to national security matters.

APPLYING THE LAW – SPECIAL EDUCATIONAL NEEDS AND DISABILITY

Local education authorities have duties to support children whose special educational needs (SEN) affect their ability to learn. These needs include physical needs or impairments, dyslexia and Attention Deficit Hyperactivity Disorder. The support may involve e.g. a special learning programme, extra help from a teaching assistant, or support with physical needs such as moving around the school.

As with any decision made by a public body that involves discretion and judgement in applying criteria, there is scope for disagreement between the citizen (the child's parents) and the state (the SEN officer and local education authority). Appeals against SEN decisions are heard by the Special Educational Needs and Disability section of the Health, Education and Social Care chamber of the First-tier Tribunal. Appeal can be on grounds including a refusal to:

- Assess a child's educational, health and care (EHC) needs.
- Create an EHC plan.
- Maintain the EHC plan.

The tribunal's website states that civil legal aid may be available,[37] but unless the appeal involves a very serious problem involving a human rights or discrimination claim by someone with very low income, then it will not be eligible. More realistically, appellants are directed to the Independent Parental Special Education Advice (IPSEA) charity. We saw above that the Leggatt Review called for support for voluntary advice groups, and IPSEA makes a virtue of its lack of governmental support. It says that it is independent because its funding comes from companies and individuals. As well as general information and advice on the law and local authority duties on SEN, it has a tribunal helpline to give specific support on preparing a case.[38] There is no direct representation by IPSEA within tribunal hearings.

---

37 Special Educational Needs Tribunal, https://www.gov.uk/special-educational-needs-disability-tribunal (last accessed 03/11/17).

38 Independent Parental Special Educational Advice, https://www.ipsea.org.uk/contact/advice-and-support/tribunal-helpline (last accessed 03/11/17).

In line with the idea of proportionate dispute resolution and a preference for problem-solving rather than just adjudication, parents are directed to take advantage of local authority SEN mediation services, involving a trained and impartial 'referee', before they bring an appeal. The deadline for appeals is two months from the decision or one month from any mediation.

The tribunal uses oral hearings, at a location reasonably near the appellant's home, and appellants can bring up to three witnesses. If the appeal succeeds, then the local authority have to act quickly, e.g. within four weeks to start assessment of a child's needs. If the appellant loses, they can ask the tribunal to review its decision if they think there has been a mistake, or seek permission to further appeal to the Upper Tribunal if they think there has been an error of law in the way the First-tier Tribunal have decided the case.

Procedure – a problem with tribunals was that their procedures had been set separately, either by the Lord Chancellor or the ministers from the relevant department. This contributed to the general lack of coherence in the tribunal system. Under section 22 of the TCEA 2007, there is now a Tribunal Procedure Committee, which issues common procedural rules.[39] There is still no single universal procedure across all tribunals (e.g. there are separate Immigration and Asylum Chamber rules), but the same rules do apply to many chambers and there is a high degree of consistency between the different procedural regimes (i.e. they only differ to the extent necessary for the particular needs of that subject matter). As an example, the Procedure Committee issued the Tribunal (Upper Tribunal) Rules 2008 (SI 2008/2698) which lays down consistent procedural rules across three chambers of the Upper Tribunal on issues such as summoning witnesses, costs orders and use of legal representatives. To further improve consistency and the profile of tribunals, there is now a post of Senior President of Tribunals (section 3 TCEA 2007). The Senior President, who is a senior judge, leads around 5,000 officeholders in the tribunal system, provides an annual report to Parliament and represents the interests and views of tribunals to the Lord Chancellor and Government.

Composition – tribunal members used to be chosen by the Government department linked to that tribunal. This was clearly unsatisfactory and undermined claims to independence. There was an interim position, up to 2007, where the legally qualified chairmen were appointed by the Lord Chancellor and other members by the relevant Government departments. Appointments are now governed by sections 4 and 5 of the TCEA 2007. Tribunal judges and chairmen need to have a legal qualification, plus at least five years (first tier) and seven years (Upper Tier) of legal experience. They are selected by the Judicial Appointments Commission (see Chapter 9, 'Separation of powers') which ensures both independence and quality control (e.g. consistent selection criteria). It has

39 The Tribunal Procedure Committee, https://www.gov.uk/government/organisations/tribunal-procedure-committee (last accessed 03/11/17).

been a traditional merit of tribunals that some of them include 'lay members' who are not lawyers but who have subject expertise, e.g. doctors in a Mental Health Tribunal or financial specialists in tax tribunals. These are recruited by the Tribunals Service directly, who specify what experience the specialist members need to have.

Appeal and review – as we have seen, there is an appeal from the First-tier to the Upper Tribunal on a point of law, e.g. failing to give adequate reasons for the decision (sections 11–12 TCEA 2007). A further appeal on a point of law from the Upper Tribunal to the Court of Appeal may be possible, but permission must be granted by either the tribunal or court (section 13 TCEA 2007). The appeal courts have indicated that it is for the specialist tribunals (particularly the Upper Tribunal), not the appellate courts, to develop a coherent approach to the interpretation and application of law in their specialist fields. The courts should not interfere with findings of tribunals unless they could clearly identify the flaw in the legal reasoning that led to an incorrect result (*Jones v First-tier Tribunal and Criminal Injuries Compensation Authority* [2013] UKSC 19). Where the citizen has already had one appeal (i.e. First-tier to Upper Tribunal), then they could only have a second appeal (i.e. Upper Tribunal to Court of Appeal) where there was an important point of principle or practice or some other compelling reason.

The Upper Tribunal also has a 'judicial review' jurisdiction (i.e. the ability to declare a public body decision as unlawful because that body has gone beyond its powers or acted unlawfully in reaching the decision). It can issue judicial review remedies, for example an order quashing a public body decision, and it largely mirrors the High Court's powers and procedures in relation to judicial review (see Chapters 12 and 13).

A question has arisen as to whether the Upper Tribunal *itself* can be subject to judicial review in the courts system. The answer is a qualified yes.

KEY CASE – *R (ON THE APPLICATION OF CART) V UPPER TRIBUNAL* [2011] UKSC 28

The Supreme Court said that there was nothing in the TCEA 2007 that tried to oust the jurisdiction of the courts to hear judicial review proceedings against tribunals. (By the way, if you want to make fascinating, and potentially original, connections between topics, then you could look at Chapter 12 on ouster clauses and consider whether any attempt to do so would have been successful.)

So judicial review of the Upper Tribunal is possible, but this leaves questions as to the *scope* of review. The Supreme Court recognised the new and more coherent system of tribunals under the TCEA 2007 which led to a 'more restrained approach to judicial review than before'. This can be interpreted as a tentative finding that the new system has better integrity and ability to follow natural justice than previous arrangements. It was noted that the High Court and Court of Appeal had been in danger of being overwhelmed by the volume of asylum and immigration judicial review claims before the introduction of tribunal 'statutory review', and that it would be counter-productive to have such a wide approach to judicial review of the tribunal system that a large number of those cases still ended up in the court system.

The Supreme Court recognised, however, that no system of decision-making is infallible and there should be an opportunity for a more experienced judge to check the decisions in some circumstances. These circumstances should not be too narrow, and the Court adopted the same test as for appeals, i.e. the Upper Tribunal should be subject to judicial review, but only where there was an important point of principle or practice or some other compelling reason.

14.16 THE ADMINISTRATIVE JUSTICE AND TRIBUNALS COUNCIL (AJTC)

The AJTC was set up in 2007 to replace the Tribunals Council and to keep the whole system of administrative justice under review, particularly with a view to making the system more accessible, fair and efficient, and to advise the Government on improvements to administrative justice.

In 2010 the Coalition Government announced a 'bonfire of the quangos'.[40] Quangos are statutory bodies providing public services but at arm's length from direct control by the Government. It was part of another attempt by another Government to roll back the frontiers of the state (a cherished ambition of the Thatcher Conservative Government of the 1980s that resulted in a larger rather than a smaller state apparatus).

In this case, the pressing need was to reduce budgets, and the first deep cuts were being made in relation to bodies such as Cycling England and the Herbal Medicines Advisory Committee. The media made great play out of the existence of hitherto little-known bodies such as the Government Hospitality Advisory Committee on the Purchase of Wines, but also on the hit-list was the Administrative Justice and Tribunals Council.

The Parliamentary Ombudsman and two House of Commons Select Committees were adamant that the Council had a very important role to play in providing an overall appraisal

---

40 'Quango list shows 192 to be axed' *BBC News*, http://www.bbc.co.uk/news/uk-politics-11538534 (last accessed 03/11/17).

of administrative justice systems, and there was no other body that could effectively carry out this function. Its abolition was more lamented than some other quangos and seemed less justified; nevertheless, abolition was carried out by the Public Bodies (Abolition of Administrative Justice and Tribunals Council) Order 2013 (SI 2013/2042).

POINTS TO REVIEW

- Tribunals carry out adjudicative functions.

- Their merits are in cost, speed, informality, accessibility and specialisation.

- The Leggatt Review reforms have both formalised the structure and procedure of the tribunal system and tried to prevent them becoming more like courts.

TAKING IT FURTHER

Parliamentary Ombudsman, http://www.ombudsman.org.uk This site, unsurprisingly, has a wealth of information on the overall role and detailed operations of the Parliamentary Ombudsman. It performs the dual role of being a public-facing advice-giving website and of holding lots of more scholarly reflection on reform and constitutional function very well.

A Abraham, 'Parliamentary Ombudsman and Administrative Justice: Shaping the next 50 years', JUSTICE Tom Sargant Memorial Lecture 2011, http://justice.org.uk/ombudsmen-administrative-justice/ Ann Abraham's tenure as Parliamentary Ombudsman from 2002–11 saw a step change in the ombudsman scheme. She revitalised the office, was unafraid of confronting Government departments and engaged the public more than ever.

J Mellor, 'The Constitutional Role of the Parliamentary and Health Service Ombudsman', speech at UCL Constitution Unit, 17 April 2013, https://vimeo.com/64628880 The former Parliamentary Ombudsman gave a thought-provoking 30-minute lecture on the role of the ombudsman scheme in checking executive power.

R Carnwath, 'Tribunal Justice: A New Start' [2009] Public Law 48 This is probably the best concise review of the changes wrought by the Tribunals, Courts and Enforcement Act 2007.

CHAPTER 15
HUMAN RIGHTS

The UK has had an interesting relationship with the subject of human rights and civil liberties. British Constitutional Law arguably provided the first major legal document on human rights protection in Europe, in the shape of the Magna Carta 1215. During much of the subsequent 800 years, British subjects have enjoyed comparatively high levels of liberty. Common law judges have been active defenders of liberties, and some common law cases are international landmarks in the limitation of state power, the development of the requirements for a fair trial, and freedom of expression.

On the other hand, the protection of rights has been patchy. The right to privacy has been neglected; the judges and the common law have, at best, a mixed record in protecting freedom of assembly (e.g. public protest) and freedom of association (e.g. the right to belong to a trade union). At times, the UK has had one of the worst records before the European Court of Human Rights and was one of the last countries in the world to introduce a positive and wide-ranging law on human rights protection (the Human Rights Act 1998). Despite the UK being one of the prime movers behind the creation of the European Convention on Human Rights, its later introduction into the UK legal system has left certain sections of the UK media and political scene profoundly uneasy.

At the heart of this is a tension within the concept of human rights. It is widely accepted that protection of basic human rights is a good thing. It makes life more bearable. It promotes human dignity. It contributes to a peaceful and stable society. To be effective, however, human rights must be universal. Your entry ticket to the protection of human rights law must come simply from being human, although how particular rights are enjoyed by individuals can be affected by their particular circumstances (e.g. the voting rights of children, prisoners or those with a mental disorder). As a consequence, human rights law can extend protection to individuals who some people may dislike, or hate, or think undeserving of protection.

AS YOU READ

This chapter focuses very much on the Human Rights Act 1998 (HRA). It sketches in some of the background to the Act and then assesses how the Act attempts to make rights effective in the UK. Some particular substantive rights, such as freedom of expression, are dealt with in the following chapters. The chapter concludes with a look at the debates on the future of, and possible demise of, the Human Rights Act 1998.

At the end of this chapter you should be able to:

- describe and evaluate the traditional UK human rights approach
- outline and illustrate how key sections of the HRA operate
- assess the overall effectiveness of the HRA scheme.

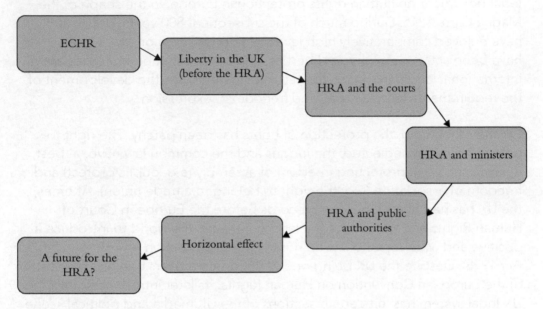

Figure 15.1 Structure of Chapter 15

15.1 LIBERTIES OR RIGHTS?

There has been a good deal of discussion on the terminology and categorisation of different forms of rights – whether something is a liberty, a freedom, a privilege or a right. Here we will set up a simple binary distinction:

- A **liberty** is where the state leaves you alone – by not intervening it gives you the freedom to decide what you want to say, or what religion to observe, or what groups you want to form or join, etc.
- A **right** is where there is a particular provision of law that guarantees your ability to do something (e.g. enter into marriage), or provides some sort of benefit (e.g. that the state cannot torture you, or that you are entitled to receive a fair trial).

This UK legal system before the HRA included many specific legal rights, but within a framework dominated by notions of civil liberty. Many of these specific legal provisions continue in force after the HRA, as do many areas where the state provides freedom by abstaining from interfering in people's lives. Following the HRA, however, they operate within a framework of human rights. The particular rights incorporated through the HRA come from the European Convention on Human Rights and Fundamental Freedoms 1950.

15.2 THE EUROPEAN CONVENTION ON HUMAN RIGHTS

APPLYING THE LAW – ASSESSMENT ADVICE

Very Important Note – the Convention was agreed in 1950 by the Council of Europe. This is *not* the same organisation as the European Union. Do not confuse the two. EU law concepts such as supremacy, direct effect, Commission enforcement, etc simply *do not* apply here.

This is one of the most common mistakes that students make in coursework and exam answers on this subject. It is particularly unfortunate because the error leads to the student spending valuable time or word space going in the wrong direction.

ECHR		EU law
47 member states		28 member states
Court in Strasbourg	vs	Court in Luxembourg
Agreement between states		Law made by EU institutions

The European Convention on Human Rights (ECHR) covers the classic civil and political rights such as freedom of speech, freedom of religion, freedom from torture and the right to a fair trial. It does not cover economic or social rights such as the right to education, to a clean environment or to medical care. You can read any human rights law textbook for a full discussion of the relative merits of including economic and social rights in human rights instruments. In summary, they can help set the agenda for political action as they are a strong indicator of what is regarded as socially fundamental, but they are difficult to enforce, particularly through court action.

The ECHR was signed in 1950 by 15 states. It is a product of the Council of Europe and its membership has grown, particularly following the end of Communist rule in Middle and Eastern Europe. It now has 47 signatories, including Russia and Turkey. Any person claiming to be a victim of a violation of a Convention right has a right of individual petition, i.e. they can bring an action against a member state before the European Court of Human Rights (ECtHR) in Strasbourg. To be admissible, the applicant must have exhausted all domestic remedies and brought the action within six months of the final national decision. Manifestly ill-founded claims, where the applicant has not suffered a significant disadvantage and repetitive cases can be declared inadmissible.

The judges of the ECtHR are drawn from the member states and are required to be independent of their national Governments. The Court normally sits in chambers of seven judges, with a possible referral for the most important cases up to a Grand Chamber of 17 judges. It has jurisdiction to hear disputes on the interpretation and application of the ECHR. The Court has developed a concept of a 'margin of appreciation' for member states. This means that there will be circumstances where the national authorities are thought to be in a better position than the Court to assess the necessity of a restriction.

The Court serves a population of around 750 million people and is struggling with its workload. In January 2014, there were 99,000 applications pending before the Court. There were a number of institutional reforms introduced through Protocol 14 in 2010, but further reform to reduce the case load and streamline the handling of cases is likely to be required.

15.2.1 THE CONVENTION RIGHTS

- The Convention includes some absolute rights which are unusual in not allowing for any exceptions or derogations. Article 3 prohibits torture and inhuman or degrading treatment or punishment. Freedom from slavery and forced labour is provided by Article 4.
- A middle group of rights only allow for very limited exceptions. Article 2, the right to life, allows the taking of life to the extent strictly necessary, e.g. in self-defence or in suppressing riots. Article 5 provides a right to liberty and security, which can be limited through e.g. imprisonment following conviction. Article 6 outlines quite detailed rules on the right to a fair trial and requires that trials are held in public, subject to limited exceptions for e.g. public order and national security.
- A number of rights are subject to very wide-ranging qualifications, including freedom of conscience and religion (Article 9), freedom of expression (Article 10) and freedom of assembly and association (Article 11). These illustrate the typically *non-absolute nature* of most human rights.

15.2.2   ARTICLE 8 ECHR – THE RIGHT TO PRIVACY

1   Everyone has the right to respect for his private and family life, his home and his correspondence.
2   There shall be no interference by a public authority with the exercise of this right except such as is in accordance with the law and is necessary in a democratic society in the interests of national security, public safety or the economic well-being of the country, for the prevention of disorder or crime, for the protection of health or morals, or for the protection of the rights and freedoms of others.

EXPLAINING THE LAW – PRIVACY

Article 8(1) therefore establishes a very general and broad-based right. The ECtHR regards the Convention as a 'living instrument', i.e. it must be interpreted according to present day conditions rather than limited to what was in the minds of the drafters six decades ago. It has, for example, interpreted Article 8 as covering sexual orientation, and the UK armed forces' policy on discharging homosexual service personnel was found to be a breach of Article 8 in *Smith v UK* (1999) 29 EHRR 493.

Article 8(2) outlines extensive exceptions to the right to privacy. In Article 8(2), the reference to 'public authority' shows that the Convention is focused on state action and on protecting people from rights breaches by the state. Any restriction on privacy must be 'in accordance with the law', which means that restrictions cannot be authorised by executive or administrative decision; they must be clearly set out in law. 'Necessary in a democratic society' provides a test of proportionality, that is, any restrictions must only go so far as is necessary and must strike an appropriate balance between the right and the state interest. A law which required police CCTV in every private home *might* further the prevention of disorder or crime but would disproportionately limit privacy. In addition, derogation is possible from most Articles (but not e.g. Article 3 torture) in times of war or other public emergency threatening the life of the nation.

The rights covered by the Convention have been extended by protocols. Protocol 1, for example, provides for a right of peaceful enjoyment of property. Each state can decide which of these additional rights it commits itself to protecting.

15.3 THE LATE BLOSSOMING OF HUMAN RIGHTS IN THE UK

The Human Rights Act 1998 came into force in 2000, a couple of centuries after the first great human rights instruments. France issued its Declaration on the Rights of Man in 1789, the same year that the US Bill of Rights was adopted. In the following 200 years, almost every state in the world laid out some positive statement of what human rights were and how they were to be protected (including those that do not respect them in practice). Why had it taken the UK so long? Two main arguments were put forward.

First, civil liberties were adequately protected by the traditional common law approach. A key case used in support of this argument was *Entick v Carrington* (1765) 19 St Tr 1030 (see Chapter 10, 'Rule of law', for a full description of the case), where Entick's ability to express his political views was protected by the ordinary law of trespass and an insistence on the rule of law. The case was used by commentators to argue that key rights and liberties were, in a concrete and practical way, protected by the English common law system. These rights were not abstract or unreal, found only in an idealistic declaration or mere words on paper. Genuine protection was delivered to people through court judgments that were both enforceable and observed in practice.

Allied to this, it was argued that the UK had a culture of democratic restraint. Whilst the Westminster Parliament could in theory pass very oppressive laws and deprive citizens of the most fundamental rights, there were an array of practical constraints including opposition parties, a free and vigorous press, and the electorate. Again, there was something in this argument. On an issue such as freedom of expression, the UK Parliament and the common law restricted freedom far less than the legal systems (and the lived reality, regardless of the printed laws) of other European countries. Karl Marx, for example, was expelled from Prussia (one of the German states) and from France due to his political writing before he sought refuge in 1849, and for the rest of his life, in the relative freedom of the UK.

Secondly, it was argued that a formal Bill of Rights could have no useful function due to the legal supremacy of the Westminster Parliament. It would be impossible to entrench a Bill of Rights as against future repeal. In other countries when there was a statement of fundamental rights, those rights were *constitutionally* protected, normally through entrenchment. You will recall from Chapter 4, 'Constitutions', that entrenchment means that it is either impossible or significantly more difficult to change or abolish a legal rule. Written constitutions can also give human rights a higher status and priority in case of conflict with 'ordinary' laws.

What is the point, the argument went, of having some grand declaration of rights for the UK when the UK constitutional system prevents any legal protection of the fundamental nature of those rights? Later Parliaments could override these rights simply by passing a new Act of Parliament. These arguments held sway until the 1990s.

15.4 PRE-HUMAN RIGHTS ACT PROTECTION IN UK LAW

People in the UK have possessed levels of liberty which have been relatively high, even in the absence of a comprehensive rights declaration. So *how were* rights protected before the Human Rights Act 1998? There are two aspects to the answer: positive protection and the residual approach.

15.4.1 POSITIVE PROTECTION

Some protections were delivered through identifiable legal provisions, either at common law or in statute. We will explore two examples.

15.4.1.1 COMMON LAW

The presumption of innocence is an important part of the right to a fair criminal trial.
It provides that the state must bear the burden of proof in showing that the accused has
committed a crime. It has come to be a significant element of Article 6 (the right to a fair
trial) of the European Convention on Human Rights. The rationale for the presumption of
innocence includes the difficulty of proving a negative, the imbalance of power between the
state and the individual and the consequences of conviction for the accused.

KEY CASE – *WOOLMINGTON V DPP* [1935] AC 462

After three months of marriage, Woolmington's wife, Violet, left home and went to
live with her mother. Woolmington went to the house to meet with Violet. He took a
stolen shotgun with him. Whilst the shotgun was pointing in the direction of Violet,
it 'went off' in his hands and killed her. He argued that he had taken the shotgun to
plead with his wife to return and threaten to kill himself if she did not. He said that
the gun had fired by accident.

Woolmington was charged with murder. The physical element (*actus reus*) for
murder is that the accused has caused the death of the victim. The mental element
(*mens rea*) is that the accused must have intended to either kill or cause grievous
bodily harm. The trial judge found that the agreed facts of the case were so
damning that the prosecution did not have the burden of proving that Woolmington
intended to cause either death or serious harm to Violet. The burden shifted to the
defendant to show that he did not have this intention.

This was overruled on appeal to the House of Lords, and Lord Sankey said that:
'Throughout the web of the English Criminal Law one golden thread is always to
be seen, that it is the duty of the prosecution to prove the prisoner's guilt'. The
common law rules of evidence therefore insisted that the burden of proof stayed
with the prosecution, which delivered a presumption of innocence and contributed
to a defendant's right to a fair trial.

15.4.1.2 STATUTE

The right of access to legal advice for those facing criminal proceedings is another aspect
of the right to a fair trial. By statute, if you are arrested and held for more than a very brief
period of time, you must be taken to a designated police station and informed of your
rights. These include your right of access to independent legal advice.

This principal right, provided for in section 58 of the Police and Criminal Evidence Act
1984, is supported by further provisions to make sure that the police do not circumvent
its effectiveness. So the police cannot try to dissuade an individual from getting access to
legal advice, and if someone asks for legal advice then they cannot be interviewed until the
arrestee has had the chance to consult with their adviser in private. The statutory provisions,

therefore, contribute to securing a defendant's right to a fair trial. A wide range of other individual legal provisions operate to protect particular rights.

15.5 RESIDUAL APPROACH TO LIBERTY

In the time before the HRA, however, the dominant approach was not found in particular provisions of law, but in an emphasis on non-interference, on liberty: 'The starting point of our domestic law is that every citizen has a right to do what he likes unless restrained by the common law or statute' (*Attorney General v Observer* [1990] 1 AC 109, Lord Donaldson).

APPLYING THE LAW – THE RESIDUAL APPROACH

Imagine that the blank space below represents your freedom to say anything. It is your freedom of expression and includes your ability to communicate through images as well as words, through text as well as speech, and your ability to receive information as well as transmit it. This is the 'starting point' referred to by Lord Donaldson above – your right to do what you like.

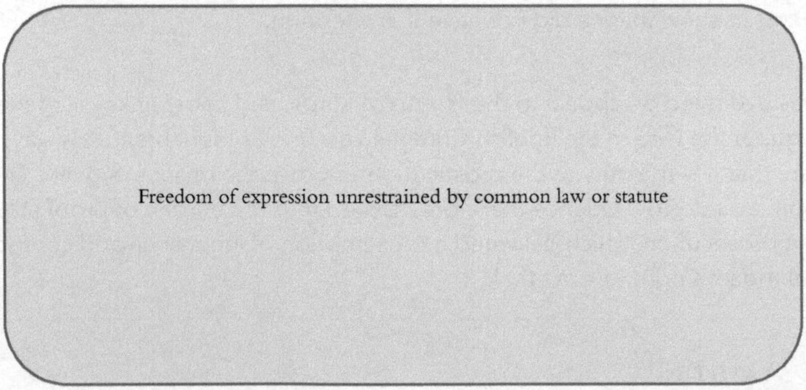

Freedom of expression unrestrained by common law or statute

Figure 15.2 Freedom of expression unrestrained

Now try to identify some of the restrictions found within common law or statute on freedom of expression. Here is one to start you off: the Official Secrets Act 1989 includes an offence of disclosing information relating to security or intelligence. This limits expression and communication. You should be able identify at least five further restrictions within a few minutes. Do not be concerned about knowing the specific provisions or precise legal rules – just identify the broad limitation.

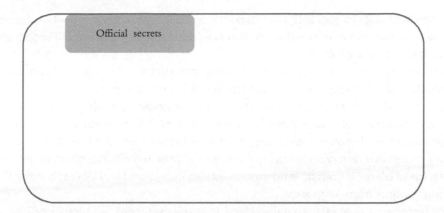

Figure 15.3 Freedom of expression with example restraint

When you add your restrictions to the space (as we have done with official secrets) you should see a pattern emerging: that there are many restrictions, but a significant area remains. This is the area of residual liberty – what you are entitled to say and communicate free of restriction. This is the irregular-shaped blank space left in the middle of the diagram below.

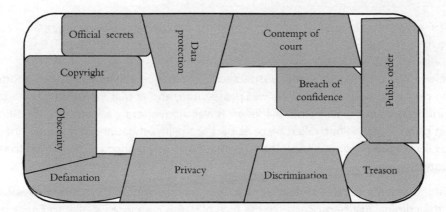

Figure 15.4 Freedom of expression with some major restraints

Weaknesses of residual approach

We can see therefore how the residual approach might work for certain issues and how it might deliver a considerable amount of liberty to citizens. There are, however, some weaknesses to the approach:

■ Uncertainty – the scope of the area of liberty is not always very clear. Have we identified all of the restrictions on freedom of expression? Some of the restrictions will be obvious (e.g. obscenity, contempt of court), but would you have readily added things like intellectual property laws (copyright restrictions) or licensing laws (such as radio station licensing) to your list? Their impact may be less obvious and serious, but they do add to the sum of expression-limiting laws and therefore change the scope and the shape of the area of liberty.

- Vulnerability – owing to supremacy of Parliament, no part of the area of liberty is free from the risk of change. *Any* law restricting *any* liberty can be introduced. There could be a huge slice of the area of liberty taken off in a single stroke (e.g. direct censorship of newspapers), but what is more likely is that liberty suffers death by a thousand cuts: that incremental change makes lots of small restrictions and the cumulative effect is a progressive reduction in liberty. Change can flow in the other direction (e.g. the offence of blasphemous libel no longer applies in England and Wales) but the trend is often towards more regulation.

- Our rights are never assured if they depend on Government self-restraint. The argument is that we need to take fundamental liberties out of the hands of the Government of the day and place them in some constitutional provision that is safeguarded from casual amendment.

- Failure to comprehensively cover rights – the residual approach works *more or less* (and subject to the concerns above) for issues like freedom of expression, freedom from arbitrary arrest or freedom of religion. It simply does not work for privacy (notice that we never use the phrase 'freedom of privacy').

KEY CASE – *MALONE V METROPOLITAN POLICE COMMISSIONER* [1979] CH 344

Malone was an antiques dealer, suspected by the police of handling stolen goods. The police tapped his phone. He was prosecuted, and at trial, whilst the phone tap evidence was not entered into evidence, it was inadvertently admitted by an officer that phone tapping had taken place as part of the investigation. At this time, there was no statute or common law authority that positively authorised the police to tap phones.

Malone argued that this amounted to a breach of his right to privacy and an abuse of the criminal justice process. On the face of it, the case looks similar to *Entick v Carrington*: a branch of the state interfering with a citizen's rights without any lawful authority. Megarry VC famously held, however, that there was no right to privacy in English law. Remember that the substance of the court action in *Entick* was not a breach of the civil liberty of freedom of expression, but the ordinary law of trespass. In *Malone*, there was no trespass. The phone tapping was physically carried out at the telephone exchange rather than at Malone's home. Since none of Malone's legally recognised interests were interfered with by the police, then the court could do nothing.

The case demonstrated that whilst the police and security services *might* choose to refrain from tapping your phone or otherwise putting you under surveillance, if they did want to place you under surveillance, and could do so in a way that did not break the law (e.g. by breaking into your house), then they were free to do so.

- Consistent failure before the European Convention on Human Rights – perhaps the most damning indictment of the residual approach is that it failed to keep the UK in conformity with the rights set out in the ECHR. Those rights were largely drafted by UK Foreign Office lawyers in 1948–50 and represent a fairly minimal set of obligations. They focus on the most fundamental human and civil rights, rather than more ambitious economic and social rights. Nevertheless, up to 1997 the UK was found to be in breach of the Convention on 35 separate occasions. At the time, this put the UK towards the top of the table for states that breached Convention rights.

As Lord Bridge said in *Attorney General v Guardian Newspapers Ltd* [1987] 3 All ER 316 confidence in 'the capacity of the common law to safeguard the fundamental freedoms essential to a free society including the right to freedom of speech [was] . . . severely undermined'.

This may seem like an historical lesson (and is none the worse for that), but it is important to note that these methods of protecting rights and liberties have not disappeared following the introduction of the Human Rights Act 1998. Your right of access to legal advice following arrest is still provided by section 58 Police and Criminal Evidence (PACE) and you still have the liberty to say anything that is not restricted by some legal provision. Both positive protection by specific legal rules and the residual approach continue to play their part in securing human rights in the UK. The real lesson of the preceding section is that the residual approach and piecemeal legal protections were insufficient by themselves to secure human rights and that a more comprehensive framework of legal protection of human rights needed to be brought into UK law.

15.5.1 ASSESSMENT ADVICE

Essay questions are the most common type of assessment in this topic. There is plenty of scope for asking questions that require the student to demonstrate both (a) knowledge of the structure and aims of the Human Rights Act 1998 and (b) analytical and evaluative skills in exploring particular areas. The sub-topics that have been most subject to lively judicial and academic debate are (a) the operation of section 3 and section 4 of the HRA and (b) the operation of section 6 of the HRA and the issue of horizontal effect. Whatever the essay question, you are likely to have to show that you grasp some of the difficulties and differences of view around these issues. A good understanding of the supporting provisions e.g. section 19, section 10 and section 7 of the HRA is also necessary.

You can review the HRA through a variety of critical lenses, including assessing the evolution and potential futures of the HRA, an overall review of the operation and effectiveness of the HRA scheme or the balance between effective rights protection and preserving supremacy of Parliament.

Problem questions where you are invited to advise a client on how to enforce their Convention rights are less common, but possible. The key here will be to have a good understanding of the operation of the individual sections (particularly ss.3, 4, 6 and 7 HRA) and how they interact.

15.6 THE HUMAN RIGHTS ACT 1998

There had been a number of unsuccessful attempts to incorporate the ECHR into UK law from the 1970s onwards; they failed because they did not have the support of a major party. In its manifesto for the 1997 General Election, the Labour Party committed to incorporating the ECHR into domestic law. Following the election, the new Labour Government released a White Paper, 'Rights Brought Home', that outlined the benefits of incorporation whilst also committing to preserving the supremacy of the Westminster Parliament.[1] The benefits included the savings in time and money of allowing UK citizens to enforce their rights within UK courts rather than having to exhaust domestic remedies and then go to the Court in Strasbourg, and potential improvements in the record of the UK before the European Court of Human Rights.

The White Paper led to the Human Rights Act 1998 which came into force in October 2000. It incorporates, in its own distinct way, most of the rights in the European Convention on Human Rights, including those additional rights in the Protocols (such as the right to peaceful enjoyment of property) that the UK has committed itself to. It omits Article 13, the right to an effective remedy, on the basis that HRA itself is the means of providing appropriate remedies.

There is a requirement for the courts to 'have particular regard' to rights of freedom of expression and religion (sections 12 and 13 HRA). Whilst this may have been politically useful in addressing concerns from certain sectors at the time the Act was passed, since the HRA requires the courts to strive to protect all rights and no right takes automatic precedence over any other, then the legal effect of these sections is bound to be very limited.

It might appear that the Human Rights Act 1998 creates an unnecessarily elaborate scheme. The key to understanding the structure and methods of the HRA scheme, however, is to keep in mind this essential point – the Human Rights Act 1998 has *two* aims.

- To make rights effective in the UK legal system, *and*
- To preserve the supremacy of Parliament.

The Act itself tries to show that the aims are not inconsistent, but there are inevitably serious tensions in accommodating both these aims.

---

1   Cm 3782, https://www.gov.uk/government/publications/the-human-rights-bill (last accessed 01/11/17).

ASSESSING THE LAW – INCORPORATING RIGHTS

Imagine that you are tasked with incorporating the ECHR rights into UK law. You have to make those rights available to, and enforceable by, people in the UK. What would be the most obvious and apparently simplest way of doing this?

You may have opted to simply enact those rights in a statute. For example, in *your version* of a Human Rights Bill you might take the right to privacy in Article 8 ECHR and use it as the basis for a section in a statute that provides that 'everyone has a right to a private and family life'. You would need a further subsection to cover the limitations to the right to privacy outlined in Article 8(2) e.g. to prevent disorder or crime. Build in some enforcement mechanisms, and once your Bill is passed and becomes an Act, then the right to privacy has been incorporated into UK law. Job done! This seems, at first glance, to be relatively straightforward.

You will see in the following sections that this is not what the framers of the HRA did. Instead, the Act imposes obligations on different parts of the state: courts, ministers in Parliament and public authorities. When they are carrying out their day-to-day functions, they have to act in ways that respect and protect the Convention rights. These obligations are far-reaching but they are not absolute, and the limits come when the obligation to protect Convention rights bumps up against the supremacy of Parliament. Simply put, the organs of the state are required to (a) obey their duty to give effect to Convention rights unless (b) this conflicts with their duty to give effect to Acts of Parliament.

We will now examine the nature of the obligations placed on the different parts of the state.

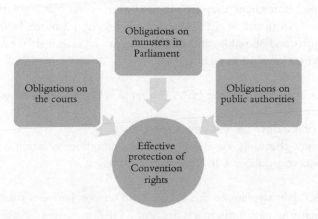

Figure 15.5 HRA obligations on the branches of state

15.7 OBLIGATIONS ON THE COURTS

The main obligations placed on the courts, found in ss.3 and 4 HRA, concern how they interpret legislation. In doing so, they must 'take into account' the judgments of the European Court of Human Rights, whenever made, so far as they are relevant to the proceedings (section 2 HRA). 'Take into account' is not the same thing as 'bound by', but the UK courts have said that 'In the absence of some special circumstances it seems to me that the court should follow any clear and constant jurisprudence of the European Court of Human Rights' (Lord Slynn, *R (Alconbury Developments and Others) v Secretary of State for the Environment, Transport and the Regions* [2001] UKHL 23).

The key obligations are:

- to interpret legislation, as far as possible, to be consistent with Convention rights (section 3 HRA), and
- if that interpretation cannot resolve the problem, then to issue a declaration of incompatibility (section 4 HRA).

15.8 JUDICIAL INTERPRETATION UNDER SECTION 3 OF THE HRA

Section 3 of the HRA states that:

> So far as it is possible to do so, primary legislation and subordinate legislation must be read and given effect in a way which is compatible with the Convention rights.

This is therefore a duty of interpretation. When the courts are carrying out their normal and day-to-day functions of interpreting Acts of Parliament and applying them to the disputes that come before them, they are required to interpret that legislation in ways which are compatible with Convention rights. Interestingly, section 3 of the HRA is not expressly limited to the courts, and all public authorities must try to read legislation in ways which are compatible with Convention rights.

The opening part of section 3 of the HRA ('so far as it is possible to do so') indicates both

- the strength of the duty, i.e. it is very strong, and
- the limitations on that duty, i.e. there will still be situations where it is not possible to interpret an Act compatibly with Convention rights.

Right at the outset then we can see this balance and tension between making rights effective and preserving parliamentary supremacy. Section 3 HRA envisages occasions when the provisions of an Act of Parliament so clearly breach Convention rights that they cannot be interpreted consistently with those rights. Even in that situation the courts are *not given the power* to invalidate or ignore the Act of Parliament.

The nature and strength of the duty under section 3 of the HRA have been subject to much judicial and academic debate. The context for this debate is that even before the HRA, the courts had to try, as a general rule of statutory interpretation, to interpret statutes in line with the UK's international obligations, including the European Convention on Human Rights. This has most impact when the UK statute is found to be ambiguous, i.e. capable of bearing different meanings. So what did section 3 of the HRA add? As a key provision of the HRA, it clearly requires the courts to go further than the existing approach, but how much further?

You will have seen throughout this subject, and in your other subjects (even in Contract Law), that there is some flexibility in how the courts can interpret statutory language. You may have covered statutory interpretation in one of your introductory modules (such as lawyer's skills, legal system, legal method etc), and seen that there are a range of broad approaches to interpretation: the literal rule, the golden rule, the mischief rule, the purposive approach and has considerable latitude in tacking the task of interpretation. A judge is not obliged to adopt any single approach. Even putting those broad approaches to one side, we know that language is a flexible tool.

A classic exercise for new law students is to consider a statutory prohibition on 'any vehicle entering a park'. We can agree that the term 'vehicle' would apply to a motorcar, or a lorry or a bus. We would probably accept that it covers a motorbike. Does it extend as far as a bicycle, or a skateboard or a pram? The courts do not have the luxury of shrugging the question off; they are regularly called on to give an answer to these sorts of questions. In practice they will look at the context of the rule in the legislation, decide the intention of Parliament, look at previous interpretations of the word and even rely on that old faithful – common sense. You will see, however, that even a simple word describing a material object, such as 'vehicle', can be interpreted in a wide variety of ways. Consider how much more scope for flexibility there is in language such as 'reasonable', 'sufficient', 'appropriate', etc.

Section 3 of the HRA is not limited in time. It applies equally to 'legislation whenever enacted', i.e. including future legislation, and it can affect well-established interpretations of statutory provisions.

KEY CASE – *R V LAMBERT* [2001] 3 WLR 206

Lambert had been convicted of possessing cocaine with intent to supply. At his trial, he had attempted to rely on a defence in section 28 of the Misuse of Drugs Act 1971: that the accused 'did not know or have reason to suspect that the material possessed was a controlled substance', e.g. if you are found with small bags of white powder on your person and you had reason to believe that they contained baking soda or talcum powder and no reason to suspect that they really contained cocaine.

For some defences, the burden of proof passes from the prosecution to the defendant (without breaching the overall presumption of innocence). There are two types of burdens relevant here:

- An evidential burden – the defendant has to establish some initial facts that support their argument. This is a very low hurdle for the defendant to clear.
- A legal burden – the defendant has to prove on the balance of probabilities that the defence is true. This is a much higher hurdle for the defendant to clear.

Since the passage of the Misuse of Drugs Act 1971, the defence under section 28 had been interpreted as imposing a *legal burden* on defendants who wished to use it. There had been 30 years of consistent interpretation of the legislation in countless cases around the country. It was a settled interpretation.

In *Lambert*, however, the House of Lords found (*obiter dicta*) that:

- The most obvious way of reading section 28 Misuse of Drugs Act 1971 was that it imposed a legal burden of proof on the defendant.
- Imposing a legal burden of proof on the defendant in these circumstances was not consistent with the right to a fair trial under Article 6 ECHR.
- The obligation under section 3 of the HRA applies to legislation whenever it was enacted, and therefore . . .
- It is possible 'without doing violence to the language or the objective of [s.28 Misuse of Drugs Act 1971], to read the words as only imposing the evidential burden of proof' (Lord Slynn).

This raises a further question of what to do if it is not possible to read the statutory words as being consistent with Convention rights without doing some 'violence to the language' of the legislation.

KEY CASE – *R V A (NO 2)* [2001] 3 ALL ER 1

In the offence of rape there is a defence of consent, or reasonable belief in consent, i.e. that the complainant agreed to the sexual intercourse. The defendant tried to bring evidence that he and the complainant had been in a sexual relationship for three weeks prior to the alleged offence, in order to help him establish his defence of reasonable belief in consent.

The difficulty facing the defendant was that under section 41 of the Youth Justice and Criminal Evidence Act 1999, no evidence may be adduced about the sexual behaviour of the complainant. The measure was introduced for very good reason: to protect rape victims from aggressive and unnecessarily intrusive questioning on their sexual history when they appear as a witness. Such questioning acted as a strong disincentive to women coming forward with rape complaints.

The protection caused a problem in this case, in that it prevented the defendant from bringing forward evidence that was necessary for him to establish his defence. He alleged that disbarring this evidence would prevent him from receiving a fair trial (as provided for by Article 6 of the ECHR).

The House of Lords agreed and found that giving section 41 of the Youth Justice and Criminal Evidence Act 1999 its normal interpretation, in these circumstances, would breach the right to a fair trial. The court turned to its duties under section 3 of the HRA and examined section 41 of the YJCEA 1999 to see if there was scope for interpreting it in such a way as to allow this evidence to be adduced.

The Lords made the following points:

- 'Subject to narrow exceptions section 41 is a blanket exclusion of potentially relevant evidence'.
- There is an exception where the sexual behaviour of the complainant is alleged to be so similar to the sexual behaviour during the alleged offence that the similarity cannot reasonably be explained as a coincidence (section 41(3)).
- There is no argument that, on *ordinary methods of interpretation*, section 41(3) could be interpreted as applying to these circumstances.

Nevertheless, the Lords ultimately found that the evidence of sexual history could be adduced in this case despite the terms of section 41 of the YJCEA 1999. Lord Steyn, giving the lead judgment, said:

- 'the interpretative obligation under section 3 of the of the 1998 Act is a strong one. It applies even if there is no ambiguity in the language . . . in accordance with the will of Parliament as reflected in section 3, it will sometimes be necessary to adopt an interpretation which linguistically may appear strained'.
- 'The techniques to be used will not only involve the reading down of express language in a statute but also the implication of provisions'.
- 'section 3 requires the court to subordinate the niceties of the language of section 41(3)(c) . . . After all, it is realistic to proceed on the basis that the legislature would not, if alerted to the problem, have wished to deny the right to an accused to put forward a full and complete defence by advancing truly probative material'.

To clarify, what the Lords did here was to take the words 'no evidence may be adduced' and imply an exception along the lines of 'no evidence may be adduced . . . (unless it is necessary for a fair trial)'. This, arguably, crossed the line between interpreting the existing words and actively rewriting legislation, particularly in its reference to 'implying provisions' (i.e. inserting words). This seems to represent a constitutional problem in the courts going beyond the judicial function and trespassing into the legislative domain, and a practical problem for the HRA scheme because it downplays the possibility inherent in the opening phrase of section 3 that there will be statutes that cannot be interpreted in line with Convention rights.

In *R v A*, Lord Hope echoed some of these concerns (whilst agreeing with the general approach laid out by Lord Steyn), saying that '. . . the rule is only a rule of interpretation. It does not entitle the judges to act as legislators'. Subsequent decisions have not explicitly distanced themselves from *R v A*, but there has in practice been a different approach. This can be interpreted as a change of emphasis from the 'subordinate the niceties of the language of [the Act]' approach of Lord Steyn to the view of Lord Nicholls in *Re S (Care Order: Implementation of Care Plan)* [2002] UKHL 10, that 'Section 3 is concerned with interpretation [and] . . . the courts must be ever mindful of this outer limit. The Human Rights Act 1998 reserves the amendment of primary legislation to Parliament'.

Finding the precise boundary of this 'outer limit' is difficult. Perhaps the only clear limit discernible from the range of judicial comment is that the courts cannot 'adopt a meaning inconsistent with a fundamental feature of the legislation', i.e. its 'underlying thrust' (Lord Nicholls in *Ghaidan v Godin-Mendoza* [2004] UKHL 30). Lord Bingham also provided a useful summary in *Sheldrake v DPP* [2004) UKHL 43:

- The interpretation obligation is 'a very strong and far-reaching one, and may require the court to depart from the legislative intention of Parliament'.
- Resolving issues through section 3 rather than a declaration under section 4 (see below) is 'the primary remedial measure'.
- The drafters of the HRA thought that a section 4 declaration of incompatibility would only be 'rarely' needed.
- 'There is a limit beyond which a Convention-compliant interpretation is not possible'.

15.9 DECLARATIONS OF INCOMPATIBILITY

Language is not infinitely flexible, and courts cannot always resolve an inconsistency between an Act of Parliament and a Convention right through interpretation under section 3 of the HRA. So what remains for the court to do? It still does not have the ability to strike the legislation down, but it can make a declaration of incompatibility under section 4 of the HRA.

Section 4(2) of the HRA states:

If the court is satisfied that the provision is incompatible with a Convention right, it may make a declaration of that incompatibility.

Courts should strive hard to resolve any apparent disparity between UK statute law and Convention rights through a process of interpretation. This is much more constitutionally harmonious than a declaration that UK statute breaches human rights law, and gives a more direct remedy to the parties to the case: 'A declaration of incompatibility is a measure of last resort' (Lord Steyn in *R v A*).

What would you imagine is the legal effect of a declaration of incompatibility? The rather surprising answer is, nothing. There is no direct legal effect on the Act of Parliament following a declaration of incompatibility. Section 4(6) of the HRA provides that 'A declaration of incompatibility a) does not affect the validity, continuing operation, or enforcement of the provision . . . and b) is not binding on the parties to the proceedings in which it is made'.

To understand why the statutory provision remains valid and in force, you need to remember the dual aims of the Human Rights Act 1998: to make rights effective and maintain Parliamentary supremacy. The courts are not, therefore, given the power to declare any Act invalid or void. The legal power of Parliament to pass an Act that breaches Convention rights is preserved. Note, also, that a declaration of incompatibility 'is not binding' on the parties to the proceedings. Litigants who are successful, to the extent of 'winning' a declaration of incompatibility, will still be subject to the same laws that they complained of, unless and until Parliament decides to amend them.

In principle, therefore, the Act will continue to apply. In practice, it will be affected by a declaration of incompatibility. It will have a shadow of doubt cast over it, not least because if Government does not move to amend that Act, then it is very likely to be subject to an action before the European Court of Human Rights. This could proceed relatively quickly; the applicant could show there was no realistic prospect of success in any further domestic litigation, and the ECtHR would have evidence that the domestic judges regard the Act as a clear breach of Convention rights. The circumstances where a declaration of incompatibility would be made were illustrated in a number of cases following the introduction of the HRA.

KEY CASE – *R(H) V LONDON NORTH AND EAST REGION MENTAL HEALTH REVIEW TRIBUNAL* [2001] 3 WLR 553

The Mental Health Act 1983 allows for the detention of persons suffering from a mental disorder such that they pose a risk either to themselves or to others. This is the process often known as 'sectioning'. At the time when the original decision to detain is made, the burden of proof is on the state. It has to show, by the written opinion of two medical practitioners, that the person is suffering from such a mental disorder. Once someone is detained and wants to be released on the basis that they are no longer suffering from a relevant mental disorder, then under the Mental Health Act 1983, the burden of proof was on the patient.

The Court of Appeal found that imposing this burden on the patient was a breach of Article 5 ECHR, the right to liberty. The right to liberty in this area of mental health law meant that the burden of proof ought to remain entirely on the public authorities to justify the continued detention of the patient.

So the Mental Health Act 1983 stated that the burden of proof is on the patient, whilst the Court found that Article 5 requires the burden to be entirely on the public authorities. Can this be resolved by interpretation under section 3 of the HRA? It could not. To take the words 'imposing the burden on the patient' and read them as meaning the very opposite would not be interpretation. It would be rewriting the statute.

Following the Court of Appeal's declaration, the Government moved to amend the law, and the Mental Health Act 1983 (Remedial) Order 2001 was passed.

KEY CASE – *WILSON V FIRST COUNTY TRUST (NO 2)* [2001] 3 WLR 42

Mrs Wilson took out a loan from First County Trust, using her car as security. The loan agreement did not contain all of the prescribed terms. This meant that under section 127 of the Consumer Credit Act 1974, the court could make no order in relation to the agreement. This resulted in First County Trust being unable to recover the money they had loaned Mrs Wilson or the security on the loan.

The company argued that this breached its right to a fair trial (Article 6) and to property (Article 1, Protocol 1). The Court of Appeal was unable to interpret the words of section 127 of the CCA 1974, that a court 'shall not make an enforcement order', to mean that a court *may make* an enforcement order. It had then to turn to section 4 of the HRA and made a declaration of incompatibility.

(This was reversed by the House of Lords on other grounds: that the agreement was made before the HRA came into force.)

The Government can respond quickly to a section 4 of the HRA declaration of incompatibility. Section section 10 of the HRA provides for a 'remedial order' which is a fast track method of amending the offending Act through secondary legislation. In practice, Governments have generally preferred to respond to section 4 of the HRA declarations through the more considered route of taking an amending Act through Parliament. Note that there is no legal obligation on the Government or Parliament to respond to a declaration of incompatibility in this way. Parliament retains the legal right, as an aspect of its supremacy, to ignore a declaration and to retain any Act on the statute book. The expectation, however, is that political pressure, and the uncomfortable position of being in open breach of human rights commitments, will lead the Government to accept the need for legal reform.

KEY LEARNING POINTS

We can see the outlines of a step-by-step method at the heart of the HRA scheme for the courts to give effect to Convention rights. They must consider:

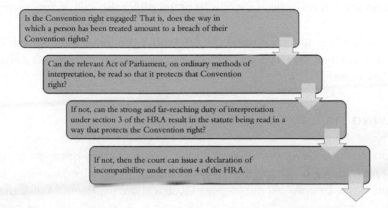

Is the Convention right engaged? That is, does the way in which a person has been treated amount to a breach of their Convention rights?

Can the relevant Act of Parliament, on ordinary methods of interpretation, be read so that it protects that Convention right?

If not, can the strong and far-reaching duty of interpretation under section 3 of the HRA result in the statute being read in a way that protects the Convention right?

If not, then the court can issue a declaration of incompatibility under section 4 of the HRA.

Figure 15.6 Method for giving effect to Convention rights in the courts

We can see that:

■ There was no intention to entrench the Convention rights. If the Convention rights had been simply translated into free-standing rights in a statute (as discussed above) then they would have been subject to the entrenchment problem of the British constitution, i.e. it is impossible to protect statutory provisions from implied or express repeal. To depart from this would involve limits on the law-making powers of Parliament.
■ Sections 3 and 4 of the HRA impose new and continuing duties on the courts. The sections sidestep the problem of entrenchment, and instead rely on this continuing duty. When the courts are carrying out their normal statutory interpretation and application functions, then for existing and for new Acts they must strive to interpret the Act compatibly with Convention rights. If this is not possible, they must issue a declaration of incompatibility.

15.10 OBLIGATIONS ON MINISTERS INTRODUCING LEGISLATION

Section 19 HRA aims to make it less likely that Parliament will pass legislation that breaches Convention rights. It provides that:

A minister must, before Second Reading of the Bill:

(a) make a statement to the effect that in his view the provisions of the Bill are compatible with the Convention rights ('a statement of compatibility'); or
(b) make a statement to the effect that although he is unable to make a statement of compatibility the government nevertheless wishes the House to proceed with the Bill.

The terminology is slightly unfortunate, being close to the language used in section 4 of the HRA. Please take careful note that these are wholly separate procedures:

- *Declarations of incompatibility* – section 4 of the HRA: role of the courts.
- *Statements of compatibility* – section 19 of the HRA: role of Government and Parliament.

The Second Reading of a Bill is when the substantive provisions are first laid before Parliament, and when MPs have a first chance to see in detail what the Government intends the new law to be.

APPLYING THE LAW

Suppose that the Government wants to restrict the rights of prisoners to receive information and to speak to journalists. After taking internal legal advice, it is clear that this would breach (without sufficient justification) the freedom of expression rights of prisoners under Article 10 ECHR, but the Government is keen to press on with the 'reform'. To achieve this, the Ministry of Justice produce a Bill to go before Parliament (a hypothetical Prison Reform Bill), and the Minister of Justice is required, therefore, to follow section 19 HRA.

Let us take a further close look at section 19. What exactly does it require in these circumstances? Are there any substantive restrictions? The answer is no; it is simply a procedural requirement to explain the Government's opinion on the consistency of the proposed new law with Convention rights. For our Prison Reform Bill, therefore, the Justice Minister would say at the Second Reading of the Bill that under section 19(b) HRA they cannot make a statement that the proposal is compatible with Convention rights but that they nevertheless wish Parliament to proceed with it, and Parliament can still pass that Bill into law.

You may wonder at the value of a merely procedural safeguard. Nevertheless, there are important benefits. The minister and their team must at least think about the human rights implications of their proposal. The requirement that the Justice Minister will have to openly declare that the Government is proceeding with a law that breaches the Convention is very likely to encourage the policy-makers and law-drafters in Government and the civil service to consider the human rights implications of their proposal at an early stage and to design out any inconsistencies. It keeps both Government and Parliament commitments to human rights visible through the law-making process.

It can also be regarded as giving a green light to courts to be active in using section 3 of the HRA to reach Convention-compliant interpretations of legislation. If the courts' main role in interpreting statute is to give effect to the intention of Parliament and a Bill passed by Parliament has been certified, by the relevant minister, as being consistent with Convention rights, then the courts are given licence to go a long way in reading the actual words of that statute in ways which protect Convention rights. Conversely, a statement of compatibility does not prevent a later court disagreeing and finding that the Act is actually inconsistent with Convention rights.

15.10.1 JOINT COMMITTEE ON HUMAN RIGHTS

The role of the Joint Committee on Human Rights is generally to consider human rights in the UK, with specific attention to remedial orders under section 10 HRA. It is a joint committee made up of 12 members drawn from the House of Commons and House of Lords. In practice, much of its work has involved legislative scrutiny of Government Bills for their human rights implications. All Government Bills are looked at, and then those with more direct human rights aspects are scrutinised in more detail, including asking questions of ministers and consulting with external groups. In 2014, for example, the Modern Slavery Bill was examined and the Committee put detailed questions to the Home Secretary and received submissions from groups such as The Forced Labour Group, UNICEF and Amnesty International.

15.11 OBLIGATIONS ON PUBLIC AUTHORITIES

Do you remember the main method that the HRA adopts to make rights effective? It is to inject those rights into the bloodstream of the legal system and to require the different limbs of the state to exercise their day-to-day functions, as far as possible, in ways which protect Convention rights. We have seen the obligations imposed on courts and ministers in Parliament; we now turn to the **executive branch** and what the HRA calls 'public authorities'. The primary obligation is outlined in section 6 HRA:

Section 6(1)

It is unlawful for a public authority to act in a way which is incompatible with a Convention right.

So when a public authority (e.g. the Prison Service) is carrying out its functions and exercising public power, it must do so in a way that is compatible with Convention rights. When prison governors are making decisions and exercising discretion on e.g. cell searches, visitation rights and penalties for misconduct, they must consider whether their decisions will breach the Convention rights of their prisoners.

You also need to keep in mind the second main aim of the HRA: to preserve the supremacy of Parliament. This means that there are limits on the duty of public authorities to act compatibly with Convention rights. Section 6(2) HRA provides:

Subsection (1) does not apply to an act if:

(a) as the result of one or more provisions of primary legislation, the authority could not have acted differently; or
(b) [for provisions that cannot be read compatibly with Convention rights] . . . the authority was acting so as to give effect to or enforce those provisions.

So if a statute *requires* a public authority (e.g. the Prison Service) to act in a way that infringes Convention rights, the public authority has to follow the Act of Parliament. We can see, again, how this preserves supremacy.

Not much attention has been given to section 6(2)(b) of the HRA but it is more wide-ranging than sub-section (a). There are relatively few binding duties imposed on public authorities, i.e. requirements to act a particular way. It is more common for public authorities to be given discretionary powers. In *Aston Cantlow PCC v Wallbank* (see below), the House of Lords indicated that if a statutory power cannot be interpreted consistently with Convention rights and it merely empowers a public authority to act a certain way (without requiring it to do so), then the public authority can *choose to act in a Convention-breaching way* to give effect to that provision.

15.12 WHAT IS A PUBLIC AUTHORITY?

The White Paper that preceded the HRA did list some examples of what the term 'public authorities' was intended to cover, including central and local government, the police, the Prison Service, and the immigration authorities. As well as this indicative list, it tried to outline the nature of the test; 'public authorities' includes bodies whose nature is governmental in a broad sense.[2]

Section 6 provides that 'public authority' includes 'any person certain of whose functions are functions of a public nature' (section 3(b)), and that 'In relation to a particular act, a person is not a public authority by virtue only of sub-section (3)(b) if the nature of the act is private'. Parliament is expressly excluded from the category of 'public authorities'.

The HRA therefore divides public authorities into two categories:

- Core public authorities – all of whose functions are covered by section 6 HRA.
- Functional public authorities – who are private in nature but have some functions of a public nature. Only their public functions are covered by section 6 HRA. (These are sometimes called 'hybrid public authorities'.)

From the 1980s onwards there has been a steady privatisation and contracting out of public services – a process that continues to this day. When public services are delivered to us they are often delivered by privately owned enterprises. This raises difficult questions of which organisations fall within the category of 'public authority'.

---

2 'Rights Brought Home', Cm 3782.

APPLYING THE LAW – CORE PUBLIC AUTHORITIES

Police forces are examples of core public authorities. If Lancashire Constabulary, for example, is policing a public protest then this is clearly a public function. It also involves competing interests of freedom of expression, public order and less fundamental concerns such as inconvenience to shoppers/commuters and the cost of policing the protest. When the police are balancing these concerns and making decisions, they must act compatibly with Convention rights (the obvious ones being freedom of expression, Article 10 ECHR and freedom of assembly, Article 11 ECHR).

The Constabulary might also be placing an order for office furniture or a new radio system. The human rights consequences of such decisions are less easy to identify (although HRA cases have included commercial relationships, see e.g. *Wilson v First County Trust* above), yet even here, the Constabulary must abide by Convention rights. Each of its actions must be Convention-compatible.

APPLYING THE LAW – FUNCTIONAL PUBLIC AUTHORITIES

Most of the work in transporting prisoners from jail to court is now carried out by private companies, such as GEOAmey and Serco. As private companies, it is only when they are carrying out their functions of a public nature that the duty under section 6 of the HRA applies to them. If a security guard employed by Serco is transporting prisoners one day, then he has to carry out his functions in a way that is compatible with Convention rights. The guard and the company are carrying out functions of a public nature.

If the next day, the guard is carrying out security duty at a shopping centre, then he (and the company) are acting in a purely private capacity and the section 6 HRA duty does not apply. When Serco is buying office furniture, it is not acting as a public authority, and similarly the section 6 HRA obligation does not apply.

15.12.1 JUDICIAL INTERPRETATION OF 'PUBLIC AUTHORITY'

The interpretation of the term 'public authority' by the courts has been controversial. Lord Hope has argued that the test to be applied under the HRA is different from the test for a 'public body' under standard judicial review and the related question of what is an 'emanation of the State' under EU law (in *YL v Birmingham City Council*, see below). The difference lies in that fact that the HRA is linked to the ECHR scheme and the liability of the UK state in that particular international agreement.

There has been an interesting interaction, although of course not a direct dialogue, between the courts and Parliament. The courts are often presented as the valiant defenders of individual liberty against an uncaring executive and compliant Parliament. This can be the case, but as this line of cases shows, it is not necessarily so.

KEY CASE – *POPLAR HOUSING ASSOCIATION V DONOGHUE*
[2001] 2 WLR 183

Local authorities have specific public duties, imposed by statute, to address homelessness in their areas. Tower Hamlets London Borough Council had transferred their social housing stock to Poplar Housing Association. Donoghue had a dispute with the housing association which she claimed involved her Article 8 ECHR right to a home and private life. The question arose: was the housing association a public authority? If so, it would have to exercise its powers in ways which were compatible with Convention rights.

The starting point for the Court of Appeal was to examine the nature of housing. It said that housing was not necessarily a governmental function. Being a landlord to someone does not mean that you are in a public authority role in relation to them. Local authorities still sometimes place homeless families in bed and breakfast accommodation. This does not turn the B&B owner into a public authority. So, a housing association was not a core public authority. The Court then went on to look at the particular details of this scheme, to assess whether this particular housing association was a functional public authority.

Function – the Court found that the housing association was 'enmeshed' with the local authority and its statutory duties. Poplar Housing Association had become the registered social landlord for this part of London. It was administering the local authority's homelessness duties on behalf of that authority. Put simply, if you were at risk of homelessness in Tower Hamlets and you rang the Council (thereby triggering the local authority's duty), then your query would be acted upon by the housing association.

Structure and control – the Court also found that the governing board of the housing association included a large number of councillors and that, to some extent, the local authority directed its work.

Speaking more generally, the Court said that section 6 HRA requires 'a generous interpretation', but did highlight a range of factors which would limit its scope, including that transferring property from the local authority to the housing association did not itself transfer the public function, and that the charitable status of an organisation does not point to it being a public authority even if it is carrying out activities of the sort generally done by public authorities.

Despite this early, and seemingly broad, interpretation by the courts, the Joint Committee on Human Rights raised concerns about the dangers of narrow interpretation. In its 7th Report of 2002, it stated that a public authority ought to include any organisation that 'exercises a function that has its origin in governmental responsibilities, in such a way as to compel individuals to rely on that body for realisation of their Convention rights'.

The judgment in *Poplar Housing* indicates that each organisation and its relationship with the core public sector has to be examined individually. The Court of Appeal in *R (on the application of Heather) v Leonard Cheshire Foundation* [2002] EWCA Civ 366 found that a charitable care home that accommodated people at public expense was not exercising statutory functions or standing in for the local authority.

KEY CASE – *ASTON CANTLOW PAROCHIAL CHURCH COUNCIL V WALLBANK* [2003] UKHL 37

Mr and Mrs Wallbank acquired a farm in the village of Aston Cantlow, Warwickshire. This land had the status of *rectorial land*. This meant that it had some obligations attached to it, not least to support the upkeep of the local parish church. The local Parochial Church Council (PCC), which is the lowest level of governance in the structure of the Church of England, asked the Wallbanks to fund some repairs to the church building. They refused. The PCC went ahead and made the repairs and presented the bill (of some £95,000) to the Wallbanks. When they refused to pay the bill, they were sued by the PCC. It is important to note that this is therefore a civil debt claim.

The Wallbanks thought that this breached their Convention right to peaceful enjoyment of their property (under Article 1, Protocol 1 ECHR), but the PCC would only be required to use its powers compatibly with this Convention right if it was a 'public authority'.

The Court of Appeal decided that the PCC was a core public authority. The Church of England is established by law with the consequence that the Church possesses powers that private individuals do not. If this was a Catholic church, a Hindu temple, Muslim mosque or a Jewish synagogue, then the neighbouring landowners could not be required to pay for the upkeep of the religious building.

On further appeal to the House of Lords, the PCC (and Church of England) was found *not* to be a core public authority. It was not a part of the state and its role was spiritual rather than governmental. The Law Lords further examined whether the PCC was a functional public authority. They decided that whilst some of the legal powers that the Church of England possessed did make it a functional public authority (for those functions), in this case the issue was simply one of civil debt and the PCC was presently not acting as a functional public authority.

The general test for finding if a body is a functional public authority is:

- Is it publicly funded in relation to this function?
- Is it exercising statutory power?
- Is it taking the place of a public authority?

This flows from Lord Nicholls's approach that section 6 of the HRA is 'essentially a reference to a body whose nature is governmental in a broad sense of that expression. It is in respect of organisations of this nature that the government is answerable under the European Convention on Human Rights'.

Aston Cantlow is a candidate for being the leading case on the section 6 test, but it had rather unusual facts. The difficulty that many more people face is the situation where their Convention rights have been breached by a private company providing a service on a contracted-out basis for central or local government.

KEY CASE – *YL V BIRMINGHAM CITY COUNCIL* [2007] UKHL 27

The claimant was an 82-year-old woman who was suffering from Alzheimer's disease. Local authorities have obligations under the National Assistance Act 1948 to provide accommodation and care to certain categories of people, and she had been placed in a private care home by Birmingham City Council under these statutory duties. The care home was close to her former family home and she was regularly visited by her husband and family. The care home wanted to evict her and she claimed that this interfered with her right to a home and family life under Article 8 of the ECHR.

The majority, by 3:2, in the House of Lords found that the delivery of housing and personal care is not inherently a public function. The care home was not exercising a governmental function, and YL therefore could not invoke her right to a home as against the private care home. Birmingham City Council retained their statutory obligations and would need to find her alternative accommodation (even though this may be some distance away from her equally elderly husband and her family).

The minority judgments were critical of the approach adopted by the majority. Lord Bingham said:

> The intention of Parliament is that residential care should be provided, but the means of doing so is treated as, in itself, unimportant. By one means or another, the function of providing residential care is one which must be performed. For this reason also the detailed contractual arrangements between Birmingham, Southern Cross and Mrs YL and her daughter are a matter of little or no moment.

> The performance by private body A by arrangement with public body B, and perhaps at the expense of B, of what would undoubtedly be a public function if carried out by B is, in my opinion, precisely the case which section 6(3)(b) was intended to embrace.

Lady Hale argued that 'the company, in providing accommodation, health and social care for the appellant, was performing a function of a public nature. This was a function performed for the appellant pursuant to statutory arrangements, at public expense and in the public interest. I have no doubt that Parliament intended that it be covered by section 6(3)(b)'. YL had no choice but to rely on private providers for the delivery of her Convention rights. Birmingham City Council remained in the background and could not escape their statutory duties, but YL was concerned with the immediate and human impact on her of the decision to evict.

The Joint Committee on Human Rights felt compelled to return to the issue. In its 9th Report of 2007, it criticised the judicial approach and recommended legislative amendment so as to include contracted services in the category of 'public authority'. The exhortations of parliamentarians to the courts to find ways of interpreting 'public authority' so as to give wider protection to the public had not worked. In direct response to *YL v Birmingham City Council*, section 145 of the Health and Social Care Act 2008 was passed, stating that a care home providing accommodation and care under arrangements with a local authority is to be taken to be a functional public authority under section 6 of the HRA. As this only applies to the residential care sector, it is only an ad hoc solution, and does not address similar contracting out issues in other sectors.

Overall, the experience of the courts in applying the 'public authority' test has not been a happy one. It has brought criticism from Parliament and from pressure groups. There have been very marked differences between senior judges on how to apply the test (as illustrated in *YL*). Often when Parliament leaves a broad and undefined phrase (such as 'public authority') in statute, then through a number of cases a judicial consensus emerges as to the criteria to be used in applying the test. This has not happened in relation to section 6 HRA. Lord Bingham in *YL* thought that it was wise to leave it open and 'leave it to the courts to decide on the facts of particular cases where the dividing line should be drawn', but the dangers of inconsistency and incoherence in such an approach point to the need for Parliament to revisit the issue.

15.13 HORIZONTAL EFFECT

One difficult area in assessing the scope and the effectiveness of the HRA has been whether the Act has a horizontal, as well as vertical, effect.

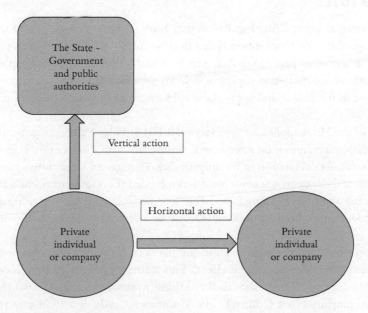

Figure 15.7 Vertical and horizontal effect

Laws have a horizontal effect when they regulate the legal relationships between private individuals, including private companies. So when an individual sues another individual (e.g. for breach of contract), that is a horizontal action; likewise, when an individual sues a private company (e.g. for personal injury caused by negligence) then that is also a horizontal action.

Vertical legal effects are the legal relationships between the state and the individual. Vertical actions are when an individual (or company) brings an action against a public authority, e.g. a judicial review of a planning decision. The main thrust of human rights law, including the ECHR, is to control state action and to protect individuals from abuses of power by the state. The key obligations are therefore placed on the state and not on private individuals. That is, they are vertical legal relationships.

It is less clear that human rights law is intended to directly impact on horizontal relationships, and the notion of 'positive obligations' has emerged to address this issue. If you consider the right to life (Article 2 ECHR), for example, it is more common for another individual, rather than the state, to take a person's life. The European Court of Human Rights has developed legal rules imposing some limited positive obligations on the state to intervene and protect life from known threats posed from other private individuals (*Osman v UK* [1998] EHRR 101). A similar obligation applies to the right to privacy. The state might spy on you, but you are as likely to have your privacy invaded by a newspaper, i.e. a private company.

The question arises then: can Convention rights be enforced against private individuals as well as public authorities? We need to distinguish between those legal relationships governed by statute law and those governed by common law.

15.13.1 STATUTE

When the courts are interpreting legislation, they must (as far as possible) do so in a way which is compatible with Convention rights (section 3 HRA). There is nothing in section 3 of the HRA, or in any other part of the Act, which indicates that this duty only applies in vertical actions. So even in actions between private individuals, where there are relevant statutory rules, the courts have to try to read and apply those rules compatibly with Convention rights.

As section 3 of the HRA applies, so does section 4 HRA. Where a statute governing a horizontal relationship cannot be interpreted consistently with Convention rights, then a court must issue a section 4 declaration of incompatibility. This has no direct impact on the parties to the case, but if the section 4 scheme works as intended (i.e. Government and Parliament pick up the issue and quickly bring UK statute law into line with Convention rights) then the future legal relationships between individuals may be affected by any legislative amendment.

It is clear then that when the legal relationship between individuals is governed by statute, the HRA does provide for horizontal effect. This is further illustrated by *Wilson v First County Trust* (see above). The parties to the dispute were a private individual (Mrs Wilson) and a private company (First County). The Consumer Credit Act 1974 governed their legal relationship and the court tried and failed to resolve the dispute through section 3 of the HRA, before moving to issue a section 4 of the HRA declaration.

Bamforth argues that this is the firmest foundation for 'giving a measure of "horizontal effect" to Convention rights'.[3] This is true, but it leaves unresolved the question of legal relationships governed by common law.

15.14 OBLIGATIONS TO DEVELOP THE COMMON LAW

The framers of the HRA were not always consistent in their views of the impact of the HRA on the common law, but the Lord Chancellor at the time did say:

> We believe that it is right as a matter of principle for the courts to have the duty of acting compatibly with the Convention not only in cases involving other public authorities but *also in developing the common law in deciding cases between individuals.*
>
> (Lord Irvine, Parliamentary debates on the Human Rights Bill 1998 (emphasis added))

Horizontal legal relationships are not only affected by statute law, and in many subject areas such as Contract, Tort, and Property law, common law remains an important source. Where the relationship is governed by common law, the impact of the HRA is more complex, and we need to return to the obligations on courts. The argument proceeds in steps:

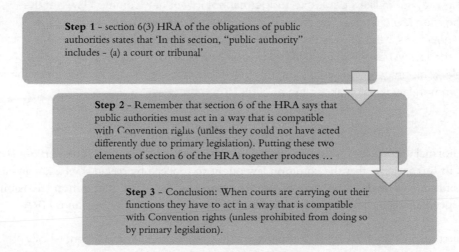

Step 1 - section 6(3) HRA of the obligations of public authorities states that 'In this section, "public authority" includes - (a) a court or tribunal'

Step 2 - Remember that section 6 of the HRA says that public authorities must act in a way that is compatible with Convention rights (unless they could not have acted differently due to primary legislation). Putting these two elements of section 6 of the HRA together produces ...

Step 3 - Conclusion: When courts are carrying out their functions they have to act in a way that is compatible with Convention rights (unless prohibited from doing so by primary legislation).

Figure 15.8 The courts as 'public authorities' under the HRA

---

3   N Bamforth, 'The True "Horizontal Effect" of the Human Rights Act 1998' (2001) 117 *Law Quarterly Review* 34.

So what are those functions? You are familiar with many of them already. They include interpreting law, applying rules of evidence, applying law to resolve disputes, giving remedies to successful parties and making costs orders. So, for example, when the courts are issuing costs orders, they must do so in ways that respect Convention rights. The next question then is: what are the courts' functions in relation to the common law? There are two propositions.

ASSESSING THE LAW

- The courts cannot simply invent new common law rules.
- The common law is not static.

The first proposition notes that there are areas of settled common law. The causes of action (the basis on which you can bring a claim to court) have already been established, e.g. a breach of contract, or a trespass to the person. Judges cannot simply consider that a whole new set of common law rules or a new cause of action would be useful and so decide to create it. The functions of a court, as a public authority under section 6 HRA, do not include inventing wholly new legal remedies.

The second proposition highlights the fact that the common law does not stay still. It changes over the course of time: the postal rule in Contract Law has evolved through the way it has been applied to new technology that has been developed, e.g. the telex machine in *Brinkibon Ltd v Stahag Stahl* [1983] 2 AC 34.

This may seem like a paradox – judges cannot invent new common law, yet the common law changes. The answer lies in the idea that applying existing rules to new facts inevitably results in an (often subtle) refinement or development of the law. When the judges had to decide how the postal rule applied to new telecommunications in *Brinkibon*, this inevitably resulted in a development of the common law rules on accepting an offer to contract.

The normal approach of judges in this role is to proceed with caution. The nervous shock cases in tort indicate that the common law ought to proceed by *evolution on a case-by-case basis* and judges ought to be wary of rapidly expanding the scope of common law liability. The speed and direction of this evolution is the key area affected by section 6 HRA:

- Section 6 of the HRA *does not mean* that judges are required to invent wholly new common law rules or new causes of action (because that is not a part of their functions).
- Section 6 of the HRA *does mean* that judges in applying and developing the common law (which is a part of their function) must do so in ways that are compatible with Convention rights.

The position adopted here is similar to that outlined by Murray Hunt[4] that *existing laws* must be applied in ways which are compatible with Convention rights. Bradley and Ewing summarise this as:

- Convention rights may not be directly enforced by one private party against another, but
- Convention rights may be relied on in *an established cause of action* to extend the rights of either party.[5]

APPLYING THE LAW

A newspaper has obtained (without hacking your phone or paying a corrupt official) a story concerning some of your private sexual conduct and intends to publish it. There is no wider public interest in the story, and after looking at Article 8 of the ECHR, the right to privacy, and the European Court of Human Rights case law, you are confident that publishing the story would be a breach of Article 8.

If you fill out your application to the High Court asking for an injunction to prevent the story being published and simply write down as the basis of the claim, 'breach of Article 8 ECHR', you would fail. Note the summary by Bradley and Ewing immediately above: Convention rights may not be directly enforced by one private party against another. You need to identify some element of UK law that can be the vehicle for your claim, the hook upon which your human rights claim can hang. There is no statute giving citizens a general right to privacy, so you would be reliant on finding some existing area of common law on which to base your claim.

If the newspaper, for example, got their story by sending someone to creep into your garden and peep through your curtains, then that would involve the tort of trespass and you could use that existing common law cause of action as the hook for your rights claim.

This process has seen the common law concept of 'breach of confidence' used to protect privacy. This is a tort that allows courts to restrict the publication of confidential information. It first developed in the context of business, employment and commercial relationships and was then extended (in a nice example of the sort of common law evolution discussed above) to family and other personal relationships. The difficulty in using this cause of action in a typical newspaper story case was that there was usually no existing relationship of confidentiality between the claimant and the newspaper journalists.

In *Douglas and Others v Hello! Ltd* [2003] 3 All ER 996, the Court of Appeal found that the HRA required it to apply the tort in such a way as to protect Article 8 privacy rights. This meant dispensing with the need for a pre-existing relationship between the parties. In

4   M Hunt, 'The "Horizontal Effect" of the Human Rights Act' [1998] *Public Law* 423.
5   A Bradley and K Ewing, *Constitutional and Administrative Law* (15th edn, Longman, 2011) 438.

Campbell v MGN [2004] 2 WLR 1232, the House of Lords formulated this evolved version of the law as: where the claimant had a reasonable expectation of privacy, and publication of that information by the defendant would cause harm, publication could be restrained. Lady Hale based this decision on the type of methodology outlined above, saying that the HRA 'does not create any new cause of action between private persons' but that 'if there is a relevant cause of action applicable, the court as a public authority must act compatibly with both parties'.

In summary then, the courts are required to direct, and speed up, the evolution of the common law. It will still grow, but the intention is that it will grow in the direction of better rights protection.

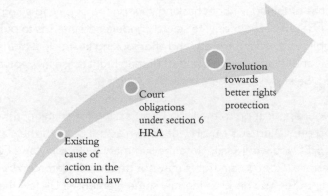

Evolution towards better rights protection

Court obligations under section 6 HRA

Existing cause of action in the common law

Figure 15.9 Court duties to develop the common law

15.15 ACTIONS TO VINDICATE CONVENTION RIGHTS

Sections 3, 4 and 6 of the HRA apply in relation to *all judicial proceedings*, so Convention rights arguments could arise in the context of any legal proceedings (section 7(1)(b) HRA). The key point here is that there is no need to launch separate litigation to vindicate Convention rights.

APPLYING THE LAW

The use of undercover police officers can in some circumstances impinge on the right to a fair trial (Article 6 ECHR). If it emerges during a criminal trial that the police have used undercover officers and the defendant feels that this breaches their right to a fair trial, then the defendant can raise the issue *in the criminal trial itself*.

If the trial judge thinks that it is necessary to exclude evidence or even stop the trial to secure the defendant's right to a fair trial, then they will do so. It is not necessary for the defendant to wait to be convicted on the basis of unfair evidence and then launch a separate action against the police (and possibly the court).

Section 7 of the HRA establishes a separate right to bring proceedings against an authority acting (or proposing to act) in breach of Convention rights. This procedure can only be used against public authorities and is very similar to judicial review. There are important differences in relation to standing, i.e. who can bring an action. For 'ordinary' judicial review, the claimant must show a 'sufficient interest' in the matter to which the claim relates. Under section 7 of the HRA, the claimant can only proceed 'if he is, or would be, a victim of that act' (section 7(3) HRA).

The concept of 'victim' is narrower than the normal approach to 'sufficient interest'. It has, however, been interpreted quite broadly by the ECtHR to include not just people directly affected by Convention-breaching decisions but also, to some extent, their families and potential victims. Whilst the victim test does seem to exclude the sort of public interest standing discussed in Chapter 12, 'Judicial review', it is still open to pressure groups to find a victim and support them in a representative action, or seek to challenge a public decision in the normal way and then incorporate human rights arguments as part of their overall case

15.16 THE FUTURE OF THE HRA?

When the HRA was passed it was widely regarded as adding to the fundamental features of the UK constitutional landscape, in both a legal and political sense. A number of its provisions, particularly section 19 and section 4, are predicated on an expectation that future Governments and Parliaments will have such a respect for Convention rights that it would be politically almost impossible to pass Convention-breaching legislation or to ignore a declaration of incompatibility.

Since its inception, however, the HRA has proved to be something of an irritant to Governments. A number of aspects of the Labour Governments' actions in the 'war on terror' had to be revised following adverse judgments. This led to Labour politicians floating the possibility (in a rather imprecise and exasperated way) of amendments to the HRA. The Conservative Party has never had an unambiguous commitment to the HRA, and a number of high-profile issues have exacerbated hostility to the HRA.

The UK has not responded to a judgment of the ECtHR that it breached Convention rights by imposing a blanket ban on prisoners voting in General Elections (*Hirst v UK (No 2)* [2005] ECHR 681). The Labour Governments 'kicked the issue into the long grass', whilst David Cameron has said that the thought of granting prisoners voting rights made him 'physically sick'. Twelve years after the judgment, the blanket ban remains in place.

Reports emerged late in 2017 that the UK was willing to end the blanket ban and allow some prisoners to vote. This would only apply to prisoners serving less than one year who are on day release.[6] It has been pointed out that such prisoners are still on the electoral roll

---

6   H Siddique, 'Government reportedly planning to allow some prisoners to vote' *The Guardian* (29 October 2017), https://www.theguardian.com/society/2017/oct/29/government-planning-to-allow-some-prisoners-to-vote-european-court-human-rights (last accessed 01/11/17).

and if they are on day release near their constituency then they could, in practice, go and vote already. The total number of prisoners affected 'could be tens'.[7] Such a cynical attempt to fob off the ECtHR would almost certainly not be accepted by the Court. Rather than illustrating commitment to the rule of human rights law, it signals the reverse.

Restrictions on the deportation of foreign nationals, either after serving a sentence and invoking the right to family life, or to face trial in countries with poor human rights records (invoking the prohibition on torture, or use of torture evidence), have also attracted considerable criticism. Elliott and Thomas point out that 'neither the HRA nor the set of rights to which it gives effect are invulnerable to the chill winds of politics; it should not be assumed that either is sacrosanct'.[8]

Conservative Party manifestos since 2010 have had a commitment to 'scrap the Human Rights Act and curtail the role of the European Court of Human Rights, so that foreign criminals can be more easily deported from Britain'. They have promised that 'The next Conservative Government will scrap the Human Rights Act, and introduce a British Bill of Rights. This will break the formal link between British courts and the European Court of Human Rights, and make our own Supreme Court the ultimate arbiter of human rights matters in the UK'.

It is not readily obvious how the UK could 'break the formal link' with the European Court of Human Rights and stay in the European Convention itself. The only European country outside of the ECHR system is Belarus, a country that is consistently rated the worst in Europe for democracy, human rights and press freedom. The Human Rights Act 1998 is also written into the heart of the devolution settlements with Scotland and, in particular, Northern Ireland. Implementing this manifesto commitment will be fraught with legal difficulties. The 2017 Conservative manifesto signaled, not a change of mind but a change of priorities in relation to the HRA, stating 'We will not repeal the Human Rights Act while the process of Brexit is underway but we will consider our human rights legal framework when the process of leaving the EU concludes'.

POINTS TO REVIEW

You will have seen that the HRA represents a significant change from the human rights position in the UK before its introduction. It seeks to impose obligations on different parts of the state to give effect to Convention rights, whilst also preserving the supremacy of Parliament.

....

7   R Allen, 'The great revolution in prisoner voting will affect . . . a few dozen' *The Guardian* (30 October 2017), https://www.theguardian.com/commentisfree/2017/oct/30/prisoner-voting-government-proposal-european-court-human-rights (last accessed 01/11/17).

8   M Elliott and R Thomas, *Public Law* (3rd edn, OUP, 2017) 812.

This has resulted in important new duties for the courts, ministers and public authorities. As ever, the scope and exercise of these duties has given rise to debate. The most intense debates have centred around the nature and extent of the interpretation duty in section 3 of the HRA, the types of organisations that are (or ought to be) within the category of 'public authorities' under section 6, and on what basis the HRA can be said to have horizontal legal effects.

TAKING IT FURTHER

D Nicol, 'Statutory Interpretation and Human Rights after Anderson' [2004] *Public Law* 27 This covers the cluster of early cases that explored the nature of the section 3 of the HRA duty. It would be an interesting exercise to compare Nicol's preferred approach (which is relatively restrictive) with the slightly wider judicial approach in the slightly later cases of *Ghaidan v Godin-Mendoza* and *Sheldrake*.

D Oliver, 'Functions of a Public Nature under the Human Rights Act' [2004] *Public Law* 32 If you want critical ideas to deepen your analysis of the section 6 of the HRA test for 'public authority' then this is for you. Oliver urges us to focus on the idea of public/private function rather than the nature of the body exercising it. Comparing her views to those of the Joint Committee on Human Rights (or the minority in *Aston Cantlow*) could be particularly insightful (and fun).

M Hunt, 'The "Horizontal Effect" of the Human Rights Act' [1998] *Public Law* 42 Out of the wide range of predictions as to how the courts would handle the issue of 'horizontal effect', this has turned out to be probably the most accurate.

British Institute of Human Rights, *The Human Rights Act – Changing Lives* (BIHR, 2008), http://www.equalityhumanrights.com/human-rights/human-rights-practical-guidance/area-generic/the-human-rights-act-changing-lives

This is a marvellous short publication that seeks to bring to life through case studies the impact of the HRA on people's lives. It directs our attention to the 'dynamic life' of the HRA outside of the courtroom. If you want to ground some of the (occasionally) esoteric debates around the HRA in real life experiences, then please do have a look at this.

CHAPTER 16
POLICE AND SECURITY POWERS

The police and security services play a crucial role in maintaining 'the good life' for citizens in the UK – a life largely (or at least relatively) free from the threat of violence and external intimidation, secure in one's possessions, and ruled by regular law and not by the caprice of some individual.

This rosy view is balanced by a more negative attitude to the police, one that is suspicious of the great powers that they wield and that is alive to the dangers of abuse. There have been long-standing questions of partiality on the part of the police and security services, and those in 'suspect communities' have suffered from police violence and injustice. These communities include ethnic minorities, political protesters, those with alternative life-styles (such as New Age travellers), and people from nationalities or religions linked to terror threats.

The balance between these two concerns (empowering those who protect us and protecting ourselves against their abuse of power) is of central importance to Public Law. So many of the key protections and celebrated features of the UK constitutional system – political accountability, separation of powers, the rule of law, human rights – would mean almost nothing if the activities of those at the sharp end of the interface between state and citizen are not controlled by law. This 'sharp end' involves a wide variety of people from soldiers and prison officers, to a private contractor carrying out a work disability assessment on a welfare claimant. Those with the most potential impact, for good or ill, are the police and security services.

AS YOU READ

This subject involves considering the careful balance between granting power and placing limitations on that power. So what are you going to do with the information covered here? In previous chapters you have been asked to consider how to use the information to perform well in assessments, or to identify what skills you are developing in thinking about the material.

This chapter gives you the same guidance, and there are assessment tips below, but you are invited to take a broader view as you read through the sections. Policing and security are important parts of civic life – the life that you are already a part of and that you will contribute to further as a law graduate. As someone trained in Public Law, you will not just have to write assessments on these issues; you will at some point form opinions on policing matters. Just as a dog is for life and not just for Christmas, your education is for life and not just for assessments.

We will examine how the police are organised and empowered and how the exercise of their powers is controlled and scrutinised.

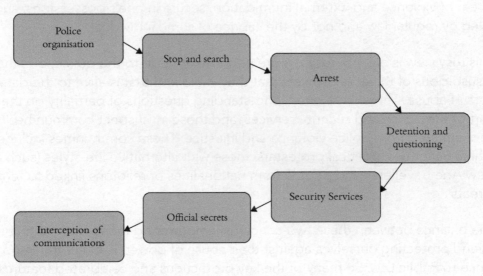

Figure 16.1 Structure of Chapter 16

16.1 POLICE ORGANISATION

There is no national police force. As established by the Police Act 1996, there are 43 police forces in England and Wales, including two in London. Both Northern Ireland and, since 2013, Scotland have single police services. A pertinent question is: who directs these forces? Who decides their goals, powers, methods and resources?

The police are an arm of the state with dramatic power to intrude into people's lives. The police can stop you going about your business, they can detain you and put you in a cell. They can start an investigation that could lead to your incarceration in jail for years; add to all this the human rights impact of the public policing role in relation to protests and marches. If this power could be deployed at the whim of individual politicians or civil servants, or even by Government as a whole, then the ramifications would be awful.

Related to these concerns of holding the police to account is the question of whether powers that can used benignly to protect people from criminality and to maintain order can also be used malignantly to give vent to prejudice and to control and punish those regarded as some kind of 'enemy within' or 'enemy of the state'.

16.1.1 INDEPENDENCE/STATUS

A police officer is not an employee, but 'a servant of the state' (*Fisher v Oldham Corporation* [1930] 2 KB 364), i.e. a holder of public office. Police officers are barred from belonging to trade unions and from political activities. They are subject to a disciplinary code. In theory, they have independence from direct political control, as Lord Denning said in *R v Metropolitan Police Commissioner, ex parte Blackburn* [1968] 2 QB 118: 'No Minister of the Crown can tell him that he must or must not, keep observation on this place or that; or that he must, or must not, prosecute this man or that one. Nor can any police authority tell him to do so. The responsibility for law enforcement lies on him. He is answerable to the law and the law alone'. Whilst there is some high-level policy direction (national policing objectives are set out by the Home Office and Police and Crime Commissioners publish more local plans), it is the Chief Constable for each force who is responsible for operational matters.

Over recent years there has been a partial civilianisation and privatisation of the forces. Following the Police Reform Act 2002, Police Community Support Officers (PCSOs) were introduced, as were other civilian support officers, e.g. for detention and escort duties. PCSOs had limited powers, for example to issue fixed penalty notices, direct traffic and deal with drug possession. These powers were significantly extended by the Policing and Crime Act 2017 and brought almost into line with those of police constables. They can use reasonable force in the exercise of their duties.

16.1.2 POLICE AND CRIME COMMISSIONERS

The Police and Crime Commissioner posts were introduced by the Police Reform and Social Responsibility Act 2011. PCCs are elected so as to 'secure the maintenance of the police force for that area and secure that the police force is efficient and effective' (section 1(6) PRSRA 2011). They are to hold their Chief Constable to account for operational matters.

PCCs issue a police and crime plan (section 32 PRSRA 2011) and an annual report. The plan sets out the main objectives, including crime reduction, and covers resource issues. Police and Crime Panels made up of representatives from local authorities, plus some independent members, have the role of holding the PCC, rather than the police directly, to account (section 30 PRSRA 2011).

The structure established by the Police Reform and Social Responsibility Act 2011 replaced the existing police authorities. The reform was introduced due to a perceived lack of accountability. It was felt that the public did not understand, or even know of, the role of police authorities. The identification of a single post (the PCC) and direct elections to that post were intended to promote public engagement with the work of holding the police to account and of setting broad priorities for policing in local areas. The success of the reforms is questionable. The first elections were held in November 2012. The turnout, at around 15 per cent, was very poor, and was the lowest ever for an election on a national scale.

APPLYING THE LAW – POLICE AND CRIME COMMISSIONERS

Find (through a simple internet search) the website for the Police and Crime Commissioner for your own area. This will tell you who your PCC is and what priorities they have identified for policing in your area.

The Police and Crime Plan for Lancashire Constabulary,[1] for example, sets out some broad-brush priorities. Some, such as to 'Champion the rights of victims', involve consultation, coordination of existing services and developing an overall strategy for victims. Others, such as 'Protect vulnerable people', appear to be more interventionist, with the PCC allocating funds specifically for domestic abuse services.

Have a read through of the Plan for your area and consider:

- Whether the role of the Police and Crime Commissioner appears to effectively promote public engagement with the scrutiny and goal-setting of policing in your area?
- The extent to which there is a focus on the accountability role. How does the PCC hold the Chief Constable to account? Where is this reported?
- Whether setting broad priorities can influence operational policing?

16.1.3 HOME SECRETARY

The Home Secretary retains overall responsibility for the police service. They answer questions in Parliament about policing matters. The Home Office sets the budget allocations for police forces. It publishes circulars that aim to harmonise approaches to specific issues across different forces. Examples from October 2017 include circulars on handling immigration cases involving those caught up in the Grenfell Tower tragedy, and on detainees who refuse to eat or drink.[2]

16.1.4 NATIONAL CRIME AGENCY

The National Crime Agency was established in 2013 by the Crime and Courts Act 2013. It is not the first body to co-ordinate national activity on serious crime, having replaced the Serious and Organised Crime Agency. It has roles in crime reduction and criminal intelligence in relation to organised crime, border policing, economic crime and child protection. Its priorities are directed by the Home Secretary, but all operational decisions are made by its Director General. The Director General can direct other police forces to assist in operations.

1 Lancashire Police and Crime Plan, http://lancashire-pcc.gov.uk/the-police-and-crime-plan/ (last accessed 01/11/17).
2 Home Office circulars, https://www.gov.uk/government/publications?departments[]=home-office (last accessed 01/11/17).

16.2 ASSESSMENT ADVICE

There are broadly two types of Public Law questions on policing:

- Essay questions on issues such as the constitutional role of policing, police powers, the accountability of the police, and particularly on the role of the discretion that is necessary for effective policing but which provides scope for abuse.
- Problem questions requiring you to outline and apply police powers relating to stop and search, arrest and detention.

The following sections will outline the key police powers in these areas.

16.3 THE GENERAL FRAMEWORK – ARTICLE 5 OF THE ECHR AND PACEE

The principal human right engaged by policing activity is Article 5 of the European Convention on Human Rights which provides a general right to liberty of the person. You will see later that the right to a fair trial (Article 6 ECHR) is also relevant. Article 5 of the ECHR sets out a series of permitted limitations on the right to liberty, including arrest on the basis of reasonable suspicion. Whilst it provides a general framework within which UK policing law must operate, it has been argued that Article 5 will have few direct implications for policing decisions on arrest and detention.[3]

Article 5(1) provides that:

Everyone has the right to liberty and security of person. No one shall be deprived of his liberty save in the following cases and in accordance with a procedure prescribed by law;

1(c) the lawful arrest or detention of a person effected for the purpose of bringing him before the competent legal authority on reasonable suspicion of having committed an offence or when it is reasonably considered necessary to prevent his committing an offence or fleeing after having done so.

Article 5 also provides procedural rights: that 'Everyone who is arrested shall be informed promptly, in a language which he understands, of the reasons for arrest and of any charge against him' and that 'Everyone arrested or detained [on reasonable suspicion of having committed an offence] shall be brought promptly before a judge or other officer authorised by law to exercise judicial power'.

---

3 D Mead, 'The Likely Effect of the Human Rights Act on Everyday Policing Decisions in England and Wales' [2000] *Journal of Civil Liberties* 5.

Until the 1980s, policing was governed by a wide range of different legal instruments. Most police powers were consolidated in 1984 in the Police and Criminal Evidence Act (PACE) 1984. PACE also tried to rebalance the relationship between police powers and suspects' rights. Police were, for example, granted clearer statutory authority to arrest without a warrant and to enter and search property. Suspects were given rights, for example, to access legal advice. There was an emphasis on regularising police conduct so as to make policing effective whilst reducing the risk of abuse of powers. This was to be achieved partly through the PACE Codes of Practice. These do not have the full force of law, but guide police behaviour in detailed ways and are relevant to whether officers have breached internal rules or their legal powers.

16.4 STOP AND SEARCH

It is socially useful to give limited powers to the police to stop people in the street and to search them. There is no general power of stop and search. The position at common law was outlined in *Rice v Connolly* [1966] 2 QB 414, that whilst there may be a moral duty to assist the police there was no legal duty to do so, including submitting oneself to a public search. In the absence of lawful authority, if the police try to stop and search someone they will be acting unlawfully and committing trespass to the person. In *Bentley v Brudzinski* (1982) Cr App Rep 217, for example, a person was informally stopped and asked questions by the police. He answered some questions in a calm way and then went to leave before the police had finished. When the police officer took hold of his arm to prevent him from leaving, the officer was acting without authority and therefore committing an assault.

Particular statutory provisions grant the police stop and search powers in two main areas: stolen or prohibited articles, and drugs. Section 1 PACE states that 'a constable may search a person or vehicle for stolen goods, offensive weapons and articles' for use e.g. in a burglary. They have the power to detain for the purposes of a search and to seize prohibited articles. Offensive weapons include articles which inherently may cause physical harm, such as a machete, and items which, although in and of themselves may be quite innocent (e.g. a cricket bat), the constable has reason to believe will be used for causing harm. Powers to stop and search are also given by section 23 of the Misuse of Drugs Act 1971 in relation to possession of a controlled drug.

There are a number of safeguards on the exercise of these powers:

- Under section 1(3) of PACE there is no stop and search power unless the constable has reasonable suspicion that the search will find prohibited articles. (See the discussion of reasonable suspicion in the section on arrest below.)
- Stop and search powers cannot be used on private premises, but can in places that the public can access, such as pubs and sports venues.
- A record of the search must be made as soon as is practicable (and if practicable, a copy given to the searched person).

- Under section 2 of PACE, the officer must identify themselves as a police officer, give their name and station, the object of the search and the grounds for proposing it.
- The person can only be stopped for the time reasonably required to effect the search.
- A person cannot be required to remove clothing, except an outer coat, jacket or gloves.

Code of Practice A gives more detailed practical guidance on using the powers fairly and responsibly, for example to reduce the public embarrassment of the search as much as possible.

There are additional stop and search powers, in relation to public order and terrorism offences, that can be exercised without the need for reasonable suspicion. Under section 60 of the Criminal Justice and Public Order Act 1994, a senior police officer can authorise the use of these powers where they reasonably anticipate serious violence in a particular locality and it is expedient to use stop and search powers to try to prevent this. The authorisation can only last for up to 24 hours.

16.5 ARREST

Ryan and Williams argue that:

> Police powers, particularly the powers of arrest, because they involve the deprivation of liberty, are highly intrusive on freedom. At the same time, it is in these areas that the element of discretion is strongest. As a result, vagueness and flexibility in this area all too easily can lead to the abuse of power and ultimately to arbitrary deprivations of liberty.[4]

This quote highlights the relevance of arrest. If you are arrested, you do not simply lose your liberty. Arrest triggers a range of other powers that can only be used against a person in lawful custody, and these powers are highly discretionary. We have seen in other chapters, such as on the rule of law and on judicial review, that discretion is a matter of some concern in Public Law. We need to give public officials choices over how they exercise their powers, but we need to remain alert to the dangers of abuse of such powers.

Arrest is a legal process but it also refers to a physical state, or perhaps more accurately a relationship between individuals. Lord Diplock in *Holgate-Mohammed v Duke* [1984] AC 437 said:

> The word arrest is a term of art. It should be noted that it is a continuing act; it starts with the arrester taking a person into his custody (by action or words restraining him from moving anywhere beyond the arrester's control), and it continues until the person so restrained is either released from custody or . . . is remanded in custody by the magistrates' judicial act.

---

4   C Ryan and K Williams, 'Police Discretion' [1984] *Public Law* 285.

In this sense, arrest is 'a matter of fact' (*Lewis v CC of South Wales Constabulary* [1991] 1 All ER 206). It is something that anyone can do. The arrestor is simply stopping someone from moving away. The question is, even when arrest is effected by a police officer – is it lawful? There are three main requirements for a lawful arrest:

- A power of arrest.
- Reasonable suspicion.
- Adherence to the procedural rules.

If any of the requirements are absent, then the arrest will be invalid. The consequences of this may be to:

- Form the basis of a complaint to the Independent Police Complaints Commission. This will be renamed as the Independent Office for Police Conduct from January 2018, following reform under the Policing and Crime Act 2017.
- Give rise to internal police disciplinary proceedings.
- Result in the exclusion of evidence at trial, although this would be exceptional rather than the norm.
- Be a defence to certain charges, e.g. assaulting a police officer in the course of his duty.
- Result in a civil action in tort for assault and false imprisonment. If a person is wrongly arrested, then they will be entitled to damages (*Roberts v Chief Constable of Cheshire Constabulary* [1999] 2 All ER 326).

APPLYING THE LAW – POWERS OF ARREST

Consider this scenario. There has been a theft from the premises of an office supplies company which has 18 employees. It was discovered that £120 had been taken from the petty cash box and that two tablet computers are missing. The police are called and Detective Constable Dawson speaks to the office manager.

- There is no evidence of a break-in.
- There are no fingerprints on the cash box. There is no CCTV footage.
- The office manager says that only someone with inside knowledge of the firm would know where the cash box and tablet computers were stored.
- She also tells the police that Sarah Jackson was dismissed from the firm recently (on unrelated grounds – persistent lateness) and that her last working day was yesterday.

DC Dawson goes to Ms Jackson's flat and speaks to her. She flatly denies that she had anything to do with the theft. She does not want to discuss the matter further as she needs to go and pick her daughter up from school. The detective is minded to arrest Ms Jackson and take her to the police station for further questioning.

We will use this scenario as a lens to look at the operation of the law on arrest.

Arrest with a warrant

Section 1 of the Magistrates' Court Act 1980 provides that 'on an information being laid before a Justice of the Peace that a person has, or is suspected of having committed an offence, the justice may issue a) [a summons to appear before a court], or b) a warrant to arrest that person and bring him before a magistrates' court'. The application must be in writing and substantiated on oath by a constable, and is only available for indictable or imprisonable offences, or where a summons cannot be served because the address is 'not sufficiently established'.

The powers are limited and the procedure is relatively cumbersome. You will see below that arrest without a warrant is readily available, so use of the warrant procedure for arrest (as opposed to search of property) is relatively rare. In our scenario above, it is very unlikely that the police would go to the trouble of trying to obtain a warrant for Ms Jackson's arrest. They would rely on their legal powers to make an arrest without a warrant.

Arrest without a warrant

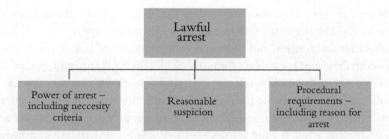

Figure 16.2 Requirements for a lawful arrest

There was a major revision to the law of arrest in the Serious Organised Crime and Police Act 2005. Previously, arrest without a warrant was very widely available for 'arrestable offences', and only available subject to much stricter conditions for 'non-arrestable offences'. Arrestable offences were those serious and middle-ranking offences for which a sentence of five years could be given (which, from our scenario, includes theft). Non-arrestable offences were the less serious offences, where arrest could only take place where the 'general arrest conditions' were present. This distinction was abolished in 2005, and arrest is now available on the same basis for all offences. The current version of section 24 of PACE provides that:

A constable may arrest without a warrant –

(a) anyone who is about to commit an offence;
(b) anyone who is in the act of committing an offence;
(c) anyone whom he has reasonable grounds for suspecting to be about to commit an offence;
(d) anyone whom he has reasonable grounds for suspecting to be committing an offence.

A constable also has arrest powers when there are 'reasonable grounds for suspecting that an offence has been committed' and, if an offence has been committed, (a) anyone who is guilty of the offence and (b) anyone whom he has reasonable grounds for suspecting to be guilty of it. This would be the power used in the scenario above. The police would base the arrest of Ms Jackson on there being reasonable grounds to suspect that an offence of theft has taken place and having reasonable grounds for suspecting Ms Jackson to be guilty of it.

A new general condition was introduced in 2005; that these powers can be exercised for any offence, but only where the constable has reasonable grounds for believing that the arrest is *necessary* for the reasons outlined in section 24(5) PACE 1984:

- To ascertain the person's name or address.
- To prevent harm, including physical harm to themselves or another, or harm to property, or to protect a child or vulnerable person.
- To achieve the prompt and effective investigation of the offence.
- To prevent a prosecution being hindered by the disappearance of the person.

These conditions are very wide-ranging and are hardly going to limit the arrest power. In our scenario, most of these 'necessity' criteria simply do not apply. The police know Ms Jackson's name and address, and there is no real evidence of risk of harm (arguably the disposal/destruction of the tablet computers?). There is no apparent risk of the disappearance of Ms Jackson. The relevant criterion (which we can now see has something of a 'catch-all' characteristic) is the prompt and effective investigation of the offence. Code of Practice G tries to structure the discretion here but arguably fails to provide any further limits. It provides that arrest for the purposes of the prompt and effective investigation of the offence may be necessary *inter alia* where the suspect has made false statements or statements that cannot be readily verified, or where it is necessary to obtain evidence by questioning. In our scenario, any of these factors appear to be available to an officer to use as justification for the necessity of arresting Ms Jackson.

The PACE Code of Practice C para 2.4 seems to indicate a strict test of necessity:

> The power of arrest is only exercisable if the constable has reasonable grounds for *believing that it is necessary* to arrest the person . . . it remains an operational decision at the discretion of the constable . . . applying the necessity criteria requires the constable to examine and justify the reason or reasons why a person needs to be arrested.

Austin, writing at the time of the reforms, thought that the introduction of the necessity test could be a significant limitation on arrest powers, arguing that Parliament had chosen the word 'necessary' knowingly and deliberately and concluding that necessary 'means there is no alternative to arrest'.[5] In *Hayes v Chief Constable of Merseyside Police* [2011] EWCA Civ 911, however, the Court of Appeal stated that there is no need to consider all the

---

5 R Austin, 'The New Powers of Arrest: Plus ça change: More of the Same or Major Change?' [2007] *Criminal Law Review* 459, 464.

alternatives to arrest in concluding that an arrest is necessary. In the scenario above, then, DC Dawson would not have to consider less intrusive options such as questioning Ms Jackson further in her own home, or requesting her attendance at the police station at a later time, before deciding that an arrest was necessary to the investigation.

There are also statutory powers of arrest without a warrant given to the general public. In comparison with a constable's powers, these are very limited. They are available only for indictable offences, i.e. those offences which can be tried at Crown Court, and only where it is not reasonably practicable for a constable to make the arrest.

Common law powers of arrest

There are very limited residual powers of arrest without a warrant at common law. These are applicable both to constables and the general public. They arise only where there is 'reasonable apprehension of imminent danger of a **breach of the peace**' (*R v Howell* [1982] QB 416, i.e. an act, done or threatened, to harm a person or property or likely to cause harm or fear of harm).

Breach of the peace is a strange beast. It is not a criminal act in itself (just a state of affairs that gives rise to certain powers), and it was stressed by the Court of Appeal in *Bibby v Chief Constable of Essex* (2000) 164 JP 297 that this power of arrest is exceptional and must only be exercised in 'the clearest of circumstances' where there is 'a sufficiently real and present threat to the peace to justify the extreme step of depriving of his liberty a citizen who is not at the time acting unlawfully'.

16.5.1 REASONABLE SUSPICION

The second element of a lawful arrest is reasonable suspicion. The powers of arrest in section 24 of PACE are conditional on there being 'reasonable grounds for suspecting . . .'. The context of our discussion of reasonable suspicion is this: the powers of arrest are very wide; the necessity criteria are not particularly restrictive; the procedural rules on arrest are not terribly burdensome. This requirement of *reasonable suspicion* is a crucial safeguard to prevent arrest powers being exercised oppressively and arbitrarily, and we need to examine reasonable suspicion as potentially the most credible constraint on the police use of their arrest powers. Despite this importance, there is no definition of reasonable suspicion given in PACE itself.

16.5.1.1 WHAT ARE THE ELEMENTS OF THE TEST?

KEY CASE – *CASTORINA V CHIEF CONSTABLE OF SURREY* (1988) 138 NLJ 180

According to the Court of Appeal in *Castorina*, there are three elements to 'reasonable suspicion':

■ A subjective element – did the constable suspect that the arrested person was guilty of the offence? In *R v Olden* [2007] EWCA Crim 726, the court would not infer that an officer had reasonable suspicion where he had not stated in evidence that he suspected the arrested person had committed an offence.

- An objective element – would the grounds have led a reasonable person to *suspect* that the arrested person was guilty of the offence? In *Castorina*, the officer did not have to have grounds for an honest belief that the suspect *was guilty*, just (a lower standard) of whether a reasonable person would suspect them of the crime.
- A discretionary element – provided that the arrest does not breach general principles of Administrative Law (e.g. improper purpose as a ground of judicial review), the constable has a discretion as to whether to arrest or not.

In our scenario then, DC Dawson must *actually suspect* Ms Jackson of the theft offence, and be able to say so in his evidence. He must also have, to his knowledge at the time of the arrest, reasonable grounds that would persuade another reasonable person to suspect Ms Jackson of the offence.

16.5.1.2 WHAT IS THE OBJECTIVE ELEMENT OF THE TEST?

PACE Code of Practice G para.2.3A states that: 'There must be some reasonable, objective grounds for the suspicion, based on known facts and information which are relevant to the likelihood the offence has been committed and the person liable to arrest committed it'. There is much more detailed guidance on the possible range of factors that can be taken into account in PACE Code of Practice A on stop and search. PACE does not state whether the more comprehensive explanation in Code A applies to arrest, but since arrest is a more serious interference with liberty, then it is arguable that the safeguards apply at least equally. It is, under Code of Practice A on stop and search, para.1.7, impermissible to take some factors into account:

Reasonable suspicion can never be supported on the basis of personal factors alone. For example, a person's colour, age, hairstyle or manner of dress, or the fact that he is known to have a previous conviction . . . cannot be used alone or in combination with each other as the sole basis on which to search that person. Nor may it be founded on the basis of stereotyped images of certain persons or groups as more likely to be committing offences.

In *O'Hara v Chief Constable of RUC* [1997] 1 ALL ER 129, the arresting officer had a briefing from a policeman which contained very limited information on which the arresting officer could form the reasonable grounds for arrest. The House of Lords rejected an argument that an order to arrest by a senior officer with no further information could be the basis of reasonable suspicion, but went on to accept that even though the information given to the officers was 'scanty', it was sufficient for them to base a reasonable suspicion on. In *Hough v Chief Constable of the Staffordshire Constabulary* [2001] EWCA Civ 39, this was extended to entries on a police database.

APPLYING THE LAW – REASONABLE SUSPICION

Apply this information on reasonable suspicion to our scenario. Try to identify the possible objective reasonable suspicion that DC Dawson held at the time of arrest. To say that the grounds must be objective means that DC Dawson must be able, at the time of the arrest and on the basis of information that he possesses at that time (and importantly, not in the light of subsequent developments), be able to explain why he thinks it is likely (to some extent) that Ms Jackson has committed the offence.

You will probably focus on two aspects. First, opportunity – she knew where the stolen materials were stored, and this was not general knowledge outside of the firm. Second, motive – she is likely to be unhappy with the firm and may also have a motive (i.e. through losing her job) to obtain further money.

You will notice that PACE Code of Practice G only indicates that there must be information that points to the likelihood of a person having committed the offence. It does not cover the strength of that likelihood; is it a near certainty or a remote possibility? The title of the test – reasonable suspicion – does imply a test of reasonableness, but this is really very vague and needs to be read in the context of the cases above, such as *O'Hara*, which allowed 'scanty' grounds to suffice.

Try to alter the facts of the scenario to the point where you think that reasonable suspicion no longer exists. You might consider changing the reason for Ms Jackson's departure from the firm (maternity leave, leaving for a better job), or the information on the 'inside job' theory (i.e. if the cash box and computers were stored in plain sight in a place that customers had access to). Each of the changes makes it less likely that Ms Jackson has committed the offence, but it is still difficult to identify a dividing line between when the highly coercive power of arrest exists and when it does not.

The purpose of arrest – *Holgate-Mohammed v Duke* [1984] AC 437 had similar facts to those in our scenario: a theft from work, with an assertion that it was an 'inside job' and the arrest of a disgruntled former employee. The court held that there were objective grounds to suspect but, in the absence of a confession, there would clearly be insufficient evidence to continuing to a successful prosecution for the offence.

The reason why the officer arrested her was that he held the honest opinion that the police inquiries were likely to be more fruitful in clearing up the case if Mrs Holgate-Mohammed were compelled to go to the police station to be questioned there.

The court of first instance, in finding that the arrest was unlawful, described the purpose of this arrest as 'to subject her to greater stress and pressure involved in arrest and deprivation of liberty'. This was condemned in the House of Lords as 'emotive phraseology'.

The House of Lords found that 'arrest for the purpose of using the period of detention to dispel or confirm the reasonable suspicion by questioning the suspect' was well established and supported by statute. This is now confirmed by PACE Code of Practice G.

The timing of arrest – In *Hussein v Chong Fook Kam* (1970) AC 942, the Privy Council stated that 'It is desirable as a general rule that an arrest should not be made until the case is complete'. The role of arrest has clearly changed in the intervening years. It is now used not simply (or even mainly) to bring the suspect before the court, or because the police cannot serve a summons, or to prevent immediate harm to others, but rather to further the investigation by the detention and questioning of the suspect, or, increasingly, to obtain physical evidence from them in custody.

PACE Code of Practice G says that: 'The power of arrest must be used fairly and responsibly'. It represents 'an obvious and significant interference' with Article 5 ECHR, the right to liberty. Paragraph 1.3 of the Code continues: 'The use of the power must be fully justified and officers exercising the power should consider if the necessary objectives can be met by other, less intrusive, means'. The conclusion of Clayton and Tomlinson, writing more than 25 years ago, that 'the law provides very scanty protection for those suspected of crime' still seems to hold true.[6]

16.5.2 PROCEDURAL RULES

Under section 28 of PACE, the fact of arrest and grounds for arrest must be communicated at the time of, or as soon as practicable after, the arrest. There are good reasons for imposing this duty. Arrest is a major step involving the loss of liberty. The moment when a person's liberty ends should be communicated clearly. If the suspect is given the reasons for the arrest, they may be able to refute these reasons and limit the amount of time when they are deprived of their liberty.

KEY CASE – *CHRISTIE V LEACHINSKY* [1947] AC 573

The appellant was a warehouse owner who the police suspected had stolen a bale of cloth. He was arrested, without a warrant, for 'unlawful possession' under the Liverpool Corporation Act 1921. The Act did not give a power of arrest in these circumstances. Leachinsky was held in custody for over two weeks and sued his arresting officers for false imprisonment. The police defence was that Leachinsky could, on the same facts, have been lawfully arrested for a different offence.

The House of Lords, finding against the police, held that 'an arrest without warrant can be justified only if it is an arrest on a charge made known to the person arrested'. A police officer must 'state at the time . . . on what charge the arrest is being made or at least inform him of the facts which are said to constitute a crime on his part. Even if circumstances exist which may excuse this, it is still his duty to give the information at the first reasonable opportunity after the arrest'.

---

6   R Clayton and J Tomlinson, 'Arrest and Reasonable Grounds for Suspicion' (1988) 32 *Law Society Gazette* 22.

This protection was put on a statutory footing with the introduction of section 28 PACE, and its importance was reiterated in *Edwards v DPP* (1993) 97 Cr App R 301: 'the arrested man is entitled to be told what is the act for which he is arrested' and 'giving the correct information of the reasons for arrest was of the utmost constitutional significance'. As well as the constitutional importance, these procedural safeguards are also reflective of human rights law obligations, i.e. Article 5(2) ECHR: 'Everyone who is arrested shall be informed promptly, in a language which he understands, of the reasons for arrest and of any charge against him'.

There is no need for the constable to formulate the precise charge that may be made, but they must communicate the required information in 'simple, non-technical language that [the suspect] could understand' (*Taylor v Thames Valley Chief Constable* [2004] EWCA Civ 858, where the arrestee was a 10-year-old boy, arrested six weeks after his alleged offence).

The consequences of not informing the arrestee of the reasons for arrest are serious: the arrest will be unlawful. The police can limit the period of unlawful arrest by providing reasons. The arrest will then be lawful from that point onwards (but not retrospectively) (*Lewis v Chief Constable of South Wales* [1991] 1 All ER 206). Code G also outlines that the officer should state the reasons why they consider the *arrest to be necessary*.

The constable may use reasonable force in making the arrest (section 3 Criminal Law Act 1967; section 117 PACE). Using unreasonable force means that the actions are not protected in law, and will render the constable liable to a civil action or criminal prosecution for their violence.

APPLYING THE LAW

Applying this to our scenario means that DC Dawson must a) inform Ms Jackson that she is under arrest and b) tell her the reasons for arrest. This does not have to be a precise indication of the statute that has been breached (section 1 Theft Act 1968). It should be precise enough for her to understand why she is being arrested and give her the opportunity to rebut the allegation, e.g. 'I am arresting you for the theft of money and computers from your former employer'.

If DC Dawson fails to do this, then the arrest is unlawful. On the basis of *Lewis*, if he remembers and informs her of the reasons for arrest e.g. an hour later, then the arrest is only unlawful for that hour. In practical terms, this means that she *would* be entitled to Civil Law damages for wrongful arrest for this hour but not for the full period of her detention.

16.6 DETENTION AND QUESTIONING

To illustrate how the different elements of detention and questioning interact we will work through a different example.

APPLYING THE LAW – POWERS OF DETENTION

Consider this scenario. There has been an assault in the street. The victim has been attacked, suffering bruises and scratches to the face. There is a wide cut above the victim's eye (of the sort that can be caused by a punch) and he has been taken to hospital (i.e. this is potentially an offence of wounding under section 18 Offences Against the Person Act 1861, an indictable offence). The victim is currently too shocked to speak. An eyewitness gives a very vague description of the attacker as a young white male wearing dark clothes.

Joseph McArdle was spotted by the police some 400 metres away from the incident and walking away from the scene of the crime. He is a young white male wearing dark clothes. He is holding his right hand as though it was uncomfortable, although there is no visible sign of blood or immediate bruising on his hands. He is arrested using the powers outlined above. We will consider the police powers of detention in the context of this scenario.

Arrestees must be taken to a designated police station and brought before a custody officer. The custody officer (usually of the rank of sergeant) plays an important role in providing procedural regularity and protection of rights. So what decisions must the custody officer make in relation to Mr McArdle? The most important is whether to charge, release or detain him.

If the custody officer decides that there is sufficient evidence to charge Mr McArdle, then he can further decide to proceed with the charge or to release him, with or without bail. If he is charged, then he must be brought before a magistrates' court as soon as practicable (section 42 PACE). If the custody officer does not think there is sufficient evidence to charge, then Mr McArdle must be released (unless the conditions for detention are present). Our focus is on the decision to detain a suspect, for the purpose of the investigation, before any charge is made.

The decision to detain – under section 37 of PACE the custody officer may authorise continuing detention if there are (a) reasonable grounds for believing that it is necessary to secure or preserve evidence relating to the offence or (b) reasonable grounds for believing that this is necessary in order to obtain evidence by questioning. As with arrest, the detention decision must be lawfully made under these powers or the police will be liable, in this case for false imprisonment.

The custody officer also has to inform a detained person:

■ Of their right to have a friend/relative informed of their arrest and detention.
■ Of their right of access to legal advice.
■ Of the grounds for detention.
■ That they can access a copy of the Codes of Practice.

The custody officer has overall responsibility for ensuring that the detained person is dealt with according to the procedures and safeguards laid down in PACE and the Codes of Practice, and that a record is kept of this.

Length of detention

We saw above that Article 5 of the ECHR gives a general right to liberty. As with arrest, detention is clearly a restriction on the right to liberty; it may be justified, e.g. for the investigation of crime, but even so it must be proportionate. Section 34 of PACE says that a suspect 'shall not be kept in police detention', except in accordance with grounds under section 34, and that if those grounds cease to exist then the person must be released. How long can Mr McArdle be detained for?

Figure 16.3 The detention clock

Section 41 PACE – the standard time limit is 24 hours. As section 34 PACE applies, then this is not an automatic period. If the grounds for detention cease to continue to exist, then the detainee must be released. The continuing justification for the detention must be reviewed within six hours and within nine-hour periods thereafter. A large majority of detained persons are dealt with within this 24-hour period.
Section 42 PACE – Mr McArdle is suspected of committing an indictable offence, so there is the potential for extended periods of detention to come into play. For indictable offences, a superintendent (i.e. a more senior police officer) may authorise an extension of the period for an additional 12 hours, i.e. up to 36 hours. The superintendent will need to believe that further detention is necessary to secure, preserve or obtain evidence. The detainee should be given the opportunity to challenge the request for further detention. Use of these extended powers of detention is relatively limited and normally occurs for more serious or more complex cases than the alleged wounding in Mr McArdle's case;

the police may want to use this power if there is the possibility that the victim will have recovered enough to speak with them in this timeframe.

Section 43 PACE – allows for extension beyond 36 hours by a magistrates' warrant of further detention. The grounds for continued detention are the same as for section 42, but the need to go to a magistrates' court injects a further level of independent scrutiny into the decision. The maximum length of the warrant is 36 hours, up to a maximum at this stage of 72 hours.

Section 44 PACE – provides for a final extension of the warrant of further detention. It is made by a magistrate, on the same criteria as for section 42, and cannot be extended by more than 36 hours and to an overall total no higher than 96 hours. There is a need to show at each stage (sections 42–44) that the investigation is being conducted diligently and expeditiously.

16.7 INTERVIEWING

There is a long and inglorious history around the world of suspects in custody being tortured, pressurised or otherwise coerced into making confessions and damaging admissions. The UK has not been immune from these forms of wrongdoing.

KEY CASE – *TREADAWAY V CHIEF CONSTABLE OF WEST MIDLANDS* (1994) THE TIMES, 25 OCTOBER

West Midlands Police were alleged to have extracted confessions in the 1980s through torturing suspects. The High Court found such allegations to be proven in *Treadaway* where the suspect had been handcuffed behind his back and then repeatedly suffocated with plastic bags.

McKinnon J said that 'What happened to [the suspect] was nothing less than torture'. The suspect's experience was 'frightening and ghastly' and the repeated assaults 'rightly put him in fear for his life'. The false confession that Treadaway made under this torture led to him being convicted of armed robbery and sentenced to 15 years' imprisonment. This was not an isolated incident.[7]

In 1975, Stefan Kiszko, who had the mental and emotional age of a 12-year-old, was arrested in relation to the murder of a child and interviewed for three days without access to legal advice or to his mother. He was told that if he confessed he could go home.

---

7   I Burrell, 'West Midlands Serious Crime Squad: Police unit to blame for dozens more injustices', *The Independent* (22 September 2015), http://www.independent.co.uk/news/west-midlands-serious-crime-squad-police-unit-to-blame-for-dozens-more-injustices-1120219.html (last accessed 22/09/15).

The false confession that this lie induced led to him serving 17 years in jail, where he suffered regular physical attacks from other inmates and developed mental illness. He died a year after having his conviction quashed. The actual murderer was convicted on the basis of DNA evidence in 2007.

PACE and the Codes of Practice try to strike a balance in allowing the police to effectively further their investigations and in preserving the rights of detainees. An important element of effective investigation is that the police can gather evidence that will be accepted by courts and juries. Any suspicion of coercion will cast a shadow over the reliability (and even the admissibility) of the evidence.

Right of access to legal representation

Under section 58 of PACE, 'a person arrested and held in custody . . . shall be entitled, if he so requests, to consult a solicitor privately at any time'. This is consistent with the obligation under Article 6 of the ECHR. Code of Practice C states that the detainee is entitled to be informed of this right and given the name of a duty solicitor. Questioning should not commence until the legal adviser has arrived and has had an opportunity to consult with their client in private. The adviser is entitled to be present during any questioning.

There are very limited circumstances when the right to legal advice can be denied under section 58(2) PACE: where the person is suspected of a serious arrestable offence and an officer of at least the rank of superintendent has reasonable grounds for believing that access to legal advice

1a)   will lead to interference with or harm to evidence . . . or interference with or physical injury to other persons; or
2b)   will lead to the alerting of other persons suspected of having committed such an offence but not yet arrested for it; or
3c)   will hinder the recovery of any property obtained as a result of such an offence.

Access to the advice can only be denied for up to 36 hours.

R v Samuel (1988) 2 All ER 135 illustrates the limited scope of these exceptions to section 58 of PACE. The police would need to be 'near certain' that a solicitor would hinder the investigation, and have objective reasonable grounds for that belief. There are special provisions under the Proceeds of Crime Act 2002 that make it easier to limit access to legal representatives where the suspect may have benefitted from drug trafficking.

Right to have someone informed of the arrest

To be held incommunicado is, in the normal course of events, unacceptable. Secret arrests and detentions are a hallmark of authoritarian regimes. Section 56 PACE provides a right to have a friend or relative informed of the arrest and detention. This can be delayed for up to 36 hours where there are reasonable grounds for believing that this information would lead to harm to other persons or interference with the investigation. It is easier for the police to invoke this restriction than it is to invoke section 58 PACE, as it does not involve impugning the professional integrity of a lawyer.

Right to silence

The right to silence was formerly regarded as a cornerstone of a detainee's rights. It has been seen as an element of the presumption of innocence and a recognition of the imbalance of power and resources between the state and the individual. It still exists, but after 1994, exercising the right comes with a potentially heavy cost.

Before any questioning begins, the suspect must be given the formal caution: 'You do not have to say anything. But it may harm your defence if you do not mention when questioned something which you later rely on in Court. Anything you do say may be given in evidence'. (PACE Code of Practice C para 10.5). Where a suspect is under caution and fails to mention any fact later relied on in his evidence, or after charge fails to mention any fact which in the circumstances existing at the time they 'could reasonably have been expected to mention', then the court/jury may 'draw such inferences from the failure as appear proper' (section 34 Criminal Justice and Public Order Act 1994). At trial, a failure to give evidence or refusal to answer can result in the same sort of negative inferences being drawn.

Conditions for interview

Code of Practice C provides a number of other safeguards for the detention and interviewing process:

- There must be an accurate record of the interview – this normally involves tape recording.
- At least eight out of each 24 hours must be free from questioning.
- There must be regular refreshment and meal breaks each 24 hours.
- The caution must be given again after each break.
- The interviewing officer must cease questioning when they believe that there is enough evidence for a prosecution to succeed.

APPLYING THE LAW

Apply these protections to Mr McArdle.

This is reasonably straightforward. He would be entitled under section 56 of PACE to have access to legal advice. The police cannot try to dissuade him from doing so or start to interview him before the adviser arrives. The legal adviser can be present when he is being interviewed. Given how narrowly the exceptions to this right were interpreted in *Samuel*, it is extremely unlikely that they would be invoked here.

Mr McArdle would also be entitled to have a friend or relative informed of the arrest under section 56 of PACE. Whilst it is possible to imagine circumstances where allowing this would result in a friend of Mr McArdle interfering with the investigations (e.g. by threatening the victim not to give evidence), there does not appear, on the information we have, to be sufficient basis for invoking an exception to the right.

A more difficult issue for Mr McArdle, and any legal adviser, is whether to stay silent or not. In practice, these are known as 'no comment' interviews, where rather than simply remaining silent in the face of repeated questions, the suspect answers 'no comment' to all questions. If he does so, he may avoid making damaging admissions, but a failure to answer questions is likely to be held against him in any subsequent court proceedings (section 34 CJPOA 1994). Finally, the police must handle him in line with the protections outlined in PACE Code of Practice C on recording the interview, refreshment breaks, etc.

16.8 IDENTIFICATION AND PHYSICAL EVIDENCE

PACE also tries to allow police to gather physical evidence from detained persons, whilst imposing rules to try to ensure that the evidence is reliable and to protect a detainee's legitimate interests.

On arrival at the police station, the custody officer must ascertain and record everything which a detained person has in their possession (section 54 PACE). Section 55 of PACE allows for intimate searches, i.e. of bodily orifices (other than the mouth). These types of searches are obviously very degrading to human dignity and there are a range of safeguards, e.g. as to who can authorise and who can undertake such searches, and they are only available in relation to Class A drugs or items that could be used to cause injury to the detainee themselves or to another person.

There are procedures for obtaining other forms of physical evidence that might be useful to the investigation (and increasingly in relation to fingerprints and DNA samples, for future investigations). Intimate samples of bodily fluids, e.g. blood, can only be obtained with the consent of the detainee, although a refusal to consent can properly result in a court drawing adverse inferences (section 62 PACE). The fingerprinting of detainees is permitted under section 61 of PACE. Section 63 of PACE allows non-intimate body samples to be taken without the consent of the detainee, that is, reasonable force can be used to obtain the sample. This covers nail clippings, plucked or combed-out hair samples, and buccal swabs, i.e. a cotton swab taken from the mouth to produce a DNA profile. The rule on retention of biometric data changed via the Protection of Freedoms Act 2012. The police had previously been able to retain samples and place profiles on the National DNA Database for an indefinite period, even if the person was found not guilty. You might be surprised to learn that these powers applied equally to people who were arrested but had not even been charged with an offence. The 2012 reform means that the police can now still take these samples, but only retain them if the person is convicted.

APPLYING THE LAW

It will be a matter of course that Mr McArdle will be fingerprinted and that a DNA sample will be taken from him. The fingerprint records and DNA profile will only be stored if he is later found guilty of an offence. There is no indication of the use of a weapon or relevant drugs, so the intimate search powers do not appear to be relevant, nor do the section 62 PACE powers to take intimate samples. If the victim has been scratched, then the police may want to take material from under Mr McArdle's nails and can do this without his consent under the non-intimate samples powers (section 63 PACE).

In this particular case, the eyewitness evidence does not seem particularly strong, but it may be appropriate to undertake an identification parade. If so, PACE Code D lays down detailed guidance on how it should be carried out in a reliable and fair manner.

16.9 ACTIONS AND COMPLAINTS AGAINST THE POLICE

You will have seen that the legal regime on stop and search, arrest and detention tries to strike a balance between effective policing and citizens' rights. This balance simply would not work if the police could exceed their powers and breach those rights with impunity. We need to examine, therefore, the range of ways in which the police can be legally held to account for their actions.

Until the passing of section 88 of the Police Act 1996, police officers were personally liable for any wrongdoing. Now the position is that Chief Constables are liable 'in respect of any unlawful conduct of constables under his direction and control in the performance . . . of their functions'. The liability is in tort (i.e. civil claims), and any damages are paid out of police funds. Typical civil actions include wrongful arrest, false imprisonment, assault and trespass. These can arise whenever the police act without lawful authority. Failing to adhere to the Codes of Practice does not directly give rise to civil liability, but can be relevant in deciding whether or not the police have stepped beyond the boundaries of their power.

Criminal proceedings against police officers are possible. If a police officer is physically violent to a suspect, in a way that goes beyond any reasonable force necessary to carry out their functions, then they have no lawful authority for their actions. They will be in the same position as a private citizen who assaults someone. In practice, it has proven difficult to successfully bring criminal proceedings against officers for allegations of brutality.[8]

Under the Police Reform Act 2002, complaints about the police are handled directly by the forces themselves. This most commonly results in local resolution through an explanation or apology. The police can initiate a local investigation which may result in misconduct charges being brought against officers. There is a right of appeal to the Independent Office for Police Conduct.

EXPLAINING THE LAW – THE INDEPENDENT POLICE COMPLAINTS COMMISSION (IPCC)

The IPCC will be renamed as the Independent Office for Police Conduct from January 2018. This reform, introduced by the Policing and Crime Act 2017, was motivated by a desire for a fresh start following the concerns and criticisms outlined below. The IPPC could investigate issues in the absence of a complaint, and serious cases (such as deaths in police custody or shooting incidents) went directly to it. The IPCC could not grant compensation but its findings may have resulted in an officer being disciplined.

The effectiveness of the IPCC in holding the police to account was questioned, particularly following high-profile deaths including that of Ian Tomlinson who died in 2009 of a heart attack after being struck and pushed to the ground without provocation by a police officer, and Mark Duggan, shot by the Metropolitan Police in 2011. The House of Commons Home Affairs Committee found in 2013 that:

Police officers are warranted with powers that can strip people of their liberty, their money and even their lives and it is vital that the public have confidence that those powers are not abused. In this report, we conclude that the Independent Police Complaints Commission is not yet capable of delivering the kind of powerful, objective scrutiny that is needed to inspire that confidence.[9]

Confessions are often an important part of a prosecution case. Establishing a case against a suspect can be a difficult and time-consuming task for the police. Eyewitness evidence may be unclear, and witnesses cannot always be relied on to appear in court or give cogent evidence if they do. Physical evidence (such as DNA evidence) has

8   P Gallagher, 'Over 3,000 police officers being investigated for alleged assault – and almost all of them are still on the beat' *The Independent* (24 September 2015), http://www.independent.co.uk/news/uk/crime/over-3000-police-officers-being-investigated-for-alleged-assault-and-almost-all-of-them-are-still-on-the-beat-10220091.html (last accessed 24/09/15).

9   Home Affairs Committee, 'The Independent Police Complaints Commission', http://www.publications.parliament.uk/pa/cm201213/cmselect/cmhaff/494/49411.htm (last accessed 15/08/15).

become more important in recent decades but is not always present at the scene or on the person of the suspect. Often the easiest way of resolving an investigation will be to obtain a confession. A confession will normally result in a guilty plea from the suspect, and even if it does not it will normally lead to a guilty verdict by the court. In other words, the temptation to obtain a confession by unfair means can be strong in some investigations, whilst the consequences of a false confession (as we saw in the *Treadaway* and *Kiszko* examples discussed above) can be catastrophic for an innocent suspect. Confessions are not simply of the 'It was all me. I am guilty. It's a fair cop' type. Under section 82 of PACE, they include 'any statement wholly or partly adverse to the person who made it'.

Section 76 of PACE applies when a confession 'was or may have been obtained (a) by oppression of the person who made it; or (b) in consequence of anything said or done which was likely, in the circumstances existing at the time, to render unreliable any confession which might be made by him as a consequence thereof'. It *requires* the exclusion of the confession in these circumstances. Oppression will include the use of or threats of violence. The section also covers inducements (some benefit in return for a confession, e.g. not to charge other offences) as well as threats.

Section 78 of PACE gives a wider *discretion* for a court to 'refuse to allow evidence if it appears to the court that, having regard to all the circumstances, the admission of the evidence would have such an adverse effect on the fairness of the proceedings that the court ought not to admit it'. The starting point for the courts' use of this discretion is that unlawfully obtained evidence is not inherently inadmissible; it can be heard in court. The question for the court is not whether the evidence was obtained lawfully, but whether its admission into court would have a sufficiently adverse effect on the fairness of the proceedings that it ought to be excluded. This is a very wide discretion and each case has 'to be determined in its own facts' (*R v Smurthwaite* [1994] 1 All ER 898). The usual approach to significant and substantial breaches of the Act or Codes of Practice has, however, been to exclude any evidence that flows from that breach (*R v Walsh* [1988] Crim LR 449). Examples include *R v Samuel* (1988) QB 615 where admissions made by the suspect following a wrongful refusal to allow him access to legal advice under section 58 PACE were excluded from evidence.

KEY LEARNING POINTS

The section above has outlined and reviewed the powers of the police in relation to stop and search, arrest and detention.

- You should be able to use this information to answer problem scenario questions along the lines of the two scenarios discussed above.
- You ought to be able to reach a reasoned conclusion on the appropriateness of the safeguards and limitations on these police powers.

16.10 SECURITY SERVICES

This will be a brief overview of the role of the security services and wider security issues such as the protection of official secrets. The issues are similar to those that we have examined in the context of police powers. We need to hand over coercive and intrusive powers to public bodies so as to allow them to protect the country for our benefit, but there are well-founded concerns over the scrutiny of and accountability for the exercise of these powers.

National security is at the heart of the duties of a Government; there is a compact between people and the state where political legitimacy and the power to act intrusively and coercively are passed to the state but only in return for the hope of safety from external threats and internal terrorism. The dangers of abuse of these powers are manifest, as we saw above in relation to police powers, with the added danger that most of the activities of these agencies are kept secret from the public and Governments can, rather too easily, invoke the necessities of national security to prevent detailed scrutiny of these activities.

The basic structure for security and intelligence is that there are three agencies focusing on, respectively:

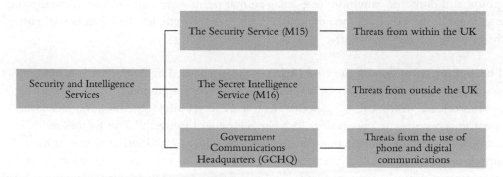

Figure 16.4 Structure of the security services

There are a number of interfaces between Government and the intelligence agencies, such as the Joint Intelligence Committee. For much of their lives the intelligence agencies operated without any statutory authority or even official acknowledgement of their existence and activities. More recently, legislation has recognised and authorised their roles and established a framework that tries to balance the need for oversight of their activities with the need for sensitive information to be kept secret.

The Security Service (MI5) – was created in 1909. It operated without statutory authority until 1989, and had no special powers; if it was necessary to arrest a suspect or search premises, then it would work in conjunction with the police, particularly Special Branch.

Its role is now outlined in section 1(2) of the Security Service Act 1989: 'The function of the Service shall be the protection of national security and, in particular, its protection against threats from espionage, terrorism and sabotage, from the activities of agents of foreign powers and from actions intended to overthrow or undermine parliamentary democracy by political, industrial or violent means'.

There are two further functions outlined in section 1 Security Services Act 1989: 'to safeguard the economic well-being of the United Kingdom against threats posed by the actions or intentions of persons outside the British Islands' and 'to act in support of the activities of police forces . . . in the prevention and detection of serious crime'. This crime investigation role, which was added in 1996, is controversial, as MI5 is not subject to the sort of accountability that police operations are (Crime and Police Commissioners, Independent Office for Police Conduct, etc.). The role, however, is to support the police who maintain the primary responsibility for criminal investigation.

The Security Services Act 1989 makes the Service the responsibility of the Home Secretary, and insists that the Service does not take action to further the interests of any political party.[10] The Director General of the Service must submit an annual report to the Prime Minister and Home Secretary. In practice, it has an important role in counter-terrorism operations against international groups such as ISIS, al-Qaida, Northern Irish dissident groups and domestic extremism (e.g. some animal rights organisations) and in countering espionage in the UK from foreign powers (which increasingly involves commercial rather than purely military espionage).

The Secret Intelligence Service (MI6) – was established in 1909. Its role is outlined in section 1 of the Intelligence Services Act 1994 as applying to information concerning persons outside of the UK. SIS describes its role as 'secret intelligence and mounts covert operations overseas in support of British Government objectives'.[11] This focuses on national security, but also encompasses economic well-being and serious crime. It has a similar role to the Security Service, but with an overseas focus. This obviously requires close co-operation with the Security Service and other domestic agencies. Its Chief is appointed by and accountable to the Foreign Secretary.

According to its website, 'Our mission is to provide Her Majesty's Government with a global covert capability. We collect secret intelligence and mount operations overseas to prevent and detect serious crime, and promote and defend the national security and economic wellbeing of the United Kingdom'.[12]

For those students wondering where James Bond fits into all this, the closest provision is section 7 Intelligence Services Act 1994 which allows the Foreign Secretary to authorise an

---

10 Security Service, https://www.mi5.gov.uk/home/about-us/what-we-do.html (last accessed 01/11/17).

11 Secret Intelligence Service, https://www.sis.gov.uk/ (last accessed 01/11/17).

12 Secret Intelligence Service, https://www.sis.gov.uk/our-mission.html (last accessed 01/11/17).

act 'done outside of the British Islands' for which a person would otherwise be liable under the law of the UK. There is no information on whether this authorisation has ever involved a licence to kill.

Government Communications Headquarters (GCHQ) – was established in 1947 and is primarily based in Cheltenham. It is now regulated by the Intelligence Security Act 1994, to monitor or interfere with communications (very broadly defined) and provide advice on languages and cryptography to the Government (section 3). Its powers are exercisable for the same three purposes as the other agencies (national security, economic well-being and serious crime). It is accountable to the Foreign Secretary. It intercepts individual communications under warrants issued by the Foreign Secretary (Intelligence Services Act 1994, sections 5–7).

Special Branch is a section of the police concerned with terrorism and other extremist activity. The Special Branches of each police force now work with the counter-terrorism police units, particularly the Counter-Terrorism Command in London. The **Joint Intelligence Committee** is a part of the Cabinet Office. It brings together staff from intelligence agencies and the relevant Government departments (e.g. Home Office, Foreign Office, Ministry of Defence, the Treasury). Its role is to produce intelligence assessments and set priorities for the intelligence agencies, together with a warning and monitoring function. A broader overview is provided by the **National Security Council**, which is chaired by the Prime Minister and meets weekly.

Oversight – as the Security Service itself says, 'In a democratic society, it is vital that a security intelligence agency should be well regulated by law and subjected to rigorous oversight. There should be as much transparency as is possible to achieve without compromising our operations'.[13] From a political perspective, this oversight comes principally through the Home Secretary. This includes through the personal authorisation of warrants to intercept communications and carry out intrusive surveillance under the Regulation of Investigatory Powers Act 2000.

Parliament also provides political scrutiny in the Intelligence and Security Committee of Parliament (ISC). Its role and membership are governed by the Justice and Security Act 2013. It has nine members from the House of Commons and House of Lords and oversees 'the expenditure, administration, policy and operations' of the three main security agencies. The main difficulty with Parliamentary oversight is the sensitivity of the information. This is governed by Schedule 1 of the Justice and Security Act 2013 which allows for classified information to be shared with members of the Committee, subject to exceptions for particularly sensitive material. The exceptions are decided by the relevant minister, not the intelligence organisation itself.

The Intelligence and Security Committee publishes an annual report. In 2015–2016, for example, the Committee focused on three issues, the development and review of

---

13 Security Service, https://www.mi5.gov.uk/law-and-governance (last accessed 01/11/17).

the Investigatory Powers Bill (see below), the potential involvement of UK authorities in mistreatment of detainees who had been subject to 'rendition' as part of the counter-terrorism efforts after 9/11, and lethal strikes in Syria.

Oversight arrangements were radically changed by the Investigatory Powers Act 2016 which replaced the three separate judicial commissioners for the intelligence services, interception of communications and surveillance with, from September 2017, a single Investigatory Powers Commissioner's Office. This oversees the use of investigatory powers by public bodies. Highly intrusive forms of surveillance, such as phone tapping, are still authorised by the Home Secretary but these decisions are then reviewed by a Judicial Commissioner before they can take effect – the 'double lock' provision. Other powers such as the bulk acquisition of internet communications data are subject to retrospective audit. The 2016 Act retained the Investigatory Powers Tribunal which deals with complaints about the security agencies and Human Rights Act claims against them.

16.11 OFFICIAL SECRETS

There is information which it is necessary to keep secret to protect the security of the country. Constitutionalism involves a balance between endowing a state with the powers necessary to carry out its functions and protecting citizens from the overuse or abuse of these powers. At the heart of the state's functions is national security: to keep the country safe from external and internal threats. More widely, the state needs to defend itself and promote national interests. There is a risk of (a) abuses being carried out behind the veil of national security and (b) the 'trump card' of national security being played in areas where that particular level of secrecy is not necessary, merely to shield governmental action from criticism and embarrassment.

The main provision through the twentieth century was the Official Secrets Act 1911. Section 2 of this Act was an example of these concerns. It was overly wide and protected even innocuous information. It was replaced by the Official Secrets Act 1989. Under section 1 it is an offence for any member of the security services, or any person who has been notified that they are subject to the Act, to disclose, without lawful authority, any information relating to security or intelligence which has been in their possession by virtue of their work. This covers all information, with no need to prove damage.

Section 1(3) of the Official Secrets Act 1989 imposes an additional lifelong duty (that also applies to Crown servants and police officers) not to make *damaging disclosures* on information relating to security or intelligence. There are also protected categories of information for defence of the realm, international relations and the investigation of crime. There is no public interest defence (*R v Shayler* [2002] 2 UKHL 11).

16.12 INTERCEPTION OF COMMUNICATIONS

In *Malone v United Kingdom* (1984) 7 EHRR 14, the European Court of Human Rights found that the phone tapping regime in the UK was in breach of Article 8 of the ECHR (the right to a private life) because police interception of communications was not authorised by law. This led to the Interception of Communications Act 1985 which a) made it a criminal offence to intentionally intercept a communication and b) granted power to the Secretary of State to issue warrants (on the grounds laid out in Article 8(2) of the ECHR, particularly national security and to prevent or detect serious crime).

These powers were updated for the electronic communications age by the Regulation of Investigatory Powers Act 2000 (RIPA). This kept the basic structure of an overall ban on communications interceptions subject to wide powers to grant particular warrants for interception. It added a requirement of proportionality; the Secretary of State had to consider that obtaining the information was necessary and that it could not be obtained by other means (section 5 RIPA 2000).

One of the problems with RIPA was that, despite it seeming to require a focus on single targets for surveillance for domestic warrants, the security agencies assumed that it gave them very wide powers to undertake surveillance of 'thematic groups'. They also used the wider power in relation to external communications to undertake the bulk collection of internet data that involved US servers. This includes information such as your interaction with Twitter and Facebook etc, search terms that you use in Google and many seemingly internal communications that happen to be routed through US servers. A very large proportion of this data is gathered from people who are not suspected of any wrongdoing. Unfortunately, those charged with oversight of the security agencies did not tell us that this was going on and it was left to whistle-blowers, such as Edward Snowden, to inform the public of these practices. This lack of transparency has been addressed, not by reining back on mass surveillance activities, but by giving clearer legal authorisation to them through 'group warrants' and 'bulk collection warrants' in the Investigatory Powers Act 2016.

POINTS TO REVIEW

- The principal issue addressed in this chapter has been whether the law provides the right balance between empowering the police and security services to do their essential work and protecting citizens from abuses of those powers.

- We have largely left it up to you to decide on whether an appropriate balance has been struck, but you should note the particular concerns about e.g. the effectiveness of reasonable suspicion.

TAKING IT FURTHER

N Parpworth, 'Reasonable Suspicion: A Safeguard in Relation to Police Powers of Arrest' (2009) 173 *Justice of the Peace* 151 This is a fascinating counter-point to some of the scepticism as to the value of reasonable suspicion as a limitation on police arrest powers. It explores the Court of Appeal decision in *Raissi v Commissioner of the Metropolitan Police* [2008] EWCA Civ 1237.

R Austin, 'The New Powers of Arrest: Plus ça change: More of the Same or Major Change?' [2007] *Criminal Law Review* 459 This is a concise and thoughtful review of the changes introduced by the Serious Organised Crime and Police Act 2005, particularly in relation to arrest and the 'necessity' criteria. It would be an interesting piece of critical evaluation to compare Austin's view on how the arrest necessity criteria might play out with subsequent court applications of the test.

The Guardian, 'Surveillance', http://www.theguardian.com/world/surveillance Surveillance issues illustrate the tensions between liberty and security. *The Guardian* has collected many of its stories on phone and internet surveillance under this heading.

CHAPTER 17
FREEDOM OF EXPRESSION

Imagine a world in which you were not generally at liberty to say what you wished, or free to read the books, newspaper or websites that you wanted. The impact of such a legal regime both on you and the society in which you lived would be both awful and enormous.

Freedom of expression is so important to the human personality and to human social relations that it is sometimes (and particularly in the United States) regarded as the most fundamental of human rights. It has a particular significance for you as a Public Law student due to its central role in supporting democracy and in allowing the press and public to hold public power to account.

As with most rights, however, this freedom cannot be limitless. Expression, as a powerful tool, can be used for socially harmful ends such as inciting violence, spreading harmful lies or publicising intimate details from someone's personal life – an appropriate balance must be struck.

AS YOU READ

- You should form a view on the value of freedom of expression at both a personal and societal level.
- You should be able to identify the main range of legal limitations on expression.
- You should be able reach a reasoned and evidenced position on whether there is an appropriate balance between freedom of expression and any socially important limitations on that freedom.

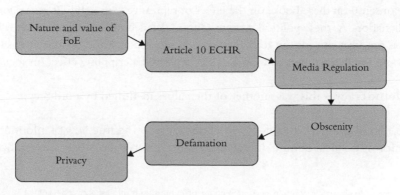

Figure 17.1 Structure of Chapter 17

17.1 THE NATURE AND IMPORTANCE OF FREEDOM OF EXPRESSION

Freedom of expression covers both the right to impart information and to receive it; it underpins a range of important things. Lord Steyn in *R v Secretary of State for the Home Office, ex p Simms* [2000] 2 AC 115 said: 'Freedom of expression is, of course, intrinsically important: it is valued for its own sake. But it is well recognised that it is also instrumentally important. It serves a number of broad objectives'.

As a 'good thing' – we can treat freedom of expression as a 'good unto itself' (*Bose Corp v Consumers Union*, 466 US 485 (1984), US Supreme Court). This means that we do not need to base its value solely on any beneficial consequences. The focus of this argument is that social and political benefits (which might need to give way too easily to other social goods, such as national security or public order) are not the only rationale for protecting the freedom; it has an independent and free-standing value. When expression is regarded as a 'good thing' for individuals, however, it is normally linked to ideas of personal development and autonomy.

Autonomy and development of personality – this was the first of Lord Steyn's broad objectives: 'First, it promotes the self-fulfilment of individuals in society'. This involves your ability to make decisions about many aspects of your life (your autonomy) and is a central part of what contributes to a 'good life'. The ability to express yourself and to select what influences to embrace and which to reject are regarded as foundational aspects of human development. As the freedom of expression pressure group Article 19 say, 'people can gain an understanding of their surroundings and the wider world by exchanging ideas and information freely with others'[1]. Elliott and Thomas make an even more fundamental point: 'To deny people the right to express themselves is to deny their humanity'.[2]

The life of individuals in a society that denies freedom of expression has been extensively explored by novelists and historians, from the dystopias of alternate realities and sci-fi nightmares such as Orwell's *1984* and *Fahrenheit 451* by Rad Bradbury to novels based on real life regimes, e.g. Hans Fallada's *Alone in Berlin* set in Nazi Germany, and historical narratives such as the survey of Communist-era surveillance in *Stasiland* by Anna Funder. There is a high degree of consensus in these books on the effect of repressive censorship. It causes loneliness, fear and alienation. As these political systems require detailed intelligence on who is breaking prohibitions on what citizens can read, they rely on secret police and denunciations by colleagues and family members causing a lack of trust and a crippling effect on social relations.

Role in democracy – this was another of the values identified by Lord Steyn:

> . . . freedom of speech is the lifeblood of democracy. The free flow of information and ideas informs political debate. It is a safety valve: people are more ready to accept

---

1   Article 19, http://www.article19.org/pages/en/freedom-of-expression.html (last accessed 01/11/17).
2   M Elliott and R Thomas, *Public Law* (3rd edn, OUP, 2014) 816.

decisions that go against them if they can in principle seek to influence them. It acts as a brake on the abuse of power by public officials. It facilitates the exposure of errors in the governance and administration of justice of the country.

This benefit of freedom of expression has a number of facets.

When parties present themselves and their policies to voters at election time, it is obviously crucial that they can impart information and try to persuade. Equally, voters need to be able to access a range of information and consider the arguments before casting their votes.

Democracy means more than election campaigns, and freedom of expression is also important to the continuing accountability of public bodies. It allows the genuine concerns of citizens to be raised and heard by the state. This makes it more likely that the interests of the state and citizens can be aligned or accommodated.

KEY CASE – *DERBYSHIRE COUNTY COUNCIL V TIMES NEWSPAPERS* [1993] AC 534

The Sunday Times published articles which questioned the propriety of some financial deals done by Derbyshire County Council and a businessman. The leader of the Council, David Bookbinder, was named in the articles as being primarily responsible for the deals, but the action was brought in the name of Council itself, on the basis that the reputation of the Council had suffered.

The House of Lords held that it ought to apply and develop the common law in accordance with fundamental rights, which in this case involved freedom of expression. The Lords thought that allowing public bodies to bring defamation actions could be an undesirable fetter on the freedom to criticise such bodies. Lord Keith said, 'it is of the highest constitutional importance that a democratically elected governmental body . . . should be open to uninhibited public criticism'. If named individuals were defamed, then they were free to bring defamation proceedings in their own names.

Wider societal role – a further objective, according to Lord Steyn was that '. . . in the famous words of Holmes J. (echoing John Stuart Mill), "the best test of truth is the power of the thought to get itself accepted in the competition of the market"': *Abrams v. United States* (1919) 250 U.S. 616, 630, per Holmes J. (dissenting)', often known as the 'whole marketplace of ideas' concept. Lord Bingham, in *R (Animal Defenders International) v Secretary of State for Culture, Media and Sport* [2008] UKHL 15, argued that 'Freedom of thought and expression is an essential condition of an intellectually healthy society . . . if competing views, opinions and policies are publicly debated and exposed to public scrutiny the good will over time drive out the bad and the true prevail over the false'. This is perhaps a rather optimistic view of marketplaces in general, in that it doesn't fully acknowledge the risk of distortions in the marketplace, particularly the role of money and power (although these issues were considered elsewhere in the judgment).

Many modern law students do not see themselves as 'political' in a party political sense, but the marketplace of ideas raises an interesting view of politics, that it is simply about decision-making. These decisions encompass your views on the whole range of social issues, such as on equality (see e.g. the Everyday Sexism website, http://everydaysexism.com/), or animal rights, on vegetarianism, on changes to the legal profession, or on 'poshness tests' for access to elite law and finance firms.[3] Your ability to receive and impart information on these issues ought to contribute to better decisions and effective change.

Freedom of expression is also important in securing other rights. There is a direct relationship with the right of assembly and public protest, and with aspects of freedom of religion, thought and conscience. It is also more likely that the human rights of a fair trial, liberty, and freedom from inhuman and degrading treatment will be secured if the press can highlight abuses. As the Guardian said, in commenting on the 2017 Turkish crackdown on journalists following the failed coup, 'Putting journalists on trial for doing their job, for informing the public or conveying opinion, is never acceptable. Like the canary in the mine, journalist can serve as an early alert to the erosion of the rights of every citizen. Where media freedom is curtailed other freedoms invariably follow'.[4]

APPLYING THE LAW

The exercise here is simply to apply some of these considerations to your life. Consider how important this free flow of information has been to you. Think about the information that has informed your intellectual, political or religious development, right the way down to the usefulness of consumer reviews on what toaster to buy, or what holiday apartment to rent.

Think about the ways in which your ability to receive and impart information has affected the development of *who* you are:

- The books you have read, the films you have seen, and the computer games you have played.
- The ideas that your family, friends and teachers (especially your Public Law teachers) have imparted to you.
- How you have been affected, concerned and influenced by news stories.
- Your ability to choose how you present yourself to the world through your clothes, texts and calls and social media postings.

3   M Weaver, 'Poshness tests block working class applicants' *The Guardian* (15 June 2015), http://www.theguardian.com/society/2015/jun/15/poshness-tests-block-working-class-applicants-at-top-companies (last accessed 01/11/01).

4   Editorial, 'Turkish press freedom: standing up for democracy' *The Guardian* (24 July 2017), https://amp.theguardian.com/commentisfree/2017/jul/24/the-guardian-view-on-turkish-press-freedom-standing-up-for-democracy (last accessed 01/11/17).

The fundamental nature of freedom of expression should emerge from this exercise. Nevertheless, and even through the considerations you have identified, it will be clear that some restrictions are necessary. If the holiday apartment reviews you read were all dishonestly and misleadingly posted by the apartment owner, you would hope for some protection from the law. If someone has received political or religious messages that have directly incited them to commit acts of terrorist violence, then we would expect that the interests of national security and personal safety would override a specific claim for freedom of expression to communicate those messages. Freedom of expression must therefore be subject to proportionate limitations in the interests of e.g. public order, national security, the administration of justice, commercial necessity and softer notions of social harmony and even public morality.

17.2 US VERSUS UK APPROACHES

The First Amendment to the US Constitution states that 'Congress shall make no law respecting an establishment of religion, or prohibiting the free exercise thereof; or abridging the freedom of speech, or of the press; or the right of the people peaceably to assemble, and to petition the Government for a redress of grievances'. Freedom of expression has always had a particularly honoured place in the US legal and political system. In general terms, there are fewer restrictions on freedom of expression in US law than in other Western countries.

If you undertook a thought experiment on imagining an organisation that would test the United States' commitment to freedom of expression, you might well come up with something like Westboro Baptist Church, based in Topeka, Kansas. This is not affiliated to mainstream Baptist churches. It avoids direct calls to violence and racial hatred, although it has praised terror attacks including the 9/11 attacks and the Boston marathon bombing. Its most high-profile activity is to conduct anti-gay protests by picketing military funerals, often using placards with the slogan 'God Hates Fags'. It regards the death of American service personnel as a part of God's judgement on a country that is permissive of homosexuality. The targets of their hatred also include Jews (and indeed all other religious groups), and their picketing activity includes funerals of murder victims of gay hate crime.

KEY CASE – *SNYDER V PHELPS*, 131 S CT 1207 (2011)

Mathew Snyder was a US Marine killed whilst on active duty in Iraq in 2006. Westboro Baptist Church (WBC) picketed his funeral, and their picketing involved their usual array of placards, including one saying 'Thank God for dead soldiers'. These actions caused serious emotional harm to Snyder's father who sued Fred Phelps, the leader of the WBC, for publicity given to private life and intentional infliction of emotional distress.

> After the case succeeded in the lower courts, the Fourth Circuit Court of Appeals found that WBC's statements were not statements of facts but rather figurative expression, i.e. a form of political speech that was protected by the First Amendment. This verdict was upheld by the Supreme Court.

It is interesting, and cheering, to note that these freedom of expression laws also allow the pressure group Planting Peace to buy the house opposite the Westboro Church compound, rename it Equality House, paint it in the gay pride colours and use it to celebrate advances in LGBT equality.[5]

In the same year, the High Court in England heard the case of *Abdul v DPP* [2011] EWHC 247 (Admin). This involved a parade to mark the return of the Royal Anglian Regiment from a tour of duty in Afghanistan and Iraq. The parade attracted a crowd of well-wishers, but also some protesters who shouted slogans such as 'British soldiers murderers' and 'Rapists all of you'. This provoked a reaction from the crowd, and the police had to keep the groups separate and escort the protesters away. They were charged under section 5 of the Public Order Act 1986 with 'threatening, abusive or insulting words or behaviour within the sight or hearing of a person likely to be caused harassment alarm or distress'.

The starting point for the High Court was freedom of expression, including the right to legitimate protest. It recognised that such protests might need to be offensive if they were to have an impact, and even distasteful minority views could be expressed. Any exceptions to this general principle must be narrowly construed.

Applying these principles, the court found that the specific context was important and that on the facts the protesters had gone well beyond the legitimate expressions of protest. There was no right to abuse and insult gratuitously, and the protesters were guilty of the public order offence.[6] The case of *Hammond v DPP* [2004] Crim LR 851 also shows that the English courts are willing to allow public order concerns to restrict freedom of expression even in less incendiary circumstances than *Abdul*; a lay minister's public order conviction flowing from responses to his 'Stop Homosexuality' placard was upheld. These contrasting examples show that two liberal democracies can both commit strongly to freedom of expression but end with very differing outcomes to similar challenges.

---

5   Planting Peace Organisation, http://www.plantingpeace.org/equality/ (last accessed 01/11/17).
6   These contrasting cases are highlighted by Jacob Rowbottom in Elliott and Thomas, above n 2, 856.

17.3 ARTICLE 10 OF THE EUROPEAN CONVENTION ON HUMAN RIGHTS

Article 10(1) of the ECHR states: 'Everyone has the right to freedom of expression. This right shall include freedom to hold opinions and to receive and impart information and ideas without interference by public authority and regardless of frontiers. This article shall not prevent States from requiring the licensing of broadcasting, television or cinema enterprises'.

This is a broad right but is subject to the potential limitations in Article 10(2):

> The exercise of these freedoms, since it carries with it duties and responsibilities, may be subject to such formalities, conditions, restrictions or penalties as are prescribed by law and are necessary in a democratic society, in the interests of national security, territorial integrity or public safety, for the prevention of disorder or crime, for the protection of health or morals, for the protection of the reputation or rights of others, for preventing the disclosure of information received in confidence, or for maintaining the authority and impartiality of the judiciary.

As we saw in Chapter 15, 'Human rights', these limitations must be clearly outlined in law, be necessary for one of the reasons listed and must be proportionate, i.e. only go as far as is necessary to meet the competing social reason and strike a fair balance between the human right and the pressing social need.

It is sometimes the case that those in most need of the protection of a human right attract the least public sympathy (and indeed attract antipathy) when trying to exercise that right. Prisoners, by the nature of their confinement, do not have ready access to the channels of free expression whilst there is sometimes a compelling need to shine a light on the circumstances of their life before prison, including their conviction, and the nature of the conditions under which they are confined.

KEY CASE – *R V SECRETARY OF STATE FOR THE HOME DEPARTMENT, EX PARTE SIMMS* [2000] 2 AC 115

Two prisoners, serving life sentences for murder, were appealing their convictions and wanted to speak to journalists who were interested in their cases. The Home Secretary had a policy that journalists could only speak to prisoners if the journalists signed an undertaking not to publish any part of the interviews. The journalists refused to make such an undertaking and the prisoners sought a judicial review based on their freedom of expression. This was not a general claim of freedom of expression for all prisoners in all circumstances, but rather was focused on the role of the journalist in investigating miscarriages of justice.

The House of Lords found that Prison Service Standing Order 5 of 1996 para.37 and para.37A, made under the Prison Rules 1964 r.33, interpreted in the light of the fundamental right of freedom of expression, did not permit a blanket ban on these interviews. Restrictions on prisoners' rights were permitted but these had to be justified by a pressing social need and the minimum interference necessary for this need. The Law Lords also noted that previous journalistic investigations, involving these sorts of interviews, had led to the uncovering of a number of miscarriages of justice.

Simms is therefore an illustration of how the proportionality test can limit state action, but it remains the case that freedom of expression is far from absolute for prisoners, and *Simms* can be contrasted with *R (Nilsen) v Governor of Full Sutton Prison* [2004] EWCA Civ 1540. Dennis Nilsen, a notorious serial killer, wanted to publish an autobiography, including details of his horrifying crimes, but was prevented from receiving related documents from his solicitor. The Prison Governor relied on prison standing orders that a prisoner's correspondence could not contain material intended for publication. The Court of Appeal held that imprisonment could involve some restrictions on freedom of expression, and in this case, as Nilsen was not making serious representations about his conviction or sentence, the interference was not disproportionate.

The Human Rights Act 1998 makes special provision for freedom of expression in section 12:

> The court must have particular regard to the importance of the Convention right to freedom of expression and, where the proceedings relate to material which the respondent claims, or which appears to the court, to be journalistic, literary or artistic material (or to conduct connected with such material), to (a) the extent to which (i) the material has, or is about to, become available to the public; or (ii) it is, or would be, in the public interest for the material to be published; (b) any relevant privacy code.

Given that courts will have to have regard to all relevant Convention rights in deciding cases anyway and that it is a core idea of the judicial interpretation of the HRA that no single right automatically takes precedence over another, it is difficult to see what practical difference section 12 can make. Its inclusion seems more like a placatory note to a press and media that was concerned that the introduction of the HRA would result in significant further limitations on freedom of the press.

Most of the rest of this chapter outlines the main limitations found in the law on freedom of expression. Before proceeding with that task, there are a number of other restrictions summarised here:

Contempt of court – recognises that media coverage of criminal investigations and of trials has the potential to prejudice legal proceedings. The laws on contempt of court, therefore, are intended to protect the administration of justice. The main offence is in section 2 of the Contempt of Court Act 1981, which prohibits the publication of material which creates 'a substantial risk that the course of justice in the proceedings in question will be seriously impeded or prejudiced'. This offence can be committed regardless of the intention of the person making the publication (section 1 CCA 1981). Whether there will be a 'substantial risk' of prejudice to the course of justice depends on a range of factors including how likely it is to come to the attention of potential jurors and the likely impact of the publication (*Attorney-General v Mirror Group Newspapers* [1997] 1 ALL ER 456).

One example relates to the coverage of the murder in 2010 of Joanna Yeates, a landscape architect from Bristol. The police originally suspected and arrested her landlord, Christopher Jefferies. Many newspapers focused on what they regarded as Jefferies's eccentricities and tried, very vigorously, to portray him as a rather weird and creepy person. He was entirely innocent of any involvement in the murder. The police ultimately found the murderer (a neighbour), and Jefferies won libel actions against six newspapers. Contempt of court proceedings were brought against the *Mirror* and *Sun* newspapers for alleged 'extreme' articles that conveyed the impression that Jefferies was a voyeur and a stalker of young women (*Attorney General v MGN Ltd* [2011] EWHC 2074). Both were found guilty and fined £50,000 and £18,000, respectively, with Lord Judge LCJ saying that 'the vilification of a suspect under arrest is a potential impediment to the course of justice'.

The main defence to a contempt charge is in section 4 of the Contempt of Court Act 1981 which protects a 'fair and accurate report of legal proceedings held in public, published contemporaneously and in good faith'.

Public order – there are a number of public order offences that can be committed by words or other forms of expression. We looked at one example (*Abdul v DPP* [2011] EWHC 247 (Admin)) involving section 5 of the Public Order Act 1986 above, and other restrictions are considered in the next chapter.

Incitement of racial and religious hatred – Sections 17–23 of the Public Order Act 1986 make it an offence to use words or behaviour which are 'threatening, abusive or insulting' and intended to incite racial hatred or are likely to do so. Any prosecution needs the consent of the Attorney General. The Racial and Religious Hatred Act 2006 extended this to incitement to religious hatred. This extension was controversial, and concerns were raised, in particular by comedians such as Rowan Atkinson, that it would prevent criticism of religious views including satire and ridicule. In response, the Bill was amended, and the 2006 Act clarifies that it does not prohibit 'discussion, criticism or expressions of antipathy, dislike, ridicule, insult or abuse' of particular religions.

Official secrets – see Chapter 16 on how the Official Secrets Act 1989 can restrict expression for the purposes of protecting national security.

Data protection – the Data Protection Act 1998 attempts to give people some control over their personal information and imposes duties on 'data holders' which include limits on when and how they can communicate that data, for example that data is not used for direct marketing (section 11 Data Protection Act 1988).

Treason – the Treason Act 1351 makes it an offence to give 'aid or comfort to the King's enemies'. William Joyce, who became known as Lord Haw-Haw, was a member of the British Fascists who fled to Germany in the 1930s. He broadcast a programme on German radio during the Second World War that sought to demoralise British listeners and promote Nazi propaganda. He was captured in 1945, convicted of high treason and hanged at Wandsworth Prison in 1946.

We will finish this brief overview with two different types of examples. First, whilst there have been a number of restrictions on freedom of expression *introduced* in recent decades (some of which are mentioned above), the traffic is not all in one direction. Limitations on freedom of expression can also be *withdrawn*. **Blasphemy** was an old, and rather erratically enforced, common law offence. It was defined by Lord Scarman in *Whitehouse v Lemon* (1979) 2 WLR 281 as: 'Every publication is said to be blasphemous which contains any contemptuous, reviling, scurrilous or ludicrous matter relating to God, Jesus Christ, or the Bible, or the formularies of the Church of England as by law established'. Following criticisms of its existence in a multi-faith and increasingly secular society, including a Law Commission recommendation for its abolition in 1985, section 79 of the Criminal Justice and Immigration Act 2008 was passed. This provided that 'The offences of blasphemy and blasphemous libel under the common law of England and Wales are abolished'.

Second, there can be voluntary, but nonetheless quite formal and powerful, restrictions on freedom of expression. The prime example is the system of **Defence Advisory Notices**.[7] These are issued by the Defence, Press and Broadcasting Committee and have no statutory basis. There are five standing DA Notices covering issues such as nuclear weapons, secure communications and military operations, which are intended to guide editors as to whether publication of particular types of defence and counter-terrorism information would damage national security. The guidance is stated to be purely voluntary, but media outlets can come under considerable pressure to follow the DA Notice guidance.

KEY LEARNING POINTS

- Freedom of expression is a fundamental, but not absolute, human right.
- Expression is particularly privileged in the US.
- There are a range of legal limits on expression.

17.4 CENSORSHIP AND MEDIA REGULATION

What does it mean to say that we have 'a free press'? It does not mean that newspapers and TV stations are free from all legal restraint. Many of the general legal constraints on

---

7   The Defence, Press and Broadcasting Advisory Committee, http://www.dsma.uk/ (last accessed 01/11/17).

freedom of expression (e.g. defamation, contempt of court) have a particular significance in restricting press activity. 'Freedom of the press' really means that there is no need, in general, to obtain the consent of a public body for publication and that media outlets are free of any direct state control or influence. We will first examine the general regulation of TV and radio, and then of the print press.

17.4.1 REGULATION OF TV AND RADIO

The BBC is partly governed under a separate legal regime. The BBC Charter was renewed in 2016, which introduced a new unitary Board, retained the 'license-fee' model of funding and required publication of the salaries of high-earning employees such as Chris Evans and Gary Lineker. The Charter sets out its public purposes whilst guaranteeing its independence from political control. Many aspects of the wider Broadcasting Code apply to the BBC.

Commercial television and radio are regulated by the Broadcasting Acts 1990 & 1996 and the Communications Act 2003. This establishes Ofcom (the Office of Communications) which issues broadcasting licences, regulates 'offensive and harmful material' (section 3 Communications Act 2003) and deals with listener/viewer complaints. Its powers were extended by the Digital Economy Act 2017 to allow it to penalise broadcasters for failure to comply with licensing conditions and to give it a wider role in regulating the BBC, effectively replacing the BBC Trust as the external regulator.

17.4.2 POLITICAL ADVERTISING

There is an obvious sensitivity to the use of TV and radio media for political advertising. It has the potential to magnify any distortions in resources between political parties. Put simply, it seems to offer the opportunity to buy influence with voters. There is very limited regulation of political advertising in the US, where we have seen there is a real premium placed on freedom of expression. Even some of the rather modest restrictions included in the Bipartisan Campaign Reform Act 2002 were found to be unconstitutional by the US Supreme Court in *Citizens United v Federal Election Commission*, 558 US 310 (2010).

The main television stations in the UK are obliged, at election times, to broadcast party election programmes (under the BBC Charter and the Communications Act 2003). The parties are allocated slots based on their previous electoral performances, and the five-minute slots are made available free of charge. This is accompanied by a general ban on political adverting on TV and radio. Section 321 of the Communications Act 2003 prohibits any advertisement which

1(a) is inserted by or on behalf of a political organisation,
2(b) is directed towards a political end, or
3(c) has a connection to an industrial dispute.

This is a wide ban that goes far beyond prohibiting direct advertisements by political parties. In the US, the limited rules on campaign spending are circumvented by the use of 'super-PACs' which can spend unlimited amounts of money on political issues, including campaigns, as long as they are formally independent from the candidates' own official campaigns, and 'issue advocacy ads' that broadcast on issues such as the environment or opposition to abortion and endorse, or criticise, specific candidates. In contrast, the wide scope of the UK ban is highlighted in the *Animal Defenders* case.

KEY CASE – *R (ANIMAL DEFENDERS INTERNATIONAL) V SECRETARY OF STATE FOR CULTURE, MEDIA AND SPORT* [2008] UKHL 15

Animal Defenders International (ADI) was a non-profit company that campaigned against cruelty to animals, including their use in commerce and science. It sought changes in the law, and as part of this campaign produced an advert focusing on the use of primates. The advert was not cleared for broadcast, on the basis that ADI were 'a political organisation' (section 321 Communications Act 2003).

ADI sought a judicial review of this decision on the basis that they were involved in social advocacy rather than direct political action, and that the ban was disproportionate ('not necessary in a democratic society') and therefore breached the human right of freedom of expression.

The House of Lords held that whilst ADI was not a political party, it was a political entity and did fall within the prohibition. The Lords also considered whether the broad ban was necessary in a democratic society and concluded that it was. Baroness Hale said, 'In the United Kingdom we do not want our government or its policies to be decided by the highest spender . . . We want everyone to be able to make up their own minds on the important issues of the day'. This calls for a free exchange of ideas. There was a recognition that some political groups do have greater resources than others, and it is not always possible to stop the influence of this disparity, but there is nevertheless a need to avoid 'gross distortions'.

A subsequent case before the European Court of Human Rights, *Animal Defenders International v United Kingdom*, [2013] ECHR 48876/08, found that the UK ban on political advertising, and the way it had been applied to ADI in this case, did not breach Article 10 ECHR.

17.4.3 THE BROADCASTING CODE 2013

The Code was issued under section 107 of the Broadcasting Act 1996, and covers standards and fairness.

The Code has also been drafted in the light of the Human Rights Act 1998 and the European Convention on Human Rights ('the Convention'). In particular, the right to freedom of expression, as expressed in Article 10 of the Convention, encompasses the audience's right to receive creative material, information and ideas without interference but subject to restrictions prescribed by law and necessary in a democratic society.[8]

There are sections on protecting under-18s, protecting people from harmful or offensive material, and material likely to encourage or incite the commission of crime or to lead to disorder. There are further obligations in relation to religious programmes. Interestingly, as well as trying to ensure that these programmes do not involve any abusive treatment of religious views, they also seek to protect people from religion 'promoted by stealth' and ban religious television programmes from trying to seek new recruits. The Code includes obligations on impartiality, particularly in news coverage. There are additional rules on election coverage, privacy and a general duty of fairness to individuals and organisations.

APPLYING THE LAW – THE 9 O'CLOCK WATERSHED

Most of you will be familiar with the 9 o'clock watershed. This a rule that certain content that it is acceptable to broadcast after 9pm cannot be broadcast earlier than that. Have a look at Section 1 of the Broadcasting Code: http://stakeholders.ofcom.org.uk/broadcasting/broadcast-codes/broadcast-code/

Think about what the phrase 'unsuitable for children' might mean. Is it sufficiently clear? Does the rest of section 1 of the Code on e.g. drugs, smoking, solvents or alcohol or on offensive language illuminate the phrase 'adult material' adequately?

The Court of Appeal considered the relationship between the Code and freedom of expression under Article 10 ECHR in the *Gaunt* case.

KEY CASE – *GAUNT V OFCOM* [2011] EWCA CIV 692

The case arose out of an interview between Jon Gaunt, a Talksport radio host, and a local authority children's services councillor on a proposal to stop people who smoke from becoming foster parents. Gaunt had written a newspaper article criticising the proposal using very robust language (including calling its proponents 'health and safety Nazis'). The judges thought the article itself was unobjectionable.

---

8   OFCOM, The Broadcasting Code 2017, http://stakeholders.ofcom.org.uk/broadcasting/broadcast-codes/broadcast-code/ (last accessed 01/11/17).

The radio interview, however, became 'a slanging match' during which Gaunt called the councillor a Nazi, an 'ignorant pig' and a 'health fascist'. Following complaints from listeners, Ofcom found that there had been a breach of the Code, specifically Rule 2.3 on offensive material including offensive language, humiliation, distress and violation of human dignity.

The Court of Appeal found that Ofcom's ruling was consistent with Article 10 ECHR. Even taking into account the often argumentative nature of this particular radio programme and the social importance of the issues being discussed, the tone and persistent aggression of the presenter's statements put it outside of the scope of protection:

> The essential point is that, the offensive and abusive nature of the broadcast was gratuitous, having no factual content or justification . . . An inhibition from broadcasting shouted abuse which expresses no content does not inhibit, and should not deter, heated and even offensive dialogue which retains a degree of relevant content.

17.5 REGULATION OF THE PRESS

It is interesting at this stage to go back to the benefits of freedom of expression identified at the start of this chapter. They include the promotion of democracy and a free 'marketplace of ideas'. It is a central tenet of defenders of a free press that these values would be destroyed by direct state regulation of newspapers; it is not only state regulation, however, that can distort the marketplace of ideas.

In the 2015 UK General Election, out of seven national newspapers (not counting Sunday or Scottish editions), five supported the Conservatives, with one each for Labour and UKIP. One might regard this as the marketplace in action; if readers do not like the political endorsement of a paper they can stop buying it and move to another. The division of newspaper support, however, in no way mirrors political preferences in the country at large. The source of the distortion, and its subsequent impact on the marketplace of ideas, is more likely to be found in the political views of owners or of major advertisers.

We live in an age of social media and multiple television channels and radio stations, where sales of hard copies of newspapers are in long-term decline. Nevertheless, the press retains a really important role in informing debates and providing information to the public. The Leveson Report, which contained stinging criticisms of press conduct, also found that the press was 'the guardian of the interests of the public, as a critical witness to events, as the standard bearer for those who have no one else to speak up for them'. It concluded that 'The press, operating properly and in the public interest is one of the true safeguards of our democracy'.

In some respects, the internet, which has been seen as the biggest threat to the existence of traditional print media, has provided new opportunities for newspapers. *MailOnline* reported in 2012 that it was the world's biggest newspaper website with 45 million unique users.[9] The *Financial Times* has made online subscriptions a financial success, whilst *The Times* and *Sunday Times* also seem to be creating a viable business model by using a pay wall.[10] Any predictions of the death of newspaper journalism seem rather premature, and so its role in securing freedom of expression and safeguarding democracy does need to be examined.

The context in which press regulation needs to be assessed has two faces. One is the incredibly valuable, but often difficult and controversial work, of investigative journalism.

There are many examples across many different newspapers, but obvious ones include the *Telegraph*'s investigation into abuses of the MP's expenses system in 2009 which led to some MPs being jailed, others suspended, and wholesale reform of the Parliamentary expenses system. Another is *The Guardian*'s continuing work on transparency and surveillance from the WikiLeaks story through the Edward Snowden revelations of mass (and unlawful) surveillance of citizens by the US National Security Agency and by the UK's GCHQ. The key point is that this type of journalism is so valuable to democracy, and so uncomfortable for those in power, that whatever system of regulation is needed, it cannot have any sort of chilling effect on the ability of journalists to 'speak truth to power'.

The other side of the coin is an inglorious history of scandalous behaviour, involving phone hacking, harassment, breaches of privacy and corrupting payments to public officials to encourage them to commit misconduct in a public office. Many of the generalities of these practices were known before 2011 and, for example, the former *News of the World* editor Andy Coulson resigned as the Prime Minister's Director of Communications in early 2011 following allegations of phone hacking. The real trigger for a more in-depth look at press practices and an appetite for reform were the revelations on the conduct of the *News of the World* when reporting the murder of Milly Dowler.

ANALYSING THE LAW – PHONE HACKING

Milly Dowler was a 13-year-old who was abducted and murdered in Surrey in 2002. Her attacker, Levi Bellfield, was found guilty of the murder in 2011. *The Guardian* published allegations in 2011 that private investigators working for the *News of the*

---

9 '*MailOnline*, the world's number one: We're the biggest newspaper website with 45.348 million unique users' *Daily Mail* (27 January 2012) http://www.dailymail.co.uk/news/article-2092432/MailOnline-worlds-number-Daily-Mail-biggest-newspaper-website-45-348-million-unique-users.html (last accessed 15/08/15).

10 P Preston, 'The Financial Times paywall is in the pink: everyone else is still in the red' *The Guardian* (3 August 2014), http://www.theguardian.com/media/2014/aug/03/financial-times-paywall-online-advertisings-subscriptions (last accessed 01/11/17); P Preston, 'Is a profit worth the price of the Times's paywall?' *The Guardian* (7 December 2014), http://www.theguardian.com/media/2014/dec/07/is-profit-worth-price-times-paywall (last accessed 01/11/17).

World had hacked into Milly Dowler's voicemail whilst she was still a missing person, and deleted messages so as to free up space for new messages. This activity on her phone led her family and the police to assume that she was still alive. There were suggestions (never conclusively proven) that this interfered with the investigation, and it was noted that Bellfield went on to kill two other women after 2002.

Other allegations quickly followed that *News of the World* journalists had hacked the voicemails of British soldiers who had been killed in action in Afghanistan and Iraq, and of victims of the 7/7 terrorist bombings in London. At the heart of the public outrage was that these were ordinary people. Previous allegations of phone hacking against members of the Royal Family and celebrities could be dismissed as part of the 'media game' or as 'keeping an eye' on people in power. These allegations could not be dismissed in the same way and showed journalists intruding on the deepest feelings of grief with not even a tenuous claim to be acting in the public interest.

In July 2011, the parent company, News International, decided to close the *News of the World* down (although it introduced a replacement, the *Sun on Sunday*, some seven months later).

All of this happened on the watch of a system of press self-regulation, the Press Complaints Commission. This voluntary organisation was dominated by members of the press themselves, whose two-thirds allocation of Commission membership included editors of national newspapers. It had no coercive controls and was funded by the newspaper industry.

In 2011, the Government announced a major public inquiry into the culture, practice and ethics of the press. Chaired by a judge, Lord Justice Leveson, this inquiry published its report in November 2012. The Leveson Report's key conclusions and recommendations were:

- On the Press Complaints Commission – that it was 'woefully inadequate' and lacked independence. Press behaviour had been, at times, 'outrageous'.
- On regulation – 'An independent self-regulatory body should be governed by an independent Board. In order to ensure the independence of the body, the Chair and members of the Board must be appointed in a genuinely open, transparent and independent way, without any influence from industry or Government . . . should contain a substantial majority of members who are demonstrably independent of the press'.
- On powers – 'The Board should have the power to hear and decide on complaints about breach of the standards code . . . should have the power to direct appropriate remedial action for breach of standards and the publication of corrections and apologies (including their nature, extent and prominence) . . . should have the power to

impose appropriate and proportionate sanctions' (including financial sanctions up to
1 per cent of turnover with a maximum of £1 million). There should be a quick
arbitration system to allow redress to the public without going to court.

- Membership – 'should not be considered sufficiently effective if it does not cover all
significant news publishers'. Membership was to be encouraged through a judicial
power to award much higher court costs against those newspapers remaining outside
of the organisation.

- On statutory underpinning – to ensure independence from press and Government, a
recognition body was needed to recognise and certify that a regulator met the requirements set out in law. In effect, this would be self-regulation but with verification of the
regulatory arrangements provided by a body with a statutory underpinning.

There was immediate controversy over any statutory underpinning for the proposed
recognition body. The Prime Minister expressed reservations about this, and most
newspapers immediately rejected this aspect of the Report, claiming that it could lead to
state censorship or control of a hitherto free press and was a threat to free expression.

After much debate, the main political parties decided to proceed by Royal Charter
rather than legislation. The Royal Charter on self-regulation of the press was signed by
the Queen in 2013. This created a Press Recognition Panel but postponed its start of
operations until 2015. In the meantime, the press went ahead with their own reform
and are continuing to operate their own form of self-regulation regardless of the Royal
Charter and Recognition Panel. The Recognition Panel gave its formal approval to
IMPRESS in 2016, but the 'official' regulator has struggled to get large publications to
sign up with it.[11]

17.5.1 INDEPENDENT PRESS STANDARDS ORGANISATION (IPSO)[12]

IPSO was established in 2014 by the newspaper industry as a replacement for the Press
Complaints Commission. It is not recognised by the Press Recognition Panel but has
nevertheless emerged as the most important regulator. Its role includes maintaining
standards of press conduct, hearing complaints and general monitoring work. The
public can seek redress for a breach of the Editors' Code of Practice. This Code covers
issues such as accuracy, privacy and inappropriate intrusion, e.g. into grief. There is
a broad public interest exception, particularly in relation to crime, public health and
safety, and preventing people from being misled.[13] This means, for example, that a
newspaper story that intruded onto sensitive personal information could be justified if
it reveals (in the public interest) criminal behaviour. IPSO has the power to require a
newspaper to print prominent corrections, and a limited power to fine for serious and
systemic failures.

---

11 IMPRESS, https://www.impress.press/ (last accessed 01/11/17).
12 The Independent Press Standards Organisation, https://www.ipso.co.uk/IPSO/index.html (last accessed 01/11/17).
13 IPSO Editor's Code of Practice 2016, https://www.ipso.co.uk/IPSO/cop.html (last accessed 01/11/17).

The composition of any 'independent' regulator was central to Lord Leveson's concerns. IPSO has a 12-person board with an official structure of seven independent members and five from the newspaper industry. Though on examining the composition of the IPSO board, as of October 2017, it seems that only three members have no background in media, journalism or publishing.[14] Of the major newspapers, the *Financial Times*, *Independent* and *Guardian* decided against joining the IPSO regulation system and have established their own complaints systems.

The media commentator, Roy Greenslade, writing in 2014, was highly critical of the post-Leveson process. He said that the three papers outside IPSO 'do not wish to sign up to a flawed regulator that, in every key respect, is little different from its predecessor because it is just not independent enough. Yet they did not want to risk joining a regulator relying on recognition through a royal charter'.[15] He also points out, without offering any real solutions, two systemic problems with the very idea of a national press regulator. First, media now has an international scope. Even monoglot readers can access English-language press reports from abroad (and some foreign-language press websites now have English versions, e.g. El *País* in English). Second, it is not just the traditional print media who are generating news stories; blogs, Facebook posts and Twitter feeds are increasingly important sources of information but are not regulated by any press regulator.

17.6 OBSCENITY

Some legal commentaries on the control of obscene material are in danger of appearing slightly quaint with the ready availability of online hardcore pornography, but the approach of the law has developed over time. The focus has shifted from representations of consensual sexual activity between adults which were the subject of many prosecutions in the 1950s and subsequent decades, to a more concentrated concern with child pornography, sexual violence and 'extreme pornographic images', although the Digital Economy Act 2017 will introduce much tighter controls over access to all pornography websites.

The law of obscenity is not confined to sexual activity; representations of drug taking or, very rarely, violence (*DPP v A & BC Chewing Gum Ltd* [1968] 1 QB 159) can also be criminalised. To be frank, however, we are generally talking about sex or, more precisely, pornography, described by the Court of Appeal as 'this filthy trade' (*R v Holloway* (1982) 4 Cr App R 128).

The basic offence under the Obscene Publications Act 1959 is to publish an obscene article, or possess an obscene article with a view to such publication. An 'article' includes

14 IPSO, 'Who We Are', https://www.ipso.co.uk/aboutipso/whoweare.html (last accessed 01/11/17).

15 R Greenslade, 'Why the Guardian's decision not to sign up to IPSO makes sense' *The Guardian* (4 September 2014), http://www.theguardian.com/media/greenslade/2014/sep/04/press-regulation-ipso (last accessed 01/11/17).

books, films and pictures. The Criminal Justice and Public Order Act 1994, section 168 extended the offence to include the transmission of electronically stored data. Downloading, in England and Wales, obscene material that has been uploaded and hosted elsewhere is covered because the download is considered to be a 'publication'. The obscene nature of material is defined in section 1 of the Obscene Publications Act 1959: 'an article shall be deemed to be obscene if its effect . . . is such as to tend to deprave and corrupt persons who are likely . . . to read, see or hear it'. This causes problems. There is no further definition of 'tend to deprave and corrupt', and it is up to the jury to decide if the material would have that effect.

Look at the words again. They are derived from a Victorian court judgment,[16] but are they clear or easy to apply to specific material? Lord Denning famously said that the legislation had misfired (*R v Metropolitan Police Commissioner ex parte Blackburn (No 3)* [1973] Crim LR 55). There is a need to consider the impact of the article on the likely readers, and the article must be likely to have a corrupting effect on 'a significant proportion of those likely to read it' (*R v Calder and Boyars Ltd* [1969] 1 QB 151).

What if the readers/viewers are already corrupted (by extensive exposure to pornography)? Can they still be further depraved and corrupted? The answer from *DPP v Whyte* [1972] AC 849 is yes. The House of Lords stated that magistrates were mistaken in finding that the articles were not obscene because the purchasers were 'inadequate, pathetic, dirty-minded men . . . whose minds were already in a state of depravity and corruption'. The Lords reversed this ruling and said: 'The Act is not merely concerned with the once and for all corruption of the wholly innocent'.

17.6.1 DEFENCE

One important feature of the Obscene Publications Act 1959 is its public interest defence: 'as being for the public good on the ground that [publication] is in the interests of science, literature, art or learning or other object of general concern' (section 4 OPA 1959).

Expert evidence, which cannot normally be called on the question of whether the material is likely to tend to deprave and corrupt, can be called on the public interest merits, e.g. a literature professor may give evidence on the literary merit of a novel. A finding that some article has scientific or literary merit does not give it *carte blanche* to be morally corrupting. The jury must balance the strength of the tendency to deprave and corrupt (including the number of people so affected) against the strength of the 'public good' merits.

As mentioned above, there is a sharper focus in current law and practice on particular types of pornographic obscene material. Section 63 of the Criminal Justice and Immigration Act 2008 makes it an offence to *possess* an 'extreme pornographic image',

---

16 *R v Hicklin* (1868) LR 3 QB 360 (Lord Cockburn).

i.e. the offence is not limited to publicising such images. 'Pornographic' means material 'produced solely or principally for the purpose of sexual arousal'. 'Extreme' means it must be grossly offensive, disgusting or otherwise of an obscene nature and shows a threat to life, serious injury to anus, breast or genitals, sex with a human corpse or intercourse or oral sex with an animal (dead or alive). The definition was extended to cover images of rape and assault by penetration (Criminal Justice and Courts Act 2015). Criminalising possession of this type of material may seem to be uncontroversial, but as the lawyer of a man acquitted of section 63 of the CJIA 2008 charges in 2012 pointed out, some of the activities represented in the contested material in his client's trial also feature in *50 Shades of Grey* (the best-selling book in British history, and with over 100 million sales worldwide) and the work of the celebrated photographer Robert Mapplethorpe.[17] The Digital Economy Act 2017 will make it easier to block websites that carry extreme pornographic material. The Criminal Justice and Courts Act 2015 created an offence in relation to 'revenge porn', i.e. disclosing private sexual photographs or films with intent to cause distress.

There are specific offences concerning indecent images of children. Section 1 of the Protection of Children Act 1978 makes it an offence to take, make or distribute indecent images of children. A child is a person under the age of 16. Section 160 of the Criminal Justice Act 1988 makes it an offence to possess an indecent photograph of a child. A computer image is not technically a photograph, but to avoid digital images falling outside the offence, the section now applies to 'pseudo-photographs'. Parpworth notes that there has been a shift from prosecution under the Obscene Publications Act 1959 to wider use of these specific child indecency provisions under the 1978 and 1988 Acts.[18]

Concerns over children accessing, rather than being the subject of, pornography led to provisions in the Digital Economy Act 2017 (sections 14–21) that will require age-verification checks for access to pornographic websites. The intention is to require users to input credit cards details before they can access sites, with controls due to be in place by 2018.

These provisions are complemented by a form of internet self-regulation. The Internet Watch Foundation has no statutory powers but has a UK hotline for reporting criminal content online. The focus is on child sexual abuse content hosted anywhere in the world and it also covers 'criminally obscene adult content hosted in the UK'.[19] The reports received from the public are 'overwhelmingly about child pornography'. The Foundation can ask the internet service provider to remove the material and can inform the police.

---

17 M Jackman, 'Extreme porn trial: consensual sex and the state' *The Guardian* (8 August 2012), https://www.theguardian. com/law/2012/aug/08/extreme-porn-trial-simon-walsh (last accessed 01/11/17)

18 N Parpworth, *Constitutional & Administrative Law* (9th edn, OUP, 2016) 435.

19 Internet Watch Foundation, https://www.iwf.org.uk/ (last accessed 01/11/17).

APPLYING THE LAW – OBSCENITY VERSUS FREEDOM OF EXPRESSION

Consider the overall relationship between obscenity and freedom of expression. Article 10(2) ECHR does allow for proportionate restrictions on freedom of expression for the 'protection of health or morals'. Yet many important works of art have been censored or controlled on this ground from the novels of de Sade, through Anaïs Nin, Henry Miller, D H Lawrence and Hubert Selby Jr. It is normally best practice to avoid Nazi analogies as the first port of call in any argument (see Godwin's Law[20]), but it is difficult to avoid mentioning the Degenerate Art Exhibition of 1937, where confiscated works of arts were displayed to highlight their morally corrupt nature. The exhibition included works by some of the greatest artists of the twentieth century: Chagal, Picasso, Klee, Kandinsky and others.

Any law on obscenity must be very alive to the dangers of impeding artistic work that can contribute to the 'public good'. This seems to have little relevance to current UK legal practice with its focus on the more extreme pornographic images and indecent images of children, but we have seen that, for example, some consensual BDSM practices that feature in art and the personal behaviour of some individuals do seem to transgress the restrictions imposed on extreme pornographic images.

17.7 DEFAMATION

The law of defamation restricts expression so as to protect reputation. A defamation is a falsehood which exposes a person to 'hatred, ridicule or contempt', or damages that reputation in the eyes of 'right thinking members of society' (*Sim v Stretch* [1936] 2 ALL ER 1237). Article 10(2) of the European Convention on Human Rights allows for proportionate limits on freedom of expression to 'protect the reputation of others'.

Defamation is a tort with two branches. Slander involves defamation through spoken words or gestures. Libel is defamation in a more permanent form. This mainly covers written words, but also applies to statements in broadcasts. English libel law has traditionally had some problematic features that meant that resulted in the wrong balance between reputation and freedom of expression.

One problem was that the only limitation on anyone using the English courts as a forum for a defamation claim was that there must have been some publication of the defamatory material in England and Wales. This resulted in 'libel tourism' where claimants with very

---

20 Oxford English Dictionary, 'Godwin's law', http://www.oed.com/view/Entry/340583 (last accessed 01/11/17).

little connection to the UK brought actions where only a few copies of the material were sold in England and Wales, or where a website had been accessed many thousands of times from another country and only a couple of dozen times in England and Wales. In 2008, for example, the Ukrainian businessman Rinat Akhmetova brought a defamation action in London against a Ukrainian news website, Obozrevtal, over an article published in the Ukrainian language. The pressure group Article 19 commented that 'Terrorist financing and corruption-related topics have often been the objects of such suits, bringing larger public-policy concerns into the equation'.[21]

English libel law was regarded as being more claimant-friendly than many other countries. All the claimant had to do was to prove that the statement was defamatory and then the defendant had to justify it. The remedies issued by English courts, such as the level of damages and orders to e.g. destroy all copies of a book, were also appreciated by claimants looking for the most advantageous forum for their action. Costs for defendants were always very high and it was general policy not to award legal aid to defendants in libel cases. It was sometimes prudent for a publisher to cancel the entire publication of a book on the basis of a mere threat of libel action.

KEY CASE – *MCDONALD'S CORP V STEEL* [1999] EWCA CIV 1144

The so-called McLibel trial was one of the longest cases in UK legal history. The case itself took around ten years. From the time the protesters handed out their leaflets to the eventual European Court of Human Rights judgment in their favour was a period of almost 20 years.

The protesters Steel and Morris handed out leaflets critical of McDonald's on the streets of London in 1986. They were sued for defamation by McDonald's, who were estimated to have spent several millions of pounds on the case. Steel and Morris had very low incomes and were denied legal aid. They received extensive pro bono support from legal professionals, and from undergraduate law students (bravo!).

The case reached the High Court in 1998, where Mr Justice Bell found that some of the allegations, for example that McDonald's endangered the health of their workers and that they exploit children, were justified by being true. Some of the allegations, e.g. on the direct dangers of eating their food, were unfounded and Steel and Morris were found liable for those and ordered to pay £60,000 damages. On appeal, the Court of Appeal found that a wider range of the allegations were justified by truth and reduced the damages to £40,000.

---

21 Article 19, www.article19.org/pdfs/publications/uk-libel-tourism.pdf (last accessed 01/11/17).

Steel and Morris took the case on to the European Court of Human Rights (*Steel and Morris v UK* [2005] EMLR 314) and won. The Court held that the operation of English defamation laws in this case had breached the right to a fair trial and freedom of expression. The imbalance between the resources of the parties was unfair, and the laws had provided insufficient protection to the strong public interest in allowing small groups and individuals to contribute to public debate particularly in relation to the social impact of big businesses who had to accept a wider limit of acceptable criticism.

The overall operation of English defamation law at this time was that it had a serious 'chilling effect' on freedom of expression. Lord Keith, in *Derbyshire County Council* described this: 'quite often the facts which would justify a defamatory publication are known to be true, but admissible evidence capable of proving those facts is not available. This may prevent the publication of matters which it is very desirable to make public'.

The Defamation Act 2013 (DA 2013) sought to address some of these shortcomings by introducing new safeguards, and by trying to prevent frivolous cases. Section 1 states that a statement is not defamation 'unless its publication has caused, or is likely to cause serious harm to the reputation of the claimant'. The test for actions brought by commercial organisations is that the defamation must cause 'serious financial loss'.

To address libel tourism, for actions against a person not domiciled in the UK a court 'shall not have jurisdiction to hear an action unless it is satisfied that, of all places in which the statement complained of has been published, England and Wales is clearly the most appropriate place to bring an action' (section 9 DA 2013).

The Act introduced a single publication rule. Previously, each time a webpage was accessed it was regarded as a separate publication. So, years after the initial statement, each 'publication' was a separate defamation. Section 8 of the DA 2013 introduces a one-year limitation period, for further publication of substantially the same statement. Section 11 of the DA 2013 reverses the presumption in favour of a jury trial. Defamation cases will be held without a jury unless the court orders otherwise.

The defences are set out in sections 2–4 of the Defamation Act 2013:

- Truth – section 2: that 'the imputation conveyed by the statement complained of is substantially true'. Note that the burden of proof is still on the defendant (to show that their statement is true) rather than on the claimant (to show that it is false). We have highlighted the chilling effect of this, but the practical difficulties of proving a negative (e.g. that I have not been dishonest in any of my financial dealings) means that it is difficult to have a complete shift in the burden.

- Honest opinion – section 3: if I say 'in my view, person X is totally unfit to hold public office', this is neither true nor false, it is opinion. Section 3 states that as long as the basis of the opinion is indicated, and an honest person could have held the opinion on the basis of the facts existing at the time, then this is not a defamation.
- Public interest – section 4: protects a reasonable belief that publishing the statement was in the public interest. The common law concept of responsible journalism will still be relevant, e.g. did the newspaper take steps to verify the story, did they give the subject of the story a chance to comment on allegations before publication? This allows to the court to give 'such allowance for editorial judgement as it considers appropriate'. The first successful use of the defence was in *Economou v De Freitas* [2017] EMLR 4, where the court said that the responsible journalism obligation would not apply as strictly to ordinary members of the public as to professional journalists.
- Absolute privilege – any fair and accurate reporting of court proceedings, proceedings of Parliament, and now also reporting of proceedings of a press conference on a matter of public interest, are protected under the concept of absolute privilege.
- Qualified privilege – the trigger for this particular reform was the case of **British Chiropractic Association v Singh** [2010] EWCA Civ 350, where after a long legal battle and at considerable personal expense the science writer Simon Singh was able to rely on a defence of fair comment in making allegations that the British Chiropractors Association 'happily promotes bogus treatments'. This defence, in relation to academic writing, was partly codified by section 6 DA 2013, protecting publication in a peer-reviewed scientific or academic journal in the absence of malice.

17.8 PRIVACY AND BREACH OF CONFIDENCE

As well as introducing a strong obligation to protect freedom of expression, the Human Rights Act 1998 also introduced similar obligations to protect privacy. Where someone (a journalist, an ex-partner) is in possession of private information about another person and wants to publicise that information, then the two rights come into conflict. This section will explore how far freedom of expression is limited by the protection of privacy.

17.8.1 DEFINING PRIVACY

Wacks wrote that 'the concept of "privacy" has become too vague and unwieldy a concept to perform useful analytical (and, hence, legal) work . . . This ambiguity has, it is submitted, actually undermined the importance of the value of "privacy" and impeded its effective legal protection'.[22] This has not prevented many writers from attempting a definition, for example Phillipson and Fenwick define privacy as '. . . the individual's interest in controlling the flow of personal information about herself . . . the right to "selective disclosure"'.[23]

---

22 R Wacks, *Personal Information: Privacy and the Law* (OUP, 1994) 10–11.

23 G Phillipson and H Fenwick, 'Breach of Confidence as a Privacy Remedy in the Human Rights Era' [2000] *Modern Law Review* 660, 662.

17.8.2 PRE-HUMAN RIGHTS ACT PRIVACY

Looking back at the condition of English law before the introduction of the Human Rights Act can provoke a curious reaction. Could it *really* be the position that there was no direct protection for privacy? The answer, as illustrated by *Kaye v Robertson*, is yes.

KEY CASE – *KAYE V ROBERTSON* [1991] EWCA CIV 21

Gorden Kaye was a very popular BBC comedy actor.[24] He was involved in a serious road traffic accident, taken to Charing Cross Hospital, placed on life support and then underwent emergency brain surgery. Tabloid journalists from the *Sunday Sport* 'newspaper' went to the hospital, avoided hospital staff and ignored notices refusing them access. They interviewed and photographed Kaye. During this time, he was in semi-conscious state and medical evidence showed that he would be incapable of giving informed consent (or even of recollecting the incident). The *Sunday Sport* intended to publish a story and pictures as though Kaye had consented.

The judges indicated that they were appalled by this behaviour, calling it 'a monstrous invasion of his privacy', but could not provide a direct remedy because there was no right to privacy in English law (there was some protection possible under the law on malicious falsehood).

Glidewell LJ stated: 'It is well known that in English law there is no right to privacy, and accordingly there is no right of action for breach of a person's privacy. The facts of the present case are a graphic illustration of the desirability of Parliament considering whether and in what circumstances statutory provision can be made to protect the privacy of individuals'. Bingham LJ bemoaned the 'failure of both the common law of England and statute to protect the personal privacy of individual citizens', and called for statutory intervention to define and limit a tort of privacy.

17.8.3 ACTION FOR BREACH OF CONFIDENCE

Kaye v Robertson also shows that some aspects of private life could, in some circumstances, be protected under existing actions; a claim in malicious falsehood was partially successfully and arguments in relation to libel, and trespass to the person, were also put forward. It was the common law tort of breach of confidence, however, that emerged as the most useful existing cause of action to serve as a vehicle for driving forward the legal protection of privacy.

The Law Commission explained the action for breach of confidence as: 'a civil remedy affording protection against the disclosure or use of information which is not publicly known and which

---

24 And I will say this only once.

has been entrusted to a person in circumstances imposing an obligation not to disclose or use that information without the authority of the person who imparted it'.[25] Three main elements were identified by Megarry J in *Coco v A N Clark (Engineers) Ltd* [1969] RPC 41:

- First, the information itself, . . . 'must have the necessary quality of confidence about it'.
- Secondly, that information must have been imparted in circumstances imparting an obligation of confidence.
- Thirdly, there must have been an unauthorised use of that information to the detriment of the party communicating it . . .

17.8.4 BALANCING THE RIGHTS

Even before the introduction of the Human Rights Act 1998, the courts were wrestling with the appropriate balance between competing rights, as illustrated in *X v Y*.

KEY CASE – *X V Y* [1988] 2 ALL ER 648

A newspaper had obtained information about two doctors who had HIV and was intending to publish this information. A local health authority obtained an injunction preventing publication.

Rose J:

On the one hand there are the public interests in having a free press and an informed public debate; on the other, it is in the public interest that actual or potential AIDS sufferers should be able to resort to hospitals without fear of this being revealed, that those owing duties of confidence in their employment should be loyal and not disclose confidential matters . . .

I keep in the forefront of my mind the very important public interest in freedom of the press. And I accept that there is some public interest in knowing that which the defendants seek to publish . . . But in my judgment those public interests are substantially outweighed when measured against the public interest in relation to loyalty and confidentiality both generally and with particular reference to AIDS patients' hospital records.

17.8.5 IS THERE ALWAYS A CONFLICT BETWEEN PRIVACY AND FREEDOM OF EXPRESSION?

The drafters of the Human Rights Act 1998 envisaged that these sorts of conflicts would be so likely that they made special provision for them in section 12, discussed above.

---

25 Law Commission, '*Breach of Confidence*' Report 110, Cmnd 8388, 1981 (HMSO) 10.

Phillipson and Fenwick argue, however, that it is 'exaggerated and simplistic' to think that these sorts of conflicts are inevitable.[26] They categorise the typical examples of invasions of privacy (i.e. in the personal, not political, affairs of people who are normally celebrities) as *not even engaging* the Article 10 ECHR values of imparting information on 'matters of serious concern' or furtherance of a democratic society.

> Thus, it will only be in a fairly narrow category of cases that any real conflict will arise –
> those where a publication relates to the personal life of a particular figure, but there is a
> serious argument that it serves a valuable purpose in revealing a matter relevant to that
> person's fitness for office, or in furthering public knowledge or debate about matters of
> legitimate public concern.[27]

This approach was supported by Lord Mance in *PJS v News Group Newspapers Ltd* [2016] UKSC 26, where a paper wanted to print a story about a celebrity's extra-marital affair. He said 'it may well be' that these sorts of stories did not engage Article 10 and if they did then only 'at the bottom end of the spectrum of importance'.

17.8.6 HOW HAVE THE COURTS RESPONDED TO THE CHALLENGE OF PROTECTING PRIVACY UNDER THE HRA?

The courts have not had the advantage of being able to rely on statutory provisions. Successive Governments since 1998 have refused to introduce comprehensive privacy legislation. Over time, as the courts have crafted privacy protections from existing rules, this has itself become the convenient excuse for governmental inaction: that the judges have the issue in hand and there is now no need for new laws.

There is a very large body of case law on the judicial development of a new tort of misuse of private information, created since the early 2000s. We will focus on just four cases. The major step in this development was that courts found that they could extend the tort of breach of confidence to situations which were previously beyond its scope. Breach of confidence developed in commercial and employment-type relationships to protect confidential information. Through the twentieth century it was extended to cover information arising from family and social relationships, but it was always an essential ingredient of the tort that there was 'an existing relationship of confidence'.

In most cases of newspapers invading a person's privacy, this existing relationship was simply absent – the tort, as it stood, could not effectively protect privacy.

---

26 Phillipson and Fenwick, above n 21, 662.
27 Ibid., 685.

KEY CASE – *DOUGLAS AND OTHERS V HELLO! LTD* [2003] 3 ALL ER 996

A paparazzi photographer disguised himself as a guest so as to gain entry to the wedding of the film stars Michael Douglas and Catherine Zeta-Jones. He surreptitiously took some photos and sold them to *Hello!* magazine. There was no existing relationship of confidence between the photographer and the happy couple. The court was willing to dispense with this requirement because of the new demands of the Human Rights Act to develop existing laws to protect fundamental rights. As long as the information was of a confidential nature and there was a proposed unauthorised use of that information that would cause harm for the claimant, the courts could intervene.

Sedley LJ commented that:

> . . . a concept of privacy does . . . accord recognition to the fact that the law has to protect not only those people whose trust has been abused but those who simply find themselves subjected to an unwanted intrusion into their personal lives. The law no longer needs to construct an artificial relationship of confidentiality between the intruder and victims: it can recognise privacy itself as a legal principle drawn from the fundamental value of personal autonomy.

The challenge for UK judges has been to develop English common law to be consistent with Article 10 ECHR as interpreted by the European Court of Human Rights. This interpretation has also changed over the years. Much tabloid journalism, across Europe, has involved simply following famous people around and taking photographs of them in public places. A question that came before the ECtHR was whether such people had any sort of expectation of privacy in these circumstances and whether this expectation could be outweighed by freedom of expression.

KEY CASE – *VON HANNOVER V GERMANY* [2004] EMLR 379

This case examined the press coverage of the life of Princess Caroline of Monaco. She had no public or political function in the state of Monaco. She was married to a German aristocrat, was patron of some charities and in support of these roles appeared at public events where she was extensively photographed.

In addition, she had been subject to a long campaign of what (to her) amounted to harassment by the press and paparazzi photographers. This involved following her and taking photographs whilst she was going about her activities of daily life such as eating out in restaurants, going jogging, going on holiday with her family etc.

The European Court of Human Rights heard that German law would not protect her because she had the status of a 'public person' and the activities that she was photographed doing were not sufficiently private. The Court held that there had been a breach of her Article 8 rights to privacy. In the balance between privacy and expression, neither right automatically took precedence over the other. Courts would have to *weigh* each right in the context of all the circumstances.

It was found that the Article 10 claim, that e.g. taking and publishing pictures of the Princess in her swimsuit whilst on holiday with her family at the Monte Carlo Beach Club, was an exercise of the human right of free expression, but was a very light, and almost insubstantial claim. On the other side of the scale was the Article 8 claim. The Court found that taking her photo in public places did engage her privacy rights. It was not the worst case of invasion of privacy, but the key to understanding why the Court put weight on the privacy claim was the relentless nature of the intrusion. The fact that she was under very extensive surveillance by the press and the consequent impact on her life made it a serious issue.

In highlighting this notion of 'weight', the Court also seemed to establish a hierarchy of value for different types of expression. Political speech, understood broadly as any contribution to a debate of public importance, had the highest value and would be the most difficult to be overborne by competing considerations. Artistic expression and, to some extent, commercial speech (as communication contributing to economic development) were also recognised as having value. The landmark case in English law also had to consider these competing notions of the public interest in imparting and receiving information.

KEY CASE – *CAMPBELL V MGN* [2004] 2 WLR 1232

The *Sunday Mirror* had obtained information and related photographs that the fashion model Naomi Campbell had been attending Narcotics Anonymous sessions in London. It appeared that Campbell had, on various occasions in press interviews, voluntarily lied to the public about her drug use. Campbell sought an injunction to prevent publication and the case was ultimately appealed to the House of Lords.

The Lords identified five elements to the proposed story:

1   That Campbell was a drug addict.
2   That she was receiving treatment for that addiction.

3   That the treatment was with Narcotics Anonymous.
4   The details of that treatment.
5   Photographs of her leaving her treatment sessions.

The Lords then framed the two questions that now form the basis for the new tort. First, was there a reasonable expectation of privacy? Second, does the public interest in publication outweigh the privacy interest?

Applying these questions to the facts, the court found:

(a) That there *was* a reasonable expectation of privacy in all aspects of the story. Campbell was reasonably entitled to expect that this sensitive and intimate information on a medical issue would be private.
(b) That the 'public interest in publication' test applied differently to different elements of the story. There was a strong public interest in correcting her deliberate mistruth. The newspaper was entitled, in the public interest, to inform its readers that Campbell actually was a drug user and a drug addict. This public interest, however, did not extend to more sensitive aspects of the story such as details of her medical addiction treatment. The photographs were similarly unnecessary to convey the public interest aspects of the story.

The consequence, as developed through many other privacy actions, was that a new tort has been developed: misuse of information in which there is a reasonable expectation of privacy. The scope of this new tort and the way in which it can restrict what would otherwise be perfectly lawful forms of expression were explored in *Murray*.

KEY CASE – *MURRAY V BIG PICTURES (UK) LTD* [2008] EWCA CIV 446

Dr and Mrs Murray (who happens to be the author J K Rowling) were photographed by a photo news agency whilst walking in the street in Edinburgh with their baby son, David. The photos were taken with a long lens and without the consent of the subjects. The parents brought the case in the name, and the interests of, their son. They claimed that even though this was a public place, the press agency should not have taken pictures of the child as he had a reasonable expectation of privacy and there was no public interest in publishing images of him. The photo agency argued that there was no general right not to be photographed in a public place.

The Court of Appeal was keen to move away from generalities and focused on the specific facts of the case. Sir Anthony Clarke MR, for example, said, 'We do

not share the predisposition identified by the [trial] judge that routine acts such as
a visit to a shop or a ride on a bus should not attract any reasonable expectation
of privacy. All depends upon the circumstances'. The Court found that the
circumstances here meant that there was a reasonable expectation of privacy for the
child which outweighed any public interest claim.

So if you were a tourist taking a picture of Edinburgh Castle and it just so happened that
J K Rowling was walking past with her son and ruined your shot, that would not even
engage Article 8. Even if you wanted to publish the picture, e.g. on a social media site,
then this would be very unlikely to impinge on anyone's reasonable expectation of privacy.
The key 'circumstance' identified by the Court in *Murray* was not the objective nature of
the pictures themselves. As in *von Hannover*, the pictures taken in isolation would be legally
unobjectionable. It was the nature of the process for finding, following and photographically
capturing the targets, and the psychological awareness of that 'constant fear of media
intrusion' that was key. In *Murray*, it was the covert and clandestine taking of photos for the
purposes of publication and then their subsequent sale and publication for profit, together
with the targeting of images of children, which ultimately pushed the images into the realm
of privacy-invading material that could be restricted by the court.

17.8.7 INJUNCTIONS

Actions for breach of confidence or reasonable expectation of privacy have a very useful
advantage for applicants. This is the notion of prior restraint. The general approach of the law to
the press is often summed up in the phrase 'publish and be damned'. This means that the press
has a general right to decide itself whether to publish material or not. If that material breaches
e.g. defamation laws, then the newspaper will have to face the damning legal consequences
but it will not have been subject to prior controls by courts or by a Government agency.

This model simply does not work in relation to privacy law. If private information is
unlawfully published, the wronged individual may be able to get damages but this remedy
does not make the information private again. Once private information is out in the public
domain it is just no longer private. In practical terms, this means that injunctions are more
common (as compared to defamation proceedings).

Injunctions on publication are clearly more of a danger to freedom of expression than
subsequent restraints. There is a further danger. The general approach to court orders
including injunctions is that such orders are public documents that can be freely reported
in the press. Imagine that instead of being a dedicated educator, your Public Law teacher
is a top international footballer. Some celebrity magazines have been speculating about the
health of their marriage and then it is reported that they have obtained an injunction from
the High Court preventing publication of a story about another relationship. You would
be spared the details, but the essence of the story, that they have been in an extra-marital

relationship, would be revealed by the very injunction that was intended to protect their privacy. The response to this conundrum was the super-injunction: an injunction that prevents the press from reporting its existence.

APPLYING THE LAW – THE TRAFIGURA SUPER-INJUNCTION

Trafigura, a Dutch commodities company, was responsible for the dumping of toxic waste in the Ivory Coast in 2006.[28] This caused death and extensive injury. *The Guardian* obtained internal emails about the extent to which the company knew the dangerous nature of the waste material. When Trafigura launched court proceedings against *The Guardian*, its privacy was protected by the court in three ways:

- There was an injunction against using the information.
- The injunction also prevented *The Guardian* from disclosing the fact that Trafigura had obtained an injunction,
- Trafigura was given random initials (RJW) in all proceedings and court documents.

A Labour MP, Paul Farrelly, tabled a question in the House of Commons about this matter. Trafigura warned *The Guardian* not to report the Parliamentary question. The response to this warning was a report confirmed by the Lord Chief Justice, the Speaker of the House of Commons and the Parliamentary Under-Secretary of State (an unusual triumvirate of the three branches of the state), that a) Mr Farrelly's statements were covered by Parliamentary privilege and b) *The Guardian*'s reporting of those statements was covered by section 3 of the Parliamentary Papers Act 1840.[29]

Super-injunctions are also undermined by the leakage and spread of information through social media, for example the super-injunction obtained by the footballer Ryan Giggs in relation to extra-marital affairs was effectively rendered useless by the revelation of his identity through Twitter in 2011. Overall, super-injunctions have attracted criticism because it is thought that they do not strike the right balance between privacy and freedom of expression.

17.9 ASSESSMENT ADVICE

There is a great deal of primary law and many interesting scenarios in this subject, but problem questions seem to be rare. It is more common for examiners to set general

---

28 R Evans, 'Trafigura fined 1m euros for exporting toxic waste to Africa, *The Guardian* (23 July 2010), http://www. theguardian.com/world/2010/jul/23/trafigura-dutch-fine-waste-export (last accessed 01/11/17).
29 A Bradley and K Ewing, *Constitutional and Administrative Law* (15th edn, Longman, 2011) 525–26.

essay-type questions, normally involving the issue of 'balance'. Are there too many restrictions on freedom of expression? Has the right balance been struck?

When you are faced with these sorts of 'balance' questions, it is particularly important to structure your argument effectively. One way of improving your reasoning and assessment skills on these issues is to use argument maps. These have a more formal structure then mind maps. Almost every assessment that you undertake as a law student, across all your subjects, asks you to create an argument. If you can map your argument, you will ensure that it is well-constructed. A simple visual representation of an argument could look like this.

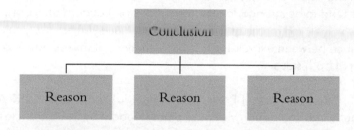

Figure 17.2 Argument mapping

You should draft an argument map in relation to all coursework assessments. This will help you to:

■ Clarify your main conclusion.
■ Check that you have a coherent set of supporting reasons.
■ Allow you to assess whether you have enough research/authority/evidence to support those conclusions.
■ Uncover any assumptions or logical flaws.

See the further detailed explanation of argument mapping and outline of its benefits by van Gelder: http://timvangelder.com/2009/02/17/what-is-argument-mapping/.

POINTS TO REVIEW

■ Press regulation has been, and continues to be, fraught with difficulty.

■ There are important areas of law – defamation and privacy – that impose limits on expression.

■ Recent reforms have seen an attempt to recast the balance between the competing interests and show a more nuanced and appreciative understanding of the place of freedom of expression in the UK legal system.

TAKING IT FURTHER

Amnesty International, Freedom of Expression https://www.youtube.com/
watch?v=geMOuJZ20Ic a clear and beautifully produced short video on rights to freedom
of expression in international law.

E Barendt, *Freedom of Speech* (2nd edn, OUP, 2005) We do not usually recommend
whole books in these 'Taking it further' sections; we want to be more focused and identify
useful and accessible material that you will actually use to enhance your work rather than
leave unloved and unseen on a long reading list. This recommendation is here, however,
because a) the book is particularly good, b) there is a good chance that there is a copy
in your institution's library and c) it addresses a deficit. Even very decent student answers
on this subject tend to be stronger on the restrictions on freedom of expression than
they are on the values and merits of expression itself. Since you are likely to be asked
about the balance between expression and its restrictions, it makes sense to have a good
understanding of both sides.

J Rowbottom, 'The Legitimacy of Press Regulation' [2015] *Public Law* 290 A very
interesting inquiry into competing visions of press freedom by the current leading
academic thinker on the subject. Use this to develop your understanding of the post-
Leveson world of press regulation.

Article 19, https://www.article19.org/ The leading international organisation defending
freedom of expression. It would be useful to browse its news and legal briefing sections
for breaking stories of the struggle to protect freedom of expression.

CHAPTER 18
FREEDOM OF ASSEMBLY AND PUBLIC PROTEST

Public protest has played a significant part in winning most of the features of modern democracy, e.g. free and fair elections for men and women. It provides access to public attention and to the media for those denied control of the press. It is therefore a fundamental aspect of freedom of expression. Poll tax demonstrations in 1990 were credited with contributing to the downfall of one of the most formidable Prime Ministers in British history, Margaret Thatcher.

However, it is also one of the most inconvenient of rights, almost always causing some form of disruption, even if only to traffic or shopping. There are direct costs in policing protests and indirect costs to business that can run into hundreds of thousands of pounds. Protest may, on occasion, lead to public disorder and violence, as seen in some of the student protests of 2010.

AS YOU READ

By the end of this chapter you should:

■ have a critical understanding of the legal rules on freedom of assembly and public order

■ be able to evaluate the impact of Article 11 of the ECHR

■ understand and assess the responses to the 'hostile audience' issue.

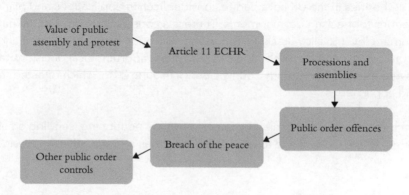

Figure 18.1 Structure of Chapter 18

18.1 FREEDOM OF ASSEMBLY

What is the relevance of public protest in an age of social media? Increasingly, campaigns take shape in an online environment through Facebook, Twitter and online petitions. An example is the campaign by Caroline Criado-Perez on the representation of women in public life. An element of this campaign in 2013 was to try to persuade the Bank of England to retain a female historical figure on UK banknotes. This campaign took place largely online, although it also involved face-to-face lobbying and a threat of a legal challenge under the Equality Act 2010. It was successful, and the image of Jane Austen on the £10 note in your pocket is a direct result of this protest.

Arguably, one of the most successful campaigning groups (or 'communities' in their words) in recent years has been 38 Degrees. It has contributed to important changes in human trafficking laws, transparency for MPs' expenses, and limitation of privatisation of health services. Does this mean that we can now assume that there are adequate avenues for dissent without the need to allow public protest on the streets, with its negative consequences of disruption and potential disorder? The answer has to be no. As 38 Degrees say, 'While our campaigns often start on the web, they rarely stay there for long';[1] the campaigns' tactics normally involve face-to-face events and public meetings. There is scepticism as to how effective 'clicktivism' (activism by clicking online links) can be in the absence of complementary 'real world' actions.

APPLYING THE LAW – FRACKING

This hand-in-hand approach of virtual and real-world campaigns can be seen in the protests around fracking. Fracking (or hydraulic fracturing) is a process where a pressurised liquid mixture is injected into rock. This fractures the rock and releases gas. Its potential in the UK is contested, but it could contribute to the UK's energy supplies. The risks, which are said to encompass water pollution and increases in seismic activity, are equally contested.

Public authorities in the UK have had to consider licence applications and planning applications for fracking developments. There is a considerable drive at the national Government level to allow fracking, but each application has been resisted and subject to protest at local levels. Some of the most important local decisions taken so far were made by Lancashire County Council in June 2015, which rejected the fracking applications.

The decisions were accompanied by intensive online petitioning, sending emails and letters to the Council and to local MPs. There was also a significant physical

---

1   38 Degrees, 'About us', https://home.38degrees.org.uk/start-here/ (last accessed 01/11/17).

element to the protests, involving placards, residents' meetings and 400–500 protesters assembled outside of Lancashire County Hall on the days of the decision. Preston Police used social media to reassure residents that they would ensure the protests remained peaceful and to warn drivers and pedestrians of some disruption in the immediate area.

The protesters felt that through these methods they were able to get their voices heard as a counterbalance to more powerful commercial interests. The key point is that the public protest was an important part of the mix of methods used in a grass-roots campaign. As of 2017, those protests are continuing. The Lancashire County Council decision was overturned by the Communities Secretary in 2016, a decision that was unsuccessfully challenged by judicial review and which is being further appealed. Fracking operations commenced in summer 2017 and there are daily ongoing protests at the site.

Other protests against fracking around the country, such as at Balcombe in Sussex, Barton Moss in Greater Manchester, and from 2017 Kirby Misperton in North Yorkshire, have been (no pun intended) much more fractious, resulting in arrests and accusations that the police have tried to break up and criminalise peaceful protest.

As with the previous chapter on freedom of expression, our main concern is balance – here it is between the right of assembly and public protest on one hand and the inconvenience, discomfort and potential threats to order that such protest can produce on the other hand. The chapter follows the same structure of seeking to outline the purpose and value of the right and then exploring the limitations on that right and assessing the proportionality of those restrictions. As Feldman explains: 'The job of the lawmakers is to decide when the interests of society in being free of unwanted persuasion or disorder outweigh the interests in free expression of opinions and persuasion'.[2]

18.2 THE VALUES OF PUBLIC PROTEST

In February 2003, the largest public demonstration in British history took place. The police estimated that over 750,000 people took part in a protest march in London against the proposed UK involvement in a war in Iraq. The organisers put the estimated number at closer to 2 million and it seems very likely that over 1 million people were involved. There were almost no public order problems.

---

2   D Feldman, *Civil Liberties and Human Rights in England and Wales* (2nd edn OUP, 2002) ch. 18.

In 2011–2012, the Occupy movement, a broad-based protest against the inequities of the global financial system and responses to the banking crisis that largely protected financial institutions, were prevented by injunction from setting up a protest camp outside the London Stock Exchange. The protesters diverted to St Paul's Cathedral, where a group of several hundred endured the English winter in tents on the pavement, maintaining the protests and setting up alternative organisations such as a 'Bank of Ideas'. The protest lasted for four months until the City of London Corporation obtained an injunction to have them removed.

In November and December 2010, there were a series of protests from student groups against cuts to further education, particularly the withdrawal of the Education Maintenance Allowance (EMA), and proposed major increases to university tuition fees in England. Over 40,000 protesters took part in an initial march in central London. A couple of hundred protesters escaped from the main march and attacked the Conservative Party headquarters in the Millbank building. Windows were broken and, notoriously, a fire extinguisher was thrown from the roof, narrowly avoiding striking people in the courtyard. This breakaway group was strongly condemned by the NUS and university lecturers' union, whilst subsequent protests were subjected to proactive, and allegedly aggressive, control by the police.

Looking through the list of recent major demonstrations (which is much longer than the small sample here), one is struck by how unsuccessful many of them seem to have been, at least in direct terms. The Iraq War went ahead with UK involvement; austerity economic policies were applied whilst major stories of incompetence and/or dishonesty in the banking sector continued to appear with depressing regularity; the EMA was cut and tuition fees went up. Even so, it is difficult to assess the indirect consequences of the actions, and at least the protests contributed to public discourse on these important issues. For the protesters, there was little alternative. If these changes could have been successfully opposed by writing letters to MPs and newspapers or having invited conversations with ministers over tea and sandwiches, then they would have been. Getting involved in public protest may be noble, but it is always inconvenient, occasionally cold and damp and sometimes quite scary, but as Lord Denning said in *Hubbard v Pitt* [1976], 'It is often the only means by which grievances can be brought to the knowledge of those in authority, at any rate with such impact as to gain remedy'.

APPLYING THE LAW – EDUCATIONAL MAINTENANCE ALLOWANCE

The Coalition Government was elected in 2010 with a mandate to reduce the financial deficit. It saw the Educational Maintenance Allowance (EMA) as a suitable target for spending cuts. The EMA was a financial support system aimed at helping young people from poorer backgrounds to stay in education, providing up to £30 a week for students from the poorest families who were in post-16 further education.

There was evidence to support the effectiveness of the EMA, but its merits were contested. In any case, there was nothing inevitable about the decision to withdraw it. Even within the same field of education, for example, taking away charitable status from public schools would end what is, in effect, a taxpayer subsidy for pupils at school such as Eton and Harrow that far exceeds the weekly support granted to the poorest students. This was never seriously considered by the Coalition Government.

Take a moment to consider how many of the people in Government and Parliament had children who relied on EMA support. How many editors of newspapers or TV news programmes had children in that position? The answer is going to be at, or close to, zero. This is not to deny that people are capable of principled positions on issues like supporting the children of poorer families to stay in education, or of empathy for young people in difficult circumstances, but it highlights the fact that that there are issues affecting large sections of society which are not directly reflected in the daily lives of those taking decisions or setting the news agenda. Getting access to this news agenda – to public discourse – must therefore be done by other means, and public protest remains potent in achieving this.

Freedom of expression is often regarded as a 'safety valve' for serious public concerns. It is in the form of public protest that this safety valve is most needed and most effective. Public protest is therefore important for democracy; it does not just indicate what people are concerned about, it says *how many* people are concerned and has a unique capacity for saying *how strongly* people feel about it.

18.3 ASSESSMENT ADVICE

The approach of examiners to freedom of assembly is similar to that in relation to freedom of expression. There is a preponderance of essay-type questions and they tend to focus on the constitutional role of the right to assemble and protest, and on questions of balance between the right and other social interests, such as public order.

Elliott and Thomas make an excellent point that it would be wise to keep in mind when addressing these sorts of questions. The balance is not normally two-dimensional (protester versus another party). It is multi-dimensional. Typically, there will be multiple competing interests to balance: protesters exercising their human right of peaceful assembly, shoppers and shop-keepers (and other residents and businesses) who are disrupted by the protest, and wider society which bears the direct costs of policing and the indirect economic costs of disruptions to travel, trade, etc.[3] Public order law can be taught as part of Public Law courses or in separate Human Rights Law options. Public order problem questions are more common in Human Rights Law options but they may appear in Public Law as well. We include some short worked examples below, particularly in relation to the Public Order Act offences.

18.4 ARTICLE 11 OF THE EUROPEAN CONVENTION ON HUMAN RIGHTS (ECHR)

This follows the typical ECHR approach of prescribing a broad general right and then outlining the limited circumstances in which it can be qualified (i.e. outweighed) by other pressing social needs.

1 Everyone has the right of peaceful assembly . . .
2 No restrictions shall be placed on the exercise of these rights other than as are prescribed by law and are necessary in a democratic society in the interests of national security or public safety, for the prevention of disorder or crime, for the protection of health or morals or for the protection of the rights and freedoms of others.

It is important to note, therefore, that the right only extends to 'peaceful assembly'. There is no human right to engage in violent protest. The ECtHR clarified in *Christians against Racism and Fascism v UK* (1980) 21 DR 138 that 'Under Article 11(1) of the Convention, the right to freedom of peaceful assembly is secured to everyone who has the intention of organising a peaceful demonstration', so any violence that is *incidental to* a protest will not automatically take that protest outside of the scope of Article 11.

Article 11 primarily imposes a negative obligation on the state – to abstain from preventing peaceful assemblies – but it also involves a positive obligation to stop hostile audiences or counter-demonstrators from denying this right.

You should note that Article 11 also protects freedom of association, including the right to form and to join a trade union. Overall, the state must not inhibit people from forming political parties, pressure groups and other associations. There are only two significant limits in English law:

• Proscribed organisations – the Terrorism Act 2000 allows the Home Secretary to proscribe (i.e. ban) any organisation they believe 'commits, participates, prepares, promotes or is otherwise engaged in acts of terrorism'. The key feature of this law is that that *membership* of the group (rather than any more direct involvement in terrorist

---

3   M Elliott and R Thomas, *Public Law* (3rd edn, OUP, 2017) ch 20.

violence) is enough for the offence. The list of organisations can change but currently includes Hamas, al-Qaida and a range of Irish groups such as the IRA and the Ulster Freedom Fighters.

- Para-military organisations – in the 1930s, the British Union of Fascists, led by Oswald Mosley, posed a significant threat to public order. The party's stewards adopted para-military clothing – the Blackshirt uniform – and were involved in violent clashes with counter-demonstrators. The Public Order Act 1936 prohibited the wearing of uniforms in public with the intention of promoting a political objective. It also banned membership of groups organised and trained for the purpose of displaying physical force. This was used against post-war fascist groups such as Spearhead, a private army established by Colin Jordan and BNP founder John Tyndall in 1963.

Freedom of association under Article 11 ECHR does not just protect membership of trade unions, professional associations and mainstream political groups. In *Redfearn v UK* [2012] ECHR 1878, a Bradford bus driver was sacked following his election as a councillor for the far-right British National Party. This was justified by his employers as being on health and safety grounds, i.e. that his identification with racist views would make him subject to attack and make the bus service unsafe. The Court of Appeal found that the dismissal was not unlawful, but the European Court of Human Rights held that UK law had not taken reasonable and proportionate steps to protect members of a lawful political party from dismissal.

18.5 PUBLIC ORDER

A number of prior restraints are possible under the Public Order Act 1986 (POA 1986), i.e. the state can impose conditions or bans on processions or assemblies before they take place. Such restraints are problematic because they undermine publicity, which is a common objective of the protest.

APPLYING THE LAW – PROBLEM SCENARIO

Here is a scenario that will we apply as we go through the different aspects of public order law.

Olivia and Salvador are students at Capital University, although they are originally from South America. They have organised an immediate protest march in response to the failure of the Court of Appeal to extradite General Augusto, formerly an oppressive leader of their country, for crimes against humanity. The police turn up at the march assembly point and tell Olivia and Salvador that they must change the route of the march so as to avoid the hospital where the General is staying and proceed up a side street, ending up in the Central Park.

On the march, some of the more radical elements avoid this side street and lead the march past the hospital. As Salvador passes the hospital he becomes inflamed and, seeing the General at his window, shakes his fist and shouts, 'Soon I will dance on your grave, you murdering scum, you are dead meat'. He is arrested. The General was laughing at the protesters, but some bystanders appeared offended by Salvador's behaviour. Olivia has been carrying a placard depicting a victim of the General's regime, horribly disfigured by torture. She is arrested.

18.6 PROCESSIONS

The archetype of a procession is a protest march, but ss.11–13 POA 1986 cover a wider range of activities, and a procession is understood to be 'not a mere body of persons; it is a body of persons who are moving along a route. Therefore, the person who organises the route is the person who organises the procession' (Lord Goddard in *Flockhart v Robinson* [1950] 2 KB 498). A static protest is called an 'assembly' – outlined below.

Notice – section 11 of the POA 1986 imposes a notification requirement on the organisers of processions, stating that 'written notice shall be given of any proposal to hold a public procession intended:

1(a) to demonstrate support for or opposition to the views or actions of any person or body of persons
2(b) to publicise a cause or campaign or
3(c) to mark or commemorate an event,

unless it is not reasonably practicable to give any advance notice of the procession'.

Processions which are commonly or customarily held (such as May Day or church parades) are exempted. The organiser must give six days' notice, which must specify the date, time and proposed route of the march and the name and address of an organiser. If the organisers fail to give this notice, they are guilty of an offence. If they fail to keep to the time and route outlined in the notice, they will be guilty of an offence. There is a defence that they had no reason to suspect that any divergence occurred or that it arose due to circumstances outside of their control.

Notification is not the same thing as permission. The rationale for the notification requirement under section 11 of the POA is that it involves the police at an early stage so that they can exercise their powers under sections 12 and 13 of the POA, but also more constructively so that they can have a dialogue with the organisers. There are no reported successful prosecutions under section 11 of the POA, even though it seems that not all processions have given the required notice. It could be argued that section 11 of the POA is uncontentious on the basis that a procession will almost always cause some disruption and a notification requirement is a proportionate rule that allows police to plan and limit that disruption.[4]

KEY CASE – *METROPOLITAN POLICE COMMISSIONER V KAY* [2007] *EWCA CIV 477*

Critical Mass is a cycling event that happens in around 300 cities across the world, often on the final Friday of each month. It could be described as a protest against the hazards (including death) of competing for road space with other cars and lorries or as a spontaneous celebration of city cycling. The London version of the event had met at the same time and place once a month since around 1994 and typically involved 300–400 cyclists. There was no planned route, and the person who happened to be at the front at any one time decided which streets to go down.

The Metropolitan Police Commissioner argued that the organisers needed to give section 11 of the POA notice of the event. The Court of Appeal held that just because the police wanted information on an event did not make it a procession. Ackner LJ doubted that the 'impromptu bike ride' amounted to a procession, and held that even if it was a procession then it was exempted from the notice requirement because it was 'commonly or customarily held' (having regularly happened for 13 years by this time). This implies that any new similar event may need to give notice (and we will see below that this judgment did not stop the Metropolitan Police from trying to regulate Critical Mass events).

So how would section 11 of the POA apply to our scenario?

APPLYING THE LAW

Is the march a procession? Yes, it is a body of persons moving along a route to demonstrate support for or opposition to the views or actions of any person or body. Olivia and Salvador have given no notice and are described as the organisers; they appear to have breached section 11; however:

■ They could argue that it was not reasonably practicable to give advance notice. The march is an immediate response to an event, and to wait six days would

---

> dissipate energies and undermine the message (the news cycle would have moved on to a new set of concerns). There is so little judicial interpretation of section 11 that it is hard to say if this would work, but it is a feasible argument.
> - With no reported successful prosecutions, and the very different facts of *Kay* as the only reported unsuccessful prosecution, it seems unlikely that they would be charged for a one-off event like this.

Conditions – the power to impose conditions on processions is provided by section 12 of the POA 1986. If the senior police officer reasonably believes that

1(a) the procession may result in serious public disorder, serious damage to property or serious disruption of the life of the community, or
2(b) the purpose of the persons organising the procession is the intimidation of others with a view to compelling them not to do an act they have a right to do, or to do an act they have a right not to do,

they may give directions imposing such conditions as appear to them necessary to prevent such disorder, damage, disruption or intimidation. Breach of a condition is an offence.

Section 12(b) of the POA relates not to the possible consequences of the march but to its *purpose*. There must be both intimidation and coercion. It was aimed at industrial disputes, with the 'act they have a right to do' being the right of those breaking a strike to cross a picket line.

A further criticism of section 12 of the POA 1986 is that the earlier law, the Public Order Act 1936, only allowed conditions to be triggered by a reasonable belief that serious public disorder (i.e. violence to people and/or property) would ensue. The 'serious disruption of the life of the community' ground appears to be a significant extension of the power and is arguably far too broad. Feldman has argued that section 12 of the POA would be unconstitutional in the US because it fails to provide 'narrowly drawn, reasonable, objective and definite standards to guide the discretion'.[5]

KEY CASE – *POWLESLAND V DPP* [2013] EWHC 3846 (ADMIN)

This is another case arising out of the Critical Mass events – see *MPC v Kay* above. On the day of the opening ceremony of the Olympic Games, the police had imposed a section 12 condition on the Critical Mass event that prohibited the ride from going north of the River Thames. When the riders did go north of the river, Powlesland was arrested and convicted of breaching the section 12 condition.

---

5 Feldman, above n 2, ch 18.

Given that *MPC v Kay* had established that there was no need to give notice for the event, Powlesland argued that there was no power to impose a section 12 condition. The High Court disagreed, and found that conditions could be imposed on unnotified processions and that whilst section 12 conditions apply to a 'route, or proposed route', this did not have to mean a specifically planned route. A condition could therefore be imposed even on Critical Mass's spontaneous and improvised routes.

So how does section 12 of the POA apply to our scenario?

APPLYING THE LAW

The police have imposed a condition on the route of the procession. The senior police officer could justify this by reference to a reasonable belief that the planned route may result in serious disorder or disruption. This seems reasonable, even under the strict approach to interpreting this statutory language (seen in *Reid* and *Baillie* below) and was borne out by later events. When the protesters, including Olivia and Salvador, departed from the route and went down the side street, they broke the condition and committed an offence.

Bans – the police have the power to ban processions. This is potentially draconian, but it is subject to a number of limits. Under section 13 POA 1986, 'if at any time the chief officer of police reasonably believes that the powers under section 12 will not be sufficient to prevent the holding of public processions in that district from resulting in serious public disorder, he shall apply to the council for an order prohibiting for a period not exceeding three months the holding of all public processions (or of any class of public processions so specified)'.

If a council wants to grant such an order, it must obtain the consent of the Home Secretary. The exercise of the police power therefore is subject to two levels of political control; both the local council and the Home Secretary must agree to it. The power is only triggered by a reasonable belief in 'serious public disorder' that cannot be dealt with by gentler means, such as imposing conditions, and any banning order has a three-month maximum duration.

It might seem strange that the power is to impose *a blanket ban* on processions rather than to ban specific dangerous marches. The rationale for this is so that the police are not open to charges of partiality. However, it will normally be patently obvious who a particular banning order is made in relation to, and in practice it has been possible to effectively ban single marches by excluding classes of marches from the ban.

KEY CASE – *KENT V METROPOLITAN POLICE COMMISSIONER* (1981)
THE TIMES, 15 MAY

The Campaign for Nuclear Disarmament (CND) was a hugely important pressure
group through the 1960s–80s, regularly holding peaceful rallies and marches
attracting hundreds of thousands of participants. The Metropolitan Police
Commissioner became concerned about the general public order situation in
London in 1981. There had been extensive rioting in Brixton involving hundreds
of injuries and damage to many vehicles and properties. There were continuing
conflicts between the far-right racist National Front and anti-Nazi protesters. The
Commissioner requested a four-week ban on all marches in London, which was
approved by the Home Secretary.

CND, which was not the target of the ban, asked for judicial review of the ban which
had caused it to lose a number of important marches and revenue. The court found
in favour of the Commissioner, even though the reasons for the ban were 'meagre',
the exercise of discretion had not been capricious or unreasonable and Parliament
had granted the Commissioner a wide discretion to decide what was necessary
to prevent serious disorder. Whilst CND was not violent, the banning order would
protect peaceful demonstrators from 'hooligans'.

Whilst there was rhetoric from the Court of Appeal on the importance of freedom of assembly (the courts will be vigilant in scrutinising the exercise of a power that limits a
fundamental freedom), the ban was allowed to stand. A similar ban on processions in
London was upheld by the European Court of Human Rights as not being disproportionate
to the risks on the basis that there was, in the specific circumstances, a pressing social need
for order (*Christians against Racism and Fascism v UK* (1980) 21 DR 138).

The Human Rights Act 1998 has superimposed some obligations on the exercise of these
powers. Under the Public Order Act 1986 there is no explicit requirement to balance
the social needs of avoiding disorder or disruption with the fundamental human right of
assembly and public protest, but section 6 HRA now means that decision-makers must
exercise their powers to give due respect to those rights.

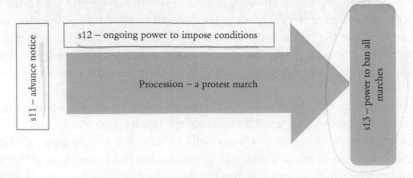

Figure 18.2 Controls over processions

18.7 ASSEMBLIES

An assembly differs from a procession by being static. It is a public meeting or a rally, or even a few people standing outside of a town hall or company headquarters holding placards.

The Public Order Act 1986 had originally imposed a minimum number of 20 persons before an assembly could be regulated by public order law, but this was reduced by section 57 Anti-social Behaviour Act 2003 to two persons. There is no notice requirement for assemblies nor any power to ban them. Under section 14 POA, a senior police officer can impose conditions on an assembly if he 'reasonably believes that:

1(a) it may result in serious public disorder, serious damage to property or serious disruption of the life of the community
2(b) the purpose of the persons organising the assembly is the intimidation of others with a view to compelling them not to do an act they have a right to do, or to do an act they have a right not to do'.

These conditions can cover 'the place at which the assembly may be (or continue to be) held, its maximum duration, or the maximum number of persons who constitute it'. The conditions must be 'necessary to prevent such disorder, damage, disruption or intimidation'.

The 'intimidation' trigger was considered in *Police v Reid* [1987] Crim LR 702, where protesters were picketing the (apartheid-era) South African Embassy to protest against the racist nature of the political system in that country. Specifically, they were shouting general slogans and wagging their fingers at guests arriving for a reception at the embassy. The senior police officer thought that this was intimidation, which he defined as 'putting people in fear or discomfort'. He imposed conditions on the spot requiring the assembly to move away. The court quashed Reid's conviction for failing to comply with the condition; 'intimidation' means more than mere discomfort or being caused embarrassment.

It is easy to imagine conditions so strict that they frustrate the entire purpose of the assembly. This was the case in *DPP v Baillie* [1995] Crim LR 426, where the defendant gave out information about a free festival. It was unclear whether he was the organiser or whether the event was even an assembly, but the police nevertheless imposed very strict conditions. The Crown Court struck down the conditions, saying that they were intended to stop the event 'not simply regulate it'. On appeal, the High Court took a relatively strict approach to section 14 and said that the event did not clearly come within the ambit of the term 'public assembly', so there was no power to impose conditions.

APPLYING THE LAW – FINDING PLACES TO PROTEST?

One of the difficult issues with public assemblies is deciding *where* they can take place.

For assemblies on private land, the organisers will need to obtain the permission of the landowner. The places where people meet are the sorts of places where protesters want to be, e.g. shopping malls. These are normally in private hands and the owners are highly unlikely to give their consent. This was illustrated in *Appleby v UK* (2003) 37 EHRR 38, where the new centre of the town of Washington, in Tyne & Wear, had been constructed by a public corporation and then sold to a private company. The centre of the town was therefore owned by a private landowner. Local campaigners wanted to collect signatures for a petition within the centre, but were refused permission by the landowner. The European Court of Human Rights found that there was no breach of Article 11. The situation was not so restrictive as to seriously limit the campaigners' rights, the ECHR did not provide any specific right to a forum for protests and the landowner's property rights (also protected under the ECHR) had to be respected. The Court noted that the campaigners could seek signatures on the streets outside of the shopping centre.

Public parks are owned by local authorities and there is a public right of access, but the use of these spaces can be limited by bye-laws. The public have the right to use the highway, but it was long thought (until *DPP v Jones*, see below) that this was simply for passage. You could use streets for passing and repassing, but there appeared to be no inherent right to use them for any other purpose (which explains the wider powers in relation to processions). This placed almost every assembly in a precarious legal position of relying on the consent, or the sufferance, of private landowners or public bodies.[6]

18.7.1 TRESPASSORY ASSEMBLIES

The late 1980s saw new challenges to public order. New Age travellers sought alternative lifestyles and sometimes congregated in unlawful campsites. Rave culture, which originated in the towns and cities of North West England, had spread across the UK and often involved unlicensed dance music events in abandoned buildings and open air spaces. The comprehensive, and controversial, response was the Criminal Justice and Public Order Act 1994. The thrust of the Act was to criminalise what had until then only been the civil wrong of trespass; but we will just focus on the elements of the Act that affect assemblies as forms of public protest.

Section 70 of the Act created new offences of trespassory assembly by amending section 14 of the Public Order Act 1986. The scheme is similar to section 13 of the POA. An order can be applied for by the chief police officer; it can be granted by the council with the consent of the Home Secretary. An order applies to all trespassory assemblies in a specified area (which is limited to a five-mile radius) for a specified time (which is limited to four days).

---

6 See D Mead, 'A Chill through the Back Door? The Privatised Regulation of Peaceful Protest' [2013] *Public Law* 100.

The power is triggered by a reasonable belief that an assembly, of at least 20 people, is intended to be held at a place on land in the open air to which the public has no right of access or a limited right of access, and that the assembly

1(a) is likely to be held without the permission of the occupier, or to exceed that permission or to exceed the public's right of access; and

2(b) may result in serious disruption to the life of the community, or in significant damage to land, or to a building or monument upon the land, where the land, building or monument is of historical, architectural, archaeological or scientific importance.

It is an offence to breach the ban, and it is possible to stop a person and direct him not to proceed if a police officer reasonably believes that they are on the way to the banned assembly. This is exercisable up to a five-mile radius. Whilst this was an extension of police power over protest, it is clearly hedged around with a number of limitations as to the number of people, the trigger of serious disorder, the trespassory nature of the activity, and the need for agreement from the council and Home Secretary.

The section also gave rise to an important case that involved the courts not merely espousing the rhetoric of fundamental rights to protest, but actually using their interpretive powers to give some effective protection to that right.

KEY CASE – *DPP V JONES* [1999] 2 AC 240

A section 14A POA order had been obtained by the police for Stonehenge and its vicinity. Margaret Jones was one of 20 protesters who were standing on a grass verge by the side of the road, i.e. on the public highway but not obstructing the highway. She challenged her arrest for breach of section 14A after refusing to follow a police instruction to move away from the site.

If she was committing trespass by standing where she was, then she would be guilty of the offence, but the order would only apply to her if she was 'at a place on land in the open air to which the public has no right of access or a limited right of access' (that she had exceeded).

In the House of Lords there were two views put forward. The minority held that the only right of access to the highway for the public was for transport, i.e. passing and repassing. The majority, led by Lord Irvine, differed; they pointed out that this narrow view would make unlawful such activities as stopping in the street for a chat with a friend or children playing. The Lords held that the statutory public order powers cannot prevent people using the highway for 'all manner of reasonable activities', and that subject to rules on causing a nuisance and obstructing the highway, 'there is a public right of peaceful assembly on the highway'.

18.8 DEMONSTRATIONS IN THE VICINITY OF PARLIAMENT

In 2005, Maya Evans stood on the pavement in Whitehall near the Cenotaph (the principal monument in the UK to those killed in conflict) and read out the names of the 97 British soldiers who had been killed in the war in Iraq up to that point. She rang a small bell after reading out each name. She was arrested for breaching public order law, held in custody for five hours and then convicted of an offence under the Serious Organised Crime and Police Act 2005.[7]

You might wonder how this action (within five years of the coming into force of the Human Rights Act 1998 and under legislation introduced by the same Government) could possibly strike the appropriate balance between defending fundamental human rights and competing pressing social needs such as national security or the prevention of disorder. You would be right to wonder; it is difficult to regard the initial attempts to regulate protest within the vicinity of Parliament as anything other than, to put it politely, misguided and disproportionate.

Sections 132–38 of the Serious Organised Crime and Police Act 2005 applied to protests in Parliament Square and its environs, that is, approximately within 1 kilometre of Parliament. This made it a criminal offence to organise or participate in a demonstration without written notification to the Metropolitan Police Commissioner and permission from the police to hold that demonstration. Under section 134(2) of SOCPA, the Commissioner had a duty to authorise demonstrations, i.e. they could not withhold permission, but could impose conditions (based on a wide range of triggers of risk), covering the place of the demonstration, the numbers involved, and the use of banners and amplified noise.

The legislation seems to have been inspired by the protests of Brian Haw, who set up a one man 'peace camp' in Parliament Square in 2001, protesting against the sanctions on, and then the war in, Iraq. This was the cause of continual embarrassment for the Government, and MPs complained of being disturbed by Haw's use of a loudspeaker. The Court of Appeal decided that the new legislation could apply to pre-existing protests, i.e. Brian Haw's peace camp (*R (on the application of Haw) v Secretary of State for the Home Department* [2006] EWCA Civ 532). The legislation meant that even if you planned to hold a small, entirely peaceful, non–obstructive demonstration against e.g. some aspect of state action, then you had, on pain of arrest and criminal conviction, to obtain the permission of the state to do so.

---

7 'Activist convicted under demo law', *BBC News* (7 December 2005), http://news.bbc.co.uk/1/hi/england/london/4507446.stm (last accessed 11/09/15).

KEY CASE – *BLUM V DPP* [2006] EWHC 3209 (ADMIN)

This case also considered the legality of the arrest and prosecution of Maya Evans (see above). Blum and others had taken part in what the High Court found were 'peaceful and good-humoured demonstrations. All behaved in a peaceful and orderly way throughout'. They were arrested and convicted under section 132 SOCPA.

They argued that the decisions of the police and Crown Prosecution Service to arrest and prosecute them were in breach of their Convention rights to freedom of expression and assembly (Article 10 and 11); the authorities ought to have considered the specific nature of the demonstrations before they decided that arrest and prosecution were necessary for public safety or to prevent disorder or crime (i.e. the exceptions listed in Article 11(2) ECHR). So their challenge was not to the legislation itself, but to the exercise of these powers by public authorities.

The starting point for the Court was that the appellants were not charged with demonstrating, but rather with failing to get authorisation to demonstrate. Looking at ECtHR case law, it found that an authorisation procedure could be compatible with Articles 10 and 11, and that it was permissible to impose sanctions to reinforce the need to obtain such authorisation. Once it was accepted that the authorisation scheme set up by section 132 SOCPA did not breach Convention rights, there was no need for public authorities to assess the specific nature of each unauthorised demonstration.

Even though the Government in 2005 had the chutzpah (or brass-neck, if you prefer) to suggest that the legislation was needed to address threats to the democratic process, it ultimately became an embarrassment to the democratic credentials of the Government itself. It was replaced by the Police Reform and Social Responsibility Act 2011, ss.141–49. This covers a smaller controlled area, and only allows the police to direct people not to engage in 'prohibited activities', in particular to erect tents and use amplified noise. Its compatibility with Convention rights was upheld in *R (on the application of Gallastegui) v Westminster City Council* [2013] EWCA Civ 28.

KEY LEARNING POINTS

- There are a range of restrictions on the right to march.
- The potential limits on public assembly are similar but less onerous.
- These laws try to balance the right to assemble and protest with the inconvenience and other harms that can flow from public protest.
- The attempt to impose a highly restrictive special public assembly zone around Parliament failed and only survives in a diluted form.

18.9 PUBLIC ORDER OFFENCES

There were very serious breakdowns of public order through the late 1970s and early 1980s, from football hooliganism, far-right-wing marches and counter anti-fascist demonstrations. The miners' strike of 1984–1985 saw extensive clashes between strikers and police. There were major riots in cities across the UK. In 1981, Toxteth in Liverpool had one of the highest levels of unemployment in the country, and young black men in the area had been subject to persistent and aggressive stop and search by the police. In July, a minor disturbance led to full-scale rioting lasting over a week. Almost 500 police officers were injured and over 500 arrests were made. Petrol bombs and paving stones were used against the police, and over 50 buildings were so badly damaged that they had to be destroyed. Similarly, serious disturbances took place at Brixton in London, St Paul's in Bristol and elsewhere. These led to reforms to public order offences in the Public Order Act 1986.

We have seen that Article 11 provides no protection for violent conduct. The right is to *peaceful* assembly and *peaceful* protest. Our focus is on the offences that potentially restrict this behaviour. The more serious public order offences are briefly outlined here only because they can arise when public protest disintegrates into violent public order problems.

There are six main offences in the Public Order Act 1986, on a sliding scale of seriousness (as seen in the sentencing options that go from maximums of ten years' imprisonment to a minor fine). There is also a sliding scale of the potential tension with Article 11 of the ECHR. The more the Criminal Law restricts relatively trivial behaviour (especially where that behaviour does not include violence) and the more that offences can be committed by words and gestures alone, then the more likely it is that they will impinge on legitimate methods of protest.

The offences are, in the literature, normally treated in two batches: sections 1–3 covering the more serious crimes, and sections 4, 4A and 5 the less serious offences. The approach here is slightly different. Sections 1–4 of the POA are all concerned with threats to public order from actual or potential violence. Sections 4A and 5 POA are concerned with the dangers of causing harassment, alarm or distress to the public. These are the provisions that could cause inappropriate limitations on the right to peaceful assembly; this is particularly so for protest which often wants to provoke and to rouse people from their torpor and indifference to a subject.

Public Order Act 1986	Offence	Maximum Sentence
section 1	Riot	10 years
section 2	Violent disorder	5 years
section 3	Affray	3 years
section 4	Fear of provocation of violence	6 months
section 4A	Intentional harassment, alarm or distress	6 months
section 5	Harassment, alarm or distress	Fine

Figure 18.3 Public Order Act offences

18.9.1 OFFENCES INVOLVING VIOLENCE

18.9.1.1 SECTION 1 – RIOT

- Where 12 or more persons who are present together
- use or threaten unlawful violence for a common purpose and
- the conduct of them (taken together) is such as would cause a person of reasonable firmness present at the scene to fear for his personal safety,
- each of the persons using unlawful violence for the common purpose is guilty of riot.

The common purpose can be inferred from their conduct.

18.9.1.2 SECTION 2 – VIOLENT DISORDER

- Where three or more persons who are present together use or threaten unlawful violence and
- the conduct of them (taken together) is such as would cause a person of reasonable firmness present at the scene to fear for his personal safety,
- each of the persons using or threatening unlawful violence is guilty of violent disorder.

18.9.1.3 SECTION 3 – AFFRAY
A person is guilty of affray if

- he uses or threatens unlawful violence towards another and
- his conduct is such as would cause a person of reasonable firmness present at the scene to fear for his personal safety.

It is important to note that it is *not* the direct violence which is the offence. It is the harm to public order that is criminalised. The offence cannot be committed by words alone (*R v Robinson* [1993] Crim LR 581), and the 'degree of violence must be such as to be calculated to terrify a person of reasonably firm character' (*Taylor v DPP* (1973) AC 964).

18.9.1.4 SECTION 4 – FEAR OR PROVOCATION OF VIOLENCE
A person is guilty of an offence if he–

- uses threatening, abusive or insulting words or behaviour, or displays any writing, sign or other visible representation which is threatening, abusive or insulting,
- with intent to cause that person to believe that immediate unlawful violence will be used against him or another by any person, . . .

Under section 4, the behaviour must be *directed* towards another person. 'Immediate' does not mean 'instantaneous', but such proximity that violence 'would result in a relatively short period of time and without any intervening occurrence' (*R v Horseferry Road Magistrates' Court, ex parte Siadatan* [1990] Crim LR 598).

The civil liberties issue with these offences of violence is not with their use, but with their potential misuse. McCabe and Wallington, for example, allege that there was a broad policy of using serious public order charges during the miners' strike of 1984–1985 as a way to intimidate the strikers and deter them from taking part in lawful picketing and protests.[8]

18.9.2 OFFENCES OF HARASSMENT, ALARM OR DISTRESS

These are the offences that lie along the border that divides legitimate and illegitimate methods of protest. It is probably inevitable (as part of any legal system's endeavour of trying to control behaviour through written rules) that attempting to criminalise this sort of relatively low-level misconduct will involve using troublesome language. This is the case with reconciling words such as 'alarm' and 'insulting' with the need to allow robust public protest and debate.

18.9.2.1 SECTION 4A – INTENTIONAL HARASSMENT, ALARM OR DISTRESS

'A person is guilty of an offence if,

- with intent to cause harassment, alarm or distress, he –
- uses threatening, abusive or insulting words or behaviour [or an equivalent sign], or disorderly behaviour,
- thereby causing that or another person harassment, alarm or distress'.

This offence was added by section 154 of the Criminal Justice and Public Order Act 1994. It is more serious than the similar section 5 of the POA because it requires intent to cause harassment etc *and* that victim did suffer that consequence. It is an imprisonable offence (up to six months).

The meaning of '*threatening, abusive or insulting*' was considered in another case which involved protests against the racist apartheid-era South African regime.

KEY CASE – *BRUTUS V COZENS* [1973] AC 834

Protesters invaded a tennis court at Wimbledon in a match featuring a South African player. They handed leaflets to the crowd, blew whistles and sat down in the court to stop the match. The crowd became agitated and threatened violence against the protesters.

The prosecution said the protesters' behaviour was insulting to the crowd; it affronted other people and evidenced a disrespect or contempt for their rights. The House of Lords rejected this definition of 'insulting'. Lord Reid said that 'an ordinary sensible man knows an insult when he sees and hears it'. The conduct was 'deplorable' but not insulting.

---

8 S McCabe and P Wallington, *The Police, Public Order and Civil Liberties* (Routledge, 1988).

More broadly, 'threatening, abusive or insulting' were to be given their ordinary meanings. It is a question of fact in each case and the courts will not attempt to lay down any positive rules of recognition, because the circumstances vary so much. The most they will do is to lay down some limits so that the section is not interpreted too widely. Threatening, abusive or insulting words or conduct are not the same as causing annoyance or offence, or the same as mere rudeness.

18.9.2.2 SECTION 5 – HARASSMENT, ALARM OR DISTRESS

By introducing this offence, the Public Order Act 1986 extended police powers to behaviour that was previously seen as too trivial to be covered by the Criminal Law. It is the offence most relevant to public assemblies, particularly those that involve forms of direct action or civil disobedience. The maximum sentence is a relatively low-level fine.

'A person is guilty of an offence if he

- uses threatening or abusive words or behaviour [or an equivalent sign], or disorderly behaviour,
- within the hearing or sight of a person likely to be caused harassment, alarm or distress thereby'.

APPLYING THE LAW – DEFINITIONAL DIFFICULTIES

Section 5 originally covered 'insulting' words or behaviour. What we are insulted by and whether we feel distressed by this perceived insult can be highly variable and subjective, and this has caused some problems.

In the early 1990s the popular Madchester band The Inspiral Carpets had a logo comprising a smiling cow cartoon and the slogan 'Cool as Fuck'. People wearing t-shirts with this logo on were threatened, by Greater Manchester Police and by West Yorkshire Police, with arrest under section 5 of the POA. In 2006, an Oxford University student said to a mounted police officer, 'Excuse me, do you realise your horse is gay?'[9] He was arrested and detained overnight. The CPS ultimately decided not to proceed with the prosecution. The US magazine *Time* reported with some amusement that: 'The following year a 16-year-old from Newcastle was charged under the same Public Order law, for saying "woof" to a dog in front of police officers'.[10]

---

9 'Gay police horse case dropped' *BBC News* (12 January 2006), http://news.bbc.co.uk/1/hi/england/oxford-shire/4606022.stm (last accessed 01/11/17).

10 M Locker, 'You may now call a police horse "gay" in the UK' *Time* (16 January 2013), http://newsfeed.time.com/2013/01/16/you-may-now-call-a-police-horse-gay-in-the-u-k/ (last accessed 01/11/17).

These incidents did not ultimately lead to successful prosecutions, but they do highlight that these are sketchy and ill-defined terms. I would like to imagine that both you (dear reader) and I are reasonable people, but if we had to separately list what we might find insulting and how alarmed or distressed we might be, then we would produce different lists. If we had to apply our own internal definitions of these terms in the heat of an altercation on the street (as police officers often have to do), then there are bound to be problems.

Section 57 of the Crime and Courts Act 2013 removed the term 'insulting' from the section 5 POA offence. This reduces the definitional difficulties associated with the offence but does not eliminate them. In *DPP v Orum* (1988) 3 All ER 449, it was held that the person caused 'harassment, alarm or distress' can be a police officer, although the court will take into account the characteristics of a police officer, and the fact that they will be 'wearily familiar' rather than distressed by some conduct and comments.

A failed prosecution in 2016 illustrates both these points. A protestor in East London was arrested and prosecuted under section 5 of the POA for refusing to take down his banner which showed David Cameron, Ed Miliband, Nick Clegg and Nigel Farage above the phrase "All Fucking Wankers". It seems that failed attempts to criminalise public representations of foul language are continuing. The arrest happened because a bystander, a school teacher, was afraid that her pupils might repeat this language. She later admitted that she already heard language like this from both her pupils and colleagues.[11] Whether or not she was personally offended by the banner is seems difficult to characterise it as a criminal threat to *public order*.

The threatening or abusive words or behaviour does not have to be directed towards another person (*R v Ball* [1989] Crim LR 579), but whilst it must be apparent from the evidence that there was someone who was able to see or hear the conduct, there is no need to call witnesses or evidence that they actually did see or hear it (*Taylor v DPP* [2006] EWHC 1202 (Admin)). Note that the offence is words or behaviour 'likely' to cause harassment, harm or distress, so a police witness can give evidence of the behaviour and that there were people present who could see or hear it; it is then up to the magistrates as to whether the offence has been made out.

Section 5 also covers 'disorderly behaviour' that is likely to cause harassment, alarm or distress. This was explored in the context of public protest in *Chambers and Edwards v DPP* [1995] Crim LR 896. The appellants were protesting the construction of a motorway. They

---

11 O Bowcott, 'Student arrested over "offensive banner" about politicians is cleared' *The Guardian* (25 February 2016), https://www.theguardian.com/world/2016/feb/25/adam-barr-arrested-offensive-banner-politicians-cleared (last accessed 01/11/17).

interfered with the work of an engineer using a theodolite (a surveying instrument mainly used for measuring horizontal angles with a laser pointer), by simply standing in front of the laser beam to prevent the measurements being taken. In line with *Brutus v Cozens*, the High Court gave the words their ordinary meaning and treated it as a question of fact.

Looking at all the circumstances, they found that there was no need for any actual or threatened violence, and that the protesters' behaviour was disorderly.

There are two main defences. First, that the conduct was reasonable (section 5(3) POA). This defence must now be read in the context of the Human Rights Act 1998 and the clearer need to acknowledge that the exercise of rights of freedom of expression and assembly are often 'reasonable'. Second, absence of an intention or awareness that a person is present who is likely to be caused harassment, alarm or distress. In *DPP v Clarke* [1992] Crim LR 60, there was a demonstration outside an abortion clinic. The protesters had placards with images of aborted foetuses that they showed to police who said they were abusive and caused alarm and distress. The court found that whilst the protesters were aware that their actions could cause distress, this did not equate to an intention to engage in threatening behaviour.

There is a distinct power of arrest attached to section 5 POA. The officer must give a warning to the individual and then there must be 'further offensive conduct' before the power comes into effect.

APPLYING THE LAW

Returning to our example scenario, remember that Salvador shakes his fist and shouts, 'Soon I will dance on your grave, you murdering scum, you are dead meat' at the General. What offences, if any, has he committed?

- section 3 – affray: no; the words are not an unambiguous threat of direct violence (with the possible exception of the 'dead meat' comment); the General is safely inside the hospital building and the level of violence is not close to being terrifying.
- section 4 – fear or provocation of violence: no; it requires a belief that 'immediate unlawful harm' will be caused. There is no reason to believe that could be the case here.
- section 4A – intentional harassment, alarm or distress: possible but unlikely; on these facts a court might find that (a) he intended to cause harassment, alarm or distress (HAD) and (b) he used threatening, abusive or insulting language. The target of his conduct, the General, is not caused HAD but it is possible that bystanders were caused HAD. The court, however, would need evidence that they actually had been so affected, which makes a prosecution unlikely.

- section 5 – harassment alarm or distress: possible; on these facts a court might find that (a) he used threatening or abusive language and (b) it was within the sight or hearing of people likely to be caused HAD. There would be no need for evidence from such people, and police evidence of Salvador's conduct and the presence of bystanders may be sufficient. Following *Brutus v Cozens*, it would be a question of fact for the court.

For Olivia, section 5 is the only realistic charge and she could argue on the basis of *Clarke* that whilst the image on her placard may cause distress, her conduct is not threatening or abusive. She could also argue that her behaviour is reasonable as an exercise of her rights of free expression.

We are not told that the police have asked Olivia or Salvador to stop their behaviour, so the power of arrest under section 5 would not arise.

18.9.3 SECTION 5 AND FREEDOM OF ASSEMBLY AND EXPRESSION

The courts have recognised the potential for section 5 of the POA to have a chilling effect on public protest. In *Percy v DPP* [2001] EWHC Admin 1125, Hallett J said, 'A peaceful protest will only come within the terms of section 5 and constitute an offence where the conduct goes beyond legitimate protest and moves into the realms of threatening, abusive or insulting behaviour, which is calculated to insult either intentionally or recklessly, and which is unreasonable'. This seems reassuring, but it throws up as many questions as it answers.

In *Masterson v Holden* [1986] 1 WLR 1017, the defendants were a gay couple who were 'kissing and cuddling' at 2am on Oxford Street, London. Despite the fact that consensual homosexual relationships were legalised almost 20 years previously, the men were convicted of insulting behaviour whereby a breach of the peace might be committed. Glidewell LJ said that the insult could be towards anyone passing, by implying that they were the kinds of people who found that sort of public behaviour acceptable. He said that overt heterosexual, as well as homosexual, behaviour could be insulting if an observer (particularly a young lady) found it objectionable. It is difficult to imagine anyone falling for the suggestion that the High Court would have upheld the conviction of a straight couple kissing on the street at 2am in the morning (even in the 1980s). The case illustrates the ability of vague terminology to act as gateway or vehicle for the particular values (and prejudices) of police, prosecutors and judges.

A seemingly opposing case actually illustrates some of the same dangers. In *Hammond v DPP* [2004] EWHC 69 (Admin), a lay Christian preacher displayed a sign in Bournemouth town centre saying, 'Stop Immorality, Stop Homosexuality, Stop Lesbianism'. This drew a hostile response and Hammond was assaulted, forced to the ground and had mud and water poured on him. When the police arrived, they arrested Hammond rather than those who had assaulted him. He was convicted under (the old version of) section 5 POA on the basis that equating homosexuality with immorality was insulting and had caused distress. He could not use the defence of 'reasonable behaviour' because of the pressing need to show tolerance to all sections of society.

This is a nice illustration of the 'hostile audience dilemma' considered below. It seems to show considerable social progress from the anti-LGBT case law of the earlier era, but the case is troublesome. You might well think that Mr Hammond was utterly mistaken in his views on homosexuality, but these views do represent mainstream thought in many of the major world religions. You might want to take part in a Pride march to tell those religious adherents that their views on the morality of homosexuality are not only mistaken but profoundly immoral in themselves. This equates their faith with immorality, but you would not want to be arrested for their reaction to that. We can be offended by what a protester is saying without that person committing a public order offence, and the law ought to recognise this.

This analysis would not be accepted by all. There is a very respectable line of progressive thought that says we ought to pay particular regard to power relationships in society and that the court in *Masterson v Holden* was wrong in reinforcing the dominant paradigm of oppression of gay people, whilst the court in *Hammond* should be congratulated on providing some long overdue protection to a gay community that is still subject to prejudice. The different line of argument in this book is openly liberal, placing particular emphasis on political liberties of expression and assembly. Elliott and Thomas sum up the choice as 'between a "pro-civility" approach (one that emphasises the importance of respecting others' sensibilities and of preserving public decorum) and one that places greater weight on free speech as a force for good and something that people must learn to tolerate, even when they disagree with the content or medium'.[12]

18.10 BREACH OF THE PEACE

Breach of the peace is such a venerable part of our legal system that it sometimes escapes notice how very odd it and its close relative, binding over, really are. You may be surprised to learn that breach of the peace is not an offence in itself; you cannot be convicted of a breach of the peace. Its significance lies in the power of arrest attached to it. A police officer's apprehension of a breach of the peace gives them the power to issue directions and conditions. In practice, it is a wide-ranging power to give orders to the public that have to be followed on pain of arrest, and the dangers of such a wide and vague power for public protest are apparent.

---

12 Elliott and Thomas, above n 3, 879.

18.10.1 DEFINITION

Parpworth argues that 'The courts had a tendency to refer to the concept in a way that suggested it was so well understood as not to require definition'.[13] The leading definition comes from *R v Howell* [1982] QB 416: 'whenever harm is actually done or is likely to be done to a person or in his presence his property or a person is in fear of being so harmed through an assault, an affray, a riot, an unlawful assembly or other disturbance', i.e. there must be some element of violence (to persons or property) involved.

A wider approach was taken by Lord Denning in *R v Chief Constable of Devon and Cornwall ex parte Central Electricity Generating Board* [1982] QB 458, that there is a breach of the peace 'whenever a person who is lawfully carrying out his work is unlawfully and physically prevented by another from doing it'. This would extend the power to cover non–violent behaviour, e.g. physically lying down in front of a vehicle, but subsequent cases have preferred the *Howell* definition: 'breach of the peace is limited to violence or threats of violence' (*Percy v DPP* [1995] 3 All ER 124).

The courts have tried to develop limits on the power of arrest. Schiemann J said in *Foulkes v Chief Constable of Merseyside Police* [1998] 3 All ER 705 that there must be a 'sufficiently real and present threat to the peace to justify the extreme step of depriving a citizen who is not at the time acting unlawfully'. The police should use breach of the peace arrest powers with 'special care' (*McQuade v Chief Constable of Humberside* [2001] EWCA Civ 1330).

18.10.2 THE OPERATION OF THE POWER

The *Howell* definition places emphasis on physical harm, so is breach of the peace in the same category as the more serious Public Order Act offences, i.e. outside of the direct scope of enquiry into peaceful assembly? This is arguable, but the case law and police practice say otherwise, and breach of the peace is also central to the 'hostile audience dilemma' considered below.

The Court of Appeal in *Piddington v Bates* [1960] 3 All ER 660 said that if an officer reasonably apprehends a breach of the peace then they may impose conditions. Failure to obey the condition may lead to arrest. Parker CJ was astoundingly expansive on the latitude this gave: 'a police officer charged with the duty of preserving the Queen's peace must be left to take such steps as, on the evidence before him, he thinks are proper'. This can justify imposing conditions when an officer is unable to under sections 12 and 14 of the POA.

In the miners' strike case of *Moss v McLachlan* [1985] IRLR 76, police stopped pickets on their way to collieries. The cars were between a mile and half and five miles from their destinations. There had been previous disturbances from picketing activity in the area. It was held that 'provided [the police] honestly and reasonably form the opinion that there

13 N Parpworth, *Constitutional and Administrative Law* (9th edn, OUP, 2016) 491.

is a real risk of breach of peace in the sense that it is close in proximity in place and time', they could impose conditions and arrest for breach of them. Here any potential trouble was some miles away and some time away.

Each of these cases turns on its facts, so direct comparison is not always easy, but it does seem that the law has moved on, under the influence of the ECHR. In *R (on the application of Laporte) v Chief Constable of the Gloucestershire Constabulary* [2006] UKHL 55, police stopped three coaches carrying protesters to a rally against the war in Iraq. On searching the buses, they found that some items carried by some of the protesters might disclose an intent to cause disorder. All the passengers were returned to the buses which were then escorted back to London. Police motorcycle outriders prevented the coaches from stopping or changing route. The House of Lords held that breach of the peace powers must be kept within proper bounds and that the Chief Constable had acted disproportionately, and therefore unlawfully. The actions were premature in not being close enough in time or place to any potential disorder, and indiscriminate in treating passengers who had only ever disclosed peaceful intentions the same as a minority who had not. The Chief Constable had struck the wrong balance between the demands of public order and the protesters' rights of freedom of expression and assembly.

18.11 THE HOSTILE AUDIENCE DILEMMA

If my organisation is promoting views, via public meeting and marches, that you and your organisation vehemently disagree with, then you might want to counter-demonstrate – you are our hostile audience. Things might get heated; at best you may want to disrupt us through noise and shouting. If the views that we are espousing cause your counter-demonstration to go further and try to physically stop or hurt us, what should the police do? You are responsible for your own actions, but should we have any responsibility for provoking you to act that way?

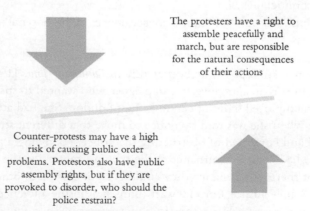

The protesters have a right to assemble peacefully and march, but are responsible for the natural consequences of their actions

Counter-protests may have a high risk of causing public order problems. Protestors also have public assembly rights, but if they are provoked to disorder, who should the police restrain?

Figure 18.4 The hostile audience dilemma

KEY CASE – *BEATTY V GILLBANKS* (1882) 9 QBD 308

The Salvation Army is a Christian organisation with a particular mission to the poor and hungry. In the Victorian era, it campaigned against alcohol and organised marches. It was opposed by a group called The Skeleton Army who sought to disrupt their marches, mainly through noise and shouting, but also by throwing objects and physical assault. The consequence of allowing both the Salvation and Skeleton Armies on the streets at the same time was 'shouting, uproar, and noise, to the great terror, disturbance, annoyance, and inconvenience of the peaceable inhabitants of the town'.

The town was Weston-Super-Mare, where the Salvation Army were first advised by police and then ordered by magistrates not to march. They refused and assembled to march. The police directed them to disperse and arrested an organiser when they did not. Beatty was convicted by magistrates of 'unlawfully and tumultuously assemble with divers other persons . . . to the disturbance of the public peace'.

The High Court found that upholding his conviction would mean that 'a man may be convicted for doing a lawful act if he knows that his doing it may cause another to do an unlawful act', which would be unsatisfactory. The Salvation Army marches were not in themselves a breach of the peace. The disturbances flowed from the actions of the counter-demonstrators. 'If this disturbance of the peace was the natural consequence of acts of the appellants they would be liable, and the justices would have been right in binding them over', but this was not the case here.

- Key point – people have a right to behave lawfully.
- If a hostile audience responds with threats of violence of disorder that does not make the original conduct unlawful.
- Only if a disturbance was 'the natural consequence' of the original acts would they be unlawful.

The hostile audience concept worked differently in *Duncan v Jones* [1936] 1 KB 218. Katherine Duncan was an anti-poverty campaigner who wanted to speak near the entrance to an unemployed training centre in East London. She had attracted a crowd of about 30 people when she was told by police to move to a different street. She refused and was arrested and convicted of obstructing the police. Following a previous speech by Duncan there had been a disturbance at the training centre, i.e. the audience was not hostile to her but there was a chance they could become hostile to others as a result of her speech. The Chief Justice, Lord Hewart (himself a hostile audience), dismissed the appeal, saying that the case held no constitutional aspects because there is no right of public meeting. He found there was 'clearly a causal connection' between the previous meeting and the disturbance, and so the police were justified in apprehending a breach of the peace and issuing instructions.

The hostile audience issue has also been considered by the European Court of Human Rights. In *Plattform 'Ärtze für das Leben' v Austria* (1985) (Case 10126/82), an anti-abortion group march and subsequent meeting had been disrupted by counter-demonstrators. There was almost no violence, and the police had separated the factions. The Court made a general statement of principle:

> A demonstration may annoy or give offence to persons opposed to the ideas or claims that it is seeking to promote. The participants must, however, be able to hold the demonstration without having to fear that they will be subjected to physical violence by their opponents . . . In a democracy the right to counter-demonstrate cannot extend to inhibiting the exercise of the right to demonstrate.

This imposes positive obligations on the state 'even in the sphere of relations between individuals'.

This principle did not seem to be applied in *Chorherr v Austria* (1994) 17 EHRR 358, which allowed the police to close down a peaceful but provocative demonstration on the basis of a possible threat to order or violence from the audience. Two men were handing out leaflets asking for a referendum on purchasing military aircraft at a ceremony to celebrate Austrian military neutrality. The ECtHR allowed Austria a very wide discretion on striking a balance between the competing interests. It found that the demonstrators must have known that their actions might lead to hostility and disturbance, and so the state was entitled to proportionately restrain their actions.

The case of *Öllinger v Austria* (2008) 46 EHRR 38 goes back to the principles from *Plattform 'Ärtze für das Leben'* and outlines a better approach to balance between demonstrators and counter-demonstrations. An organisation of former SS members, the *Kameradschaft IV*, held an annual funeral commemoration in Salzburg cemetery. A Green Party MP wanted to organise a meeting at the same time and place to remember the Jews of Salzburg who had been murdered by the SS. The meeting would involve six people simply holding placards, with no shouting or chanting. The Austrian authorities found that the meeting aimed at confrontation with *Kameradschaft* and banned it.

The ECtHR held that Austria should have given more consideration to the ability of the police to keep the groups apart, which would protect the free expression and free assembly rights of both. It had given too much weight to the rights of *Kameradschaft* to be protected from rather limited disturbance. The demonstration might make the attendees at the funeral commemoration uncomfortable or even angry, but it did not interfere with their ability to publicly remember and honour their former comrades.

This approach, which goes back to *Beatty v Gillbanks*, now seems the dominant view in the UK. In *Redmond-Bate v DPP* [2000] HRLR 249, three Christian fundamentalists were preaching on the steps of Wakefield cathedral. A crowd gathered, some of whom showed signs of hostility. A police officer feared there may be a breach of the peace and directed them to stop. When they refused, they were arrested.

It was held that fearing a breach of the peace is not enough for an officer to be able to give lawful directions to a person. The constable needs to identify 'where the threat is coming from, because it is there that the preventive action must be directed'. In this case, the women were preaching about morality and the Bible; to say that a violent response was the natural consequence would be illogical and illiberal. The court said, 'Free speech includes not only the inoffensive but the irritating, the contentious, the eccentric, the heretical, the unwelcome and the provocative provided it does not tend to provoke violence. Freedom only to speak inoffensively is not worth having'. This was confirmed by the House of Lords in *Laporte*, that the first duty of the police in handling peaceful protest is to 'protect the rights of the innocent rather than compel the innocent to cease exercising them' (Lord Brown).

18.12 OBSTRUCTION OF THE POLICE

This is an offence under section 51 Police Act 1951. The test from *Rice v Connolly* [1966] 2 QB 414 is that

- the officer is acting in the course of his duty
- the defendant did an act that made it more difficult for officer to carry out duty and
- the defendant behaved wilfully.

This offence can interact with breach of the peace. If an officer gives a valid breach of the peace direction, they are acting in the course of their duty. If a person wilfully refuses to act on that direction (e.g. by refusing to move along) then they are guilty of a substantive criminal offence.

18.13 BINDING OVER

If a person is suspected of causing (or about to cause) a breach of the peace, they can be arrested without warrant and bound over to keep the peace and/or to be of good behaviour, even though they have not been found guilty of any criminal offence. If the person refuses to be bound over or breaches their promise to keep the peace, they can be imprisoned. The courts' powers arise under common law, section 115 of the Magistrates' Court Act 1980 and (rather improbably) the Justice of the Peace Act 1361.

What is particularly troublesome is that an individual can be bound over to be 'of good behaviour', or not to act *contra bones mores* (against good moral, or against the moral welfare of society). The Law Commission recommended the complete abolition of binding over powers in 1994.[14] It thought the power was too vague, that orders were potentially oppressive, that the imprisonment power was anomalous and that it was procedurally unfair.

18.14 BAIL CONDITIONS

Conditions can be attached to bail for any alleged offence. If a person breaches the conditions, they can be imprisoned. In the miners' strike of 1984–85, it became common practice to attach a list of usual bail conditions with no reference to the facts of the case. These were directed at stopping involvement in picketing, and therefore the exercise of the miners' rights of association and assembly. The legality of these 'usual conditions' was upheld in *R v Mansfield Magistrates' Court, ex p Sharkey* [1985] 1 All ER 193.

18.15 OBSTRUCTION OF THE HIGHWAY

Under section 137 of the Highways Act 1980, it is an offence if 'a person without lawful authority or excuse in any way wilfully obstructs the free passage of the highway'. The highway is not limited to the roadway and includes the pavement.

This has been used to limit peaceful protest, but case law has usefully clarified what the highway can reasonably be used for. In *Arrowsmith v Jenkins* [1963] 2 QB 561, 2 All ER 210, the offence was interpreted strictly. A protest was held that caused a minor blockage to a street. The organiser had given notice of the meeting to police, and other meetings had been held in the same street previously without incident, but Arrowsmith was still convicted. This seemed to indicate a strict liability approach: that any organiser of an assembly could be criminalised for minor or even partial obstruction of a highway by people who turned up to the meeting. *Nagy v Weston* [1965] 1 All ER 78 introduced a more nuanced approach. The court would look at the overall reasonableness of the behaviour including the length of any obstruction, the purpose of the event that caused obstruction, its place and whether actual or potential obstruction took place.

The notion that *the purpose* of the event causing any obstruction is relevant was taken up in *Hirst and Agu v Chief Constable of West Yorkshire* (1986) 85 CR App Rep 143 where animal rights protesters were handing out leaflets outside a fur shop. In applying the reasonableness test, 'the courts have long recognised the rights to free speech, to protest

---

14 Law Commission, 'Binding Over', Cm 2439, 1994.

on matters of public concern and to demonstrate on the one hand and the need for peace and good order on the other'. This position was confirmed by House of Lords in *DPP v Jones* (see above).

18.16 PROTECTION FROM HARASSMENT

The Protection from Harassment Act 1997 creates various offences including causing another to fear violence and knowingly engaging in a course of conduct that amounts to harassment. A separate offence of using harassment to try to persuade someone not to do something that he is entitled or required to do was added by section 125 of the Serious Organised Crime and Police Act 2005. The 1997 Act was introduced primarily to address stalking and domestic violence, but has been used in relation to animal rights campaigns and, to a lesser extent, environment protests. In animal rights campaigns feelings run particularly high, and some groups have tried to use threats and harassment to persuade employees of animal testing companies to leave their jobs, and to persuade companies to change their activities (*Huntingdon Life Sciences v Curtin* (1997), The Times, 11 December). Harassment is not defined, although following the Human Rights Act it must be interpreted in accordance with Convention rights. Proceedings under the Act can lead to courts imposing wide-ranging restraining orders (*Oxford University v Broughton* [2004] EWHC 2543).

POINTS TO REVIEW

- The statutory public order offences, ss.1–5 POA 1986, outline a series of crimes of descending seriousness.
- Only the less serious ones have a significant and potentially difficult relationship with the right to peaceful protest.
- These offences are supplemented by a range of common law powers, such as breach of the peace.
- These common law powers have been interpreted, in more recent years, in ways that reflect the importance of freedom of assembly, but are still problematic in their scope and discretion.

TAKING IT FURTHER

NUS & Liberty, Protest Your Rights, https://www.liberty-human-rights.org.uk/sites/.../ nusliberty-rights-document-a5.pd (last accessed 01/11/17). A guide for students on how to undertake public protest in a lawful manner. This provides an accessible review of the laws covered in this chapter and applies it to the modern practicalities of protesting.

D Mead, 'Strasbourg discovers the right to counter-demonstrate – a note on *Öllinger v Austria*' [2007] *European Human Rights Law Review* 133 Mead is the leading contemporary writer on public order issues and considers how the 'hostile audience' issue has played out before the European Court of Human Rights.

S Laville, 'Sussex police under fire for "criminalising" fracking protests', *The Guardian* (15 May 2014) http://www.theguardian.com/environment/2014/may/15/sussex-police-criminalising-fracking-protest-acquittals-balcombe This gives an interesting insight into the 'on the ground' application of some of the powers covered in this chapter, including controversial use of section 14 of the POA 1986 and bail condition powers.

INDEX